PARTY POLITICS
IN AMERICA

PARTY POLITICS IN AMERICA

Eighth Edition

Paul Allen Beck

The Ohio State University

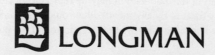 LONGMAN

An imprint of Addison Wesley Longman, Inc.

New York • Reading, Massachusetts • Menlo Park, California • Harlow, England
Don Mills, Ontario • Sydney • Mexico City • Madrid • Amsterdam

Acquisitions Editor: Leo Wiegman
Project Coordination: Electronic Publishing Services Inc.
Cover Designer: Kay Petronio
Art Studio: Electronic Publishing Services Inc.
Electronic Production Manager: Eric Jorgensen
Manufacturing Manager: Hilda Koparanian
Electronic Page Makeup: Americomp
Printer and Binder: RR Donnelley & Sons Company
Cover Printer: Phoenix Color Corp.

Library of Congress Cataloging-in-Publication Data

Beck, Paul Allen.
    Party politics in America / Paul Allen Beck. — 8th ed.
        p.   cm.
    Includes biographical references and index.
    ISBN 0-673-99578-X (pb)
    1. Political parties—United States. I. Title.
JK2265.S65   1996   96-13789
324.273—dc20   CIP

ISBN 0-673-99578-X

12345678910—DOC—99989796

Contents

Preface

The contemporary scene provides dramatic evidence of the central role political parties play in the American political process. In the very months before this book went to press, the federal government experienced two partial shutdowns because of half a year's delay before the adoption of the fiscal year 1996 operating budget. This stalemate over the federal budget was the immediate result of intense and continuing partisan conflict between a Republican Congress and a Democratic president over which programs to cut in reducing the federal budget deficit. Over the longer term, it is the product of the battle over governmental priorities between a more ideologically unified and aggressive Republican party in the Congress than we have seen in a century and an unusually cohesive Democratic competitor, both supported by energetic national party organizations. No better illustration can be found in the annals of American history of cohesive programmatic parties battling one another over consequential matters of public policy.

The contemporary situation also illustrates how much the influence of political parties has waned within the American electorate. The current budget stalemate came about because voters elected a Democratic president in 1992 but a Republican Congress in 1994—the first in four decades. Once rare, divided government has now become the norm, albeit with a Republican in the White House and Democrats running the Congress rather than the situation after 1994. Even though Bill Clinton won the White House in 1992, his popular support fell far short of a majority of those voting, as independent Ross Perot was preferred by almost one voter in five. The diminished partisan fidelity of American voters, symbolized by volatility in both vote results from election to election and ticket splitting to vote for candidates from different parties or an independent, has been another prominent feature of the last few decades. Isn't it ironic that the congressional parties have become more partisan and the national party organizations more active just as voters have become less partisan?

Party politics in the 1990s requires a new chapter in the almost two-hundred-year story of political parties as key actors in the American political process. Both in what they are and what they do, parties have contributed mightily to the shape of American politics. At the same time, they have been themselves shaped by this politics and the broader sociocultural environment in which it has operated, which have made them unique among their counterparts in the democratic world. The longevity of the American two-party system and of the Democratic and Republican parties within it, in a nation that has seen enormous changes in the party environment since its founding, are testimony both to the remarkable staying power of the parties and to their capacity to adapt to changes around them. This new chapter, then, to return to the metaphor, echoes many of the themes of the old ones.

Recent decades, though, have posed perhaps the sternest tests yet to the adaptability of the American parties. The quintessential party organization, the local party machine, has been driven to the brink of extinction. With the rise of television as the political medium of choice by politicians and voters, the quickening of the antiparty reform spirit which has robbed the parties of their control over nominations and vital campaign resources, the increasing personalization of candidates for office, and the shrinking of the party-oriented electorate, American politics had become more candidate- and less party-centered than ever before—and candidates always have enjoyed more independence of operation here than in other democracies. The unusually party-oriented contest of 1994, with its Republican Contract with America and repudiation of many leading Democratic incumbents, brought an abrupt halt to this trend. Whether it signals a reversal of recent patterns or merely a pause in the steady march of party decline, though, remains to be seen.

Even before 1994, the parties had responded to these new challenges, as they have done time and time again throughout their history. They confronted some of them directly—by, for example, becoming television producers themselves, investing millions of dollars in party building at the grass roots, and vesting more power in the party leadership in Congress. Other challenges were dealt with indirectly, by adapting what they do and ultimately what they are to the new realities. For example, the parties countered the increasing candidate centeredness of campaigns by becoming an important service provider to the candidates, and they responded to declines in party loyalty by redoubling their efforts to involve loyalists in party fund-raising.

The eighth edition of *Party Politics in America* continues the story told in earlier editions of the role of political parties in the American political process. As any comprehensive treatment of the American parties must, its focus embraces both continuity and change. Continuity in the essential features of the American parties and party system, including its domination by the same two giants for well over a century, allows the same theoretical framework that has molded past editions to shape this one as well. In particular, the parties remain tripartite combinations of sometimes cooperating, sometimes conflicting organizations, public officials, and electorates. This tripartite structure and the interaction of parts within it endures as a principal characteristic of the American parties and the central organizing theme of the eighth edition.

The book has been substantially revised, however, to reflect changes in the American parties and the burgeoning research literature on them since 1991. An unusually large number of important works on the parties, many of them adopting a rational chice perspective, have been published in the 1990s; their insights are well reflected in the eighth edition. Events too have overtaken the parties—chief among them the Perot insurgency, the rise of programmatic parties in the Congress, and the emergence of a Republican Congress—and their influence too may be seen in the following pages. All of the book's chapters have been substantially updated and revised. Two chapters have been eliminated—one to acknowledge the declining role of the national party conventions, the other to recognize that theoretical points which have been integrated into the appropriate substantive chapters do not need to stand alone at the end. The new edition also employs more comparisons with other times and other countries so as to gain an even better appreciation of the contemporary American parties. *Party Politics in America* has always been designed as a comprehensive treatment of the American parties and party system, and I believe that this goal has been attained yet again.

The contributors to this book were many, even if I alone bear responsibility for converting their contributions to prose. My greatest debt is to Frank Sorauf, who a decade ago generously passed on to me the book that had been so formative of my own understandings of American political parties. Even though the eighth edition of *Party Politics in America* no longer bears his name, it still carries his powerful imprint. Much of its organization and many of its ideas I inherited from him, and I have tried to satisfy his exacting standards for factual accuracy and felicitous prose. I always will be grateful to Frank for inviting me to gain a deeper understanding of American parties by taking over responsibility for this book and for providing me with such an excellent foundation from which to work.

A substantial debt also is owed to many professional colleagues, inside and outside of academia, who are too numerous to mention. The community of political-parties scholars provided me with much of the raw material for this book. Because of their scholarly contributions, which have become even richer in recent years, I have had a lot to say about the parties. My department colleagues have been a valuable source of intellectual nourishment and stimulation. Ohio State University has provided an exciting intellectual environment for me, which has enabled me to continue to grow as a political scientist, even in areas beyond those of my immediate expertise. The readers HarperCollins enlisted to review my proposal for a new edition— David Canon (University of Wisconsin), Mary Ellen Balchunis (LaSalle University), Robert Sittig (University of Nebraska), and Ronald Busch (Cleveland State University)—provided valuable suggestions. This book was improved by their contructive criticism.

Special debts of gratitude are owed to my collaborators in another long-standing project, Russell Dalton of the University of California at Irvine and Robert Huckfeldt of Indiana University, and to Dean Burnham of the University of Texas, John Bibby and Tom Holbrook of the University of Wisconsin at Milwaukee, Majorie Hershey of Indiana University, Kathleen Frankovic and her staff at CBS News, Masanori Hashimoto in the Department of Economics at Ohio State University, and staff members at the Democratic and Republican National Committees as well as at the Federal Elections Commission. Among my Ohio State colleagues, Larry Baum, Dick Gunther, John Kessel, Pat Patterson, Brad Richardson, Rip Ripley, Elliot Slotnick, and Herb Weisberg were especially valuable contributors to my thinking about the political parties. I am deeply appreciative also to Wayne DeYoung for his excellent work in preparing the index.

My students, undergraduate and graduate, always have been an important source of inspiration for me. By challenging me to present my ideas carefully and clearly, they have helped to sharpen my thinking and my writing. By asking the one question that I have not anticipated on many of the book's topics, they have pushed me to new understandings of party politics. By sharing with me their own insights about American politics and their experiences working within the parties and government, they have served as valuable sources of material for the book. Several graduate students—Joel Blumberg, Audrey Haynes, Sally Healy, Steve Nichols, and Peter Radcliffe—have made extraordinary contributions to the book as my research assistants. I am grateful to them for both their careful work and what they have taught me about the parties.

In an era of seemingly incessant change in the publishing industry, authors are greatly advantaged when they have a first-rate editor who stays with them over a considerable period of time. I have been associated with five different publishing companies and a multitude of editors, some lasting only a few months, in the decade since I started to write *Party Politics*. My current editor, Leo Wiegman, stayed with me for the longest time. I am deeply indebted to him for his guidance in writing the eighth edition of *Party Politics* and hope to be able to work with him in the future. I am also grateful for the professional service rendered me by members of the HarperCollins production staff and to Patty Andrews of Electronic Publishing Services Inc.

Finally, members of my immediate family have been important silent (well, not always so silent!) contributors to this book. Tere, Dan, David, and now Gabe have patiently endured my late arrivals for dinner and nightly and weekend disappearances into my study with the understanding that this book had to be finished before I could resume a normal life. Our regular discussions of politics also have been a valuable source of my understanding of American politics. That I have become the author of a book on political parties seems almost a natural part of my inheritance from members of my more extended family—especially my parents Frank and Mary, my aunts Irene, Maryana, and Luallen, my uncle Randy, and my grandmother Lucille. They instilled in me early in life an abiding interest in party politics; my uncle and my grandmother also provided me with early experience in its practice. In its small way, this book is a tribute to their abiding commitment to a democratic party politics.

Paul Allen Beck
Columbus, Ohio
May 1996

PARTY POLITICS IN AMERICA

PART
One

PARTIES AND PARTY SYSTEMS

The pervasiveness of politics is a central fact of our times. We have seen in the twentieth century an enormous expansion of governmental activity. The demands of a complex society and the dictates of an increasingly interdependent world do not easily permit a return to limited government. For the foreseeable future, therefore, most of the important conflicts over the desirable things in American society will be addressed by the political system, and their resolution primarily will come through the political process, if it is to come at all. This makes how influence and power are organized within the political system, who wins the rewards and successes of political activity, and to whom the people who make the decisions are responsible the really meaningful issues of our time. It is the political system that plays the crucial role in deciding, in the apt phrase of Harold Lasswell, "who gets what, when, how."[1]

In the United States, these political contestations are directed largely at the regular institutions of government. Few political scientists believe that the real and important political decisions are made clandestinely by murky, semivisible elites and are merely ratified by the governmental bodies they control.[2] It may happen, to be sure, that political decisions in a local community are made by a group of influential local citizens rather than by a city council or a mayor or a school board. Nonetheless, one is reasonably safe in looking for the substance of American politics in the legislatures, executives, and courts of the nation, the fifty states, and localities. Considerable activity is directed, therefore, to influence either the making of decisions within these governmental bodies or the selecting of the men and women who will occupy them.

This struggle for influence is not unorganized, however confusing it may seem to be at times. Large political organizations attempt to mobilize influence on behalf of aggregates of individuals. In democracies, the political party is typically the most important and pervasive of these political organizations. It is not, however, the only one. Interest groups, such as the National Rifle Association and the AFL-CIO, and their political action committees (PACs) also mobilize influence. So do smaller factions and cliques, charismatic individuals, and nonparty political organizations such

1

as United We Stand America, the Christian Coalition, and the Americans for Democratic Action. Even ostensibly nonpolitical organizations, for example, churches,
civic clubs, and ethnic group associations, may from time to time play important
roles in the political process.

All these political organizations work as intermediaries between the millions of
political individuals and the often-distant policymakers in government (Figure I.1).
They build influence into large aggregates in order to have a greater effect on the
selection of policymakers and the policies they will make. At the same time, they
codify and simplify information about government and politics as it moves back to
the individual. In a very real sense, therefore, these political organizers are the informal agents by which individuals are linked to government in the complex democracies of our time.

In any political system, these political intermediary organizations develop an
informal division of labor. Political parties concentrate on contesting elections and
organizing governing majorities as a way of aggregating influence. Others, especially interest groups, pursue the avenues of direct influence on legislators or administrators in articulating the demands of narrower groups. Still others seek mainly to
propagate ideologies or build support on specific issues of foreign or domestic policy. Indeed, the nature of the division of labor among the various political intermediaries says a great deal about any political system and about the general processes of
mobilizing influence within it.

This division of labor also speaks meaningfully about the political parties.
Among the parties of the democracies, the American political parties are preoccupied
to an unusual extent with the activity of contesting elections. The parties of Western

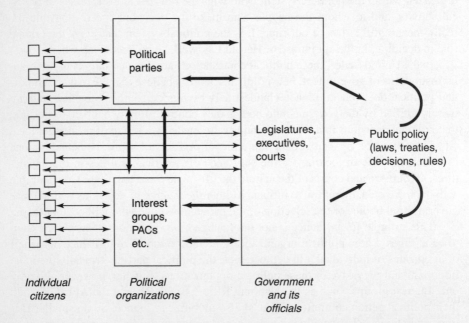

Figure I.1 Political organizations as organizing intermediaries in the political system.

Europe, on the other hand, have been more committed to spreading ideologies and disciplining legislators as well as trying to win elections. Those of developing countries sometimes play important roles in transmitting political values and information to a citizenry that lacks other avenues of political socialization and communication. On the other hand, the American parties do not monopolize the contesting of elections as much as parties do in some other nations. They must share the electoral politics stage, increasingly it seems, with independent groups and independent candidates as well as with party nominees who want little association with their party.

The division of labor among political organizations is neither clear nor permanent. There is always an overlap and hence a competition among political organizations over the performance of their activities. That competition is most obvious when it takes place within the party system, the competition of one party against another. It also takes place between parties and other political intermediaries—for example, in the competition of parties and powerful interest groups for the attention and support of legislators or for the right to name a candidate in a primary election. Furthermore, the extent to which any one kind of political organization controls or participates in any one kind of organizing activity may change radically over time. Certainly, no one would argue that the American political parties today control as much of the business of campaigning as they did a century ago.

All of this competing for a role in American politics implies another kind of competition. The political organizations compete among themselves for political resources: money, skills, expertise, the efforts of men and women. All of these resources are necessary for the fueling of organizational activity, but none of them is in particularly abundant supply in the American society. Then, with those resources in hand, organizations compete for the support of individual citizens—that is, they seek their support for the goals and leadership of the organization. In sum, the parties and other political organizations compete first for the capacity to organize influence and then for the influence itself.

Although this is a book about political parties, excursions beyond the subject of political parties are necessary to understand them fully. The broader survey of politics and political organizations, for example, introduces two themes that will recur throughout the book. The first is that the political party is not the unique political organization we have conventionally thought it to be. On the contrary, it is frequently similar to other political organizations, and the difficulty of coming to a clear, agreed-on definition of a political party illustrates that point only too well. Parties do have their distinctive qualities and it is important to know them, but there is little point in denying their similarity and, in some cases, their functional equivalence to many other political organizations.

Second, a broad perspective is essential in assessing the role and position of political parties in the American democracy. American writers about political parties have not been modest in their claims for them. They have celebrated the parties as agents of democracy and even as the chosen instruments through which a democratic citizenry governs itself. Some have gone a step further to proclaim them the architects of the democratic processes that they now serve. E. E. Schattschneider opened his classic study of the American parties this way in 1942:

> The rise of political parties is indubitably one of the principal distinguishing marks of modern government. The parties, in fact, have played a major role as makers of democratic government. It should be stated flatly at the outset that this volume is devoted to the thesis that the political parties created democracy and that modern democracy is unthinkable save in terms of the parties.[3]

Other scholars, and many thoughtful Americans too, agree that American democracy presumes the two-party system of today. Similar paeans to the role of political parties in democracy are sounded by some observers of the development of democracy in new nations.[4]

This heroic view of parties stands in stark contrast to recurrent expressions of antiparty sentiment and the general ambivalence about the parties in the American political culture. The Republic's Founding Fathers were wary of organized factions in political life, as is exemplified by James Madison's famous peroration against the "mischiefs of faction" in *Federalist* 10. The Progressive reforms a century or so later were directed in large part against the perceived evils of entrenched political parties and their control over the political process. Antiparty sentiment has intensified once again in recent years, providing fertile ground for yet another series of party reforms. Many Americans today, among them certainly many readers of this book, are skeptical of the value of parties and even may go so far as to view them as adversaries rather than guardians of political democracy.[5]

Nor do the immodest claims for political parties give adequate recognition to the fact that the major American parties have changed and continue to change both in the form of their organization and in the pattern and style of their activities. Political parties as they existed a century ago scarcely can be found today, and the political parties we know today may not exist even twenty years from now. In this book, a vigorous case will be made for the proposition that the political parties have lost their preeminent position as political organizations and that competing political organizations and other institutions now perform many of the activities traditionally regarded as the parties' exclusive prerogatives. If this is really the case, we must face the question of whether political parties are indeed indispensable and inevitable shapers of democratic politics.

These two suspicions—that the parties may be less distinctive and their activities less pervasive than we have thought—add up, perhaps, to no more than a plea for modesty in the study of the American political parties.[6] It is perfectly natural for scholars to identify with the objects of their study and thus to exaggerate their importance. Medievalists often find the late Middle Ages to be the high point of Western civilization, and most scholars of hitherto obscure painters and philosophers find the objects of their study to have been sadly neglected or tragically underestimated. So, too, has it been with students of political parties, and this sometimes leads them to claim more for the parties that they can deliver and to neglect how the parties may have adapted to changing conditions.

In spite of these qualifications, though, there is no question that political parties have played an important role in American politics and seem destined to continue as important players into the future. Their long lifetime of involvement at the center of the politics of the world's oldest representative democracy requires this conclusion.

The plea here is merely for a careful assessment of their role and how it may have changed. Assertions that political parties are essential to American democracy may or may not be true, but simply as assertions they advance our understanding of politics and parties very little. The same is true of predispositions to the contrary—that political parties are unnecessary or baneful influences upon a democratic politics. To even begin to evaluate such propositions requires a detailed examination of what the political parties are and what they do, now and in earlier times. That examination is the task of this book.

Chapter
1

In Search of the Political Parties

The dramatic explosion of democracy at the turn of the decade in Eastern Europe and the former Soviet Union introduced a multitude of new intermediary groups into a political scene that long had been dominated by only one, the Communist party. As these groups quickly prepared to play a role in the first democratic elections their nations had held in more than forty years, fundamental questions arose about them. What kind of groups were they—movements, interest groups, leadership factions, or political parties? Which of them would turn out to be viable or enduring electorally? If electorally successful, could they master the challenges of governing in this demanding and dynamic environment? Could they avoid the stigma widely attached to organized political groups because of the monopolizing history of the Communist party? For these nations, how such questions were to be answered became fundamental to the development of the new democratic institutions that might fulfill their hopes and dreams.

This early experience in the democratization of the former Warsaw Pact nations raises anew the question of what is a political party. How can a party be distinguished from a temporary grouping of like-minded officials, an interest group, or a mass movement? What is encompassed in the concept of party? Is a party the politicians who share a party label in seeking and filling public offices? The functionaries and activists who staff the offices and work in the campaigns? The ordinary citizens who possess similar political loyalties and who regularly vote alike in elections? A group of people who are like-minded in ideas, values, or stands on issues? Whatever entity, however organized, that performs a prescribed set of activities, especially centered on the electoral arena? Or is a party any grouping that chooses to call itself a party?

Political parties can be different things to different people, as the sample of alternative definitions in the following box illustrates. How they are defined matters for scholarly purposes, for it identifies the object of study and differentiates it from its environment. Because of the important role political parties have played in the operation of democracies, determining their essential features is more than a mere academic exercise. It is a quest for understanding democracy itself and how it may be fostered.

WHAT IS A POLITICAL PARTY? SOME ALTERNATIVE DEFINITIONS[1]

(A) party is a body of men united, for promoting by their joint endeavors the national interest, upon some particular principle in which they are all agreed.

Edmund Burke (1770)

In the broadest sense, a political party is a coalition of men (sic!) seeking to control the governing apparatus by legal means. By coalition, we mean a group of individuals who have certain ends in common and cooperate with one another to achieve them. By governing apparatus, we mean the physical, legal, and institutional equipment which the government uses to carry out its specialized role in the division of labor. By legal means, we mean either duly constituted elections or legitimate influence.

Anthony Downs (1957)

(W)hat is meant by a political party (is) any group, however loosely organized, seeking to elect governmental office-holders under a given label. Having a label (which may or may not be on the ballot) rather than an organization is the crucial defining element.

Leon Epstein (1979)

(A) political party in the modern sense may be thought of as a relatively durable social formation which seeks offices or power in government, exhibits a structure or organization which links leaders at the centers of government to a significant popular following in the political arena and its local enclaves, and generates in-group perspectives or at least symbols of identification or loyalty.

William Nisbet Chambers (1967)

A fundamental difficulty in talking about political party is that the term is applied without discrimination to many types of groups and near-groups. . . . Within the body of voters as a whole, groups are formed of persons who regard themselves as party members. . . . In another sense the term party may refers to the group of more or less professional political workers. . . . At times party denotes groups within the government. . . . Often it refers to an entity which rolls into one the party-in-the-electorate, the professional political group, the party-in-the-legislature, and the party-in-the-government. . . . In truth, this all-encompassing usage has its legitimate applications for all the

(box continues)

types of groups called party interact more or less closely and at times may be as one.

V. O. Key (1958)

Political parties can be seen as coalitions of elites to capture and use political office. . . . (But) a political party is . . . more than a coalition. A major political party is an institutionalized coalition, one that has adopted rules, norms, and procedures.

John H. Aldrich (1995)

TOWARD A TRIPARTITE CONCEPTUALIZATION OF THE POLITICAL PARTY

The various conceptions of party for most purposes quickly reduce to three. The ideological approach, exemplified by Edmund Burke's idea of parties, defines the parties in terms of commonly held ideas, values, or stands on issues as a group of like-minded people. That view has not enjoyed much favor among students of the American political parties. Ideological homogeneity or purpose has not been a hallmark of major American parties, even if it may have fit some traditional European parties, particularly those on the left. A conceptualization of parties solely as ideologically like-minded individuals also makes it difficult to distinguish parties from more narrowly drawn and often evanescent factions.

Most of the attempts at definition vacillate between two other options. Numerous scholars, such as Anthony Downs and Leon Epstein, see parties as teams of elites unified by a common purpose, namely the control of government through electoral victory and other means. Others, like William Nisbet Chambers and V. O. Key, prefer a broader conception that encompasses elites, organizational activists, and even ordinary voters. So important have these alternative conceptualizations been to the treatment of the American political parties that they should be considered more fully.[2]

At a minimum, the major American parties include current or prospective officeholders who are willing to be identified together under the same label. Many parties in democratic nations, including the United States, originated in this fashion. So it is understandable that some conceptions of party are content to restrict its meaning to just these leaders and their electoral organizations.

But most conceptions of modern parties see them as broad-based organizations that transcend the office seekers and officeholders. In some localities, the parties have offices and phone listings as political parties and virtually everywhere they have official standing under state law (see box on p. 10). It is possible to join them, to work within them, to become officers in them, to participate in setting their goals and strategies much as one would do within a fraternal organization or union without ever seeking or holding governmental office or even directly supporting a particular can-

WHAT IS *NOT* A POLITICAL PARTY: WEST VIRGINIA LAW

Under West Virginia law, a party that receives at least 1 percent of the vote for governor has the right to place its nominees on the ballot in the subsequent statewide election. After a write-in candidate for governor received 7 percent of the vote in 1992, the political action committee that had organized her campaign declared itself the Mountaineer party and claimed direct access to the 1994 ballot rather than having to gain it through a petition drive. The West Virginia Supreme Court ruled that this so-called party did not qualify for an automatic ballot position because it did not have a partylike organization prior to the 1992 election, had not presented itself as a party to the electorate in 1992, and did not include its 1992 candidate as a party member.

This incident is a reminder that the definition of a party is not only a matter for scholarly debate. Through their laws, the American states define what political parties are—and are not—and can thereby determine which groups will have the privileges generally accorded to official political parties, such as a listing on the ballot and access to public funding where it is available.[3]

didate. Some of these activists are even selected as the official representatives of the party under the statutory authority of the state.

There is a tendency for many scholars to close their conceptions of what the political party structures are at this point—to view them as teams of political specialists actively involved in competing for and exercising political power. This view is also common among ordinary citizens, who may desire to put some distance between themselves and these political entities. Moreover, it has allowed scholars to define parties in a neat, well-structured fashion and to analyze changes in the form they have taken over the course of American history.[4]

Yet, however attractive this simple definition may be, other scholars contend that it ignores a fundamental reality about political parties, especially the American parties. As intermediary organizations, political parties reside in both citizen and elite political circles. Many ordinary voters develop such strong and enduring attachments to a particular party that they are publicly registered with it on state registration rolls and loyally support its candidates; without any requirements for formal membership in the party, such as paying dues, this is a strong measure of belonging. Moreover, it is common in discussing the electoral fortunes of the political parties to treat them as coalitions of voters rather than simply groupings of political elites. Talk of political realignment or mere references to Democrats and Republicans, for example, recognize parties as including voters as well as officeholders and office seekers, functionaries and activists.

The Progressive tradition, by instituting party registration and nomination through primary elections as regular practices, has strengthened further the case for a conceptualization of American parties that includes a citizen base. Party voters in the United States are directly involved through primary elections, usually qualifying for participation by simply affirming their party loyalty, in what is probably the single most important party decision—selecting which candidates will run under the party label in elections. This function is performed by a thin stratum of party activists and leaders elsewhere in the democratic world.

By involving voters directly in the nomination process, the line between elite and mass that demarcates political parties in some political systems is blurred in the American setting, very much as the Progressives intended. This creates a situation in which voters as consumers not only choose among competing products in the political marketplace but also assume the management responsibility to determine just what products will be introduced in the first place—an arrangement that would revolutionize market economies just as it has transformed political parties. Perhaps this makes for a messier concept of political party, but it nonetheless is a more realistic one for the American parties.

The major American political parties are, in sum, best conceptualized as tripartite systems of interactions that embrace party leaders and officials, the thousands of anonymous activists who work for candidates and party causes, the people who loyally vote for the party's candidates, and the men and women elected to office on the party's label. Simply put, parties are the somewhat unwieldy combination of a party organization, a party in government, and a party in the electorate (see Figure 1.1).[5] Although breaking the parties down into these separate parts may facilitate their study, it is important not to lose sight of the fact that much of the character of the American parties is defined by how they are combined by the dynamic interaction among the parts. The reality of this interaction pervades the American parties and is especially noticeable as the parties operate in the electoral process.[6]

The Party Organization

In the party organization, one finds the formally chosen party leaders, the informally anointed ones, the legions of local captains and leaders, the ward and precinct workers, the members and activists of the party—that is, all those who give their time, money, and skills to the party, whether as leaders or as followers. The organization operates in part through the formal machinery of committees and conventions set by the laws of the fifty states and in part through its own informal apparatus. Here one finds the centers of party authority and bureaucracy, and here one also observes the face-to-face contacts and interactions that characterize an organization of any kind.

The Party in Government

The party in government is made up of those who have captured office under the label of the party and of those who seek to do so. The chief executives and legislative parties of the nation and the states are its major components. Although in many ways they are not subject to the control or discipline of the party organization, they do, in the broadest sense, speak for the party. Their pronouncements are the most audible

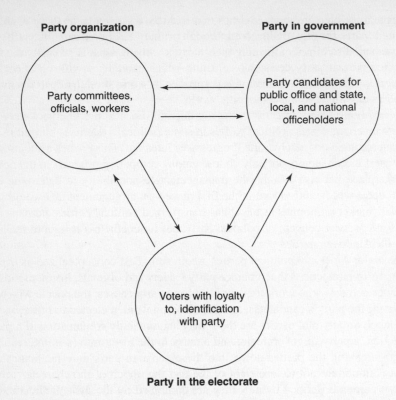

Figure 1.1 The three-part political party.

party statements and carry the greatest weight with the public. A party's president or leader in the Congress claims more attention than its national chairperson. Its governor or state legislative leader usually has more visibility as a party spokesperson than its state chairperson. Even though these two components of the party regularly work together to achieve their many common goals, there sometimes arises a tension between the party organization and the party in government because the goals of holding particular offices and achieving maximal party strength are not always compatible. The existence of such a tension, as the two components compete for scarce resources in pursuit of somewhat different goals, is ample testimony to the need to treat them as separate parts of the party.

The Party in the Electorate

The party in the electorate is the party's least well-defined part. It comprises the men and women who affiliate casually with it, show it some degree of loyalty, participate in the selecting of its candidates for office, and vote habitually for it, even if they are not active participants in the party organization or do not interact with its leaders and activists. Many of these "partisans" may be registered officially with the party where the state prescribes party registration (and more than half do), but many others are no less a part of the electoral party, even though they have not taken the official step of declaring a party for registration purposes. These individuals are not subject to the incentives and disciplines of the party organization and, in the case of party nominations, often vie with the organization for influence. They are, in effect, the regular consumers of the party's candidates and appeals. As such, they make up the coalitions necessary for effective political power in the American political system. Their association with the party is a passive one, however—accepting here, rejecting there, always threatening the party with the fickleness of their affections.

In their three-part structure, therefore, the major American parties include mixed, varied, and even contradictory and conflicting components. Each party, for example, is a political organization with active, even disciplined participants. It is also an aggregate of unorganized partisans who may begrudge the party organization even the merest public gesture of support or loyalty. The party thus embraces the widest range of involvement and commitment. It is a reasonably well-defined, voluntary political organization and, at the same time, an open, public collection of loyalists.

Perhaps the most telling characteristic of the major American parties, therefore, is the relationship that their clientele—the party in the electorate—has to them. Other political organizations, such as interest groups and ad hoc campaign organizations, usually work to attract supporters beyond their members and workers, but this wider clientele remains outside the political organization. This is not so with the political party. The party in the electorate is more than an external group to be wooed and mobilized. State laws usually permit it a voice in the selection of the parties' candidates in the direct primary, and in many states it helps select local party officials such as ward and precinct committeepersons. Consequently, the major American party is an open, inclusive, semipublic political organization. It includes both a tangible political organization and its own political clientele (as well as the party in government, of course). In this combination of exclusive organization and inclusive clientele, of organization and electorate, the American political party stands apart from the other political organizations and parties elsewhere.

A complicating reality of American politics is how much each major party differs from state to state in the relationships and interactions among its three sectors. The Republicans and the Democrats are so decentralized and so diverse that virtually every state party has its own distinctive mix of the three. Party organizations, for example, differ in form from state to state; in a few the party organization may dominate the party in government, whereas in others the reverse is the case. Also, party electorates differ in composition and in the bases of their loyalties; in some states the two parties in the electorate divide roughly along social class lines, but in others they do not. The parties also differ from state to state in their inclusivity for the purpose of nominating candidates for office. In some states, a voter can participate in a party's nomination process merely by voting for a candidate of that party on a ballot that includes candidates from both parties. In others, the act prior to election day of registering with the party is necessary for a voter to participate in that party's nomination process. Indeed, much of the distinctive quality of a state party is a reflection of the form and composition of each of the party sectors and of their relationships with each other.

THE PARTY AS A CLUSTER OF ACTIVITIES

Political parties also can be viewed from the perspective of what they do rather than what they are. In varying degrees, the competitive political parties of every democracy perform three sets of activities: They select candidates and contest elections, they propagandize on behalf of a party ideology or program, and they attempt to guide the elected officeholders of government to provide particular policy or patronage benefits.[7] The degree of emphasis that any particular political party puts on each of these individual activities varies within and between countries, but no party completely escapes the necessity of any of them.

Parties as Electors

It often appears that the American parties are little more than regular attempts to capture public office. Electoral activity so dominates the life of the American party that its metabolism follows almost exactly the cycles of the election calendar. Party activity and vitality reach a peak at the elections; between elections, the parties go into hibernation. Party activity is goal oriented, and in American politics most of the general goals as well as the goals of the individual sectors depend ultimately on electoral victory. It is, in fact, chiefly in the attempt to achieve their often separate goals through winning public office that the three sectors of the party are brought together in unified action.

Parties as Propagandizers

Second, the American parties carry on a series of loosely related activities that perhaps can best be called education or propagandization. There is, of course, a school of thought that argues that the American parties fail almost completely to function on behalf of ideas or ideologies. The Democrats and the Republicans, to be sure, do not espouse the all-inclusive ideologies of a European Marxist or proletarian party. They do, however, represent the interests of and the issue stands congenial to the groups that identify with them and support them. In this sense, they become parties of business or labor, of the advantaged or the disadvantaged. Moreover, events since the 1960s suggest that ideology in a purer sense may be playing a more prominent role for the American parties. In presidential politics alone, one merely needs to mention the Goldwater conservatism of 1964, the McGovern liberalism of 1972, and the Reagan conservatism of the 1980s as indicative of how ideas can guide the activities of the political party.

Parties as Governors

Virtually all officeholders in American national and state governments were elected as either Democrats or Republicans. Not surprisingly, these partisan perspectives pervade the governmental process. The legislatures of forty-nine states (the exception is nonpartisan Nebraska, but even there clear partisan ties are obvious to close observers and to many voters) and the United States Congress are organized along party lines, and the voting of their members shows party discipline and cohesion. To be sure, on controversial issues that cohesion is irregular, sporadic, and often unpredictable in most legislatures. Yet, in the aggregate, an important degree of party discipline does exist. In executive branches, presidents and governors depend on their fellow partisans for executive talent and count on their party loyalty to bind them to the executive programs. Even the American judiciary cannot escape the organizing and directing touch of the parties, although the effects of this touch are highly muted.

These, then, are the chief overt activities of democratic political parties generally and of American parties in particular. They are the activities that the parties set out consciously to perform. Any book on American parties must examine them.

To list these activities of the parties, however, is not to suggest that the American parties monopolize any or all of them. The parties compete with nonparty political organizations over the ability and the right to perform them. The American parties, having organized the legislatures, battle constantly and often with little success against interest groups and constituency pressures in order to firm up party lines for votes on major bills. In attempting to nominate candidates for public office, especially at the local level, the party faces often insurmountable competition from interest groups, community elites, and powerful local personalities, each of whom may be sponsoring pet candidates. In stating issues and ideologies, they are often overshadowed by the fervor of the minor (third) parties, the ubiquitous interest groups, the mass media, public figures, and political action groups.

These patterns of party activity also affect the party structure and its three sectors. The emphasis on the electoral activities of American parties, for example, elevates the party in government to a position of unusual power, even dominance. It frequently eclipses the party organization for the favor of the party in the electorate. In parties more strongly linked to issues and ideologies—such as those of continental Europe—party organizations, by contrast, often have been able to dictate to legislative parties.

On the other hand, individuals from all three sectors of the party may unite in specific activities. Party organization activists loyal to officeholders may unite with those persons, with other individuals of the party in government, and with individuals in the party electorate to return them to public office. When the election is won or lost, they very likely will drift apart again. Therefore, one finds within the parties certain functional clusters or nuclei, certain groups of individuals, drawn together in a single, concerted action.[8] Small and informal task groups cut across the differences in structure and goals that characterize the three party sectors. In American politics, alliances and coalitions are far more common within the parties than between them.

THE INDIRECT CONSEQUENCES OF PARTY ACTIVITY

The goal-seeking behavior of any individual or organization has indirect, sometimes even unintended, consequences. By pursuing its legislating activities, for example, Congress may be said to be either resolving or aggravating great areas of social conflict, depending on the judgment of the observer. Similarly, interest groups, in pursuing their particular goals in the legislative process, are also providing an informal, auxiliary avenue of representation. The same search for the indirect consequences of party activities is an old tradition in the study of the American parties. It produces rich insights into the contributions of the parties to the American political system. Yet it can be frustrating because it is much easier to prove or establish the activity itself than the results or consequences it brings about.[9]

It is not surprising, then, that scholars of the American political parties have seen and recorded differing sets of these indirect consequences or functions, as many refer to them. What follows is a discussion of some of the most readily identifiable and thus most frequently mentioned of these consequences of party activity. Each contributes in important ways to the operation of the American political system and to the democratic process.

The parties participate in the political socialization of the American electorate by transmitting political values and information to large numbers of current and future voters. They preach the value of political commitment and activity, and they convey information and cues about a confusing political system. By symbolizing and representing a political point of view, they offer uninformed or underinformed citizens a map of the political world. They help them form political judgments and make political choices, and, in both physical and psychological terms, they make it easier to be politically active.

The American parties also contribute to the accumulation of political power. They aggregate masses of political individuals and groups and thereby organize blocs that are powerful enough to govern or to oppose those who govern. For the confused and confounded citizen, they simplify, and often oversimplify, the political world into more comprehensible choices. By using attachment to the party as a perceptual screen, the voter has a master clue for assessing issues and candidates. Thus, both within the individual and in the external political world, the political party operates to focus political loyalties on a small number of alternatives and then to accumulate support behind them.

Because they devote so much effort to contesting elections, the American parties dominate the recruitment of political leadership. One needs only to run down a list of the members of any legislature, a cabinet, or even the courts to see how many of them entered public service through a political party or through partisan candidacy for office. Because the American parties pervade all governmental levels in the federal system, they may recruit and elevate leadership from one level to another. Furthermore, the orderly contesting of elections enables the parties to routinize political change, especially change of governmental leadership. More than one commentator has noted the disruptive quality of leadership changes in those countries in which no stable political parties compete in regular elections.

Finally, the American parties are a force of unification in the divided American political system. The fragmentation of government is an incontestably crucial fact of American politics. To the fragmentation of the nation and the fifty states, multiplied by the threefold separation of powers in each, the two great national parties bring a unifying, centripetal force. They unify with an obviously limited efficiency; for example, they often fail to bind the president and the Congress together in causes that can transcend the separation of powers. Their similar symbols and traditions, however, are a force for unity in governmental institutions marked by decentralization and division.

THE SPECIAL CHARACTERISTICS OF POLITICAL PARTIES

It now is time to end these excursions into related topics and to narrow the search for political parties. The goal is not to produce a memorable, one-sentence definition, for no such rendering could hope to capture the fullness of the meaning of party. Rather, it is important to come to an understanding of what characterizes the political parties and sets them apart from other political organizations—to have a firm grasp, in short, of what the political parties are and what they do.[10]

All political organizations exist to organize and mobilize their supporters either to capture public office or to influence the activities of those already in public office. If the term *political party* is to have any meaning at all, however, there must also be clear lines of differentiation between parties and other political organizations, especially the large national interest (or pressure) groups. The differences are there, however, even if they are really only differences among species of the same genus.

Commitment to Electoral Activity

Above all, the political party is distinguished from other political organizations by its concentration on the contesting of elections. Although the major American parties do not monopolize the contesting of elections, their preeminence in this activity cannot be questioned. Other political organizations do attempt to influence American electoral politics. Some seem to do little else. In many localities, interest groups encourage or discourage candidates, work for them within parties, contribute to campaign funds, and get their members to the polls to support them. Other nonparty organizations may raise funds, organize endorsements, and recruit workers for some candidate's campaign for public office. The parties, however, are occupied with the contesting of elections in a way and to a degree that the other political organizations are not. Indeed, their names and symbols are the ones the states recognize for inclusion on most ballots, and their presence is felt throughout the nation, intruding even into its remotest corners.

Mobilization of Numbers

Commitment not only to electoral activity but also to its organizational consequences characterizes the political party. Because the party chooses to work toward its goals largely in elections, it must recruit an enormous supportive clientele. Organizations that attempt to influence legislative committees or rule making in administrative agencies may succeed with a few strategists and the support of only a small, well-mobilized clientele. The political parties, in order to win elections, must depend less on the intricate skills and maneuverings of organizational strategists and more on the mobilization of large numbers of citizens. Party appeals must be broad and inclusive; the party cannot afford either exclusivity or a narrow range of concerns. It is at the opposite pole from the "single-issue" group or organization. To put it simply, the major political party has committed itself through its concentration on electoral politics to the mobilization of large numbers of citizens in large numbers of elections, and from that commitment flow many of its other characteristics.

Devotion to Political Activity

The major American political parties and similar parties elsewhere are characterized by a full commitment to political activity. They operate solely as political organizations, solely as instruments of political action. Interest groups and most other political organizations, by contrast, move freely and frequently from political to nonpolitical activities and back again. The AFL-CIO, for example, seeks many of its goals and interests in nonpolitical ways, especially through collective bargaining. It may, however, turn to political action to support sympathetic candidates or to lobby before Congress when political avenues appear to be the best or the only means to achieve its goals. Every organized group in the United States is a potential political organization. Still, the interest group almost always maintains some sphere of nonpolitical action.

Endurance

Political parties also are marked by an uncommon stability and persistence. The personal clique, the faction, the ad hoc campaign organization, and even many interest groups seem by contrast almost political will-o'-the-wisps, which disappear as suddenly as they appear. The size and the abstractness of the political parties, their relative independence from personalities, and their continuing symbolic strength for thousands of voters assure them a far greater longevity. Both major American parties can trace their histories for much more than a century, and the major parties of the other Western democracies have impressive, if shorter, life spans. It is precisely this enduring, ongoing quality that enhances their value as reference symbols. The parties are there as points of reference year after year, election after election, and candidate after candidate, giving continuity and form to the choices Americans face and the issues they debate.

Political Symbols

Finally, the political parties are distinguished from other political organizations by the extent to which they operate as cues or symbols or even more vaguely as emotion-laden objects of loyalty. For millions of Americans, the party label is the chief cue for their decisions about candidates or issues. It is the point of reference that allows them to organize and simplify the buzzing confusion and strident rhetoric of American politics. It shapes their perceptions and structures their choices; it relates their political values and goals to the real options of American politics.

Resemblance to Other Organizations

To reemphasize a previous point, however, the differences between parties and other political organizations are often slender. Interest groups certainly contest elections to some degree, and the larger ones have achieved impressive stability and duration and considerable symbolic status. They can recruit candidates and give political clues and cues to their members and fellow travelers. The unique American nomination process enables them to play an important role in selecting party candidates for office. Interest groups also promote interests and issue positions, try to influence and organize officeholders, and (through their political action committees) contribute to their campaigns. They do not, however, and in most localities cannot, offer their names and symbols for candidates to use on the ballot. That difference and the whole question of size and degree separates their activities and political roles from those of the parties.

So similar are the major parties to some other political organizations that in important respects they resemble them more closely than they do the minor or third parties. The minor political parties are only nominally electoral organizations. Not even the congenital optimism of candidates can lead Socialists or Prohibitionists to expect victories on the ballot. Lacking local organization, as most of them do, they resemble the major parties less than do the complex, nationwide interest groups such as the Chamber of Commerce or the AFL-CIO. Also, their membership base, often dependent upon a single issue, may be just as narrow, just as exclusively recruited, as that of most interest groups. Even so, minor parties do appear on the ballot, and their candidates can receive public funding where it is available—assuming that they have qualified, typically by attaining a certain number of votes in previous elections. In these respects, they are more like the major parties than are the large interest groups.

THE EVOLUTION OF AMERICAN PARTIES

To see the special role and character of political parties and how they may have changed as their environment changed, it is useful to look at their origins and evolution in the United States—the country credited with the development of the world's first parties. This history is one of an almost 200-year alliance with popular democracy. (For a summary of American party history, see the box on p. 32.) The American parties grew up in response to the expansion of the adult suffrage and to all the changes it brought to American politics. It is also a history of change in the relative positions of the three different parts of the party, as first the party in government, then the party organizations, and then the parties in government and in the electorate enjoyed their period of ascendancy.[11]

The Founding of American Parties

In the first years of the Republic, the vote was limited in almost every state to those free men who could meet property-holding or tax-paying requirements. Furthermore, the framers of the new Constitution of 1787 intentionally limited the power of individual voters at elections. The president was to be chosen, not by a direct vote of the electorate, but indirectly by the electoral college. The method of selection of each state's electors, was left to the individual state legislatures. Also, although election to the House of Representatives was entrusted to a direct popular vote, that of the Senate was not. Its members were to be chosen by the respective state legislatures. It was, in short, a cautious and limited beginning to democratic self-government.

In their first years, the organizations that were to become the American parties reflected this politics of a limited suffrage and indirect elections. Their incipient national form, in fact, was largely as caucuses of like-minded members of the Congress, involving only the men and the issues of politics in the nation's capital. These congressional caucuses nominated presidential candidates and mobilized groups of political figures supportive of or opposed to the administration of the time. Gradually, during the 1790s, these factions began to take on the permanence commonly associated with political parties as they struggled to keep their members focused on their collective purpose. The Federalists, as the dominant group came to be called, were organized around Alexander Hamilton and championed a measure of central direction of the economy. The opposition, rallying around Thomas Jefferson and James Madison (see box on p. 21), favored the protection of states' rights from national government interference. These nascent "parties" were dominated by their party in government at the national level.

Party organization at the grass roots by the congressional caucuses initially was restricted to "committees of correspondence" between national and local leaders, although each side did establish a newspaper to propagandize on behalf of its cause. These were the first formal outreaches to the leaders and voters "back home," and through them officeholders organized and communicated with the electorate. The party impetus was not wholly one sided, however, flowing from the capital to the grass roots. Organized popular protest against the Jay Treaty and other unpopular administration measures, as well as protoparty conflict within the various states, provided fertile ground for the development of parties on a national scale.

One of these incipient parties, the Democratic-Republicans, was transformed into the first semblance of a modern-style party by organizing efforts in the states and localities in advance of the 1800 presidential elections. On the other hand, the Federalists, their elitism preventing parallel organizational efforts, virtually disappeared in most states shortly after the defeat of their last president, John Adams, in 1800. The pressures for democratization already were powerful enough by the early 1800s to vanquish an infant party whose leaders in the government were unable to adapt to the necessity for organizing a mass electorate, especially in the growing states of the frontier.[12]

The Democratic-Republicans, the new party of agrarian interests and the frontier, quickly established their superiority and enjoyed a twenty-year period of one-party monopoly. So thorough was their domination by the time of James Monroe's presidency that the absence of party and political conflict was dubbed the "Era of Good Feelings." Despite the decline of one party and the rise of another, however, the nature of the parties did not change. It was a time during which government and politics were the business of an elite of well-known, well-established men, and the parties reflected the politics of the time. In both of his successful races for the

JAMES MADISON: ANTI-PARTY THEORIST, PARTY FOUNDER

James Madison, the fourth president of the United States and one of the most important framers of the American Constitution, was a paradoxical combination of theorist and activist when it came to political parties.

Writing in No. 10 of *The Federalist* to justify a new constitution of which he was one of the prime architects, Madison railed against political parties in his famous warning against the "mischiefs of faction:"

> Complaints are everywhere heard from our most considerate and virtuous citizens, equally the friends of public and private faith and of public and personal liberty, that our governments are too unstable, that the public good is disregarded in the conflicts of rival parties, and that measures are too often decided, not according to the rules of justice and the rights of the minor party, but by the superior force of an interested and overbearing majority.[13]

Just a few years later, locked in conflict with the administration over deep policy disagreements, however, Madison became a founder and key organizer of what some scholars have seen as the world's first political party, the Democratic-Republicans. He was the leader of the congressional opposition to the Washington administration in the early 1790s and especially to its guiding figure, Alexander Hamilton. After leaving the Congress in mid-decade, he worked with his lifelong friend and ally, Thomas Jefferson, to organize the increasing opposition to the administration in the countryside. Their efforts met with extraordinary success—with Jefferson's presidential victory in 1800 and with the ensuing dominance of their Democratic-Republican party into the 1820s.

Madison probably would not have seen any contradiction between his thoughts and actions. In *The Federalist,* he justified the Constitution as necessary to contain the natural emergence of factions and to prevent them from undermining democracy. In founding the Democratic-Republicans, he was exercising his right to oppose the policies of one faction by organizing another.

presidency (1816 and 1820), Monroe was the only nominee of the Democratic-Republican caucus in the Congress. The absence of party competition, moreover, made extensive grass roots organization unnecessary, thus stalling further development of the parties.

The early politics of the country began, however, to undergo sharp changes in the 1820s. The struggle for universal white male suffrage, focused primarily on eliminating real property qualifications for voting, was over in most states by that decade, at least where state and federal elections were concerned. (Property qualifications lingered in local elections, in some places into the twentieth century, where revenues were raised from assessments on property.) The growing tide of democratization also made more public officials subject to popular election.[14]

The most obvious change in the 1820s, occurring so precipitously at the national level that its evolutionary foundation in the states often is obscured, was the emergence of the presidential election process that has endured to this day. The framers of the Constitution had crafted a curious arrangement for the selection of the president, known as the electoral college. They prescribed a method of indirect election in which each state, in a manner determined by its legislature, would choose a number of presidential electors equivalent to the size of its congressional delegation; these electors in turn would meet in the state to cast their votes for president, with the national winner being the candidate who received a majority of the states' electoral votes. If no candidate received a majority, the president was to be selected by the House of Representatives, with one vote per state.

With the electoral college arrangement, the Constitutional convention was able to sidestep some difficult and divisive questions regarding selection of the chief executive. Leaving the choice of electors to the state legislatures avoided the setting of uniform election methods and suffrage requirements (involving also the contentious matter of slavery), issues on which the framers themselves were divided and on which federal intervention to dictate state practices where the states had hitherto enjoyed autonomy might have produced state opposition. Requiring electors to meet simultaneously within their respective states also prevented a cabal among electors from different states to put forward their own choice for president.

In the early years of the Republic, state legislatures adopted various methods for selecting presidential electors. From the first, a few states adopted popular elections, albeit typically with electorates restricted to property owners or taxpayers. This number grew during the next three decades, although unevenly as partisan majorities within the state legislatures engaged in the time-honored practice of manipulating election laws to their short-term advantage. Lame-duck Federalist legislatures were especially active around 1800 in turning to popular election to avoid the sure results of a transition in legislative control to the Democratic-Republicans. By the 1820s, though, popular election had come to predominate, and after 1828 only in South Carolina were presidential electors selected by the state legislature.[15]

The move in the states to popular election of presidential electors in the 1820s coincided with and contributed to the demise of the congressional caucus in the presidential selection process and, more generally, as the predominant force within the parties. With their hegemony in Congress and the country in the two decades after 1800, the Democratic-Republicans were able to select the president through their control of the nomination process. As the tide of democratization strengthened, however, the practice of caucus nominations fell under increasing criticism as the work of a narrow-based and self-perpetuating elite in the nation's capital.

Quite apart from criticism, however, the caucus system began to decline from its own infirmities. The attempt of the Democratic-Republicans to nominate a presidential candidate in 1824 was a shambles. The chosen candidate of the caucus, William Crawford, ran fourth in the race, and because no candidate won a majority in the electoral college, it was left to the House of Representatives to choose among John Quincy Adams, Henry Clay, and Andrew Jackson. The House chose Adams over

Jackson, the popular and electoral vote front runner in the election. When Jackson, in turn, defeated Adams in 1828, the nation entered a new phase of party politics.

The Emergence of a National Two-Party System

This "new" party politics emerged in the 1830s, partially as a product of powerful centrifugal tendencies in American politics. First, the nonparty politics of the Era of Good Feelings gave way to a two-party system that has prevailed ever since. Andrew Jackson took the frontier and agrarian wing of the Jeffersonians into what is now thought of as the Democratic party. The National Republicans, whose candidate in 1832 was Henry Clay, merged with the Whigs, and bipartyism in the United States was born. Second, and just as important, the parties as political institutions began to change. The Jacksonian Democrats held the first national nominating convention in 1832 at which, appropriately, Jackson himself was nominated for a second term. (The Whig and Anti-Masonic parties had both held more limited conventions a year before.) The campaign for the presidency also became more "popular" and especially less dominated by a national political elite, as new campaign organizations and tactics brought the contest to more and more people. As a consequence, Jackson came to the White House for a second term with a popular mandate as the leader of a national political party. Larger numbers of citizens were voting than had ever voted before as the tide of democratization seemed irresistible.

At the same time, party organization in the states had a new burst of growth, and conventions of state and local leaders increasingly replaced the narrower caucuses as the means of nominating candidates for state and local office. Before the middle of the century, therefore, party organization was developing throughout the nation, and the party convention—an assemblage of state and local party leaders held both in the states and nationally—became an increasingly common way of picking party candidates. Also, by 1840, the Whigs and the Democrats established themselves in the first truly national party system, one in which both parties were established and competitive in all the states.

Modern political parties pretty much as they are known today—with their characteristic organizational structures, bases of loyal voters, and enduring alliances among governmental leaders—had thus arrived by the middle of the nineteenth century. The American parties were, in fact, the first modern parties in Western history, and their arrival reflected, above all, the early expansion of the electorate in the United States. The comparable development of parties in Great Britain did not occur until the 1870s, after further extension of the adult male electorate in the Reform Acts of 1832 and 1867.[16]

The Golden Age of the Parties

Just as the parties were reaching their maturity, they and American politics received another massive infusion of voters from a new source: immigration from Europe. Hundreds of thousands of Europeans—the great majority from Ireland and Germany—came to the country before the Civil War. So many immigrated, in fact, that their very coming and their entry into American politics became a political issue. The newcomers found a ready home in the Democratic party, and a nativist third party, the American party (the so-called Know-Nothing party), sprang up in response in the 1850s. The tide of immigration was only temporarily halted by the Civil War. New nationalities came from 1870 on in a virtually uninterrupted flow until Congress closed the door to mass immigration in the 1920s. More than five million arrived in the 1880s (they comprised one-tenth of the 1880 resident population), and ten million came between 1905 and 1914 (one-eighth of the 1900 resident population).

The political parties played an important role in assimilating these huge waves of immigrants. The American cities offered industrial jobs to the newcomers from abroad, and they settled heavily in them. It was there in the cities that a new kind of party organization, the city "machine," developed in response to the immigrants' problems and vulnerabilities. The machines were more than impressively efficient organizations. They were social service mechanisms that helped the new arrivals cope with a new country and with all the problems of urban, industrial society. They softened the hard edge of poverty, they smoothed the way with government and the law, and they taught the immigrants the ways and customs of their new life. Moreover, they were in many instances indistinguishable from the government of the city; theirs was the classic instance of "party government" in the American experience. They also were the vehicle by which the new urban working class won control of the cities away from the largely Anglo-Saxon, Protestant elites who had prevailed for so long. Thus, the parties again became an instrument of the aspirations of new citizens, just as they had been in the 1830s. In doing so, they achieved their high point of power and influence in American history.

The American parties—with their organizational component now predominant—thus had reached their zenith, something of a "golden age" indeed, by the beginning of the twentieth century. Party organization now existed in all the states and localities; it positively flourished in the industrial cities. Parties achieved an all-time high in discipline in the Congress and in most state legislatures. They controlled campaigns for public office—they held rallies, did door-to-door canvassing, and brought the voters to the polls. They controlled access to a great deal of public employment, often including who would represent the state in Washington. They were an important source of information and guidance for a largely uneducated and often illiterate electorate. Indeed, they rode the crest of an extraordinarily vital American politics; the latter half of the nineteenth century featured the highest voter turnouts in the history of American presidential elections. The parties suited the needs and limitations of the new voters and the problems of mobilizing majorities in the new and raw industrial society. If ever a time and a political organization were well matched, this was it.[17]

Parties after Their Golden Age

To be sure, the democratic impetus was not spent by the turn of the century. The electorate continued to expand with the enfranchisement of women, with the delayed securing of the vote for blacks, and with the lowering of the voting age to eighteen. The move toward direct, popular elections and away from the indirection the Founding Fathers favored also continued its inexorable course with adoption of the Seventeenth Amendment which decreed the direct election of senators. Just as important for the parties, however, were the changes wrought in them in the name of the continuing commitment to egalitarianism and popular democracy.

What was a golden age for parties in terms of their influence over the American political process was seen disparagingly by many as a "gilded age," in which party control of politics had bred rampant corruption and inefficiency in government.[18] Fat, powerful, and even arrogant at the end of the nineteenth century, the parties fell under attack by the Progressive reformers and never have regained the exalted position they enjoyed in the three decades after the Civil War. The reformers enacted the direct primary to give the citizenry a voice in party nominations, and large numbers of state legislatures wrote laws to define and limit party organizations. The business of nominating a president was made more popular by the establishment of presidential primaries in the states, and activists within the parties reformed their national conventions. All in all, the Progressive reforms succeeded in wresting control of the parties from their professional organizations. As the twenty-first century approaches, Americans have a party politics born and shaped in the triumph of the democratic ethos and its expectations—but, some would say, increasingly incapable of playing the role it once played in American politics.

These reforms were to some extent intended to diminish the power and position the parties, and especially their organizational part, had achieved by the end of the 1800s. To that extent, they succeeded. For these and a number of other reasons, the heyday of the American parties passed. The theme of the decline of the parties runs through many commentaries on the American parties these days, and it certainly will be addressed in this one.[19]

It would be too pat to conclude that these changes mark the next shift in power within the party—beginning with the "party in government," then to the party organization during the golden age of the parties, and now to the "party in the electorate." The Progressive reforms indeed did empower ordinary citizens in party affairs at the expense of the party organizations and their leaders who had played the predominant role in intraparty politics before. In many cases, these citizens had little if any attachment to the party itself, however, making it difficult to conceive of them as the party electorate. The effect of the Progressive reforms also was to free candidates for office from party control or discipline and, by weakening the party's campaign capabilities overall, make the party less relevant to them. Some would contend that this change strengthened their position vis-a-vis the party organization and perhaps even made them less vulnerable to popular control.

Not all reforms in traditional party practices, though, have undermined the organizational component of the parties. Beginning many decades ago and increasing in crescendo in the 1960s, party rules for the selection of candidates for office, especially the presidency, have become more uniform across the nation. Especially active in promoting this nationalization of party practices was the Democratic party, through its national committee and quadrennial national convention. Simultaneously, the Republicans were enhancing the capacity of their national party organization to support candidates for office throughout the country, an activity soon emulated by the Democrats. The result of these two nationalizing thrusts, the one rules-based and the other organizational, has been to strengthen the national party organizations at a time when state and particularly local organizations had atrophied. Whether this new nationalization of the parties represents a fundamental alteration in their nature is not yet clear, but it has shifted the balance of organizational power from the grass roots to the center.

Even amidst all these changes, the parties remain to a significant extent what they were eighty or a hundred years ago: the preeminent political organizations of mass, popular democracy. They developed and grew with the expansion of the suffrage and the popularizing of electoral politics. They were and remain the invention by which large numbers of voters come together to control the selection of their representatives. They rose to prominence at a time when a new electorate of limited knowledge and limited political sophistication needed the guidance of their symbols. Thus it was that the modern American political party was born and reached its time of glory in the nineteenth century. When one talks today of the decline of the parties, it is the standard of that Golden Age against which the decline is measured.

THE PARTY IN ITS ENVIRONMENT

This brief excursion into the historical development of American parties calls attention to forces in their environment that shape both their form and their activities. There is a temptation in a book on political parties to treat them more or less in isolation. Yet, useful as this isolation is for focusing attention, it may give the false impression that political parties are autonomous structures, moving without constraint within the political system. Once the importance of environmental pressures is recognized, though, one must resist the opposite temptation to imagine a party environment that includes virtually every other structure and process in the political system and a great deal outside it. Some influences on the parties clearly are more powerful and insistent than others. It will suffice to limit a discussion of the parties' environment to these.

Electorates and Elections

As the preceding section indicates, the expansion of the American electorate shaped the very origin and development of the parties as political organizations. Furthermore, each new group of voters that enters the electorate challenges the parties to readjust their appeals. The parties must compete for the votes and support of new voters, and the necessity of doing so forces them to reconsider their strategies for building the coalitions that can win elections.

Similarly, the fortunes of the parties are also bound up with the nature of American elections. The move from indirect toward direct elections transformed both the contesting of elections and the parties that contested them. Should American presidents ever come to be directly elected, that change, too, would have its impact on the parties.

The election machinery in a state may indeed be thought of as an extensive regulation of the parties' chief political activity. At least, it is often difficult to determine where the regulation of the party ends and reform of electoral practices begins. Consider, for example, the replacement of nomination by conventions with the direct primary. It is both a significant addition to the machinery of American electoral processes and a sharp regulation of the way a party selects the candidates who bear its label in an election, and it was aimed by its originators, the Progressives, at diminishing party power. Even the relatively minor differences in primary law from one state to another—such as differences in the form of the ballot or the time of the year in which the primary occurs—are not without their impact on the parties. In short, the collective electoral institutions of the nation and of the fifty states set a matrix of rules and boundaries within which the parties compete for public office.

The Political Institutions

Very little in the American political system escapes the influence of the two most prominent American institutional features—federalism and the separation of powers. At the national level and in the states, American legislators and executives are elected independently of one another, and sometimes (frequently in recent years) the legislature and executive have come under the control of opposing parties. Most of the world's democracies, by contrast, have parliamentary systems in which the legislative majority chooses executive officials from among its own members. When that parliamentary majority dissolves, its control of the executive ends, and a new government must be formed. An important consequence of this institutional arrangement is that American legislative parties rarely even approach the degree of party discipline and party cohesion that is common in parliamentary systems.

The American institutional arrangement often exacerbates conflict between legislators and the executive of the same party. One reason is that the chief executive and cabinet secretaries are not simultaneously legislative party leaders as they are in a parliamentary system. Another is that legislative defiance of the executive on key party issues does not threaten to bring down the entire government and force new elections. Support for and opposition to executive programs often cut sharply across party lines in the American system to a degree rarely found in the parliamentary democracies.

The decentralization of American federalism, with its islands of state autonomy from national control, also has left its imprint on the American parties. It has instilled in them local political loyalties and generations of local, often provincial, political traditions. It has spawned an awesome range and number of public offices to fill, creating an electoral politics that in size and diversity dwarfs that of all other political systems. By permitting local rewards, local traditions, even local patronage systems, it has sustained a whole set of semiautonomous local parties within the two parties. The establishment of these local centers of power has worked mightily against the development of strong permanent national party organs.

Statutory Regulation

No other parties among the democracies of the world are so entangled in legal regulations as are the American parties. It was not always this way. Prior to the Progressive reforms near the beginning of the twentieth century, American parties essentially were self-governing political organizations, virtually unrestrained by state or federal law in pursuit of their core activities. During their golden age, for example, the parties nominated candidates for office by their own rules. The arrival of the direct primary around 1900 and recent reforms of the presidential nomination process at the behest of national party commissions but under the aegis of state laws have severely circumscribed this autonomy. Before the introduction of the secret ballot, the parties printed, distributed, and with a wary eye upon one another often even counted the ballots. The Australian (or secret) ballot reform changed all of this, vesting the responsibility for running elections in government, where it has remained ever since. The parties even played an active role in the distribution of government jobs, a practice that has largely disappeared under successive waves of civil service reform and recent judicial intervention.

Both state and, to a still limited degree, federal laws govern the parties today, producing an almost bewildering fifty-state variety of political parties. The forms of their organization are prescribed by the states in endless, often finicky, detail. The statutes on party organization set up grandiose layers of party committees and often chart the details of who will compose them, when they will meet, and what their agenda will be. State law also defines the parties themselves, often by defining the right to place candidates on the ballot. Numerous states also undertake to regulate the activities of parties; many, for example, regulate their finances, and most place at least some limits on their campaign practices. So severe can these regulations be, in fact, that in some states the parties have tried various strategies to evade the worst of the burdens. In recent years, the parties increasingly have been subjected to federal regulation in campaign practices and finances as well as through federal proscriptions against certain state practices, especially involving primary and general elections.[20]

The Political Culture

It is one thing to specify such tangibles in the parties' environment as regulatory statutes, electoral mechanisms, and even political institutions. It is quite another, however, to pin down so elusive a part of the party environment as the political culture. A nation's political culture is the all-enveloping network of the political norms, values, and expectations of its people. It is, in other words, the people's view of what the political system is, what it should be, and what their place is in it.[21]

The feeling that party politics is a compromising, somewhat dirty business has been a major and persistent component of the American political culture. Public opinion polls give evidence of that hostility toward partisan politics in recent years. A number of polls have found, for example, that American parents prefer that their sons and daughters not choose a full-time political career. In their estimation, politics as a vocation compares unfavorably with most occupations. The polls report a similarly low level of popular support for the parties, even in comparison with other governing institutions such as Congress, the Supreme Court, or the president which do not enjoy particularly high favor in these times. A 1994 survey demonstrated that support for the prevailing two-party system was so low that a total of 53 percent of the sample called for a third major political party.[22]

Suspicion of things partisan is only one element, however, in a multifaceted political culture that shapes the American parties. The views of Americans are relevant on such broad points as representative democracy itself. A constituency-centered view of representation, which holds that the representative ought to decide public questions on the basis of the interests of his or her local district, certainly retards the development of party discipline in American legislatures. More detailed public attitudes govern even such matters as the incentives for party activity and the kinds of campaign tactics a party or candidate chooses. Indeed, the whole issue of what we consider fair or ethical campaigning is simply a reflection of the norms and expectations of large numbers of Americans.

The Nonpolitical Environment

Much of the parties' nonpolitical environment works on them through the elements of the political environment. Changes in levels of education, for example, affect the political culture, the skills of the electorate, and the levels of political information. It is well known that less-educated Americans seem to accept party loyalty and discipline more easily than the better educated do, so overall educational levels affect the electorate's dependence upon political parties. Perhaps no force has been more important for party politics than the emergence of the modern mass media, especially television. By providing alternative sources of information to voters, the media have weakened party control over political campaigns—and, ironically, over the contacts between their own candidates and voters. With the importance it attaches to visual images, television too has elevated individuals over institutions in its coverage of politics.

Whether the impact of the nonpolitical environment is direct or indirect, however, may be beside the point. The impact is strong and often disruptive. The advent of a recession, for example, may have important repercussions on the parties. It may make raising money more difficult; it will certainly make patronage positions more attractive and perhaps even shift the incentives for recruiting the workers on whom the party organizations rely. It will also certainly define a very important issue for the electorate. If the crisis is especially severe, as was the Great Depression of the 1930s, it may even fracture and reorganize the pattern of enduring party loyalties, thereby changing the electoral standings of the parties.

What began in this chapter as a search for what parties are and what they do has concluded by looking at how they became what they are. To be sure, it is important to have a firm grasp of what is meant in referring to a political party, especially to understand its peculiar three-part nature: the party organization, the party in the electorate, and the party in government. Answers to the questions about party transformation or decline, so prominent in recent years here and in the former Communist nations of Eastern Europe and the Soviet Union, depend upon what is meant by *party*. The search for the parties, however, is, paradoxically, a search for more than the parties. It requires a grasp of the context, the environment, in which they are set and by which they are shaped.

Chapter
2

The American
Two-Party System

The most common party systems have been those in which either one political party dominates political life or many parties compete with one another for control of government. One-party systems have appeared in such diverse places as China, where the Communist party continues to exercise undiluted control; the Soviet Union and Eastern Europe, which the Communist party dominated until the 1990s; and Mexico, where the Partido Revolucionario Institucional's (or PRI) decades-long monopoly of elections only recently has received a serious challenge. By contrast, the European democracies typically harbor multiparty systems in which three, four, or more parties compete with one another, often without any single party being able to win a majority of the votes.[1]

One-partyism and multipartyism are not alien to the American experience. Some states or cities have had a long tradition of one-party hegemony that, if not as total as that characterizing Eastern Europe and the USSR a decade before or China today, nonetheless rivals the single-party control enjoyed by Mexico's PRI. In other areas, at certain times multipartyism has flourished. Minor or third parties and independent candidates have played important roles in American politics, and they seem to be increasingly important today. These varieties of multipartyism have been most visible at the presidential level in recent years. George C. Wallace came within 32 electoral votes of throwing the entire election into the unpredictable hands of the House of Representatives in 1968. In 1980 John Anderson, running without any party label, won almost 6 million popular votes. Ross Perot's independent presidential bid in 1992 gained the support of almost 20 million Americans for about 19 percent of the popular vote—the third highest percentage for a candidate outside of the major parties in history—and was transformed into a third party in 1996.

However colorful or captivating past incursions into two-party control may have been and however tempting it may be see the Perot challenge as a harbinger of the future, we must not let them divert our attention from the routines of American politics. For most of our history in most elections, two parties—not one or many—have fought only one another for victory. Even the rapid rise of the Republican party from its founding in 1854 to become one of two major parties two years later, displacing the Whig party in the process, is the third party exception that proves the rule. First Democrat versus Whig and then, since 1856, Democrat versus Republican, the United States has had a two-party system—a duopoly in national party competition.

For all its elegant simplicity, this conventional classification of party systems into one-party, two-party, and multiparty has a number of significant shortcomings, not the least of which is that it characterizes only past and present while ignoring trends toward the future. It focuses solely on the electoral dimension of political competition. Consequently, it overlooks the possibility that minor parties compete ideologically or programmatically with major parties, even if they do not compete electorally. By focusing only on the political parties, it ignores the full range of competition among all kinds of political organizations. By classifying parties exclusively by electoral competition, it ignores any differences in organization the parties may have and centers its measurement on the size of the party's electorate. Finally, by counting parties, it tends to ignore the implications of the word *system*. It overlooks the relationships and interactions one expects in any system and settles merely for the presence of competitive parties and their presumed competings in elections. This concept of the party system is deeply ingrained in both everyday use and scholarly literature in spite of its limitations. One has little choice but to work within its terms while bearing in mind that it may oversimplify, as most classification schemes do, a more complex political reality.[2]

THE NATIONAL PARTY SYSTEM

The American party system is and has been essentially a two-party system for at least 160 years. Beyond all subtle variations in competition, there is the inescapable, crucial fact that almost all partisan political conflict in the United States has been channeled through two major political parties. They rise and fall, they establish their seats of strength, they suffer their local setbacks and weaknesses, but they endure. Perhaps even more remarkable is the fact that one does not easily find another democracy in which two parties have so long and so thoroughly dominated politics.

The Republic, though, has not always had such two-party hegemony (see box on p. 32). The period before 1836 was one of party system instability. The Federalists established a short period of superiority during the presidency of George Washington but, failing to become a true political party, faded quickly with the rise and success of the Democratic-Republicans. They rode their success to a brief period of dominance that culminated in the one-party (or nonparty) politics of Monroe's two presidential terms. As the Washington-centered caucus method of nominations crumbled in the 1820s, however, new national parties appeared, and by 1836 a stable two-party system had emerged. For the almost sixteen decades since then, one party—the Democratic party—has sustained a place in the party system. In opposition, the Whigs survived until the 1850s and were replaced almost immediately by the infant Republican party. Both the Democratic and the Republican parties were briefly divided by the events of the Civil War along sectional lines, but the old party labels survived the war and, indeed, survive to this day.

THE AMERICAN MAJOR PARTIES

The list of the American major parties is short and select. In almost 200 years of history, only five political parties have achieved a competitive position in American national politics, and one of these five does not fully qualify as a party. Three lost it; the Democrats and Republicans maintain it to this day.

1. **The Federalist party, 1788–1816.** The champion of the new Constitution and strong national government, it was the first American political institution to resemble a political party, although it failed to fulfill all of the conditions of a full-fledged party. Its strength was rooted in the Northeast and the Atlantic seaboard, where it attracted the support of merchants, landowners, and established families of wealth and status. Limited by its narrow electoral base, it quickly fell before the success of the Democratic-Republicans.

2. **The Democratic-Republican party, 1800–1832.** Opposed to the extreme nationalism of the Federalists, although many of its leaders had been strong proponents of the Constitution, it was a party of the small farmers, workers, and less-privileged citizens who preferred the authority of the states. Like its leader, Thomas Jefferson, it shared many of the ideals of the French Revolution, especially the extension of the suffrage and the notion of direct popular self-government.

3. **The Democratic party, 1832–Present.** Growing out of the Jacksonian wing of the Democratic-Republicans, it was initially Andrew Jackson's party and the first really broad-based, popular party in the United States. On behalf of a coalition of less-privileged voters, it opposed such commercial goals as national banking and high tariffs; it also welcomed the new immigrants and opposed nativist opposition to them.

4. **The Whig party, 1836–1854.** This party, too, had roots in the old Jeffersonian party—in the Clay-Adams faction and in enmity to the Jacksonians. Opposed in its origins to the strong presidency of Jackson, its greatest leaders, Henry Clay and Daniel Webster, were embodiments of legislative supremacy. For its short life, the Whig party was an unstable coalition of many interests, among them nativism, property, and the new business and commerce.

5. **The Republican party, 1854–Present.** Born as the Civil War approached, this was the party of northern opposition to slavery and its spread to the new territories. Therefore, it was also the party of the Union, the North, Lincoln, the freeing of slaves, victory in the Civil War, and the imposition of Reconstruction. From the Whigs, it also inherited a concern for business, mercantile, and propertied interests.

Thus, the two-party drama is long, but its cast of major characters is short. Minor parties have briefly pushed themselves into competitiveness but have not yet been able to sustain themselves at the level of these five over several elections. The Democratic and Republican parties also have changed, of course, in their issues and appeals and in the coalitions that are their "parties in the electorate." All of those hedges, however, do not hide the fact that for over 140 years the Democratic and Republican parties have together made up the American two-party system.

The longevity of the two major parties, exceptional in itself, is paralleled by the closeness of their national competition. Of the thirty-two presidential elections from 1868 through 1992, only six were decided by a popular vote spread of more than 20 percent between the two major parties, and four of these occurred between 1920 and 1936; that is, in the twenty-six other elections, a shift of 10 percent of the vote or less would have given the other party's candidate the lead. Also, only four of the winners of those thirty-two presidential elections received more than 60 percent of the total popular vote: Warren G. Harding in 1920, Franklin Roosevelt in 1936, Lyndon Johnson in 1964, and Richard Nixon in 1972. The shade over 61 percent with which Lyndon Johnson won in 1964 set a new record for a president's percentage of the popular vote.[3] Fourteen of these thirty-two presidential elections were decided by a spread of less than 7 percent of the popular vote, and presidential elections have generally been so close that Dwight D. Eisenhower's 57.4 percent of the popular vote in 1956 was widely called a landslide. Recent decades have seen some of the closest presidential contests in American history (1960, 1968, 1976) but also some of the largest landslides (1964, 1972, 1984), although not all of the latter were won by the same party.

As close as the results of the presidential elections have been, the elections to Congress have been even closer. If we move to percentages of the two-party vote for ease of comparison, we quickly note the remarkable balance between the aggregate votes cast for Democratic and Republican candidates for the House of Representatives from across the United States for more than fifty years (Table 2.1). From 1932 through 1994, in none of the biennial House elections was there a difference greater than seventeen percentage points between the two parties; in twenty-four of the thirty-two elections, the spread between the major party candidates was less than 10 percent. The mean absolute percentage spread between the candidates of the two parties for the House was considerably less than that for the presidential candidates in the same period. Perhaps even more telling, in every year except 1948, 1960, 1968, 1976, and 1988, the margin between the two parties' congressional votes was smaller than that between their presidential aspirants.

The closeness and persistence of party competition in national politics is apparent, therefore, in even the quickest survey of recent electoral history. Even more impressive is the resilience of the major parties. Although from time to time the parties have lapsed from closely matched competitiveness, in the long run they have shown a remarkable facility for restoring balance. The Democrats recovered quickly from their failures of the 1920s and regained the White House after their electoral reversals in the 1980s. By the same token, the GOP (or Grand Old Party, a nickname that developed for the Republican party in the late 1800s) confounded the pessimists

Table 2.1   PERCENTAGE OF TWO-PARTY VOTE WON BY REPUBLICAN CANDIDATES
AND SPREAD IN PERCENTAGE OF TOTAL VOTES, FOR PRESIDENT AND
HOUSE OF REPRESENTATIVES: 1932–94

Year	Presidential Elections		House Elections	
	% Republican of Two-party Vote	% Republican Minus % Democratic of Total Vote	% Republican of Two-party Vote	% Republican Minus % Democratic of Total Vote
1932	40.8	−17.8	43.1	−13.1
1934			43.8	−11.9
1936	37.5	−24.3	41.5	−16.2
1938			49.2	− 1.6
1940	45.0	− 9.9	47.0	− 5.7
1942			52.3	4.5
1944	46.2	− 7.5	48.3	− 3.4
1946			54.7	9.3
1948	47.7	− 4.4	46.8	− 6.4
1950			49.9	0.0
1952	55.4	10.7	50.1	− 0.4
1954			47.5	− 5.5
1956	57.8	15.4	49.0	− 2.4
1958			43.9	−12.8
1960	49.9	− 0.2	45.0	− 8.8
1962			47.4	− 4.9
1964	38.7	−22.6	42.5	−15.3
1966			48.7	− 2.7
1968	50.4	0.7	49.1	− 1.7
1970			45.6	− 8.3
1972	61.8	23.2	47.3	− 5.3
1974			43.0	−17.0
1976	48.9	− 2.1	42.8	−14.1
1978			45.6	− 8.7
1980	55.3	9.7	48.7	− 2.4
1982			43.8	−12.7
1984	59.2	18.2	47.2	− 5.1
1986			44.9	− 9.9
1988	53.9	7.8	46.0	− 7.8
1990			46.0	− 7.9
1992	46.5	− 5.6	47.3	− 5.2
1994			52.4	4.7

Sources: Presidential data in 1932 from the *Statistical Abstract of the United States: 1992.* Congressional data for 1932 through 1992 and presidential data for 1936 through 1992 calculated from Harold Stanley and Richard G. Niemi, *Vital Statistics on American Politics* (Washington, D.C.: CQ Press, 1994), Tables 3–13 (President) and 3–17 (House). Data on 1994 are from *Congressional Quarterly Weekly Report,* December 3, 1994, p. 3460.

by springing back from the Roosevelt victories of the 1930s, landslide defeat in 1964, and the Watergate-related setbacks of the mid-1970s.

Is this aggregate record of winning and losing in national elections what we mean by a two-party system? Well, yes and no. It does express the vote support for national candidates under national party labels. Indeed, the struggle for the presidency every four years is undoubtedly the one occasion on which we actually do have national parties and a national party system. On the other hand, such measures are only aggregates, and they obscure the possibility of other types of party systems at a more localized level. That is, statements about national competitiveness gloss over the issue of how evenly competitiveness is spread across the states and localities.

THE FIFTY AMERICAN PARTY SYSTEMS

The closeness of both presidential elections and the aggregate vote for the House of Representatives often has been the product of considerable one-partyism below the national level. It was not until 1964, for example, that Georgia cast its first electoral votes ever for a Republican presidential candidate and Vermont voted Democratic for the first time since the Civil War. Moreover, although one may talk of the aggregate closeness of the biennial elections to the House, the aura of competitiveness in recent decades vanishes if one looks at individual races. Significant numbers of candidates win election to the House of Representatives with at least 60 percent of the total vote, although their number has declined somewhat in the last few elections. In 1994, for example, more than 60 percent of them did; 31 of these candidates were elected without any major-party opposition.[4]

If we are to discuss the varying degrees of competitiveness of the fifty state party systems, however, the practical problem of measuring competitiveness must be faced. It requires resolution of several difficult issues. First, which offices should be counted—president, governor, senator, statewide officials, state legislators? Singly or in what combination? A state may show strikingly different competitive patterns between its national and its state and local politics. Second, should we count vote totals and percentages or simply the offices won? Do we regard a party that averages 45 percent of the vote but never wins office any differently than one that averages around the 25 percent mark but occasionally is victorious? Third, how can we take into account the relative standings of more than two parties? Measuring two-party competition is easy because it can be summarized by a single number. Beyond two parties, the representation necessarily becomes more complex.

Fortunately, in categorizing the party systems of the American states, multiparty systems have been rare. The most conspicuous examples of them in the American experience are to be found in the states of the upper midwest. In the 1930s and 1940s, remnants of the Progressive movement—the Progressive party in Wisconsin, the Farmer-Labor party in Minnesota, and the Non-Partisan League in North Dakota—competed with some success against the major parties. In these and a few other instances of statewide multipartyism in the recent American past, however, the period of multipartyism was brief and ended with a return to two-partyism. Even the independent candidacy of Ross Perot in 1992 creates little problem of measurement. Although he polled between 9 and 30 percent of the popular vote across the fifty states, he ran alone. Whether the Perot movement will become an enduring third force in American electorate politics remains to be seen, but for now it does not require modification of a bipartisan framework.

The Ranney Index

The most familiar approach to measuring interparty competition below the national level is an index originated by Austin Ranney.[5] The Ranney index is an average of three indicators of Democratic strength over the specified time period: the percentage of the popular vote for Democratic gubernatorial candidates, the percentage of seats held by Democrats in the legislature, and the percentage of the time the Democrats held both the governorship and a majority in the state legislature. The resulting scores range from 1.00 (complete Democratic success) through .50 (Democratic and Republican parity) to .00 (complete Republican success).

Like any other summary measure, the Ranney index oversimplifies and some-times distorts the nature of competition. In particular, it is based wholly on state offices. While this protects the measure from abnormal patterns of national politics that may accompany landslide victories, it ignores national electoral patterns that may foreshadow what will occur in voting for state offices. In the South, for exam-ple, growing GOP strength was reflected first in competition for national offices and only later worked its way down to the state and local level. In these states, the Ran-ney index has shown less interparty competition than really exists. A second problem is that the dividing lines between categories are purely arbitrary. There is no magic threshold that separates competitive from one-party. Finally, any index score of course will vary depending upon the years on which it is calculated and the offices it covers, so one must beware of reifying a state's level of competition using its Ranney index number.

Snapshots are of great descriptive value, though, even if they cannot capture fully a complex and dynamic reality. Table 2.2 presents the calculations for the Ran-ney index through the 1994 elections. It shows much more balanced party competi-tion at the state level than had appeared in Ranney index compilations for earlier periods going all the way back to World War II. The principal change has been the movement of the southern states away from one-party Democratic status toward two-partyism—a movement that is paralleled on the other side by the most one-party Republican states from earlier times. The result is that interparty competition is more uniform throughout the fifty states than it probably has ever been.[6]

Variations in two-party competition among the fifty states have provided useful raw material for explanations of how competition develops and is sustained. Not so long ago, the states exhibiting the greatest degree of competition had a more edu-cated citizenry, stronger local party organizations, and larger and more urbanized populations.[7] As the states have become more uniform in their degree of interparty competition, the social and political differences between the more and less competi-tive states surely have narrowed as well.

Table 2.2 THE FIFTY STATES CLASSIFIED ACCORDING TO DEGREE OF INTERPARTY COMPETITION: 1989–94

One-Party Democratic (none)	California (.537)
	Oregon (.534)
Modified One-Party Democratic	New York (.530)
Arkansas (.831)	Maine (.528)
Louisiana (.828)	Delaware (.519)
Hawaii (.814)	Indiana (.518)
West Virginia (.798)	Connecticut (.518)
Rhode Island (.776)	——— .50 (perfect competition) ———
Maryland (.776)	Wisconsin (.496)
Kentucky (.741)	Pennsylvania (.496)
Georgia (.739)	Iowa (.481)
Mississippi (.709)	Alaska (.467)
Alabama (.666)	Illinois (.462)
Nebraska (.660)	Montana (.453)
Oklahoma (.659)	Colorado (.438)
Massachusetts (.658)	Michigan (.421)
	New Jersey (.410)
Two-Party	North Dakota (.394)
Tennessee (.649)	Ohio (.384)
New Mexico (.645)	Kansas (.359)
North Carolina (.636)	
Missouri (.633)	Modified One-Party Republican
Texas (.618)	Idaho (.338)
Virginia (.617)	South Dakota (.322)
Minnesota (.608)	Arizona (.316)
Florida (.594)	Wyoming (.313)
Washington (.568)	New Hampshire (.259)
Vermont (.568)	Utah (.232)
South Carolina (.550)	
Nevada (.548)	One-Party Republican (none)

Source: John F. Bibby and Thomas M. Holbrook, "Parties and Elections," in Virginia Gray and Herbert Jacob, eds., *Politics in the American States, Sixth Edition* (Washington, D.C.: CQ Press, 1995).

Competitiveness and Candidate Security

In a chapter focused on overall levels of interparty competition, it is easy to lose sight of the level of competitiveness for particular offices and how it has varied across time. For much of the history of the United States, especially throughout the nineteenth century, the prospect of victory for a candidate depended upon what party he or she represented. Candidates of the dominant party in one-party areas virtually were assured of victory. In more competitive constituencies, candidate fates were tied to the vicissitudes of fortune for their parties in response to national or statewide forces. Even though candidates have been better able to insulate themselves from their party's misfortunes in American elections than elsewhere, during this period a good many of them came from constituencies that could easily turn to the other party as the political winds changed. The result was considerable party turnover in seats and insecurity for the candidates.

Candidates for office in the twentieth century, particularly in the years since World War Two, have faced a more certain fate as incumbency has become a critical electoral resource. Between 1954 and 1992, the average success rates for incumbents seeking reelection were 93 percent in the House of Representatives and 82 percent in the Senate. These rates peaked in 1988 for the House when 402 (99 percent) of a historically high 409 incumbents were reelected, and in 1990 for the Senate when 30 of 31 senators running for reelection were victorious. Similarly high rates of incumbency success appeared in most of the state legislatures. It is not entirely clear why incumbency came to be such a valuable resource in running for office—the perquisites of congressional office, the personal services and visibility of the officeholder, the incumbent's ease in raising campaign contributions are all plausible reasons—but it is clear that incumbency provided great electoral security during this period, even as interparty competition seemed to be increasing.

There are signs in the 1990s that incumbency is not the electoral resource that it was just a few years before. In 1990, the aggregate popular vote for incumbent House members dropped below the levels achieved in the 1980s, even though incumbent success rates remained high. The elections of 1992 and 1994 were even less favorable to incumbent representatives. Because of redistricting, special incentives for retirement, especially strong challengers, and a prevailing mood of anti-incumbency, fewer incumbents (368) sought reelection to the House of Representatives in 1992 than at any time since 1954, and their success rate of 93 percent, although still impressive, was the lowest since 1982. More House incumbents sought reelection in 1994, but their electoral fortunes fell well below earlier levels, as only 90.1 percent were able to win reelection—the lowest reelection rate since the post-Watergate election in 1974. This decline in incumbency success rates in 1994, though, was entirely a Democratic phenomenon; all Republican incumbents were reelected, but only 84.4 percent of the Democrats were successful, which suggests that party considerations overrode incumbency. The movement toward term limitations in a number of states surely will place additional restrictions on the power of incumbency, at least for the nonfederal offices to which term limits have been applied, although it may have the ironic effect of increasing incumbency success rates in elections before the limit expires.[8] Moreover, even at the height of their reelection success, though, it is questionable that incumbents enjoyed the kind of electoral security that their rates of return to office would suggest.[9]

THE CAUSES AND CONDITIONS OF TWO-PARTYISM

Whereas a two-party system has distinguished American politics for more than 160 years, two-party dominance has been rare in the world's other democracies. The contrast leads to an obvious question: Why should the politics of this one nation among so many others have revolved around only two parties? Scholars have offered several different explanations for this American uniqueness.

Institutional Theories

By far the most widespread explanation of the two-party system, often called Duverger's law, ties it to the effects of American electoral and governmental institutions.[10] It argues that single-member districts with plurality electoral systems produce two-party systems. A corollary of Duverger's law is that multimember constituencies and proportional representation result in multipartyism. Plurality election in a single-member district means simply that one candidate is elected and that the winner is the person who receives the largest number of votes, even if it is not a majority. There are no rewards for parties or candidates that run second, third, or fourth. In a system of proportional representation, on the other hand, candidates typically are elected on party slates in multimember districts in proportion to the strength of the vote for their parties (see box on p. 40). The American election system offers no reward of office to any but the single plurality winner in most cases and, so the theory goes, thus discourages the minority parties.[11]

Many institutional theorists also argue that the importance of the single executive in the American system strengthens the tendencies toward two-partyism. The American presidency and the state governorships are the main prizes of American politics, and they are indivisible offices which go only to a single party. That they can be won with a plurality rather than a majority[12] further advantages the strongest contenders at the expense of the weaker ones. On the contrary, a cabinet in a parliamentary system may be formed by a coalition that includes representatives of minority parties; indeed, the main prize of chief executive can go to even a small party if it provided the crucial votes to produce the majority. (Giovanni Spadolini, the premier of Italy in the early 1980s, came from a party that held less than 3 percent of the parliamentary seats.) Beyond the loss of the executive office, moreover, the minor party is denied the national leadership, the focus of the national campaign, and the national spokespersons who increasingly dominate the politics of the democracies. The necessity to contend for a national executive, in other words, works against local or regional parties, even those that may elect candidates in their own bailiwicks.

Leon Epstein identifies a third, frequently neglected, institutional factor that has prevented the development of third parties in areas of single-party dominance during the twentieth century—the direct primary.[13] By offering dissident groups an opportunity to compete for nominations within the dominant party, the direct primary keeps them from forming a third party. Thus, in the one-party Democratic South or the one-party Republican Wisconsin of an earlier era, where traditional animosities kept most voters from supporting the other major party, factional disputes that under other conditions would have led to third-party development were contained within the dominant party by existence of a direct primary. Similarly, the movement that has developed around Ross Perot could be absorbed by a major party if Perot chose to seek its nomination for president, as George Wallace did after his third-party challenge in 1968.

PLURALITY VS. PROPORTIONAL REPRESENTATION RULES IN OPERATION

The difference between plurality and proportional representation (PR) rules in the American context is illustrated best by contrasting their operation in the selection of delegates to the presidential nominating conventions through primary elections. Under current rules, the popular vote for a candidate and the vote-to-delegate translation rules determine how many delegates who prefer that candidate will go to the national nominating convention. Currently, both winner-take-all (plurality) and proportional representation rules are used for this translation, with the Democratic party requiring PR and the Republicans favoring plurality selection.

If a congressional district is to elect four delegates to the convention, for example, the distributions of delegates under proportional representation (with at least 15 percent of the vote required to earn one delegate) and plurality rules would be:

		Delegates Won	
	% of vote	PR	Plurality
Candidate A	40%	2	4
Candidate B	30%	1	
Candidate C	20%	1	
Candidate D	10%	0	

Obviously, the plurality rule overrepresents the support of the leading candidate at the expense of all other candidates. The second-place candidate wins nothing, but the chance of overtaking the victor is ample incentive to compete for the office. Under PR rules, three candidates are rewarded with delegates in rough proportion to their popular support. In the 1992 presidential nomination contests, to cite a real-life example, attaining about 20 percent of the popular vote won Jerry Brown more than 600 delegates under the Democrats' PR rules but awarded Republican Pat Buchanan fewer than 100 delegates under the Republicans' plurality rules.

The contrast between PR and plurality election rules is even sharper in comparing single-member district elections in the United States and the other Anglo-American democracies with the multimember district systems of most European nations where legislative elections are concerned. Through PR, the European systems promote multipartyism and coalition governments in which two or more different parties often share control of the executive. In the British parliamentary system, by contrast, single-member districts operating under plurality rules almost inevitably produce a parliamentary majority for one party, giving it sole control of the executive, even if it fails to win a majority of the popular vote.

Dualist Theories

Some theorists maintain that an underlying duality of interest in the American society has sustained the American two-party system. V. O. Key suggested that the initial sectional tension between the eastern financial and commercial interests and the western frontiersmen stamped itself on the parties in their incipient stages and fostered a two-party competition. Later, the dualism shifted to the North-South conflict over the issue of slavery and the Civil War and then to urban-rural and socioeconomic status divisions. A related line of argument points to a "natural dualism" within democratic institutions: government versus opposition, pro and anti the status quo, and even the ideological dualism of liberal and conservative. Thus, social and economic interests or the very processes of a democratic politics or both reduce the political contestants to two great camps, and that dualism gives rise to two political parties.[14]

Tendencies toward dualism even are apparent in multiparty systems, as the construction of governmental coalitions produces an inevitable dichotomy between government and opposition. In France and Italy, for example, the Socialists and other parties of the left or the various parties of the right and center often compete against one another initially but then coalesce along largely ideological lines to contest run-off elections or to form a government. What distinguishes two-party from multiparty systems, in short, may be where this inherent tendency toward dualism is expressed.

The two major American political parties also play an important role in sustaining this dualism. Their openness to new groups and their adaptability to changing conditions—a permeability rare among democratic parties—undermines the development of strong third parties. Just when a third party rides the crest of a new issue or popular concern to the point where it can challenge the two-party monopoly, one or both of the major parties is likely to absorb the new movement, as the experience of the Populists and the Progressives can attest. As discussed earlier, such absorption has become even more likely in the twentieth century as the direct primary has come to be the principal method for selecting party candidates. Disgruntled groups are more likely to pursue opportunities within one of the major parties when those parties offer the possibility of nomination to outsiders.

Social Consensus Theories

Finally, the American two-party system has been explained in terms of a wide-sweeping American social consensus. Despite a diverse cultural heritage and society, Americans early achieved a consensus on the fundamentals that divide other societies. Virtually all Americans traditionally have accepted the prevailing social, economic, and political institutions. They accepted the Constitution and its governmental apparatus, a regulated but free-enterprise economy, and (perhaps to a lesser extent) American patterns of social class and status.

In the traditional multiparty countries such as France and Italy, substantial chunks of political opinion have favored radical changes in those and other basic institutions. They have supported programs of fundamental constitutional change, the socialization of the economy, or the disestablishment of the national church. Whether it is because Americans were spared feudalism and its rigid classes, because early widespread enfranchisement obviated the need for American lower classes to organize to gain entry to the system, or because they have had an expanding economic and geographic frontier, they have escaped the division on fundamentals that racks the other democracies and yields deep political divisions. Because the matters that divide Americans are secondary, so the argument goes, the compromises necessary to bring them into one of two major parties are easier to make.[15]

In appraising these explanations of the American two-party system, one has to ask some searching questions. Are the factors proposed in these explanations causes of the two-party system, or are they effects of it? The chances are that they are, at least in part, effects. Certainly, two competitive parties will choose and perpetuate electoral systems that do not offer easy entry to minor parties. Through their control of the legislative process, for example, they have made it difficult for third parties to qualify for the ballot or for third party candidates to receive public funding when it is available. The major parties do what they can to channel opinion into alternatives, reducing and forcing the system's complexities into their dual channels. The two-party system will also create, foster, and perpetuate the political values and attitudes that justify and protect itself. It will even encourage some measure of social consensus by denying competitive opportunities to movements that challenge the great consensus of the status quo.

Although these factors may be effects of the two-party system to some degree, they certainly are also causes. The most important cause no doubt is the institutional arrangement of American electoral politics. Without single-member districts, plurality elections, and an indivisible executive, it would have been far easier for third parties to break the virtual electoral monopoly enjoyed by the two major parties. Although third parties play a less subdued role in the other Anglo-American democracies, which share the American institutional arrangements, these systems too tend to be dominated by two parties. The other forces, especially the long-run American consensus on fundamental beliefs and its consequent lack of deep ideological divisions, have contributed to the development of the unique American two-party system as well. Moreover, once the two-party system was launched, its very existence fostered the values of moderation, compromise, and political pragmatism that ensured its perpetuation. It also created deep loyalties within the American public to one party or the other and attachments to the two-party system itself.

DEVIATIONS FROM TWO-PARTYISM

That the American party system is essentially a two-party system does not mean that electoral competition is organized around the two parties in every place and at every time. We already have seen that one-partyism has been common within some states and localities. Moreover, some areas have experienced a uniquely American brand of no-party politics, and third parties or independent candidates occasionally have made their presence felt on the political scene, most recently in the 1992 presidential election. Any exploration of the nature of the American party system is incomplete without consideration of these deviations from the predominant two-party mode.

Nonpartisan Elections

One of the crowning achievements of the Progressive movement was to restrict the role of parties in elections by removing party labels from many ballots, mostly in local elections. Roughly three-quarters of American towns and cities conduct their local elections on a nonpartisan basis. One state, Nebraska, elects state legislators on a nonpartisan ballot, and many states elect judges in this manner. These many islands of nonpartisanship constitute a structural anomaly in the prevailing pattern of two-partyism.

While this reform certainly has made politics less ostensibly partisan, by itself it probably has not removed partisan influences where parties already are strong. The nonpartisan ballot did not prevent the development of a powerful political-party machine in Chicago—or, for that matter, a highly partisan British politics. A resourceful party organization still can carry out its candidate selection and election functions in the presence of a nonpartisan ballot, even if the task of communicating party endorsements to voters is made more difficult by the absence of a party label on the ballot. Nonpartisanship, though, surely has contributed to the erosion of local party strength.

What makes it difficult to assess the effects of nonpartisanship is the tendency for it to have been adopted under conditions that muted partisanship in elections to begin with. The reform took root more commonly in cities and towns with weak parties and for offices, like judgeships and school boards, in which the traditional American aversion to party politics is most pronounced. Most northeastern cities, where strong party machines were the most visible targets of the Progressives, by contrast, were able to resist the reforms and retain partisan local elections to this day.

Beyond the obvious changes in the role of parties, what are the consequences of nonpartisanship? The traditional view among political scientists was that a move to nonpartisan elections shifts the balance of power among contending partisan forces in a pro-Republican direction rather than rendering politics any less partisan or more high-minded. Without party labels on the ballot, the voter is more dependent upon other cues. The greater resources and community visibility typically enjoyed by higher-status candidates can fill the void left by the absence of party. In contemporary American politics, these higher-status candidates are more likely to be Republicans.[16] A subsequent study of council races in cities across the nation, though, has challenged the conventional wisdom by showing that the GOP advantage disappears once the partisan nature of the city is taken into account.[17]

Pockets of One-Party Monopoly

To argue the existence of only two competitive parties is not to argue that their competitiveness is spread evenly over the country. Historically, there have been substantial statewide and local pockets of one-partyism in the United States, and vestiges of these tendencies remain to this day (see earlier Table 2.2). The states of the Deep South have been the country's most celebrated area of one-party domination. Much the same could be said in the past of the rocklike Republicanism of Maine, New Hampshire, and Vermont. Also, scattered throughout the country today are thousands of one-party cities, towns, and counties in which the city hall or county courthouse comes perilously close to being the property of one party. Parallel to the question of the causes of the two-party system, therefore, is the question of the causes of one-partyism within it.

One-partyism set within the context of broad, two-party competitiveness often reflects a "fault" in the distribution of the electorates of the competitive parties. Since the 1930s, the major American parties, especially in national elections, have divided the American electorate roughly along lines of socioeconomic status. One-partyism may result from a maldistribution of these characteristics that normally divide the parties. The local constituency may be too small to contain a perfect sample of socioeconomic status (SES) characteristics and thus of competitive politics—hence the noncompetitiveness of the "safe" Democratic congressional districts of the older, lower-middle-class or black neighborhoods of the cities and the "safe" Republican districts of the more fashionable and spacious suburbs. In other words, the more heterogeneous are its people, the more likely the district is to foster competitiveness.

Alternatively, one-partyism may result from some potent local basis of party loyalty that overrides the SES dualism. In the classic one-partyism of the American South, regional loyalties long overrode the factors that were dividing Americans into two parties in most of the rest of the country. Reaction to the Republican party as the party of abolition, Lincoln, the Civil War, and the hated Reconstruction was so pervasive, even generations after the fact, that the impact of the SES division was greatly diluted. It was thus a one-partyism based on isolation from the factors that normally produced two-party competitiveness and designed to preserve racial segregation. Competitiveness also may reflect the influences of local personages, of powerful officeholders, of local traditions, or of local political conflict, such as that between a dominant industry and its disgruntled employees.

That the two parties are not of equal strength in every constituency creates the competitive disadvantages that can enhance one-partyism. These competitive disadvantages begin with stubborn party loyalties. Voters are not easily moved from their attachments to a party, even though the reasons for the original attachment have long passed. Also, a party trying to pull itself into competitiveness may find itself caught in a vicious circle of impotence. Its inability to win elections limits its ability to recruit resources, including manpower, money, and attractive candidates for office, because as a chronic loser it offers so little chance of achieving political goals. It may even find itself without an effective appeal to the electorate. The Republican party in the South, for example, found for many years that the Democrats had recruited the region's most promising politicians and had preempted its most salient political issues.

Today, the would-be competitive party finds disadvantage taking another form: the formation of party loyalties along lines determined by national political debate. If the Democratic party is identified nationally with the aspirations of the poor and minority groups, its appeal in a homogeneous, affluent suburb may be limited. Thus, a nationalized politics may increasingly rob the local party organization of the chance to develop strength based on its own issues, personalities, and traditions. To the extent that party loyalties and identifications grow out of national politics, as many Democrats in the South have learned in recent years, competitiveness (or the lack of it) may be beyond the reach of the local party organizations.

There are, to be sure, other sources of competitive disadvantage. Once domi-nant, a party may shore up its supremacy by carefully calculated legislative district-ing, which is why parties are especially concerned with winning state legislative majorities at the beginning of each decade when district lines are to be redrawn. Another traditional device for preserving majority party dominance was the malap-portionment of legislative districts to overrepresent voters of the party in power, a decades-long practice halted by the Supreme Court in the 1960s. In the past, south-ern Democrats also stifled competition by maintaining election laws that disenfran-chised blacks and poor whites. In addition to these institutional buttresses to one-partyism, of course, the normal processes of socialization and social conformity work to the disadvantage of a weak local party trying to become competitive. That force of conformity, a number of observers have argued, works especially against competitiveness in closely knit, socially sensitive communities.

The Third Parties

Two-partyism occasionally is challenged from the other side—by a third force rather than by the absence of competition or of party labels, by a new minor party or a par-ticularly attractive independent candidate that flashes on to the scene. During most of American history, these challenges have come from other parties, understandably dubbed "third" or, referring to their impact, "minor" parties. In recent years, a new kind of challenge has appeared, from "independent" candidates running alone with-out any party label, and it will be considered separately below.

Except for the rapid movement of the Republicans from third-party to major-party status between their founding in 1854 and the 1856 presidential election, dis-placing the Whigs in the process, the third-party challenges have been short-lived, and the attention they have received exaggerates their electoral impact. Only seven minor parties in all of American history have carried so much as a single state in a presidential election, and only one (the Progressive party) has done so twice (see box on p. 46). (Even the independent candidacy of Ross Perot in 1992 failed to win a sin-gle state.) More important, no minor party has come close to winning the presidency. Their best showing so far came in 1912 with Teddy Roosevelt and the Progressives, who won 17 percent of the electoral vote and 27 percent of the popular vote. That candidacy was, in fact, the only minor party candidacy ever to run ahead of one of the major party candidates in either electoral or popular votes.

Between these peaks of third-party influence are the long valleys. In most pres-idential elections, minor parties have received barely noticeable shares of the popu-lar vote. In 1964, for example, the leading minor party, the Socialist Labor party, attracted fewer than 46,000 voters, and the minor parties altogether polled only one-sixth of one percent of the popular vote. After the George Wallace phenomenon of 1968—almost 10 million votes for Wallace—minor party strength ebbed once again. The combined minor or third party vote for president, excluding votes for indepen-dent candidates, was only 872,638 in 1988 and 605,021 in 1992 (Table 2.3), or about 1.0 and 0.6 percent, respectively, of the total popular vote.

Third-party successes also can be found below the presidential level, but they are as rare as they are captivating. For every example of third-party success in local elec-

THE BIG LITTLE PARTIES

To put the minor parties in some perspective, we need some point of calibration—some measure by which we can compare their electoral strength to that of the major parties and by which we can separate the stronger and weaker minor parties. If we choose as a test of strength the ability to carry just **one** state in a presidential election, only eight minor parties in American history qualify:

1. **Anti-Masonic party, 1832:** 7 electoral votes; 8 percent of the popular vote. A party opposed to the alleged secret political influence of the Masons; later part of an anti-Jackson coalition that formed the Whig party.

2. **American (Know-Nothing) party, 1856:** 8 electoral votes; 22 percent of the popular vote. A nativist party, often in alliance with the fading Whigs, opposed to open immigration and in favor of electing native-born Americans to public office.

3. **Constitutional Union party, 1860:** 39 electoral votes; 13 percent of the popular vote. The southern remnant of the former Whig party, organized to deny Lincoln and the Republicans an electoral college victory and dedicated to preserving the Union by preventing the abolition of slavery.

4. **People's (Populist) party, 1892:** 22 electoral votes; 8 percent of the popular vote. An outgrowth of a movement of agrarian protest opposed to the economic power of bankers, railroads and fuel industries and in favor of a graduated income tax, government regulation, and currency reform (especially free silver coinage).

5. **Progressive (Bull Moose) party, 1912:** 88 electoral votes; 27 percent of the popular vote. An offshoot of the Republican party organized around the candidacy of former Republican President Theodore Roosevelt, it favored liberal reforms such as expanded suffrage, improved working conditions, conservation of resources, and antimonopoly laws.

6. **Progressive party, 1924:** 13 electoral votes; 17 percent of the popular vote. A continuation of the 1912 Progressive tradition with the candidacy of Robert La Follette, who had been one of its founders and leaders.

7. **States Rights Democratic (Dixiecrat) party, 1948:** 39 electoral votes; 2 percent of the popular vote. A southern splinter of the Democratic party, it ran as the Democratic party in some southern states on a conservative, segregationist platform.

8. **American Independent party, 1968:** 46 electoral votes; 14 percent of the popular vote. The party of George Wallace; traditionalist, segregationist, and opposed to the authority of the national government.

If we adopt a more stringent measure, the ability to draw at least 10 percent of the popular vote for president, only six minor parties qualify—numbers 2, 3, 5, 6, and 8 above plus the Free Soil candidacy of Martin Van Buren in 1848.

Table 2.3   POPULAR VOTES CAST FOR MINOR PARTIES IN 1988 AND 1992
PRESIDENTIAL ELECTIONS

1988		1992	
Parties	Vote	Parties	Vote
Libertarian	431,616	Libertarian	291,628
New Alliance	217,200	Populist	107,002
Populist	46,910	New Alliance	73,708
Consumer	30,903	U.S. Taxpayers	43,398
American Independent	27,818	Natural Law	39,163
Right to Life	20,497	Socialist Workers	23,091
Workers League	18,662	Grassroots	3,875
Socialist Workers	15,603	Socialist	3,064
Peace and Freedom	10,370	Workers League	3,050
Others and Scattered	53,059	Others and Scattered	17,042
Total	872,638	Total	605,021

Note: Lyndon LaRouche ran as an independent in 1988, and in 1992 there were six independent candidates including Ross Perot. Their totals (25,530 for LaRouche in 1988; 19,741,048 for Perot, and 61,356 for the others in 1992) and those for write-in candidates are not included in this table.

Sources: 1988 Congressional Quarterly Almanac (Washington, D.C.: Congressional Quarterly, Inc., 1989), p. 7-A; and Federal Election Commission, *Federal Elections '92* (Washington, D.C.: Federal Election Commission, 1993), pp. 15–32.

tions, there are thousands of cases where the major parties have enjoyed unchallenged hegemony. The picture at the state level is even clearer. Of more than a thousand governors elected since 1875, only seventeen ran solely on a third-party ticket; another six, all since 1921, were independents.[18] Third-party candidates have been more successful in running for Congress, but the impression gained at high tide when they have won more than ten seats (in 1878, 1880, 1890, 1898, 1912, 1934, and 1936) must be qualified by the low proportion of third-party seats even then and the paucity of third-party representatives in other years. All in all, the Democratic and Republican parties have monopolized American electoral politics even more fully at the state and local level than at the national level.

The very looseness with which we customarily use the term *third party* to designate all minor parties may indicate that third place is as good (or bad) as last place in a two-party system. It would be a serious mistake, however, to treat the minor parties as indistinguishable. They differ in origin, purpose, and function, and American political history affords plentiful examples of their activities to illustrate those differences.[19]

Differences in Scope of Ideological Commitment   Although it is true, first of all, that most minor parties are parties of ideology and issue, they differ in the scope of that commitment. The narrow, highly specific commitment of such parties as the Prohibition, Vegetarian, and Right to Life parties is apparent in their names. In the 1840s, the Liberty party and its successor, the Free Soil party, campaigned largely on the single issue of the abolition of slavery. At the other extremes are the parties that have the broadest ideological commitments—the Marxist parties and the recent profusion of conservative parties. The leading minor party in recent years, the Libertarian party, for example, advocates a complete withdrawal of government from most of its present programs and responsibilities.[20] In the middle ground between specific issues and total ideologies, the examples are infinitely varied. The farmer-labor parties of economic protest—the Greenback and Populist parties—ran on an extensive program of government regulation of the economy (especially designed to counter concentrations of economic power) and social welfare legislation. The Progressive party of 1948 combined a program of social reform and civil liberties with a foreign policy of friendship with the Soviet Union and reduction of cold-war tensions.

Difference of Origins   The minor parties differ, too, in their origin. Some were literally imported into the United States. Much of the early Socialist party strength in the United States came from the freethinkers and radicals who fled Europe after the failures of the revolutions of 1848. Socialist strength in cities such as Milwaukee, New York, and Cincinnati reflected the concentrations of liberal German immigrants there. Other parties—especially the Granger and Populist parties and their successors—were parties of indigenous social protest, born of social inequality and economic hardship in the marginal farmlands of America. Other minor parties began as splinters or factions of one of the major parties. For example, so great were the objections of the Progressives (the Bull Moose party) of 1912 and the Dixiecrats of 1948 to the platforms and candidates of their parent parties that they contested the presidential elections with their own slates and programs.

The Dixiecrats symbolized the entry of a new variety of southern minor parties in the several decades after World War Two. These were dissident movements within the Democratic party, opposed to the civil rights liberalism of the national party and its presidential nominees, that have refused to run as separate parties on the ballot. In some instances (the Dixiecrats in 1948, George Wallace's presence on the 1968 Alabama ballot as the Democratic candidate for president), they substituted their own candidate for the one chosen by the party's national convention as the official presidential candidate of the Democratic party in the state. In other cases (Louisiana and Mississippi in 1960 and Alabama in 1964), these movements have run unpledged slates of presidential electors.

Differing Tactics   Finally, the third parties differ in their tactics. For some, their mere existence is a protest against what they believe is the unqualified support of the status quo by the major parties. Operating as a political party also offers a reasonably effective educational opportunity. The publicity value of the ballot is good, and with it often goes mass-media attention the party could not otherwise hope for. Indeed, many of these parties have freely accepted their electoral failures, for they have chosen, by their very nature, not to compromise ideological principles for electoral success. The Prohibition party, for example, has contested presidential elections since 1872 (winning but 935 votes in 1992) with unflagging devotion to the cause of temperance but equally strong indifference to electoral success; it peaked in 1892 with little more than 2 percent of the popular vote.

Other minor parties, however, do have serious electoral ambitions. Often their goal is local, although today they find it difficult to control an American city as the Socialists once did or an entire state like the Progressives. More realistically, they may hope to hold a balance of power in the presidential election between the major parties as was the goal of the Dixiecrats of 1948 and Wallace's American Independent party of 1968. Both parties hoped that by carrying a number of states, most likely southern states, they might prevent the major party tickets from winning the necessary majority of votes in the electoral college, thus throwing the stalemated election into the House of Representatives. The Wallace effort of 1968 faltered because Richard Nixon carried an unexpected number of large states.

The Question of Impact   Their variety is endless, but what have the minor parties contributed to American politics? For better or for worse, they have influenced, perhaps even altered, the courses of a few presidential elections. By threatening about once a generation to deadlock the electoral college, they probably have kept alive movements to reform it. Beyond their role as potential electoral spoiler, however, can they count any significant accomplishments? The answer, to be candid, is that they have not assumed the importance that all the attention lavished on them suggests.

One line of argument has maintained persistently that the minor parties' early adoption of unpopular programs ultimately has forced the major parties to adopt them. Its proponents point to the platforms of the Socialist party in the years before the 1930s. The issue is whether or not the Socialists' advocacy for twenty or thirty years of such measures as a minimum wage had anything to do with its enactment in the 1930s. Unfortunately, there is no way of testing what might have happened had there been no Socialist party. The evidence suggests, however, that the major parties grasp new programs and proposals in their "time of ripeness" when large numbers of Americans have done so and when such a course is therefore politically useful to the parties. In their earlier, maturing time, new issues need not depend on minor parties for their advocacy. Interest groups, the mass media, influential individuals, and factions within the major parties may perform the propagandizing role, often more effectively than a minor party. More than one commentator has noted that the cause of prohibition in the United States was served far more effectively by interest groups such as the Anti-Saloon League than by the Prohibition party.

In view of their limited impact on American politics in the past, then, why do some voters nonetheless find a third-party alternative attractive? The immediate answer to this question is that few voters have supported third-party candidates under even the most auspicious of circumstances. They labor under a number of constraints on their electoral potential, not the least of which is the self-fulfilling prophecy of many voters that a vote for a third party is wasted.[21] Yet, some voters do end up casting a third-party ballot. An investigation of third-party presidential voting from 1840 to 1980 explains their behavior as the result of major party failures "to do what the electorate expects of them—reflect the issue preferences of voters, manage the economy, select attractive and acceptable candidates, and build voter loyalty to the parties and the political system."[22]

Of course, continued dissatisfaction with the major parties ultimately can provide an opening for a formidable third party, as the rise of the Republicans in the 1850s illustrates. When this occurs, though, the normal operations of American electoral system make it likely that the "third" party will displace one of the major parties (as the Republicans did with the Whigs in 1856) or be absorbed by changes in one of the major parties (as happened with the Democrats in 1896 and 1936). What this suggests is that the power of the American two-party system embraces its alternatives, permitting their development only when the major parties are failing.

The Rise of Independent Candidates

In recent years, dissatisfaction with the two major parties has been vented in a new way—in support for candidates running as independents rather than as third-party standard bearers. The independent campaign of John Anderson in 1980 drew more than 5.7 million votes; he polled four times the votes of the minor parties combined, almost 7 percent of the popular vote nationwide, and more than 10 percent in nine states. The independent candidacy of Ross Perot in 1992 achieved a new milestone among non-major-party candidates. He received a larger share of the popular vote than any "third" candidate in history who was not a former president; only Theodore Roosevelt and Millard Fillmore did better than Perot. With 19.7 million popular votes, Perot also outdrew all of the third party candidates combined by more than 19 million ballots. Much of Perot's support, though, seemed to come from voters who were more dissatisfied with Bush and Clinton than they were drawn into an enduring commitment to another party or candidate.[23]

Even some third-party candidates in recent times have run more as individuals than as leaders of an organized political party. George Wallace's American Independent party in 1968 was dedicated to his own ambitions and had little more than the degree of organization required by the states for a place on the ballot. When he backed away from the party's leadership to contest for the Democratic presidential nomination in 1972, the party slipped into ineffectuality. In a similar vein, Lowell Weicker won the governorship of Connecticut in 1990 as the candidate of A Connecticut Party, but he proved unable to build it into an organization capable of sustaining itself in succeeding elections and for other offices.

The common denominator in all these efforts is that they were vehicles for a single candidate and thus were not devoted to fielding a party ticket or building a party organization. In this important respect, they differ from earlier third-party movements, such as the emergence of the Republican party before the Civil War, the Populists several decades later, and even the Progressive campaigns of the second and third decades of the twentieth century—all of which were aimed at creating a new major party. These recent independent (rather than truly third-party) presidential bids are another indicator of how candidate centered American politics has become, and they may signal a transformation of the very nature of third-partyism.

Because of its record success in 1992 and its continuing presence on the political scene, the Perot movement warrants special attention. In that election, it achieved a degree of organization that other independent candidacies and even minor parties have lacked. Through his organizational efforts, Perot gained a presidential ballot line in all fifty states and mounted an active campaign throughout the nation. The key ingredient to the Perot challenge to the major parties, however, was money—the millions of dollars from his own personal fortune that Perot was willing to invest in his quest for the presidency. This money financed the organizational efforts at the grass roots and, more important, purchased large blocks of expensive television time for the candidate's widely viewed "infomercials."[24] No minor party or independent candidate for president in American history, with the exception of former presidents such as Theodore Roosevelt, has achieved the national visibility of Ross Perot.

The Perot movement has remained a major force in American presidential politics. Its organizational expression, United We Stand America, has paid executive directors in all fifty states, elected state chairs, elected leaders in many of the nation's congressional districts, and numerous dues-paying members across the nation. In keeping with its status as a nonprofit educational organization, in the 1994 midterm elections United We Stand did not endorse or field candidates for office, although Perot did urge his followers to vote against Democrats in the congressional contests (but for at least one Democratic governor, Roy Romer of Colorado). This organization could provide the foundation for a new third party on the American scene. That was the course pursued in advance of the 1996 elections as Perot forces sought to qualify for the ballot as a third party in the states. With the continued willingness of Americans to consider supporting candidates outside the mainstream of the major parties like Ross Perot or Colin Powell, independent candidacies and third parties should continue to be a visible part of the American political scene.

WHITHER THE AMERICAN TWO-PARTY SYSTEM?

These considerations of two-partyism and its exceptions leave us with somewhat contradictory signs about the future of the two-party system. In important respects, the two-party hegemony seems to be becoming more complete. The competition between the two major parties at both the national level and within the states is more spirited than it has been in decades. Below the presidential level, third-party deviations are less common today than perhaps ever before. Yet recent developments threaten the two-party dominance. Voter loyalties to the two major parties and support for the two-party system itself have withered in recent decades, providing an opening to independent candidates, exploited most recently by Ross Perot and contributing to an increased volatility in electoral outcomes. Moreover, the barriers to ballot access for minor party and independent candidates, once so formidable, have been lowered in recent years to make it even easier for alternatives to the major parties to emerge. What these diverse signs augur for the future of the two-party system, though, requires more substantial consideration.

The Decline of Minor Parties and the Rise of Independents

It may seem paradoxical to chronicle the demise of third parties in the aftermath of record levels of support for an independent presidential candidate in 1992, but the record so far is clear. Third-party members of Congress, quite common in the early decades of the two-party system, have been rare throughout the twentieth century, but never so rare as in recent years (Figure 2.1). Since 1952, only one member of Congress has been elected on a third-party ticket—James Buckley in 1971 as a Conservative party Senator from New York, and he aligned himself with the Republicans after taking office. One other, Bernard Sanders of Vermont, was elected as an independent member of the House of Representatives. Minor-party candidates also have fared poorly in state legislative contests during this same period, and local enclaves of significant minor party strength have been reduced to a small, albeit colorful, handful.

As minor party strength has declined, independent candidates have been more successful than ever before, and several major figures (among them Jesse Jackson, Ross Perot, and Colin Powell) considered making independent bids for president in 1996. It is the presence of independents that was responsible for major party candidates receiving the lowest percentage of the 1992 congressional vote since the 1930s, although this percentage remained in the high 90s.[25] In presidential politics, independents Anderson and Perot, not minor party candidates, have mounted the most effective challenges to the major party candidates in recent years. Independents pose a different threat to the two-party system than minor party candidacies. There is perhaps no better gauge of the candidate-centered nature of recent American politics than voters' recent preferences for independents rather than minor-party candidates when they are inclined to deviate from a major-party vote.

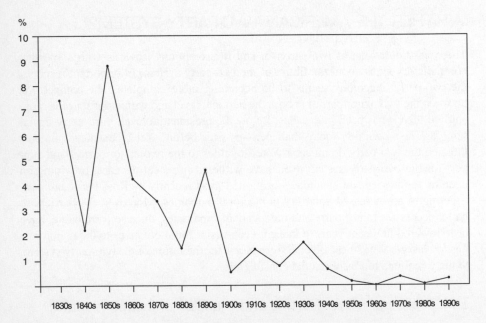

Figure 2.1 Third-party and independent members of Congress: 1830s–1990s.

Note: Figures are percentages of third-party and independent senators and representatives during each decade. The 1990s data are through 1996.

Ironically, independent candidates have been the primary beneficiaries of recent reductions in barriers to ballot access that the third parties battled for so long. In many states, third-party and independent candidates traditionally have had to gather thousands of signatures just to earn a place on the ballot (see box on pp. 54–55). A minor-party or independent presidential candidate still must satisfy a patchwork of different state requirements to qualify for the ballot nationwide, but the process has been eased by facilitative court decisions. Even so, the electoral process remains far less open to minor-party or independent candidates than to those of the major parties who automatically qualify for the ballot.[26]

Financial barriers to challenges from outside the two major parties seem less imposing today as well. The Wallace campaign astounded experts by raising and spending some $7 million, by far the largest sum ever spent by a minor party campaign in American history. His achievement demonstrated that a nationwide third-party campaign could attract substantial financial backing, just as Perot's showed the advantages of great personal wealth. Public funding of presidential campaigns adds another possibility for funding by opening the public treasury to candidates outside the major-party mainstream. John Anderson was the first "outside" candidate to receive such federal financing. By polling more than 5 percent of the popular vote as an independent, he qualified for more than $4 million in public funds. This money was dispersed to him after the election, but his vote total made him eligible for public funding in the next election—an opportunity he passed up by choosing not to run. Offsetting the advantages of this new campaign finance environment, though, is the enormous cost of modern campaigns, which probably restricts the opportunities to only a few highly visible or personally wealthy third-party or independent candidates.

For non-major-party candidates with financial resources, though, the modern campaign environment offers advantages which were absent in earlier times. The traditional third parties were regionally based—building their grass-roots organizations around local loyalties, interests, and troubles. The appeals of such parties increasingly have lost out in a mobile society that receives the same political messages via the same radio and television networks, the same magazines, and the same press services and syndicated columnists. The access to a nationalized media that money can buy, coupled with the 1980 precedent for opening the televised debates to serious candidates beyond the major-party nominees, though, has enabled candidates to reach a national audience of voters without extensive grass-roots organizing as Ross Perot did in 1992.

What, then, can we predict for minor parties and independents in American politics? There may continue to be a few local third parties that reflect special local conditions, especially quirks in local election laws. The classic instance is the New York minor parties—notably the Liberals and Conservatives—that continue to exist because they can nominate candidates of a major party to run under their party labels.[27] For national impact, minor parties generally must ride the coattails of a well-known, charismatic candidate, but such candidates may find it more advantageous to be independents rather than partisans or, if they run as a third-party candidate, to stand alone on the party ticket. The challenge of fielding a full slate of candidates, after all, is not one that recent third parties have accepted. What seems most likely, though, is that minor parties and independents will have divergent futures as they compete for space in the American electoral arena.[28]

GAINING ACCESS TO THE BALLOT: A TALE OF FOUR CANDIDATES

George Wallace, 1968

George Wallace had to devote considerable resources to gaining a position on the ballot in his presidential bid in 1968. In most states, his supporters organized the petition drives necessary to gain the required number of signatures. In Ohio, where the difficulties in gaining ballot access were particularly formidable, he took his battle to the courts. To gain a place on the ballot under Ohio law, Wallace would have needed 433,000 signatures very early in his campaign. He sued instead. The Ohio law had been passed, the state argued in its defense, for legitimate purposes—to preserve the existing two-party system and to make sure small pluralities would not win elections. By a vote of six to three, the Court disagreed. It ruled that the Ohio law violated the equal protection clause of the Fourteenth Amendment in restricting the rights of voting and association of supporters of minor parties.[29]

John Anderson, 1980

A substantial part of John Anderson's independent campaign for the presidency in 1980 involved prodigious efforts to gain a position on each of fifty state ballots. Petitions with large numbers of signatures were required in most states, and formal legal action was necessary in at least ten. The Anderson campaign in many states was built around the drive to gain access to the ballot in the hope that these activities would gain attention and help to create a strong organization. Unfortunately, the ballot access campaign spent $2.5 million and left little money for candidate advertising in the ensuing general election. Anderson also faced a second hurdle. Some states imposed early filing deadlines on nonparty, independent candidates. Ohio was one of them, and Anderson took the state to court. The issue finally was resolved in Anderson's favor in 1983—three years after the election—when the Supreme Court ruled that Ohio and other states could not discriminate against independent candidates seeking a place on the presidential ballot by imposing early deadlines.[30]

H. Ross Perot, 1992

The Perot independent candidacy for president benefited from the gains made in ballot access by non-major-party candidates before him, but it still faced a difficult task when Perot declared to the Federal Election Commission that he was interested in organizing a run for the presidency in April 1992. In his home state of Texas, for example, Perot had to collect nearly 40,000 signatures by a May 11 deadline from registered voters who had not voted in the March 10 primary. In New York, 20,000 signatures from registered voters who had not voted in the April 7 primary were necessary, but they had to be gathered no sooner than July and no later than August 18. By mid-September, after spending $18 million to collect about 5.5 million signatures nationwide, he had qualified

(box continues)

for a place on the ballot in all fifty states and the District of Columbia. Ironically, while his petition campaign was winding up its efforts, Perot had withdrawn as a presidential candidate, only to return to the race in October.

H. Ross Perot, 1996

As the 1996 presidential election approached, Ross Perot was at it again. This time his goal was to qualify a new political party for the ballot in all fifty states—a much more formidable task than qualifying as an independent candidate. He started too late to gain the 890,000 petition signatures necessary to meet the October 1995 deadline for the prized California ballot, and his petition drive initially fell short in Ohio. Only California and Ohio, with a November 20 deadline, required a new party to qualify before the election year had begun, and no state had such an imposing requirement for the sheer number of signatures or registrants as California. New party-qualifying deadlines came much later in the remaining states—no earlier than April in the election year—so the new Perot-led party had better chances there. Where it failed to qualify as a third party, though, the Perot movement pursued the presidency via the comparatively easier independent route.

Increasing Major-Party Competitiveness

Paradoxically, the unprecedented successes of independent candidates have paralleled a second recent trend in the American party system—the increasing competitiveness between the major parties. No regions of the country, and very few states, can be thought of as wholly one-party areas any longer. Contests for state offices are more competitive now than they have been in decades, perhaps ever (Table 2.2), and presidents increasingly have been winning with popular vote percentages that vary less and less from one state to another (Figure 2.2). They are no longer carrying some states by fat margins while losing others in a similarly lopsided way. This trend of increasing uniformity in presidential vote patterns across the country, then, parallels the declining number of states that are one-party bastions in state party competition. The result is a more competitive two-party politics throughout the nation.

The spread of major party competitiveness reflects the same nationalization of life and politics in the United States that threatens local minor parties. It is increasingly difficult for one major party to maintain its dominance on the basis of regional appeals and traditions as the Democrats did in the South from 1876 to 1950. Furthermore, the social and economic conditions that support one-partyism are disappearing. As Americans move about the country, as industry comes to formerly agrarian states, as more and varied people move to the urban centers, each state increasingly becomes a microcosm of the diversity of life and interest that undergirds national party competition. National mass media and national political leaders also

Figure 2.2 The growth of national two-party competitiveness: Interstate differences in the presidential popular vote 1896–1992.

Note: The measure of interstate differences is called the *standard deviation*. It measures the amount of dispersal of items around the average. It discriminates, therefore, among dispersals in the following three series: 3,6,9; 4,6,8; and 5,6,7. Even though the means and medians of each series are identical (6), the standard deviations decline in the order in which the three series are listed. The data on which the calculations are based are the percentages of the total vote in each state won by the winning candidate.

bring the conflict between the Democrats and the Republicans to all corners of the country. Thus, the party electorates are increasingly recruited by the appeals of national candidates and issues regardless of whatever special appeals the local party makes. The shifting of important state contests away from presidential election years, now extended to about three-quarters of the states, can mute the influence of national forces to some degree, but it is only a small counterweight to their inexorable power.

Ironically, the increasing degree of two-party competition may create a set of vexing problems for the American parties. By reducing pockets of one-party strength, the new competitiveness threatens a source of stability in the party system. When a party holds noncompetitive strongholds of its own, it can survive even a catastrophic national loss through victories and continued officeholding in its own areas of strength. Without those one-party strongholds to fall back on, a losing party in the future may find its loss more sweeping and devastating. Furthermore, the spread of two-party competitiveness expands the scope of party activity and thus makes extra demands on the resources the parties must employ. When one-party areas could be written off in a presidential campaign and election, the area of political combat was reduced. Now the parties must mobilize and organize more resources than ever across more of the states.

As we pass the 140th anniversary of the current party duopoly, the reign of the existing parties and the two-party system faces a new challenge. The major parties' popularity may not be what it was, but their resilience and their dominance of the electoral system continues. The Republicans quickly regained their strength after the defeats of 1964 and the Watergate losses of 1974 and 1976, just as the Democrats rebounded from the Reagan era with the defeat of incumbent President Bush in 1992. Nor have third parties seized recent opportunities to cut into the Democratic-Republican duopoly. The principal contemporary threat to the two-party system, instead, has come from independent candidates like John Anderson and especially Ross Perot, rather than from full-fledged third parties.

How serious is the independent threat to the longstanding Republican-Democratic duopoly? The presence of strong independent candidates, at the presidential level and below, raises the unpredictability of election outcomes and occasionally the instability of governing coalitions. Running by themselves, without anyone else on their "tickets" and often with no clear indication that they stand for anything more than alternatives to the major party candidates, their very independence prevents them from presenting a pervasive challenge to the two-party system. Unless these independents organize to confront the major parties across the ballot, therefore, they will be relegated to the interstices of the two-party framework—periodically threatening its hegemony but not offering the kind of sustained challenge to it that could fundamentally transform the parties or the party system. But if they do coalesce in this way, what is to distinguish them from a new political party—and is a new party really likely in an antiparty, candidate-centered age?

PART
Two

THE POLITICAL PARTY AS AN ORGANIZATION

I t is often easier to see the political activity than the actor. The yard signs and television ads of a bitterly fought election, the carnival antics and revival-meeting fervor of national conventions, the interelection feuding of party leaders in a legislature, and the other activities of the political parties could not be more obvious. There is a palpable actor behind the activity, however—a political party with characteristics not unlike those of large national corporations, trade unions, and fraternal societies. The political party is no mere bundle of activities, no disembodied ideology, no unseen hand in the political process. It is a definable, observable social structure that must itself be organized in order to organize political interests.

The party organization has the stable relationships and rough division of labor and responsibility that we commonly associate with an organization of any kind. While organizations also appear in another sector of the tripartite party, the party in government, the party organization alone has the organizational capacity to plan and initiate the major share of party activities. It also has the most systematic network of relationships and roles of all the party sectors. It speaks in the name of the party, governs it, and under law is responsible for it. It is the sector in which active partisans most often work to set the goals of the party and to mobilize and deploy its resources. In that sense, it is the part of the party most concerned with party governance and priorities.

In concrete terms, the party organization is the formal apparatus of the precincts, wards, cities, counties, congressional districts, and state that results from the legislation of the state itself. In addition, each party has set up a national committee, which peaks the pyramid of committees the state has created. The party organization is thus the totality of the machinery operated by party officials, leaders, members, and activists. The three chapters that follow analyze it.

The public life of the party organization—its espousal of ideas and recruitment of candidates for public office, for instance—will receive treatment in later chapters. It is the "private life" of the party organizations that will be the immediate concern.

This life involves the kinds of internal relationships and behavior one might find in any complex organization, such as:

- *The formal structure of the organization:* its committees and machinery; the selection of its leadership.
- *The centers of power:* the relative centralization or decentralization of power within the organization; the locus of authority within it.
- *The patterns of decision making:* the processes by which decisions are made, especially the degree of intraorganizational democracy.
- *Cohesion and consent:* the maintenance of unity, discipline, and morale within the organization.
- *The recruitment of resources:* the ability of the organization to attract people, money, and skills and the incentives it uses to do so.
- *The division of labor:* the various roles and relationships among people within the organization.

The private life of the party is far less obvious than its public life. Although we may separate them, however, the two are obviously related. To a considerable extent, the internal, organizational characteristics of the party determine its capacity to carry on its external, public activities.

A comparison with large business organizations is, if not pressed too far, a valid one. The party organization competes with other political organizations, both within the party and outside of it, for such political resources as personnel, knowledge, and money. Its rewards or incentives bring together varied groups of men and women who seek their often differing goals through collective party action. What are considered rewards and incentives to induce activity from the viewpoint of the party organization are merely the goals for which their activists have come together in the party. Many of the party organization's activities, therefore, may be viewed in terms of its attempts to win those goals and thereby reward the faithful for their investment of resources, loyalties, work, and support.

Ultimately, the most important questions about party organizations concern their effectiveness, vitality, and capacity. These characteristics can be summed up as strength, and the strength of the party organization has two dimensions: its ability to hold its own in its relationships with the two other sectors of the party and its ability to function efficiently and consistently in mobilizing resources and making decisions. In other words, the party organization must be able to function successfully both within the political party and within the broader political system.

In its relationships with the party in government and the party in the electorate, the party organization rarely achieves any permanent supremacy within the American political party. All three sectors of the party struggle for control of its symbols and its political capabilities. All three have goals—at times, competing goals—and each seeks control of the party as a means to its own particular ends. The states and to a limited degree even the national government, through laws defining and regulating the parties, substantially influence the balance of power in this struggle. Rarely is the party organization able to dictate to the party in government, although there have been times in American history when it certainly seemed so. It is far more common for the organization to be dependent on and even submissive to this other sector which, after all, writes the laws that regulate the organization. It must also conduct an almost endless wooing of its own party electorate, most of whom are neither formal members nor unfailingly loyal voters.

In addition to these sometimes strained, often dependent, usually symbiotic relationships with the other sectors of the party, the organization confronts formidable problems in maintaining its internal vitality. Contrary to popular impression, which has been shaped by the colorful urban political machines and their critics, party organizations are not unified, omnipotent monoliths. They have within them men and women of different values and goals, and they have always been plagued with dissidents and competing factions. They or parts of them often display amazing degrees of organizational disintegration. It is not unusual, for example, to find entire county organizations of the Democratic or Republican party in total dormancy.

Over time and across the many states and localities, there is tremendous variation in the strength and vitality of the American parties' organizations. The next few chapters will illustrate these many varieties, and it is crucial to bear in mind how extensive this variation is in assessing overall party strength or how it has changed. By the standards of political parties of most Western democracies or of the past century here at home, though, it is well to remember that the American party organizations are comparatively weak. To a considerable extent, the problem is in the very nature of the animal. The party organization is an expression of some very special qualities of the American political party and of the American political ethos.

At the risk of considerable oversimplification, one can say that, among democratic political parties, two types of organization appear most frequently: the cadre and the mass membership. In the cadre party, the organizational machinery is run by a relatively small number of leaders and activists. These officials and activists perpetuate the apparatus of the organization, make decisions in its name, and pick the candidates and strategies that will enlist large numbers of voters. In the mass membership party, on the other hand, the party organization grows out of and is more continuously responsible to the party membership. In such parties, substantial portions of the party electorate are involved in the party organization as dues-paying members and even as participants in year-around activities. The party organization therefore has a continuous responsibility to its membership, often providing such nonpolitical benefits as insurance and leisure-time activities.

In a mass membership party, the three sectors of the party are drawn together, with the party organization often occupying a central, dominant position. What we think of as the party in the electorate becomes an integral, even guiding, part of the party organization, with the right to pick officers and to vote on policy questions. Because of its great power in the selection of candidates—no primary elections limit it—this organization of the mass membership party exerts far greater control over the party in government. In short, the mass membership party resembles a continuous, participatory organization; the cadre party, on the other hand, is far more a momentary, pragmatic coalition of interests and people brought together in a temporary way to win elections, only to wither to a small core once the elections are over (see Table II.1).[1]

The major American parties usually are cited as prime examples of cadre parties, and in key respects they fit this mold. American parties possess few dues-paying

Table II.1 COMPARISON OF CADRE AND MASS MEMBERSHIP PARTY ORGANIZATIONS

Organizational Feature	Cadre Party	Mass Membership Party
Members	Generally few	Many dues-paying members
Activities	Predominantly electoral	Ideological and educational, as well as electoral
Organizational continuity	Active chiefly at elections	Continuously active
Leadership	Few full-time workers or leaders	Permanent bureaucracy and full-time leadership
Position in party	Usually subordinate to party in government	Generally some influence over party in government

members. Their activities are almost exclusively electoral. Involvement in the organization is rarely a full-time occupation for either leaders or activists. The organization also makes little attempt to influence the party in government. Yet, the modern American parties depart from the cadre-party mold in a few important ways. In recent years, they have solicited mass memberships, although more as a means for raising money than as a way to create a party community. Those willing to declare themselves as party members in closed primaries—and they number in the millions—select the party nominees for most offices. The major parties now are affluent enough to maintain a full-time professional staff in their national and state offices, as well as in a few local offices. Even these movements in the direction of mass parties, though, leave them a far cry from the European Socialist or Labor parties of the early 1900s. However, with the dulling of their ideological edge and the massive falloffs in their mass memberships in recent years, even those exemplars of the mass party about which Duverger wrote no longer stand in such stark contrast to the American parties.

Still, the major American parties are much more cadre than mass parties, and the American style of party organization is shaped by this reality. It expresses the organizational needs of parties that are preoccupied—indeed, obsessed—with contesting elections. It reflects the organizational needs of parties that must appeal to majorities rather than to 10, 20, or 30 percent of the electorate. It reflects the needs of parties that traditionally have not been concerned with ideology, with vast political causes, or even with taking specific stands on political issues. Finally, it reflects a political system in which the electorate is already organized by a wealth of interest groups and other nonparty political organizations. The party organization of the American parties does not reflect the politics of a multiparty system, the politics of a deeply ideological political system, or a political system in which the parties have monopolized the organization of political interests.

There is an insubstantial, even unimpressive quality to the organizations of the American parties, especially in comparison with their counterparts in other democracies or, even more, with large business organizations. In this era of a widely acknowledged decline of parties, their organizations, if anything, perhaps have been spared because they were so weak to begin with. American party organizations were not always so enervated, as the zealous assaults on them by Progressive reformers around the turn of the century suggest.[2] Nor has the demise of the powerful urban machine so hated by the reformers been a fatal blow, for recently there are compelling signs of a strengthening of the state and national party organizations and an unprecedented centralization of party organizational power. In spite of their comparative weakness and varying health, the American party organizations nonetheless command our attention, for they are at the very center of the political parties. More than the party in government or the party in the electorate, they control the parties' lives, their names, and their symbols. If their organizations are in decline, it may change the nature of the American parties and of American politics. If they are possessed of a new and growing robustness, the consequences may be felt far and wide. Any study of the American political parties must take the measure of the party organizations.

Chapter
3

The State and Local Party Organizations

The popular vocabulary of party organization suggests almost menacing strength. "Machines" headed by "bosses" keep the local "captains" toeing a "party line" and mobilize vast "armies" of workers and seekers of "spoils" to vote the "party slate" at election time. Their power or strength has become their "clout." This vocabulary expresses a pervasive American fear of politics and politicians. In what has become virtually a conspiratorial theory of American politics, the party organization or "machine" is the prime conspirator or corrupter in a wider net of political intrigue.

Even the most cursory experience with American party organizations suggests that behind this extravagant vocabulary lies a vastly less imposing reality. Machine imagery may have aptly characterized the party organizations of some major American cities and an occasional rural area or town at the beginning of the twentieth century. Exaggerated claims by machine leaders in boasting of their prowess or by their Progressive opponents in whipping up public indignation against their enemy, though, must be discounted. Even in their heyday, the machine epitome of party organization hardly characterized the organizations that prevailed in most locales. Today, as the last remnants of machines have all but disappeared from their once-secure urban outposts, the machine image of the party organization seems ever more anachronistic.

This truth about their party organizations may be difficult for many Americans to accept, for it involves not only a recognition of reality about the parties but also a modification of some dim views of politics in general. Nonetheless, it is necessary to sweep this tenacious myth away in order to gain a clear view of the state and local party organizations. To gain this view requires the blending into focus of three different lenses on reality—the party organizations as they are stipulated in state legislation, the party machines as they have traveled into modern times, and the party organizations as they operate across a wide array of American locales.

THE STATUTORY DEFINITION
OF THE PARTY ORGANIZATIONS

A good place to begin to come to grips with the reality of the party organizations is with the constitutions and statutes of the fifty states, which bulge with detailed prescriptions defining the nature of party organizations and the duties they are to perform. The states have, in fact, enacted such a kaleidoscopic variety of legislation on the parties that it defies easy summary or classification. In scope and extent, the laws range from those which specify party structure in detailed and full-blown provisions of more than 5,000 words to those of states that dispose of the parties in a few sentences or paragraphs. In between are all grades and degrees of statutory specificity.

State Regulations

A study by the Advisory Commission on Intergovernmental Relations (ACIR) indicates the rich variety found in these regulations as recently as the 1980s.[1] (See Table 3.1.) Most states attempted to regulate both internal party organization and the party role in the electoral process. (Electoral regulations will be considered later in discussing the electoral process.) Organizational regulations range from specifying the composition of party committees at the local level to stipulating the internal rules under which the parties will operate. Some of the strongest party organizations in the nation are also the most tightly regulated, so state activity here should not be viewed as necessarily weakening the parties.

The variety and detail of state approaches contained in Table 3.1 illustrate the cardinal fact that the definition and regulation of political party organization in the United States have been left largely to the states. The United States Constitution makes no mention of parties; it does not have even an oblique reference to them in its elegant paragraphs. Nor has the Congress attempted very often to define or regulate them. Only in the 1970s legislation on campaign finance is there a substantial body of national legislation that affects the parties in important ways.

In regulating the parties, though, the states cannot do entirely as they wish. Over the years, the federal courts have frequently intervened to protect citizens' voting rights (in cases to be discussed in Chapter 8) and to restrict the states from unreasonably limiting access to the ballot by third-party and independent candidates for office (see Chapter 2). Recently, the courts have even begun to overturn state regulation of party organizational arrangements and practices. In *Tashjian v. Connecticut,* the Supreme Court ruled that the state could not prevent the Republican party from opening up its primary to independents if it wanted to. In *Eu v. San Francisco County Democratic Central Committee,* the Court unanimously invalidated California's statutory requirements that the state chair's term be two years, chairs be rotated between southern and northern Californians, and party endorsements be prohibited in primaries. In 1994, a federal court judge blocked enforcement of yet another feature of California law restricting party endorsements—the prohibition on endorsements in nonpartisan elections. If the parties choose to challenge the state laws that

Table 3.1   STATE LAWS REGULATING POLITICAL PARTIES

State	State Committee Rules				Local Committee Rules			Cumulative Regulatory Index Score[h]
	Selection[a]	Composition[b]	Meeting Date[c]	Internal Rules[d]	Selection[e]	Composition[f]	Internal Rules/ Activities[g]	
Light Regulators[i]								
Alaska								0
Delaware								0
Hawaii								0
Kentucky								0
North Carolina								0
Alabama							X	1
Georgia							X	1
Minnesota							X	1
New Mexico							X	1
Oklahoma							X	1
Virginia							X	1
Connecticut						X	X	3
Maine	X		X		X		X	4
New Hampshire	X				X		X	4
Moderate Regulators[i]								
Arkansas	X				X		X	5
Florida		X	X	X		X	X	5
Nebraska	X				X		X	5
Rhode Island				X	X	X	X	6
Pennsylvania	X	X	X	X			X	7
Colorado	X	X	X	X	X	X	X	8
Idaho	X	X			X	X	X	8
Iowa	X	X			X	X	X	8
South Carolina	X	X		X		X	X	8
South Dakota	X	X			X	X	X	8
Utah	X	X		X	X	X	X	8
Mississippi	X	X		X	X	X	X	9
Montana	X	X			X	X	X	9
Nevada	X	X		X	X	X	X	9
Vermont	X	X	X	X	X	X	X	9
Washington	X	X			X	X	X	9
Wisconsin	X	X			X	X	X	9

(continued)

Table 3.1 (continued)

State	State Committee Rules				Local Committee Rules			Cumulative Regulatory Index Score[h]
	Selection[a]	Composition[b]	Meeting Date[c]	Internal Rules[d]	Selection[e]	Composition[f]	Internal Rules/ Activities[g]	

Heavy Regulators[i]

State	Selection[a]	Composition[b]	Meeting Date[c]	Internal Rules[d]	Selection[e]	Composition[f]	Internal Rules/ Activities[g]	Index Score
Indiana	X	X	X	X	X	X	X	10
Michigan	X	X		X	X	X	X	10
New York	X		X	X	X	X	X	10
North Dakota	X	X	X	X	X	X	X	10
Oregon	X	X	X	X	X	X	X	10
Arizona	X	X	X	X	X	X	X	11
California	X	X		X	X	X	X	11
Maryland	X	X	X	X	X	X	X	11
Massachusetts	X	X	X	X	X	X	X	11
Missouri	X	X	X	X	X	X	X	11
Tennessee	X	X	X	X	X	X	X	11
West Virginia	X	X	X	X	X	X	X	11
Kansas	X	X	X	X	X	X	X	12
New Jersey	X	X	X	X	X	X	X	12
Texas	X	X	X	X	X	X	X	12
Wyoming	X	X	X	X	X	X	X	12
Illinois	X	X	X	X	X	X	X	13
Ohio	X	X	X	X	X	X	X	13
Louisiana	X	X	X	X	X	X	X	14

[a] Does state allow or require the manner of selecting the parties' state central committees?

[b] Does state law require the composition of the parties' state central committees?

[c] Does state law regulate when the parties' state central committees will meet?

[d] Does state law regulate any of the internal procedures of the parties' state central committees?

[e] Does state law regulate the manner of selecting the parties' local organizations?

[f] Does state law regulate the composition of the parties' local organizations?

[g] Does state law regulate any of the internal rules or activities of the parties' local organizations?

[h] Scores are determined by state regulatory actions in the seven areas examined. Scores of 0 (no regulation), 1 (medium regulation), or 2 (strong regulation) are possible on each action. Minimum score is 0; maximum score is 14.

[i] "Light" regulators are defined as having an index score of 0-4; "moderate" regulators are those states having index scores of 5-9; and "heavy" regulators are those states having index scores above 10.

Source: Modified from Timothy Conlan, Ann Martino, and Robert Dilger, *The Transformation in American Politics* (Washington, D.C.: Advisory Commission on Intergovernmental Affairs, 1986), pp. 141–42.

DEREGULATING THE PARTY ORGANIZATIONS

The 1980s was a decade of widespread deregulation of private activity. In the *Eu* case, drawing upon precedents in *Tashjian* and earlier cases, Justice Thurgood Marshall applied the logic of deregulation to state governance of the parties. In his opinion for the Court, he concluded:

> . . . a State cannot justify regulating a party's internal affairs without showing that such regulation is necessary to ensure an election that is orderly and fair. Because California has made no such showing here, the challenged laws cannot be upheld. . . . For the reasons stated above, we hold that the challenged California election laws burden the First Amendment rights of political parties and their members without serving a compelling state interest.

Protecting the integrity of the electoral process, therefore, may be a compelling state interest. When the state turns to regulating the structure and rules of the party organization, however, the Court has found the interest far less compelling and has given the parties more freedom to govern themselves as private associations.

govern them, it now appears that a significant part of the regulatory framework in which parties currently operate could be dismantled (see box above).[2]

An Organizational Pyramid

Amidst all this variety, the party organizations created by the states have a common structure, which matches the geographically-defined voting districts of the state. They form great step pyramids of the myriad, overlapping constituencies of a democracy committed to the election of vast numbers of officeholders (Figure 3.1). At the bottom, their base usually is the smallest voting district of the state and their basic functionaries are the local committeeperson, representing a precinct, a ward, or a township. Then, in a succession of layers which vary in name and size from state to state, the ward and city committees, county committees, and sometimes even state legislative and congressional districts are piled on top of each other.[3] At the apex of the state pyramid, there is invariably a state committee, usually called a state central committee in the idiom of these statutes. The degree to which this entire structure is actually specified by the statutes differs from state to state. Statutes generally ordain the county and the state committees; some then mandate the other levels, whereas others leave the filling out of the organizational hierarchy to the parties themselves.

The Elected Committeeperson   At the base of this pyramid is the local committeeperson (or captain or chairperson) who is chosen from the precinct or whatever is the smallest voting district in the states. Because there are more than 100,000 precincts in the United States, a fully staffed, two-party system would assume the

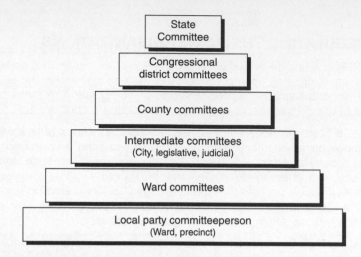

Figure 3.1 A typical pyramid of party organization in a state.

participation of at least some 200,000 men and women. In truth, of course, many of the local committee positions are either vacant or only nominally occupied.

The local committeepersons generally are selected in one of three ways. Most are chosen at local party caucuses or in the primary elections of the party, but in a few instances, higher party authorities appoint them. In states that choose them in the primaries, any voter may place his or her name in nomination for the party position with a petition signed by a handful of local voters (see box on following page). If, as often happens, there are no nominees, the committeeperson may be elected by an even smaller handful of write-in votes. In other states, the statutes direct or permit the party to hold local caucus meetings in the wards and precincts to which any voters of the area who declare themselves attached to the party may come. These party loyalists then elect the committeepersons in the caucuses; they also generally elect delegates to county and/or state conventions.

The duties of the local party officials are not often fully spelled out in the statutes. In areas where local parties are active, the officials naturally develop organizational responsibilities that the statutes never mention. In the past, the fabled local committeemen or "ward heelers" of the American political machine knew the local voters, catered to their needs and problems, introduced the party candidates to them, and propagandized the parties' issues—all with the ultimate purpose of turning out a bloc of votes for the party on election day. In the less active local parties, the committeepersons may do little more than occasionally attend meetings and campaign for a party candidate or two.

The Local Committees   A welter of party committees rises above the local committeepersons. Collectively, they often make up the city, town, village, legislative, county, and congressional district committees, or they elect the delegates who do. In a few cases, these committees, or some of them, are chosen at county conventions or

THE OCCURRENCE OF A RARE EVENT: CONTESTS FOR THE COUNTY COMMITTEE

Spirited competition for positions on the county committee is a rare occurrence. Every once in a while, though, an organized attempt emerges to take over the local party organization through penetration of its base. These challenges typically involve battles over the ideological direction of the party. The challenges are resolved in favor of the group that most successfully mobilizes its supporters in the low turnout elections in which party officials are selected.

Such an event occurred in Columbus, Ohio, in 1990, when challenges were mounted for a number of the 133 seats on both the Democratic and Republican county central committees by people identified as Christian conservatives. By seizing these positions, they hoped to be able to move the county parties, in their words, more in the direction of preserving "traditional family values." That the challenges came in the May primaries for statewide offices in a year when there was no competition within either party for most offices made the outcome especially dependent upon mobilization efforts on both sides. In the end, the insurgents won only a handful of seats on each committee.

Christian conservatives have been more successful in transforming the ideological posture of the Republican party in other states. A study by the editorial staff of the magazine *Campaigns and Elections* in Summer 1994 found the "Christian right" to be dominant in eighteen state Republican party organizations (including such states as California, Florida, Iowa, Minnesota, Oregon, South Carolina, and Texas) and of substantial strength in thirteen others.[4]

by the party's candidates for public office. Regardless of this profusion of committees and the various mechanics of their formation, the chief committee is generally the county committee, although in some states the congressional district committees assume a comparable importance.

Some states specify the fine details in their regulation of party activities and its internal processes. They may require that local committees meet within thirty or forty-five days after the primary elections, that they notify the secretary of state or the county clerk of the election of officers within a set time, that they not permit the voting of proxies, that they observe a fixed order of business at their meetings, or that they hold their conventions in certain types of public buildings. Under state law, in short, the political parties are not, in the usual sense, merely private associations. As Leon Epstein has put it, they are public utilities, sometimes subject to a considerable amount of state direction.[5]

The State Central Committees   The state central committees, too, come in fifty state varieties. In some states, the lawmakers have left the composition to the discretion of the parties, but in most they have decided the matter for themselves. The sources of variation center on two points: the lower party unit from which state committee members are chosen and the ways in which this choice is made. The unit represented may be the county, the congressional district, the state legislative district, the state convention, cities, or a mixture of these. The methods of choice include election in the party's primaries, election by a lower committee, ex officio representation, or selection by a party convention.

The activities of these state committees often are set down in almost painful detail. It is common to assign the committees responsibility for calling and organizing party conventions, for drafting party platforms, for supervising the spending of party campaign funds, and for selecting the party's presidential electors, representatives to the national committee, and at least some of the national convention delegates and alternates. A number of states assign to statewide conventions many of the powers and responsibilities that other states leave to the state central committees. Indeed, some states provide that the state convention select the state committee itself. In a few states, the state convention of the party actually nominates candidates for some statewide offices—a reminder of the power of conventions in the days before the direct primary.

Such, then, are the formal organizational structures created for the parties in the states. Three general observations about them are in order. First, the organizational layers relate to voting districts and to the constituencies in which public officials are chosen, and the duties assigned to them are mostly concerned with the contesting of elections. The political party organization as seen in the statute books of the states is clearly an auxiliary to the state's regulation of nominations and elections, tasks that before the turn of the century belonged almost exclusively to the parties. Second, the statutes betray legislators' ambivalence about the parties as organizations. Many regulations view the parties as cadre organizations run by a small number of party officials. By opening the election of local committeepersons (and of other party officials) to the electorate in the primary election, though, they have defined the parties' voters as a quasi-membership group—subject to the ultimate participation and authority of all voters. Thus, the party that results is not a private association whose participating members choose its leaders and chart its affairs; it is the semipublic, easily permeable hybrid of which we have already spoken.

Finally, although the formal organization of the parties appears to be hierarchical, it is not. Throughout much of their history, the state party hierarchies were best described as "a system of layers of organization"[6] or as a "stratarchy."[7] In some states, for example, the state central committee's members are chosen directly by the voters; the committee, therefore, does not grow out of the committees below it. Even when the linkage between the layers of organization is direct, the power traditionally has flowed from bottom to top. Such a system hardly would appear to be designed to produce the centralization of power at the apex that the very concept of hierarchy presumes.[8] Basically, the party organization is a system of party committees close to and growing from the political grass roots. The result is to retain in the party organizations a great deal of localism and decentralization even in the face of recent trends toward stronger state and national committees.

PARTY MACHINES, THEN AND NOW

American images of party organizations have been influenced heavily by their "ideal type"—the acme of vigorous and disciplined party organization embodied in the classic urban political machine—and it is useful to judge local party organizations from the standard they defined. The heyday of the machine was in the several decades around the turn of the twentieth century when, by one account, a large majority of American cities were governed by machines.[9] Its characteristics were substantial autonomy in its operations, durability, a hierarchical internal structure, control over nominations, reliance upon material incentives to build loyalty and support among the electorate, and overall control of government in a city or county.[10] The almost mythical proportions of its reputation have been fueled by the colorful histories of Tammany Hall in New York, the knaveries of the Pendergasts in Kansas City and Frank ("I am the law") Hague in Jersey City, the cheeky threats of Chicago's "Big Bill" Thompson to punch the King of England on the nose, and the genial rascality (and mail fraud conviction) of Mayor James Curley of Boston.

For all their power in shaping how we may think of party organizations, the great urban machines of yore were uncommon and only temporary residents of the political scene. The most recent and most visible symbol of their decay has been the decline of the Chicago machine after the death of Mayor Richard J. Daley in 1976 (see box on p. 74). All manner of problems beset other traditional urban machines before they brought down Chicago's Democratic machine. Some, such as the ones in Pittsburgh and New York, never recovered after being upset by middle-class reformers. Others, such as those in Philadelphia and Gary, Indiana, were displaced by the succession to power of new ethnic groups, especially blacks, who had become the more effective practitioners of the old ethnic politics.[11]

The Foundations of the Party Machines

Urban machines such as Chicago's have depended fundamentally upon their ability to provide tangible material benefits to their clients. The most visible of these benefits have been patronage jobs, which numbered in the thousands in many cities during the heyday of the machine. These appointments won the indispensable loyalty and service of the city workers to the machine. Their efforts, in turn, created the vitality that drove the local party organization and produced the party vote—their own votes plus those of their friends, family, and neighbors. Local party workers also won voter loyalties by coping with the problems of their constituencies. Often, those problems were personal—unemployment or a delinquent child—as well as public or governmental. The machine and its workers could earn political gratitude by finding social welfare agencies for the troubled, jobs for the jobless, contracts for local merchants, or even the storied Christmas baskets or deliveries of coal for the needy.

Public jobs and the cadre of loyal party workers they create were only one of the machine's resources. Governments purchase many goods and services from the private sector, which can be exchanged for political support as well. Banks that hold city money, insurance agents who write city policies, lawyers who are retained to

THE END OF MACHINE POLITICS, CHICAGO STYLE

The difficulties of the last great party machine—in Chicago during the 1970s and 1980s—have signaled the vanishing of that special breed of party organization. In its heyday under the leadership of Mayor Richard J. Daley, the Chicago machine controlled nominations, elections, and the making of public policy in the city. Its dominance was based on control over an estimated 35,000 patronage jobs in government and access to another 10,000 in the private economy. Building from this loyal base by adding their families, friends, and relatives, the organization could deliver 350,000 disciplined votes at election time.

With Daley's death in 1976, the machine lost its already-eroding control over Chicago politics and government. Machine candidates were defeated in two successive Democratic primaries, the second of which saw the party polarize along racial lines. It took black Mayor Harold Washington, the narrow victor of the 1983 primary and general election contests, several years to gain even majority support on the Democratic-dominated Board of Aldermen (Chicago's city council). Washington's reelection in 1987 further consolidated his power but over a Democratic party riven by racial conflict, a government with declining numbers of patronage jobs, and a city with debilitating economic and social problems. It is doubtful that Washington could have overcome these troubles to reconstruct a Democratic party machine, and his untimely death in 1987 initiated a new round of sharp internecine conflict. When the dust had settled, Chicago had a new mayor, Richard M. Daley, Jr., elected by a substantial majority in 1989 and reelected without serious opposition in subsequent years. Even with all of his electoral strength, there seems to be little chance that the junior Daley can resurrect the Chicago party machine.

No simple explanation will suffice for the demise of Chicago's heralded machine. Was it the inevitable result of the death of Daley, whose consummate skill had been the only glue binding together antagonistic ethnic, racial, and class groups? Was it just another phase in the inexorable process of ethnic succession, as blacks flexed their muscles in pursuit of their share of political power? Was it the product of a changing political culture in which machine politics was less acceptable and patronage jobs less plentiful? Or was it the simple electoral reaction to a deterioration of city services? As is so often the case, each of these probably has contributed to the decline of machine politics in Chicago.[12]

conduct city business or to take private cases on assignment by judges, newspapers that print city notices, even suppliers of soap to city washrooms all could be drawn into the web of the party machine. Government also influences economic opportunities in the private sector by zoning and public works decisions. Individuals advantaged by these decisions can be induced to feel a debt of gratitude to political leaders, which will be called in at election time. Finally, city hall regulates a good deal of the economic activity of a city by giving or withholding building permits, health certificates, zoning variances, and so on. Political leadership dedicated to the extraction of political support in exchange for these so-called "preferments" can use them rather ruthlessly to build its political power.

Machines overcame the inherent scarcity of benefits by reducing electoral competition through restricting the electorate, by using force and intimidation if necessary, and through manipulation of election rules and (if all else failed) the vote count. Their ability to appeal to ethnic loyalties also should not be discounted. Evidence from studies of the development of machinelike organizations in a variety of nations illustrates this source of support nicely. Political machines are found to develop and flourish where competitive elections with mass suffrage occur in a parochial social context in which loyalties to family, neighborhood, or ethnic group accompany the strong needs for immediate, short-term benefits. Thus, the rise and fall of the American political machine cannot be disassociated from changes in ethnic group loyalties in our cities. The urban machine has been a vehicle for ethnic group integration and succession in American politics, especially for the Irish.[13] It has atrophied where outlooks are more cosmopolitan or where it cannot satisfy the aspirations of competing ethnic groups or where the government bureaucracy was insulated from party control, depriving the party organization of patronage resources.[14]

Thus, the classic urban machine has always been part electoral organization, part "informal government," part social-service agency, and part ladder for upward social and economic mobility. To a significant degree, it resembles the local organization of a European mass-membership party, except that the American machine has no membership base and few, if any, ideological concerns. Its focus on the immediate needs of its constituents has driven it to look almost completely inward and to ignore the issues and ideologies of the political world beyond. It is provincially concerned with the city, and its politics are almost completely divorced from the issues that agitate our national politics.

Even though the most colorful and certainly the most visible American party machines developed in our largest cities, it would be a mistake to view political machines as exclusively urban phenomena. The conditions conducive for the development of machines, especially a large parochially-oriented population with short-term material needs, also have existed outside of urban environments, such as in small towns in the South or in one-company towns. Even some affluent suburban areas, in defiance of the general rule about the social conditions for machines, have spawned strong machine-style party organizations. In the affluent Long Island suburbs of New York City, for example, there developed in recent decades a Republican Nassau County political machine that controlled local government and local politics "with a local party operation that in terms of patronage and party loyalty rivals the machine of the famed Democratic mayor of Chicago, Richard J. Daley."[15]

It is difficult to discern how powerful party machines really were even in their heyday. Contemporary evidence from areas of machine strength casts doubt on the vaunted efficiency of the machine. A Chicago study found little evidence that public services were distributed by the party machine to reward political support in either

1967 or 1977. Rather, historical factors and bureaucratic decision rules governed the allocation of services.[16] A New Haven study found that an Italian-led machine distributed summer jobs disproportionately to Italian youths from nonmachine wards who rarely engaged in subsequent political work, not to youth from strong machine areas—supporting Steven Erie's observation (see note 13) that ethnic loyalties often overwhelm the machine's devotion to organizational maintenance and expansion.[17]

By the same token, one must not lose sight of the near consensus among scholars that the conditions conducive to the maintenance of political party machines have withered away in recent years. Contemporary evidence, even from the most putatively machine-dominated cities, may not reflect what machines were like in their heyday. It is incontrovertible that the patronage resources now available to local parties cannot match what they once commanded. The extension of civil service protection to municipal employees, through legislation and court decisions as well as the growth of public-sector unions, has sharply reduced the number of jobs that can be used to reward the party faithful (as will be discussed more fully in Chapter 5). The institutionalization of social services through federal entitlement programs has eroded another important source of machine power. Moreover, post-World War Two prosperity raised many Americans to levels of economic security that ended their dependence upon government, reduced the attractiveness of public employment, and increased their ability to fend for themselves in a complex bureaucratic society.

A Future for Political Machines?

Nonetheless, we must be careful not to underestimate the persistence of conditions conducive to machine-style party organizations in some locales. Dependent populations remain in our major cities. Indeed, many cities are experiencing growth in the numbers of the disadvantaged at the same time that they are losing their tax base and middle class to the suburbs. As government has become more bureaucratized, furthermore, the needs of many citizens for intervention have grown rather than declined. Even the ethnic strains that figured so prominently in the electoral strength of some machines have not disappeared, although they may now take different forms—e.g., recent immigrants vs. long-term residents, whites vs. blacks.

Where the demand for their services exists, political organizations will respond, even if they have to adapt their ways to work within new and tighter constraints. Political machines have demonstrated great creativity in subverting civil service regulations to create patronage jobs (for example, Mayor Daley hired thousands of long-term "temporary" employees) and in brokering federal benefits for the poor (for example, the summer jobs distributed by the machine in New Haven were provided through the federal CETA program). More fundamentally, because local governments continue to have large budgets, provide a complex array of services, and play an active regulatory role, ample opportunities remain to sustain a patron-client form of politics in a supportive political culture.

Consequently, while political machines in their classic (and often exaggerated) form undoubtedly are artifacts of an earlier time, it may be premature to announce their death. Party organizations will learn how to adapt to the new realities, and functional equivalents to the machines of old may well emerge. It also is conceivable that their recent demise is just another chapter in the battle over ethnic succession, this time between blacks and white ethnics in many cities, and is but a temporary interlude in party organizations' centralization of political authority in American cities.[18]

THE REVITALIZATION OF LOCAL PARTY ORGANIZATIONS

The machines of the big cities have never been and are not now typical of party organizations in the United States. They set the standard for effective party organizations, but it is a standard rarely achieved, in the past and especially now. At the other extreme—essentially unrepresented in the scholarly or popular literature because it offers so little to study—is virtual disorganization. In such cases, most of the party positions are unfilled or are held by completely inactive incumbents. A chairman and a handful of loyal party officials may meet occasionally to carry out the most essential affairs of the party. Their main activity occurs shortly before the primary elections, as they plead with members of the party to become candidates or step in themselves as candidates to "fill the party ticket." They are largely without influence or following, for theirs is often a chronic minority party. They meet infrequently, raise little money for election campaigns, and create little or no public attention. This type of organization probably always has been more common than the machine. Most American local party organizations lie between these two extremes.

A comprehensive picture of local organizations is provided by a 1979–80 study (Table 3.2), which surveyed several thousand county (or the equivalent where there were no counties) leaders.[19] This study found that most county organizations had formal rules or bylaws and were headed by a chair and executive committee who met regularly and were most active during election campaigns. These party leaders, plus a few associated activists, made decisions in the name of the party, raised funds, sought out and screened candidates (or approved candidates who selected themselves), and got involved in election campaigns. Most were volunteers, with meager resources with which to work. Virtually none received salaries for their efforts, and only a few had paid staff to assist them or enjoyed such basic organizational support as a regular budget, a year-round office, or even a telephone listing.

When the various indicators of organizational strength at the local level were combined in this study, Democratic and Republican organizations differed little on average. Considerable variation in local organizational strength, though, was found among the states. Some states in the 1979–80 study—for example, New Jersey, New York, Pennsylvania, Indiana, and Ohio—had relatively strong local organizations in both parties, while others—for example, Louisiana, Georgia, Nebraska, Kentucky, Alabama, and, Texas—had relatively weak parties at the county level. In a few states, such as Arizona and Florida, one party was considerably stronger at the local level than the other party, but divergence in organizational strength is the exception to a more natural symbiosis: Strong organizations of one party were typically matched with strong organizations in the other party.[20]

There is persuasive evidence that the average county organization today is better organized and more active in political campaigns than it was just a few decades ago. By comparing data on the same counties between 1964 and 1979–80, these researchers found increases in organizational activity levels for five important campaign activities—literature distribution, arranging campaign events, fund raising, publicity, and registration drives. For most activities, the increase was substantial. These increases continued in subsequent elections. A 1984 resurvey of a sample of the local organizations assessed in 1980 showed that, if anything, the organizations had become even more robust, perhaps as a result of intensive efforts by national and state parties to invigorate local parties.[21] A national survey in 1988 showed yet even higher levels of activity. Studies over time of Detroit and Los Angeles show similar growth in local party activities.[22]

A study of the county party organizations in forty representative counties across the nation during the 1992 presidential election further corroborates this trend toward an increasing organizational presence at the local level. As shown in Table 3.2, the basic ingredients for organizational viability (a permanent office, an office during the campaign, a budget, a telephone listing, a staff) were more widespread in 1992 than they had been just a few years before, although the local parties remained heavily dependent upon volunteer efforts. The big change seems to have come in the things money can buy, which supports the observation that more money has flowed to local party organizations in recent years. Moreover, these county organizations exhibited considerable involvement in the 1992 election campaign. Only one of the eighty Democratic and Republican organizations sampled failed to perform any campaign activities. A majority of organizations in each party conducted registration drives, transported voters to the polls, ran campaign events, telephoned voters to urge them to support the party ticket, and distributed yard signs and slate cards.[23]

Thus, there seems to be no doubt that county party organizations are stronger and more active in the 1990s than they had been just a few decades before.[24] More difficult to determine because of the scarcity of reliable records before the 1960s is whether this revitalization has brought local organizations to the levels of strength achieved by the local organizations a century ago. Certainly no modern-day local organizations can match the vaunted urban party machines of that earlier era, so this extreme end of the organizational strength continuum now is empty.[25] But the party machines never were the typical party organizations. For each one of them, there were surely scores, maybe hundreds, of local parties that were little more than skeletal in form. Few contemporary organizations seem to fall at this inert end of the organizational strength continuum. Consequently, many locales now may have stronger party organizations than ever before, even if the typical local party is but a pale imitation of the storied political machine. It also is conceivable that what we are witnessing here is the growing strength of organizations at the county level, which typically were not very strong, to fill (albeit only partially) a void created by the demise of strong *city* organizations. However, one cannot help but wonder how much this growing county organizational presence matters in an age of candidate-centered campaigns and less party-oriented voters.[26]

Table 3.2 THE ORGANIZATIONAL STRENGTH OF LOCAL PARTIES, 1979–80 VS. 1992

	Democrats		Republicans	
Attribute	1979–80	1992	1979–80	1992
Percent with complete/near complete set of officers	90	85	81	65
Percent with year-round office	12	45	14	64
Percent with telephone listing	11	68	16	75
Percent with paid staff				
Full-time	3	22	4	26
Part-time	5	18	6	36
Percent with paid chair	—	2	—	5
Percent with regular volunteer staff	—	80	—	79
Percent with regular annual budget	20	95	31	97
Percent operating a campaign headquarters	55	85	60	65

Note: The 1979–80 figures are based on responses from a total of 2,021 Democratic and 1,980 Republican organizations to a mail survey; the 1992 figures are based on telephone and mail responses to a survey of 40 Democratic chairs and 39 Republican chairs in 40 counties nationwide. Some of the differences between the figures may be the result of the different timing of the two surveys in the election cycle. The 1992 study reports on the situation during the general election campaign; the 1979–80 study covers the period before the general election campaign began.

Source: For the 1979–80 study, Cornelius P. Cotter, James L. Gibson, John F. Bibby, and Robert J. Huckshorn, *Party Organization in American Politics*, (New York: Praeger, 1984), p. 43; for the 1992 study, Paul Allen Beck, Russell J. Dalton, and Robert Huckfeldt, Comparative National Election Project, United States study.

STATE PARTY ORGANIZATION

Sitting atop the apex of the pyramid of party organization described in state statutes and conventional depictions of the party hierarchy such as in Figure 3.1 is the state committee and its organizational structure. This exalted location of the state party organization has been illusory for most of the history of the American parties. Examples of powerful, patronage-rich state party organizations could be found in the industrial heartland in the late nineteenth century, where they served as the organizational base for U.S. senators (who were appointed rather than elected prior to 1913), and in Huey Long's Louisiana several decades later. But in most states most of the time, the state committee has not been the major locus of organizational authority.[27] Recent years have seen a growing importance of the state organizations, however, in a centralization of activity throughout the party hierarchy.

Traditional Weakness

Traditionally, state party organizations have been federations—and loose ones at that—of semiautonomous or autonomous local baronies and baronial county chairmen. Added to the fragmentation of this decentralization is the fragmentation of factionalism. Parties are divided internally by regions of the state, by rural-urban differences, along ethnic and religious lines, by loyalty to local leaders, and especially by liberal and conservative preferences. Any consolidation of power at the state level seriously threatens the various factions. It is a prize that can be won by only one of them rather than shared. In the past, with but the few exceptions mentioned above, this threat was avoided through a variety of devices, not the least of which has been to vest few resources in the hands of the state party organization. That, in turn, reinforced their tendencies toward decentralization, which meant that power and authority within them resided in the most viable of the local organizations.

The pervasive localism of American politics was reinforced by other forces that weakened the state party organizations at the same time that local political machines were vanishing from the scene. Progressive reforms early in the twentieth century sapped the influence of state parties over nomination and election campaigns for state offices. Since then, candidates have found it increasingly easy to win nominations in primary elections without party organization support and to raise money for their own campaigns and thus run them without party help. Since 1968, the state party's role in the national presidential nominating conventions has been diminished by internal party reforms, especially among the Democrats. Convention delegates now are mostly chosen by voters, and almost all come to the convention pledged to a particular candidate for the nomination rather than under the thumb of state party leaders. Continuing extension of civil service protections, unionization, and judicial intervention to prevent even the firing of patronage workers when the party controlling government changes all contributed to the erosion of the patronage base for many state parties. It is little wonder that the state organizations seemed feeble by the 1950s and 1960s.

Strengthening in Recent Years

In spite of these impediments, state parties seem to have become organizationally stronger in recent years, although the present strength of no one of them rivals that achieved by few powerful state machines of the late 1800s, by Long's Louisiana machine, or probably even by the modal state machine of a half-century ago. In 1960–64, only 50 percent of a sample of state organizations had a permanent state headquarters, compared with 91 percent in 1979–80. The number with a full-time, salaried chairman or director grew from 63 percent to 90 percent during the same period, and average staff size in the off-election years increased from 3.5 to 5.9. The non–election-year budgets of the state parties were higher in absolute dollars as well, climbing from an average of $188,125 in 1960–64 to $340,667 in 1979–80.[28] By the mid-1980s, with the Republican party leading the way, their average expenditures had risen to $424,700 in the off years and more than $1 million in election years, and most of them had paid executive directors.[29] In addition, state legislative campaign committees, operating either through the party caucus or the leadership, have come to play an increasingly important role in legislative campaigns.[30]

The increased strength of the state parties has enabled them to play a more important role in political campaigns. Their organizational resources principally have been devoted to supplying campaign services in the form of training, advertising, polling, and voter-mobilization drives that supplement those of the candidates' own organizations. Coordinated campaigns, emphasizing the sharing of campaign services among a variety of candidates, also are increasingly being run through the state party organizations. These state parties, it thus appears, have at last allied themselves with the new campaign skills to recapture a role in the election campaigns.[31]

Most of this activity takes place, of course, not in the unwieldy state central committees, but in the bureaucracies they create. We are therefore seeing the first real signs of the institutionalization of the state parties—their dominance, or at least the dominance of their activity, by full-time, paid, professional staffs (see Table 3.3). From the early 1960s to 1980, for example, the average number of paid staff members in the state parties doubled, and there is every reason to believe that their growth has continued. These party bureaucrats cannot easily exert much influence over the party in government; nor do they exert much control over local party units in the state. Theirs is a service organization that brings useful skills and information to party candidates in the election campaigns. Their services will certainly win the appreciation and gratitude of the candidates, which leads one to wonder about the ultimate uses of growing state party organization strength: Can the state parties convert the obligation of their successful candidates to support for party positions or programs?

Data from the 1979–80 study and a similar 1984 study[32] also show that, unlike the situation at the county level, Republican state organizations were considerably stronger than their Democratic counterparts. The Republicans had more paid leaders, larger and more specialized staffs, and substantially bigger budgets. This relative advantage in organizational strength enabled the GOP to perform more services for the party and its candidates. For example, twice as many Republican as Democratic state organizations provided public-opinion polling services. The GOP organizational advantage is uniform rather than regional, reflecting to a considerable degree the extensive subsidies the national party has been able to provide to all of the state parties. It is an advantage that surely has persisted into the 1990s.

To build a powerful state organization is to overcome both the grass-roots localism of American politics and the widespread antipathy to strong party discipline. Understandably, it is not easy. Strong and skillful personal leadership by a governor,

Table 3.3 COMPARISON OF STATE PARTY ORGANIZATIONS: EARLY 1960S AND 1979

Organizational Feature	Percentage of Democratic and Republican State Parties that Have Each Feature	
	1960–64	1979–80
Permanent state headquarters	50	91
Full-time chairman or director	63	90
Voter mobilization programs	39	75

Sources: Data from Robert J. Huckshorn and John F. Bibby, "State Parties in an Era of Political Change," in Joel L. Fleishman, ed., *The Future of American Political Parties* (Englewood Cliffs, N.J.: Prentice-Hall, 1982) and James L. Gibson, Cornelius P. Cotter, John F. Bibby, Robert J. Huckshorn, "Assessing Party Organization Strength," *American Journal of Political Science* 27 (1983): 193–222.

a senator, or a state chairman[33] helps. So do political resources—especially money, which is the essential fuel for the modern campaign. It also helps to have a tradition or culture, as well as state regulations embodying it, that accept the notion of a unified and effective party. Similarly, it makes a difference whether the state parties retain important political responsibilities. It is no coincidence that central party organization has flourished in the states in which primary elections are least extensive and in which the party organization determines much more directly who the statewide and congressional candidates will be. An environment conducive to strong party organizations is rarely found in the American states. But where it is present (such as in Pennsylvania for both parties; Ohio, Minnesota, and South Dakota for the Republicans; and North Dakota for the Democrats[34]), state organizations have flourished.

By far the most important ingredient in the vitalization of state party organizations, though, has been the party-building efforts of the national parties. With more energetic leadership and more bountiful financial resources than ever before, the national party committees since the 1970s have been dedicated to building the organizational effectiveness of the state parties—and local parties too. The full story of these efforts will be told in Chapter 4, but what is important for this chapter is how the state parties have benefited from national party investments. Millions of dollars (since 1980, increasingly in the form of "soft money"[35]) have been channeled from the Democratic and Republican national committees to state party committees to be used in building up organizational capacity and running party campaigns. In the 1991–92 election cycle alone, the national parties transferred approximately $18 million directly to state parties ($9 million each for the Democrats and Republicans) and spent another $41 million in joint activities ($23 million by the Republicans, $18 million by the Democrats) to support a variety of "party-building" activities and services. With these new-found financial resources, the state parties have gained an importance seemingly more commensurate with their formal position in the organizational hierarchy. Whether their new status has cost them their independence, this time from the national parties, is a question only the future can answer.[36]

PARTY ORGANIZATION IN PERSPECTIVE: TRENDS AND CHANGES

Local party organizations are indisputably weaker today than they were a hundred years ago when the parties could be described as:

> ... armies drawn up for combat (in which) financial and communications "sinews of war" were provided by an elaborate, well-staffed, and strongly motivated organizational structure. In the field of communications, a partisan press was dominant. . . . The "drilling" of voters in this period by their party captains was intense.[37]

While this description surely did not apply uniformly to party organizations throughout the nation, it might be impossible to find a local party organization that would earn this characterization today.

Since their heyday in the latter part of the nineteenth century, the local parties have been buffeted by numerous forces, some explicitly directed at weakening them and others eroding the parties in their wake. Progressive-movement reforms adopted around the turn of the century sapped party strength by limiting their control over nominations and general elections as well as over treasured patronage resources. In recent decades, a number of disparate forces—reforms in presidential nominations, bureaucratization of the welfare state, the integration of ethnics into American life, the almost total demise of the patronage system, national regulation of previously state-controlled party activities, and greater education of the electorate—have threatened further the viability of the local parties.[38]

Yet, local parties have exhibited such great resiliency in adapting to these changes that one must be careful not to exaggerate the extent of their demise. County party organizations seem to have moved to fill at least some of the void created by the absence of the urban machines. It may even be premature to announce the death of the machines, considering the ample rewards local governments still offer to the resourceful political entrepreneur and the continuing dependency of city residents. The local party organizations, in short, are adapting to meet the new challenges posed by a changing environment, demonstrating once again the resiliency that has enabled them to survive throughout much of the history of the American Republic.

The state party organizations have followed a different route to where they are today. Traditionally weak in all but a handful of states, little more than vessels that could barely contain vibrant and often warring local organizations, the state organizations appear to have achieved an unprecedented robustness in recent years, becoming more professionalized than ever before and servicing grass-roots local organizations, which in an earlier era rarely looked to their state headquarters for assistance. Recent trends within the states, then, seem to have undermined the long-standing decentralization of the party organizations.

In fact, the flow of money, resources, and to some degree leadership from the national party to the state party and in turn from the state to the local parties signifies a reversal, at least in part, of the traditional flows in the party hierarchy. Through most of their lives, the American parties have been remarkably decentralized, with power and influence lodged at the base of the organizational pyramid, and hollow at the top, dependent upon the base for whatever influence and resources they had. This extreme decentralization is now gone, a victim of the death of urban machines and the birth of vigorous state and national party organizations. The nationalization of American society and politics has embraced the political party organizations as well.

Yet for all of this rejuvenated party power, it is clear that the formal, statutory party organizations at the state and local level are less consequential for our politics than they once were. They have been muscled aside by a motley assortment of new and old actors in the electoral process. Membership clubs, candidates and their organizations, ambitious or wealthy individuals, campaign technocrats, donors of political money, issue groups and caucuses, and even some traditional interest groups also work the election campaigns. Many of them ally themselves with a party label and, to some extent, with a party organization. Therefore, state and local party organizations are far looser and more flexible today than the words of the statutes would suggest.[39]

In other words, the party is a flexible and somewhat undisciplined pool of active groups and individuals. They are recruited to the party for different reasons, and they are activated by different candidates, different issues, and different elections. A hotly contested school-board election will activate one cluster of partisans, and a congressional election will activate another. What we have thought of as the party organization is really a reservoir of organizations and activists from which are drawn the shifting organizational coalitions that speak and act in the name of the party.

In searching for change in American party organization, however, one ought not lose sight of what does not change. The American state and local parties remain largely skeletal, cadre organizations, run by small numbers of activists and involving the great masses of their supporters only at election time. The shift away from the organizational forms inherent in the statutes of the states has largely been a shift from a well-defined cadre organization to a looser, more amorphous cadre organization. Yet, the American parties are still a long way from becoming mass-membership parties, and they are still some distance from achieving the continuously active, year-round tempos of parties elsewhere in the world. By the standards of those parties, American party organization continues to be characterized by unusual fluidity and evanescence, by failure to generate activity at nonelection time, and by the ease with which a handful of activists and public officeholders dominate it.

Chapter
4

National Organizations: A New Presence at the Summit

South of Capitol Hill, a few blocks from the House and Senate offices, stand the national headquarters buildings of the Democratic and Republican parties. These are the offices of the national committees, which occupy the apex of the American party organization pyramid, and their professional staffs under the day-to-day direction of the national party chairs.

The two buildings are palpable signs of the current standing of the national parties. These modern national headquarters manifest levels of financial well-being, independence, and permanence unprecedented in the annals of the national parties. Only a few decades ago, the national committees were poor and transient renters—often moving back and forth between New York and Washington and all but disbanding between presidential campaigns. Location of the offices closer to Congress than to the White House symbolizes movement of the national party beyond its traditional position as handmaiden to the president and into a new role of party building in the states and localities. A more imposing and older GOP headquarters, purchased in 1970 compared with 1985 for the Democrats, testifies to the earlier beginning and continuing lead the Republicans have enjoyed in building an effective national party organization.

All of this supports the realization of close observers of American political parties that the national committees are stronger in modern times than at any time since their creation by the Democrats in 1848 and by the Republicans in 1856. Stronger, too, are the congressional campaign committees and, with respect to their influence over the state parties, the national party conventions. Only early in the development of party politics, before 1828 when presidential nominations were made by the congressional caucus, were the national parties as important in American politics. Moreover, the national parties seem to be gaining in strength with each passing year and now play ever more vital roles in national, state, and local party politics.

What a contrast the present-day status of the national party committees is to their situation only a few decades ago, which leading students of the national committees could accurately characterize as "politics without power."[1] For most of their history, in fact, the national parties were merely nominal summit organizations in a heavily decentralized party system. As one noted scholar of American party politics put it in characterizing the old arrangement:

> Decentralization of power is by all odds the most important single characteristic of the American major party; more than anything else this trait distinguishes it from all others. Indeed, once this truth is understood, nearly everything else about American parties is greatly illuminated. . . . The American major party is, to repeat the definition, a loose confederation of state and local bosses for limited purposes.[2]

The bases for the traditional decentralization are obvious. State and local party organizations of the major parties pick their own officers, nominate their own candidates, take their own stands on issues, and raise and spend their own funds without much interference from the national party. For most of their long history, the national committees served only as arenas for the bargaining and jockeying among powerful local and state organizations and presidential candidates within the party. Indeed, it was often said that, in reality, there were no national parties, that what we blithely call the national parties were merely coalitions of jealous, wary, and diverse state and local party organizations.

Since the 1970s, however, there have been incontestable signs that the national committees are emerging into the light after decades of eclipse. Their resources and staffs have grown, and they have undertaken new roles and activities. They have become more active, vital, and influential. There also have been successful attempts to limit the autonomy of state and local organizations in their one collective function—the selection of delegates to the national conventions.

These changes have led some to revise the traditional picture of a decentralized party by claiming that the national parties have become "federations" rather than "confederations" of the state and local parties—a subtle but meaningful shift in terminology that is meant to signify an enhanced potential for national authority similar to that following the replacement of the Articles of Confederation by the Constitution in the early days of the American Republic.[3] While the American party system remains decentralized in many significant respects and one must be careful not to exaggerate present trends, it is impossible to ignore the signs of unprecedented national vitality and even centralization in the major parties.

But one is compelled to ask what took them so long. Most other aspects of American life have long since been nationalized. The mass media bring the same reporters, TV images, and commentators into homes in all parts of the country. By almost any other measure, government in the American federal system has been increasingly centered in Washington since the 1930s, although this trend may now be reversing. Even the other two sectors of the party have been nationalized in the past few decades. The party electorates respond increasingly to national issues, to national candidates, and to national party symbols and positions; the 1994 midterm contest was the most nationally centered congressional elections in years. Attention now centers as well on the national parties in government; the president and the congressional leadership of the parties are more than ever the prime spokespersons for their parties.

The party organizations responded belatedly to nationalizing forces for a number of reasons: the state regulation of parties, the thousands of public officials chosen in the states, and the domination of local organization by those officials. All those localizing pressures still exist, of course, and they will continue to restrain the centralization of authority within the parties, but they show little sign of being able to reverse the trend toward more centralized American party organizations.

THE NATIONAL COMMITTEES AND NATIONAL OFFICERS

Before investigating how the national party has changed, though, it is important to establish what it is. Technically speaking, the nominating convention each party holds midway in a presidential election year is the party's supreme national authority. The convention's role, however, rarely goes beyond the selection of presidential and vice-presidential candidates and the formulation of party platforms and party rules. It does specify the structure and powers of the national committee, but because the convention adjourns *sine die* (i.e., without setting a time for a future meeting) until four years later, it can exercise no continuing supervision over the national organizational apparatus of the party.

The Committees

Between conventions, the national committees are the primary governing institutions of the two major parties. For years, they were similarly composed. Traditionally, each state (as well as certain territories) was represented in both national committees on an approximately equal basis, regardless of the size of its electorate or the extent of its support for the party. Under this arrangement, states, not populations or number of party supporters, were the basis of representation, much as Alaska and California are represented equally in the United States Senate. That system overrepresented the state organizations of the smaller states, however, and it also gave roughly equal weight in the national committees to the winning and the losing parts of the party. The practical consequence was a strengthening of the southern and western segments of each party, which tended to be more conservative.

With the drastic revision of the Democratic body in 1972, the parties now apply contrasting principles in structuring their national committees. After a brief flirtation with unequal state representation in the 1950s, the Republicans have retained their traditional confederational structure by giving each of the state and territorial parties three seats on the committee; the state party chairperson plus a committeeman and committeewoman from each state. By contrast, the Democratic National Committee (DNC), now virtually four times the size of its Republican counterpart (RNC), has abandoned the confederational principle by giving weight both to population and to party support in representing the states. California, for example, has twenty seats on the committee, and Alaska has four. The Democrats also give some representation to groups of officeholders and affiliates as well as have at-large members to better represent their minority constituencies (Table 4.1).

Table 4.1   MEMBERS OF DEMOCRATIC AND REPUBLICAN NATIONAL COMMITTEES: 1995

	Number of Members
Democratic National Committee	
Chair and vice-chair from each state and from American Samoa, Democrats abroad, D.C., Guam, Puerto Rico, and Virgin Islands	112
Members apportioned to states, etc., on same basis as delegates to national convention (at least two per state, etc.)	212
Party leader and one other member from each house of Congress	4
Chairperson of Democratic Governors Conference and two additional governors	3
Chairperson of Democratic Mayors Conference and two additional mayors	3
Chairperson of Democratic County Officials Conference and two additional officials	3
Chairperson of Democratic State Legislative Leaders Association and two additional leaders	3
Chairperson of Democratic Municipal Officials Conference and two additional officials	3
Chairperson of Democratic Lieutenant Governors Association and one other member	2
Chairperson of Democratic Secretaries of State Association and one other member	2
Chairperson of Democratic State Treasurers Association and one other member	2
Chairperson of Young Democrats and two additional members	3
Chairperson of National Federation of Democratic Women and two additional members	3
Chairperson of College Democrats and one other member	2
Officers of National Committee	10
Additional at-large members to implement full participation goals for blacks, Hispanics, women, youth, Asians, and Native Americans	65
	430
Republican National Committee	
National committeeman, national committeewoman, and state chairperson from each state and from D.C., American Samoa, Guam, Puerto Rico, and Virgin Islands	165
	165

Note: Two Democratic committee officers also are state committee representatives.

National committee members are selected by the states and, for the Democrats, also by the other constituencies. The state parties differ from one another in how they make their decisions, and in many states, the two parties choose their national committee representatives differently. They use four main methods—selection by state party convention, by the party delegation to the national convention, by the state central committee, and by election in a primary. In this welter of selection processes, one point is worth noting. Although the parties' state organizations usually can control the selection of committee members when they are chosen by the state committee and by the state conventions, they are less effective when the selection is by primaries or by national convention delegates. Especially in states that choose delegates in presidential primaries, the delegation to the national convention may represent voter support of a momentarily popular candidate more than it represents the leadership of the state party. A number of Democratic delegations in 1972, for example, were composed of party newcomers and mavericks who were pledged to George McGovern. The old-line party leaders in those states had supported other contenders and thus were not delegates.

The Officers

The chairpersons and other officers of the national committees do not have to be—and often are not—members of the committees. They are elected and removed by the committees. Immediately after the conventions, however, tradition recognizes the right of the parties' presidential candidates to name the national chairpersons for the course of the presidential campaign in recognition of the important role the national committee once played in the campaign. The committees ratify their choices without question. Moreover, because the party of the president will continue to respect his choice of a national party chairperson after the election, only the committee of the "out" party actually selects its own national chairperson. The committees generally have much greater freedom to select other committee officials—vice-chairpersons, secretaries, and treasurers—some of whom may come from the committee itself. In addition, both national committees select executive committees, which include the officers and some other members of the committee.

Within this apparatus—supplemented, of course, by the national committees' permanent staffs—the chairpersons dominate. The full committees usually meet only two or three times a year. Cotter and Hennessy's classic description still applies:

> Collectively the national committee is not much more than a categorical group. . . . The national committee members have very little collective identity, little patterned interaction, and only rudimentary common values and goals. Except for occasional meetings—largely for show and newsmaking purposes—the national committees may be thought of not so much as groups, but as lists of people who have obtained their national committee memberships through organizational processes wholly separate in each state.[4]

The other officers of the party are not especially influential, and the executive committees meet only a little more often than the full committees. Like the full committees, the executive committees are composed of men and women whose concern is state (and even local) organizational work rather than the building of a strong national-party apparatus. Traditionally, therefore, the national chairperson, with a permanent staff that he or she has chosen, has in effect been the national party organization.

Shifting Roles with Presidential Control

In reality, the role of the national committees and chairpersons depends upon whether the president is from their party. When their party does not hold the presidency, the national chairperson and committee often provide what national leadership the party has. To them falls the responsibility for binding up wounds, healing intraparty squabbles, helping pay debts from the losing campaign, raising new money, and revivifying the party organization around the country. The chairperson of the opposition party may also speak for the party and as an alternative to the president's party. There is little doubt that the national committees are more important national players the less control their party has over the national government.

With a party leader in the White House, on the other hand, the national committee's role is what he wants it to be. Presidents came to dominate their national committees early in this century. Their control reached a new peak in the 1960s and 1970s[5] and has remained strong ever since. Some presidents have turned their national committees into little more than managers of the president's campaigns and builders of the president's political support between campaigns. During the Nixon years, for example, the president and his staff handled his political affairs, and Rogers Morton and Robert Dole, the Republican national chairmen, did little more than serve as liaisons between the president and party leaders around the country. After his landslide election in 1964, adopting an even more adversarial posture toward his national committee, President Lyndon Johnson used his control to slash its staff and programs. By contrast, other modern presidents—especially Eisenhower, Kennedy, Reagan, and Bush—have used their control to build up the national committees to achieve party, not just presidential, goals.

As the role of the committee and its chairperson shifts, so too do the job specifications for a national party chairperson (see Table 4.2). Within the party of the president, he or she must be congenial to the president, representative of the president's ideological stance, and willing to be loyal primarily to the president. Bill Clinton's selection of David Wilhelm, his 1992 campaign manager, for the post in 1993 is the most recent bit of evidence to that effect. In the aftermath of the Democrat's stunning electoral defeat in 1994 and in preparation for the 1996 campaign, President Clinton tried a different approach—paralleling the one favored by President Reagan a decade earlier—by engineering the selection of a sitting senator, Christopher Dodd of Connecticut, as the party's general chairman and a veteran party official, Don Fowler from South Carolina, as the DNC chair in charge of handling the day-to-day operations of the national committee.

Within the opposition party, the chairperson will often be congenial to or at least trusted by the various factions or segments of the party. Frequently, he or she is chosen for ideological neutrality or for lack of identification with any of the individuals seeking the party's next presidential nomination. Experience in the nuts and bolts of party and campaign organization is also desirable. In this respect, it is hardly coincidental that, as the 1996 election cycle began with the Republicans trying to recapture the White House and the Democrats attempting to rebound from their defeats in 1994, the chairpersons in both parties were veteran political operatives. As the job specifications vary, so too do the hunting grounds for prospective chairpersons (see box on p. 92).

Table 4.2 NATIONAL COMMITTEE CHAIRPERSONS OF THE MAJOR PARTIES: 1961–96

Name	Tenure	Previous Political Position
	Democrats	
John M. Bailey	1961–68	State party chairman in Connecticut
Lawrence F. O'Brien	1968–69	U.S. postmaster general
Fred R. Harris	1969–70	U.S. senator from Oklahoma
Lawrence F. O'Brien	1970–72	Former national party chairman
Jean Westwood	1972	McGovern campaign activist
Robert S. Strauss	1972–77	Democratic national treasurer
Kenneth M. Curtis	1977	Former governor of Maine
John C. White	1977–81	Deputy secretary of agriculture
Charles T. Manatt	1981–85	Finance chairman of Democratic National Committee
Paul G. Kirk, Jr.	1985–89	Former national party treasurer
Ronald H. Brown	1989–93	Jesse Jackson's 1988 campaign convention manager
David Wilhelm	1993–95	Bill Clinton's 1992 campaign manager
Don Fowler	1995–	Executive committee member of Democratic National Committee
	Republicans	
William E. Miller	1961–64	U.S. representative from New York
Dean Burch	1964–65	Barry Goldwater campaign activist
Ray C. Bliss	1965–69	State party chairman in Ohio
Rogers C. Morton	1969–71	U.S. representative from Maryland
Robert J. Dole	1971–73	U.S. senator from Kansas
George H. Bush	1973–74	U.S. ambassador to the United Nations
Mary Louise Smith	1974–77	Co-chair of Republican National Committee
William E. Brock	1977–81	Former U.S. senator from Tennessee
Richard Richards	1981–83	Regional coordinator for Reagan campaign
Frank J. Fahrenkopf	1983–89	Republican state chairman in Nevada
Harvey Leroy Atwater	1989–91	George Bush's 1988 campaign manager
Clayton Yeutter	1991–92	Secretary of agriculture
Rich Bond	1992–93	Former deputy chief of staff for Vice-President George Bush
Haley Barbour	1993–	Republican National Committee member

LEE ATWATER AND RON BROWN: ALTERNATIVE ROUTES TO THE TOP

Lee Atwater and Ron Brown were installed after the 1988 presidential election as chairpersons of the Democratic and the Republican national committees. Both had spent most of their adult lives in politics and public affairs. Until assuming their duties as the head of their national parties, though, they had pursued almost diametrically opposed political careers and provide contrasting examples of the routes which can be taken to the leadership of the parties.

Harvey Leroy Atwater began his meteoric rise to national prominence as a college intern in the office of South Carolina Senator Strom Thurmond, and seven years later he became the director of Thurmond's 1978 reelection campaign. In between, he had served as national director of the College Republicans at the same time that George Bush was chairman of the Republican National Committee. By 1988, he was managing the Bush presidential campaign, drawing the barbs of the Democrats for his "hardball" and combative campaign style, and still practicing his populist brand of conservatism and playing blues guitar at every available opportunity. Only his debilitating illness and death in 1991 at age 40 prevented him from leading the RNC well into the 1990s.

Ronald Harmon Brown traveled a different route to the top of his party. His first taste of politics came as a child in a politically active Harlem family well linked into the black political elite. Educated at prestigious schools, he was the only black in his college class and the first black in his college fraternity. Instead of toiling in the vineyards of grass-roots campaign politics like Atwater, Brown enjoyed early success as a Washington insider in the roles of chief lobbyist for the National Urban League, counsel for the Senate Judiciary Committee, and first black partner in a prestigious Washington law firm. His ties to Edward Kennedy (as deputy manager of his 1980 presidential campaign) and Jesse Jackson raised suspicions in moderate and conservative Democratic circles. His insider credentials and responsible performance in 1988 as Jackson's convention floor manager, however, were sufficient to blunt worries that he might lead his party to the left and to turn a close early contest for chairperson into a runaway Brown victory. Brown left the DNC to become secretary of commerce in the Clinton administration, then tragically died in a plane crash in Croatia.

THE SUPPORTING CAST OF NATIONAL GROUPS

Clustered around the national committees are a set of more-or-less formal groups which also purport to speak for the national party or for some part of it. Some of them are creatures of the national committees, but some are not. Taken together with the national committee in each party, they come close to constituting that vague entity we call the national party.

Special Constituency Groups

The national party committees occasionally have given formal recognition to certain constituencies, especially supportive groups that might not be well represented otherwise. For a long time, both the Democratic and the Republican national committees have had women's divisions within their structures. In addition, both have had national federations of state and local women's groups: the National Federation of Democratic Women and the National Federation of Republican Women. Within the past thirty years, however, the importance of these women's divisions and organizations has declined markedly as women have entered regular leadership positions in the parties and served more frequently as convention delegates. Quite simply, they now want a role in the regular party organizations, or else they prefer to become active in nonparty organizations, such as the National Women's Political Caucus.

The Young Republican National Federation and the Young Democrats of America also have a long history. Both federations traditionally have been represented in their party's national councils, and support for both is provided by the senior party. The organized youth of both parties, however, are not controlled by the national committees, and often they have taken stands and supported candidates in opposition to the senior party organization. The Young Republicans, for instance, had an infatuation with Goldwater conservatism long after the regular leadership of the party had tried to reflect a more centrist position. In the late 1960s and 1970s, their loyalties turned increasingly to the conservatism of Ronald Reagan. The Young Democrats often stood to the left of their senior party organization. In 1969, for instance, their national convention called for repeal of all legal limits on abortion, for liberalization of marijuana laws, for recognition of Cuba and Communist China, and for an "immediate and total withdrawal of all American troops in Vietnam." In recent years, however, the ranks of the Young Democrats have dwindled at the same time as the Young Republicans attracted unprecedented numbers of members by capitalizing on the popularity of President Reagan and the party's enhanced electoral strength. This illustrates how much the strength of the youth groups depends on the fortunes of the party in general.

The Party's Officeholders in the States

Although they are not part of the official national organizations of their parties, the state governors invariably speak with authority in them. They have the prestige of high office and electoral success. Many lead or command the support of state party organizations, and a few inevitably contend for their party's presidential nomination.

The organization of the gubernatorial presence in the national parties, however, is relatively recent. The Republicans were first. After the Goldwater defeat of 1964, the moderate Republican governors wanted primarily to create a counterweight to the party's conservatives. A few years later, they established a full-time Washington office with financial help from the party's national committee, but their influence waned after the Republican victory of 1968. Like many such groups within the national parties, the governors operate most tellingly in the power vacuums of a party out of power. By the 1970s, the Democratic governors, then in the party of opposition, began to press for a role in national party affairs. By 1974, they had achieved that voice and had won representation, although in modest numbers, on the national committee. By the late 1970s and early 1980s, therefore, the governors of both parties had Washington offices and staffs. The Democratic Governors Conference even was represented on the national committee. Their organizational influence in the national parties, however, has continued to vary inversely with the party's presidential fortunes.

State legislators and local officials in both parties also are organized; moreover, they are formally represented on the Democratic National Committee. It would be hard to argue, though, that they greatly influence the national business of either party. A group with perhaps more influence is the Democratic Leadership Council. Founded in 1985, it brings together elected officials, led by influential members of Congress and governors and some prospective candidates for president. The DLC represents the moderate to conservative wing of the party and is attempting to make the party appeal more to southern and western voters. It played an important role in Bill Clinton's rise to national prominence leading up to his 1992 nomination for president.

The Congressional Campaign Committees

The most important of all the supporting cast are each party's House and Senate campaign committees. The House committees were founded in the immediate aftermath of the Civil War; the Senate committees came into being with the popular election of senators in 1913. The Democratic Congressional Campaign Committee (DCCC), the National Republican Congressional Committee (NRCC), the Democratic Senatorial Campaign Committee (DSCC), and the National Republican Senatorial Committee (NRSC) are organized to promote the reelection of their members and the addition of new members to their ranks. They are the campaign organizations of the congressional party in government, much as the national committee serves as the campaign organization of the presidential party.

The congressional campaign committees provide party candidates for office with many varieties of campaign assistance, from production facilities for television spots to that most valuable of all resources, money. They also have become increasingly active in channeling contributions from political action committees to the party's candidates for office. Although controlled by incumbent officeholders, they have nonetheless been able to resist inevitable pressures to serve only the reelection interests of incumbents and have concentrated considerable resources where they will have the greatest marginal payoff for the congressional party, such as in supporting their party's challengers to incumbents or candidates for open seats.

The new vitality of the congressional campaign committees derives from their increasing ability to raise campaign funds (see Table 4.3). The Republican committees are by far more successful in this endeavor. Together they raised $254 million for the campaigns in the 1991–92 election cycle and another $246 million for 1993–94. Indeed, the stunning success of GOP candidates in the 1994 midterm contests in part may be credited to aggressive fund raising and candidate recruitment by their congressional committees. Some of the funds raised by the committees went directly to candidates, but the larger part went for candidate recruitment, candidate training,

Table 4.3   POLITICAL PARTY NET RECEIPTS: 1975-76 TO 1993-94 (IN MILLIONS)

	National	Senate	House	State/Local	Total
		Democratic Committees			
1975-76	$ 13.1	1.0	0.9	0.0	$ 15.0
1977-78	$ 11.3	0.3	2.8	8.7	$ 23.1
1979-80	$ 15.1	1.7	2.1	11.7	$ 30.6
1981-82	$ 16.4	5.6	6.5	10.6	$ 39.1
1983-84	$ 46.6	8.9	10.4	18.5	$ 84.4
1985-86	$ 17.2	13.4	12.3	14.1	$ 60.0
1987-88	$ 52.3	16.3	12.5	35.0	$116.1
1989-90	$ 14.5	17.5	9.1	35.8	$ 76.9
1991-92	$ 65.8	25.5	12.8	58.1	$162.2
1993-94	$ 41.8	26.4	19.4	43.6	$131.3
		Republican Committees			
1975-76	$ 29.1	12.2	1.8	0.0	$ 43.1
1977-78	$ 34.2	10.9	14.1	20.9	$ 80.1
1979-80	$ 76.2	23.3	28.6	33.8	$161.9
1981-82	$ 83.5	48.9	58.0	24.0	$214.4
1983-84	$105.9	81.7	58.3	43.1	$289.0
1985-86	$ 83.8	84.4	39.8	47.2	$255.2
1987-88	$ 91.0	65.9	34.7	66.0	$257.5
1989-90	$ 68.7	65.1	33.2	39.3	$206.4
1991-92	$ 85.4	72.3	33.6	63.5	$254.8
1993-94	$ 87.4	65.4	26.7	66.1	$245.6

Note: Figures exclude receipts of miscellaneous national committees.

Source: Federal Election Commission.

research on opponents and issues, media, opinion polling, ads, and other campaign services. The Democrats now function in a similar but much more modest way, raising almost $162 million in 1991–92 and another $131 million in 1993–94. In both parties, the committees of the Hill are vastly more active and effective than they were in the 1970s. In resources and campaigning skills, they have begun to challenge the importance of the national committees of their parties. Their strength also insulates them and the congressional party very well from the national party organization, their sometime competitor.

TWO PATHS TO POWER

These national organizations have been the scene of considerable ferment in recent decades, as the hollow organizational shells that once were the national parties have been filled in. Movement has come along two separate "service" and "procedural" paths. The result is two national party organizations that are stronger than ever before—and that in an era that was supposed to have been characterized by the "decline of parties."[6]

The key to the recent development of the national parties has been a growing and independent financial base (Table 4.3), largely achieved through thousands of small contributions solicited by mass mailings to likely party supporters.[7] The Republican committees were the first to experience this new affluence, which grew most dramatically in the 1979–80 electoral cycle, peaked in 1983–84, and has leveled off since. A comparable surge in the income of the Democratic committees followed in 1983–84, succeeded by a second surge in the early 1990s. What began as a 3-to-1 financial advantage for the Republicans now has been cut in about half. These changes in party income have occurred simultaneously for the Republican's national and congressional campaign committees, with the latter's fund-raising successes quickly outpacing the former's. For the Democrats, on the other hand, the congressional committees led the way in the midterm election of 1982. This illustrates the principle for party development that adversity breeds change. The greatest advances in party organizational innovation have come when the party does not hold the presidency.[8] With this new financing in hand, the Republicans and belatedly the Democrats have developed strong and active national party organizations, which in turn have devoted themselves to supporting party candidates and state and local organizations throughout the nation. By the mid-1980s, the national parties had become institutionalized as "service" parties.[9]

Beginning in the 1960s, through party action often ratified by state law and court decisions, the Democrats pursued another goal: To better represent new party constituencies, they vested authority over the presidential nomination process in the national parties. The GOP choose not to take advantage of their competitor's precedent, reinforced in the courts, for centralizing party authority out of deference to their longstanding confederational structure, but it remains available to them should they ever want to pursue it.

The Service Party Path

The service party was born when, at some point in the 1960s, a quiet revolution began in the Republican National Committee. The committee's chairman of those years, Ray Bliss, involved the committee more and more in helping state and local parties with the nuts and bolts of party organizational work. Chairman William Brock carried the work forward in the late 1970s, turning the national party into an extraordinarily effective service organization for the parties of the states and localities. Bliss and Brock, more than anyone else, revived and strengthened the Republican national party by fashioning a new role for it. Charles Manatt generally is credited with turning the Democratic National Committee to the same path in the early 1980s.[10]

The keys to success in performing the new service role were two: new money and mastery of the new campaign technologies. Using direct-mail solicitations, which in turn used computer-based mailing lists, the Republicans began to generate ever higher levels of income (see Table 4.3). By the 1983–84 election cycle, the Republican National Committee, along with its subsidiary funds and committees, had raised $105.9 million—a record for national committee fund raising that still stands. (Campaign finance is discussed more fully in Chapter 12.) These resources enabled the RNC and its affiliates to engage in programs of aid to candidates and local party organizations without parallel in American party history.

The Democrats, long mired in debt, found themselves doing better but still badly overmatched in organizational and service capacity in the 1980s. The good news for the Democrats was that they had dramatically improved their fund-raising capacities (see Table 4.3) and their activities in the states and localities since 1979 or 1980. The bad news was that the Republicans were far ahead of them to begin with and were increasing their strength and capacity. Whatever the degree of Democratic success in becoming a service party, there was certainly no doubt that the party, under the national chairmanship of first Charles Manatt and then Paul Kirk had seen that as the only feasible course for party development. Indeed, the national Democrats made no secret of their attempt to mimic the Republican success in fund raising and in performing the services those funds could buy.

By the mid-1980s both parties were providing unprecedented levels of assistance to candidates and state parties. This assistance included a broad array of services—candidate recruitment and training, research, public opinion polling, data processing, computer networking and software development, production of radio and television commercials, direct mailing, expert consultants, and legal services—and millions of dollars to finance campaigns and to build party organizations. Concerned with the weakness of party organizations at the grass roots, Republican efforts even have turned to party building there. The Republican National Committee, breaking with its tradition of working only with the state parties, lavished money and assistance in 1984 on 650 key counties containing a majority of the nation's voters. What money made possible, a growing professional staff in the national headquarters was able to implement (see Table 4.4). Both national parties have emerged as well-staffed, institutionalized political organizations.

The Democrats' Procedural-Reform Path

Becoming a service party was not, of course, the path the national Democrats initially pursued. Instead, in the late 1960s and the 1970s, they were concerned with establishing their authority over the states' selection of delegates to the national nominating conventions. Beginning with efforts in the 1960s to enforce the loyalty of southern delegations to the national party ticket and continuing with the nomination process reforms of the McGovern-Fraser Commission and its successors, the Democrats restricted the autonomy of the state parties and the authority of state law in determining how delegates were to be selected for the presidential nominating conventions. Key court decisions upheld these actions, further solidifying the new-found authority of the national party. The immediate intent of the reformers was to make the nomination process more open and democratic. To achieve that goal, the confederated structure of the party, in which each state was sovereign in internal affairs, had to give way. That the reformers were successful in realizing their goals is testimony to the unusual politics of the period, the inattentiveness of state party leaders to the potential threat posed by the reforms, and the vacuum of power at the

Table 4.4 THE GROWTH OF NATIONAL PARTY COMMITTEE STAFF, 1972–92

	1972	1976	1980	1984	1988	1992
Democratic Party Committees						
National Committee	30	30	40	130	160	270
House Campaign Committee	5	6	26	45	80	64
Senate Campaign Committee	4	5	20	22	50	35
Republican Party Committees						
National Committee	30	200	350	600	425	300
House Campaign Committee	6	8	40	130	80	89
Senate Campaign Committee	4	6	30	90	88	135

Note: These numbers fluctuate considerably from month to month and year to year. As a general rule, however, size of the national committees peaks in the presidential election year and is smaller in the interelection period.

Source: 1972–84: Paul S. Herrnson, *Party Campaigning in the 1980s* (Cambridge, Mass.: Harvard University Press, 1988), p. 39; 1988: Paul S. Herrnson, "Reemergent National Party Organizations," in L. Sandy Maisel, ed., *The Parties Respond: Changes in the American Party System* (Boulder, Colo.: Westview Press, 1990), pp. 41–66 at p. 51. 1992: Paul S. Herrnson, "The Revitalization of National Party Organizations," in L. Sandy Maisel, ed., *The Parties Respond: Changes in American Parties and Campaigns* (Boulder, Colo.: Westview Press, 1994), pp. 45–68 at p. 54.

national apex of the traditional party organization. (This story is told in more detail in Chapter 10.)[11] Ironically, the GOP, innocent of any strong desire to alter its nomination process rules,[12] was carried along nonetheless by the tide of Democratic party reform because of the bipartisan nature of the state implementing legislation.

By the early 1980s, the national Democratic party had decided to soft pedal organizational reforms and move toward the Republican service model. All of its centralization of national authority on questions of representation and participation, even the overriding of the procedural preferences of state parties and state laws, had done little to win elections. Moreover, it had divided the party and alienated a good part of the Democratic party in government, much of which was conspicuously absent from party conventions and midyear conferences in the 1970s. Thus, in the early 1980s the Democrats shifted course. The national committee adopted rules for the 1984 national convention that guaranteed a much greater representation of the party's leaders and officeholders. (See Chapter 10 for an extensive discussion of Democratic reforms of the delegate selection process.) The midyear conference was refocused from issues to party building in 1982 and then scrapped in 1986. In addition, in the 1980s, the party rushed to broaden the base of its fund raising and to provide the means and know-how to recruit candidates and revitalize local party organization. When the dust from all of this effort settled, the signs of change were everywhere, authority over party rules had been nationalized, and what had been two models for national party strengthening were rapidly converging into one.[13]

POWER AND AUTHORITY IN THE NATIONAL PARTY

It is clear that there has been a strengthening of the national parties in the last two decades and that the most apparent and important strengthening has been in the activities that would regain some of the parties' lost roles in nominating and electing candidates. To an important degree, the parties (especially the Republicans) have begun to "muscle in" on the campaign support functions monopolized just a few years before by political action committees (PACs) and private political consultants, although it is as yet unclear whether parties can displace them. But it is not inconceivable that, when viewed in retrospect, the major significance of these competitors to parties will be found to be their service as temporary bridges between the old party, centered at the grass roots, and the new national service party. The buttressing of the national parties also has the potential to alter the relationships within the parties: between the national party and state-and-local party organizations, the president, and the Congress, as well as among the various representatives of the national parties.

The State and Local Connection

The increased resources and activities of the two national parties, without question, have increased their visibility and presence. The extent to which that kind of nationalization of the parties also has contributed to a centralization of authority within them is not yet clear. The Democrats approach the service party role with far more experience than the Republicans have in drafting and enforcing national rules and a stronger will to assert centralized authority, although the centralizing actions have been taken by the convention and its committees rather than the national committee.[14] Moreover, the structure of representation on the DNC can sustain and legitimize more centralized authority. The Republicans, on the other hand, remain a confederation of equal state parties; they are also, by political philosophy, more wary of centralized authority. Due to its vastly superior resources, however, the Republican national party has penetrated more to the state and local level.

Philosophies and organizational formalities aside, it is difficult to imagine that the national subsidization of state and local party organizations and the national intervention into their nominations and elections will not be accompanied by some centralization of authority (see box on pp. 100–101). The temptation to guide and direct from above is strong, given the expertise and resources of the national parties. However lightly and informally it is exercised, it is most likely that a national imprint on issues, on the kinds of candidates recruited, and on the way things are done organizationally will follow. Resistance in the state and local organizations might come at the price of starvation. Those who pay the pipers more often than not call the tune.[15]

The Presidential Connection

When a party holds the presidency, the president's program and record become the party's. It is the president who interprets the party's platform and the mandate of the

TWO CASES OF TENSION BETWEEN THE STATE AND THE NATIONAL PARTIES

Increased national party activity and authority can produce conflict between traditionally autonomous state parties and assertive national parties. An example from each party illustrates how national party incursions into areas traditionally left to states have led to tensions between state party leaders and their national parties.

RNC FAVORITISM IN CONTESTED PRIMARIES

In its efforts to field the strongest party ticket, the RNC under William Brock adopted a policy of picking one candidate to support in contested state primaries. Occasionally, RNC efforts backfired, such as in 1978 when it supported the primary opponent of the candidate, Lee Dreyfus, who went on to become governor of Wisconsin—and no friend of the national party establishment. In response to criticisms from the state party leaders, the party revised this policy in 1980 to require approval by the state party chairperson and the national committee members from the state before the RNC could support a candidate for nomination.[16]

DNC EFFORTS TO REDUCE "PARTY BASHING"

Recognizing that candidates were undermining their own party by running against the national Democratic party, in 1986 DNC Chairperson Paul Kirk asked state Democratic leaders who wished to participate in a DNC-financed program for state party building to sign an agreement that would require them, in the words of the DNC memorandum,

> to insist that Democratic candidates who benefit from this program do not run campaigns against, and instead run with, the national Democratic Party. This means exerting all of the state party's influence and bringing to bear all of the pressure it can to ensure that a positive, unified Democratic party campaign develops. It also means that the state party and state committee shall disagree with and disavow any remarks by a candidate or campaign that attack the national party.

Not surprisingly, the Republicans gleefully attacked the Democrats for attempting to impose an undemocratic loyalty oath, and some state Democratic leaders expressed dismay that the national party was overreacting to what was a minor problem.

For right now, such examples are exceptions to the usual cooperation between the state and national parties. Candidates for office, often thankful for assistance of any sort, have welcomed the technical and financial resources offered by the national parties. State and local organizations,

(*box continues*)

recognizing the value of national assistance, usually have been more receptive to than threatened by national intervention in party building and candidate support. To be sure, state and local party leaders and candidates occasionally resent the intrusion of the sometimes brash and arrogant national party operatives into their local affairs, but cooperative relationships have been the norm.

voters. His preferences, whether embodied in the formal measures of the State of the Union address or tossed off more casually at a press conference, impose a policy and a record on his party. He may consult the party chairperson or other party notables, but it is his decisions, his successes or failures, that form the party record.

Every president in recent memory has kept his national committee on a short leash, but White House dominance of the national party reached its zenith in the presidency of Richard M. Nixon. The Watergate tapes reveal that the president's principal assistants, John Erlichman and H. R. Haldeman, were deeply involved in the decisions of the 1972 campaign—a campaign headed, in fact, by another close Nixon associate, former attorney general John Mitchell. So marginal to the 1972 campaign were the Republican party bodies and officials that they remained ignorant and innocent of the wrongdoing and scandals of the campaign. Democratic presidents, too, have wanted the national committee under their control. In 1980 President Jimmy Carter angered party people by diverting crucial DNC personnel and resources to his own reelection campaign.

During the 1980s the national committee of the president's party, here the Republican National Committee, really came into its own as an important independent actor in party politics. Federal funding of presidential campaigns, with its strict limitations on party expenditures for presidential politics, freed the national committees from their traditional concentration on presidential elections and allowed them to dedicate their now considerable resources to party building at the state and local level. This inclination was reenforced by the emergence of a party committee role in raising soft-money contributions to the presidential-year campaign and channeling this money to the state and local parties for grass-roots mobilization activities (see Chapter 12 on soft money). At the same time, the selection of close advisors to the president as its recent chairs has given the RNC a status it had not enjoyed before, even as presidential influence was being asserted. Designation of President Reagan's longtime friend, Senator Paul Laxalt of Nevada, to the post of general chairman and the appointment of Nevada's party chairman, Frank Fahrenkopf, to the party chairmanship eliminated the tensions between the White House and the national committee that inevitably follow a transition from the leaderless party out of power to a presidential party. The move also brought the party leader into the inner circle of White House advisors. This relationship continued with the selection of Lee Atwater, George Bush's principal campaign advisor, to the RNC chairmanship in 1989. President Clinton's choice of Christopher Dodd as general chair and Donald Fowler as national chair of the DNC in 1995 was similarly designed to integrate the national committee more fully into the presidential reelection effort.

By contrast, in those four long years after presidential defeat, a national party suffers an almost incessant jockeying for the right to lead. The defeated presidential candidate, depending on his ties and popularity within the party, may achieve an important voice in the party. Gerald Ford did, but George Bush, Jimmy Carter, Walter Mondale, and Michael Dukakis did not. A strong and vigorous national chairperson may help to fill the void in national leadership; those with substantial financial and organizational accomplishments, like the RNC's Haley Barbour, are more likely to succeed. Most commonly, however, leadership of the "out" party falls to its leaders in the Congress. The visibility of the party's leadership in Congress is matched by the political support and power of its campaign committees. Above all, the congressional party, simply because its legislative responsibilities force it to take policy stands, formulates the party position and challenges the program of the opposition's president.

It seems safe to predict that strengthened national party committees will assume a more prominent party role in the party out of power. The same is true of their chairpersons. That much seems clear when one considers the Republicans under William Brock in the late 1970s and the Democrats under Charles Manatt, Paul Kirk, and Ron Brown since then. But what of a strengthened party and its president? It seems likely that presidents will continue to worry about independent party voices and that they will want the new party power to be at their service. They will certainly want the party committees to mobilize behind their programs all those members of Congress they recruited, trained, financed, and helped elect. Also, if presidents are in their first term, they will very likely want to draw on the assets of the national party for their reelection campaigns as much as the Federal Elections Campaign Act permits. If presidents feared and used the national committees when the committees were weak, they have even more reason to turn to them when the committees are more formidable. Even as the national parties continue their party building, it will be in the service of presidential goals.[17]

The Congressional Connection

Nationalizing forces, this time emanating from the congressional party itself rather than the national party committees, have overtaken the Congress as well. Congressional campaign committees elected by the party congressional caucuses have become increasingly active in recruiting and supporting party candidates for office. This assistance is more valuable to challengers and contenders for open seats than to incumbents, who are easily able to raise their own campaign resources.

The expanded role for the congressional party greatly increases the potential for greater control of the rank and file, particularly newly elected members, by the party leadership in each chamber. There is a temptation to attribute the greater intraparty voting cohesion manifested in recent years (see Chapter 13) in part to the congressional party's financial prowess. The party leadership so far has refrained from allocating campaign funds and services on the basis of support for the party's program, but it has not been bashful in reminding members that the party played some role in their electoral success. One factor in the party cohesion of the post-1994 Republican majority in the House surely is the role the party leadership played in supporting Republicans for office in the 1994 contests. Constituency pressures will always be paramount in the Congress, but the more senators and representatives can count on campaign support from the congressional party, the more open they will be to party-based appeals.[18] This campaign support also may, to some degree, counterbalance pressures on Congress from PACs and competing centers for party power in Washington—the president and the national party committees.

The Connections Within the National Party

When it comes to election campaigns, each national party has three committees that are of significance—the national committee and the Senate and House campaign committees. As we have seen from Table 4.3, each raises millions of dollars to support its activities. There are, to be sure, many opportunities for cooperation among them, and such cooperation has increased greatly in recent years. All benefit, for example, from voter registration and get-out-the-vote drives, and there often are economies of scale to be realized in a dovetailing of effort in candidate recruitment and campaigns. In raising and spending their money, however, the committees within each party to some degree are competitors (see box on p. 104). They seek financial support from the same contributors (and jealously guard their contributor lists), recruit political talent from the same limited pool, and pursue sometimes incompatible goals. Where resources are as scarce as they are in party organizing, it should not be at all surprising that different organizations from the same party will struggle over them.[19]

THE LIMITS OF PARTY ORGANIZATION

Amid all the talk and reports of new strength in the national party organization, it is well to remember that the parties seem to have lost their vitality for many Americans. More professionalized, service-oriented parties may be better at assisting candidates in their races for office than in stimulating voter attachments to parties or at involving the faithful at the grass roots. The strengthening of parties at the center, then, may have contributed little to a heightening of their role in American politics.[20]

Moreover, American party organizations remain weak by most standards. They are an anachronism in this era of large-scale organizations. In business, government, universities, and voluntary organizations, it is a time of complex social structures and of the bureaucrats who have become their symbols. We have every right to include the parties among them, but it is an inescapable fact that the parties, almost alone among our major social institutions, have resisted the development of large, centralized organization.

Even by the standards of the parties of some other democracies, the American party organizations cut an unimpressive figure. They lack the hierarchical control and efficiency, the unified setting of priorities and strategy, and the central responsibility we often find in parties in other nations. Instead of a continuity of relationships and

CONFLICT AMONG THE PARTY COMMITTEES: ED ROLLINS AND THE WHITE HOUSE IN 1990

Conflict over strategy during the 1990 midterm campaigns pitted Edward Rollins, co-chairman of the National Republican Congressional Committee and a well-respected campaign strategist, against the White House and the Republican National Committee. In a memo to Republican House candidates early in the campaign, Rollins advised them to distance themselves from President Bush's recent support for a tax increase in violation of his 1988 campaign pledge of "no new taxes." This repudiation of their president's action, urged by Rollins to protect Republican House candidates from electoral retribution, infuriated the White House and led to Rollins' resignation on the eve of the RNC meeting in January, 1991—a victim of the conflict between the interest of House candidates to desert their president on a controversial issue and the interest of the national party committee and the White House to protect the president's authority and national standing. Rollins turned up in 1992, for a short stint at least, as a top campaign advisor to independent candidate Ross Perot.

of operations, the American party organizations feature only improvisatory, elusive, and sporadic structure and activities. Also, whereas the party organizations of other Western democracies have had permanent, highly professional leadership and large party bureaucracies, the American organizations have generally done without a professional bureaucracy or leadership cadre. Except at the national level in recent years, the business of American party organization is still largely in the hands of part-time activists and inexperienced professionals, which is perhaps to say that its business and its organizational relationships require little specialization or high-level professional care. Even at the national level, as Epstein has observed: "The very word 'committee' suggests limited national structure."[21]

One is compelled to wonder at the reasons for the stunting of American party organization, even in these times of unprecedented strength at its national level. In part, it results from statutory limits and the federal structure of our polity. Traditional fears of political parties and party strength have certainly contributed as well. (There is little in American political values that would welcome an efficient or "businesslike" operation of the parties.) So has a candidate-centered politics and the American system of separation of powers. Even recent reforms in campaign financing contribute to the weakness of the party organizations by denying them their traditional position as a major source of campaign funds. By restricting party contributions to $5,000 per federal candidate, the statutes now treat parties as just another source of candidate support along with political action committees, which can also give only $5,000, and individuals, who are limited to $1,000 per candidate rather than organizations that are integral to the electoral process.[22]

In large part, however, the underorganization of the American parties results from their fundamental character. They have been pragmatic electoral parties, involved chiefly in supporting candidates for public office and active mainly during campaigns. As such, they have long been led and dominated, not by career bureaucrats, but by public office seekers and holders. Perhaps too the degree of pragmatic flexibility to which Americans have carried their party politics rules out the routine and the fixity of a large organization. Organization is to some extent routine and unchanging, and it is therefore more compatible with the party of unchanging ideology or principle than with one committed to the adjustments necessary for electoral success. Thus, the electoral preoccupations of the American parties have tipped the scales against the party organizations.

Chapter
5

The Political Party of the Activists

Behind the imposing facades of its formal, statutory organizational structures are the living, human realities of the political parties. The party organization is a grouping of people, most of them contributing their time and energy on a purely voluntary basis. Even the paid professional party workers who increasingly staff the national and state offices share many of the attributes of volunteers. The statutes ignore these men and women of the party, their goals and motives, their interactions and relationships, the contributions they make to the organizations, and the price they exact for those contributions. Yet, the activity and motivations of those men and women are closer to the real world of party politics than all the statutory paragraphs put together.

As an organization, the political party is a mechanism for uniting people in pursuit of goals. It is vastly committed to the winning of elections. In addition, it may seek to spread an ideology, enact a set of public policies, or ease regulations affecting its activities. Goal seeking also goes on within the party organization on a personal, individual level. Individual party leaders, workers, and members are involved for some identifiable, if covert or implicit, set of reasons. They seek some reward or payoff for devoting their time to party activity rather than to their church, their service organization, or even their golf game.

The major task for the party organization is to convert the raw materials of people, resources, and expertise into activity that is oriented toward fulfilling the party's goals. How it accomplishes this is determined by the private life of the party—its internal division of labor and allocation of authority, its internal system of communication, and the internal decision-making processes through which it chooses how to mobilize its resources, deploy its assets, and set its strategies. To be effective, above all else, the party must be able to fulfill its organizational goals while simultaneously allowing its individual members to realize their goals. Many are the party organizations that are incapable of meeting that challenge.

INCENTIVES FOR POLITICAL ACTIVITY

The American political parties have never operated primarily in a cash economy. They have rarely bought or hired more than a small proportion of the millions of labor hours they need. Even today, in spite of the increasing professionalization of the national and state party headquarters, paid staffs are small or nonexistent in most local party organizations, and it is a rare local chairman who draws any salary.[1]

The great number of Americans who are active in the parties receive no cash in return for their considerable time and skills. Even the earthy old customs of paying precinct workers on election day or using government employees as the party's workers at election time are vanishing. What is it, then, that induces party workers to lavish their hours and efforts on the affairs of the parties? If the parties' payments are not made in cash, in which coin are they made?

In their seminal theory of motivations for organizational involvement, Peter B. Clark and James Q. Wilson identified three different types of incentives for activity. *Material incentives* are tangible rewards for activity—if not direct cash payments for work, they often involve implicit understandings that involvement will be rewarded with some kind of material benefits. *Solidary incentives* are the intangible benefits derived from association and fellowship, from being "one of the group." *Purposive incentives* are intangible rewards of a different kind—based on the sense of satisfaction that accompanies involvement in a worthwhile cause or in activities that promote some collective principle. This typology has been widely and fruitfully employed in the study of incentives for party activity.[2]

Material Incentives

Historically, the principal material inducement to party activity has been the opportunity to share in the "spoils" obtained when a party is in control of government. These "spoils" are generally of two types—patronage and preferments. *Patronage* refers to appointment to governmental positions as a reward for party work. *Preferments* involve, more generally, the discretionary granting of the favors of government to party supporters. Both patronage and preferments have played important roles in building and sustaining the American party organizations.[3]

Patronage   Since the beginning of the Republic in the 1790s, but especially since the presidency of Andrew Jackson when federal patronage jobs doubled, Americans have been attracted to party work by the prospect of being rewarded with governmental employment. The use of patronage is hardly unique to American parties, but no other party system has over its history relied so systematically on patronage as has the American system. In the heyday of the political machine, for example, city governments were staffed almost entirely by loyalists of the party in power, all of whom faced the prospect of being thrown out of work should their party be turned out of office.[4]

As the price to be paid for their "political" jobs, patronage appointees traditionally "volunteered" their time, energy, and often even a part of their salary to the party organization, particularly to help in political campaigns. In many places, the cadres of activists in political campaigns have been filled with public employees. Tales of the entire staff of certain government departments being mobilized in support of their boss's reelection are not uncommon in the annals of American party politics. Money, too, always has been an important resource in campaigns, and patronage workers have been called upon to "invest" in the party through which they received their jobs. Even in modern times when such directly partisan practices are increasingly frowned upon and sometimes even illegal, the pressures remain compelling in some places for government employees to contribute their time or money to the party that helped them to get their job. The line between voluntary and expected, even required, activities, though, is a fine one.

Despite the explosive growth of government in this century to more than 18 million public employees today (3 million federal, more than 4 million state, and almost 11 million local), the number of patronage jobs available to the parties has declined dramatically as civil service and merit systems have expanded. The first major step in this process was the establishment of the federal civil service system by the Pendleton Act in 1883, which removed almost 14,000 of the more than 131,000 federal employees from patronage appointment.[5] The number of full-time federal positions filled by political appointees has dwindled over the years to only several thousand today, many of them high-level policy-making positions.[6] Similar declines have come, albeit more belatedly, to the states and localities; although, in New York City, new Republican Mayor Giuliani still had 1,500 positions to fill in 1994. Any number of states, counties, and cities—the great majority surely—have virtually abolished patronage, moving to merit systems of some sort, at least for nonpolicy-making positions.

While these changes traditionally have been the products of antimachine reform movements and the unionization of public employees, recent Supreme Court decisions also have administered some of the final blows against patronage at the state and local level. In 1976 the Court barred dismissal of sheriff's employees in Cook County, Illinois, just because of a change of the party in power. Four years later the Court blocked political dismissals of assistant public defenders in Rockland County, New York. Then, in a 1990 Illinois case, the Supreme Court moved beyond protecting government employees from political dismissal to rule that politically based promotion and hiring violated the First Amendment freedoms of speech and association. In each case, the Court appreciated that party affiliation might be a relevant condition in filling policy-making positions but found such considerations inappropriate for lower-level offices (see box on following page).[7]

Even where patronage positions remain, the party often encounters formidable problems in exploiting them as incentives for party activity. Evidence from a variety of locales shows that the parties achieve only a partial return in party work or contributions from their patronage appointees. Also there is frequently a poor fit between the available patronage jobs and the kinds of activists the party wants to recruit. The politics of patronage have always worked best among the depressed and disadvantaged; most patronage positions do not tempt the educated, "respected" middle-class leadership the parties would like to attract. Furthermore, in an age of candidate-centered politics, elected executives are more interested in using patronage to build their own political followings than to strengthen the party apparatus, and, of course,

---

THE DISMANTLING OF CHICAGO'S "PATRONAGE ARMY"

Unable to defeat a candidate of Chicago's Democratic machine in a race for delegate to the state's 1969 constitutional convention, frustrated reformer Michael Shakman sought judicial relief. He challenged the constitutionality of the city's patronage system in the federal courts. His suit triggered a series of court rulings and subsequent consent decrees between 1972 and 1988 through which the city agreed, albeit grudgingly, to eliminate political hiring and firing for all but the top policy-making positions and to protect city employees from being forced to do political work or make political contributions. To implement these agreements, the courts required the city to develop stringent plans for compliance and to submit to yearly external audits of its personnel practices. While politics still influences personnel decisions in Chicago government, the large "patronage army" that once was the hallmark of Chicago politics seems to have been dismantled.[8]

---

as the supply of valuable patronage positions dwindles, the old aphorism that each appointment creates one ingrate who gets the job and many malcontents who do not becomes even more apropos.[9]

Nonetheless, patronage is likely to endure as long as it is attractive to both political leaders and their followers. The consequences of antipatronage court rulings will diffuse slowly, case by case, through the decentralized political system. Top policy-making positions should continue to be reserved for loyal supporters of a mayor, a governor, a president. Legislative bodies at all levels of government will remain loathe to bring their staff employees under the protection of civil service systems. Civil service regulations for governmental employees will be bypassed by the hiring of politically loyal temporaries outside of the civil service system or by channelling political workers into the growing number of quasi-governmental organizations. Honorary positions on government advisory groups will linger on as coveted rewards for loyal party service. Ambassadorial appointments still will be tendered to a few important campaign supporters. Wherever political leaders retain discretion over personnel appointments, in short, they will find a way to award them to their trusted political supporters. The promise of such awards, in turn, will inevitably attract people to political activity—though not the large numbers who once served as the "foot soldiers" of the traditional political machines.

Although the decline of patronage surely suits the current norms of the American political culture, some thoughtful observers mourn the passing of a practice that has been central to American political life since early in the nineteenth century. The parties may find it more and more difficult to recruit the labor and talent they need to retain their strength, and those who value strong parties as instruments of democracy will lament this trend. The activists whom parties do recruit may demand more ideological payoffs for their participation—diverting the parties from the pragmatic, inclusive postures they have assumed during most of their histories. By the same token, with the replacement of political appointees by neutral professionals, governmental bureaucracies may become less responsive to elected political leaders and perhaps even less sympathetic to their clienteles. Also, it is virtually impossible in a civil service system for reform-minded leaders to replace a stodgy or ineffective public bureaucracy with more efficient workers. With the stigma attached to patronage in current times, it is easy to forget that patronage practices were first promoted at the federal level by Andrew Jackson to produce a more democratic and less elitist government and that career civil service employees today are often criticized as unresponsive to the public they are supposed to serve.[10]

Patronage jobs in government, though, are not the only employment opportunities a party can offer. In recent years, the party organizations at the state and national levels have become important employers themselves of paid professional campaign workers, and numerous activists are attracted to party work in the hopes of landing these jobs.

Elected Office   The party also offers an efficient and in a few cases the only avenue to elective office, so it is inevitable that the possibility of a career in public office should recruit new party activists or sustain activity after other incentives have worn off. About 40 percent of the county chairpersons interviewed in a 1979–80 national survey aspired to hold public office, and an earlier study found that one-third of all state party chairs were candidates for elective office after serving the party.[11] Involvement in the party, like activity in various community organizations, remains an attractive way for aspiring politicians to build a base from which to launch a political career.

A few party organizations enjoy such disciplined control over their primaries that they can and do "give" public office, especially at the state and local level, to loyal party workers. That degree of control over nomination and election to office, however, is rare today. It is far more common for candidates for office to see the party as one of the bases, in some areas the most important one, of support for election or reelection. Candidates need advice, know-how, people (staff and volunteers), and money, and the party remains a likely source of them. Nonetheless, candidates sometimes remain aloof from the party, in part because they may not need the resources it commands and in part because, in an antiparty age, they do not want to be identified too closely with a political party.

Preferments   The tangible, material rewards of politics may take forms other than appointive or elective office, perhaps increasingly so with the decline of patronage. Because public officials always can exercise at least some discretion in the allocation of government services and the granting of government contracts, the potential for political favoritism exists. Many people are attracted to party activity and party financial support in search of these favors. The active partisan or the financial "fat cat" may, for example, seek preference in the awarding of public contracts. It is no accident that leaders of the construction industry are so active politically in states and localities that spend millions every year on roads and public buildings. Preference may take other forms: a tolerant application of regulatory or inspection policies, unusually prompt snow and garbage removal, the fixed traffic ticket, or the granting of admission to crowded state universities. It may also involve the granting of scarce opportunities such as liquor licenses or cable television franchises or calculated ignoring of prostitution, bookmaking, the numbers game, or traffic in drugs in return for some form of political support. By "preferment," in other words, one means the special treatment or advantage that flows from the party's holding the decision-making positions in government.

Various procedures (such as tight regulations, active oversight, inspectors general, competitive and sealed bidding, conflict of interest statutes, privatization, even affirmative action) have been adopted over the years, often at the behest of "good government" reformers, to constrain the exercise of this political discretion in the allocation of government benefits and the procurement of goods and services by government. Nonetheless, where the benefits to be realized are great and the desire to create political support is compelling (and where are they not?), there always seem to be ways to evade even the most stringent controls. There is understandable resistance, in the name of both democracy and efficiency, to sacrificing all discretion to eliminate political discretion. The result is that preferments may have taken the place of patronage as the principal material incentive for political activity. In the process, though, party leaders have lost an important source of leverage over officeholders, at whose discretion preferments are granted.[12]

Solidary Incentives

The personal, nonmaterial rewards of party activity are not easy to identify and certainly are not easy to measure. One can sense, however, the social rewards of politics in the camaraderie at party headquarters or the courthouse. Such solidary incentives are evident at a party dinner as the workers press around the great and near-great of the party, hoping for a word of greeting or a nod of recognition. Even in the amateur political clubs of some large cities, the attractiveness of the social life and friendship circle is important. Although the parties' regularly rely on social incentives of this sort, those incentives are probably secondary to the pursuit of political goals. Perhaps one can say more simply that party politics is a splendid vehicle for gregariousness. Almost all reported research on the motivations of party activists has found a substantial number who cite the social life of party politics as a valuable reward.[13]

Social satisfactions merge almost imperceptibly into the psychological. "Like the theater, politics is a great nourisher of egos," writes one observer. It attracts men and women "who are hungry for attention, for assurance that somebody loves them, for the soul-stirring music of their own voices."[14] Party work may also offer the individual a cause with which to identify, a charismatic leader to follow, a round of activities that can lift him or her above the personally unrewarding tasks of the workday world. Even though party politics may seem out of fashion in this antiparty era, for some Americans it provides the small island of excitement in a sea of routine. It may even offer an occasion for the manipulation or domination of others, a chance to decide or command, even an avenue for the projection of aggression and hostility.

Purposive Incentives

Even the most casual soundings of party rhetoric indicate an increasing identification of partisans as "liberals" or "conservatives." Behind these phrases lies a potent purposive motivation to party activity: a commitment to clusters of related attitudes about government and politics, especially about the proper role of government in contemporary society. On a more modest and limited scale, the spur to activity may be concern for a single issue or interest (e.g., tax cuts, the war in Vietnam, abortion, religious values, gun control) or a single area of policy concern (foreign policy, civil rights, the environment). The "causes" of involvement may, indeed, be the reform or rehabilitation of the political party itself.

Just as the importance of the immediate, material, personal rewards of politics has recently declined, that of issue and ideology has increased. These issue concerns in the local parties have paralleled the ideological triumphs in the national parties: the capture of the Republicans by Goldwater conservatives in 1964, the success of the liberal Democratic ideologues on behalf of Eugene McCarthy (1968) and George McGovern (1972), the victories of Ronald Reagan in 1980 both within the Republican party and throughout the nation, and the rise of the religious fundamentalists in the GOP of the 1990s. As these particular movements suggest, the mobilization of issue and ideologically motivated workers into the party often depends upon the drawing power of an attractive leader who champions the cause. We must not underestimate the importance of a Kennedy, a Goldwater, or a Reagan in attracting citizens into party politics. Nor can we ignore the importance of ideological motivations when party activists resort to the extreme measure of switching parties in pursuit of greater harmony between their personal views and the positions of their party.[15]

Party activists may also be drawn to the party by a more general civic commitment—a sense of obligation and duty as a citizen or a belief in the democratic values of citizen participation. Scholars who have questioned party workers about their motives for service in the party know the familiar answers. They were asked to serve, and they assented because it was their civic duty. Often that response, in whatever words it may be couched, merely masks what the respondent feels are less acceptable motives. Often, however, it is an honest reflection of deeply ingrained civic values, developed perhaps from parents who themselves were party activists or acted upon in political cultures in which good citizenship is expected. Often, too, it may be combined with honest, if vague, commitments to "good government" and political reform.

Mixed Incentives

No party organization depends on a single incentive, and very few partisans labor in the party for only one reason. Most party organizations rely on a variety of incentives. Patronage workers may coexist with workers attracted by policy issues or by a middle-class sense of civic responsibility. Both may gain the satisfactions of social interaction with like-minded people. The mixture of incentives may vary between levels of the party organization, with higher-level activists sustained more by purposive incentives and lower-level activists attracted by material or solidary rewards,[16] or the mix may differ by political culture, with more traditional cultures conducive to parties built around material motives and reform-oriented cultures attracting purposive activists.

For all the subtleties of the mix and variety of incentives, however, general comments about their overall frequency are possible. Scholarly evidence on the point comes from sporadic studies of parties in scattered parts of the country, but what evidence there is points to the dominance of ideological or issue incentives. Put very simply, the desire to use the party as a means to achieve policy goals appears to be the major incentive attracting individuals to party work these days.[17] Although similar data are unavailable for earlier periods, there is reason to believe that this generalization was far less true of party workers a generation or two ago.[18] This is not to say, however, that personal material interests are unimportant as sources of involvement in parties. Parties and political activity continue to offer many attractive material rewards in spite of the declining availability of patronage jobs.

Incentives may change, moreover, for any individual; that is, the incentive that recruits people to party activity may not sustain them in that activity. Several studies suggest that a shift in incentives takes place in those party activists attracted by the purposive incentives—those who seek to achieve issue, ideological, or other impersonal goals through their party activity. To sustain their involvement in party work, they tend to depend more on incentives of social contact, identification with the party itself, and other personal rewards and satisfactions.[19] Perhaps an electorally pragmatic party—one traditionally committed to the flexibilities necessary to win elections—has difficulty providing the ideological successes necessary to sustain workers whose incentives remain ideological for any length of time.

THE PROCESSES OF RECRUITMENT

The mere existence of incentives for work in the party organization will not automatically produce a full roster of active workers. The political party, like any other organization, must recruit actively to ensure for itself useful and compatible members. Potential activists may lack either the knowledge of the opportunity or the stimulus to act or both. Therefore, there must be some process of recruitment that will join opportunity and stimulus to incentives in order to attract them.

Nonetheless, except at the national level and in some states where the recent profusion of paid positions and exciting work have transformed dull and inconsequential positions into attractive professional opportunities, the parties do not find it easy to recruit. Frequently, their incentives are not attractive enough to compete even with the modest pleasures of activity in a local service club. They often lack any effective mechanism for recruiting new personnel, and they may even ignore the necessity for self-renewal. Furthermore, state statutes often take at least part of the recruitment process out of their hands; open party caucuses and the election of party officials in primaries tend to encourage self-recruitment at the expense of the party initiatives and control. Above all, the chronic need for personnel of any kind disposes the parties to accept whatever help is available. Even patronage-rich organizations in job-poor communities tend not to be proactive in recruiting new activists. Friendship and contacts within the party organization may speed the entry of the new activist more effectively than political skills or promise of performance.

The Recruitment System

In the absence of regular and rigorous recruitment by the party, opportunities for party work come in a haphazard way. Initially, a certain degree of awareness of the parties is necessary, as are strong political goals and commitments. Then, at the time of recruitment, there must also be some more immediate stimulus for the individual to enter party work. Sometimes that stimulus is internal, and the individual in effect recruits himself or herself. In other cases, the stimulus is external, most often the invitation or persuasion of some other individual. Over the years, activists have tended to ascribe their initial recruitment largely to these external stimuli.[20]

Events in the larger political world also play an important role in the recruitment of party activists. Specific candidates for office and political causes often provide the first attraction to party work, which for some is sustained long after the initial reason has disappeared. Just as the Democratic party has been heavily influenced by the influx of liberals activated by the New Deal in the 1930s and the Vietnam War, the civil rights movement, and Jesse Jackson's candidacy in more recent times, the GOP has been energized by a mobilization of conservatives by Barry Goldwater, Ronald Reagan, and fundamentalist ministers such as Pat Robertson. This process of political recruitment, depending as it does upon the presence of magnetic personalities and powerful issues, is episodic rather than continuous. It produces a generational layering within the party cadres, in which political outlooks may differ considerably by formative experiences and time of initial activation, and it, more than any other single factor, defines the ideological direction of the parties (see box on following page).[21]

The result is an extensive, informal recruitment system—a complex of interrelated factors that selects out of the American population a particular group of men and women. Its chief elements are:

- The motives, goals, and knowledge of the men and women whom the parties want to recruit.
- The incentives to party activity that the party can offer and the value of those incentives.
- The role the party is allowed by state statutes to play in recruitment.
- The contacts, opportunities, events, and persuasions that are the immediate, proximate occasions of recruitment.[22]

The components of this system change constantly, and as they do, they affect the supply of personnel entering the organization. Recruitment in any form, however, is a matching of the motives and goals of the individual with the incentives and expectations of the party organization.

Recruitment from Within

An auxiliary recruitment system may work within the organization to promote especially successful party workers to positions of greater responsibility. A study of

PRESIDENTIAL CAMPAIGN GYPSY: A CASE STUDY IN POLITICAL RECRUITMENT

Modern politics has seen the emergence of a cadre of professional campaign specialists who hone and apply their skills in campaign after campaign. One such "political gypsy," as described by John Homans, is Steve Murphy, who worked for Richard Gephardt's campaign for the Democratic presidential nomination in 1988. His history of political activism typifies a common recruitment pattern in recent decades.

> Steve Murphy, the Gephardt organizer, proudly calls himself a child of the 60's, a member of the generation that was going to change the world. He volunteered for George McGovern's campaign while he was a student at the University of Delaware. After he graduated, he worked as a VISTA volunteer, doing community organizing on New York's Lower East Side. The work satisfied his idealism, but he came to feel that changing Christie Street and changing the world were two different propositions. "I guess I'm much too impatient," he said. "I figured out that if I wanted to have a real impact, electoral politics was the way to do it." In 1976, he joined Jimmy Carter's campaign as a paid organizer, corralling votes in the South and the Middle West, sacrificing the minuscule but concrete increments of change that community organizing can produce for the gamble that his man would get to the White House. He loved it. The results were measurable. "Elections have consequences," said Murphy.
>
> *John Homans*

Source: *The New York Times Magazine,* March 13, 1988. Copyright © 1988 by *The New York Times* Company. Reprinted by permission.

Detroit showed this system at work in the 1950s: Party leaders had risen exclusively through the avenues of party and public office. One group came up through the precinct positions, another came through the auxiliary organizations (e.g., women's groups, youth organizations, political clubs), and a third and smaller group moved from the race for public office to a career within the party.[23] More recent data on the political careers of party activists, however, do not suggest that party activists invariably inch up the career ladder in the party, position by position. Almost half of a national sample of Democratic and Republican county chairs in 1979–80, for example, had held no party office before becoming chair.[24] In general, the most that can be said is that the way stations of a political career vary with the nature of the political organization. In party organizations that have relatively open access and easy mobility, careers in the party are developed easily, almost spontaneously. In disciplined, hierarchical party organizations, party activists must inevitably work up the hierarchy in carefully graded steps and expectations. Over time, with the decline of the old-style hierarchical organizations, career paths surely have become more varied.

THE RECRUITS: AMATEURS AND PROFESSIONALS

The diverse incentives and recruitment processes combine to produce the party cadres, the men and women who do the work of the parties. These activists play a wide variety of roles in party affairs from campaigning on behalf of party candidates and serving as delegates to party-nominating conventions to staffing the party offices.

Common Characteristics

In spite of their different motivations and activities, American party activists have two characteristics in common that set them apart from the general population of adults. First, they tend, rather uniformly, to come from families with a history of party activity. Study after study indicates that large numbers of party activists had an adult party activist in their immediate family as they were growing up. Second, activists are marked by their relatively high socioeconomic status (SES), whether one measures SES by income, by years of formal education, or by occupation. Lawyers are especially common among the active partisans, just as they appear with great frequency among political officeholders.[25] The parties thus attract men and women with the time and financial resources to afford politics, with the information and knowledge to understand it, and with the skills to be useful in it.[26]

Some local organizations provide exceptions to this general pattern of activists coming from the relatively higher status ranks. The patronage-oriented, favor-dispensing machines in the center cities have drawn party workers and leaders in a more representative fashion from the populations with which they work. For many lower-status Americans, the kinds of material incentives the machines could provide probably were the crucial inducements for activism. As patronage and other material incentives have dwindled, the social character of these parties has changed. A comparison of county committee members from both Pittsburgh parties in 1971, 1976, and 1983 illustrates this transformation of party cadres into a more and more educated group as machine control declined. The mix of incentives that parties can provide, in short, has clear implications for the social composition of the activists it can recruit.[27]

The social characteristics of the activist cadres differ between the Democrat and Republican parties as would be expected from the divergent social bases of the parties' electoral coalitions. Democratic activists are more likely than their Republican counterparts to be black, union members, or Catholic. But differences in education, income, and occupation, once perhaps substantial, appear to be negligible in recent years. Although they may come from different backgrounds and certainly possess different political views, the leadership cadres of both parties seem to be drawn disproportionately from the higher status groups in American society.[28]

Professionals versus Amateurs

Beyond their social characteristics, it also matters what goals, expectations, and skills the activists bring to the party organizations. The goals and activities of the party and the men and women it recruits reflect one another. In fact, observers of the American party organizations have developed a two-part typology of party activists, based not only on their personal characteristics but also on the role they play in the organization and the expectations they have for it. One type of party activist is the professional—the traditional party worker whose prime loyalty is to the party itself and whose operating style is pragmatic. Its antithesis is the amateur—the issue-oriented purist to whom party activity is only one means for realizing important political goals. Professionals and amateurs are seen to differ in virtually all of the characteristics important for party activists (see Table 5.1).

Yet, these polar types are abstractions rather than descriptions of specific individuals. They tend to be purer and more extreme than one finds in reality, and most party workers probably harbor a mixture of professional and amateur orientations. They also have become pejorative labels for the opposition in intraparty factional disputes. Nevertheless, the typology has been usefully employed to distinguish between machine politicians and reformers in city politics, between party regulars and ideological insurgents at the party nominating conventions, and even between "old"- and "new"-style party activists (see box on p. 118).[29]

The implication of having amateurs versus professionals populate the party organization is clear. A different party is assumed to emerge with one type or with its predominance than with the other. Above all, the amateur activists are thought to be more issue-oriented and to insist on participation and agenda setting within the organization in order to bring those issue concerns to the party. They are seen as less comfortable with the traditional electoral pragmatism of the parties—that is, with making compromises in their positions in order to win elections. They are drawn into the

Table 5.1 PROFESSIONALS AND AMATEURS: A TYPOLOGY

	Professionals	Amateurs
Political style	Pragmatic	Purist
Incentives for activism	Material (patronage, preferments)	Purposive (issues, ideology)
Locus of party loyalty	Party organization	Officeholders, political clubs, other auxiliaries
Desired orientation of party	To candidates, elections	To issues, ideology
Criterion for selecting party candidates	Electability	Principles
Desired process of party governance	Hierarchical	Democratic
Support of party candidates	Automatic	Conditional on issues, principles
Recruitment path	Through party	Through issue, candidate organizations
SES level	Average to above average	Well above average

O'BRIEN AND LOWENSTEIN, PROFESSIONAL AND AMATEUR

Lawrence O'Brien and Allard Lowenstein epitomized the leadership of the antagonistic sides in the struggles over the direction of the Democratic party in the 1960s, particularly in the tumultuous 1968 nomination contest when they organized the campaigns of competing candidates. Their paths crossed many times in Democratic party politics, especially during the turbulent 1960s, but their different styles give real-life meaning to the terms *professional* and *amateur*.

Lawrence O'Brien was the party professional "extraordinaire." Twice chairman of the Democratic National Committee and top campaign advisor to four presidential candidates (John and Robert Kennedy, Lyndon Johnson, and Hubert Humphrey), O'Brien was known for his expertise in winning elections rather than promoting causes. The candidates he worked for were insiders with good chances of winning election to begin with. The interests he brokered on their behalf were the core groups within the Democratic party.

O'Brien's antithesis and sometime adversary was Allard Lowenstein, who entered politics as an issue-oriented amateur and spent a lifetime working for unpopular political causes. From civil rights activism as a young college student in North Carolina in the 1940s, on behalf of an independent Namibia in the 1950s, and in Mississippi in the early 1960s, Lowenstein turned to the anti-Vietnam movement in the mid-1960s. He spearheaded Eugene McCarthy's challenge to President Lyndon Johnson in the 1968 New Hampshire primary, which was pivotal in Johnson's withdrawal from the presidential race, and was elected as an antiwar candidate to Congress later that year.

party, in short, for purposive goals and often disdain material incentives. To the extent that their orientations mold the party organizations, they bring a profound change to the American parties. They also work a change of similar magnitude by bringing to the parties a strong impetus for reform, not only in the internal business of the party but also in its external environment, by favoring, for example, the adoption of presidential primaries and simplified voter registration.

Differences that are clear in theory, however, do not always carry over into practice. Amateurs may be distinguishable from professionals in their incentives for party activity. They may exhibit different attitudes on such key matters as the importance of party loyalty and the use of patronage. But there is persuasive evidence that these differences in motives and attitudes do not necessarily carry over into key realms of behavior. Among delegates to the 1980 state nominating conventions, amateurs were no less likely than professionals to sacrifice ideology for electability in their support of candidates.[30] Among county party chairs in 1972, at the height of the presumed ascendancy of the amateurs, the amateurs were no different from professionals in working to communicate within the party, maintain party morale, or run effective campaigns.[31] One needs to be careful, in short, not to exaggerate the contrast between professionals and amateurs and the implications of changes in their relative numbers for the parties.

VITALITY OF THE PARTY ORGANIZATION

Party organizations are apparatuses for assembling political resources and mobilizing them in the pursuit of political goals. Some do it with strength and vitality; others are ineffective. For decades, the American model or ideal in local party organization has been the classic urban machine. Its organizational hierarchy, its full range of year-round services and activities, and its army of eager workers in the wards and precincts have traditionally represented the apex of organizational strength. It is an organizational form which is dedicated throughout the year to earning the support of the electorate, thus enabling the activists and office seekers of the party to deliver its vote and achieve their political goals through victory at the polls.

As Chapter 3 suggested, the urban machine ideal has never been the norm for the performance of the party organization. Even in heyday of machine politics, at the turn of the twentieth century, party organizations in many locales fell far short of the vote-mobilizing efficiency of the classic machines. Despite recent evidence that the local parties have rebounded from their lull in activity during the 1950s and 1960s, party grass-roots activity, by any measure, still falls far short of the storied efficiency of the urban political machine.

The problem extends, however, beyond inert or underactive local organizations. Modern parties often cannot maintain the nexus of roles and relationships on which the organizational paradigm depends. In spite of improved integration among national, state, and local parties through centralized party-building efforts and funding, communications remain poor within many organizations, and leaders at each level commonly operate independently of others. A national survey of local party efforts in the 1992 presidential campaign, for example, found that 22 percent of the county party chairs did not communicate with their local counterparts in the presidential campaign organizations, 21 percent had no contact with their state parties, and a majority (61 percent) had no contact with their national parties.[32]

The principal difficulty for the modern party in attaining organizational efficiency is attributable, as it always has been, to the people of the party. Local workers enter and remain in party service for a splendid variety of motives—perhaps more so than ever without the glue of patronage to hold them together. They pursue different goals and harbor different political values, perceptions of political reality, and commitments to the party and its leaders. Unable to harness their energies in united pursuit of a common goal, many local parties barely qualify as organizations in the conventional meaning of the term.[33]

If the private life of the party were all that mattered, the vitality of the party organization would be of little concern. But the party's effectiveness in the political marketplace, measured by the currency of votes, depends crucially on its organizational vitality. Over the years, from locales with and without political machines, the evidence has cumulated consistently that a well-organized and active local party can win extra votes for its candidates for office, typically by mobilizing its supporters. The margin is not large, but in competitive electoral environments, such a small margin may be the critical difference between winning and losing.[34]

It is because organizational effectiveness matters in the quest for electoral victory that the search for the strong, vital party organization goes on. This search, however, is hampered by the lack of agreement on what the ideal ought to be. For many, the ideal remains the classic, turn-of-the-century urban machine. It is an ideal rooted in time, in the methods of campaigning, and in the electorate of a past era. Its operations are not acceptable, however, to the new activists and the reformers; furthermore, voters can be reached by means other than the ubiquitous precinct workers. What we need but haven't found is some common conception of strength and effectiveness for the political realities of the late twentieth century.

Variations in Organizational Strength

Although the shades of vitality in party organization are not easy to sort out, it is possible to generalize roughly about the conditions under which organizational strength develops. First, because of the density of cities and the special needs of urban populations, it is not surprising that the acmes of party organization have been reached in the nation's metropolitan centers. Differences in political culture also affect the development of party organizations. Persistent canvassing by committee members and patronage practices are acceptable in some quarters but not in others. Even the mix of amateur and professional orientations within the party organization may vary by political culture. The parties of Berkeley, Manhattan, or suburban Minneapolis may contain more amateurs than those of Columbus, Queens, or Chicago.[35] The greatest number of a party's defunct organizations appear where it is an entrenched minority party. One-partyism has the tendency to enervate the majority party as well. Until the 1950s, for example, Republican organizations in the Deep South were largely defunct and their Democratic counterparts were little stronger. Finally, the statutory regulations of some states are more burdensome than those of others. State laws that make it difficult for the party to remove or replace inactive officials, to use patronage as an inducement for party work, or to decide which candidates will carry its label hamper the development of strong party organizations.[36]

POWER AND DISCIPLINE IN THE PARTY ORGANIZATION

Organization requires discipline—at least enough discipline to coordinate its parts and to implement its decisions. It also implies some well-established system of authority for making those decisions. Many Americans have gone beyond these implications, however, and have imagined virtually authoritarian control within the party organization. Some leader, generally identified as the boss, has widely been thought to rule the party apparatus by a combination of cunning, toughness, and force of will. The boss, in fact, became something of an American folk hero, feared for his ruthlessness and admired for his rascality and intrepid daring. He has been celebrated

THE BOSS IN CARTOON

At the turn of the century, Walter Clark's pen captured, for all time, the enduring American image of the urban political boss.

Source: Walter Appleton Clark, "The Boss," From *Collier's Weekly*, November 10, 1906. Reprinted from Ralph F. Shikes, *The Indignant Eye* (Boston: Beacon Press, 1969), p. 321.

in the public arts,[37] and if he had not existed, it might have been necessary to create him, if only to justify Americans' instinctive demonizations of concentrations of power (see box above).

Very few organizational leaders ruled absolutely by personal magnetism, tactical adroitness, or the use of sanctions. Even in the era of boss rule, the boss's power was shared with influential underlings, and the terms of that sharing were deeply rooted in all of the hierarchical traditions of the organization. Much of what centralization there was existed because the foot soldiers in the ranks accepted the hierarchical system of authority. To many, the party's hierarchy may have seemed natural and inevitable. If they sought patronage jobs, they cared little about what else the party did or did not do.

More recently, however, party activists have come to demand a voice in the affairs of the party. A good portion of the ideological fervor of the amateurs has been directed at reforming the party's authoritarianism and bossism, and probably nothing divides amateurs from professionals more than their attitudes toward the political machines and lack of obedience to party authorities. Amateurs are committed to the norms and imperatives of democracy. Their commitment to intraparty democracy also follows logically from their desire to move the party to ideology because achievement of their own political goals hinges directly on the party's achievement of congruent goals. Thus, they must reform the American parties if they are to reform American society.[38]

It is not only participation, however, that is cutting into the discipline of the party organization. Discipline depends also on the ability of the organization to withdraw or withhold its incentives. Much of the discipline of the classic machine resulted from the willingness and ability of party leaders to manipulate material rewards. A disobedient or inefficient committee member sacrificed a public job or the hope for it. The newer incentives, however, cannot be given or revoked so easily. The party is only one among many organizations pursuing policy or ideological goals, and given the party's very imperfect control of its elected officials, it may not even be the most efficient means to these ends. The ideologically oriented activist may find substitute outlets for his or her activities in interest groups or nonparty political associations, such as neighborhood associations, professional groups, or issue-based causes.

Other powerful forces in the American polity resisted the creation of centralized, disciplined party organizations even before the changes in their activist cadres took root. Whether or not irresponsible power has been a fact within the party organizations, the American political culture is haunted by fear that a few people, responsible to no one, will control the selection of public officials and set the agendas of policy making in "smoke-filled rooms." Understandably, the search for mechanisms with which to control that power has been a long and diligent one. The results fall into two broad categories: mechanisms that impose controls from outside the parties and those that look to internal controls.

External Controls

Political laissez-faire suggests that two competitive parties will set limits to each other's exercise of organizational powers by their very competition.[39] One-party monopoly of the political system negates the automatic corrective action assumed in laissez-faire theory, however, and some of the centers of greater organizational power have emerged in areas without serious two-party competition. The current spread of two-party competitiveness may expose more party organizations to the discipline of the electoral market.

Anti-organization reformers have generally preferred statutory controls on party power to the unseen hand of competition, but their disappointments have outnumbered their successes. Where voters in the primary pick precinct committee members and other party officials, there are rarely contests for offices. Frequently, there is not even a candidate. Attempts to regulate the holding of party caucuses and conventions have not always guaranteed access to all qualified comers. The reformers have not been without their successes, however. Statutorily guaranteed access has opened party organizations to competition by other factions and oligarchies or to reinvigoration by new party personnel. Patronage has been massively curtailed. Moreover, in all of the states, the direct primary has at least forced the parties to face the scrutiny of voters on one key decision: the nomination of candidates for office. Some scholars have argued, in fact, that the introduction of the direct primary into American politics in this century is primarily responsible for the atrophy of local party organizations throughout the country.[40]

Internal Controls

In his sweeping "iron law of oligarchy," Robert Michels declared more than 80 years ago that complex organizations are by their nature oligarchic or "minoritarian," for only a few leaders have the experience, interest, and involvement necessary to manage their affairs.

> Organization implies the tendency to oligarchy. In every organization, whether it be a political party, a professional union, or any other association of the kind, the aristocratic tendency manifests itself very clearly. The mechanism of the organization, while conferring a solidity of structure, induces serious changes in the organized mass, completely inverting the respective position of the leaders and the led. As a result of organization, every party or professional union becomes divided into a minority of directors and a majority of directed.[41]

To the extent that we are all believers in the myths of the bosses, the smoke-filled rooms, and the deals between oligarchs, we are all disciples of Michels.

Michels' "iron law" of oligarchy has had little relevance, however, to the organizations of the American major parties. The distribution of power within most American party organizations is best described as a stratarchy rather than a hierarchy. It is "the enlargement of the ruling group of an organization, its power stratification, the involvement of large numbers of people in group decision making, and, thus, the diffusion and proliferation of control throughout the structure." Various levels of party organization operate at least semi-independently of other levels, even superordinate ones. Precinct committee members, district leaders, and county officials freely define their own political roles and nourish their separate bases of party power. Thus, "although authority to speak for the organization may remain in the hands of the top elite nucleus, there is great autonomy in operations at the lower 'strata' or echelons of the hierarchy, and . . . control from the top is minimal and formal."[42]

What accounts for stratarchy and the failure of top party leaders to centralize organizational power in the hierarchy? Weighing against the pressures for a centralized party oligarchy are these factors:

- *Participatory expectations.* Large percentages of party activists expect to participate in the decision-making processes of their political party. Therefore, the organization may have to tolerate or even create intraparty democracy (or consultation) to maintain vitality, to lift morale, and to achieve cohesion.
- *Controls of lower party levels over higher levels.* The chieftains of the lower-level party organizations typically make up the conventions or consultative bodies that select party officialdom above them. County chairpersons who choose state officers are forces to be reckoned with in the state party organizations. Similarly, precinct workers or delegates often form or choose county committees.

- *Internal competition.* Party organizations rarely are monoliths. They often embrace competing organizations or factions. Differences in goals and political styles produce continuing competition in the selecting of party officials and the mapping of party activities.
- *Independence of officeholders.* Because they do not need to rely upon the party organization for nomination or election, public officials often create their own power bases within the party, which enable them to compete with organizational leaders for control over the party. The most powerful political machines have emerged where the leaders of the party organization were also the top elected officials. In Chicago during the 1950s and 1960s, for example, Richard Daley was both mayor and chairman of the Cook County Democratic Party.

Diffusion of power marks all but the exceptional party organizations. Top party leaders engage in much mobilizing and placating of support within the organization; their consultations with middle-level leadership are endless. Even the ward or precinct leader with a small electoral following and a single vote at an important convention must be cultivated. Above all, party leaders in modern times rarely command, for their commands no longer carry potent sanctions. They plead, they bargain, they cajole, and they reason, and they even learn to lose gracefully on occasion. They mobilize party power not so much by threats as by the solidarity of common goals and interests.

Recent years, though, have witnessed one development with the potential for counteracting these powerful forces for stratarchy and decentralization. The growth in capabilities of the state and especially the national parties, through their abundant treasuries and their cadres of skilled professional operatives, has converted them into effective organizational forces for the first time in American history. With such resources available at the top of the party hierarchies, there is a temptation for local party organizations to turn away from uncontrollable volunteers and labor-intensive grass-roots activity toward a dependence upon professional campaign organizers and capital-intensive campaigning, especially heavy use of television. This greater dependence on the higher organizational levels may bring with it more control and direction from the top. It has not happened yet and may never happen given the powerful forces mitigating against centralization of authority in the American parties, but it should not come as a complete surprise if these new sources of skilled labor and money were to create new pressures for centralized authority and discipline within the organization.

In a sense, however, these concerns over power, discipline, and control in American party organization seem misplaced and out of date. Whereas earlier generations may have worried about the excesses of party power, particularly in local party machines, we increasingly worry about the weakness and withering of party organization. Many reformers have turned their energies from curbing the parties to saving them, and there is even an organization called The Committee for Party Renewal, comprised of party activists and scholarly specialists on the parties, dedicated to this end.

American party organizations probably have never commanded incentives and rewards at all equal to their organizational goals and ambitions or to their reputations. In that sense, they have been chronically "underfinanced." They never have been able to recruit the kinds of resources they would need in order to flesh out the party organization that the state statutes create. The thousands of inactive precinct workers and unfilled precinct positions testify to that poverty of incentive. The parties, therefore, have had no alternative but to tolerate organizational forms that have permitted them to live within their means and to draw upon activists with diverse motives, backgrounds, and styles. They are, after all, the products of their people.

Three

THE POLITICAL PARTY IN THE ELECTORATE

The separation between the party organization and the party's faithful voters is great in the American parties. They have largely failed to integrate the party's most loyal supporters into the party organization, especially since the decline of the machine-style organizations and their armies of devoted followers. Even the membership cards exchanged for party contributions in modern times are but a nominal reward in that they bring with them little meaningful organizational involvement. Nor have the American parties traditionally mounted any substantial program to educate their loyal electorates into the principles and traditions of the party. They view even the most sympathetic voters as a separate clientele to be reinforced anew at each election but largely ignored between elections. Those faithful voters, for all their protestations of loyalty to the party, also stand apart from its organization. Many consider their obligation to the party amply fulfilled if they support its candidates in a substantial majority of instances. In these important respects, then, the American parties resemble true cadre parties, top-heavy in leaders and activists without any significant mass membership, not the mass parties that have been such an important part of the European democratic experience.

This "party in the electorate," unlike the party organization, is largely a categorical group. There is no interaction within it, no structured set of relationships, no organizational or group life. Also, like any categorical group, it is an artifact of the way we choose to define it. There has been widespread scholarly agreement that the party in the electorate is defined by loyalty to or identification with the party. In the American political context, partisans are the men and women who consider themselves Democrats and Republicans, regardless of what else they do for the party—just as Presbyterians or Catholics are commonly regarded as those who profess a preference for that religious denomination regardless of whether they attend its services or make any other commitment to the church.

Party loyalty has been measured quite simply by asking people with which party, if any, they identify. A variety of different questions have been utilized over the years and, as is typically the case, the answers vary to some degree depending upon the precise question wording that is employed.[1] The two-part question that has dominated research on partisanship, though, comes from surveys conducted by the University of Michigan since 1952, now under the heading of the American National Election Studies (ANES), which asks:

> Generally speaking, do you usually think of yourself as a Republican, a Democrat, an independent, or what? [IF REPUBLICAN OR DEMOCRAT] Would you call yourself a strong [Republican or Democrat] or a not very strong [Republican or Democrat]? [IF INDEPENDENT, NO PREFERENCE, OR OTHER PARTY] Do you think of yourself as closer to the Republican party or to the Democratic party?

Answers to this question have allowed researchers to classify people into seven different categories of party identification—strong Democrats, weak Democrats, independent Democrats, independents, independent Republicans, weak Republicans, and strong Republicans—plus, for a handful of people, apolitical or third party groupings.[2]

This measure of the party in the electorate is based upon the psychological identifications of American adults with a party. One can easily imagine other working definitions of partisans. For example, the party in the electorate might be defined as the party's regular voters, regardless of whether they declare any loyalty to the party per se. This approach typically has been rejected by analysts of partisanship, however, because it is too much affected by candidate appeal. The loyalties of the party in the electorate are thought to transcend such candidate-based deviations. In the American electoral setting with its many elections and strong norm of voting for "the person, rather than the party," someone can remain a committed partisan even while defecting to vote for the opposition party's candidate. An alternative measurement of party affiliation may be sought in the official act of registering with a party. The utility of this approach is compromised, though, by the absence of party registration in almost half of the states (and many of the most populous ones), the instrumental value of registering with the majority party regardless of one's true loyalties in one-party areas, and the tendency for some voters to retain their original registration long after their party identification has changed.[3]

In addition to the frailties of alternatives, there are good reasons for preferring the concept of party identification and its conventional measure. Strong party identifiers do tend to be the party's faithful voters, but they are more than straight-ticket voters. They have a degree of loyalty and emotional attachment to the party that substitutes in some measure for the formal act of membership in a party system in which membership is not common. They are also more apt to be active participants in the party nomination process and active workers in the party. In short, the party identifiers bring fairly predictable votes to the party, but they also bring it loyalty, activity, and even public support.

Despite their expressions of party loyalty, the members of the parties in the electorate can be fickle, and they sometimes waver in their support of the party of their choice. The party organizations and candidates know that their electoral support cannot be taken for granted; other appeals and loyalties may occasionally override even the staunchest party loyalties. Also, some loyalists express a loyalty that is little more than an empty formula. They may be Democrats or Republicans in the same sense that many individuals call themselves members of a religious denomination even though they have not stepped inside the church for years. For all of this, however, the members of the party electorates do vote for the candidates of "their" party and support its public positions with a faithfulness far beyond that of the rest of the electorate. They tend, in other words, to be the party regulars and straight-ticket voters. They are the men and women who, in the argot of Madison Avenue, display the greatest partisan "product loyalty."

For all its uncertainties, the party in the electorate does provide the party organization and candidates with a stable, hard core of electoral support. Its reliability releases the organization and its standard-bearers from the intolerable burden of convincing and mobilizing a full majority of the electorate in every campaign. The party in the electorate also performs additional services for the party. It largely determines who the party's nominees for office will be. It is a reservoir of potential activists for the organization. Its members may also make financial contributions to the party, or they may work in a specific campaign. Those people who attend party rallies, who talk about politics and persuade friends, or who express any form of political enthusiasm in the community very probably come from its ranks. Its members are most active in perpetuating the party by socializing their children into loyalty to the party and possibly activity in it. In sum, party identifiers give the party an image and a presence in the community, and the most involved among them constitute something of an auxiliary semiorganization that supports the work of the loyal party organization.

Yet, the party in the electorate is an alarmingly diverse group, largely because the simple gesture of loyalty that defines it—an attitude measured by a word or two in response to a stranger asking questions—means different things to different people. Understandably, the boundaries of the party electorate are indistinct. Individuals also move freely in and out of it, either to or from the more active circles of the party organization or the less committed circles of the electorate at large.

A party in the electorate is more, however, than a categorical group or even a quasi organization. It is also an aggregate of cognitive images within large numbers of individual voters, a loyalty or identification ordinarily so strong that it structures the individual's cognitive map of politics. In this sense, it is the party in the elector. It acts as a reference symbol, a political cue giver, and a perceptual screen through which the individual sees and evaluates candidates and issues. For voters and citizens, the political party of their cognitions may be far more real and tangible than any overt political activity or any observable political organization, because they react to what they believe and perceive.

Because the American parties are still cadre parties without important membership contingents, the party in the electorate gives the party its mass popular character. It is to the party in the electorate that people generally refer when they speak of Democrats and Republicans. It is certainly to the party in the electorate that the casual observer refers when he says, for example, that the Democratic party is the party of the disadvantaged or that the Republican party is the party of business. Many of the differences in the programs and the public images of the major parties spring from differences in the segments of the American electorate that they are successful in enlisting. In fact, the interplay between the appeals of the party (that is, its candidates, issues, and traditions) and its loyal electoral clienteles—each one shaping and reinforcing the other—comes very close to determining what the parties are.

All of this is not to suggest that the rest of the American electorate is of less concern to the American party. Rarely can a national party or its candidates find within its party electorate the majorities needed for election to office. Even though the voters outside the loyal party electorates have lighter commitments to party and issues, competition for their support is keen. The two American parties cannot, as can some of the parties of the parliamentary democracies, fall back on a safely committed and heavily ideological 15 or 25 percent of the electorate. They must mobilize majorities partly from a vast pool of fluid, heterogeneous, often disinterested voters beyond the parties in the electorate.

The individuals of the American electorate, therefore, range along a continuum from heavy, almost blind commitment to a political party to total lack of commitment, not only to a party but to any political cause or object. The competitive American parties do not ignore or take for granted any segment of that total electorate. Their base, though, is the millions of voters who, by psychologically identifying with that party, comprise its coalition of supporters. These coalitions, loose as they may sometimes be in a two-party system, nonetheless give important definition to the parties by aggregating in common cause very diverse peoples.

The three chapters in Part III examine the variety and importance of these parties in the electorate. Chapter 6 deals with them as coalitions of voters, asking who the Democrats are and who the Republicans are. It is concerned, as suggested earlier, with the party electorate as a categorical group, as an aggregation of identifiers. Chapter 7 takes up the party within the elector—the party as a set of cognitive images in the citizen's mind. It deals with the impact of party identification on the political behavior of the individual. Chapter 8 focuses on the differences, large in American elections, between the total eligible electorate and the active electorate. This difference affects the role that party loyalists play in any election and defines the challenges the parties face in mobilizing their faithful and recruiting new supporters.

Chapter
6

The Loyal Electorates

Who are the Democrats? Who are the Republicans? In a political culture that often disparages political parties, there is a tendency for some people to view them solely as the candidates and officeholders who carry the party label and the activists who run the party organizations—that is, as entities distant from ordinary citizens. But for millions of Americans, the people and groups who loyally support the party and profess identification with it define the political parties as much as do the candidates and the activists.

In the vernacular, then, the political parties are seen as residing in the electorate. Much of the written history of American parties and politics has reinforced that impression. It has recorded the successes of the parties, not in terms of party organization, strategy, or activity or even of who holds particular offices but in terms of the enduring blocs or coalitions of voters that support them. Thus, the parties have been defined at various times as parties of the East or West, the North or South, the city or country, the rich or poor, the white or black, the "Sun Belt" or "Rust Belt."

PARTY REALIGNMENTS AND THE AMERICAN PARTY SYSTEMS

Throughout the life of the American party system, the coalitions of voters that define the parties in the electorate seem to have been rearranged every generation or so. If we had survey data with which to measure party identifications since about 1800, we could expect to find long periods of relative stability in the membership of each party coalition punctuated by brief periods of change or what is called "realignment."[1] Unfortunately, survey data were not available until the late 1930s. Prior to this time, the composition of the parties in the electorate can only be estimated from aggregated voting returns. The changes in both levels and geographical distributions of party support at regular intervals followed by long periods of relative stability that these voting returns show provide the major justification for dividing American electoral politics into a series of electoral eras.[2]

From these patterns of vote stability and change and more recent survey data on partisanship, scholars have concluded that the United States has experienced at least five different periods of partisan politics or, as many call them, party systems.[3] Each party system has begun with a realignment of the parties in the electorate (or, for the first party system, an initial alignment), followed by a long period of relative stability in the voter coalitions. Each of these party systems is distinguished by a unique coalitional structure, even when the parties remain the same and, as circumstances would have it, by a different overall balance of partisan forces. Each party system is also distinctive in its success in controlling the national government and in the substantive directions of government and public policy.[4] (See Table 6.1 for a summary of each party system.)

The First Party System

The first party system (1801–28)[5] originated in the conflict between opposing groups within the Washington administration and was ushered in by the hotly contested 1800 election in which Thomas Jefferson was elected president. For the first time in American history, one of the factions in the nation's capital, with Jefferson and Madison as its leaders, had organized support for its presidential candidate in the country at large. The partisan balance of each electoral period is signified by party control of the presidency and Congress. Beginning in 1801, the party of Jefferson—or the Democratic-Republicans as they came to be called—enjoyed more than two decades of virtually unchallenged hegemony over American national politics.

The Second Party System

The second party system (1829–60) emerged from the inability of the one-party system that prevailed after the Federalists' demise to contain the issues and conflicts of a rapidly changing nation. The Democratic-Republicans split into an antiadministration populist western faction under Andrew Jackson, which later grew into the Democratic party, and a more elitist and eastern faction represented by John Quincy Adams, which eventually was absorbed in the Whig party.[6] With the controversy over the 1824 presidential election, in which Jackson received the most popular votes in a four-candidate contest but lacked an electoral college majority and was denied the presidency by the House of Representatives, development of a new party system to reflect the growth and democratization of the nation seemed inevitable. Its first signs appeared in Jackson's election to the presidency four years later—the first time popular voting played the key role in determining the winner. As this party system matured, the nation experienced its first prolonged two-party competition, which the Democrats dominated as the majority party. Their hegemony over the national government was disrupted only twice, both times by the election of Whig war heroes to the presidency. The second party system was, to a considerable degree, a class-based electoral alignment, with the more privileged supporting the Whigs and the less privileged identifying as Democrats.

The Third Party System

The rapid ascendancy of the abolitionist Republican party from its birth in 1854 to major party status by 1856, replacing the Whigs in the process, brought about the end

Table 6.1 YEARS OF PARTISAN CONTROL OF CONGRESS AND THE PRESIDENCY: 1801–1996

	House		Senate		President	
	D–R	Opp.	D–R	Opp.	D–R	Opp.
First party system						
(1801–28)	26	2	26	2	28	0
	Dem.	Opp.	Dem.	Opp.	Dem.	Opp.
Second party system						
(1829–60)	24	8	28	4	24	8
	Dem.	Rep.	Dem.	Rep.	Dem.	Rep.
Third party system						
(1861–76)	2	14	0	16	0	16
(1877–96)	14	6	4	16	8	12
Fourth party system						
(1897–1932)	10	26	6	30	8	28
Fifth party system						
(1933–68?)	32	4	32	4	28	8
Sixth party system?						
(1969–80)	12	0	12	0	4	8
(1981–96)	14	2	8	8	4	12
(1969–92)	26	2	20	8	8	20

Note: Entries for the first party system are Democratic-Republicans and their opposition, first Federalists and then Jacksonians; for the second party system, Democrats and their opposition, first Whigs and then Republicans; for subsequent party systems, Democrats and Republicans.

of the second party system. The intense conflict of the Civil War ensured that the new third party system (1861–96) would have the most sharply defined coalitional structure of any party system before or since. War and Reconstruction divided the nation roughly along the Mason-Dixon line—the South becoming a Democratic bastion after the return of white southerners to the polls in the 1870s, the North remaining a reliable base for Republicanism. So sharp was the sectional cleavage that northern Democratic strength was restricted to the cities controlled by Democratic machines (for example, New York City's Tammany Hall) and areas settled by southerners (such as Kentucky, Missouri, and the southern portions of Ohio, Indiana, and Illinois). In the South, only blacks (who were largely disenfranchised as the century drew to a close) and people from mountain areas originally opposed to secession supported the GOP. By 1876, when southern whites finally were reintegrated into national politics, the Civil War party system had become highly competitive in presidential voting and in the House of Representatives as a product of offsetting sectional monopolies.[7]

The Fourth Party System

While the imprint of the Civil War shaped southern politics for the next century, the Civil War system soon moved toward obsolescence elsewhere. Under the weight of agrarian protest and the economic panic of 1893, the third party system dissolved. It was replaced by a fourth party system (1897–1932) that basically pitted the eastern economic "center" against the western and southern "periphery"—with the South even more Democratic than before—in part reflecting antithetical agrarian and industrial economies and ways of life. Beginning with William McKinley's defeat of populist William Jennings Bryan in 1896, the Republican party achieved a hegemony over American national politics, broken only by an intraparty split in 1912 which produced eight years of Democratic rule, that lasted into the 1920s.

Just as earlier party systems began to weaken a decade or two after their establishment, the fourth party system showed signs of deterioration in the 1920s, even in the midst of unparalleled Republican successes. The Progressive party made inroads into major party strength early in the decade, and in 1928 Democratic candidate Al Smith, the first Catholic ever nominated for the presidency, mobilized Catholic voters into Democratic ranks in the North and drove Protestant southerners temporarily into Republican voting.

The Fifth Party System

But it took the Great Depression of 1929 and the subsequent election of Franklin Delano Roosevelt to produce the fifth, or New Deal, party system. As is evident in the pattern of voting results that had emerged by 1936 and in the present-day vestiges of partisan feelings from that time, the new Democratic majority party was a grand coalition of the less privileged minorities—industrial workers (especially union members), poor farmers, Catholics, Jews, blacks—plus the South, where the Democratic hegemony established in the aftermath of the Civil War continued to prevail. This New Deal party system has shaped the parties into modern times.[8]

Lacking the clarity of hindsight, it is more difficult to identify the partisan directions of contemporary politics even with an abundance of survey evidence on partisan loyalties of the electorate. What can be said for sure is that the coalitional basis of the New Deal party system has eroded in recent decades. Since the mid-1960s, more Americans than before have failed to join the electorate of either party—answering "independent" or "no preference" in response to the familiar question eliciting partisan loyalties. The American electorate was clearly less partisan by the 1990s than it had been thirty years before. These changes first became apparent in 1968, although the seeds for them may have been sown in the 1950s and obscured by the landslide Democratic victory in 1964. They mark an important turning point in the American party system.

A Sixth Party System: Dealignment or Realignment?

Scholars observing this pervasive decline in the size of the partisan portion of the electorate have characterized it as a "dealignment" to bring out the contrast to realignment, which is a rearrangement rather than a diminution of partisan loyalties. Some scholars see dealignment (and its corollary characteristics of higher levels of third-party voting and ticket splitting) as a recurrent sign of aging within each American party system, including the most recent one. In their view, dealignment is the final stage of a party system, signaling the obsolescence of the electoral conflicts that established it and making it possible for new party coalitions to emerge. Leading the way in dealignment, in the 1960s as well as perhaps in earlier eras, are the newest members of the electorate. Because they lack the experiences that shaped the partisanship of the older generations as the party coalitions were being established, they increasingly find the major parties irrelevant to their present needs.[9]

What will follow the dealignment? In each previous party system, the dissolution of the old alignment was soon followed by realignment and the emergence of a new party system. Yet, such a return to party-centered politics is not inevitable. The forces that lead to dealignment (that is, a withdrawal from party loyalties) are not the same ones that produce realignment (that is, the development of new party loyalties). Indeed Walter Dean Burnham has argued that the American party system, weakened by the loss of party control over nominations and the insulation of many state and local elections from national forces by scheduling them in off-years, may no longer be capable of realignment.[10] The dealignment that began in the 1960s, the duration of which seems unparalleled in American history, lends credence to Burnham's view.

The Democratic dominance of the fifth party system and its recent decline are well portrayed in the measurements of the party loyalties of the American electorate taken before each presidential election since 1952 by researchers at the University of Michigan[11] (see Table 6.2). Throughout the entire 1952–64 period, more Americans identified themselves as Democrats than as either Republicans or Independents. This Democratic partisan advantage was perpetuated with an amazing regularity from one presidential election to another. Not even a popular president of the minority party, General Dwight D. Eisenhower, could disturb it. The Democratic edge eroded considerably after 1964, though, but not to the immediate advantage of the Republicans. Even Richard Nixon's landslide victory in the 1972 presidential contest failed to add party loyalists to GOP ranks. In fact, the Republican party in the electorate did not even regain its 1950s levels until the 1980s.

The most recent readings in the Michigan ANES series, from 1984 through 1992, show the highest levels of weak and strong Republican identifiers since 1960. Perhaps we are now finally experiencing the new realignment following the long period of dealignment. Whereas Eisenhower and Nixon, for all their vote-getting prowess, did not strengthen the Republican coalition, Ronald Reagan seemed to have been able to translate his popularity into growth for his party. The Democrats show a corresponding decline, dropping below the 40 percent level in 1984 for the first time in the entire data series. While it is perilous to infer realignment solely from such changes in partisan standings, these figures raise the possibility that the 1980s may have signaled the long-heralded realignment of the fifth party system—a possibility that receives the careful consideration it deserves at the close of this chapter.[12]

Just as important as the question of how many Democrats and Republican identifiers there are now or were at earlier times in the New Deal party system, however, are the questions of who they are and why they identify as they do. What is the com-

Table 6.2   ANES MEASUREMENTS OF PARTY IDENTIFICATION: 1952-92

	1952	1956	1960	1964	1968	1972	1976	1980	1984	1988	1992
Strong Democrats	22%	21%	20%	27%	20%	15%	15%	18%	17%	17%	17%
Weak Democrats	25	23	25	25	25	26	25	23	20	18	18
Independents, closer to Democrats	10	6	6	9	10	11	12	11	11	12	14
Independents	6	9	10	8	10	13	14	13	11	11	12
Independents, closer to Republicans	7	8	7	6	9	10	10	10	12	13	13
Weak Republicans	14	14	14	13	14	13	14	14	15	14	15
Strong Republicans	13	15	15	11	10	10	9	8	12	14	11
Others	4	4	3	2	2	2	1	3	2	2	1
	101%	100%	100%	101%	100%	100%	100%	100%	100%	101%	101%
Cases	1793	1762	1928	1571	1556	2707	2864	1614	2236	2033	2478

Note: Based on surveys of the national electorate conducted immediately before each presidential election—in recent years as part of the American National Election Studies (ANES) program. Due to rounding, the percentages do not always add up to exactly 100 percent.

Source: American National Election Studies, Center for Political Studies, University of Michigan; data made available through the Inter-University Consortium for Political and Social Research.

position of the Democratic and Republican party coalitions—their parties in the electorate? From what educational backgrounds, what regions, what occupations, what religions, what social groups do they come? On what bases of interest do the parties attract their supporters? Why do Americans align themselves with one party rather than the other? Each of America's party systems has had a distinctive coalitional structure as the cleavage lines through the electorate have changed in response to transformations in the dominant issue concerns and group loyalties of the period. To understand contemporary electoral politics and assess the possibilities for realignment, we need to know what these coalitions have been and what they may be becoming. Before addressing these questions, though, it is important to consider how and why people adopt particular party identifications.

THE ACQUISITION OF PARTY LOYALTIES

It is a commonplace among Americans to say that they are Democrats or Republicans because they were brought up that way, just as one was raised as a Methodist, Catholic, or Christian Scientist. The processes of partisan socialization begin early in life as the child begins to become aware of political parties and to absorb judgments about them. He or she soon realizes that one party is the family's party and that it is "good."

Childhood Influences

Even though they do not often consciously indoctrinate their children into loyalty to a political party, parents are the primary agents of political socialization in the Amer-

NATURE VS. NURTURE IN PARTY IDENTIFICATIONS

One wit, no doubt with Democratic genes, has written about the recent "discovery" that

> . . . affiliation with the Republican Party is genetically determined. The finding has been greeted with relief by parents and friends of Republicans, who have tended to blame themselves for the political views of otherwise lovable people. . . . Despite the near-certainty of the medical community about Republicanism's genetic origins, troubling issues remain. . . . [T]he startlingly high incidence of Republicanism among siblings could result from the fact that they share not only genes but also psychological and emotional attitudes, being the products of the same parents and family dynamics. And it remains to be explained why so many avowed Democrats are known to vote Republican occasionally. . . . [T]he discovery opens a window on a brighter tomorrow. In a few years, gene therapy could eradicate Republicanism altogether.

Source: These excerpts are taken from a longer article by Daniel Mendelsohn in *The New York Times,* July 26, 1993.

ican culture (see box above). Their casual conversations, their references to political events, and the example of their political activity are sufficient to convey their party loyalties to their children. So powerful are these influences that strong intergenerational similarities in party loyalty persist when the children reach adulthood, even during recent times when young adults are pulled toward independence (see Table 6.3). Furthermore, parental pairs with consistent, reinforcing party loyalties are more likely to produce strong party identifiers among their children. Those without party loyalties or with mixed loyalties are more likely to produce independents.[13]

The acquisition of party loyalties normally comes early in childhood. For example, more than 60 percent of the fourth-grade children in a New Haven, Connecticut, study were able to state a party preference. Few of the children, however, supported their identification with much information about party leaders, issues, or traditions. Not until they were eighth-graders did they develop the supportive knowledge that permits party identification to become fully operative in the political world. Students at that age began, for example, to associate the parties with general economic interests or groups—with business or labor, with the rich or the poor. The sequence of this childhood learning is critical: First comes party loyalty and afterwards, at least partially filtered through it, is added the content of politics.[14]

Individuals' party loyalties are also supported by a homogeneous circle of family, friends, and secondary groups. Friends, associates, relatives, and spouses typically have the same partisan loyalties that they do.[15] Some offspring, to be sure, do leave the parties of their parents. Those whose initial identification is weak are more likely to change, and when their mother and father themselves identify with different parties or when their identification is not congruent with their social setting—that is,

Table 6.3 INTERGENERATIONAL SIMILARITIES IN PARTY IDENTIFICATION: 1982

Party of Child as Young Adult (1982)	Party of Parent, 1965		
	Democrat	Independent	Republican
Democrat	51%	27%	10%
Independent	39	51	46
Republican	10	22	44
	100%	100%	100%
Cases	295	192	211

Note: Democrats and Republicans include strong and weak identifiers. Independents include all respondents answering independent or no preference to the initial party identification question, regardless of whether they later located themselves closer to one of the parties. The young adults had all been high school seniors in 1965 and were aged 34–35 in 1982 when the party identification shown above was measured.

Source: Three Wave Parent-Child Socialization Study. Provided by its principal investigator, M. Kent Jennings.

when political signals are mixed—their children are more apt to develop an identification with the other party.[16]

In part, the stability of these party loyalties results from the relative absence in the American political system of other agencies of political socialization that might challenge the early influences of the family. Where they are involved in partisan politics, these other agents more often reinforce than challenge a person's inherited partisanship. But most potential agents leave the field of partisan socialization clear for familial influence. Schools typically avoid partisan politics; if anything, they probably are more inclined to inculcate political independence than partisanship. During most of the twentieth century, American churches generally steered clear of partisan conflict while their counterparts in Europe sometimes had their own church-connected political parties. In recent years, many churches and other religious organizations have entered the political fray, but it is unlikely that they lead preadults away from parental partisan influences. The American parties themselves engage in very little direct socialization; they do not maintain the youth groups, the flourishing university branches (which may have offices, lounges, and eating facilities), the social or recreational activities, or the occupational organizations that some of their European counterparts do.

Adult Influences

Carrying a party identification from childhood to adulthood, however, is a complicated process. Initially, the individual acquires it in a process of early socialization dominated by parents. Subsequently, the individual maintains or changes the identification in an increasingly complex set of adult experiences. At this point in the life cycle, adults have tested their party loyalties against political reality. They have evaluated the performance of their favored parties and party leaders, and they also have watched the performance of the "other party." Events and experience may reinforce these loyalties, but they may also undermine them. Thus,

> . . . there is an inertial element in voting behavior that cannot be ignored, but that inertial element has an experiential basis; it is not something learned at mommy's knee and never questioned thereafter.[17]

Beyond the processes of acquiring and maintaining the party identification, there apparently is also a process of strengthening or intensifying existing party attachments for some adults. Party loyalties are most strongly held by older adults, and they are the least likely to change them. That strengthening across the life cycle may reflect an ongoing process of reinforcement in decades of political observation or activity; it may also reflect the usefulness of a party loyalty as a cue that will simplify choice and cut the cost of political decision for older voters.[18]

Nothing threatens the inherited partisan loyalties of large numbers of voters more than a realignment, when the issue bases of partisanship and with them the party coalitions themselves are being transformed. Unless the realignment is wholly produced by the mobilization of heretofore nonpartisan groups into partisan politics, at least some voters must desert the partisan tradition of their parents. Evidence from the New Deal realignment of the 1930s as well as from partisan changes in recent years suggests that this desertion may be considerable. Young adults seem to be highly susceptible to the pressures of the times. Childhood socialization alone proves to be a fragile foundation for adult partisanship and often cracks under the intense challenges of adult experience, especially in response to the powerful forces of electoral realignment. Older adults may be caught up in the momentum of the moment, but their partisanship, typically reinforced by years of consistent partisan behavior, is much more resistant to intense counterpressures. Thus, it is typically young adults who act as the "carriers" of realignment and, consequently, to whom we should look for early signs of partisan change.[19]

The processes of political socialization do not, however, explain the allocations of party loyalties in the United States. They describe how an individual may acquire a party loyalty but not what particular loyalty is acquired. For an accounting of why one party attracts some people but repels others, and why each party assumes a distinctive shape, we must turn in another direction—to the role of social groups and issues.

THE SOCIAL BASES OF PARTY IDENTIFICATION

There is a long and hallowed tradition of viewing the political parties as representatives of the various social groups contained in a society. Sectional or regional animosities, ethnic and religious divisions, conflicts between agriculture and industry, and differences in social class and status are common ingredients in the politics of the western democracies. While the United States may have been spared the intensity of some of these conflicts because of its newness, its isolation from the old world, and its social pluralism, many of them have been important sources of party cleavage here as well.[20]

Social Status and Class Cleavages

Most democratic party systems reflect political cleavages along social class lines, even if they may have softened over the years, so the search for the social bases of party loyalties probably should begin with social class, or its more general synonym, socioeconomic status (SES). *Socioeconomic status* is simply the relative amount of economic and/or social deference the individual can command based on his or her social and economic characteristics. In the modern industrialized world, it is best measured objectively by a combination of income, education, and occupation. Also, individuals identify with different social classes, and this can be employed to assess their subjective socioeconomic status. Regardless of the rubric one chooses, status differences underlie the party electorates of most of the mature, industrial democracies with which one can most reasonably compare the United States.[21]

The signs and marks of SES conflict are scattered throughout American history, even in the preindustrial decades. James Madison, one of the most knowing observers of human nature among the Founding Fathers, wrote in the *Federalist Papers* that economic differences are the most common source of factions.[22] Early political conflicts in the American polity often were most noticeable along sectional lines, but section typically connoted status differences as well. Social and economic status differences underlay the battle between the wealthy, aristocratic Federalists and the less privileged Democratic-Republicans and became even sharper between the Jacksonian Democrats and the Whigs a few decades later. In the 1890s, SES conflicts surfaced again in the presidential contest between Republican William McKinley and William Jennings Bryan, who converted the Democratic party into the vehicle for protests by discontented and disadvantaged farmers and tried but failed to join urban workers with them in common cause. Despite his defeat in the general election of 1896, the Democrats twice (1900 and 1908) returned to him as their presidential candidate for the crusade against corporate wealth, eastern banking interests, and what Bryan liked to call the "plutocracy."

The SES stamp on the parties became even more pronounced in the 1930s. Franklin Roosevelt rebuilt the Democratic party more firmly than ever as a party of social and economic reform. His New Deal programs—labor legislation, social security, wage and hours laws—strengthened the Democratic party's image as the party of the relative have-nots. Even groups such as blacks, long allied with the Republicans as the party of Lincoln, were lured to the Democratic banner; the strength of SES issues even kept them as allies of southern whites in the Roosevelt coalition. In brief, Franklin Roosevelt buttressed the class divisions of industrialism by adding to its conflicts the consequent response of government: the welfare state. Its programs and expenditures heightened the stakes of socioeconomic status politics.

The relationship between party and SES established in the New Deal party system underlies the partisan preferences of different social groups as recently as the 1992 presidential election (Table 6.4, panels A-C). It is immediately apparent in the data on occupation and income. SES even contributes to other partisan differences, especially with education. There is little reason to suspect that formal education itself leads young men and women overwhelmingly to Republicanism (or to the Democrats), so the higher levels of Republicanism among the better educated more surely result from the meaning of education in SES terms: A higher percentage of upper

Table 6.4 SOCIAL CHARACTERISTICS AND PARTY IDENTIFICATION: 1992

| | Democrats | | Independents | | | Republicans | | | |
	Strong	Weak	Closer to Demo.	Closer to Neither	Closer to Rep.	Weak	Strong	Dem.–Rep.	Cases
A. Income									
Lower 3rd	27%	15	17	15	9	10	7	25	505
Middle 3rd	17%	24	14	12	10	15	8	18	703
Upper 3rd	13%	16	13	10	16	18	15	–4	1053
B. Occupation									
Service	20%	21	16	11	9	11	12	18	227
Blue collar	18%	16	12	16	16	15	8	11	402
White collar	12%	22	15	11	15	15	11	8	448
Professional	13%	18	14	9	15	17	14	0	496
Farm	10%	2	16	13	20	14	25	–27	37
C. Education									
No high sch.	26%	21	13	14	9	9	8	30	414
High sch. grad	18%	18	16	12	13	13	9	14	815
College	14%	18	13	10	14	17	14	1	1156
D. Subjective Class									
Working	21%	19	13	14	13	14	7	19	1218
Middle	14%	18	15	9	12	16	16	0	1156
E. Region									
South	21%	18	11	13	12	13	11	15	659
Non-south	16%	18	15	11	13	15	11	8	1792
F. Religion									
Jews	28%	41	18	5	4	2	2	65	48
Catholics	19%	22	14	10	14	13	7	21	591
Protestants	18%	16	12	11	13	16	14	4	1430
White "Born-again"									
Protestants	11%	14	10	11	16	18	20	–5	502
G. Race									
Blacks	41%	24	14	12	3	3	2	60	310
Whites	14%	18	14	12	14	16	13	3	2045
H. Gender									
Female	19%	21	15	11	11	14	9	17	1277
Male	16%	16	13	12	15	15	13	4	1174

Note: Totals add to approximately 100 percent reading across (with slight variations due to rounding). Dem.–Rep. is party difference calculated by subtracting the percentage of strong and weak Republicans from the percentage of strong and weak Democrats. Negative numbers indicate a Republican advantage in the group.

Source: 1992 American National Election Study, Center for Political Studies, University of Michigan; data made available by the Inter-University Consortium for Political and Social Research.

SES parents send their sons and daughters to college, and the college degree leads to higher SES. Also, given the somewhat higher SES of Protestants in the United States, their relationship with Republicanism reflects, in part, status differences, and there certainly is no need to elaborate the enormous SES differences between whites and blacks. Furthermore, to the extent that Americans see themselves in different social classes, those differences (panel D) relate strongly to their party loyalties. Those who see themselves as middle class tend to be more Republican than those who perceive themselves as working class.

Yet, the lines of SES difference between the American parties, even during the heyday of the New Deal party system, have been less distinct than the parties' rhetoric and campaigns might lead one to expect. Socioeconomic status has been less important as a basis for party loyalty in the United States than in many other western democracies.[23] The electorates of both American parties contain a significant number of people from all status groups. Consequently, the parties find it difficult to formulate overt class appeals or to enunciate ideologies that reflect sharp class differences. The heterogeneity of their loyalists is perfectly consistent with the parties' pragmatic, relatively nonideological tone and with their mission as brokers among diverse social groupings. Thus, the lines of SES division between the major American parties are indistinct and overlapping, and although SES is one explanation of interparty differences, it is by no means the only one.

Sectional Cleavages

Historically, the greatest rival to SES as an explanation for American party differences has been sectionalism. Varying geographic areas or sections of the country sometimes have had separate and deeply felt political interests, which when honored and favored by a political party, united large numbers of otherwise different voters.

The most enduring sectionalism in American party history has been the one-party Democratic control of the South. Even before the Civil War, the interests of the South in slavery and in an agriculture geared to export markets had unified it. The searing experience of that war and the reconstruction that followed made the South into the "Solid South" and delivered it to the Democrats for the better part of the next century. United by historical experience and by a desperate defense of a way of life against threats from the national government, the eleven states of the Confederacy cast all their electoral votes for Democratic presidential candidates in every election from 1880 through 1924, except for Tennessee's defection in 1920. Al Smith's Catholicism frightened four of these states into the Republican column in 1928, but the Roosevelt economic programs reinforced the region's economic interests and in no way greatly challenged its way of life and brought the South back to the Democratic party for the four Roosevelt elections. Only with the successes of the Dixiecrat ticket in 1948 and the beginnings of the civil rights movement did the South begin to move away from its traditional party loyalties. Yet, as we saw in Chapter 2, vestiges of this sectional unity have survived into modern times at the state and local level and in partisanship (Table 6.4, panel E),[24] even if not in presidential voting.

Similarly, strong East-West differences have periodically marked American party conflict, reflecting the competition between the economically dominant East and the economically dependent South and West. In the first years of the Republic, the fading Federalists held to an ever-narrowing base of eastern seaport and financial interests, while the Democratic-Republicans expanded westward with the new settlers. Jackson pointed his party appeals to the men of the frontier, and the protest movements that thrust William Jennings Bryan into the 1896 campaign sprang from the agrarian discontent of the western prairies and the South. Many of the Populists' loudest complaints were directed at eastern capitalism, eastern bankers, and eastern trusts. Indeed, the geographical distribution of the presidential vote of 1896, with the Democrats winning all but three states in the South and West but losing all northern and border states east of the Mississippi River, is striking affirmation of sectional voting.

The pull of sectionalism has eroded steadily within the past several generations. The isolation and homogeneity of life which perpetuated sectional subcultures have yielded to a nationalization of life and interests in the nation. Sectional loyalties have not completely disappeared, of course. Southern sectionalism awakened in a new guise in 1964 as five states of the deep South supported Barry Goldwater, the Republican presidential candidate. Then, in 1968, George Wallace carried five southern states on the American Independent ticket: Alabama, Arkansas, Georgia, Louisiana, and Mississippi. Even in the South, however, sectional loyalties now appear to have receded into a secondary position in the development of political party loyalties.

In the 1970s and early 1980s, some observers of American politics thought they saw the emergence of a new sectionalism—that of the Sun Belt. Evidence for it is not strong, however. The Republicans have indeed improved their position in a number of the states of the South, Southwest, and West, but the result of that improvement has generally been to increase rather than diminish two-party competition. Moreover, the regional distribution of party loyalties in 1992 offers no support for the emergence of a distinctive Sun Belt section. Nor, for that matter, was there a distinctive sectional thrust to the Perot insurgency, marking him as one of the few non-major-party candidates for president not to have drawn upon a sectional base of support.

In retrospect, it is difficult to say what force sectionalism had even at its zenith. The great difficulty with sectional explanation is that the term *section* may simply be an obscuring shorthand for a geographic concentration of other identifiable interests—ethnic, economic, or possibly SES. Much sectional voting in the past, for instance, reflected conflicts among crop economies in the various agricultural sections. Thus, the central question is whether the sections themselves are the basic source of sectional interest or whether they merely signify categories or concentrations of voters who identify with a party for other reasons. In this vein, it means little to say that the Midwest supported Franklin Roosevelt in 1936 or that the West backed Reagan in 1980 and 1984. The South, though, has been more than a descriptive category; its political behavior has been sectional in the sense of unified interests and an awareness of the region and its distinctiveness. The case for sectional explanations weakens greatly, however, as soon as one looks beyond the South.

Religious Cleavages

From the beginnings of the American Republic, there always have been religious differences between the party coalitions—just as there are in many other democracies.[25]

Since the inception of the New Deal party system, Catholics and Jews were among the most loyal supporters of the Democratic party (Table 6.4, panel F). Some of the relationship between religion and party loyalty is no doubt attributable to the socio-economic status differences among religious groupings. Yet, it does appear that religious conviction and group identification also are involved. A Jewish internationalism and concern for social justice, rooted in the religious and ethnic traditions of Judaism, has disposed many Jews toward the Democratic party as the party of international concern, support for Israel, and social and economic justice.[26] The longstanding ties of Catholics to the Democratic party have been in great part the result of a greater openness within that party to participation by Catholics and their political advancement. Most of the national chairmen of the Democratic party in this century have been Catholics, and the only Catholic presidential nominees of a major party have been Democrats.

The sources of white Protestant ties to the Republicans are less obvious, probably in part because of the enormous diversity of sects and orientations that Protestantism embraces. Very possibly, the theological individualism of more conservative Protestantism disposes Protestants to Republicanism, although it was obscured for decades by the dominance of SES and sectional interests. In recent years, however, it has been the political conservatism of white Protestant fundamentalists, anchored to such nonindividualistic issues as abortion and school prayers, that has stimulated a surge in Protestant fervor for the GOP.[27]

Racial Cleavages

Some decades ago, the Republican party as the party of Lincoln, the Civil War, and Reconstruction was associated with racial equality in the minds of both black and white Americans. In the generation between 1930 and 1960, however, the partisan direction of racial politics turned 180 degrees. It is now the Democratic party, the Kennedy and Johnson administrations, the candidacy of Jesse Jackson, and Democratic Congresses that blacks see as advancing racial equality and integration. As a result of this, and the correlative concern of the Democratic party for disadvantaged minorities in general, blacks identify as Democrats in overwhelming numbers today, as they have since at least the 1960s, and regardless of any other set of social characteristics (Table 6.4, panel G). In fact, there is no major social group more tied into a party than the association of blacks with the Democrats. Moreover, the racial cleavage has been responsible for the transformation of party conflict in the South, and perhaps in the rest of the nation as well.[28]

Gender Cleavages

In the last decade or so, the votes and stands of adult women have diverged from those of men. Women voted about 6 percent more than men did for Jimmy Carter in 1980, and following the 1980 election, the differences between the sexes grew. Women were considerably less approving of President Reagan, and they differed from men on a number of issues beyond the specifically "women's" issues of abortion or equal rights for women. Their position on those issues, moreover, was the

Democratic (or anti-Reagan) position: supportive of a nuclear freeze and spending for social programs and critical of increased defense spending. By the mid-1980s, the gender difference had enveloped partisanship, with women more supportive of the Democratic party than men. This partisan gender gap has persisted through the 1992 election (Table 6.4, panel H) and into the mid-90s.[29]

The Changing Partisan Complexion of Social Groups

This picture of the contemporary social group basis of the American parties bears the strong imprint of the cleavage structure of the New Deal party system. Even as late as 1992, the partisan ties of the various social groups (with the possible exceptions of gender and racial groups) resembled those established in the 1930s when the New Deal system was first established. But these relationships have weakened in recent years, as the bases for the New Deal party system have eroded.

The changing social group bases of the parties is evident when the 1992 figures are compared with those from 1960 (Figure 6.1).[30] The SES and sectional differences in partisanship that were so important in the aftermath of the New Deal realignment had narrowed by 1992, especially the contrast between the South and the North. In their place had emerged sharper cleavages along racial, religious, and even gender lines than in earlier years. Based on this evidence, the New Deal party system still casts its shadow over contemporary American politics, but that shadow no longer dominates as it once did and, in the view of many scholars, the New Deal coalition is now dead.[31]

This view of parties as coalitions of distinctive groups in the society and the ease with which the partisan loyalties of such groups can be determined, if one is not careful, can lead to a misleading social deterministic view of party identification. Party coalitions cannot be assembled by any simple process of combining group voting blocks. Nor can groups be delivered in block to a party or a candidate. Rather, the group basis of partisan politics is rooted in the common reactions of individuals to the major issues and candidates of the day. These orientations may be shared by members of particular groups, although the pluralism of American society prevents most groups from being very cohesive. It is party differences on political issues and in the representation of the aspirations and interests of particular groups, not some sort of unadulterated "group-think," that underlie the partisan distinctiveness of groups in American politics.

Yet, there is a strong inertial element to partisan loyalties and therefore to the party coalitions. In ordinary times, the group bases of politics are transmitted, perhaps without much reflection, from parents to children. Moreover, people are slow to reject their inherited party loyalties even when the basis for this loyalty has deteriorated. Inertia, though, can be overcome. Parties change their postures, especially in realignment periods, and their traditional supporters may forsake them as a result. While party identifications and the coalitional bases of the party system are durable, they are not immutable. In recent years, for example, there is ample evidence that negative party images and votes for opposition candidates have "fed back" upon partisanship and influenced many Americans to change their loyalties. It is these individual decisions, not the lockstep march of groups, that have weakened the New Deal Democratic coalition.[32]

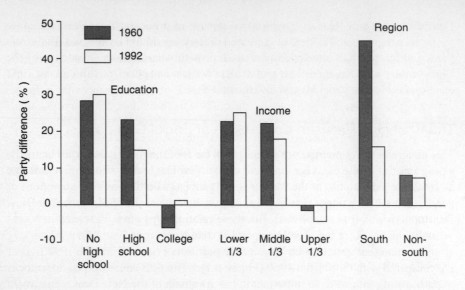

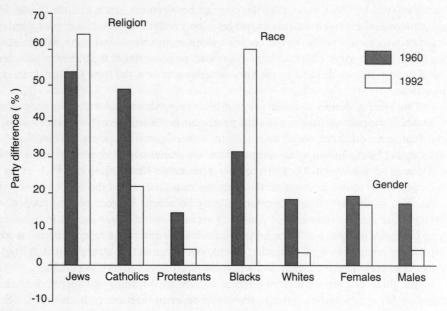

Figure 6.1 The changing social bases of partisanship.

Note: Entries are % strong/weak Democrat minus % strong/weak Republican within each group in each year

THE ISSUE AND IDEOLOGICAL BASES OF PARTY IDENTIFICATION

These considerations lead us to examine the issue and ideological bases of the different parties in the electorate. The party conflicts that appear among various social groups typically are rooted in different views of what government should do on particular matters and in general what kind of society we should have. Sometimes, these attitudinal differences are strongly related to social characteristics, and much political analysis is based on this assumption. But often social characteristics are an imperfect guide to what someone thinks about the issues of the day, especially in modern pluralistic societies. The value of the information on individuals that surveys can supply is that individuals with the same positions on issues and ideology can be identified directly rather than inferred by assuming group homogeneity.

Positions on the major policy issues of the 1992 presidential election campaign had variable relationships to partisan loyalties (Table 6.5). Party identification seems most closely related to individual stands on the issues of the welfare state, the ones touching the government's role in spending for services and providing jobs for the unemployed (panels A and B). Fundamentally, these issues involve questions of equality and the distribution of wealth. They are SES issues, one might say, because they propose different benefits for people of different economic status.

Clearly, much of the partisan rhetoric and conflict of American politics since the 1930s has run along SES lines—whether it is a debate over jobs, medicaid, how to resolve the budget deficit, or taxes. The American electorate, even in its distribution of partisan loyalties, responds to SES issues. The response comes, however, not as the response of specific social classes or groups but from individuals who, for one reason or another, have come to hold different attitudes or views about the role of government and its social responsibility for the less advantaged. For many these views have status roots, but others exhibit issue attitudes that are not necessarily congruent with their own socioeconomic status. They may reflect some sympathy for the socioeconomic "underdog," some deference to the socioeconomic "overdog," or some identification with an earlier status of their own. They may even be acting on some personal vision of the good society. Thus, the relationship is not always between socioeconomic characteristics and party identification. It may be between attitudes and party, and socioeconomic status is not always a good guide to attitudes.[33]

The influence of issues on party identification is more complex than all of this suggests. For one thing, attitudes on SES-type issues are for many voters absorbed into broader, liberal and conservative ideologies. As one might expect, there is a considerable correlation between self-described liberals and Democrats and, conversely, between conservatives and Republicans (Table 6.5, panel H). Second, recent elections have seen the rising importance of non-SES issues—issues of American involvement in the world, spending for defense, crime and drugs (and thus "law and order"), racial and gender equality, and such moral issues as abortion. Some of these issues have joined SES issues as sources of party differences (see Table 6.5, panels C–G). Since the 1960s, for example, the parties have been sharply differentiated along racial policy lines, and in 1992, defense and foreign policy issues and the relatively recent concerns about women's rights and abortion separated Democrats from Republicans to a significant degree. Just four years before, however, these issues were unrelated to political party identifications and, in fact, cut across party lines, dividing Democrats and Republicans against themselves.[34] Because they do not coincide with existing partisan divisions, cross-cutting issues such as these strain the coalitional foundations of a party system and sometimes can even lead to

Table 6.5 ISSUE POSITIONS, IDEOLOGICAL SELF-IDENTIFICATION, AND PARTY
IDENTIFICATION: 1992

| | Democrats | | Independents | | | Republicans | | | |
	Strong	Weak	Closer to Demo.	Closer to Neither	Closer to Rep.	Weak	Strong	Dem.–Rep.	Cases
A. Government spending on services									
More	26%	21	18	11	9	9	7	31	763
Same	17%	21	16	12	13	15	8	15	622
Less	8%	10	9	8	20	23	23	–28	635
B. Government role in providing jobs and a good standard of living									
Gov. help	26%	24	16	12	9	9	5	36	658
In between	17%	20	17	13	10	14	9	14	481
Help self	11%	13	11	10	18	20	18	–14	1017
C. Government role in improving position of minorities									
Gov. help	28%	23	16	10	8	8	7	36	499
In between	15%	20	20	12	10	15	9	11	576
Help self	13%	15	11	12	16	18	15	–5	1142
D. Government spending on defense									
Decrease	21%	19	18	11	12	13	6	21	1004
Same	14%	18	11	11	15	17	16	–1	703
Increase	15%	15	10	12	14	16	18	–4	441
E. Willingness to use force to solve international problems									
Unwilling	22%	16	19	15	10	14	5	19	516
In between	16%	20	15	11	14	15	10	11	1345
Willing	16%	17	8	10	14	14	21	–2	555
F. Should men or women have more influence in government and industry?									
Women	20%	28	28	7	10	5	2	41	33
equal	18%	18	15	12	12	15	10	11	1872
Men	16%	13	11	8	14	16	23	–10	275
G. Abortion									
Own choice	19%	21	16	12	11	14	7	19	1141
In between	13%	22	13	12	14	15	11	9	339
Illegal	17%	14	12	10	15	16	16	–1	907
H. Ideological self-identification									
Liberal	27%	25	22	10	7	7	2	45	817
Moderate	17%	19	9	22	10	17	6	13	172
Conservative	11%	13	10	10	18	20	19	–15	1290

Note: Totals add to approximately 100 percent reading across (with slight variations due to rounding).
Dem.–Rep. is party difference calculated by subtracting the percentage of strong and weak Republicans from the percentage of strong and weak Democrats. Negative numbers indicate a Republican
advantage in the group. Individuals who were unable to describe themselves in ideological terms were
not included in the data in panel H.

Source: 1992 American National Election Study, Center for Political Studies, University of Michigan;
data made available by the Inter-University Consortium for Political and Social Research.

the development of a new party system. That women's rights and abortion now differentiate Democrats from Republicans, in short, portends important changes in the parties in the electorate.

TOWARD A SIXTH PARTY SYSTEM?

The parties in the electorate have changed significantly since the 1950s and early 1960s. As we have seen, the Democratic share of the electorate is considerably smaller than before, even if the GOP has not realized comparable gains by capitalizing upon the Democrats' losses (Table 6.2). Among the most recent generations of young adults, the inheritance of partisanship from parents, both Democratic and Republican, seems not nearly as strong as it was for earlier generations. It is also clear that the social group and issue foundations of the New Deal party system have eroded. Socioeconomic status differences continue to separate the Democratic and Republican coalitions, but they now must vie for center stage with powerful social, racial, and foreign policy cleavages.

That the parties in the electorate have changed significantly in the last three decades there can be no doubt. Just what that change means is more difficult to determine. One interpretation emphasizes a dealignment that has undermined the foundations of the New Deal party system without building a new party system in its place. An alternative view, which has gained new life after the 1994 elections, is that recent changes signify the emergence of a new party system led by an ascendant Republican party. Recent politics lends some credence to each alternative, so scholars remain divided over whether we have witnessed dealignment or realignment in recent years.

The dealignment scenario emphasizes the erosion of the New Deal party system but the failure of the Republican party to capitalize fully upon the troubles of that system's majority Democratic party. Despite the decline in Democratic loyalists in the last three decades, the GOP has been unable to increase its partisan share of the electorate beyond levels achieved before 1964. At the state and local level, a sizable majority of public officials still come from the Democratic party. At the national level, despite more-frequent Republican control of the presidency in recent decades, GOP presidents invariably have had to deal with a Congress in which at least one and often both houses were under Democratic control. The 1994 election produced Republican majorities in each house of Congress for the first time in forty years—but ironically, this time with a Democrat in the White House.[35]

The realignment alternative dwells upon the successes of Republican presidential candidates, the growth of the GOP in the once one-party Democratic South, and—more recently—Republican gains in the Congress, most notably their control of the Senate in the early 1980s and their stunning victories in 1994. Only Jimmy Carter and Bill Clinton have been able to break the Republican hold on the White House since 1968. Carter barely won in the aftermath of the Watergate scandal[36] and was defeated for reelection, while Clinton claimed the White House in 1992 with only 43 percent of the popular vote in a three-candidate race. Republican growth in the South, in particular, has been just short of phenomenal—from a beachhead at the presidential level established in the 1950s, the party soon was able to compete with the Democrats in statewide races and in 1994 secured majorities among the region's U.S. representatives, U.S. senators, and governors for the first time since Reconstruction.[37]

In the end, though, it is to changes in partisan loyalties—the relative size and composition of the parties in the electorate—that one should look for conclusive evidence of realignment. No sign of realignment can be found in the partisan totals of the late 1960s and the 1970s, as both parties lost supporters (see Table 6.2) and their group and issue coalitions frayed but did not basically change. The 1980s, however, were a different story. With Ronald Reagan's defeat of Carter and GOP capture of the Senate in 1980 followed by victories of their presidential candidates in 1984 and 1988, the Republican party was ascendant throughout the decade, while the Democratic share of the electorate declined. Just as significant for a realignment interpretation was the GOP surge among young voters, who in the 1980s became more Republican than Democratic for the first time in the fifty-year annals of public opinion polling.[38]

So far the 1990s, if anything, have seen a recurrence of this ebb-and-flow pattern of partisan change. By the eve of the 1992 presidential election, the total of Democratic identifiers had reached its lowest level since the beginning of the ANES series; yet, the GOP party identification surge of the 1980s had not continued, leaving the electorate even less partisan than before. Since that 1992 contest, the regular soundings of *The New York Times*/CBS News poll, which uses the ANES party identification question, show even more Democratic decay with little compensating growth in GOP loyalties. Against this backdrop, the magnitude of the Republican *partisan* victory in the 1994 midterm contests was unexpected. Whether it signals a decisive step toward a pro-Republican realignment or merely a continuation of the electoral volatility inherent in dealignment remains to be seen—or, more likely, remains to be determined by how effectively Democratic and especially Republican party leaders can seize the current opportunities for mobilizing voters in the 1996 election and beyond.

As the twentieth century comes to an end, then, the American electorate has divided into three groups of roughly equal size—Democrats, Republicans, and independents.[39] Whether signifying a realigned sixth party system or the continued dealignment of the New Deal system, and this surely will be a subject of dispute for some time, it is an electorate which possesses markedly different partisan loyalties from those of a generation or two before. Yet, it is an electorate still dominated by party loyalists, by the Democratic and Republican parties in the electorate. As long as it contains so many nonpartisans and a near parity between the partisan camps, it also is an electorate capable of producing unprecedented inconsistency in electoral results, both within and across elections, and thereby sustaining third party and independent candidacies for president as well as the divided control of government that has been so characteristic of the American system for the last three decades (see Table 6.1).

Chapter 7

The Party within the Voter

The hyperactive world of American politics is difficult to understand, at best. The contest of parties and candidates, the cacophony of interests and views, the hyperbole of political charge and countercharge may baffle even highly attentive political activists. The confusion is inevitably greater among the less experienced and involved members of the party electorate. Their best guide to this trackless political world is their party identification.

For many individuals the political party exists in two forms. Obviously, they can see the party of the real world—the party of conventions, candidates, campaigns, and organizations. But they also come to depend on a cognitive party—the party of attitudes, perceptions, and loyalties, the party within the voter. This party is an organizing point of view, a screen or framework through which individuals see political reality and in terms of which they organize it in their own minds. We all perceive the world about us selectively, and for the committed partisan—the member of the party electorate—party loyalty is the key to this selectivity. Because the party identification will very likely be the individual's most enduring political attachment, it serves as something of a political gyroscope, stabilizing political outlooks against the buffetings of short-term influences.

For all the attention focused on the declines in partisanship since the 1960s, it is easy to lose sight of the fact that these parties in the electorate continue to dominate the electoral landscape. Committed partisans may not be as large a share of the American electorate as they were in the 1950s, but almost three-tenths of the electorate identify themselves as strong Democrats or Republicans, and about a third profess weak party identifications. Among the remaining independents, more than two-thirds confess to some partisan leanings. However partisanship is measured (see box on p. 152), the unmistakable result is that most Americans depend upon party as an important guide to politics. Knowing this one fact about people tells us more about their political perceptions and behavior than any other single piece of information.

THE PARTY IDENTIFICATION CONTROVERSY

The ANES measure of party identification categorizes people into one of seven types of identification (ranging from strong Democrat through independent to strong Republican) plus apoliticals, don't-knows, and identifiers with minor or third parties who are so few that they may be ignored. Although widely used by scholars who study elections, this measure has engendered two sorts of controversies.

First, because the seven categories of the party identification continuum measure degrees of partisanship, scholars have disagreed on where partisanship ends and independence begins. How this controversy is resolved is consequential: It estimates the percentages of Democrats and Republicans in the electorate. In most tables in this volume, therefore, the full seven categories are presented so that readers can draw their own line between partisan and independent. In the book's interpretations and analyses, the line most often is drawn between strong and weak identifiers on the one hand and independents on the other, even though most independents profess closeness to one or the other of the major parties.

Second, this controversy is compounded by a paradox. The party identification index treats weak Democrats and Republicans as more partisan than independents who lean toward a party. Yet in reality, independent leaners often exhibit more partisan behavior than weak partisans, especially in voting for their party's candidates. This seemingly illogical behavior has led some scholars to conclude that the party identification measure is capturing more than a single attitude toward the parties. One argument is that the illogical partisan behavior of independent leaners and weak partisans is the result of an attempt by researchers to force onto a single continuum three different and only partially related orientations to politics—Democratic, Republican, and independent identifications. In particular, independence is not always the opposite of partisanship; some voters seem attracted both to a party and to independence.

Scientific controversies over the measurement of key concepts are not uncommon. While the controversy over party identification may grip the research community, it is fought out over a relatively narrow ground focused on refining, not dismissing, the idea of party loyalties. Moreover, the traditional measure of party identification emerges from the debate as still a valid and reliable measures of party loyalty.[1]

THE STABILITY OF PARTY IDENTIFICATIONS

For a large number of Americans, partisanship is a stable anchor in an ever-changing political world. By the standards of political attitudes, party identifications do indeed exhibit a remarkable consistency over time. The partisan shares of the electorate have shown a remarkable durability over a forty-year period. Even more impressive is how strongly individuals cling to the same party loyalties from year to year in the face of powerful challenges. Most Americans, once they have developed such loyalties, retain them without change. When partisanship does change, moreover, the changes almost always are registered in intensity of partisan feeling (for example, from strong to weak) rather than in wholesale conversions from one party to the other.

It is not often that the opportunity arises to gauge the consistency of party identifications across a series of elections. The most recent such opportunity was provided in the early 1970s by the repeated interviewing of the same individuals in three successive ANES surveys conducted in 1972, 1974, and 1976. Almost two-thirds of the respondents remained in the same broad category of party identification (44 percent were stable strong/weak Democrats or Republicans, 20 percent stable independents) across all three time points. A third changed from one of the parties to independence. Only 3 percent actually changed parties.[2]

These results can be represented in a single number, an index of the degree of which similar positions were taken at two time points called the *coefficient of correlation*. In the language of correlations, where maximum consistency attains a value of 1.00, partisanship during that period was shown to be more stable than evaluations of prominent political figures or policy issues (Figure 7.1). No better testimony could be provided to the stability of partisanship than its consistency during the turbulent period in which the Watergate episode turned a landslide victory for Richard Nixon in 1972 into his ignominious resignation from office two years later and the defeat of his Republican successor Gerald Ford in 1976.[3]

THE COGNITIVE SCREENING FUNCTIONS OF PARTY IDENTIFICATIONS

Because of their early development (as discussed in Chapter 6) and their stability, partisan loyalties are in a position to function as a filter through which the voter views the political world. Even if voters may form or adjust a partisan loyalty because of a particular issue or candidate or use their party loyalty as a running tally of party-related evaluations, as will be shown momentarily, many voters also accommodate their images of issues and candidates with their more fundamental and enduring association with a party. In many instances, of course, these images reflect the realities of the party coalitions, and the voter can reasonably use them as information shortcuts in a complex political world. Candidates are drawn to the parties because of what they stand for, and the parties stand for certain things because of what their coalitions have been. Beyond this, though, voters **project** favorable personal characteristics and acceptable issue positions onto the candidates of the party they favor and are **persuaded** to support particular candidates or issues because they are associated with their party.[4]

Perceptual Projection

Party identification provides a perceptual predisposition for candidate evaluations. For most members of the parties in the electorate, the knowledge that a candidate for office is a Democrat or a Republican alone induces a positive or negative evaluation. "The stronger the voter's party bias, the more likely he is to see the candidate of his

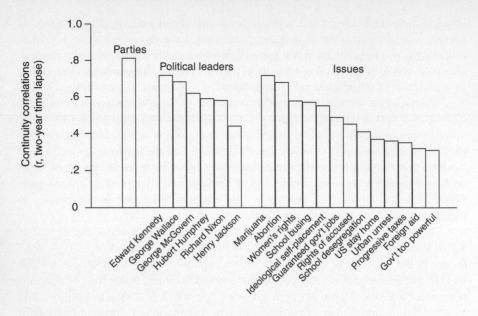

Figure 7.1 Consistency in political orientations, 1972–1974–1976.

Note: Entries are the average correlations, across a two-year interval. Complete continuity = 1.0; no continuity = 0.0; complete reversal = − 1.0.

own party as hero, the candidate of the other party as villain."[5] Every once in awhile, for example, a popular nonpolitician like Colin Powell becomes the subject of discussion as a possible candidate for office. Evaluations of that person quickly diverge along partisan lines once the name is associated with a party.

There is no better guide than the voters' partisanship to how they view the candidates. Even in the face of strong counter pressures, partisanship proves influential. In the 1960 presidential election, for example, competing perceptual predispositions were at work. Catholics tended to perceive John F. Kennedy more favorably than did Protestants. Nonetheless, party identification kept its organizing power. Among those with similar religious loyalties, party identification still had its effect on the perception of Kennedy. Among those with the same party identification, the religious loyalty had its effect. When one says that a candidate is attractive or compelling, therefore, one says something about the electorate as well as about the candidate. In politics, too, beauty is in the eyes of the beholder.[6]

The control that party identification exercises in the perception of candidates may be somewhat selective, however. Partisan projection appears to extend to the candidate's political traits but not to such purely personal matters as personality, appearance, or social characteristics (for example, religion).[7] The partisan view of candidates is selective in another sense: It is not without limits. Candidates for president who have gone down to defeats of landslide proportions—for example, Goldwater in 1964, McGovern in 1972, Mondale in 1984—have suffered from low evaluations among their fellow partisans. Yet, even here partisanship remains important: however low the candidate's standing may have sunk, he could count on more sympathy from members of his party than from other voters.

The impact of party identification on political issues is not as easy to determine as its impact on the perception of candidates. The candidate is a tangible person, but an issue is an abstraction, with far more subtle components and often a degree of longevity that makes it difficult to discern whether issues or party came first. We have already seen in Chapter 6 that identifiers with the parties take divergent positions on issues. Of course these patterns reflect the natural affinity of people to a party that champions their causes. But they also reflect a tendency for partisans to adopt their party's positions on issues, especially complicated and remote policy concerns. To an important degree, then, the electorate's policy positions do follow the partisan flag.

Feedback on Party

The metaphor of party identification as a perceptual screen, however, does not apply to all partisans or at all times. It assumes that a one-way relationship exists between the individual and political reality, that the individual's party loyalty colors his or her perception of that reality. Recent studies have shown, however, that perceptions of candidates and issues can influence party identifications too. In particular, the evidence is powerful that retrospective evaluations of performance, especially negative assessments of an incumbent president's management of the economy, can feed back on party loyalties and cause them to weaken or change or that partisanship can function more generally as a "running tally" of party-related evaluations.[8]

Thus, we confront a complex two-way process in which loyalty to party affects one's evaluations, and yet those evaluations shape the way one views the parties. Even if one concedes that party identification is usually stable and basic enough to withstand a number of conflicting short-term observations and evaluations, it is clear that the inertial force of party loyalty as a perceptual screen can be overcome. An accumulation of perceptions hostile to it can overwhelm its barriers and register on the individual. Under adverse conditions, then, party loyalty within the voter cannot turn unfavorable observations of reality into reinforcements of that very loyalty.

There is good reason to believe that the force of party loyalties as cognitive instruments, as shapers of political reality, has diminished in recent years. With the decline in partisanship that characterized American politics after the mid-1960s, of course, the share of the electorate lacking the partisan lenses through which political reality is colored has increased. Among partisans, moreover, there has been a moderation in the strength of loyalties, which has the effect of reducing the distorting power of the partisan lenses for those who use them. These trends have been paralleled by a diminution of partisan cognitions in recent years among even the strongest of partisans. Party remains an important source of political orientations, but it is not as important as it once was.[9]

PARTY IDENTIFICATION AND VOTING

The primary significance of the parties in the electorate lies in their patterns of voting. Partisans provide the core support for the candidates of their party. The nature of the American electoral setting—its long ballots and frequent elections, its traditional emphasis on person over party, and the ambivalence of even its partisans about strong parties—discourages absolute party regularity. Nevertheless, partisans support their party with considerable fidelity, which strengthens as the intensity of partisan loyalty grows.

Party Voting

Partisan voting fidelity has been high during the entire 1952–1992 period of the ANES surveys. A majority of each partisan category have voted for their party's candidate for president in every year except for weak Democrats in 1972 and independent Democrats in 1980 (both GOP landslide years), and strong partisans always have been more faithful than weak or independent partisans (Table 7.1). Even in the Reagan landslide victory of 1984, almost nine out of ten strong Democrats voted for Walter Mondale. Strong Republicans, though, have compiled the most enviable record of party fidelity (see box on following page): Only twice in forty years has their support for the GOP standard bearer dipped as low as 90 percent—in the Democratic landslide of 1964 and in the three-candidate race of 1992.

These patterns extend to voting for Congress (Table 7.2). A majority within each group of partisans have voted for their party's congressional candidates in each election, with the strong partisans exhibiting the greatest regularity. One key to the Democrats' ability to continue to win congressional majorities in the 1970s and 1980s, even as their electoral base was eroding, moreover, may be found in their greater fidelity than their GOP counterparts to their party's congressional candidates.

Similar results appear in voting at the state and local level through 1984, which is the last year for which such figures are available (Table 7.3). Straight-ticket vot-

Table 7.1 VOTING FOR THEIR PARTY'S PRESIDENTIAL CANDIDATES AMONG PARTY IDENTIFIERS: 1952–92

	1952	1956	1960	1964	1968	1972	1976	1980	1984	1988	1992
Strong Democrats	84%	85%	90%	95%	85%	73%	91%	86%	87%	93%	93%
Weak Democrats	62	62	72	82	58	48	74	60	67	70	69
Independents closer to Democrats	60	68	88	90	52	60	72	45	79	88	71
Independents	—	—	—	—	—	—	—	—	—	—	—
Independents closer to Republicans	93	94	87	75	82	86	83	76	92	84	62
Weak Republicans	94	93	87	56	82	90	77	86	93	83	60
Strong Republicans	98	100	98	90	96	97	96	92	96	98	87

Note: The table entries are the percentages of each category of partisans who reported a vote for their party's candidate for president. To find the percentage voting for the opposing party's candidate or some other candidate, subtract the entry from 100 percent. Individuals who did not vote for president are excluded from the table.

Source: American National Election Studies, Center for Political Studies, University of Michigan; data made available by the Inter-University Consortium for Political and Social Research.

THE FAITHFUL REPUBLICANS

Republicans historically have supported the candidates of their party more than Democrats have, especially at the presidential level. Popular impressions of their fidelity are nicely captured in this *New Yorker* cartoon.

"Tell me, sir, is there any such thing as just a plain Republican, or are they all staunch?"

Source: Drawing by Stan Hunt, © 1984 *The New Yorker* Magazine, Inc.

ing at that level occurs mostly among the partisans. Strong Democrats and strong Republicans have also been more inclined than weaker partisans to vote only for members of their party. For these contests, in fact, rates of party regularity steadily increase with strength of partisanship.[10] The higher level of party voting among independent partisans than among weak partisans, which appeared as a curious anomaly in presidential and congressional voting, though, is absent at the state and local level.[11]

Voting patterns such as these are the product of the push of an enduring partisan loyalty and the pull of the candidates and issues particular to each year. Typically, this push and pull are reinforcing; they incline the voter in the same direction. On the

Table 7.2 VOTING FOR THEIR PARTY'S CONGRESSIONAL CANDIDATES AMONG PARTY IDENTIFIERS: 1952–92

	1952	1956	1960	1964	1968	1972	1976	1980	1984	1988	1992
Strong Democrats	89%	94%	93%	94%	88%	91%	89%	85%	89%	88%	86%
Weak Democrats	77	86	86	84	73	80	78	69	70	82	82
Independents closer to Democrats	64	83	84	79	63	80	76	70	78	87	74
Independents	—	—	—	—	—	—	—	—	—	—	—
Independents closer to Republicans	81	83	74	72	81	73	65	68	61	64	65
Weak Republicans	90	88	84	64	78	75	66	74	66	70	63
Strong Republicans	95	95	90	92	91	85	83	77	85	77	82

Note: The table entries are the percentages of each category of partisans who reported a vote for their party's candidate for Congress. To find the percentage voting for the opposing party's candidate or some other candidate, subtract the entry from 100 percent. Individuals who did not vote or did not vote for Congress are excluded from the table.

Source: American National Election Studies, Center for Political Studies, University of Michigan; data made available by the Inter-University Consortium for Political and Social Research.

occasions when they conflict, however, the short-term force of candidates and issues may lead the partisan to defect from his or her party. In fact, the most powerful influence in leading voters to defect from their party loyalty is a highly visible candidate, most often an incumbent, from the opposing party.[12]

Like reeds in a pond that bend as the wind blows, though, the likelihood that voters will temporarily desert their ordinary partisan location more generally depends upon the strength and direction of that election's "wind" and how firmly their partisan roots are anchored. In a year during which short-term forces are running in a

Table 7.3 STRAIGHT-TICKET VOTING AMONG PARTY IDENTIFIERS: 1952-84

	1952	1956	1960	1964	1968	1972	1976	1980	1984
Strong Democrats	86%	84	87	80	72	66	—	62	69
Weak Democrats	69	72	74	53	43	38	—	39	46
Independents closer to Democrats	56	58	56	37	32	28	—	23	38
Independents	56	43	65	53	24	28	—	21	25
Independents closer to Republicans	65	56	51	33	43	30	—	28	33
Weak Republicans	72	69	68	44	49	40	—	35	41
Strong Republicans	85	83	79	71	74	60	—	61	59

Note: The table entries are the percentages of each category of partisans who reported voting a straight ticket in state and local elections. To find the percentage splitting their tickets, subtract the entry from 100 percent. Individuals who did not vote or did not vote in state and local elections are excluded from the table. The question was not asked in 1976, 1988, or 1992.

Source: American National Election Studies, Center for Political Studies, University of Michigan; data made available by the Inter-University Consortium for Political and Social Research.

Republican direction, for example, many Democrats will defect to vote for GOP candidates, but the strong identifiers will remain most steadfast. Of course, the longer these short-term forces continue in the same direction, the greater is the chance that defection may turn into conversion as voters change their partisanship to bring it into line with their vote just as, to extend the metaphor, reeds may be uprooted by continuously strong winds to be transplanted in a different part of the pond.[13]

A Party-in-the-Electorate-Based Typology of Elections

These notions underlie the main typology of American presidential elections which specifies three election types:

1. The **maintaining** election, in which the party attachments of the recent past prevail without any great change or divergence. In these elections, the candidate from the largest party in the electorate wins.

2. The **deviating** election, in which the basic distribution of party loyalties is not changed, but in which short-term candidate or issue forces cause the defeat of the majority party.

3. The **realigning** election, in which a new coalition of party loyalists emerges and governs the outcome. These elections typically produce a new majority party.

Since 1952, deviating elections have become common at the presidential level. Only in 1960, 1964, 1976, and 1992 did the majority Democratic party win the presidency in a maintaining election. In the other years, Republicans were victorious, and they earned their victories by inducing considerable defection among Democrats; in three of these contests, in fact, the GOP candidate won by the landslide proportions of more than 15 percent of the popular vote.

No other period of American history can match the past forty years in terms of the success of the minority party at the presidential level. Whether this era represents a new brand of American politics without strong party alignments (or without party playing much of a role in presidential politics), the prolonged unraveling of the New Deal party system, or the advent of realignment (in which case some of the contests described as deviating would instead be realigning), of course, is the subject of considerable debate. However this debate is resolved, it is unmistakable that in recent American politics party identifications have not played the role in elections traditionally ascribed to them.

One reason for the diminished role of partisanship in voting is that since the mid-1960s, there simply have been fewer partisans—especially fewer strong partisans. But this is not the whole story. Partisan fidelity in voting has also declined within both parties. Through 1992, Republican presidential and congressional voting by Republican partisans had not returned to the levels it achieved in the 1950s, even in the 1984 Reagan landslide (Tables 7.1 and 7.2). Partisan voting among Democrats in presidential election years peaked a decade later, in the 1960 and 1964 elections, and has not attained those levels since.[14]

Viewed from this long-term perspective, the patterns of partisan fidelity in the 1994 contests for Congress stand out. Unlike their typical behavior since the 1960s, more Republicans (93 percent and 79 percent among strong and weak identifiers, respectively, in the 1994 ANES survey) than Democrats (88 percent and 74 percent) "stayed home" to support their parties' candidates for the House of Representatives. Republicans also won a clear majority of the support of independents, but it probably was that extra boost in loyalty from their own partisans that gave them control of Congress for the first time in forty years.

Party Versus Candidates and Issues

Scholars of voting behavior have found it useful to break the influence on the voting decision into party, candidate, and issue components and then to determine the relative influence of each on the vote. Analyses along these lines focused on elections through the 1970s provided evidence that the relative influence of party identifications on the vote indeed had declined, as we know it must have given the decreasing numbers of partisans and their waning party fidelity, and there is no reason to assume that the previous importance of party has been restored.[15]

Because the three factors are so strongly interrelated themselves, however, it is difficult to separate their effects. Conclusions about relative importance often depend upon how well each of the factors is measured and what one is willing to assume about the causal priority of one over the other. The classic accounts of the dominant role of party identification in the 1950s assumed that party was causally prior to candidates and issues, influencing them but not in turn influenced by them, and the early measures of issue positions were not adequate for determining how close the voter felt to the candidates on the issues.[16] With new measures of issue closeness and an allowance for reciprocal influences of issue, candidate, and party orientations upon one another, the role of party identifications has been found to be dwarfed by that of short-run issue and candidate evaluations in the 1970s.[17]

This is not to say that party was no longer important then—or now. Rather, in modern times it has come to be dominated by short-run, election-specific forces—as quite possibly would have been the case in the two deviating-election Eisenhower victories of the 1950s as well if better issue measures had been available. When a longer-term perspective is adopted by looking at changing orientations across a four-year period among the same voters, though, party identification keeps coming back as a background force of continuing importance in structuring the immediate context of the electoral decision.[18] If it is the general trends of American electoral politics that we want to explain, then, party identification still must play a prominent role.

PARTY IDENTIFICATION AND POLITICAL ACTIVITY

American politics is dominated by the two major parties, so it should hardly be surprising that individuals with attachments to these parties have high rates of involvement in political life. It is the strongest partisans, in fact, who are the members of the electorate most likely to actively follow and participate in politics.

Over the years, strong partisans have consistently exhibited more interest than other citizens in politics in general and in particular in election campaigns. The 1992

ANES survey shows, for example, that strong Democrats and strong Republicans were more likely than weak identifiers or independents to be attentive to politics and highly interested in the campaign (Table 7.4). Strong partisans also were more inclined than weak partisans or independents to follow reports about politics and the campaign on television and in newspapers.

The most partisan members of the parties in the electorate match their greater cognitive involvement with relatively higher levels of political activity. A total of 87–88 percent of the strong partisans reported having voted in 1992—more than 10 percent higher than the turnout levels among other partisans or independents.[19] They also were significantly more likely than the remainder of the electorate to try to persuade other people to vote a certain way; to wear campaign buttons, display bumper stickers, or use yard signs; to attend political meetings or rallies; and to contribute money to a candidate or party. The combatants of American electoral politics, in short, come disproportionately from the ranks of the strong Democrats and strong Republicans.

PARTY IDENTIFICATION AND PARTY PERCEPTIONS

The strong party identifiers also see the parties in sharper terms than do weak identifiers and independents. They are considerably more likely to perceive differences between the Democrats and Republicans in general (Table 7.5) and on specific pol-

Table 7.4   POLITICAL INVOLVEMENT OF PARTISANS AND INDEPENDENTS: 1992

	Democrats		Independents			Republicans	
				Closer to...			
	Strong	Weak	Dem.	Neither	Rep.	Weak	Strong
Very much interested in politics	54%	33	36	30	39	32	56
Follow public affairs most of time	37%	18	24	19	26	23	42
Great deal of attention to campaign via TV	35%	19	19	16	18	17	30
Read about campaign in newspapers	74%	61	71	57	65	61	78
Voted	87%	75	74	61	75	78	88
Tried to persuade people to vote certain way	43%	32	37	25	43	38	61
Displayed button, bumper sticker, sign	15%	10	14	8	9	9	16
Attended rally or meeting	16%	11	10	8	10	9	13
Contributed money to:							
Candidate	7%	3	7	3	5	5	12
Party	5%	3	2	2	3	5	10

Source: 1992 American National Election Study, Center for Political Studies, University of Michigan; data made available by the Inter-University Consortium for Political and Social Research.

Table 7.5 DIFFERENCES BETWEEN THE PARTIES AS PERCEIVED BY PARTISANS
AND INDEPENDENTS: 1992

	Perceived differences between Democratic and Republican parties
Strong Democrats	79%
Weak Democrats	65
Independents closer to Democrats	59
Independents	39
Independents closer to Republicans	63
Weak Republicans	61
Strong Republicans	78

Source: 1992 American National Election Study, Center for Political Studies, University of Michigan; data made available by the Inter-University Consortium for Political and Social Research.

icy issues. Paralleling this are their more strongly differentiated evaluations of the two parties and their candidates, as well as of the parties' abilities to govern for the benefit of the nation. Strong partisans are even more inclined than weaker partisans and independents to perceive that their party's president has performed his job well and that a president of the opposing party has performed poorly.[20] In the mind of the strong partisan, in sum, the political parties stand in bold relief, sharply polarized along the important dimensions of politics.

Such relationships, by themselves, are no reason to leap to the conclusion that party identification alone produces greater activity or sharper party images. Behavioral and cognitive involvement in political affairs has diverse roots. Higher socioeconomic status, and the greater political sophistication and easier entry into political participation that it often brings, contribute considerably to involvement. The relatively stronger involvement of partisans (and, in most years although not 1992, of Republicans), in fact, springs in part from their generally higher socioeconomic status levels as well as from their more ideological commitment to politics.[21] Nonetheless, loyal commitment to a party figures prominently in inducing involvement in the world of partisan politics.

PARTISANSHIP, THIRD PARTY CANDIDATES, AND PEROT

Alongside the defeat of an incumbent president by the little-known governor of a small state, the principal story of the 1992 presidential elections was the unprecedented showing of independent candidate H. Ross Perot. Flourishing rather than fading as the campaign came to an end, Perot finished with almost 20 million votes, 19 percent of the total cast. Poll results from late spring of 1992 suggested that he might have done even better had he not temporarily withdrawn from the contest.

A look at the presidential vote patterns of voters with different party identifications shows how little of this surprising outcome is attributable to the most partisan

Table 7.6   VOTES FOR ROSS PEROT AMONG PARTY IDENTIFIERS
AND INDEPENDENTS: 1992

	Voted for Perot
Strong Democrats	4%
Weak Democrats	18
Independents closer to Democrats	23
Independents	37
Independents closer to Republicans	27
Weak Republicans	25
Strong Republicans	11

Source: 1992 American National Election Study, Center for Political Studies, University of Michigan; data made available by the Inter-University Consortium for Political and Social Research.

members of the electorate. Perot drew his support preponderantly from the middle of the party identification continuum (Table 7.6) as had third-party candidates John Anderson (in 1980) and George Wallace (in 1968) before him.[22] Based on the ANES estimates, a majority of Perot's total vote came from self-identified independents.

Electoral conditions were especially ripe for a strong independent or third-party candidate in 1992. Never before in forty years of presidential election polling by the ANES group had such a high percentage of the electorate refrained from expressing either weak or strong partisan loyalties. Coupled with the dissatisfaction many voters felt with their incumbent president, this situation provided ample opportunity for a candidate who could appeal to both independents and disgruntled Democrats and Republicans. Perot proved to be such a candidate, although in the end his appeal was not strong enough or widespread enough to construct a winning coalition from among such a diverse set of voters.[23] Partisanship and the continued fidelity of partisans to their party's standard-bearer were able to overcome even the well-financed Perot challenge.

THE MYTH OF THE INDEPENDENT

That party loyalties should govern so much political behavior in a culture that so warmly celebrates the independent well-informed voter who is moved by issues and candidates, not parties, is too striking a paradox to ignore. There clearly is a disjuncture between the American myth of the high-minded independent and the reality of widespread partisanship. The problem is with the myth. Before the myth is finally put to rest, however, we ought to be clear about what myth we are burying.

Attitudinal Independents

If we mean by the term *independent* those Americans who prefer not to identify with a political party, then the myth is a casualty of survey research. Although by definition these independents must vote for candidates and issues (because they do not have a party) and it is true that they split their tickets more frequently and wait longer in the campaign to make their voting decisions, they fall short of the mythical picture of the independent in most other respects. They are less concerned about specific elections than identifiers are, less well informed, and less active politically. Also, they are more likely not to vote at a given election. In 1992, for instance, independents once again had a higher frequency of nonvoting than did party identifiers, and "pure" independents voted less often than independents who leaned toward one party or the other. As a group, the pure independents, in fact, are the least involved and least informed of all American citizens (Table 7.4). They look especially pallid in comparison to the strong partisans.[24]

Behavioral Independents

There is no reason, however, why we cannot define the political independents in terms of their behavior or activity. In his last work, published posthumously, V. O. Key attempted to reclaim the independents from their obloquy by dealing not with the self-styled independents but with voters who switched their party vote in a consecutive pair of presidential elections. The picture of the American voter that emerged from American political folklore and from the electoral studies of the time, Key thought, was not a pretty one; it was one of an electorate whose voting decision was determined by deeply ingrained attitudes, perceptions, and loyalties without its having grasped the major political issues and alternatives.[25]

Key's search for electoral "rationality" centered, therefore, on the switchers—the voters who did not keep voting for the same party in consecutive elections. Key's switchers came much closer to the image of the independent than did the self-described independents. He found their levels of political interest no lower than those of the stand-patters, who remained firm in their voting allegiances. By his definition, of course, switchers are not nonvoters. Above all, they are marked by an issue-related rationality that fits well the usual picture of the independent. They agree on policy issues with the stand-patters toward whom they shift, and they disagree with the policies of the party from which they defect.

Debunking the Myth

It is the attitudinal independents, however—the ones who voice no party preference or assert their independence—who are the subject of most scholarly inquiry. As their numbers among American voters have increased in recent years (Table 6.2), more attention has been paid to those who profess no party loyalty. The contemporary view is that they are, and always have been, a rather diverse group containing many of the least involved and least informed voters, but also including some who come close to matching the mythological independent. In fact, when a distinction is made between independents who feel closer to one of the two parties (independent "leaners") and those who do not ("pure" independents), the independent leaners often turn out to be more politically involved (Table 7.4) and sometimes even more partisan in voting (especially for president) than weak partisans (Tables 7.1–7.3). It is only in comparison to strong partisans that these partisan-oriented independents fall short.

By contrast, the pure independents typically have the most dismal record, with relatively low levels of political interest and information, turnout, and education.[26] The myth that they are a sophisticated and involved group of voters operating above the party fray indeed has been debunked by survey research. But it also is survey research, by its relentless measurement of partisan loyalties, that has brought renewed attention to independence.

THE LOYAL ELECTORATES AND CHANGING PARTY POLITICS

The leaders of the party organizations scarcely know the men and women of the parties' loyal electorates. They know them largely in the same way that political scientists do—in some abstract, aggregate profile. They know that members of the party in the electorate see the issues and candidates through party-tinted glasses. They know that the party electorate has a somewhat unified and reinforcing view of politics, that it is more likely to vote the party ticket, and that it is easier to recruit into activity for the party or for a candidate. Party strategists know, in other words, that the party electorate is a hard core of party supporters. In a general, if vague, way, they see—as do political scientists—that party identification is a commitment that is often strong enough to affect other commitments and pervasive enough to color and codify perceptions of political reality.

Toward a Candidate-Centered Electoral Politics

The size and loyalty of the party electorates are critical elements in defining the style of American politics. For a century after the establishment of the current two-party system, the Democratic and Republican parties in the electorate had a great stabilizing influence on party politics. Because large numbers of people had party identifications, because they rarely changed them, and because those identifications strongly governed their voting decisions, patterns of voting support for the two parties were remarkably stable. In election after election, many individual voters voted straight party tickets. The patterns of party support also were stable geographically. When the votes shifted enough to tip balances of victory and defeat they usually shifted so evenly that they did not greatly alter those overall patterns of support. A party's state-to-state profile of support was raised or lowered, but not changed greatly.[27]

The events of recent years have jolted this long-term stability to the point that a different style of party politics seems to have emerged. Since 1964, the relative sizes of the parties in the electorate have declined as many Americans rejected partisan loyalties. The remaining Democratic and Republican partisans have become less loyal to the candidates of their party as well. The consequence is that, across the nation, electoral politics has become less party centered and more candidate centered.[28]

In terms of both professed identification with a party and loyalty among partisans to party candidates, then, political parties are less important to the electorate today—possibly less important than they have been since the emergence of the

PARTY ELECTORATES AND PARTY CAMPAIGN STRATEGIES

The nature of these loyal party electorates shapes the strategies of American political campaigning. The cardinal rule of campaigning is to stimulate and reinforce the party loyalties of one's own partisans while making candidate and issue appeals to independents and partisans of the other party.

How this rule applies depends upon the relative sizes of the party electorates. The majority party's emphasis will be placed on mobilizing loyalists through appeals to the tried and true issues of the reigning party cleavage. Democrats since the 1930s, for example, have stressed over and over again the economic and SES issues that had given them their majority status. The minority party, by contrast, is reduced to trying to divert attention from these issues of party cleavage with candidates who transcend partisan politics (a popular general like Dwight Eisenhower in 1952) or by raising issues that crosscut the party coalitions (such as GOP emphasis on racial and social issues in the 1960s). When the minority party does attempt to confront the majority party on its own ground, it runs the risk of suffering a defeat of historic proportions—as the example of 1964 Republican candidate for president Barry Goldwater shows.

Campaign strategies also vary with the absolute size and loyalty of the party electorates. Appeals to party loyalty are effective in a party-committed electorate, but can undermine candidate support in an electorate with weak party attachments. Just as Richard Nixon and especially Ronald Reagan were willing to forsake traditional GOP ties in their attempts to enlarge their electoral base, Jimmy Carter and Bill Clinton showed a willingness to defy established leaders of the Democratic party and desert traditional party issues in dealing with the erosion of the Democratic electoral party. In general, a less partisan-aligned electorate inclines party candidates to craft their own unique electoral appeals, occasionally even running against the party, and, as the Perot showing illustrates, opens up the electoral system to candidates from outside the major-party mainstream.

American two-party system. Whether this situation will survive a putative realignment only time will tell. Declines in party loyalists and partisan fidelity among loyalists no doubt are natural as one party system dies and another takes its place. But, for the present—a present that now has lasted for at least two decades, the parties in the electorate play less of a leading role in American electoral politics. One important result is that elections now turn more than ever on short-run forces—candidates, issues, and the particular events of the immediate campaign, and this consequence itself has consequences for the party organizations and their campaign strategies (see box above) as well as for the role of the parties in government.

The Continuing Significance of Party

Yet, it is important not to exaggerate the declining role of the party in the electorate. Most Americans—a clear majority using only strong and weak identifiers, almost all if leaners are included as well—still profess some degree of loyalty to either the Democratic or the Republican party, and many Americans are faithful to these loyalties in voting for candidates for office. Voters may stray from the party fold here and there, defections which the very abundance of contests for office encourages, but they continue to perceive candidates, issues, and elections in partisan terms and often vote accordingly. Although challenged by strong antiparty forces since the mid-1960s, the party within the voter continues to exert a powerful force on electoral choices and the parties in the electorate remain significant players in American elections.

Finally, there are signs that we may have reached the nadir of candidate-centered politics, although these signs must be interpreted cautiously lest passing fancies be mistaken for enduring change. The 1994 midterm elections were the most party-oriented contests in some time, as the GOP was able to overcome the localism that protected incumbents by appealing to national issues, especially dissatisfaction with the Democratic president. The new Republican majority in the Congress, rallying around its "Contract with America," again has demonstrated the power of a cohesive party. If these are premonitions of the future rather than yet another ephemeral symptom of the electoral instability of the recent past, then the party in the electorate may assume an even more important role in American party politics.

Chapter
8

The Active Electorate

The political parties in the electorate are defined by those people who profess party attachments, and we have naturally focused our attention upon them. Their composition as well as their place in the party system and American politics more generally, though, depend upon the nature of the electorate itself, in particular what portion of the electorate is actively involved in elections. Both the legally defined electorate and the active electorate among it have varied greatly in size and composition over the course of American history, and both still differ considerably across the fifty states. These variations have had a profound effect on party politics.

The nature of the electorate determines what parties enjoy prominence in the party system, which has meant what two parties will dominate in the American two-party system. Much of the early history of political parties can be written in terms of their responses to expansion of the suffrage. Parties first appeared as essentially aristocratic instruments for mobilizing very homogeneous and limited electorates. As electorates were expanded by enfranchising lower-status citizens, disadvantaged minorities, and women, the parties were forced to alter their organizations and appeals. Some early American parties, like the Federalists, suffered extinction because they were unable to adjust their appeals to accommodate the new electorates. Parties in other democracies, largely of the European socialist and labor variety, fought to secure the suffrage for lower-status voters and then rode their enfranchisement to prominent positions in the party system. What the parties are, to the degree to which they are defined by their electoral coalitions, depends upon what the electorate is.

But it is the nature of the **active** electorate that has determined the relative standing of the parties and the extent to which the parties in the electorate have dominated the electoral system. If the participating members of the electorate were a representative sample of the adult citizenry, then the issue of their composition would not arise. The effective electorate, however, usually is nothing of the sort. It almost always overrepresents some groups in the society at the expense of others. Because of the preferences of various groups for one party or another, the composition of the active electorate is a matter of differential advantage for the parties.

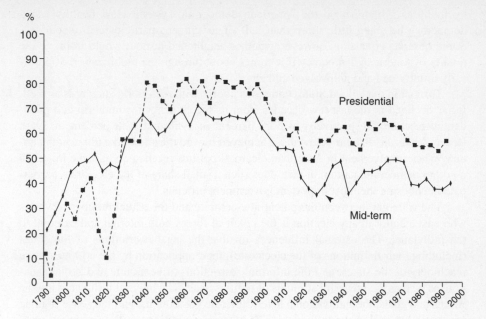

Figure 8.1 Turnout in American elections: 1828–1994.

Note: These are the percentages voting for president and for the office with the highest vote in midterm elections. Because the base is the total of eligible votes, which is somewhat less than the voting-age population, these turnout rates are somewhat higher than are commonly reported.

THE LOW TURNOUT IN AMERICAN ELECTIONS

In the American system, there is a wide gap between the potential electorate and the active electorate. Only 56.9 percent of the eligible electorate cast a ballot for president in 1992; four years earlier the presidential turnout figure had fallen to the bare majority of 52.7 percent. Since 1828, only the first two elections of the 1920s, before many women had become accustomed to their new right to vote, have recorded lower levels of presidential turnout. Considerably less participation occurs in midterm elections; in 1994, only 40 percent of the eligible voters cast a ballot for the top office on the ballot (see Fig. 8.1).[1]

As low as they may seem, these figures are *maximum* turnout rates for any year. They hide the considerable state variation that appears in any election. In the 1992 presidential contest, for example, only 39 percent of the voting-age population voted in South Carolina in comparison to almost 66 percent in Minnesota. The figures ignore roll-off, or voting for the most important office on the ballot but not lesser offices; turnout in the 1992 congressional elections, for example, was 4 percent less than presidential turnout. They also neglect the even lower levels of participation in contests for local offices and party primaries.

By whatever standard is employed, turnout in American elections is low. By the norms of democratic theory, such extensive noninvolvement in elections is regarded by many as a blemish on the American democratic system. How healthy can a democracy be when little more than half of its citizens participate in elections?[2] Some observers question, however, whether heightened turnout would improve the quality of American democracy if it comes about through the mobilization of politically uninformed and uninvolved citizens.

Turnout in the United States compares poorly with real-world standards as well. It has declined in the last few decades from its recent peaks for midterm and presidential elections, respectively, of 55.0 percent in 1958 and 72.8 percent in 1960. Recent levels are also far below those achieved toward the end of the nineteenth century, when involvement in American electoral politics reached an all-time high.[3] In no other democratic nation, in fact, does such a small share of the electorate participate in choosing the most important government officials.[4]

The wide gap between the potential electorate and the actual number of voters who cast a ballot in any election is the result of forces both internal and external to the individual. The external influences involve the legal restrictions of the states (including their definitions of the electorate), their application by the administrative machinery of the states, and the informal restrictions of economic and social sanction, as well as the powerful stimulus of politics itself. The internal influences are the values and goals, the motivational levels, the role perceptions, and the sense of civic responsibility within the individual. The external definitions of the American electorate are more tangible, so they will be considered first.

CHANGING LEGAL DEFINITIONS OF THE ELECTORATE

It was undoubtedly the intention of the framers of the Constitution to leave control over the definition of the electorate to the states. The only provision for suffrage in the original document is Article I, Section 2, which provides that, for elections to the House of Representatives, "the electors of each state shall have the qualifications requisite for electors of the most numerous branch of the state legislature," and these were left for the states to set. The inevitable result over the years was the absence of a uniform national electorate, even for national elections.

National Protections for the Right to Vote

Since the time of the Civil War, though, the national government has been given the authority—most often through constitutional amendments—to prevent states from imposing particularly objectionable restrictions on voting. Thus, the definition of the electorate over the past 150 years has expanded and occasionally even contracted through the curiously American interlacing of national and state action.

The enfranchisement of white males was accomplished earlier in the United States than in any other democracy. In the early nineteenth century, the states themselves gradually repealed the property, income, and tax-paying qualifications for voting by which they had so severely restricted male suffrage.[5] By 1860 no states required property holding and only four required substantial tax paying as a condition for voting. About a century later, the Supreme Court and then the

Twenty-fourth Amendment, finally ended even the small poll tax as a requirement for voting.[6]

Complete women's suffrage did not come until the twentieth century, and it required federal action. By the mid-1870s, women had begun to work through the states for their right to vote; in 1890 with its admission to the Union, Wyoming became the first state to grant the full franchise to women. The push for women's suffrage then bogged down, especially in the eastern states, and women shifted their hopes to the United States Constitution. The Nineteenth Amendment, forbidding states to deny the vote on grounds of gender, was finally ratified in 1920.

The right to vote for black Americans has a more checkered history. The expansion of black suffrage began by state action in some of the states of New England before the Civil War and culminated after the war with the passage of the Fifteenth Amendment, which prohibited abridgments of the right to vote on account of race. As the federal government turned its attention to other matters, however, southern states effectively restricted the franchise for blacks through poll taxes, literacy tests, and outright intimidation. By the early 1900s, black turnout in the south was negligible, and it remained that way in most southern states until the 1960s, when the federal government began to enforce the Fifteenth Amendment and new voting rights laws on the reluctant states.

Lowering the voting age to eighteen has been the most recent change in the legal definition of the electorate. In the 1960s, only a handful of states allowed young people under the age of twenty-one to vote. Then, in June 1970, the United States Congress passed a law lowering the minimum voting age to eighteen in both state and federal elections. Less than a half-year later, the Supreme Court decided by a five-to-four vote that the act was constitutional as it applied to federal elections but unconstitutional as it applied to state and local elections.[7] Congress then passed and sent to the states for ratification an amendment to the Constitution lowering the age to eighteen for all elections. That amendment, the Twenty-sixth Amendment, was ratified by 1971.

In recent decades, the national government, through both the Congress and the Supreme Court, has expanded its role even more in defining the American electorate. By ordinary statute rather than by constitutional amendment, Congress extended the vote to younger voters in federal elections; banned literacy, understanding, and character tests for registration; and waived residence requirements for voting in presidential elections. In the still-controversial federal "motor voter" law, which was first implemented in 1995 (see box on p. 172), the national government also has required the states to automatically offer citizens the opportunity to register to vote when they apply for driver's licenses and to provide registration by mail and through agencies which disburse federal benefits.

The Supreme Court has enlarged its own powers in the application of constitutional guarantees, that expansion culminating in 1972 in its decision sharply restricting state residence requirements. The Court also has relied upon the Fourteenth Amendment's equal protection clause ("no state shall make or enforce any law which shall . . . deny to any person within its jurisdiction the equal protection of the laws") to prevent states from discriminating against blacks in defining their electorate. Presumably, this same clause would similarly protect the voting rights of other social groups.[8]

THE "MOTOR VOTER" LAW CONTROVERSY

The continuing controversy over the National Voter Registration Act (the so-called "motor voter" law), which was passed in 1993 to take effect at the beginning of 1995, illustrates the issues involved in attempting to ease restrictions on turnout. Many states refused to implement the new law. They protested the costs of yet another unfunded mandate imposed upon them by the national government and were especially opposed to easy registration through welfare offices and to limits on purges of registration rolls for nonvoting. State leaders, as well as Republicans in Congress and political commentators, also expressed the concern that easier access to voting would open up the electoral process to fraudulent registration. In early 1995 the Justice Department announced it was prosecuting states—among them California, Illinois, and Pennsylvania—that had refused to comply with the new law.

With the post-1994 changes in the partisan balance of power in Washington and in the state capitals, it is hardly surprising that a bill passed by a Democratic Congress and signed into law by a Democratic President would encounter such fierce opposition as it was taking effect in the states. Yet, this debate is more than a simple partisan matter, fueled by differences in the expected partisan benefits from an enlarged electorate. It is another round in the long-running disagreement between those who would make voting as cost-free as possible to stimulate greater participation and those who, in the tradition of the Progressives, are concerned with guarding the electoral process against fraudulent voting.

Early returns on the effects of the new law provide evidence on both sides of this normative controversy. After the new law took effect in 1995, registration surged in many areas of the nation—adding up to perhaps the most pronounced increases in the registration rolls ever. Research on "motor voter" laws in states which had adopted them prior to the federal legislation shows that they indeed were associated with increases in turnout.[9] On the other hand, anecdotal accounts of fraudulant registration have been reported as well, including the enrollment of aliens as voters along the U.S.-Mexican border and in large cities like Chicago and New York. Ironically the early registration surges seemed to favor the Republicans, but the increased registration rates have not necessarily boosted turnout.

Between the constitutional territory of the states and that of the nation there is a tiny no-man's-land, the District of Columbia. For almost all of American history, the citizens of the district remained voteless, even in their own local affairs. Since the passage of the Twenty-third Amendment to the Constitution in 1961, however, the voters of the District of Columbia have had three votes in the electoral college. They also elect a nonvoting delegate to Congress and a series of local officials on the authorization of the Congress.

LEGAL-INSTITUTIONAL BARRIERS TO VOTING

Over the years, the various states have converged upon legal definitions of the suffrage that are surprisingly similar given their traditional discretion in this area. In part, the negative controls of the constitutional amendments have hemmed them in. So, too, have the political pressures for universal adult suffrage, the examples of other states, and increased supervision by the Congress and the Supreme Court. In any event, it is now possible to deal with the state definitions of the suffrage in a small number of categories.

Citizenship

Since the 1920s all states have required that voters be citizens of the United States. As surprising as it may now seem, prior to 1894 at least twelve states permitted aliens to vote,[10] although some required that the individual had begun to seek American citizenship. Without any doubt, the requirement of citizenship is the major legal barrier to voting for adults now living in the United States. There are millions of adults living in the United States—most of them concentrated in such states as California, Florida, Texas, and New York—who are ineligible to vote until they qualify as citizens. The states presumably could enfranchise their resident aliens, and some cities have proposed doing this, but with the current mood toward immigrants they are hardly likely to do so.

Residence

For most of the history of the Republic, the states were free to require that citizens live in the state and locality for a certain period of time before they could vote. Indeed, most states devised three-layer residence requirements: a minimum period of time in the state, a shorter time in the county, and an even shorter period in the local voting district. The longest residence requirements were those of the southern states (where migrant farm labor was disenfranchised), but long waits for eligibility were not uncommon elsewhere. As recently as 1970, the median residence requirement among the fifty states was one year in the state, three months in the county, and one month in the voting district.

These substantial residence requirements began to crumble in the 1950s and 1960s in response both to the demands of a physically mobile society and to its rising democratic expectations. States lowered their residence requirements, and many also set up even lower requirements for newcomers wishing to vote in presidential elections. In 1970, Congress settled the latter issue by establishing a national uniform residence requirement of thirty days within a state for voting in its presidential election. Then, in 1972, the Supreme Court struck down Tennessee's one-year residence requirement for voting in state and local elections, indicating a strong preference for a thirty-day limit.[11] Subsequently, almost half of the states have dropped residence requirements altogether, and most of the rest have fixed them at one month.

Despite the uniform reduction in the length of residence necessary to qualify for registration, residency requirements still impose a barrier to voting. The United States is a nation of movers. About 16 percent of the population moved within the

United States between 1990 and 1991, with about 6 percent moving to a different county and 3 percent to a different state.[12] One study shows that those who have recently moved are far less likely than nonmovers to vote in elections, even if they are identical on other characteristics related to turnout. With the depressing effects of mobility removed, this study estimates that turnout would be about 9 percent higher.[13]

Disqualifications

Many states restrict the suffrage for reasons of crime or mental incompetence. Institutionalization for insanity or severe mental illness temporarily removes an individual from the suffrage in all states. In the great majority of states (but not in Maine, Massachusetts, or Vermont), so does conviction for certain categories of crimes, the most common being felonies and electoral corruption. The disqualification for felonies lasts indefinitely in some states, even after release from prison. Only gubernatorial pardon or some formal administrative or legislative action will restore the franchise to these citizens.

Registration

One of the most effective external barriers to voting is the requirement in most states that voters themselves must take the initiative to register in order to participate in an election. Placing the responsibility for registration on the shoulders of the individual was a reform of the Progressive movement, implemented in most states toward the end of the nineteenth century to limit illegal voting in the teeming cities. Before then, voters only had to show up on election day or to be listed on an electoral roll compiled by the government to be able to cast a ballot, which is the practice in most European democracies. The adoption of registration requirements is widely credited with reducing the high turnout levels of the late nineteenth century because it both increased the motivation necessary to vote and reduced the fraudulent padding of voter rolls.[14]

Different provisions for registration among the states produce considerable variation in how much of a burden registration places on the individual. The provisions most affecting the ease of registration are the closing date for registration (which range from none to thirty days prior to the election), the frequency of purges of the registration rolls (a few states remove voters from the rolls after missing one election, but most do it only after four years of nonvoting), and the accessibility of registrars through regular office hours during the week as well as in evenings and on Saturdays.[15]

Restricting the right to vote only to those who have registered under the myriad provisions of the various states imposes additional "costs" on the exercise of the franchise. The higher these costs, the more citizens will choose not to participate in elections. While registration requirements have been greatly liberalized in recent years, they still pose a formidable obstacle to higher turnout. Studies have consistently estimated that turnout in presidential elections could be raised considerably if all states allowed election day registration, set regular as well as evening and Saturday hours for registration offices, and did not purge for nonvoting. The greatest gains would be realized by elimination of the closing date, which would enable citizens who are stimulated by the last weeks of the election campaign to cast a ballot.[16]

Registration laws, however, are not the insurmountable barriers to the vote that the hard-and-fast provisions defining the electorate are. Rather, they make voting only more difficult by increasing its "costs"—the amount of time, effort, and even knowledge required to gain access to the polls. Like voting, then, registration is a matter of individual choice. Because of this, in calculating turnout rates we should not restrict the definition of the potential electorate only to those who are registered, as some have suggested, however much that might improve American turnout levels relative to other democracies.

THE SPECIAL CASE OF VOTING RIGHTS FOR AMERICAN BLACKS

Nowhere have legal-institutional barriers to voting been more effective than in denying suffrage to southern blacks. Before slavery was abolished at the end of the Civil War, most blacks of course could not vote; only a few free blacks in a handful of northern states enjoyed that privilege. With the defeat of the Confederacy and the passage of the Reconstruction amendments to the Constitution to extend to blacks the rights of citizenship, black males were enfranchised nationwide. Once Union occupation troops withdrew from the South as the Reconstruction came to an end, however, southern states set about systematically to remove blacks from the active electorate and, by the beginning of the twentieth century, they had succeeded.

Systematic Disenfranchisement

The story of the disenfranchisement of the southern black electorate is a tale of blatant manipulation of the electoral system to control political outcomes. Legal restrictions on voting, capricious administration of the laws, and outright intimidation and violence when these "nicer" methods were not effective combined to reverse the tide of democratization for blacks—and often for poor whites as well—in the former Confederacy and some neighboring states. Only in contemporary times have southern blacks regained this essential right of democratic citizenship.

Southern states employed an arsenal of weapons to restrict the black vote. Residence requirements were most stringent in the South. Most states in that region required payment of a poll tax as a qualification for voting. Only one or two dollars a year, its disenfranchising effect was often increased by a stipulation that it be cumulative, that it be paid well in advance of the election, or that the taxpayer keep a receipt and present it at the voting booth. Many states also required passage of a literacy test, often of both reading ability and understanding (frequently as judged by a hostile registrar), as a condition for voting. These laws were intentionally directed at the poor, uneducated, and often itinerant black population. They created huge barriers to voting.

If the law did not prove sufficient to discourage black participation, other devices were available. Faced with the threat of black voting in the Democratic party's primary elections, some states declared the party a private club open only to whites. Blacks who were able to negotiate the legal maze traditionally found themselves blocked by the administration of registration and election laws. Endless delay, unavailable or antagonistic registrars, niggling technicalities, and double standards were formidable barriers (see box on following page). To those who nonetheless persevered, the threat—and all too often the reality—of economic reprisal (the loss of a job or a home) and of physical violence proved a powerful deterrent. Left alone to pursue their constitutionally given voting rights in an unremittingly hostile and threatening environment, it is little wonder that only 5 percent of voting-age blacks were registered in the eleven southern states as recently as 1940.[17]

The Long Struggle for Voting Rights

The struggle for the black franchise began in the classic American way as a constitutional issue. For years after the end of Reconstruction, in fact, the states and the United States Supreme Court played a game of constitutional "hide and seek." The states would devise a scheme of disenfranchisement, the Court would strike it down as unconstitutional, and the states would find another—ad infinitum. The states sometimes were careful not to disenfranchise poorer whites along with blacks—hence their devising of grandfather clauses, which automatically registered all persons whose ancestors had been eligible to vote before the Civil War. The ingenuity shown by southern states determined to avoid black registration is perhaps best illustrated by the white-primary cases. The white primary was simply a party primary in which blacks were forbidden to vote; it arose at a time in which the candidate who won the Democratic primary in southern states was assured of victory in the general election against an enfeebled Republican party. It finally expired, but only after twenty-one years of litigation and five cases before the Supreme Court.[18]

Court action is not nearly so effective, however, for dealing with informal administrative evasions. Increasingly, the most useful remedies were legislative and administrative—a fighting of fire with fire. The federal Voting Rights Act of 1965 and its extensions in 1970, 1975, and 1982 all made this kind of attack on discrimination against black would-be voters. The 1965 act and the 1982 extension involved the national government directly in local registration practices:

- The U.S. Justice Department was authorized to seek injunctions against individuals who prevented blacks from voting in primaries or general elections. When it could convince a federal court that a "pattern or practice" of discrimination existed in a district, the court could order registration and send federal registrars and observers to the area.
- The Justice Department acquired authority to supervise voting procedures in states and counties in which less than 50 percent of potential voters had voted in the most recent presidential election. Any changes in voting procedures had to be approved by the attorney general or by the United States District Court in the District of Columbia. The attorney general could also send registrars and observers into supervised states or counties.

ADMINISTRATIVE BARRIERS TO BLACK REGISTRATION IN THE SOUTH

In their account of the civil rights movement in the South, Pat Watters and Reese Cleghorn describe how blacks were prevented from registering by mundane, yet very effective, administrative practices:

> Slowdowns were common. Separate tables would be assigned whites and Negroes. If a line of Negroes were waiting for the Negro table, a white might go ahead of them, use the empty white table, and leave. In Anniston, Alabama, a report said the white table was larger, and Negroes were not allowed in the room when a white was using it. Another variation was to seat four Negroes at a table, and make three wait until the slowest had finished, while others waited outside in line. These methods were particularly effective when coupled with the one or two day a month registration periods. . . . In one north Florida county, the registrar didn't bother with any of these refinements, and didn't close his office when Negro applicants appeared. He simply sat with his legs stretched out across the doorway. Negroes didn't break through them.[19]

- Local registrars were brought under greater regulation and control. They were required to keep voting and registration records for twenty-two months and were prohibited from applying voting requirements unequally. Nor were they permitted to seize on immaterial errors or omissions in the application process as a reason for refusing registration.[2]

The Growth of Black Registration in the South

This unprecedented federal government intervention in state electoral practices and the resolute efforts of the civil rights movement in mobilizing black voters have enabled the black electorate to grow enormously in the South. Black registration increased from 5 percent of the black voting-age population in 1940 to 29 percent in 1960 on the eve of the massive efforts to protect black voting rights and then surged dramatically to 64.5 percent in the 1992 election—a level that came close to that achieved by white southerners. Variation in black registration levels remains among the southern states, however, reflecting differences in the size and socioeconomic characteristics of their black population, in their political traditions, and in the legal and extralegal barriers they continue to raise to black participation (Table 8.1).[21]

Virtually erased by now is the systematic exclusion of blacks from the electorate by legislation or administrative delay. Nonetheless, blacks have continued to face barriers in gaining an effective political voice in many areas of the South, as the frontier of discrimination has shifted from preventing black voting to limiting the impact of black votes.

Table 8.1 BLACK AND WHITE VOTER REGISTRATION IN THE SOUTH: 1960 AND 1992

State	1960			1992		
	Whites	Blacks	Whites–Blacks	Whites	Blacks	Whites–Blacks
Alabama	63.6%	13.7%	+49.9%	79.3%	71.8%	+ 7.5%
Arkansas	60.9	38.0	+22.9	67.8	62.4	+ 5.4
Florida	69.3	39.4	+29.9	64.5	54.7	+ 9.8
Georgia	56.8	29.3	+27.5	67.3	53.9	+13.4
Louisiana	76.9	31.1	+45.8	76.2	82.3	– 6.1
Mississippi	63.9	5.2	+58.7	80.2	78.5	+ 1.7
North Carolina	92.1	39.1	+53.0	70.8	64.0	+ 6.8
South Carolina	57.1	13.7	+43.4	69.2	62.0	+ 7.2
Tennessee	73.0	59.1	+13.9	63.4	77.4	–14.0
Texas	42.5	35.5	+ 7.0	66.1	63.5	+ 2.6
Virginia	46.1	23.1	+23.0	67.2	64.5	+ 2.7
Total	61.1	29.1	+32.0	68.0	64.5	+ 3.5

Note: Table entries are the percentage of each group in that year who are registered to vote.

Source: For 1960 figures, U.S. Bureau of the Census, *Statistical Abstract of the United States*, 99th edition (Washington, D.C.: U.S. Government Printing Office, 1980), p. 514; for 1992 figures, U.S. Bureau of the Census, *Current Population Report* P20–466, Table 4.

From Voting Rights to Representation

In the debate over the extension of the 1965 Voting Rights Act in 1981 and 1982, the major issue was the inclination of governmental bodies to dilute black voting power or to limit the opportunities for blacks to choose black officeholders by such devices as shifts to at-large local elections, legislative redistricting to divide black voters among a number of districts, or the annexation of white suburbs to offset black majorities in the cities or towns. Any such change now must be approved ahead of time, and the Justice Department's basis for rejecting a change was broadened somewhat in 1982.

Appropriately, in the 1990s attention has shifted away from registration and voting to the representation of black voters in the new legislative districts drawn up after the census. Under pressure from the Bush administration's Justice Department to create more minority districts in the South and through legislative alliances of black and Hispanic Democrats with white Republicans, a number of southern states redrew legislative district lines so as to concentrate black voters in often-odd-shaped "majority-minority" districts. The effect has been to increase the number of black seats but also to enhance Republican prospects in neighboring districts through concentration of the Democratic vote. The Supreme Court has questioned the constitutionality of the most flagrantly gerrymandered of these majority-minority districts. In a case challenging a congressional district in Georgia represented by a black Democrat, a slim majority of the Court found gerrymandering that violated the equal protection clause of the Fourteenth Amendment because race was the "predominant" factor in the redistricting. The controversy over redistricting plans for the 1990s that increase minority representation is sure to continue.[22]

POLITICAL INFLUENCES ON TURNOUT

Often ignored among external influences on turnout, so manifest are the legal-institutional barriers to voting, is politics itself. Through such features as the amount of competition between the parties, the attractiveness of the specific candidates for office, the importance and salience of the electoral contest, and the grass-roots efforts of political organizations themselves, voters can be drawn to or driven away from the polls. A logical explanation for the considerable variation in turnout levels across constituencies and across years may be found in the inherent variability of our politics.

Differential Interest among Elections

The attention and interest of American voters flag as they face the four-year cycle of American politics, and many of them respond only to the elections of greatest prominence. Probably no electorate in the democratic world is more frequently called to the polls than the American electorate. Within four years, it confronts national, state, and local elections for legislative and executive offices (and for the judiciary in a majority of the states), not to mention elections for school boards and assorted other local authorities. Most of these elections are preceded by primaries; and initiatives, referenda, and even an occasional recall election further complicate the calendar. Thus, whereas voters in other democracies may go to the polls only a few times in a four-or five-year cycle, civic obligation may call their beleaguered American counterparts to the polls for many primaries and general elections across any four years.

Voter participation varies substantially across these different elections. It is generally highest in presidential elections and lowest in local elections. For each office level, moreover, general elections normally attract far more voters than primaries. Initiatives and referenda, the Progressives' devices for allowing voters to decide issues and constitutional questions directly, elicit much lower levels of participation than ordinary elections, although an occasional emotionally charged issue can stimulate substantial turnout. The absence of a personal clash in these questions may reduce their interest and immediacy, and their frequent complexity confuses many would-be voters.[23]

The reasons for these variations in turnout are not hard to imagine. The more intense general election campaigns for the presidency and the governorships unquestionably spark greater voter interest and involvement. The personalities are well known, and the issues seem more momentous. Furthermore, party fortunes are involved and party loyalties are inflamed—contrary to the case in many nonpartisan local and judicial elections. To put it very simply, one should hardly be surprised that a presidential election in which two national political figures and two national parties engage in an intensive mass-media campaign draws three or four times more voters to the polls than does either a nonpartisan judicial campaign in which the candidates talk discreetly and a bit dully of the efficient administration of the courts or a primary for local offices.[24]

Competition

Competition in elections heightens voter participation. Turnout is higher in areas where the parties and candidates regularly compete on a fairly even basis—for example, in the states in Table 2.2 that fall into the two-party range.[25] Turnout also tends to be higher in elections that have hotly contested races.[26] This relationship between competition, in its various forms, and turnout appears in contests for a variety of different offices and holds up even when differences in the characteristics of the electorate and all historical voting trends in the district are held constant. Understandably, voters seem to be stimulated politically by the excitement of closely contested elections and by the fact that their votes may well affect the outcomes. Conversely, there is little appeal in trying to undo a foregone conclusion.

Historical changes in electoral turnout also have been linked to interparty competition. After the realignment of 1896, participation in presidential elections declined precipitously—from almost 80 percent of the voting-age population in prior elections to about 65 percent in the early 1900s. Some scholars have attributed this decline to the realignment of 1896. Electoral politics in the two decades before 1900 was fiercely competitive at the national level, where control of government turned on razor-thin margins of victory, and in many states and localities as well. The realignment of 1896 brought an abrupt end to all of this—in the South with the absorption of the Populist movement into the Democratic party and outside of the South with the declining appeal of the Democratic party. Even the realignment of the 1930s failed to restore the highly competitive and participative politics of that earlier era.[27]

Other scholars have countered with a legal-institutional explanation of the turnout declines registered after 1896. At that time, the electorate was constricted by a series of devices designed to increase the "cost" of voting—poll taxes, literacy tests, heightened residency requirements in the South, and the introduction of the secret ballot and tight registration requirements throughout the nation.[28] Even though it may be impossible to reconstruct the causal sequence of events in full, and the increased restrictions on voting surely played an important role, it seems undeniable that the decline in competition produced by the realignment of 1896 reduced turnout to at least some degree.

The Representativeness of the Party System

More generally, how effectively the party system gives voice to citizen interests and needs seems to be related to turnout. In European multiparty systems, where each sizable group in the society often is represented by its own party, turnout tends to be much higher than it is in two-party systems where so-called "catch-all" parties contain broad electoral coalitions. One price the United States may pay for its two-party system, then, is lower turnout.[29] Which of the various possible social, economic, and religious conflicts are represented by the dominant party cleavages also affects citizen participation. It should hardly be surprising that those citizens who perceive they have no stake in the prevailing political game refrain from voting.[30]

Organizational Efforts at Voter Mobilization

Aiding and abetting these various political influences on turnout is effort by political leaders and organizations in mobilizing voters to support their causes actively. As we have seen in Chapter 5, the political party organizations have long played an important mobilization—and, sometimes, demobilization (see box on p. 182)—role through their grass-roots campaigning. But the payoffs from mobilization in an electoral system lacking anything near full participation have been too attractive to be left entirely to the parties.[31]

From the traditional efforts of labor unions to the civil rights movement and Christian conservatives in modern times, American history is replete with examples of how turnout has been enhanced within particular groups by organized effort outside of the political parties. Dramatic increases in black voting during the postwar period can be attributed in no small measure to the registration and get-out-the-vote efforts of the civil rights movement and, more recently, to the excitement of the candidacies of Jesse Jackson for president and legitimate black contenders for other offices, especially big city mayors.[32] By the same token, the increasing influence of Christian conservatives in the Republican party is attributable to the efforts of Christian organizations to develop a base of loyal enthusiasts and then to mobilize them in partisan politics.

Organizational mobilization is inherently difficult, which is why successful mobilization effort has waxed and waned so much over the course of American history. Uniting a group of citizens in common cause often is challenge enough. Among other things, it requires them to subordinate their real differences to emphasize what they have in common. Convincing people to pursue this cause through politics is a big second step, but when it is taken, considerable opportunities open up for political involvement and influence.

TURNOUT: THE PERSONAL EQUATION

Turnout can also be explained from the point of view of the individual citizen. He or she bears the burdens and the costs of voting—costs not in cash but in energy, attention, time, and self-esteem. Indeed, when viewed as the result of a strictly rational calculation of costs and benefits, it is surprising that so many people make the effort to vote when the impact of their single vote seems so small.[33] More generally, it seems that the willingness to bear these burdens is a function of the individual's own motivations.

Personal Aversions to Voting

For the nonvoter, the many and varied costs of voting very likely outweigh any total of satisfactions or achievements that the act of voting brings. For some nonvoters, in fact, the act of voting is often a threatening act. For adults whose political cues are mixed—those, for example, who were raised as Democrats but had Republicanism urged on them by persuasive spouses—the necessity of voting threatens a personal turmoil. Similarly, the uneducated and unsophisticated voter may very well find the imposing facade of the voting machine more than a little intimidating. Some people even refuse to register because the registration rolls are used to choose citizens for duties they want to avoid, such as serving on a jury, and, of course, some nonvoting can be accounted for by unanticipated election day problems such as illness or bad weather (see box on p. 183).

PARTY DEMOBILIZATION IN NEW JERSEY

Mobilizing strategies target voters for special efforts—for example, a phone call or personal visit from a local leader or friend, the whipping up of enthusiasm at a rally or in church, a mailed appeal to action—designed to increase their motivation to vote. Parties and other organizations also sometimes work to demobilize voters, either by consciously refraining from rallying them to a particular cause or by actively undermining their desire to participate. Examples of demobilization abound in American history. For a century, a wide variety of devices were employed to demobilize black voters in the South as well as Hispanics in the Southwest, and in recent years well-advertised efforts to challenge voters' credentials in some states have dampened turnout.

The most recent example of a possible demobilization strategy at work involves allegations of Republican attempts to depress black turnout in the 1993 New Jersey gubernatorial election. The allegations arose when GOP strategist Ed Rollins told reporters that so-called "walking-around money" was passed out by the Republicans to black ministers and Democratic precinct workers to induce them to refrain from their usual voter-mobilization efforts in black neighborhoods. These comments created a firestorm of controversy, leading to a retraction by Rollins, denials of wrongdoing by Republican leaders, and a subsequent state and federal investigation. The investigation found no evidence to support the allegations.

SES

Explanations for voting turnout due to personal factors begin with an identification of the differences between voters and nonvoters. The principal contrast between them involves socioeconomic status.[34] Lower-status Americans are considerably less likely to vote, even somewhat more so in recent years. Interestingly, the strong relationship between status and voting participation so familiar in the United States is muted in many other democracies. Outside of the United States, it appears that the initial disadvantages of low status can be overcome through a lowering of the costs of voting and a mobilization of lower-status citizens by political parties and other electoral organizations.[35]

The most careful study of voting attributes the relationship between status and turnout almost solely to education level, finding that the effects of income and occupation are meager once education is taken into account (Table 8.2, panel A). According to this study:

> Education . . . does three things. First, it increases cognitive skills, which facilitates learning about politics. Schooling increases one's capacity for understanding and working with complex, abstract, and intangible subjects such as politics. This heightens one's ability to pay attention to politics, to understand politics, and to gather the information necessary for making political choices. . . . Second, better educated people are likely to

EXCUSES FOR NONVOTING

The advertisement below appeared as a full page in *The New York Times* the day before the 1977 local elections (Monday, November 7, 1977). It carried no title or heading, and, indeed, it hardly needed one. Barney's is a clothing store in New York City.

THE NEW YORK TIMES, MONDAY, NOVEMBER 7, 1977

I only vote for President.
The polls are too far away.
I don't want to be called for jury duty.
I had to work late.
I was too tired when I got home.
It's raining.
I didn't know I had to register.
I have a headache.
I hate making decisions.
Whenever I vote, they lose.
I forgot.
Tuesday's my bowling night.
I hate waiting on lines.
The voting booth gives me claustrophobia.
I didn't know where to vote.
My company doesn't give me off.
I was out of town.
There's no one to watch the kids.
I broke my glasses.
The polls were closed when I got there.
I hate crowds.
The Knicks were playing.
I'm moving anyway.
My car broke down.
Everyone knows who's gonna win.
I had a doctor's appointment.
When was the election?
I already voted in the primaries.
I had to study for a test.
It was my vacation day.
My vote won't make the difference.

A collection of the classics from Barney's.

Polls will be open tomorrow from 6:00 AM to 9:00 PM

Source: Courtesy of Barney's, New York.

get more gratification from political participation. They are more likely to have a strong sense of citizen duty, to feel moral pressure to participate, and to receive expressive benefits from voting. Finally, schooling imparts experience with a variety of bureaucratic relationships: learning requirements, filling out forms, and meeting deadlines. This experience helps one overcome the procedural hurdles required first to register and then to vote.[36]

Youth

After SES explanations, the next most-powerful personal factor in accounting for differences between voters and nonvoters is youth. For a long time, younger Americans have voted at rates well below the average (Table 8.2, panel B). This tendency is largely attributable to the high "start up" costs the young must pay—the difficulties of settling into a community, registering for the first time, and establishing the habit of voting, all at a time when other, more personal interests dominate their lives.[37] The lowering of the national voting age to eighteen in 1971 and the entry of the unusually large "baby boom" generation into the electorate magnified the impact of youthful nonvoting well into the 1980s.

Gender and Race

Education and age have not been the only important demographic differences between voters and nonvoters. For many decades after their enfranchisement in 1920, women voted less frequently than men. With the changes of recent decades in the role of women in society and their growing education levels, especially among the youngest generations, though, that difference has disappeared (Table 8.2, panel C). Traditionally, too, blacks have been less likely to vote than whites, a gap that has narrowed but still persists into the most recent elections (Table 8.2, panel D). But whites on the average have considerably more education and higher status than blacks, and differences in turnout between the races vanish if their status disparities are taken into account.[38]

Social Connectedness

Rivaling demographic characteristics as a source of motivation to vote is the integration of individuals into the social world around them. People who are embedded in dense social networks are considerably more likely to participate in elections. One reason is that those who possess other personal characteristics conducive to voting also tend to be more socially integrated. A more direct reason is that social interaction itself enhances political involvement. People who belong to secondary organizations exhibit considerably higher rates of turnout than those who do not, which illustrates from a different perspective the great potential of organizational mobilization. Voting is also more common among people who are well integrated into the

Table 8.2 PERSONAL CHARACTERISTICS AND VOTER TURNOUT: 1992

	Percentage Voting	
	ANES Survey	US Census Survey
A. Education		
No high school degree	50%	39%
High school graduate	73	58
Attended college	89	74
B. Years of Age		
Under 35	68	49
35 or more	82	68
C. Gender		
Females	76	62
Males	77	60
D. Race		
Blacks	71	54
Whites	78	64
E. Interested in politics		
Very much	91	—
Somewhat	75	—
Not much	44	—
F. Party identification		
Strong Democrat	87	—
Weak Democrat	75	—
Independent closer to Democrats	74	—
Independent closer to neither	61	—
Independent closer to Republicans	75	—
Weak Republican	78	—
Strong Republican	89	—

Note: Table entries are the percentages of each group who reported having voted in the 1992 presidential election. The Census survey does not ask attitudinal questions, so it provides no data on partisanship or interest.

Source: The ANES data are from the 1992 American National Election Study, Center for Political Studies, University of Michigan; data made available by the Inter-University Consortium for Political and Social Research. The US Census data are from the U.S. Bureau of the Census's Current Population Reports, P20–466, *Voting and Registration in the Election of November 1992* (Washington, D.C.: U.S. Government Printing Office, 1993), Table A, Table C, and Table 1.

community—through longevity of residence, church attendance, working outside the home, or even owning their own home. Even marriage seems to be conducive to voting participation, as acquiring a spouse or losing one both have consequences for participation.[39]

Political Attitudes

Certain personal attitudes toward politics itself also contribute to higher levels of voting participation through their effects on the motivation to vote. Voters and nonvoters also are clearly differentiated by basic interest in politics (Table 8.2, panel E) and by strength of party loyalties (Table 8.2, panel F). It should hardly be surprising that Americans who find politics more interesting and who are more firmly committed to its major players, the Democratic and Republican parties, are more involved in elections. In addition, a cluster of so-called "civic attitudes" have proven to be conducive to voting participation in study after study. The most important of them are the citizen's perceptions that government is responsive to them (or what is termed *external political efficacy*), can be trusted to do what is right (*trust in government*), and a sense of responsibility to take part in elections (*citizen duty*).[40]

THE PUZZLE OF DECLINING VOTER TURNOUT

Since the 1960s, turnout in American elections has declined substantially. Presidential voting steadily fell from its postwar peak of 72.8 percent in 1960 to a low of 52.7 percent of the eligible electorate in 1988—and then rose to 56.9 percent in 1992. Turnout in midterm elections suffered a similar free fall from a postwar high of 56.8 percent in 1966 to a historic low of 37.5 percent in 1990—and 39.9 percent four years later.

Explaining the Decline

In some respects, this has been a puzzling change because it occurred in the face of powerful forces that should have propelled turnout in the opposite direction. Southern blacks won much greater access to the ballot and voted in increasing numbers after 1960. Southern whites, stimulated in part by the presence of blacks at the polls, increased their turnout levels as well. Throughout the nation, restrictive residency and registration requirements were lifted, vastly reducing the costs of voting. The generation of women who had come of voting age in an earlier era when women were not accustomed to voting shrank in size and was replaced by a new generation for whom voting was unquestionably consistent with their expected role. Finally, the educational levels of the electorate have grown enormously since 1960, as the percentage of the population continuing on to college doubled in a generation. Yet, in spite of all of these boons for turnout, it declined—at least outside the South![41]

   This change is primarily attributed to declines in participation-inducing political attitudes and in social connectedness. Two political attitudes have played an especially important role in these changes—beliefs that government is responsive to its citizens, or what is called external (because its source is external to the individual) political efficacy, and party identification. Both efficacy and partisanship decreased substantially after 1960. Because turnout falls off with each step decrease in each, as the levels of efficacy and partisanship in the electorate decrease, turnout should decline. These two attitudes contributed separately to the turnout declines from 1960 through 1992, with efficacy accounting for more of the change than partisanship, as can be seen in Table 8.3, and their combined effects were even stronger.[42]

Other factors appear to have been at work as well in lowering voting participation over the last three decades. During this period, the American electorate has become younger, less married, less inclined to attend religious services on a regular basis, and more mobile. These are indicators of a general erosion in social connectedness, in the integration of Americans into the social networks that are conducive to participation. This also has been a time of reduced electoral mobilization. After the 1960s, labor-intensive campaigning and social-movement activism declined, and electoral competition fell off. With this slackening of effort to arouse the electorate, voters had less motivation to go to the polls.[43]

Is Turnout On Its Way Back Up?

The downward drift in turnout did not continue through the 1992 and 1994 elections. While participation in them was still low by most standards, it reached its highest levels in a decade for midterm contests and in two decades in presidential contests. Whether this situation is temporary or presages significant changes in electoral involvement of course remains to be seen, but there are characteristics of each election that suggest a quickening of political participation in America for some years to come.

The surge in presidential turnout in 1992 is best explained by the political forces operating in that contest. This was the closest election since 1976, with public opinion polls showing a tight race through the entire fall campaign and most states recording only a small plurality for the winner on election day. It also was a three-way contest, full of dramatic campaign events, in which independent Ross Perot posed a serious challenge to the major-party standard-bearers. As a consequence, interest in the election was considerably higher than the 1964–1988 average, and this heightened interest buoyed turnout. The Perot candidacy itself contributed significantly to the rise in interest. Not only did his presence add a level of excitement and

Table 8.3   VOTING PARTICIPATION AMONG CATEGORIES OF PARTISAN STRENGTH AND EXTERNAL POLITICAL EFFICACY: 1992

External Political Efficacy	Strong Partisans	Weak Partisans	Independents Closer to Party	Independents	Total
High	93%	81	81	72	84
Medium	84	80	78	54	78
Low	84	72	70	56	72
Total	88	74	74	61	

Note: Table entries are the percentage of each combined efficacy-partisan group from the ANES survey who were recorded in the official records as having voted in the presidential election.

Source: 1992 American National Election Study, Center for Political Studies, University of Michigan; data made available through the Inter-University Consortium for Political and Social Research.

drama to the campaign, but it succeeded in mobilizing into the active electorate many disaffected Americans who were looking for an alternative to the two traditional parties and found it in Perot.[44]

Heightened midterm participation in 1994 also can be traced to political factors intrinsic to the election. As the campaign proceeded, it appeared that the GOP had its best prospects in decades to capture the Congress and to win a disproportionate share of statehouses and state legislative seats. Many Republicans campaigned on national issues, widely advertised through an issue-based Contract for America, rather than allow the inherent localism of midterm contests to redound to the benefit of incumbent Democrats. The consequence was an unprecedented mobilization of Republican voters: GOP House candidates drew almost 9 million more votes than four years before, whereas Democrats lost nearly 1 million votes from 1990 totals. Such one-sided mobilization is a rare occurrence, having last appeared in the 1934 election—during the realignment which created the New Deal party system.

Whether the turnout surge of the 1990s will continue into the second half of the decade remains to be seen. If Ross Perot, Colin Powell, Jesse Jackson, or some other independent (or third-party candidate) joins the fray in 1996 and puts the presidency as much up for grabs as it was in 1992, interest and hence turnout may reach—or even surpass—previous levels. If 1994 was a harbinger of realignment, voting participation should increase, as it has in previous realignments. Without the stimulation of an interesting contest or the mobilization of partisans in a quest for political hegemony, however, turnout levels could retreat to earlier levels.

CONSEQUENCES FOR THE POLITICAL PARTIES

The American parties operate within an American electorate that is neither a representative sample of the full American adult population nor of that segment of it eligible to vote. Moreover, this electorate constantly shifts in size and composition. The strategies of the parties in pursuing their goals, especially the contesting of elections, must take account of those facts.

Long-Range Consequences

The long-run consequences for the parties of changes in the electorate spring from basic changes in its legal definitions. Because electorates in democracies usually expand rather than contract, the changes most often result from the addition of new groups to the eligible electorate. Most recently, the American parties have absorbed two major groups: previously disenfranchised American blacks and young adults between the ages of eighteen and twenty-one. With the flood of Hispanic and Asian immigrants in recent years, the amnesty for illegal aliens in the 1986 immigration reform law, and recent incentives for immigrants to become citizens as quickly as possible, the need to absorb other major groups may be on the horizon.

The effects of these newly enfranchised groups on the parties have been substantial. Blacks have flowed into the Democratic party: three-quarters of them identify as Democrats, and in each presidential election since 1964 more than 80 percent have given their vote to the Democratic candidate. The mobilization of blacks has been a mixed blessing for the party, though, because it seems to have triggered a countermovement of whites away from the Democrats, particularly in the South.[45] The impact of young voters entering the electorate in recent years is more complex. In the first few years after the voting age was reduced to eighteen, the newly of-age voters exhibited more pro-Democratic than pro-Republican dispositions. In 1984 and 1988, the youngest voters became more favorable toward the Republicans, however, only to return to favor Democrats in 1992 and 1994. On balance, youthful voters in recent decades usually have been more responsive to the short-term forces of a particular election setting than to any fundamental appeals of the parties.[46]

Long-range consequences for the parties also stem from changes in the composition and distribution, rather than the size, of the American electorate. Population growth and migration are a case in point. The parties of ten states—Alaska, Arizona, California, Florida, Georgia, New Hampshire, New Mexico, Nevada, Texas, and Utah—faced increases in state populations in excess of 20 percent between the 1980 and 1990 censuses. Similarly, the aging of the American population has enlarged the group of over-sixty-five voters in each successive presidential election. These shifts and growths are differential: the groups (and their goals) added in each case are not a representative sample of the entire American electorate. Change in the electorate of any magnitude necessitates a party response if the parties are to preserve, much less enhance, their standing.

The long-term standing of the parties also is affected by the difference between the potential and actual electorates. There were about 60 million adults of voting age in 1992 who were not registered to vote—whether for reasons of disqualification or their own unconcern. Those adults are widely considered more likely recruits for the Democratic party than for the Republicans because of their lower SES characteristics. Therefore, legislation that would expand the electorate—for instance, by permitting registration at the polls, by making illegal aliens eligible for citizenship and thus for the suffrage, or (as with the "motor voter" law) by making it easier to register—might benefit the Democrats, although perhaps not the Democratic party as it is presently constituted. On the other hand, surges in registration most often are induced by political forces, not pure demographics. Recent trends from 1988 through early 1996 show dramatic gains in Republican registration in a variety of different states, with the largest increase coming in the so-called Sunbelt, at the same time that Democratic registration was barely increasing at all.[47]

The most basic of all the consequences of voting and nonvoting concerns the distribution of political influence in the American political system. Citizens who fail to register or vote deny themselves a potent voice in American politics, and the implications of that loss are all the more serious when the nonvoters differ markedly from the voters. Reduced levels of turnout among low-status Americans likely limit the attention elected officials pay to their needs and concerns. To some degree, then, increases in the marginalization of the disadvantaged in American society may be attributable to their failure to participate in the electoral process.[48]

Yet, this observation must be tempered by the finding of meticulous studies that nonvoters, despite their social backgrounds, tend not to have very different views on the issues from those of voters.[49] What their political views and goals might be if they were mobilized into political involvement is the fundamental question, however, and on that point scholars are of necessity reduced to speculation.

Short-Range Consequences

In addition to the long-range consequences of changes in the basic structure of the eligible electorate, the political parties must deal with the possibilities of short-range changes in turnout from election to election. Because increases or decreases in turnout are unlikely to benefit all parties and candidates equally—because nonvoters as a group have different political characteristics from voters—these changes too have potent political consequences. The increasing or decreasing of voter turnout and the exploiting of variations in turnout between various elections frequently become focal points in party strategy. If nothing else, the quest for Perot voters by both the Democratic and Republican parties illustrates how much political strategists appreciate the consequences of mobilization and demobilization.

The conventional wisdom has it that big turnouts favor the Democrats. There is little room to quarrel with the underlying logic of that maxim. The greatest percentage of nonvoters in the United States comes from groups ordinarily disposed to the Democratic party. It is for this reason that effective registration or get-out-the-vote campaigns are thought to help the Democrats more often than not. The maxim explains the money and manpower that organized labor spends in registration campaigns. It explains the ancillary maxim that rainy weather is Republican weather. It also suggests why, in some states, Republicans prefer an electoral calendar in which gubernatorial elections are held in the nonpresidential years and therefore in a smaller electorate that may be a bit more favorable to Republican candidates.

Despite the general appeal of the maxim linking big turnouts with the Democrats, the relationship is more subtle and complicated than that—particularly because it fails to take the one-sided nature of defections from party among peripherally involved voters into account. Three of the last five presidential elections with turnouts exceeding 60 percent—in 1952, 1956, and 1968—were won by the Republicans, and until 1994 Republicans have fared better in presidential election years than at mid-term. Especially because nonvoters are less partisan, they also may be more responsive to the momentary, dramatic appeal of issue or candidate. Since 1952, in fact, nonvoters have favored the ultimate presidential victor even more than did voters in eight of the ten presidential contests, including those in 1984, 1988, and 1992 (Table 8.4).[50]

Party strategists cannot fail to consider the likely voting electorate as they prepare their campaigns. They nourish the often fragile hope that turnouts can be affected selectively and differentially, and they attempt, therefore, to mold the size and makeup of the participating electorate itself in the campaign. When they must contest a primary election, they may hope by discreet and selective campaigning to minimize the turnout—for (generally) the smaller the turnout, the larger will be the proportion of it accounted for by the party's most loyal electorate. In general elections, the strategists may try to concentrate campaigns in areas of known party strength, thus maximizing that turnout. Individuals planning a congressional career always confront the fact that they will seek reelection by different electorates in alter-

Table 8.4 PRESIDENTIAL CANDIDATE PREFERENCES OF NONVOTERS: 1952–92

	1952	1956	1960	1964	1968	1972	1976	1980	1984	1988	1992
Would have voted Democratic	52%	28%	51%	80%	45%	35%	57%	47%	39%	45%	49%
Would have voted Republican	48	72	49	20	41	65	43	45	61	55	30
	100%	100%	100%	100%	86%	100%	100%	92%	100%	100%	79%

Note: The figures in 1968, 1980, and 1992 add to less than 100 percent because some nonvoters preferred the third-party candidate Wallace in 1968 and independents Anderson in 1980 and Perot in 1992.

Source: American National Election Studies, Center for Political Studies, University of Michigan; data made available by the Inter-University Consortium for Political and Social Research.

nate elections—the large turnout of the presidential election followed by the smaller turnout of the midterm elections two years later—as well as in their party's primary and general election.

THE BROADER ISSUES

The democratic ethos assumes the desirability of full popular participation in the affairs of democratic self-government. The case for democracy itself rests on the wisdom of the widest possible sharing of political power and political decision making within the society. It is precisely this ethos that is offended by the relatively low voting percentages of American adults. The affront to the democratic ethos seems all the greater in view of the fact that voting percentages are higher in most other democracies and in countries that Americans would like to think have less stable and responsive democracies.

Widespread nonvoting also casts some doubt on the effectiveness with which the political parties—the political organizations primarily concerned with contesting elections—manage to involve the total eligible electorate. Presumably, the parties, heralded so often as the instruments of democratic politics, should maximize political participation in the American society. The political parties themselves are, after all, the political organizations that developed to mobilize the new democratic masses. All of their capabilities are directed to recruiting large political aggregates, and much of the case for their superiority as political organizations rests on that ability.

Clearly, the record of the parties in mobilizing and involving the American electorate is mixed. We can cite examples of effective competition for the support of new groups entering the electorate. Even so, the hands of the parties are not completely clean. They often appear not to relish the challenges of new voters, especially those of low status. The experience of political power has made them (especially their parties in government) sympathetic to the comfortable status quo of two-party competition. They do not welcome the uncertainties that a radical alteration in the electorate would bring. The party in government, which after all makes the changes in the formal definition of the electorate, has won office with the support of the electorate as it now exists, and it is understandably not anxious to alter it greatly.

All in all, the American parties work within a somewhat homogeneous active electorate. That electorate reduces the totality of political conflict and the range of political interests to which the parties must respond. The parties find it easier to be moderate and pragmatic because the electorate to which they respond is largely settled in and committed to the present basic social arrangements. Compromise and tactical movement come more easily when the effective electorate is homogeneous and agrees on fundamentals. In brief, although it has been fashionable to say that the moderate, pragmatic, nondoctrinaire American parties are the result of an electorate that agrees on the fundamental questions, it is probably also true that the pragmatic, majoritarian parties in a two-party system do not easily draw into their ambit the low-status, alienated, dissident individuals who are not a part of that moderate consensus. In a predominantly middle-class society, that may be the price of a two-party system.

Some devotees of political democracy may be comfortable about paying that price. They fear the dilution in the quality of voting that might come from the sudden influx of an army of uninformed new voters. The annals of history contain sobering examples of extremist movements such as the German Nazi's in the 1920s and 1930s, which rejected the norms of civility and tolerance for minority opinion on which democracy rests, that were supported by the less-informed and involved citizens. Thus, democracy itself is seen to be threatened by the mobilization of large numbers of new voters. Even though most other Western democracies with fuller electorates seem to have avoided such problems, the possibility that a rapid enlargement of the American electorate might threaten the very foundations of political democracy cannot be entirely dismissed, especially in the aftermath of the unprecedented success of an independent candidate for president. How this concern can be reconciled with the primacy of participation in the democratic ethos is one of the perplexing normative issues of our time.

PART
Four

THE POLITICAL PARTIES IN THE ELECTORAL PROCESS

Separate treatment of the party organization, the party in the electorate, and the party in government obscures the very real and important interactions among them at key moments of American party politics. At no time is this interaction more visible than in the role the parties play in the electoral process.

The party organization, the party electorate, and the elected officials and candidates wearing the party label all contribute to the selection of the candidates for office to an extent unrivaled in the other democracies. Both the struggle among the various parts of the party to satisfy their preferences and the momentary reconciliation of these differences in uniting around the party nominees are contained within the American candidate selection process. Once a candidate is chosen, the various parts of the party also combine, albeit not always smoothly or wholeheartedly, their efforts in the ensuing campaign. American political campaigns always have been more candidate centered than most, but the party organizations play important roles in mobilizing support across the party ticket.

The contesting of elections unites the American parties in yet another crucial way. However briefly, it overcomes their decentralized and fragmented character. The choice of a presidential candidate and the following campaign bind the state and local parties into a fleeting coalition with the national party. A statewide election similarly focuses the activities and energies of local organizations and leaders within the state. With the infusion of soft money into the party organizations, central funding now is even provided to support activity on behalf of the party *ticket* generally. These joint ventures introduce the primary centripetal tendencies into an otherwise decentralized party system.

The pursuit of victory in elections unites the party for a number of reasons. The election is the event that elevates the business of politics to a visibility that can stimulate even the least involved voters. The candidates personify and simplify the difficult choices of American politics. Furthermore, the recruitment of resources for the party organization depends on the party's establishment of a possibility of electoral victory. In the long run, the incentives that lure resources to the party flow only to those parties that win. Electoral victory is a critical condition for the patronage, the triumph of an interest or an ideology, and the social and psychological rewards that motivate involvement.

Because the American parties are parties that must win elections, they must mobilize pluralities in the electorate. The conventional references to the American parties as electoral parties are, however, a little too glib and hackneyed. For one thing, these references imply that the parties carry out their electoral activities with ease. To the contrary, the party organizations find it difficult to control the selection of candidates, to take stands on issues, to fix campaign strategies, even to raise money. Those aspects of election politics are controlled, in the name of the whole party, by its candidates—its party in government and the candidates hoping to join it—and the candidates themselves are not always the choices of the organization.[1] Increasingly, it is these party candidates who have organized their own campaigns, recruited their own workers, hired their own campaign advice, and raised their own campaign funds. If it is true that the party in government controls the central, most visible activities of the party (at the expense of a frustrated party organization), can the party organizations reasonably achieve the goals set by their activists?

At the same time that the party stages an internal competition over the control of its electoral strategies, it also faces the competition of other political organizations. They increasingly seek their political goals in the electoral process. Over the past twenty years, the nonparty political organizations have played aggressive, overt roles in the nomination and election of candidates. It is not uncommon now to see accounts of electoral activities by trade unions, religious organizations, candidate organizations, public relations firms, reform groups, and political action committees.

The continuing contest for influence in American electoral politics raises questions about the very role and viability of the parties that will be addressed in the chapters that follow. The outcomes of the competition for the election role within the parties and between parties and other political organizations determine, in great measure, what the parties are and what they do in the political system.

Throughout the coming chapters, there also runs a related theme: the impact of political institutions on the nature of the parties. Nowhere are the effects of political institutions on the parties clearer than in the electoral process. The direct primary, for example, touches every attempt the parties make to control the nomination of candidates. In fact, it is the primary that so often turns the control of nominations from the party organization to the candidates themselves or to other political organizations. In so doing, primaries have changed the very nature of American electoral and party politics.

The chapters of this section, therefore, take a temporary detour from a focus on the separate parts of the party to deal with the interrelationship among these parts as the parties participate in the electoral process. This is the process that produces the government, so full treatment of the party in government naturally is reserved for the following section. But members of the party in government of course are deeply involved in the electoral process and will appear as prime players in the next several chapters.

The parties are involved at two key points in the electoral process. First, the parties nominate the candidates for office who will carry the party label. The process of nomination will constitute a major focus of this section in terms of both its general nature and the fascinating and peculiar practices through which the parties select their presidential candidates. The second point of party involvement in the electoral process comes in the contesting of the general election. The electoral campaign and the party's multifaceted role within it, therefore, will be the topic of another chapter.

The final chapter of Part Four discusses the key resource for the contesting of elections at all levels—money. Campaign money has come to pay an increasingly important and controversial role in the American electoral process. Amidst extensive efforts to reform campaign financing practices, the inexorable quest for dollars to run campaigns continues. A focus on the role of money highlights how much financial capabilities and constraints influence what the parties do and do not do in electoral campaigns and how this affects the place of parties in the electoral process.

Chapter
9

The Naming of the Party Candidates

Few Americans realize the uniqueness of their principal system of nominating candidates for office, in which through primaries ordinary citizens rather than party leaders select the party's candidates. Having devised the direct primary and adopted it almost universally for the nomination of candidates, they seem unaware that the rest of the democratic world uses a very different method—placing the choice of the party's candidates in the hands of party activists or the party's elected officials. No other single factor goes so far to explain the differences between American party politics and those of other democracies as their contrasting methods for nomination. The direct primary has forced upon the American parties a different set of strategies in making nominations, in contesting elections, and in attempting eventually to maintain responsibility over their successful candidates in office.

In the irresistible advance of the direct primary in the twentieth century, no state has been untouched. The great majority of states employ it in all nominations, and the rest use it in most. It has even now been adopted by most states in the presidential nomination process (see Chapter 10). Suffice it to say, its domination of the American nomination process now seems unquestioned. In essence, the direct primary (or, more simply, the primary) is a special election in which the party electorate, variously defined, chooses candidates to run for public office under the party label. At a subsequent general election, the total electorate then makes the final choice from among the nominees of the parties.

Even though the nomination does not formally settle the electoral outcome, its importance is great. The major screening of candidates takes place at the nomination; the choice is reduced to two in most constituencies. Especially in areas of one-party domination, the real choice is made in the primary. Moreover, the nominees of the party bring their images and visibility, their priorities and positions on issues, to the party. In the eyes of many voters, they are the party. Their quality and ability also determine, to a considerable extent, the party's chance for victory in the general election.

THE EVOLUTION OF THE NOMINATION PROCESS

The almost universal reliance upon the direct primary for the selection of party candidates in the United States is an achievement of the twentieth century. For the first
110 years of the Republic, first the party caucus and then the party convention dominated the nomination of candidates for public office. Each gave way successively
under the criticism that it permitted, if not encouraged, the making of nominations by
self-chosen and often irresponsible party elites. Finally, early in the twentieth century, the primary triumphed on the belief that the greatest possible number of party
members ought to take part in the nomination of the party's candidates. This triumph
became complete only in the 1970s when a majority of states turned to primaries in
the selection of party candidates for president.

Nominations by Caucus

The different systems of nomination developed in the United States along with and
as a part of the development of the party system. In fact, parties as parties (rather than
as legislative associations) emerged and evolved largely as nominators of candidates
for public office. In the early years of the Republic, local caucuses (or meetings)
were held to select candidates for local offices, and, frequently, caucuses of like-
minded partisans in legislatures met to nominate candidates for governor and other
statewide offices. Similarly, congressional caucuses nominated presidential and vice-
presidential candidates. Whatever their form, the caucuses were self-selected and
informal. There was no procedure for ensuring even the participation of all the major
figures in the party.

Nominations by Convention

The caucus method of presidential nomination could not withstand the spread of the
democratic ethos in the early years of the Republic. "King Caucus" was an inviting
target for the Jacksonians, who attacked it as an aristocratic device that thwarted popular wishes. In 1832, the Jacksonian Democrats met in a national convention—
the first for a major party—and, appropriately, nominated Andrew Jackson for the
presidency. From then on, the convention system quickly triumphed along with Jacksonian popular democracy, whose values it shared. It dominated the making of nominations for the rest of the nineteenth century. Broadly representative at its best, the
nominating convention was composed of delegates chosen by state and especially
local party leaders, often at their own lower-level conventions (referred to as "caucuses" even if organized around formal rules and procedures).

Even though they were representative in form, however, the large and chaotic
conventions were scarcely that in reality. Both in the picking of delegates and in the
management of the conventions, the fine, guiding hands of party leaders were too
obvious and oppressive. Party insurgents, unhappy with bossism at the conventions
and with the alliance of the bosses and "the interests," attacked the convention sys-

tem with considerable fervor and cunning. The Progressives led the anticonvention movement, and their journalistic allies, the muckrakers, furnished the often shocking, often piquant, corroborative details of democracy denied.[1]

Nominations by Direct Primaries

The cure offered by the Progressives—the direct primary—comported easily with their democratic norms. It was an article of faith among them that to cure the ills of democracy, one needed only to prescribe larger doses of democracy. Appropriately, it was one of progressivism's high priests, Robert M. La Follette, who authored the country's first statewide primary law in Wisconsin in 1902 (see box on following page). Some southern states had adopted primaries at the local level in the years after the Civil War, often to introduce some competition into a prevailing system of one-party politics, but in the first two decades of the twentieth century, all but four states turned to them statewide for at least some of their nominations.

Although the primary was designed to reform the nominating processes by "democratization," many of its supporters saw in it an instrument for crippling the political party itself. For them, the primary was a device to reduce the power of the parties and their "bosses" by striking at their chief activity as a party organization: the nomination of candidates. Party leaders had done the nominating under the caucus and convention systems, but primaries took from them the control of who would run under the party name and symbols by vesting the power to nominate in a broad party electorate. Extending this principle to its logical extreme, some states such as Wisconsin adopted so permissive a definition of the party electorate that it included any voters who chose to vote in the party's primary on election day.

Regardless of the motives of the enactors of the primary laws, there is little doubt that the laws undermined the power of party organizations. Not only did they greatly circumscribe the influence of party leaders on nominations, but they also opened up the party to possible penetration of its top leadership echelons by officeholders without any loyalty to the party organization or party principles. Largely because of the existence of primaries, party leaders have less control over who will receive the party nomination in the United States than in any other democratic political system. With the extension of the primary to the selection of leaders of the party organization itself, the parties even were threatened with loss of control over their own internal affairs.

The quick success of the direct primary happened during the years of the greatest one-partyism in American history immediately following the realignment of 1896. In the early years of the twentieth century, sectionalism was pervasive, and one party or the other dominated the politics of many states. One-partyism made the nomination of the dominant party crucial. Although the failings of the conventions might be tolerated when a real choice remained in the general election, they were more difficult to bear when the nomination of one party was equivalent to election. The convention could choose the weariest party hack without fear of challenge from the other party. Thus, the Progressives, who fought economic monopoly with antitrust legislation, used the direct primary as their major weapon in combatting political monopoly.

LA FOLLETTE AND THE PRIMARY

No one has captured the rhetoric and fervor of the movement for the direct primary as well as its leader, Robert M. La Follette, governor and then United States senator from Wisconsin. Writing in his autobiography, in the chapter "Struggle with the Bosses," La Follette reports his speech in February 1897 at the University of Chicago. Here are some excerpts from its conclusion:

> Put aside the caucus and convention. They have been and will continue to be prostituted to the service of corrupt organizations. They answer no purpose further than to give respectable form to political robbery. Abolish the caucus and the convention. Go back to the first principles of democracy; go back to the people. Substitute for both the caucus and the convention a primary election . . . where the citizen may cast his vote directly to nominate the candidate of the party with which he affiliates. . . . The nomination of the party will not be the result of "compromise" or impulse, or evil design . . . but the candidates of the majority, honestly and fairly nominated.

Source: Robert M. La Follette, *La Follette's Autobiography* (Madison: R. M. La Follette, 1913), pp. 197–98.

THE PRESENT MIX OF PRIMARY AND CONVENTION

The convention as a device for nominating candidates has faded in the face of the democratic appeal of the direct primary. Decline has not meant death, however, and the convention as a nominating device lingers in a few states and most conspicuously in the contest for the presidency.[2] Because the legal authority for devising nomination practices resides with the states, the result is a mosaic of primary and convention methods for choosing candidates for state offices.

All fifty states now provide for the nomination of statewide officials through the direct primary in some fashion, and thirty-eight of them (plus the District of Columbia) use this method exclusively.[3] In Alabama and Virginia, the party may choose to hold a convention instead of a primary, but only in Virginia is the convention option currently used (see box on p. 200).

Some combination of convention and primary is employed in the remaining states. Iowa requires a convention when no candidate in the primary has won at least 35 percent of the vote. Three additional states (Illinois, Indiana, and Michigan) use primaries for the top statewide offices but choose other nominees through conventions. Six states (Colorado, Delaware, New Mexico, New York, North Dakota, and Utah) hold conventions to screen candidates for the primary ballot. Finally, Connecticut employs a challenge primary in which the convention's choice may be challenged in the primary by candidates who received at least 15 percent of the convention vote; if there is no challenge, no primary is held.[4]

THE LAST STATE-CONVENTION NOMINATING SYSTEM: VIRGINIA AND "OLLIE" NORTH IN 1994

Virginia stands alone among the states in recent times in nominating some major statewide candidates by convention. Under Virginia law, parties are to nominate their candidates by primaries in federal elections if they had used primaries the last time for that office, unless the incumbent chooses a different method. In the 1996 Republican nomination process, the provisions of the law were interpreted as giving incumbent Senator John Warner the right to run for renomination in a primary rather than in a state convention where his intraparty opponents would have had the advantage.

Two years earlier, though, it was to a convention that the Virginia GOP had turned to select its nominee for the Senate seat held by Democrat Charles Robb. Attending the convention were more than 14,000 Republicans who had secured their delegate status by paying a $45 fee. Each of the state's counties were allocated a share of the votes using a formula favoring counties that had voted Republican in recent elections. The majority of these votes (55 percent) went to Oliver North over James Miller, former budget director in the Reagan Administration.

Using this anachronistic method of nomination, Virginia Republicans had chosen as their nominee one of America's most visible and polarizing political figures. "Ollie" North had been convicted on three felony counts for his role as a Reagan White House aide in the Iran-Contra affair, although the conviction was later overturned by a federal court because he had been granted limited immunity from prosecution in a congressional inquiry. Through his dramatic performance before the congressional committee investigating Iran-Contra and his passionate defense of core conservative values, North had emerged as a hero to many conservatives, especially Christian conservatives, who flocked to his cause at the convention.

In a tight contest with equally controversial Democratic incumbent Charles Robb, which may have been decided by the withdrawal of former Democratic governor and independent candidate Douglas Wilder from a four-candidate race, North went down to a slender defeat in the general election. The devotion of his followers, so critical in winning him the nomination at the convention, had proven inadequate to provide him with a plurality within the large general November electorate—just as, polls had suggested, it would not have won him the GOP nomination had the party used a primary instead of a convention.

VARIETIES OF THE DIRECT PRIMARY

The states also vary in the criteria they impose to determine eligibility to participate in their primaries. While each state's criteria seem unique in some respects, the basic distinctions boil down to three. In the states with so-called "closed" primaries, only voters who have publicly expressed party allegiance are able to participate. In states with "open" primaries, public expression of party allegiance is not a requirement for participation. Voters there can decide in which party's primary to participate in the privacy of the voting booth. Finally, a few states with "blanket" primaries allow voters to choose from among all the candidates for office, Democratic and Republican— in effect, not restricting voters to the nomination contests of a single party.[5]

The Closed Primary

The closed primary—which is found in an overwhelming majority of the states— requires voters to publicly declare their affiliation with a party before they can vote in that party's primary. Most of these states require voters to specify their party affiliation when they register in advance of the election. Then, at the primary election, they are given only the primary ballot of their party. Voters may change their party affiliation on the registration rolls, but most states require that this be done sometime ahead of the date of the primary. A few states do, however, permit a change of party registration at the polls.

In the other closed-primary states, voters simply declare their party "membership" or, more accurately, their party attachments or preferences at the polling place. They are then given the primary ballot of their declared party. In some states, their declarations can be challenged by one of the party observers at the polls, and they may be required to take an oath of party loyalty. Some states require voters to affirm that they have voted for the candidates of the party in the past; some demand that they declare themselves sympathetic at the moment to the candidates and principles of the party; and others ask nothing at all. These latter provisions make it possible for independents to participate in party primaries.

The Open Primary

Citizens of a few states are able to vote in the primary of their choice without ever disclosing which party's contest they have selected.[6] Upon entering the polling booth, voters are given either ballots for every party (one of which is selected in the privacy of the booth) or a consolidated ballot on which the part with the party of the voter's choice is selected. A voter may not, however, participate in the primary of more than one party.

The Blanket Primary

The blanket primary—found in Alaska, Louisiana, and Washington—goes one step in freedom beyond the open primary. Not only do the voters not need to disclose any party affiliation, but they are free to vote in the primary of more than one party; that

DAVID DUKE AND THE LOUISIANA BLANKET PRIMARY

The operations of the Louisiana blanket-primary system—as well as the dilemma posed to a party when the primary rules do not enable it to control its own nominations—can be illustrated by the state's 1990 U.S. Senate election. This contest received national attention because one of the contestants was former Ku Klux Klan leader and American Nazi party member David Duke, who had been spurned by Republican leaders in his successful campaign for a state legislative seat in 1989.

The five major-party candidates who vied for votes in the October Senate primary included incumbent Democrat J. Bennett Johnston, Republican state senator Ben Bagert, and Duke. Bagert carried the endorsement of prominent Republican party leaders, including President Bush, and had received considerable financial support from the party. On the eve of the election, however, public opinion polls showed that Duke was running second to Johnston and might even receive enough votes to deny Johnston the majority required to win the election outright, thus necessitating a run-off between Democrat Johnston and Republican Duke and further embarrassing the GOP. At the last moment, though, Bagert withdrew and (along with major GOP leaders) reluctantly threw his support to Johnston, who won the resulting four-way contest, albeit with only 54 percent of the vote. Duke received 44 percent of the total and more than half of the white vote.

is, they may choose a Democrat for one office and a Republican for another. Louisiana's version of the blanket primary, called by some the unitary primary, is the most radical of the blanket primaries in two respects. Any candidate who wins a majority of votes in the primary is elected to the office. If no candidate wins an outright majority, then the general election serves as a runoff between the top two vote getters, regardless of party (see box above).

Primary Types and the Role of Parties

These varieties of primary embody contrasting conceptions of the role of party in selecting candidates for office in a democracy. The open primary, long the darling of the Progressives, and the blanket primary implement a view of parties and rigid party loyalties as detrimental to democratic practice. The closed primary, by contrast, finds considerable value in ceding the choice of party candidates to loyal party followers. Whether democracy is realized more in the competition between disciplined parties or in a system that virtually bypasses organized parties has been a long-standing debate in American politics, and among democratic theorists.

Among these forms of primaries, the party organizations clearly prefer the closed primary with party registration prior to the primary. It pays greater respect to the right of the party itself to make nominations by limiting the party's primary electorate to voters willing to make a public declaration of party loyalty in advance of any particular election. Prior registration of party affiliation also gives the parties an added bonus: published lists of their partisans. It is not quite that simple, however. Party registration is, at best, an approximation of party loyalties at the moment. People are slow to change their party affiliations, and the party totals lag behind the pattern of voting. Furthermore, the registration figures of the majority or leading party tend to be swollen by conformists and by a few "political strategists," who register in a party solely to vote in its crucial primary.

The parties would gladly accept these uncertainties, however, in preference to what they regard as the more serious perils of the open primary, and the blanket primary enjoys even less favor. Party leaders level two charges against the open primary: crossing over and raiding. The terms are sometimes used synonymously, but there is an important distinction between them in the motivations of the voter. *Crossing over* is participation by voters in the primary of a party they do not generally support or feel a loyalty to because of the excitement of a primary battle or a more appealing candidate. *Raiding* is a conscious attempt on the part of one party or its partisans to weaken the opposing party in the general election by helping to nominate that party's least attractive candidates.

Studies of primary contests in Wisconsin, cradle of the open primary and home of an especially rambunctious political tradition, and other open primary states leave no doubt that crossing over is common, especially for independents. Crossing over generally is low in gubernatorial primaries for partisans, because of the need to stay in one's party's primary to decide other party contests. Because only one office is at stake in the presidential primaries, though, both independents and partisans may cross over; in some years the figure reached as high as a majority of the primary electorate. Moreover, the candidate has preferences of crossover voters may differ substantially from those of regular party voters. In 1964, for example, Wisconsin crossover voters favored George Wallace by a two-to-one margin; regular voters, by contrast, opposed Wallace by a margin of more than nine to one.[7]

As for organized raiding, there is little evidence to suggest that it is more than a worrisome myth. Every party fears that voters drifting to the other party's primary will develop bad voting habits. Furthermore, the party must also be watchful lest the migration from its primary permit its contests to be settled by unrepresentative minorities. But a party's greatest fear of course is that its opponents will make mischief in its own primaries by voting for weak candidates. Careful studies of open primaries have uncovered little basis for these fears. Voters cross over to vote their true preferences, rather than acting strategically to weaken the party in whose primary they are participating.[8]

PRIMARIES: RULES OF THE GAME

The states also vary in candidate access to the primary ballot and in the support required to win the nomination.

Candidate Access to the Primary Ballot

First of all, the states must deal with the problem of how a candidate gets on the primary ballot. Most states permit access to the ballot by petition (called *nomination papers* in some states). State election laws vary considerably in what is required for nomination by petition. Statutes fix the number of required signatures generally at either a specific number or a percentage of the vote for the office in the last election. New York, with its complicated 369-page law that favors party insiders, has by far the most stringent requirements for filing (see box on following page). At the other extreme, in some states it is sufficient for the would-be candidates to present themselves to the clerk of elections and pay a usually modest fee. A few states even put candidates on the ballot if they have formal party support, as demonstrated in party conventions or public opinion polls.

Even such mundane matters as access to the primary ballot have consequences for the parties. The easier access is, the more likely crank or dissident candidates will engage the party organization's candidates in costly primary battles. Sometimes, such candidates even win. For example, ease of access to the Illinois primary ballot permitted the stunning nomination of followers of Lyndon LaRouche as Democratic candidates for lieutenant governor and secretary of state in 1986 (see box on p. 207).[9]

Runoff Primaries

At the tail end of the nomination process, some states have tried to cope with primaries that are settled by less than a majority of the votes. In cases in which candidates win only a 35, 40, or 45 percent plurality, most states simply hope that the general election will produce a majority winner. Nine states, all from the South and its borders, have runoff primaries, however, if the winner in the regular primary wins less than 50 percent. In these second primaries, the two candidates with the highest vote totals face each other. This southern institution, first adopted in Mississippi in 1902, reflects the long period of Republican impotence in which the Democratic nomination was, in effect, election and in which intense Democratic factionalism often produced three, four, or five serious candidates for a single office. Two northern states provide for runoffs if no candidate receives at least 35 percent of the vote. Iowa conducts its runoff through a party convention; South Dakota uses a second primary.

In recent years, the southern runoff primary has been the subject of considerable controversy. Citing instances in which black winners of the first primary in the South have lost to whites in the subsequent primary, some have charged that runoffs discriminate against minority groups in violation of the Constitution and the federal Voting Rights Acts. Defenders of this form of primary have countered that the electorate rather than the runoff is the source of minority disadvantage in electoral politics and, furthermore, that its presence is valuable in forcing southern parties, especially the Democrats, to build biracial coalitions. It hardly should be surprising that the position one takes in this debate over runoffs often is determined by the results one prefers: More black elected officials in a less successful Democratic party versus Democrats, many of them white, who have built successful coalitions across racial lines.[10]

THE FORMIDABLE BARRIERS TO BALLOT ACCESS IN NEW YORK

The continuing difficulties in gaining a place on the New York primary ballot are well illustrated in the story of Agustin Alamo's numerous attempts to gain access to a ballot line so that he could run for the state legislature from the Bronx. As recounted in an October 18, 1990, article in *The New York Times* by Martin Gottlieb with Dean Baquet:

> . . . Seven times he has entered Democratic primaries for the State Senate and Assembly . . . and seven times he has failed, defeated not only by his opponents . . . but by an election process that many consider the worst in the nation. . . . In his ten years as a candidate, Mr. Alamo has been thrown off the ballot for omitting five words from the cover sheet of his nominating petitions. Yet, when he discovered two missing words on the cover sheets of his Bronx Democratic organization opponent, the Board of Elections and the courts let the petitions stand. . . . He has had to engage in costly and wearying challenges to his nomination petitions. Withstanding these, he has rarely bothered to press flesh on street corners and outside subway stations because most of the people he would meet are not registered, and legal restrictions make it next to senseless to sign them up. He has visited numerous polling places where the inspectors hired to preside over the balloting are political allies of his opponents. And in election districts where he has tallied well, the Board of Elections has moved polling places to less convenient locations. . . . All of which may explain why other candidates describe their efforts as a cause or a passion but Mr. Alamo forlornly and accurately calls his "an addiction."

New York politics is unusual in the protection afforded its parties from insurgent candidates in primary elections. Even candidates in presidential primaries who are not supported by party leaders, such as Bob Dole's opponents in the 1996 GOP contest, face substantial difficulties in qualifying for the ballot. In this extreme case, New York illustrates how far parties sometimes have gone to cope with the challenges to their control over nominations posed by the direct primary.

Source: Copyright 1990 by *The New York Times* Company. Reprinted by permission.

THE THREAT OF THE DIRECT PRIMARY

The Progressives intended that the direct primary would end the party organization's monopoly control of nominations for office, and in important respects it did. It created problems for the parties which have compromised their effectiveness in the electoral process. Some of the party's problems, in turn, have led to problems in the electoral process itself.

The Problem of Unattractive Party Nominees

The parties' worst fear about a direct primary is that a candidate will win the nomination who, because of poor qualifications or repugnant issue stands, has no chance of gaining much party support in the general election. Every election year seems to bring forth a few nominees, usually for low-level offices, whose only electoral advantage is that they possess a famous name. Every once in a while also, a candidate can ride strong feelings on a controversial issue to the nomination in spite of the more sober judgments of party leaders or the electorate in the general election. Imagine the discomfort of party leaders, for instance, when in 1990 conservative Reagan-supporter John Silber upset the party's endorsed candidate to win the Democratic nomination for governor in Massachusetts or in 1994 when Oliver North won the GOP nomination for senator in Virginia over a far more electable conservative. The classic example of the damage a direct primary can do is the nomination of two followers of Lyndon LaRouche for top state offices in the 1986 Illinois Democratic primary (see box on following page).

The Problem of Divisiveness

In addition, there is an impression that the primary exacerbates party rifts. It often pits party worker against party worker, party group against party group.

> A genuine primary is a fight within the family of the party and, like any family fight, is apt to be more bitter and leave more enduring wounds than battles with the November enemy. In primaries, ambitions spurt from nowhere; unknown men carve their mark; old men are sent relentlessly to their political graves; bosses and leaders may be humiliated or unseated. At ward, county, or state level, all primaries are fought with spurious family folksiness and sharp knives.[11]

The resulting wounds are often deep and slow to heal. The cost to the health and strength of the party is considerable.

The effects of primary divisiveness on the party are easier to gauge in the short term, at the subsequent general election, than over the long haul. First, party activists who have campaigned for the losing candidate in the primaries are unlikely to work for their party's nominees. The damage is mitigated to some extent, however, because a contested primary recruits new activists into party politics.[12] Second, victors in a contested primary cannot always count on the voters of their party opponent to support them in the general election. It is natural perhaps for those committed to a losing candidate to be so disgruntled that they may withdraw from political activity or even vote for the other party's candidate. Because the fight is out in the open, moreover, the wounds inflicted by the candidates upon one another and their followers in the heat of battle seem more difficult to heal.[13]

The Problem of Candidate Recruitment

A special responsibility for recruiting candidates for office in American politics is assumed by the political parties. In fulfilling this responsibility, they face two major

A PARTY'S WORST FEARS REALIZED: ILLINOIS, 1986

In the 1986 Democratic primary in Illinois, two followers of Lyndon H. LaRouche, Mark J. Fairchild and Janice Hart, upset the party-endorsed candidates to win nominations for lieutenant governor and secretary of state. These two political unknowns, running on a platform hostile to Democratic party principles, had spent a total of $200 on their campaigns. Cited as reasons for the surprising outcome were the LaRouchites' "all-American" names (their Anglo-Saxon flavor was seen as more attractive than Pucinski and Sangmeister, the endorsed candidates), a media that ignored them and their political philosophies, a Democratic party organization in Chicago that was so distracted by internal squabbles that it failed to list the regular candidates on its slate card and took the contests for granted, and general voter inattention.

This electoral outcome began the ill-fated odyssey of Democratic gubernatorial nominee and former U.S. Senator Adlai Stevenson III, who refused to run on the same ticket with the LaRouchites. First, he sought to purge his unwanted running mates from the party ballot; failing that, he renounced his party's nomination and attempted to gain a ballot position as an independent. Failing in these efforts too, he ran as a third-party candidate but lost with only 43 percent of the vote.

problems: How can they find party candidates for offices the party has little hope of winning? How can they prevent the candidates they have so actively recruited and supported from facing credible and even successful challenges in their own primaries?

The direct primary has exacerbated each of these problems. By giving attractive candidates the opportunity to challenge party favorites in the primaries of the dominant party in one-party areas, they make it more difficult for the minority party to recruit good candidates and thereby reinforce the dominant one-partyism.[14] By their inability to control access to their own primaries or to guarantee the outcome, they also have less to offer to candidates whom they are trying to recruit.[15]

The most intractable problem is that where the odds of winning a contest are especially remote, the parties often are unable to find a willing candidate—and the race goes to the other party's nominee by default.[16] Over the years uncontested elections traditionally have been common in such one-party areas as the South or major cities. With the increasing competition throughout the American system, though, the frequency of uncontested offices has declined. Uncontested races for statewide office and, in the last two elections, for the U.S. House of Representatives now are rare. But they occur regularly in elections for the state legislature and other less visible offices in many states.[17]

The inability to field any candidate, even a weak one, for an office surely is a mark of party failure. It is one of the unintended consequences of this Progressive reform that the direct primary contributes to such failures on the part of the minority party. While the Progressives surely intended to destroy the party monopoly in nominations, they hardly imagined that their cherished institution might have the effect of dampening competition for office in the general election. It is conceivable that term limits, another reform designed to heighten competition for office and thereby increase turnover in office, may have a similar unintended effect. By preventing one officeholder from staying in office decade after decade, term limits may produce more competition—but probably only in the year when the term limit has been reached and then only in the primary of the majority party in a one-party area. In the other years, competition may be reduced as attractive candidates bide their time waiting for that date certain when the term limit will have expired.

Other Problems

Beyond the possibilities of nominating an unacceptable candidate, creating deep divisions within the party electorate, and finding candidates to run in unpromising contests, the primary often causes the party many lesser inconveniences, disruptions, and problems. Consider the threats the primary poses to the well-being of a political party organization:

- For the party that wants to influence nominations, the primary greatly escalates the costs of politics. Supporting candidates in a contested primary is almost always more expensive than holding a convention. Spending in the primaries, moreover, leaves less money for the party to commit in the general election.
- By curbing party control over nominations, the primary denies the party a powerful lever for ensuring the loyalty of its officeholders to the party. If the party cannot control or prevent the reelection of a maverick officeholder, it really has no effective sanction for enforcing loyalty.
- The primary permits the nomination of a candidate hostile to the party organization and leadership, opposed to the party's platforms or programs, or out of step with the public image that party leaders want to project—or all of the above!
- The primary creates the distinct possibility that the party will find itself saddled with an unbalanced ticket for the general election if voters at the primary select all or most of the candidates from a particular group or region.

THE PARTY ORGANIZATION FIGHTS BACK

Not even the gloomiest Cassandra expects all these misfortunes to result from any given primary or even from a series of them. They are distinct possibilities for any party, however; especially a relatively weak and passive one. The parties recognize the danger, but they recognize too the futility of a direct assault on the primary. Thus, in the best American tradition of "joining 'em if you can't beat 'em," the parties have developed strategies for dealing with the primary. These strategies have not been pursued everywhere, of course. Some local parties have lacked the will or the strength to do so, or have lost ground to local political cultures that disapprove of a party role in the primary. The result is a range of party responses to the primary that extends from no response at all to complete party domination.

Party Influence on Candidate Entry

One axiom and a corollary deriving from it govern party strategy when it has recruited a candidate for the primary. The axiom is simple to the point of truism: The surest way to control the primary is to prevent competition with the party's choice. The corollary is equally clear: The party must act as early as possible in the preprimary jockeying of would-be candidates if it is to choke off unwanted competition.

Within some party organizations, a powerful party leader or a few party oligarchs make the preprimary decisions for the party organization—or it may be a party executive committee or a candidate selection committee. If their sources of information are good, they will know who intends to run and who is merely considering the race. They may arbitrate among them, or they may coax an unwilling but attractive candidate into the primary. If they command a strong and winning organization, their inducements to the nonfavored candidates to withdraw may be considerable. They may be able to offer a patronage position or a chance to run in the future. On the negative side, they may threaten to block a candidate's access to funds for the campaign (see box on p. 210). Such control of nominations by the party organization and its leadership is difficult to achieve in American primary elections, but it is the **norm** in most of the world's other democracies.

This informal and often covert selection of candidates—communicated to the party faithful by the "nod" or by the "word"—has been replaced within some parties by representative, publicized party conventions. Nine states have formalized them; but in some of those cases, state law usually prevents an unqualified endorsement. Colorado laws provide that all candidates who poll more than 30 percent of a convention endorsement vote shall go on the primary ballot in the order of their vote percentage. Utah directs the parties to nominate two candidates for each office. Conversely, a few states have attempted by law to minimize the possibility or the power of endorsing conventions. In 1963, California prohibited party organizations from "officially" endorsing candidates for office, but the state supreme court in 1984 overturned this ban as an unconstitutional interference with party control over its internal affairs.

In some states, party-endorsing bodies act informally and extralegally—that is, without the laws of the state taking notice of them. This form of endorsement has proved less effective, however, because it is not communicated on the ballot. Only the most attentive voters, as a consequence, are likely to know that the party is supporting a particular candidate; yet, they are the ones least in need of the guidance provided by an official party endorsement.[18]

CREATING THE STRONGEST PARTY TICKET

In early 1990, the Ohio Republican party faced a dilemma. Its two best-known candidates for statewide office that year—former Cleveland Mayor George Voinovich and Hamilton County (Cincinnati) Commissioner Bob Taft, scion of Ohio's most famous political family, had both announced their intention to run for governor. The Republican candidates for the other statewide offices on the ballot that year, on the other hand, seemed relatively weak.

The Republicans resolved their dilemma in the time-honored fashion of pressuring one of the two contenders out of the governor's race and into another contest. The party's state central committee unanimously passed a resolution asking the state chair to meet with both Voinovich and Taft to persuade one of them to run for another office. This action was aimed at Taft, target of a less conciliatory resolution passed a day earlier by the party's finance and policy committees naming him as the party's choice for secretary of state. At the request of state party leaders, Republican National Chairman Lee Atwater also intervened by trying to persuade Taft to shift to secretary of state. But the most effective pressures were financial. Following the state party's threat that it would not provide him with financial support if he persisted in his campaign for governor, Taft's financial supporters announced they would not bankroll his campaign.

These efforts paid handsome dividends for the GOP. Voinovich and Taft easily won the party's nominations for governor and secretary of state, respectively, in the primary and went on to be elected to those positions in November. Coupled with their control of the state senate, the gain of these two offices gave the Republicans a majority of seats on the state apportionment board that determined the congressional districts for the next ten years. In the long run, his willingness to "wait his turn" for governor gave Taft the inside position in winning his party's support for governor in 1998 after Voinovich had served out his two terms. Well in advance of this election, in fact, Voinovich endorsed Taft for governor.

Party Support for Preferred Candidates

The most effective party control over the nomination process is attained by preventing viable challenges to the party's preferred candidates from emerging in the first place. But if a primary contest does develop despite all its plans and strategies, the party then falls back on its resources in conventional ways. It may urge party committeepersons to help the anointed candidates circulate nominating petitions and leave the other candidates to their own devices. It may make available to the chosen ticket money, know-how, party workers, and the party bureaucracy. It may print advertisements announcing the party endorsees or may issue handy reference cards that the forgetful voter can take right into the polling booth. On the day of the primary, the party organization may help to get the party's voters to the polls. Whether the party organization acts overtly or covertly in the primary campaign depends both on the local political culture and on the candidates' own appraisals of it. The party and/or the candidates may feel that voter sensitivity to party intervention (that is, to "bossism") may dictate that the candidates appear untouched by party hands.

It is impossible to write authoritatively of the frequency of party attempts to manage or influence American primaries. Practices vary, not only from state to state but within states, and descriptions of local party practice are hard to come by. One is probably safe in generalizing that the most common nominating activity is the recruiting of candidates to seek the nomination. Surely less common are attempts to dissuade would-be nominees. Moreover, in most parts of the country, the political party is only one of a number of agencies seeking out and supporting men and women to run for office. It shares their recruitment with local business, professional, farm, and labor groups, with civic and community associations, with ethnic, racial, and religious organizations, with interest groups, and with officeholders. There are some party organizations, however, that do control the recruitment of candidates and the other preprimary processes. Generally, they are the parties that also intervene in the primary itself.

CANDIDATES AND VOTERS IN THE PRIMARIES

What the parties can accomplish in the primaries depends to a considerable extent on the candidates and on the electorate. To put it simply, the primaries are more "manageable" because more than one serious candidate does not often contest them and because the vast majority of voters do not vote in them. Very possibly, one or both of these conditions is of the party's making; the absence of candidates, for example, may reflect the skill of the party's preprimary persuading and dissuading. Regardless of cause, however, the result tends to be a nomination politics of a limited scope more easily controlled by aggressive party organization.

The Candidates

Simple countings will confirm that, in every part of the United States, large numbers of primary candidates win nomination without a contest. A study of state legislative primaries in fourteen states from 1972 to 1978 found that a majority of the Democratic and Republican primaries had no contests.[19] Competition appears to be much more plentiful for the more prestigious statewide offices, but that competition falls off in races with an incumbent and where there are party endorsements.[20]

Generally speaking, competition in American primaries is enhanced by certain rather predictable circumstances. As we already have seen, the chief factor is probably the party's prospects for victory in the general election; candidates are not inclined to fight for the right to go down to almost certain defeat. The attractiveness of the office and the ease of getting on the ballot also affect competition. Finally,

MICHAEL HUFFINGTON'S POLITICAL INVESTMENTS

The best example of a challenger using his own money to wage success-ful primary campaigns surely is Michael Huffington of California. Multimil-lionaire Huffington spent more than $3 million—almost all of it his own money—to wrest the Republican nomination from nine-term incumbent Robert Lagomarsino and then went on to win the general election to rep-resent California's 22nd District. Two years later, Huffington invested more than $6 million of his own fortune to win the GOP nomination for the U.S. Senate and at least an additional $20 million in his narrow loss to Dianne Feinstein in the general election.

competition seems to thrive in primaries in which no incumbent officeholder is seek-ing nomination and in the absence of effective party control or endorsement.[21]

The power of incumbency in discouraging competition is another of the ironies of the primary. By placing a premium on popular appeal and exposure that often only the well-known incumbent can muster, the primary fosters the conditions that dimin-ish its own effectiveness. By weakening party control of nominations through the direct primary, therefore, reformers may have achieved the unanticipated (and surely to them undesirable) consequence of strengthening the hold of incumbents on their positions. Where the hold of incumbents on their party's renomination is broken, though, one typically finds it to be the work of challengers who are able to spend large sums of money, often their own (see box above). This too would surely be a dis-appointment to the Progressive reformers.

The Voters

If competition is scarce at the primaries, so are voters. All evidence points over-whelmingly to one cardinal fact about the participation of the American electorate in primaries: Most do not vote. Even the study of gubernatorial primaries (1960–86) that identified a relatively high incidence of contested races found modest turnout levels. In all of the contested races in that period, only 30 percent of voting-age adults voted.[22] Turnout in races for less important offices is even lower.

How is this low turnout to be explained? In large part, it reflects the lower interest in intraparty contests for nomination, which lack the inherent drama of a general election. Turnout also is dampened by the absence of a real primary contest (a lack of competition within the majority party or in contests dominated by an incumbent), by the relative unimportance of the minority party primary in states with low levels of interparty competition or of primaries held separately from the presidential primaries, and by closing primaries to independents and members of the other party.[23]

Along with its restricted size, indeed because of it, the primary electorate pos-sesses some distinctive characteristics. A substantial sector of it generally comes from party loyalists and activists, which of course makes it more likely to respond to party endorsements and appeals on behalf of certain candidates. Primary voters, as one might expect, have higher levels of political interest and higher educational attainments. Conventional political wisdom has also held that primary voters represent more extreme ideological positions than those of the party's full electorate. While early studies of Wisconsin's open primary found little support for that assumption, more recent research (coming largely from presidential primaries, which will be considered later) suggests otherwise.[24] Even if the ideological positions of primary voters turn out not to be distinctive, the intensity of their ideological commitment may be.

Even this generally interested electorate often lapses into unpredictable voting behavior. For large numbers of voters in the primary, the choice is more difficult than the one at the general election. Because all the candidates come from the same party, party loyalties cannot guide decisions. The primary campaign is brief, the candidates are often not well known, and the issues, if any, are unclear. Therefore, the voter's choice is not so well structured or predictable; the presence of an incumbent in the race may be the only continuing, stabilizing element. Consequently, many voter decisions are made right in the polling booth; the effect of the ballot position and the success of candidates with famous names indicate that. Small wonder, then, that parties are never confident in primaries and that public opinion pollsters prefer not to predict primary outcomes.

Historically, there has been one great exception to the generalizations on competition and voter turnout in American primaries: the South. From the end of Reconstruction to the years right after World War Two, the South was securely and overwhelmingly a one-party Democratic area. For most offices, therefore, winning the Democratic nomination was tantamount to winning the office itself. The effective competitive politics of the southern states thus centered in the Democratic primary and produced relatively high turnout levels there—often even higher than in the general elections.

As the Republican party has built strength and competitiveness in the South, however, the Democratic primaries have lost their special standing. As the general election has become more significant, participation has declined in primaries, even at a time when the mobilization of blacks into Democratic party politics should have increased intraparty competition. In spite of the greater prospects for Republican candidates, however, the GOP primaries have not attracted a compensating increase in participation, although participation in them certainly has risen. The result is that turnout in southern primaries has become less and less distinctive.[25]

THE DIRECT PRIMARY IN RETROSPECT

American experience with the direct primary is approaching a century. What difference has it all made? Has the primary democratized nominations by taking them out of the hands of party oligarchs and giving them to voters? Has it weakened the party organizations overall? These, after all, were the principal intentions of its architects, the Progressives, and it seems reasonable to inquire whether they have been realized.

The Impact on Democratization

Basically, the democratic hopes behind the direct primary have been jeopardized by low levels of participation by both candidates and voters. Participation by both is necessary if there are to be meaningful choices based on meaningful alternatives. By its very nature, however, the primary tends to diminish such participation. The need for broad public appeal, the cost of the contest, and the sheer difficulty of getting on the primary ballot discourage candidacies. The multiplicity of primaries, with their unstructured, confusing, and unclear choices, reduces both the quantity and the quality of voter participation. Clearly, if widespread competition for office and extensive mass participation in the nominating process were goals of the reformers who initiated the primary, their hopes have not been realized.

Nor has the direct primary fully displaced party leaders in the making of nominations. Vestiges of the caucus-convention system remain, most visibly in presidential nomination politics, even if the democratization impulses present in the movement to primaries have made them more open as well. Moreover, although the parties can no longer strictly prevent competition where primaries operate, they can sometimes modulate it. They may control the money, symbols, and organization essential for primary victory. The party organization often commands the chief political loyalty of a significant share of those who vote in the primary. If only 30 or 40 percent of registered voters vote in the primary, some 15 or 20 percent will be sufficient to nominate a candidate. Parties count on the fact that a substantial part of that group is likely to be loyalists who respond to the cues of party leaders or endorsements. Thus, strong party organizations— able to mobilize voters, money, and manpower—still can be very effective determiners of primary outcomes.

Yet, the parties control over the primaries is fleeting and imperfect. The sheer size of the task is overwhelming. The Jacksonian tradition of electing every public official down to the local coroner has confronted the parties with numerous contests. The expense of supporting a number of candidates—not to mention the expenditures of organizational energy—forces many organizations to be selective in their primary interventions. In other instances, parties stand aside because a role in the primary would threaten their internal harmony and cohesion. They may be paralyzed by the fear that their activity in the primary will open new wounds or heat up old resentments or run the risk of offending the possible victor. Many parties are stymied by their own weakness or by local political cultures that resist party activity as a violation of the spirit of the primary.

Yet, to argue that the primary has not fulfilled the most optimistic hopes is not to argue that it has had no effect. In competitive districts—especially when an incumbent has stepped down—voters often do play the kind of role the reformers envisioned. Also, even for a strong party organization, the primaries set tangible limits. Many no longer find it possible to whisk just any "warm body" through the nomination process. The direct primary perhaps can best be thought of both as creating a veto body that passes on the work of party nominators—and thereby disciplines them—and as affording an opportunity for intraparty dissidents to take their case to the party's electorate.

The Impact on the Parties

What has been the more general impact of the primary on the political parties? V. O. Key argued that the primary encourages one-partyism by increasingly drawing both the voter and the attractive, prestigious candidates to the primary of the dominant party. Little by little, the majority party becomes the only viable instrument of political influence and the minority party atrophies, a victim of "the more general proposition that institutional decay follows deprivation of function."[26] The burden of opposition is then shifted to contests within the primary of the majority party. However persuasive this argument may once have been, it is of questionable validity today. One-partyism has receded in recent years, bringing with it a demise in a single party's monopoly on political talent. The success of candidates who run without party support, moreover, signals that opportunities exist outside of the normal party channels.[27]

It is more likely that the direct primary has been a prime contributor to a general atrophy in party organization in dominant as well as minority parties. The stronger and more centralized party organizations appear in those states in which conventions either nominate candidates or the parties make preprimary endorsements.[28] Even in these states, though, the inability of parties to control effectively who carries the party label into the general election contest has deprived the party organization of one of its key resources.

Furthermore, the direct primary unquestionably has altered the distribution of power within the party. When one speaks of party control of nominations, one means control by the party organization, and any weakening of that control obviously weakens the organization and enhances the power of the party candidates and the party in government. Their ability, especially as incumbents, to defy the organization and to win primary battles frees them from its discipline and, indeed, often opens up to them positions of party leadership. In fact, the inability of the party organization in the United States to control the party in government (as it does in so many other democracies) begins with its failure to control its nominations. Just as the direct primary undercuts the ability of the party organization to recruit to public office those partisans who share its goals and accept its discipline, it prevents the organization from disciplining partisans who already are in office.

The goal of the Progressives and the other proponents of the primary was to substitute the party electorate for the party organization as the nominator. With the primary, they thwarted the organization's quest for its own goals. Instead of achieving any genuine mass control of party nominations, however, they facilitated a shift in control from the elites of the organization to the elites of the party in government. Their greatest success was in multiplying the party oligarchies rather than in democratizing them.

Recent trends in American politics have added a new dimension to the Progressives' achievement. Incumbents are not the only ones to benefit from restricted party-organization control over primaries. With the increased role of television, especially as a substitute for the kind of labor-intensive door-to-door campaigning that strong party organizations traditionally supplied, television image-building and the need for funds to pay for it have come to dominate campaigns—particularly primary campaigns, where party labels do not function to guide voter choice. It would be the supreme irony if, in their quest to free the electoral process of control by party bosses, the Progressives were to vest that control in the hands of an even more invisible and unresponsive group of bosses—media consultants and the special interests who are the most likely to finance political campaigns—or to restrict primary elections to contests between incumbents and wealthy or special-interest challengers.[29]

A Force for Decentralization

Finally, the direct primary has buttressed the prevailing decentralization of power in the American parties. So long as the candidates or incumbents can appeal to a majority of local primary voters, they are free from the control and discipline of a state or national party or its leaders. Even so powerful a president as Franklin Roosevelt in 1938 met his greatest political defeat in trying to purge a number of Democratic senators and representatives in their local Democratic primaries; only one of his conservative targets was defeated. The primary plays on local loyalties and appeals to the local electorate, and its localism puts it beyond the control of a central party organization.

If the advocates of the direct primary wanted to aim beyond the nomination process and strike the parties themselves, they found their target. In many instances, the direct primary has weakened the control of nominations by the party organizations—even robbing them of an important raison d'être and liberating their officeholders. In many important ways, it has made the American political parties what they are today.

Who Should Select the Party Candidates?

How party candidates should be nominated has been a controversial matter since political parties first appeared in the United States in the early 1800s. At base, the question of who should make party nominations raises the question of what a political party is. Is it merely an alliance of officeholders, the party in government, as reflected by the early system of caucus nominations? Or does it also embrace the activists and party officials, the party organization, who played their greatest role in the convention system? Or should the party mantle be extended, well beyond the limits of most other democracies, to include the great mass of party voters? If so, which ones—only the ones willing to officially register a party loyalty or anyone who decides to vote for a party candidate in a primary election? Even though political scientists continue to debate this question, the American answer to it has evolved over the years toward the most inclusive definition of party. In the states with an open or blanket primary, the party indeed has become so permeable that no one can be excluded—raising the possibility that a party could become coterminous with the entire electorate.

Behind the scenes, of course, what we have here is no less than simply another venue for the eternal struggle over the distribution of power within the parties and, more generally, within the American political system. The Progressives and their modern-day counterparts, however high-minded their idealism, have used party reform as a weapon with which to wrest control of the party, and ultimately of government, from party organization regulars—just as the Jacksonians used the convention system to overturn control by the congressional leaders. To the degree to which the nomination process defines voter choices in American elections, those who control this process have substantial influence over the agenda of politics and consequently over who gets what in the political system. The stakes of the controversies over party nominations, then, are considerable.

Chapter 10

Choosing the Presidential Nominees

In the naming of their candidates for president, the American parties stand at the crossroads between the old and the new. Unlike nominations for virtually all other offices, which are handled through the direct primary, the Democrats and Republicans continue to choose their nominees in national party conventions. This makes the presidential nomination process the last redoubt of the old convention system. Yet, this continuity in structure masks a transformation in function. Now that most delegates to the conventions are committed to the presidential candidates well before the conventions, the national conventions in recent years have merely confirmed a predetermined result and, consequently, function to realize goals other than the selection of the party's presidential candidate.

The transformation of the traditional system for presidential nominations has been intermittent and, in the last analysis, not quite complete. Under the lead of its Progressive Governor Robert La Follette, Wisconsin adopted the first presidential primary in 1905, and by 1916 a total of twenty-five states had followed suit. This early enthusiasm for primaries, however, soon waned. Advocates may have lost faith in them because they did not prove to be decisive in the nomination contests. Opponents may have redoubled their efforts to get rid of them because they nonetheless made party control of nominations more difficult. Whatever the cause, by 1936 only fourteen states had retained primaries for selecting delegates to the party's national nominating conventions—the same number (and virtually the same states) that used them as recently as 1968.[1] In the furor over the 1968 Democratic nomination, though, the direct-primary movement was given new life. By the 1980s, most states had adopted presidential primaries and, more significantly, a decisive majority of the delegates were selected by this method. Even where the primary was not used, essential features of the old caucus-convention system had been reformed.

Even though it can be said that primaries now dominate the presidential nomination process, their domination is far from complete. The primaries (and the caucus-convention systems in the few states which retain them) continue to operate as mechanisms for apportioning delegates to the national nominating conventions among the various presidential candidates. This apportionment is based on popular support for presidential candidates in primaries; selection of the delegates themselves is the task of the candidates or the parties. Moreover, the ultimate nomination decision still remains in the hands of the convention, even if that outcome now seems preordained.

Compared to how candidates for virtually every other major office are selected, then, the presidential nomination process is unique—and requires special treatment. Considering the attention it commands in the press and the public at large, a comprehensive treatment is in order.

FIRST STEPS TOWARD THE NOMINATIONS

It is very difficult to say just when that nominating process begins. Officially, the campaigns of candidates for president begin when they announce their candidacies in the year preceding election year so that they can begin to raise money that will qualify them for federal matching funds. (For more on campaign funding, see Chapter 12.) By this measure, the contests for the 1996 nominations began when Senator Phil Gramm formally became a candidate on February 24, 1995. In reality, the campaigns are off and running long before they become official; within the party defeated in a presidential election, they may begin as early as the morning after that defeat. The object of this campaign, as it has been for a century and a half, is to secure the support of delegates to the national nominating convention. But little else about the campaigns is the same.

The Post-1968 Reforms

For years, the national parties, in preparing for the conventions, had stipulated only the number of delegates the states would have. It was left to the states or their parties to decide how the delegates would be chosen. Beginning in 1972, the Democrats ended that tradition in their party's nomination process. They began to control a number of the other aspects of delegate selection.

The means through which the national Democratic party took control of the delegate selection process away from the state parties is a fascinating tale of political reform. After their tumultuous 1968 convention in which insurgent forces within the party protested that the nomination of Hubert Humphrey betrayed the wishes of Democratic voters in the primaries, the national party attempted to mollify its internal critics by altering the methods of delegate selection. A commission chaired by Senator George McGovern of South Dakota and Representative Donald Fraser of Minnesota recommended, and the Democratic National Committee and the 1972 Democratic convention subsequently approved, numerous changes for the 1972 nominating process. What is remarkable about the politics of the reform process is how readily Democratic party leaders acceded to rules changes that significantly reduced their influence in awarding the party's greatest prize, the presidential nomination.[2]

In attempting to comply with the complex new regulations imposed by the national Democratic party, many states substituted primary elections for their traditional caucus-convention systems, which had begun with party meetings or caucuses at the local level and culminated in statewide conventions. In the process, not only were the delegate selection rules radically transformed, but the principle was established that the national parties (acting through their national committees and presidential nominating conventions) rather than the state parties or even the states themselves determine the rules of presidential nomination.[3]

Once the reform genie was let out of the bottle, it proved difficult to contain. The Democrats have tinkered with their presidential nomination process in advance of virtually every election since 1972. Initially they used national party leverage to make the process more open and more representative of the various party constituencies—although sometimes the means, such as delegate quotas for women, young people, and blacks, occasioned such bitter debate that they ultimately were discarded. More recently, the Democrats have focused their attention on "fine tuning" their new rules so that voter support for candidates is more faithfully represented in delegate counts (see box on following page) and that uncommitted elected and party officials can be guaranteed a place at the convention.

The legacy of this reform era is nothing short of a stunning transformation in how the Democrats select their nominees for president. The traditional caucus/convention method favored by most states in 1968, and often tightly controlled by a small group of party leaders, is now governed by stringent party rules requiring selection of delegates in timely, open, and well-publicized meetings and proscribing the techniques (for example, unannounced meetings, proxy votes, slate making) traditionally employed by party organizations to control the process. Even more important, the predominance of the caucus method has ended as more states have turned to primaries.

The GOP hardly has been immune from the Democratic reform efforts because many state legislatures responded to new Democratic party requirements by changing state election laws for both parties. For example, when states decided to run a primary for one party, they typically did it for both. The Republicans have continued to adhere to their tradition of giving state parties wide latitude in developing their own rules, however, which has kept the national party out of issues of rules reform. Consequently, many Republican state parties have retained statewide winner-take-all elections. Nor have the Republicans followed the Democratic lead in formally setting aside seats for party and public officials or maintaining affirmative action programs for women or minorities.[4]

The Presidential Primaries

Since 1968, primaries have come to dominate the presidential selection process. They are now utilized in more than two-thirds of the states, including most of the largest. As the easiest way for states to comply with the new Democratic reforms, primaries were increasingly popular from 1968 through 1980. Their attractiveness ebbed in 1984, but rose again in 1988 (Table 10.1). The proportion of delegates from primary states seems to be stabilizing at about two-thirds for the Democrats, but it has continued to climb for the GOP.[5] Because the decisions to use primaries or cau-

THE MOVE TO PROPORTIONAL REPRESENTATION: DEMOCRATIC RULES CHANGES IN 1992

For the 1992 contests, the Democrats ratified the move to full proportional representation that was negotiated between the forces of Michael Dukakis and Jesse Jackson at the 1988 convention. In spite of previous reform efforts to eliminate winner-take-all primaries, in 1988 fifteen states still were exploiting "loopholes" in the rules to give a plurality winner more than a proportionate share of the delegates. Ten states awarded a bonus delegate to the winner of each congressional district, and another five used winner-take-all rules at the congressional district level.[6] With the change to strict proportional representation in 1992, candidates in primaries or caucuses who win at least 15 percent of the vote now are awarded a share of the state's delegates proportionate to their vote total.

cuses are made by states and state parties, though, these relative numbers may continue to fluctuate.

In the primaries, it is the popular vote that determines how many delegates are won by the presidential candidates. How these delegates are chosen has changed over the years, but the common practice now is for the candidates or their agents within the states to select the members of the delegate slates to which they are entitled. This all but guarantees, in the absence of legal requirements that delegates cast their vote for any particular candidate, that the popular result in the state will be faithfully translated into delegates committed to the respective candidates at the national convention.[7]

Although most primary states use one form or another of the closed primary, the open primary has survived vigorous assaults by successive Democratic party reform commissions, which were determined to ban open primaries because they permit participation by voters who lack loyalties to the party. After succeeding in 1984 in shutting down Wisconsin's open primary as a means for selecting convention delegates, the national party relented in adopting its rules for the 1988 convention. Wisconsin was allowed to return to its cherished open primary, and the handful of other states that hold open primaries need no longer fear reproach by the national party.[8]

The Party Caucuses

The drama of the presidential primaries is reported every four years in the most intricate detail. Nonetheless, the parties of a significant number of states allocate and choose delegates by assorted internal party processes. Those processes usually begin with local caucuses. Unlike primaries, these meetings require face-to-face interaction among participants, can take several hours to conclude their business, and usually conduct their balloting in the open. As a result of these features, the caucuses and primaries also differ in levels of participation and, often, in outcome (see box on p. 223).

Table 10.1 THE USE OF PRESIDENTIAL PRIMARIES: 1968–96

Year	Democrats		Republicans	
	No. of states	Percent of delegate votes	No. of states	Percent of delegate votes
1968	17	37.5%	16	34.3%
1972	23	60.5	22	52.7
1976	29	72.6	28	67.9
1980	35	71.8	34	76.0
1984	25	62.1	30	71.0
1988	34	66.6	35	76.9
1992	36	69.6	39	79.1
1996	36	62.8	43	88.3

Note: Includes all convention constituencies (50 states plus D.C., American Samoa, Guam, Puerto Rico, Virgin Islands, and Democrats abroad). Excludes states with nonbinding preference ("beauty contest") primaries in which delegates were chosen by caucus/convention methods. Delegate percentages exclude Democratic superdelegates.

Source: William Crotty and John S. Jackson III, *Presidential Primaries and Nominations* (Washington, D.C.: CQ Press, 1985), p. 63, for 1968–84; and *Congressional Quarterly Weekly Report* (Washington, D.C.: Congressional Quarterly, Inc.) convention issues for 1988 and 1992. Figures for 1996 are based on calculations from figures reported in the *Congressional Quarterly Weekly Report*, August 19, 1995, p. 2485, and January 13, 1996, pp. 98–99.

The caucus is only the first stage of a long process; delegates chosen there typically select delegates to represent them at conventions. The well-publicized Iowa precinct caucuses, for example, are only the first of four stages used to select the Iowa delegates to the national nominating conventions. Delegates elected at the precinct meetings attend a county convention some weeks later to elect delegates for a subsequent congressional district convention, which then determines the delegates to the state convention where the final delegate slate for the national convention is determined.[9] Most caucus states are similar to Iowa in using a multilayered process. By contrast, a few small states (Maine, Delaware, and Vermont) select delegates for the state convention at local caucuses without any intervening meetings. State conventions typically are held late in the nominating process—a few, like Iowa's, fall after the primaries have been concluded.

For years, the selection of delegates in the caucus states was relatively invisible. The events of 1976, however, changed all that. A virtually unknown Democratic candidate, Jimmy Carter, vaulted himself into serious candidacy by a strenuous campaign in Iowa that netted him both media attention and about 30 percent of the state's Democratic delegates. Within the Republican party in that year, Gerald Ford and Ronald Reagan emerged from the primaries almost deadlocked in the delegate count, and they consequently turned all of their considerable persuasive efforts toward the remaining state conventions and their uncommitted delegates.

As a result, the caucus states probably will never be invisible again, and party officials in them will find it harder to control their outcomes or keep their delegations

CAUCUSES VS. PRIMARIES IN 1992

With incumbent President George Bush sure to win his party's nomination, the only real presidential selection contest in 1992 took place within the Democratic party. Spirited competition occurred in the early primaries and caucuses before Bill Clinton opened up what proved to be an insurmountable lead in mid-March. Comparing their results for the leading candidates and their turnout rates, therefore, illustrates well the differences between these two types of nomination process, especially the restricted turnout of the caucuses. In these contests, delegates were apportioned among the contenders in proportion to their vote totals in accordance with Democratic rules; consider what would have happened under winner-take-all-rules.

	Turnout (000s)	Clinton	Brown	Harkin	Tsongas
Caucuses*					
Iowa (Feb. 10)	30,000	2.8%	1.6%	76.4%	4.1%
Maine (Feb. 23)	13,500	14.8	30.3	5.2	29.0
Idaho (Mar. 3)	3,090	11.4	4.5	29.7	28.4
Minnesota (Mar. 3)	50–60,000	10.3	8.2	26.7	19.2
Utah (Mar. 3)	31,638	18.3	28.4	4.0	33.4
Washington (Mar. 3)	60,000	12.6	18.6	8.2	32.3
Primaries					
New Hampshire (Feb. 18)	167,819	24.7%	8.1%	10.2%	33.2%
South Dakota (Feb. 25)	59,503	19.1	3.9	25.2	40.2
Colorado (Mar. 3)	239,643	26.9	28.8	2.4	25.6
Georgia (Mar. 3)	454,631	57.2	8.1	2.1	24.0
Maryland (Mar. 3)	567,224	33.5	8.2	5.8	40.6

* turnout figures for caucuses typically are estimates

uncommitted. For 1988, Michigan GOP leaders, for example, began their nomination process with precinct caucuses (in 1986) two years before the state convention in order to boost the influence of their brand of moderate Republicanism in national nomination politics. Their efforts backfired, however, when supporters of Pat Robertson flooded the local caucuses and threw the entire process into turmoil for the next two years. Caucuses will remain a focus of attention, in particular, because the "great delegate hunt" traditionally begins for both parties with the Iowa caucus—although the Republicans elevated Louisiana to this favored position by allowing it to have its caucuses a week earlier than Iowa in 1996. Buchanan's showing in Louisiana in that year buoyed his Iowa efforts, enabling him to claim second place there and to relegate Phil Gramm to a distant fifth-place showing. Nonetheless, Iowa should continue to receive early and intense scrutiny.

THE POLITICS OF DELEGATE SELECTION

The politics of winning a presidential nomination obviously depends upon enlisting the support of a majority of the delegates at the national convention. While the remote possibility still exists of a deadlocked convention turning to a newcomer for the nomination, it now seems inconceivable that any candidate could come to the convention with significant delegate support who had not actively contested the primaries and caucuses. Every presidential nomination in both parties since 1956 has been won on the first ballot of the convention, and not since 1968 has that first ballot nominee been someone other than the leader in delegates gained through the primaries and caucuses. Since 1976, in fact, the party nominee has led the field in primary election votes.

Indeed, so much has the politics of nomination shifted to the preconvention phase, and within it to the struggle to win delegates in the states, that many observers feel the convention no longer plays an important role in presidential selection. In its place is a dynamic process of primaries and caucuses with even more surprising vicissitudes. About the only certainty in the new nomination process, in short, is its unpredictability (see box on following page).

Candidate Strategies

In their competition to "sew up" the nomination before the convention meets, the candidates face a number of strategic choices. They have to decide when to begin the planning for their campaign and when to officially enter the fray. The foundation for many campaigns is laid as early as the presidential election four years before, and virtually all serious candidates now enter the race a year before the presidential election year—and begin their fund raising even earlier. Candidates also must choose which states to contest and what pace or timing to adopt for their campaign, although no candidate can safely ignore the contests at the front end of the nomination calendar.

In making their many strategic choices, potential contenders for the party nominations for president must weigh a number of factors. Their viability depends principally upon the nature of the opposition they can expect to face. If their party's president is seeking reelection, their prospects are dim; even vulnerable presidents enjoy great advantages in gaining renomination—as was shown by Ford in 1976, Carter in 1980, and Bush in 1992. Clinton, in fact, faced no competition in 1996. Front-runners have no alternative but to go all out in the preconvention campaign; those who do not risk an erosion of confidence among supporters, and (as Ed Muskie discovered in 1972) early difficulties can completely derail the campaign. A candidate with less support in a crowded field, on the other hand, can improve his or her

THE ULTIMATE "DARK HORSE" CANDIDATE?

The dynamics of the contemporary nomination process, as the following cartoon illustrates in humorists' hyperbole, can produce unexpected results. While the Republican nomination of Mick Jagger certainly would be a shock compared even to the Democrats' surprise selection of Jimmy Carter in 1976 or Bill Clinton in 1992, because both of the latter were experienced if relatively unknown political leaders, the point is that it is hard to predict victors or even front-runners in advance.

BLOOM COUNTY   by Berke Breathed

Source: © 1986 Washington Writer's Group, reprinted with permission.

chances for the nomination simply by exceeding expectations in an early contest—like Lamar Alexander did in Iowa in 1996.

Money and organization also are critical to a candidate's chances. Candidates must build nationwide campaign organizations to take the seemingly necessary step of qualifying for public funding. Then they must decide to which contests to allocate their resources in personnel and money. The early state contests necessarily receive the greatest investments, but because public funding is inadequate for full-blown campaigns in every state, candidates must set their priorities. Last-minute campaigns may be a relic of the past because legal restrictions on financial contributions prevent candidates from raising funds quickly from a few sources, unless they are willing to use their own money as Malcolm Forbes, Jr. did in his unsuccessful quest of the GOP nomination in 1996.

All these decisions are made, of course, in the context of the varying rules set down by the parties and the various states. Thus, more resources will be needed, for example, to organize and contest a state primary which chooses delegates by congressional district than one that elects at large. Moreover, these rules of the game differ from party to party. Because Democrats require a "fair reflection" of candidate strength in the selection of delegates, no front-running candidate risks a total shutout in any state any more. In many Republican primaries, however, it is still possible for a candidate to win 49 percent of the votes and still come away without a single delegate.[10]

The Critical Importance of Timing

Of all the strategic imperatives, none has been stronger than the need to win early. Victories in the early primaries and caucuses win attention in the mass media and name recognition in the wider public. They create credibility for the campaign and make it easier to raise money, and, above all, they create that mysterious psychological advantage, momentum. Early victories, in short, bring the support and resources that increase the likelihood of later victories.

Victors in the early stages thus become increasingly difficult to overtake, and so the pressure increases to spend much, work hard, and do well in the first primaries and caucuses. Thus, in the contested Democratic race of 1984, the field of five recognized contenders was winnowed to Walter Mondale, Gary Hart, and Jesse Jackson after the March 13 primaries. By the time the dust had settled after the March 8 contests in 1988, only Dukakis and Jackson remained viable among the seven serious aspirants who began the race. In 1992, Clinton had built an overwhelming lead by the end of the day on March 17.

The importance of early contests has not been lost on other participants. Some states, not wanting the selection of their delegates to come too late, have moved their contests forward to the early weeks of the campaign. For 1996, in fact, there was such a stampede among states to occupy an early position in the electoral calendar that the party contests were decided earlier than ever. Bill Clinton, never challenged, wrapped up the Democratic nomination right away. Bob Dole clinched the GOP nomination with his March 26 victory in California (see box on p. 227).

Party Interests

The party organizations also have interests at stake in the selection of delegates, and their interests often clash with those of the aspiring presidential nominees. For the local and state parties, a hotly contested contest often heightens intraparty conflict, which can weaken the party effort in the general election.[11] Moreover, a state party organization (or one of its leaders) may want to preserve its bargaining power to affect the platform, win a cabinet seat for a notable of the state party, influence the vice-presidential choice, or be able to provide pivotal support for the winning candidate. Parties also are conscious of how much a weak presidential candidate may hurt their chances in other contests.

Historically, the state parties protected their interests by selecting delegates uncommitted to any candidate and mobilizing those delegates as a block in convention decisions. The bargaining power of such a delegation enhanced the power of the state party at the convention. This ability of the parties to engineer the selection of an uncommitted delegation has been a casualty of the new system. In most primary states, it is the candidates who choose the delegates, whose primary loyalty is to the candidate. In the caucuses, delegates committed to a candidate simply have a greater appeal to the voters and party activists. Moreover, for delegates to remain uncom-

"FRONT-LOADING" THE NOMINATION PROCESS

As the years have passed and more experience has been gained with the post-1968 system, states and state parties have recognized that their influence over the outcome is diluted if they hold their primaries or caucuses too late in the process.

The first recognition of this came in 1988 with the movement of most southern and border state caucuses and primaries to March 8, so-called Super Tuesday because a total of twenty-one contests were scheduled for that day.[12] Early hopes that this would increase the influence of the southern states on the Democratic nomination outcome were dashed by the results of the contests. The big winners were Michael Dukakis and Jesse Jackson, hardly the kind of candidates moderate-to-conservative southern leaders expected to boost by concentrating their states' elections early in the process. The unanticipated consequences of the Super Tuesday contests in 1988 temporarily dampened the enthusiasm of state party leaders everywhere for moving up their primaries or creating a regional primary.

This reticence proved to be short lived as 1996 produced a stampede to the front of the nomination process. By the end of March 1996, voting had taken place in a sizable majority of the states, containing almost two-thirds of the convention delegates, and the nominees for both parties had been determined. California had moved its primary from its traditional June date to March 26; Ohio, New York, Wisconsin relocated theirs to March as well. After the traditional back-to-back Iowa caucus and New Hampshire primary in February, the 1996 calendar featured a varied assortment of states (including most other New England states) holding contests in late February and early March, a southern-dominated Super Tuesday on March 12, a series of midwestern contests a week later, followed by delegate-rich California at the end of the month.

This front-loading of the calendar has important implications for the nomination process. It increased the importance of early money; Republican candidates in 1996 raised more money before the election year than they ever had before and spent it more quickly; Dole was virtually out of money by the end of March. With so many states to contest in such a brief period of time, it also enhanced both the incentives to run national, rather than state-specific, campaigns and the costs of strategic miscalculations in where to invest both time and money. Ironically, it also boosted the importance of the Iowa caucuses and New Hampshire primary, positioning them as the launching pads for momentum to carry a candidate through the frenzied gauntlet of thirty-some contests in the following six weeks. Finally, if 1996 is any example, the early clinching of the nomination due to front-loading has altered the dynamics of the nomination process by building in a long and (for the candidates who have spent their money) quiet interlude between winning the nomination and receiving it at the summer convention.

mitted while one of the contenders for the nomination is locking up a majority of the convention votes is to squander all influence over the nomination and perhaps also some influence over the business of the convention. In a process dominated by the candidates, refusing to take sides carries considerable risk.

Protecting the interests of the party in a nominating process that increasingly reflects popular sentiments has been a concern for both the Democrats and the Republicans. For the Republicans, this no doubt has been one of the considerations in allowing state parties to maintain winner-take-all principles and other practices of the pre-reform era. Faced with rules changes that eradicated past bases for party organization influence, the Democrats responded in 1984 by setting aside uncommitted delegate slots for elected and party officials. These "superdelegates" include all Democratic members of Congress and their former party leaders, all Democratic governors, current and former presidents and vice-presidents, and all members and former chairs of the Democratic National Committee. Even though they now total nearly 20 percent of all delegates, the early closure of the race for the nomination in recent years has denied them an independent role in the nomination process.[13]

CITIZEN PARTICIPATION AND CHOICE IN PRESIDENTIAL NOMINATIONS

With the reforms of the presidential selection process in recent years has come increased attention to citizen participation and to the bases for voter choice. The move to primaries has increased citizen participation in presidential nominations to unprecedented levels. Many more people vote in primaries than in the caucuses, although turnout in the primaries still falls far short of levels attained in the presidential elections—even in Iowa and New Hampshire, which usually show the highest caucus and primary participation rates, respectively (Table 10.3).[14]

Variations in Turnout

There is a considerable variation in primary turnout among the different states in any one year and across different years in any one state. Not unsurprisingly, the traditionally first caucus (Iowa) and first primary (New Hampshire) usually have among the highest participation rates because of the interest those contests regularly generate. More generally, turnout tends to be higher in states with a better-educated citizenry, higher percentages of registered voters, and a tradition of two-party competition—the same states that enjoy higher general-election turnout. But voters also are differentially mobilized by the nature of the contest. The hotly contested primaries, where candidates spend more money and there is the excitement of competition, and contests held before the nomination is decided attract many more voters.[15] When the focus turns from state participation levels to individual decisions to participate, similar factors are involved. In general, participation is a function of the perceived closeness of the primary contest and voter interest in the race.[16]

Table 10.3   TURNOUT IN FIRST REPUBLICAN CAUCUS AND PRIMARY, 1996

	Iowa Caucus	New Hampshire Primary
Total number of participants	96,451	206,014
Participants as % of 1992 Republican presidential voters	19%	102%
Participants as % of 1992 total general election voters	7%	39%
Participants as % of 1996 registered Republicans	16%	82%
Participants as % of 1994 registered Republicans, third party, and unaffiliated	6%	46%

Note: Because the states with the first major caucus and primary usually stimulate the greatest voter turnout, if they are contested, participation figures for the Iowa Republican caucus and the New Hampshire Republican primary are presented. (Neither was contested on the Democratic side.) Iowa's caucus was open, meaning that any registered voters (including independents and Democrats) willing to register with the Republican party on caucus night were eligible to participate along with registered Republicans. New Hampshire's primary was open to registered independents, who became registered Republicans by participating in the GOP primary, in addition to Republicans. Which voters are eligible for participation in these contests is important of course, because it determines the relevancy of various bases in calculating turnout rates. Turnout relative to several different bases is provided for purposes of comparison.

Source: The 1994 registration figures are provided by Michael Barone and Grant Ujifusa, *The Almanac of American Politics 1996* (Washington, D.C. National Journal, 1995), pp. 506 and 834. The 1996 registration figures for Republicans are reported by Rhodes Cook, *Congressional Quarterly Weekly Report*, January 13, 1996, p. 100. Participation figures come from the *Congressional Quarterly Weekly Report*, February 17, 1996, p. 399, and February 24, 1996, p. 438.

Representativeness of Voters

In spite of the lower turnout in primaries than in general elections, there is little evidence to support the common charge that primary electorates are unrepresentative. Primary voters are better educated, better off, and older than nonvoters, but so are general-election voters. The more appropriate comparison is between primary voters and political party followers, however, because primaries are devices through which the party in the electorate chooses *its* nominees. When this comparison is made, few important differences emerge. Primary voters may be slightly older, better educated, more affluent, better integrated into their communities, less black or Hispanic, and less attentive to politics, but their positions on key policy issues are little different from those of party followers.[17] On empirical grounds, then, it is difficult to sustain the argument made by some critics of recent party reforms that primary electorates are less representative of the party than those people who chose party nominees several decades ago. They may be less representative of the party organization per se, but the organization is only one component of the party.

Bases of Voter Choice

Another criticism of the primaries is that voter choices are guided by rather trivial considerations. Primary electorates have been found to have lower levels of attentiveness to the campaign and of knowledge about the candidates than is the case in the general elections—and often they make their decisions at the last minute. Candidate momentum plays an important role in the formation of voter preferences, as bandwagons form for candidates who have demonstrated their viability and electability by winning, or merely exceeding expectations, in the immediately preceding contests. Especially in the early contests, voters are heavily influenced by media interpretations of results in "horse-race" terms. Of demonstrated importance, too, in the voter's calculus are candidates' personal characteristics, defined in large part by the themes stressed in the candidates' own campaigns. Ideology, issues, and of course (because the primaries are within-party contests) party attachments may play only minor roles in primary-election voting behavior. The result, so this argument goes, is a series of electoral contests decided principally on the basis of short-run and inherently more fickle considerations.[18]

Most scholars believe that this indictment of the primaries goes too far. They see voters—without the powerful guidance provided by party labels and having to choose among multiple candidates in a short campaign—responding to what Samuel Popkin has referred to as "low-information signaling" based on candidates' chances of winning, personal and demographic characteristics, and whatever inferences can be drawn about their policy positions.[19]

Larry Bartels' sophisticated modeling of primary voting[20] emphasizes that candidate momentum, developed through performance that exceeds expectations in previous primaries, can be a rational basis for sorting through a pack of low-visibility candidates, especially for those voters who are searching for an alternative to the front-runner. Candidates favored by momentum, though, are quickly subjected to more searching evaluations. The dynamics of the campaign matter most where they begin with no well-known front-runner (for example, the Democratic contests in 1976, 1988, or 1992), and here strategic considerations of who among the acceptable candidates is most likely to win become strong.[21] Voters' evaluations of well-known candidates such as incumbent presidents or vice-presidents, by contrast, are less likely to be affected by the vicissitudes of the campaign, unless that candidate's chances of winning diminish substantially.

Even though primary voters often make their decisions with less information than do general election voters, then, there is an emerging view that these choices are not uninformed or irrational. In intraparty contests, issue, ideological, and of course party differences among candidates are necessarily muted. It should not be at all surprising that, in their place, various candidate characteristics would loom large and issue priorities rather than issue positions might become important. Moreover, taking candidate viability (that is, chances of winning the nomination) and electability (that is, chances of winning the presidency) into account is a rational act of the strategic voter who leavens preferences with realistic calculations in determining how to make the most effective use of his or her vote, not an indication of irrationality or ignorance. Primaries provide a different institutional context for voting behavior, but beyond that the bases for voter decision making in primaries may differ little from those in caucuses or in general elections.[22]

The debate over the quality of electoral decision making in primaries will doubtlessly continue as long as unexpected nominees emerge and one's own favorite is defeated. Of course, this questioning is hardly unique to primaries. The same doubts could be raised about the quality of judgment of voters in general elections or of party leaders in making nominations under the earlier caucus-convention system.

PRIMARY VERSUS PARTY SELECTION

Apart from the interests of parties and candidates, however, has it really made any difference whether delegates to the national conventions have been chosen by primaries or by party processes? Do the delegates chosen by a primary behave any differently from those chosen through party bodies? Do the presidential primaries have an impact on the nominations commensurate with the time and money spent in them?

Not too long ago in American politics, the processes of delegate selection were sharply bifurcated. In the states of the presidential primaries, a more open, popular candidate-centered politics worked to the advantage of well-known personalities and antiorganization insurgents. In the other states, the party organization controlled delegate selection and could apply, with few exceptions, tests of party acceptability both to delegates and ultimately to the seekers after the party's nomination. Estes Kefauver in 1952 and 1956 and Eugene McCarthy in 1968 used the primaries to challenge the party apparatus for the nominations. They failed, as did all other challengers with little support outside the primary states, if for no other reason than that there were not enough primaries; the delegates selected in the primaries were 40 percent or less of the total. Before the 1970s, the party nominees invariably fell into two categories: those, such as John Kennedy in 1960, who mixed victories in primary and nonprimary states, and those, such as Wendell Willkie in 1940, Adlai Stevenson in 1952, and Hubert Humphrey in 1968, who sat out the primaries and won the nomination in brokered conventions.

As the differences between the primary and nonprimary processes have diminished since the 1970s, however, the situation has changed. On the one hand, it now seems necessary for a successful candidate to win many primary victories, and it is even possible to succeed by winning largely primary victories. That is so if for no other reason than that most of the convention delegates are now chosen in primaries. On the other hand, the comparison between primary and nonprimary selection is losing its importance simply because the politics of choosing delegates is now more similar in all states, primary and nonprimary alike. National candidates, media coverage, and more open and better-publicized processes make for a continuous and homogeneous preconvention politics. As a consequence, the results of the primaries and the caucuses do not greatly diverge. The shift to a more-open process has touched the traditional presidential preliminaries as well.

Still, the primaries maintain their special role and appeal. Because of their openness to the voters, their results confer great legitimacy on the winners. Victories in primaries may still be as important for these symbolic purposes as for the number of delegates acquired. The primaries also provide an opportunity for candidates to show their appeal, to build a following and raise campaign funds, and to show their stamina and adaptability under various pressures. Cruelly, too, they help weed out the nonviable candidates. As Lyndon Johnson discovered in 1968, disappointing results in the primaries may even help drive an incumbent president from office.

THE FINAL ACT: THE NATIONAL PARTY CONVENTIONS

For several days every four years, the Democrats and Republicans assemble as national parties to make decisions on a national scale. The conventions draw together for collective action the different parts of the party—the party organization, the party in the electorate, and the party in government. They serve as a primary reference for millions of Americans when they think of the political parties. Yet, with their traditional purpose of selecting the party's nominee for president now compromised, one wonders how important they are for party politics in America.

The Origins and Development of the Party Conventions

The national party conventions are venerable institutions. They first emerged as vehicles for the decentralization and, hence, the democratization of the party system—as the means through which the state parties and their leaders could wrest control of the presidential selection process from congressional leaders. In 1832, the Democratic-Republican party, soon to be transformed into the Democratic party, became the first major party to hold a convention. Because the nomination of Andrew Jackson was a foregone conclusion, its principal purpose was to enable state political leaders to secure the vice-presidential nomination for Martin Van Buren over Henry Clay, the favorite of the congressional caucus. By the time the Republican party emerged in 1854, the convention had become the accepted means through which a major party's candidates for president and vice-president were to be selected; the GOP held its first convention in 1856.[23]

Every four years since their birth, then, America's two major parties have held national party conventions to nominate their candidates for president. Even though this core function has been undermined with the post-World War Two nationalization of politics and the use of the direct primary, especially since 1968, the conventions remain visible party institutions.[24]

The Structure of the Convention

The conventions are creatures of the parties themselves. They are subject to no congressional or state regulation, and even the federal courts have been loathe to intervene in their operation. Responsibility for them falls to the national party committees and their staffs, although an incumbent president strongly influences the planning for his party's convention.

Months before the convention, its major committees begin their work. Like other American institutions, both political and nonpolitical, the conventions function, in part, through committees (see box on following page). What these committees decide can be overruled by the convention itself, which acts as the ultimate arbiter of its own structure and procedures. Consequently, some of the most famous battles on the floor

KEY COMMITTEES OF THE NATIONAL PARTY CONVENTIONS

Over the years, there have been four important committees of the national conventions:

Credentials considers the qualifications of delegates and alternates. Once the scene of some of the fiercest battles over delegate seating, it has become less important in recent years as delegate contests are resolved through regularized state procedures approved by the national parties.

Permanent Organization selects the officials of the convention, including the chairperson, secretary, and sergeant at arms.

Rules sets the rules of the convention, including the length and number of nomination speeches. It often is the scene for a struggle over the procedures for future conventions.

Platform (or Resolutions) drafts the party's platform for action by the convention. As intraparty struggles leading into the convention have focused more on issues, it has emerged in recent years as the most important of the committees.

of the convention have involved disputes over committee recommendations, which have served as initial tests of strength for contending candidates.

The Business of the Conventions

The convention begins in low key, with stiff formalities and the business of organizations. It warms up with the keynote address by a party luminary, tries to maintain momentum and expectation through consideration of the platform, and reaches a dramatic peak in the nomination of the presidential and vice-presidential candidates. This general format has remained basically the same convention after convention. Declining television coverage in recent years has necessitated some rearrangement into a more compact convention, with the events of major interest reserved for prime evening transmission time and short news reports, but the tempo of the meeting is still governed by the pace of business more than by any dramatic considerations.

The Platforms   Aside from the rites of nomination, the approval of the platform is the convention's chief business. The platform committees begin public hearings long before the convention opens, so that the platform can be in draft form for convention hearings. The finished platform is then presented to the convention for its approval. That approval is not always pro forma, and the platform has occasioned some spirited convention battles because many of the delegates care deeply about construction of the party's one statement of what it stands for. In 1968, forces supporting Hubert H. Humphrey engaged Eugene McCarthy's delegates in a three-hour floor debate over Vietnam while a battle between Chicago police and antiwar protestors raged on the streets downtown. More recently, the Democrats' seventeen-hour debate over economic policy in 1980 was the last gasp of Ted Kennedy's ill-fated challenge to President Carter.[25]

Few products of American politics so openly invite skepticism, even cynicism, as do the party platforms. They are long, prolix, rarely read, and often ignored by party leaders after they have been adopted. Rather than statements of continuing party philosophy, the platforms are really an expression of the policy concerns and preferences of majorities that can be assembled around each of its planks. The platforms also are campaign documents in which positions are taken to promote the assembling of a majority coalition and to position the party favorably for the general election in the fall.

Vague or artful as the platforms may be in their attempt to satisfy multiple interests and constituencies, they do define the issue, even philosophical, differences between the parties. In recent years, the Democratic and Republican platforms have disagreed on a number of issues, most notably abortion, tax policy, collective bargaining rights, gun control, racial policy, deficit spending, and American involvement in the world. (See Chapter 15 for specification of some of their differences.) The party platform is important, its leading scholar says,

> but not as an inspired goal to which politicians resort for policy guidance. It is important because it summarizes, crystallizes, and presents to the voters the character of the party coalition. Platform pledges are not simply good ideas, or even original ones. In their programs, Democrats and Republicans are not typically breaking new paths; they are promising to proceed along one or another path which has already become involved in political controversy. The stands taken in the platform clarify the parties' positions on these controversies and reveal the nature of their support and appeals.[26]

Finally, the platforms are what they are largely because they are drafted and approved in conventions mainly concerned with picking a presidential candidate. Every convention vote tends to become a test of the strength of the various candidates, and votes on the platform are no exception. Because the party's presidential nominee generally controls the convention, the platform ordinarily has been a reflection of his views—or at least the bargains he has been willing to strike for other gains or to preserve party harmony.[27]

Selecting the Presidential Candidate   The pièce de résistance of the convention, the selection of the party's nominee for president, starts with the nominations from the floor, the formal speech of nomination and shorter seconding speeches, and the floor demonstrations by the candidate's supporters. The realities of modern television coverage—its concern with short "bites" of information and its rendering of the traditional hijinks as parodies of a bygone time—have forced the parties to limit these ceremonious events and thereby deprive the conventions of much of the drama, the sense of carnival, that was so much a part of their tradition. Modern party conventions are sedate affairs compared to the riotous conventions of yore.

Once all the nominees have been presented to the convention, the secretary calls the roll of the states (and other voting units), asking each delegation to report its vote. If no candidate wins a majority on the first ballot, the convention will continue voting until the necessary majority is obtained. All nominations since 1952 have been settled on the first ballot, and the recent reforms have increased the likelihood that one candidate will come to the convention with the support of a majority of delegates. When the Democrats required a two-thirds majority for nomination, prior to 1956, though, multiple ballots were not unusual; in 1924 the Democrats plodded through 103 ballots in sultry New York's Madison Square Garden before nominating John W. Davis.

In spite of the modern-day norm of first ballot nominations, a multiballot convention remains possible—and perhaps now is even more likely for the Democrats because of their wholesale move to proportional representation. While experience may not completely portend the politics of a divided convention under reform rules, the past does contain useful lessons. If the first ballot was inconclusive, intense negotiations would emerge in pursuit of a majority. The leading candidates would need to prevent a chipping away of their supporters, which is a genuine danger if they are seen as having little hope of winning. New support for front-runners would come most easily from the delegates preferring minor candidates or from uncommitted "superdelegates" because delegates of the candidates still in contention likely will be too loyal to those commitments to be lured away. Because today's delegates are tied to candidates rather than to state party leaders, however, it is uncertain who would play the traditional role of broker. One possibility, of course, is that the leading candidates, in command of their blocks of committed delegates, would negotiate among themselves for the prize. Another is that the uncommitted "superdelegates" would become the new power brokers.[28]

Selecting the Vice-Presidential Nominee   The day after the naming of the presidential nominee, the secretary calls the roll again to select the vice-presidential candidate. This process too is largely ceremonial, as presidential nominees almost always choose their own running mates and conventions routinely ratify their choice. This method of selecting vice-presidential candidates has drawn criticism. It is not so much that they are hand picked by the presidential candidate but that the decision is made by a tired candidate and tired advisors in so short a span of time and then sprung at the last minute upon an often-unsuspecting convention. The withdrawal of the initial Democratic vice-presidential nominee Thomas Eagleton in 1972 because of controversy over his treatments for depression and the forced resignation of scandal-plagued Vice-President Spiro Agnew a year later illustrate the pitfalls of hurried and superficial screening. But without any viable procedure to replace it, the choice of vice-presidential nominee and the responsibility for a poor selection will remain in the hands of the party's presidential nominee.

Launching the Presidential Campaign   The final business of the conventions is to introduce their party's presidential choice to both assembled delegates and the American electorate. Of course, after many grueling months of public campaigning, the nominees are hardly unknown to either party faithful or the public. But the speeches on their behalf at the convention and their own address accepting the party's call are the first salvos of the general election campaign. Coming out of their conventions, nominees generally receive a boost in popular support (a "convention bounce") as they appear before the public for the first time as their party's standard-bearer. For the presidential candidates at least, then, the convention as a campaign "event" is probably its most important role.

THE DELEGATES

The nomination contests in the fifty states (and several other convention constituencies) do not select the presidential nominees but rather choose delegates to attend the party's national conventions to render this decision. For the many Americans watching these quadrennial spectacles on television, it is the delegates assembled in the convention hall who provide their image of the party. After all, the conventions are designed to represent the parties—even if, in recent years, this representation is shaped by the relative standings of the various party candidates for president. Thus, who the delegates are says a great deal about what the parties are.

Apportioning Delegate Slots among the States

The first step in determining the delegates for the national conventions is taken by the parties themselves in advance of the presidential election year, when they define how many delegates will be apportioned to each state and other convention constituency. Recent apportionment formulas have been based upon a state's population and its record of support for the party's candidates, but the parties' give different weights to each component. The Republicans allocate delegates more equally among the states; the Democrats have tended to represent population size and strength of Democratic voting more heavily.

The intricacies of delegate apportionment formulas are subjects of occasional intraparty struggle because they play a critical role in determining the voting strength of the various groups within the party coalitions. The GOP's decision to represent the states more equally has advantaged its conservative wing. By giving relatively more weight to the larger states with stronger Democratic voting traditions, by contrast, the Democrats have favored the more liberal interests in their party. Even if variations in delegate allocation formulas have only marginal effects on the balance of forces within the parties, many a nomination has been won—and lost—at the margin.

The Representativeness of the Delegates

The delegates to the Democratic and Republican conventions have never been a cross section of American citizens, or even of their party's rank and file. Whites, males, the well educated, and the affluent traditionally have populated the convention halls. Reflecting their different coalitional bases, since the 1930s Democratic delegations have had more Catholics, Jews, and trade unionists, whereas the Republican conventions have drawn more Protestants and business entrepreneurs. Convention-goers, not unsurprisingly, also have tended to be veteran party politicians with extensive involvement in party affairs.

Demographic Characteristics In recent decades, both parties, but especially the Democrats, have broadened the representativeness of their delegations. The

Democrats employed affirmative action plans after 1968 to increase the presence of women, blacks, and for a brief time, young people; since 1980, they have required that half of the state delegates be women. The percentage of female delegates at Republican conclaves has increased during this period as well, albeit through more natural causes. The Democratic National Committee also has urged its state party organizations to recruit more low- and moderate-income delegates, but the low political involvement levels of these groups plus the exorbitant costs of attending a convention pose powerful barriers to their participation. Thus, the conventions have remained meetings of the affluent and well educated (see Table 10.4).[29]

A Self-Perpetuating Elite?   Some critics have felt that the conventions had become conclaves for a self-perpetuating set of party elites. Careful attention to turnover in convention delegates, however, makes this charge hard to sustain. Well

Table 10.4 REPRESENTATIVENESS OF THE NATIONAL PARTY CONVENTIONS: 1968–1992

	Blacks	Women	Age <30	Income Low	Income High	Education Low	Education High
			Democratic Delegates				
1968	5%	13%	3%	—	—	37	44
1972	15	40	22	—	—	43	36
1976	11	33	15	—	—	36	43
1980	15	49	11	5	27	35	45
1984	18	49	8	15	44	30	50
1988	23	48	4	6	56	27	52
1992	16	48	—	7	66	28	52
			Republican Delegates				
1968	2%	16%	4%	—	—	—	34
1972	4	29	8	—	—	—	—
1976	3	31	7	—	—	35	38
1980	3	29	5	2	42	35	39
1984	4	44	4	10	57	37	35
1988	4	33	3	6	56	33	37
1992	5	43	—	—	—	—	—

Note: Income is annual family income. Low income = <$12,000 in 1980, and <$25,000 afterwards; high income = >$50,000 in each year. Low education is some college or less; high education is postgraduate work. "—" indicates that the question was not asked or the data are otherwise unavailable.

Source: The estimates for 1968-88 are from figures provided in *The Public Perspective* 3 (1992), p. 97; they come from surveys of a random sample of convention delegates conducted by CBS News (with *The New York Times* in 1988). The Democratic estimates for 1992 come from a survey reported in *The New York Times*, July 13, 1992; Republican estimates for 1992 are drawn from a survey conducted by CBS News.

before the reforms of the post-1968 era, a comfortable majority of delegates were attending each party convention for the first time. With the move to primaries, the percentage of newcomers increased after 1968—to about 80 percent—before declining steadily to pre-reform levels of about 60 percent for both parties in 1988. The increased representation of Democratic "superdelegates" even brought the total for their newcomers to less than a majority in 1992.

Yet, for all of this infusion of new blood every four years, the party conclaves have a constancy in kind: They remain the domain of party activists and officials. In 1992, for example, 69 percent of a random sample of Democratic delegates reported that they "worked year after year" for the party, 45 percent held party office, and 24 percent held elected office. Comparable Republican figures may be even higher, as they were in previous years.[30] In short, regardless of high delegate turnover from convention to convention, these national party meetings still bring together the activists of the state and local party organizations and the leaders of the party in government.

Issue and Ideological Representativeness   A focus on the demographic and political backgrounds of the delegates overlooks a critical element of representativeness. The political views and preferences of the delegates are just as important as who they are. There is no question that convention delegates are more politically involved, more aware of issues and political circumstances, than the ordinary voters of their party. They also tend more to the ideological poles than do the party rank and file. As expected, Democratic delegates cluster toward the liberal end and Republican delegates toward the conservative end of the liberal-conservative ideological continuum.

Comparison of the ideological tendencies of a party's convention delegates with those of its rank-and-file members addresses a central issue in the debate over reforms in the presidential nomination process. Democratic reformers attacked the old caucus-convention system as unrepresentative of the views of regular party supporters. Their critics, in turn, have charged that the reformed system has produced a set of convention delegates who are ideologically out of step with ordinary party voters and the general electorate.

The reality is that reforming the delegate selection process has not necessarily made the conventions more representative of the views and values of the parties in the electorate. Prior to 1972, it was the Republican conventions whose delegates appeared to be more ideologically out of step with party voters—and even more so with the general voting public.[31] At first blush, ironically, the Democratic party reforms seemed to reverse that pattern. Democratic delegates in 1972 were more ideologically distant than Republican delegates from their party electorate—and even farther away from the public. This result led to an initial conclusion that the Democratic reforms had made Democratic conventions less rather than more representative.[32]

Comparisons of delegates with party supporters in subsequent conventions have shown, though, that the 1972 Democratic convention was an anomaly in the degree of liberal overrepresentation. Later Democratic delegations were more in line, ideologically speaking, with Democratic party identifiers. The infusion of "superdelegates" since 1984 seems to have reduced the ideological gap between Democratic party delegates and party voters even more.[33]

The real effect of the post-1968 reforms on the ideological composition of the delegations was to decrease the tie between any particular convention and the party rank and file rather than rendering either of the party delegations naturally more ideological. By linking the selection of delegates more tightly to candidate preferences, the new nomination system opened the convention doors to more members of the ideologically committed cadre of the parties when its candidates fared well. Without the leavening effect of a strong party organization presence, then, ideological front-runners will probably bring in more delegate ideologues—and, in that respect, conventions that may be less representative of the party in the electorate. But not every nomination contest will find ideologically extreme candidates in the lead. Nor will the differences among conventions always be as great as those among delegates at the same convention.

Amateurs or Professionals?   The differences among delegates extend to style and approach to politics as well. Using the typology described in Chapter 5, some convention delegates can be described as amateurs, others as professionals. Amateurs are more attracted by programs and issues, more insistent on intraparty democracy, less willing to compromise, and less committed to the prime importance of winning elections. Professionals, by contrast, are more likely to have a long-term commitment to the party and to be willing to compromise on the issues in the interest of winning the general election.

The division between amateurs (or purists) and professionals in any particular delegation has interested scholars because of the presumption that a changing mix of professionals and amateurs affects the continuing vitality of the party. A comparison of amateurs and professionals between the unreformed 1968 Democratic convention and the reformed 1972 conclave gave credence to the view that the reforms had, as intended, reduced the presence of party professionals.[34] Subsequent research, though, concludes that the supposed threat to the parties posed by the diminished role of professionals and infusion of amateurs is greatly exaggerated. Even after the reforms, convention delegates have remained strongly committed to their parties and to enduring party goals.[35] What else might we expect from Americans who have been so active in party politics on a continuing basis?

Who Controls the Delegates?   The question of representativeness is irrelevant if the delegates are mere pawns of powerful party bosses. For most of their history, state delegations at the national party conventions indeed were dominated by a few leaders. Lore has it that the top state Democratic leaders and some big city mayors were commanding presences indeed for many years, and there is ample anecdotal evidence to back this up. For most of the twentieth century, in fact, a large proportion of the Democratic senators and governors came as delegates to their quadrennial party conclave. Such Republican elected officials have been less represented in the convention hall and less visible as power brokers, but they too have played an important role.

Domination of the convention by strong party leaders through control of their state delegations is now an artifact of the past. When the Democrats eliminated their long-standing unit rule in 1968, through which a majority of a state delegation could secure all of its votes for one candidate, they removed one powerful instrument of leadership control. By opening up the delegate selection process after 1968, both parties also made it difficult for elected leaders to claim delegate seats without committing early to a presidential candidate, which they were reluctant to do. Representation of Democratic elected leaders declined rather dramatically after 1968 until the Democrats started to give them spots as uncommitted "superdelegates" in 1984.[36] Perhaps the most powerful and enduring restriction on control of conventions by a few state leaders, though, is the fact that many delegates in both parties come to the conventions today already committed to a candidate and unavailable for "delivery" by party leaders. If anyone controls the modern conventions, then, it is the party's prospective nominee for president, not leaders of the state parties.

CONVENTIONS IN THE NEW NOMINATING PROCESS

It is unlikely that small bands of national kingmakers bargaining in smoke-filled rooms ever did dominate the national conventions to the extent that popular myth has it. Even the celebrated negotiations at the Republican convention of 1920—in the course of which Warren G. Harding emerged as the party's nominee—took place in a convention deadlocked by other candidates with large popular and delegate followings. Whatever power the kingmakers may have had in the past, however, is gone. In that and in a number of other important ways, the national nominating conventions are not what they were even a generation ago.

New Preconvention Politics

The eventual nominee now is usually known well before the convention begins; in this case, all the convention does is officially confirm the choice of the primaries and caucuses. This is the product of the progressive nationalization of American politics in the last half century and the post-1968 reforms of the nominating process, especially the move to primaries and the commitment of delegates to a particular candidate that followed it. More-effective candidate organization and closer media scrutiny also ensure that both candidates and delegates have fuller information about the standing of the candidates before the convention than they ever did before. Consequently, the convention no longer functions as the key forum for the bargaining and trading of support, the committing of delegates, and the weeding out of candidates.[37]

New Centers of Power

Political power also has shifted away from the state and local party leaders, who once came as state ambassadors to the convention in control of blocs of votes to use in negotiating within a fragmented, decentralized party. Power in the parties now is less decentralized as national issues and national party figures—and party identifications shaped by national politics—have cut into the autonomy of state parties and leaders. So, too, has the increased power of potential candidates in the convention, power that is a consequence of their preconvention success in rounding up committed delegates. The battle between party regulars and anti-Vietnam insurgents over the Democratic nomination in 1968, seen now in retrospect, was the "last hurrah" for the old centers of power around state and local leaders.

The choices in the conventions also are structured more around issues and ideologies. By requiring candidates to mobilize grass-roots constituencies in their quest for the nomination, the post-1968 reforms made issue and ideological considerations, never absent from pre-reform conventions, even more likely to motivate convention delegates. Many delegates arrive at the convention not only committed to a candidate but also to a cause—as is illustrated in the ideological pressures exerted by feminists and Jackson supporters on the Democratic side in 1980s or Christian conservatives at Republican conventions in the 1990s. Ideological factions or tendencies and their associated interests, thus, also have become new centers of power.

Changing Media Coverage

The conventions also have been transformed to better suit the needs of the mass media, and media coverage of them has significantly changed as well. The result, as Byron Shafer has put it, is a "bifurcated politics" in which the convention is one thing to delegates in the meeting hall and quite another to the millions catching a glimpse of it on television.[38]

Live gavel-to-gavel televising of the meetings, beginning in the 1950s, turned them into national political spectaculars, intended as much for a national television audience as for the delegates. Party officials gave key roles to telegenic partisans, quickened the pace of proceedings, and moved the most serious business into prime-time hours. The strategic moves of major candidates, the actions of powerful figures in the party, and the defections of individual delegates came to be reported fully, as reporters swarmed through the convention halls. Even the formerly secret hagglings of platform and credentials committees came to be done in the public eye. For the party, television coverage offered a priceless opportunity to reach voters and party workers and to launch its presidential campaign with maximum impact. For television news, the convention became a prime event, like a natural disaster or the Olympic games, through which it could demonstrate its proficiency and provide its public service. Thus, the media spotlight shifted the role of the convention—not completely but perceptibly—from the conduct of party business to the stimulation of wider political audiences.

Yet, as media attention to it increased, the convention began to lose its audience appeal. Because post-reform nomination contests were settled before the proceedings began, the drama and suspense of the conventions waned. With the proliferation of competing programs, viewers also could tune to alternatives as the convention droned on and on. It is little wonder, then, that media reporters, searching for color and drama to hold an audience, became actors in the event themselves—more than willing to fan the flames of conflict or to turn base rumors into full-fledged stories. Nor should it be surprising that, in response to declining audiences, major network coverage of convention proceedings was reduced from gavel-to-gavel treatment through the 1960s and 1970s to only significant developments in the 1980s and 1990s (see Table 10.5). That convention "junkies" still can turn to C-SPAN or CNN for comprehensive coverage does not lessen the significance of the major networks' desertion of the convention.[39]

Media coverage is thus a two-edged sword, and its results are not always the ones the parties want. Television's capacity to dramatize and personalize can make a convention come to life for its audience, as it did in its coverage of the struggles in the convention hall and streets of Chicago in 1968. But it also underplays the more subtle and more essential processes of negotiation and compromise in decision-making institutions. Media exposure is also problematic in other ways. It encourages some participants to use the convention as a podium to advance their own causes, even if they may undermine the candidacy of the party nominee. The public visibility given to defeated candidates Jesse Jackson at the 1984 and 1988 Democratic conventions or to Patrick Buchanan at the 1992 Republican conclave, for example, was thought by some to have threatened the subsequent general-election campaigns of the party's nominees. Occasionally, the media even manage to participate directly in party decisions. While Ronald Reagan was trying to persuade former President Gerald Ford to be his vice-presidential candidate at the 1980 Republican convention, CBS anchorman Walter Cronkite's use of the phrase *co-presidency* in a live interview with Ford probably made reaching an agreement between them more difficult, perhaps even impossible.

Conventions in Future Party Politics

The conventions have therefore lost much of their deliberative character and independence in fulfilling their original purpose—selecting the presidential nominees.

Table 10.5 HOURS OF NETWORK TELEVISION COVERAGE OF THE NATIONAL PARTY CONVENTIONS, 1952–1992

Year	Democrats	Republicans
1952	61.1	57.5
1956	37.6	22.8
1960	29.3	25.5
1964	23.5	36.5
1968	39.1	34.0
1972	36.7	19.8
1976	30.4	29.5
1980	24.1	22.7
1984	12.9	11.9
1988	12.8	12.6
1992	8.0	7.3

Note: Figures are the number of hours of televised party conventions on the major networks (ABC, CBS, NBC). In 1988, CNN televised 30 hours of the Democratic convention and 14.5 hours of the Republican convention; in 1992, it televised 8 hours of each convention.

Source: Harold W. Stanley and Richard G. Niemi, *Vital Statistics on American Politics* (Washington, D.C.: Congressional Quarterly Press, 1994), Table 2–13, p. 75.

Genuinely brokered conventions and last-minute compromise candidates seem now to belong to the past. The unlikelihood of lightning striking the unknown statesmen does not, of course, signal the end of the convention. If no candidate has won a majority prior to the convention, delegates still may have to choose from among a small number of candidates who have established themselves in the preconvention stages. Even if the choice must be made among these well-known hopefuls, though, it will be made by a freer, more-open bargaining that involves the majority of delegates as well as the prominent party leaders.

The conventions simply reflect, as never before, a heterogeneous mix of political roles and expectations. To traditional state and local leaders, representing the interests of their party organizations, are now added the new national party leaders, national officeholders, and powerful candidates with blocks of loyal delegates. Old organizational styles also mix incongruously with new styles of media-based politics; professional party leadership rubs elbows with volunteer, amateur party activists. The old electoral pragmatism—the traditional convention emphasis on picking the winning candidate—can sometimes clash with the unwillingness of the ideologues to compromise. In reflecting all these conflicting forces, the party conventions only mirror the broader conflicts and divisions of American party politics.

Although change and declining significance may beset the conventions, the parties are not likely to abandon them. Even in its eviscerated condition, the national convention is too precious an institution to surrender. It is the only real, palpable existence of a national political party. It is the only occasion for rediscovery of common traditions and common interests, the only time for shared decision making and a coming together to celebrate old glories and achievements. It stimulates the workers and contributors to party labors, it encourages party candidates in the states and localities, and it launches the presidential campaigns. Its rites may not mean a great deal to the majority of Americans who occasionally peer at it on the TV screen, but they do mean something to the men and women of the party.

PARTIES IN THE PRESIDENTIAL SELECTION PROCESS

The story of changes in the presidential nomination process is a variation on an old theme in American politics. During the last three decades, various reforms, sustained by an aversion to concentrations of party power, have wrested away from the party organizations their control over the selection of candidates for the principal prize in American politics. The parties have devised strategies to retain some influence in the process—Democrats by selecting superdelegates, Republicans by continuing some of the old rules—but the truth is that their efforts have borne little fruit. It now is difficult for the party organizations to exert much influence over the presidential nomination, perhaps even more difficult than for them to affect other party nominations.

The sources of the party organization's problems are obvious. The presidential primary weakens organizational control and shifts it to the candidates, as primaries have for other offices. The organizations are weak too because they are unable to unite or coordinate their own preferences prior to the nominating conventions. Thus, candidates with comparatively rational and unified national strategies increasingly find it easy to take the initiative from individual state party organizations in this phase of presidential politics. To the extent that they are able to win the commitments of enough delegates to capture the nominations, they capture the nomination before the party organizations ever gather themselves together to act as a national party at the convention.

Pros and Cons of the Current System

The briefs against both the old system and the new are long and weighty. In fact, they seem to outweigh the case for each process to such an extent that the observer might easily conclude that, once again in American politics, one must choose between the lesser of two evils.

The drawbacks to the current presidential nominating system are increasingly apparent: It requires such an enormous investment of time, energy, and money before the presidential campaign has even begun that the ultimate winner can arrive at the party convention personally and financially exhausted. It puts a premium on campaign strategy and candidate image making rather than presidential leadership abilities. The results of a few early contests, in states hardly representative of the nation, have disproportionate weight in the national outcome.[40] The presidential primaries also frequently create internal divisions in state party organizations, and the resulting wounds may not be healed in time for the general election. The serial nature of the new nomination process too creates its own dynamic in which minor campaign events and the unexpected replace the deliberative decision making of a national convention—and raise the risk that a party will select a nominee who is doomed to failure in the fall election.

Yet, the old system fell under the weight of its own disabilities. In the nonprimary states, it excluded the party electorates and even many of the party activists from the crucial first step in picking a president. It often was controlled by local and state party leaders who seemed increasingly out of touch with the electorate, even within their own party. It also violated the strong American yearning for a more open, democratic politics—and gave every appearance of being run from the backrooms. All that, and it failed to produce candidates for president who were necessarily well suited for the most powerful leadership position in the world.[41]

Debating points aside, recent years have been a time of a great revival of interest in the primaries and of declining interest in the party conventions. The states have adopted primaries with enthusiasm, and the media have spotlighted their role in the nomination process while deemphasizing the conventions. Most critically, the basic rationale of the current system—achieving the twin democratic norms of mass popular participation and weakened party oligarchies—seems more attractive to the American public and to political activists than ever.[42] Whatever its problems, the basic structure of the new nomination system seems secure.

Possible Reforms

If we cannot live without the primaries, is it possible that we might learn to live more comfortably with them? The most drastic reform proposal of recent years was to do away with the national nominating conventions altogether and to choose the presidential nominees in a single national primary. Another proposal was to schedule primaries on the same day in each region, with a few weeks separating the different regional election days.

The regional coordination of state primary and caucus dates in 1996 represents a major step in the direction of regional primaries. Most southern primaries have been held on Super Tuesday for more than a decade. What was new in 1996 was the shifting of primaries to the same early March date in New England and later in the month in the Midwest. If this reform proves to have been beneficial to the states, in the sense of increasing their influence in the 1996 nomination process, it may spread to states in other regions in future years.

It is hard to imagine the states or the parties, though, moving to a national primary. The motivation behind the recent reforms was to enhance the influence of the individual states—not to pave the way for a national primary. A national primary would serve the interests of neither the parties nor the states. States would lose their individuality and their chance of becoming a pivotal player in nomination contests. The parties would completely lose control over presidential selection, throwing the contest for the presidency wide open to any candidate who could mobilize a national constituency. Instituting a national primary, under these conditions, could only be accomplished by ending the long tradition of state and party control over the presidential nomination process—and, for all of the reforms we have seen in recent decades, there seems to be little chance that will happen.

Chapter 11

Parties and the Campaign for Election

The formidable Democratic party organization of Pennsylvania had long had a reputation for controlling primaries. At the outset of the campaign in the gubernatorial primary of 1966, therefore, few observers gave any chance to Milton Shapp, a Philadelphia industrialist who was challenging the organization's candidate—thirty-four-year-old lawyer and state legislative leader, Robert B. Casey. In what was billed as a battle of "exposure versus organization," the Shapp campaign challenged the organization with some 7,000 spot radio commercials, thirty-four half-hour television shows in prime time, an assortment of thirty or so pamphlets and leaflets, more than sixty campaign headquarters across the state, and a mailing of one large brochure to a million and a half voters. The total cost of the primary campaign, financed in large part from Shapp's personal fortune, ran to more than a million dollars—at 1966 value! Shapp won the primary and was elected subsequently as governor.

After it was all over, a reflective Robert Casey observed about the campaign he had lost:

> Politics is changing tremendously. The old ways no longer work. From that election, I learned that these days you need a combination of two things. First, the traditional grass-roots effort, the telephoning and the door-knocking. But more than that, you have to use the new sophisticated techniques, the polling, the television, the heavy staffing, and the direct mail. You can't rely any more on political organizations. They don't work any more. These days, who wants a job in the courthouse or with the highway department? Why, the sons of courthouse janitors are probably doctors or professional men. You can't give those jobs away any more. We're at the tag end of an era in Pennsylvania.[1]

The final chapter in this story was written sixteen years later. In 1986, this time using an effective media campaign, Robert Casey upset William Scranton III to win the Pennsylvania governorship and went on to serve as the state's governor for eight years. He had adapted to the new media era.

Stories such as this one typifying the clash of old and new campaigning were news in the 1960s and 1970s. They heralded a great change, a watershed, in the contesting of American elections that we increasingly take for granted. It is clear to us now that the professional managers, media specialists, pollsters, and advertising and public relations people have become a powerful and regular force in American political campaigning. They have replaced the state and local party organizations as the major planners and executors of campaigns.

It is easy to understand why many have come to the conclusion that the traditional grass-roots party organization has become technologically obsolete—that it has been superseded by newer, more efficient, and more timely avenues and techniques of campaigning. Therefore, the argument continues, the old-style party organization has lost an important measure of control over the contesting of American elections and, ultimately, over its candidates when they are elected to public office. But this conclusion overlooks the great adaptability of the party organizations. Throughout their history, the Democratic and Republican parties have a record of being responsive to new realities, which in part accounts for their longevity. Before relegating the parties to the sidelines, then, we need to examine their current role in political campaigns carefully.

The impact of changing technologies also illustrates a fundamental fact of political campaigning: A campaign for election operates within a much broader context, a context determined by a variety of forces beyond the immediate control of the campaigners themselves. Before we can understand the nature of campaigning and the changes in it, the full extent of this context must be considered. Previous chapters have examined the nature of the party system; the organizational strength of the local, state, and national parties; the motivations and skills of political activists; the party loyalties and participation of the electorate; and the rules governing selection of party candidates—and weighed the impact of each of these forces, and changes in them, on the candidates and their campaigns. Other contextual forces, especially campaign finance and the role of the party in government, will be dealt with in later chapters. For right now, we turn to the legal context of campaigns—the regulation and definition of the electoral process itself. The strategies of the electoral game make sense only if one first understands the context set by its particular rules.

THE ELECTORAL INSTITUTIONS

Each part of the legal framework, each rule of the electoral game, places a strategic limit on the campaign. Each adjustment in any one rule may affect one party or candidate more than another, and it may enlarge or reduce the party's role in the electoral process. Thus, electoral institutions, however much they are taken for granted, are much more than a neutral presence in the campaign and election.

Political parties around the world have been quick to realize the possible advantages to be gained by selective tinkering with this framework, and the major American parties are no exception. In the United States, though, to the parties' efforts to gain strategic advantage in this fashion must be added the efforts, often quite successful, to weaken the political parties through changes in the electoral framework. American electoral institutions bear an even stronger imprint of the Progressives and their descendants than of the parties.

The Secret Ballot

The American ballot is now uniformly secret, but it was not always so. Until the late nineteenth century, the oral vote was common in many states and jurisdictions. The voter simply stated to the electoral officials which candidates he preferred. During the nineteenth century, the oral vote was gradually replaced by ballots printed by the parties or candidates. The voter brought the ballot of his candidate or party to the polling place and deposited it in the box. Because the ballots were by no means identical, the vote was often apparent to observers. Moreover, this type of ballot discouraged ticket splitting.

The secret ballot was introduced as a way of curbing election corruption, especially vote buying; with a secret ballot, the corrupter could never be sure the "bought" vote would be delivered. Called the Australian ballot after its country of origin, the secret ballot quickly swept the nation in the 1890s. By the beginning of the twentieth century, its success was virtually complete; only South Carolina waited, until 1950, to adopt it and make its usage uniform across the country. The Australian ballot is prepared at public expense by public authorities, and it lists all candidates for office on its single, consolidated form. It is made available at the polling places only to bona fide voters, who then indicate their choices in the seclusion of a voting booth. Especially now that paper ballots have given way to electronic ballots, the secret ballot has curtailed vote buying. By involving the government in the running of elections, it has opened the door to its regulation of the parties. It also has enabled voters to split their tickets easily by voting for candidates from different parties for different offices.[2]

Ballot Form

Now that voting is done uniformly through secret ballot, it is the format of the ballot itself that has the greatest impact on the campaign, especially in how it affects the connection between candidates and their parties in the voter's mind. Two basic types of ballots are in use in the United States. In many states, the party-column ballot prevails. The grouping of all the candidates from each party together, so that voters can perceive them as a party ticket, is the distinguishing feature of the party-column form (see the Michigan ballot in Figure 11.1). A number of other states have adopted an alternative form—the office-block ballot, which groups the candidates according to the offices they seek (see the Nebraska example in Figure 11.1). By their very nature, of course, nonpartisan elections employ the office-block ballot. But they take its detachment from party cues one step further by providing no information on the ballot about the candidates' party attachments, even if they may actually have them.

The format of the ballot affects the way the voter sees the electoral contest and the nature of the choices in it. All evidence indicates that the parties are correct in their belief that the party-column ballot encourages straight-ticket or party-line voting (that is, voting for all of a party's candidates for all the offices being filled at the election). The amount of straight-ticket voting also hinges on the presence or absence on the ballot of a single square or circle (or a single lever on machines) by which the voter can, in one action, cast a vote for the entire party ticket. These squares or circles appear on most of the party-column ballots, in about twenty states at last count, but rarely are they found on the office-block ballot.[3]

Michigan party-column ballot

DEMOCRATIC PARTY | **REPUBLICAN**

NAMES OF OFFICES VOTED FOR: | ○ | ○

	Democratic	Republican
STATE GOVERNOR AND LIEUTENANT GOVERNOR (VOTE FOR NOT MORE THAN ONE)	JAMES J. BLANCHARD / MARTHA W. GRIFFITHS	RICHARD H. HEADLEE / THOMAS E. BRENNAN
SECRETARY OF STATE (VOTE FOR NOT MORE THAN ONE)	RICHARD J. AUSTIN	ELIZABETH A. ANDRUS
ATTORNEY GENERAL (VOTE FOR NOT MORE THAN ONE)	FRANK J. KELLEY	L. BROOKS PATTERSON
CONGRESSIONAL UNITED STATES SENATOR (VOTE FOR NOT MORE THAN ONE)	DONALD W. RIEGLE, JR.	PHILIP E. RUPPE
REPRESENTATIVE IN CONGRESS, DISTRICT		
LEGISLATIVE STATE SENATOR, DISTRICT (VOTE FOR NOT MORE THAN ONE)		
REPRESENTATIVE IN STATE LEGISLATURE, DIST. (VOTE FOR NOT MORE THAN ONE)		
STATE BOARDS MEMBERS OF THE STATE BOARD OF EDUCATION (VOTE FOR NOT MORE THAN TWO)	CARROLL HUTTON / BARBARA ROBERTS MASON	RONALD G. ERICKSON / JACQUELINE McGREGOR
MEMBERS OF THE BOARD OF REGENTS OF UNIVERSITY OF MICHIGAN (VOTE FOR NOT MORE THAN TWO)	SARAH GODDARD POWER / THOMAS A. ROACH	ROCKWELL T. GUST, JR. / ELLEN M. TEMPLIN
MEMBERS OF THE BOARD OF TRUSTEES OF MICHIGAN STATE UNIVERSITY (VOTE FOR NOT MORE THAN TWO)	JOHN B. BRUFF / BOBBY D. CRIM	LAURA HEUSER / GEORGE A. McMANUS, JR.
MEMBERS OF THE BOARD OF GOVERNORS OF WAYNE STATE UNIVERSITY (VOTE FOR NOT MORE THAN TWO)	MICHAEL EINHEUSER / MILDRED JEFFREY	NANCY BOYKIN / SAM TRENTACOSTA

Form No. P-881

Nebraska office-bloc ballot

Senatorial Ticket

FOR UNITED STATES SENATOR
Vote for ONE

☐ Jim Keck .... Republican
☐ Edward Zorinsky .... Democrat
☐ Virginia Walsh .... By Petition
☐

Congressional Ticket

FOR REPRESENTATIVE IN CONGRESS FIRST DISTRICT
Vote for ONE

☐ Doug Bereuter .... Republican
☐ Curt Donaldson............. Democrat
☐

FOR REPRESENTATIVE IN CONGRESS SECOND DISTRICT
Vote for ONE

☐ Hal Daub .... Republican
☐ Richard M. Fellman .... Democrat
☐

FOR REPRESENTATIVE IN CONGRESS THIRD DISTRICT
Vote for ONE

☐ Virginia Smith .... Republican
☐

State Ticket

FOR GOVERNOR
Vote in ONE Square Only

☐ Charles Thone — Governor / Roland A. Luedtke — Lieutenant Governor } Republican
☐ Bob Kerrey — Governor / Don McGinley — Lieutenant Governor } Democrat
☐ .... Governor / .... Lieutenant Governor }

FOR MEMBER OF THE STATE BOARD OF EDUCATION SEVENTH DISTRICT
Vote for ONE

☐ Daniel G. Urwiller
☐ Gerald L. Clausen

FOR MEMBER OF THE STATE BOARD OF EDUCATION EIGHTH DISTRICT
Vote for ONE

☐ William C. Ramsey
☐ Eileen Dietz
☐

FOR MEMBER OF THE LEGISLATURE SECOND DISTRICT
Vote for ONE

☐ Calvin F. Carsten
☐ Boyd Linder
☐

FOR MEMBER OF THE LEGISLATURE FOURTH DISTRICT
Vote for ONE

☐ Gary E. Hannibal
☐ Bev Laing

FOR MEMBER OF THE LEGISLATURE SIXTH DISTRICT
Vote for ONE

☐ Gayle L. Stock
☐ Peter Hoagland

FOR MEMBER OF THE LEGISLATURE EIGHTH DISTRICT
Vote for ONE

☐ Wayne Hohndorf
☐ Vard Johnson
☐

FOR MEMBER OF THE LEGISLATURE TENTH DISTRICT
Vote for ONE

☐ Carol McBride Pirsch
☐ James S. Beutel
☐

Figure 11.1 The party-column and office-bloc ballots: selected portions of the Michigan and Nebraska general-election ballots, 1982.

Three other aspects of ballot form deserve mention. First, almost every ballot makes some provision for voters to write in the names of persons not listed on the ballot. The success of write-in candidates is so rare, however, that it is hardly a real question in American politics.[4] Second, the order in which candidates' names appear may affect the outcome of the election. American voters have shown a notorious disposition to vote for the first name on a list of candidates.[5] Ballot position probably confers the greatest advantages in primaries and other nonpartisan contests in which no information about the candidates is included on the ballot. Recognizing the value of being listed first on a ballot, some states randomly select the candidates' placements, while others rotate positions throughout all the ballots so that each candidate is first on an equal number. But the prize of appearing first on the ballot sometimes is awarded to the incumbents, further heightening their electoral chances. In the general election, at issue is party position. The states frequently give the preferred position to the majority party and virtually always give more prominence to the major parties than the minor parties.

Finally, the American ballot traditionally has been a long ballot. It reflects the American tradition of electing, rather than appointing, a great number of state and local officials. The major observable effect of the long ballot is voter fatigue. With so many contests on the ballot at the same time, voters must gather a considerable amount of information about the candidates to cast a meaningful vote. In 1990, for example, San Francisco voters faced a ballot containing seventeen initiatives and constitutional amendments, eleven bond measures, eleven local propositions, plus an array of statewide elected offices. The ballot guide provided voters by the California Secretary of State was more than 200 pages in length. In such an election, it is hardly surprising that many voters find that the price of acquiring the requisite amount of information exceeds their sense of the worth of some offices and selectively abstain from voting. Such partial voting (or roll-off) is most common for minor offices (and referendum issues) and can be practiced by as many as 20 or 30 percent of the voters at a given election.[6] Voter fatigue of course also leads voters to employ various heuristics or shortcuts in making their choices, such as voting for a particular party or for the right-sounding names (as was exemplified in the votes for LaRouche supporters in Illinois discussed in Chapter 9, p. 207).

Structure and Rules of the Choice

Overwhelmingly, American officeholders are elected from single-member constituencies by plurality election. Typically, only one person per constituency is elected to a city council, to the legislature, to the local mayoralty; and the candidate who wins the most votes (that is, the plurality) is elected. Even in cases of multimember districts, the principle often is not altered: Usually the voter casts the same number of votes as there are officials to be elected from the district, so that the plurality principle still governs. In a two-member state legislative district, for example, each voter casts two votes; and the two candidates with the greatest number of votes are the winners.[7]

Conducting elections under plurality rules has important consequences for the American parties. First, as discussed in Chapter 2, plurality rules and single-member districts discourage minor political parties (and candidates) by giving them no share of the elective offices. Receiving 10 or 20 percent of the vote will rarely win any public offices in the plurality elections of American politics, but in several European democracies which employ proportional representation, it can win parliamentary seats and cabinet positions. Second, by withholding any share of political representation from parties that cannot hope to capture a plurality, the plurality rule affects all of the parties. It increases both the electoral risk of being ideologically distinctive and the need to broaden the party's appeal in quest of a plurality victory; thus, it is less conductive to programmatic (or ideological) parties. Third, plurality elections weaken the hand of the party vis-a-vis its candidates. In many elections in multimember districts operating under proportional representation rules, the voters cast a ballot for a list of party candidates rather than individual candidates. In drawing up their list and determining what position on it each candidate will have, the parties directly affect the chances of election for each of their candidates. The prevailing single-member, plurality structure of American elections, on the contrary, reinforces both the two-party system of broadly based parties and the independence of candidates and officeholders from the parties.

The American states have experimented very little with the systems of proportional representation (PR) that so often enchant the other democracies of the world. In these systems, which are of necessity based on multimember constituencies, the voter casts his or her vote for a party slate of candidates. The parties then share the seats according to the percentage of the votes they polled, as was described in Chapter 2.[8] Proportional representation, though, is not a complete stranger to the American context. New York City adopted a variety of proportional representation from 1938 to 1947, with a resulting growth and representation of minor political parties. In modern times, proportional representation has been employed in state presidential nomination contests. The Democratic party now requires it, and the GOP has followed suit in many states (see Chapter 10). Understanding the complexities and the strategic options of proportional representation and thereby taking full advantage of its particular virtues has not come easy to many American voters, however, unaccustomed as they are to anything other than "first past the post" or plurality elections.

Election Calendars

Even a feature so seemingly innocuous as when elections are held can have important consequences for the candidates and the parties. Since 1845, when the Congress exercised its constitutionally granted power (in Article I, Section 4, and Article II, Section 1) to determine the dates of presidential and congressional elections, federal elections have been held almost uniformly on the first Tuesday after the first Monday in November of the even-numbered years—every two years for congressional contests and every four years for the presidency. Considerations of economy have dictated that statewide elections and many local elections be held at the same time, so an early November election day has become the norm. Many state and even more local elections, though, are held in the odd-numbered, non-federal-election, years.

Scheduling elections for various offices at the same time, on the same ballot, links the electoral fates of their contestants. Politicians and political analysts long have recognized that a voter's decision on one contest can influence other choices on the same ballot.[9] Such so-called coattail effects—the ability of a candidate at the top of the ticket to carry into office "on his coattails" his party's candidates on the same ticket—are usually thought to flow from the more important to the less important office, thereby linking the fate of party candidates to the candidate at the top of the party ticket and giving candidates for lesser offices an incentive to want strong candidates for the leading offices.

It generally is in the parties' interest to enhance this linkage, for it fosters party cohesion. Progressive reformers, as well as some incumbent officeholders and candidates for office, however, have not shared this interest. They have worked to weaken this linkage through electoral devices such as nonpartisan elections, office block ballots, and the scheduling of state and local contests in the nonpresidential years. Most states now hold their elections for governor and other top state officials on the second November after the presidential election in conjunction with the midterm congressional contests, and a few even have chosen years when no federal contests at all are on the ballot. Most local elections are scheduled at some other time. This practice of insulating elected officials from one another limits the possibilities for coattail effects and has had the understandable effect of reducing the cohesive-ness of the party in government.[10]

The Electoral Districts

The size and composition of the districts from which officials are elected also affects campaign strategies. Small, compact districts encourage a kind of face-to-face cam-paigning that simply is not possible in a large, sprawling constituency; voters in the lat-ter may be reachable only through the mass media. The partisan composition of a district influences what the parties and candidates do in a different way. By setting the initial odds of victory or defeat, it determines the quality of the candidates who are attracted to the race and, quite often, the level of effort that will be expended by candi-dates and parties in the quest for victory. Districts with lopsided majorities in favor of one party discourage minority-party activity, just as districts that are well balanced between the parties can be scenes of spirited campaigns by both candidates and parties.

The peculiar American institution of the electoral college produces another kind of electoral district effect. Since the 1830s, American presidents have been chosen by a faceless group of electors in each state, who in turn are selected in accordance with which presidential candidate wins the most popular votes in that state. Victory comes from winning a majority of the state electoral votes rather than compiling the highest national vote total, and the strategies of presidential candidates are adjusted accord-ingly. Candidates tend to concentrate their attention on the states with the largest num-ber of electoral votes and the highest degree of interparty competition, which generally turn out to be the largest and most diverse states. They typically write off the less pop-ulous states or states in which the result is predictable regardless of their efforts.[11]

POLITICAL CONSEQUENCES OF ELECTORAL LAW

Perhaps the chief impact of American electoral laws on the politics of campaigning has been to focus attention on the candidates rather than on the parties. The Ameri-can electoral process is relatively free from such institutions as parliamentary-cabinet government or proportional representation, which encourage the voter to see elections as contests between parties for control of government. On the contrary, such details of electoral law as the office-block ballot and even single-member dis-tricts (in the absence of a parliamentary system) tend to structure the electoral choice as a series of contests between individual candidates and not as a single, multifaceted campaign between two or more great parties. Nonpartisan elections for lower-level office have even further reduced the visibility of the party in elections, and the sepa-rate scheduling of contests at different levels of government makes it difficult for the parties to coordinate their programmatic activities.

Who Benefits?

The details of American electoral law often do not touch the parties or candidates equally. If voting machines confuse less–well-educated, lower SES voters, and if office-block ballots encourage greater voter fatigue (roll-off) among less-educated voters,[12] then the disadvantages may accrue more to the Democratic party. If the state refuses absentee ballots to travelers, whether on business or pleasure, the disadvantages may strike mainly the upper-status Republicans. If the state encourages and facilitates absentee voting as some have recently done, by contrast, it can redound to the benefit of these Republicans or any well-organized local party. Any ballot form that facilitates party-ticket voting works to the advantage of the majority party in the constituency. Prime ballot position helps the incumbent and the majority party; so do designations of incumbency printed on the ballot. Even the hours and places for polling may have some marginal benefits for one party or the other.

Just how aware the parties and state legislators are of the possible advantages in refining electoral law is not easy to say. It is always difficult to establish the motives of legislators, especially when those motives may not be of the highest type. Occasionally, however, an attempt is so persistent, so transparent, that the motivation clearly is party or political advantage. For example:

> In the state of Ohio . . . the Republican majority tried to gain an advantage for itself by tampering with the election machinery. In 1940 Governor Bricker tried to avoid the influences of F.D.R.'s "coattails" by calling a special session of the legislature which approved a separation of the ballot carrying national races from the one on which state and local races appeared. Bricker reasoned that if a normally Republican voter who was determined to vote for Roosevelt had to use a second ballot in state races he would be less likely to vote a straight Democratic ticket (the ballots were later consolidated once again to capitalize on Eisenhower's coattails). In 1949 over $85,000 was spent in a campaign to substitute the Office Block ballot for the Party Column ballot in an effort to save Senator Robert Taft from defeat in the bitter 1950 election. . . . The Taft forces thought that by eliminating the party lever they would substantially reduce the number of straight Democratic votes and thus increase the Senator's chances among normally Democratic, working class voters.

Key quotes Taft as claiming that the change "was responsible 'for something between 100,000 and 200,000' of his total majority of 430,000."[13]

Legislative Districting and Redistricting

The primary institutional device through which American parties and politicians— but rarely their counterparts in other nations—have sought an advantage in electoral politics has been through the drawing of constituency lines. The changing population sizes of various constituencies, documented through each decennial census, have provided regular opportunities to redraw district lines, as is mandated in federal and state constitutions. How these opportunities have been turned to political advantage is a continuing story of the creativity and resourcefulness of American parties and politicians.

Partisan Redistricting through Malapportionment and Gerrymandering   Traditionally, there have been two general tactics for turning redistricting opportunities into political gains. The first and more obvious of the two has been simply to ignore population changes and the often-constitutional obligation to redistrict. Many states pursued this tactic for the better part of the twentieth century as they refused to transfer political representation, and hence political power, from the shrinking rural and small town populations to the growing cities. By the 1960s, many state legislatures and the U.S. House of Representatives better represented the largely rural America of 1900 than the urban nation it had become. Such "malapportionment" worked to the disadvantage of Republicans in the South and Democrats elsewhere—and of the needs of cities everywhere. In a series of decisions in the early 1960s, however, the United States Supreme Court put an end to these inequities by requiring districts of equal population size to divide up a state's congressional and state/local legislative seats. As the courts have applied the "one person, one vote" rule to constituencies of all varieties, they have closed off this classically American way of exploiting the rules of the electoral game.[14]

More subtle and less easy to detect, the gerrymander survives, and even seems to have been resuscitated in recent years. It consists of one party's drawing district lines in such a way as to use its own popular vote most efficiently while forcing the other party to use its vote inefficiently. That goal can be achieved either by dividing and diluting pockets of the other party's strength to prevent it from winning office, or (if the other party's strength is too great for dilution) by consolidating its voters into a few districts and forcing it to win elections by large, wasteful majorities. Sometimes, the resulting constituencies, instead of being compact and contiguous, have bizarre and fanciful shapes. Which party reaps the advantage of the gerrymander traditionally has depended on which party controls the redistricting process (see box on following page).

Federal Involvement in Redistricting   As in so many areas, the states' traditional control over the redrawing of district lines has been eroded by federal action. Beginning in the 1960s, federal courts have taken an increasingly active role in the task, in response to suits charging legislatures with evading constitutional standards of equal representation. Invoking a "one person, one vote" standard, as discussed earlier, the courts first struck down long-standing apportionment schemes (some of which had not been changed in decades) that had resulted in districts of greatly unequal population size. Subsequently they worked their way, case-by-case, toward the standard of "precise mathematical equality" in district sizes in giving meaning to the prescription of one person, one vote. But the courts resisted, at least for a time, the temptation to invade the "political thicket" of gerrymandering—that is, to reject plans for equal-sized districts because of how the lines were drawn.[15]

With the passage of the voting rights acts and its extensions, especially the 1982 version, the U.S. Justice Department also became an active player in the redistricting process. To protect the voting rights of minorities, who had suffered from decades of disenfranchisement and discrimination, the Voting Rights Act and its court interpretations required many states, including all southern states, to "preclear" proposed electoral changes—from redistricting plans to voting laws—with Justice Department officials. Nine state redistricting plans were rejected by Justice after the 1980 census.[16]

The reapportionment process and federal involvement in it have taken a new turn in the 1990s. Under the 1982 Voting Rights Act, the states were required to go

THE ART OF GERRYMANDERING, THEN AND NOW

Gerrymandering is the nickname given to the artful drawing of legislative district lines by the party in power so as to give it a greater share of legislative seats than its share of votes.

> The term is derived from the name of Governor Gerry, of Massachusetts, who, in 1811, signed a bill readjusting the representative districts so as to favor the Democrats and weaken the Federalists, although the last named party polled nearly two-thirds of the votes cast. A fancied resemblance of a map of the districts thus treated led [Gilbert] Stuart, the painter, to add a few lines with his pencil, and say to Mr. Russell, editor of the *Boston Centinel,* "That will do for a salamander." Russell glanced at it: "Salamander?" said he, "Call it a Gerrymander!" The epithet took at once and became a Federalist warcry, the map caricature being published as a campaign document.[17]

Because redistricting is an inherently political process, gerrymandering is practiced every ten years when the states set about to redraw their legislative district lines to take into account the new distribution of population as determined by the census. Even within the strict requirement of equal population sizes, the creativity of those drawing district lines, now guided by computer programs designed to maximize whatever goal they seek, is impressive. In the 1990s, for example, new districts were created which rival Gerry's original "salamander" in their bizarre shapes. For example, in describing North Carolina's 160-mile-long twelfth Congressional District, it is joked that a car driving down Interstate 85 with its doors open would strike every eligible voter; and Louisiana's originally drawn fourth Congressional District was labeled the "mark of Zorro" because it cut a Z-shaped swath from the top nearly to the bottom of the state to find enough black voters for a black-majority district.

one step further in their reapportionment efforts. They were to construct legislative districts so as to maximize the opportunities for black and Hispanic candidates to win office. Many states, operating through a legislative coalition of Republicans and black Democrats and with the encouragement of the Bush administration Justice Department, met this requirement by creating new districts with clear black and Hispanic majorities—so-called majority-minority districts. These districting schemes have come under critical scrutiny by the courts. Recently, the Supreme Court has taken a dim view of using race as the "predominant factor" in drawing district lines. It has required the states to redraw existing district lines and has upheld subsequent reductions in the number of majority-minority districts. Whether this signals a wholesale judicial assault on racial gerrymandering or merely a judicial fine-tuning of the most blatant gerrymanders remains to be seen.[18]

Are There Still Political Gains from Gerrymandering?　The conventional wisdom is that effective gerrymandering can greatly advantage those interests that are drawing the district lines. Usually this is thought to be the majority party in the state, which typically controls the reapportionment process, but plans also have seemed to protect incumbent officeholders. Empirical research conducted in the 1970s and 1980s, however, found that in most states redistricting had minimal partisan or proincumbent effects, especially after the first few years. The notorious congressional gerrymanders of the 1980s in California and Indiana, however, stood out as exceptions to the minimal-effects rule. The California plan clearly advantaged the Democrats, while the GOP's effort in Indiana seemed to benefit the Republicans— although not nearly as decisively or longlastingly (the state's congressional delegation, 6–5 Democratic in 1981, was 8–2 Democratic 10 years later!). With these exceptions, then, by the 1980s it seemed that the traditional advantages from control over redistricting had diminished.[19]

The apparent erosion of the partisan advantages in redistricting may be a result of the scrutiny the courts and the Justice Department have been giving to reapportionment plans. Their involvement no doubt has stimulated more challenges and thereby more public attention to state plans which appeared to have gerrymandered for party advantage or to protect incumbents. Legal authorities are also more willing to draw district lines across the lines of civil subdivisions (for example, counties) and thus across the lines of local party organization. The result is to make it harder in yet another way for party organizations to maintain a role in electoral politics.

But the apparent decline of the advantages of the gerrymander has been proven premature by events of the 1990s, as ostensibly nonpartisan legal requirements have been turned to partisan advantage by the clever tactics of strategic politicians. In implementing the Voting Rights Act's charge to increase electoral opportunities for members of minority groups, Republicans in many states (especially in the South and Southwest) joined with minority leaders to create the new majority-minority districts referred to above. For minorities, these new districts promised an increased group presence in Congress and state legislatures. For Republicans, the concentration of black and Hispanic voters into a few majority-minority districts offered increased electoral opportunities in the now less-Democratic adjacent districts. This compact initially produced the expected benefits for both groups: American legislatures had more minority group members than ever before, and the Republicans made significant gains in previously Democratic strongholds, especially in the South.[20] Whether this increase in black and Hispanic representatives at the cost of decreased Democratic strength in legislative chambers is in the end beneficial to these minority groups remains a subject of intense debate, although the issue may become moot as federal courts are forcing a redrawing of district lines under less racially-conscious rules.

CAMPAIGN STRATEGY

The folk wisdom about all aspects of American politics is more than ample, but on the subject of campaign tactics it is overwhelming. Much of it has been brought together into little books on campaigning that read like modern how-to-do-it manuals. Because many of the books have been written by advertising and public relations specialists, much of the wisdom has a modern tone. Candidates are advised on dress and makeup for TV, and there is a good deal of emphasis on catchy phrases and slogans.[21]

There is much of value in the received wisdom about American campaigning. Generally, it represents the distillation of concrete experience. Yet, it suffers from two deficiencies that themselves are generally warnings about the crafts of political campaigning. The conventional wisdom seems to suggest, first of all, that most political campaigns are run on a master battle plan adhered to with almost military discipline and precision. In reality, most American political campaigns lurch along from one improvisation to another, from one immediate crisis to another. They are frequently underorganized, underplanned, underfinanced, and understaffed; consequently, they often play by ear with a surprising lack of information.

The folk wisdom also suggests that there are principles of good campaigning that have an almost universal applicability. In truth, however, optimum campaign strategy depends on a great number of variables, and the only general rule is that there is no general rule. The most critical variables probably are the skills of the candidate, the nature of the constituency and its electorate, the office being sought, the nature of the electoral system, the party organizations in the constituency, and the availability of political resources. The chief early task of campaign strategists is the sober evaluation of these various factors and of the consequent demands and limits they place on the campaign.

The nub of the strategic task in a campaign is selectivity in the expenditures of scarce time, energy, and resources in order to achieve the maximum effect on the electorate. The candidate and his or her managers must decide how to spend each unit of campaign resources so that it will return the maximum number of votes. Will they work on areas normally loyal to the other party in hopes of cutting losses there, or will they hammer at their own party strongholds? They must also decide how to tailor their appeals to different parts of the electorate. For some of the voters, there must be stimuli to party loyalty; for others, appeals of issue or personality are necessary. The problem is to know the variety and diversity of the voters, the likely bases of their decisions, and the ways of reaching and stimulating them differentially.[22]

All these decisions must be made within the context of political reality, and the political characteristics of the election race probably set the chief limits of campaign strategy. The presence or absence of an incumbent in the race and the competitiveness of the constituency exceed all other considerations in significance. Those two factors, perhaps, determine whether there is a possibility of victory. They affect the ability of the candidate to recruit workers and resources, to line up the support of groups to attract the attention of voters. The fact that a candidate is an incumbent running for reelection in a competitive district or a nonincumbent of the minority party in a noncompetitive district, for example, sets major limits on campaign strategy before the imaginations of the candidate and his or her advisors even begin to work.

Finally, the very nature of the office being sought places important constraints on the nature of the campaign and its strategies. The most visible campaigns are those for the most important offices—for governorships, major city offices, for president of course, as well as Congress. Candidates for them tend to have name recognition already, and the attention given to the campaign increases it. They can raise large sums of money for splashy media campaigns aimed at reaching the mass of voters. The great majority of campaigns in the United States, however, are far less visible. Candidates whose names are hardly household words and whose campaign resources are modest must run far less ambitious campaigns. They must seek different ways to reach the voter, in fact. One study finds, for example, that such candidates tend to campaign indirectly—that is, to rely on the building of voter support through intermediary devices, such as the endorsement by better known political figures or the support from organized groups, whether of the party or not.[23]

THE NEW CAMPAIGNING

Within less than a generation, changes amounting to a revolution have altered much of American political campaigning. The skills of the mass-media specialists have brought new persuasive techniques to bear on the American electorate with attendant fears that presidents and lesser officials are now sold to the electorate much as Madison Avenue sells a new mouthwash or toothpaste. With the new techniques have also come the new technicians—the campaign-management specialists, a new breed of sophisticated, hard-headed advisors who, as political mercenaries, deploy their troops and artillery for a suitable fee.

The New Campaign Professionals

Professional campaign consultants have been drawn from the worlds of advertising and public relations, as well as from political work of one kind or another. Not only have they prospered in American politics, they have also exported their campaign expertise to the rest of the democratic world.[24] Campaign firms and specialists come in all sizes and shapes. Some are experts in the development of mass-media messages; others in how to place media ads. Some can provide organizational skills, sometimes even lists of local party people and possible volunteer workers; they can organize rallies, coffee parties, phone banks, and hand-shaking tours of shopping centers. Some provide lawyers and accountants to steer the campaign away from legal shoals and to speed the reporting of campaign finances to the appropriate regulatory bodies. Some are publicists who write speeches and press releases, some sample public opinion, and some are very skilled in raising money. Some can offer virtually all of those services. It is a profession of both specialists and generalists, of both contractors and subcontractors. In it there is a scope and a skill for every candidate's need. There is no better testimony to the takeover of modern campaigns by "hired-gun" specialists, displacing the candidate loyalist of previous times, than the fact that the names of some of these campaign professionals—for example, Roger Ailes, Charles Black, Patrick Caddell, James Carville, David Garth, Peter Hart, Mary Matalin, Ed Rollins, Robert Squier, Bob Teeter, Richard Viguerie—have become as familiar as some of the candidates for office.[25]

The existence of this new breed of campaign professionals signifies a major departure from past practices, at least in contests for major offices, when campaign expertise was drawn from a candidate's loyal staff or from political party workers.

Instead, these professional campaign consultants work as independent political entrepreneurs in the service of different candidates, often several in the same year. Their skills are available to candidates who can pay their fees, although they almost always restrict themselves to clients from only one of the parties and some may impose an ideological criterion as well. Even though the parties in recent years have built impressive in-house campaign expertise and often play an important intermediary role in bringing together consultants and candidates, campaigns for the most visible offices still are dominated by these independent consultants. Neither from the party in government nor from the party organization, the new professionals occupy a political niche on the periphery of the political parties.

The New Sources of Information

Modern technology and its social science applications have opened up new sources of information and knowledge to the political campaigner. Computers permit a party to keep records about constituencies and to process that information rapidly. Carefully kept records usually yield a faster and more accurate answer to how the twenty-first ward went four years ago, for example, than even the most experienced party workers can. Wily parties and candidates have similarly used scholarly data and findings on the demographic bases of Republican and Democratic strength. Perhaps the first sophisticated use of computers in campaigns occurred when the managers of John F. Kennedy's presidential campaign commissioned a simulation of the 1960 electorate as an aid to campaign planning.[26] Other candidates have computerized records of canvassing so that they can quickly compile lists of voters to contact on election day. Computers also have been used to great advantage to produce lists of potential contributors and to locate positions taken by opponents on almost every conceivable campaign issue.

No new avenue to political knowledge has been more fully exploited than the public opinion poll. It may be employed at the beginning of a campaign to assess the political issues uppermost in the minds of voters. Early polls can also develop information about how the voting public views the candidates; the campaign then can devote its attention to overcoming the unflattering parts of the candidate's profile. Polls can also indicate whether the campaign ought to capitalize on party loyalties or whether the candidate would be better advised to ignore an unpopular party or candidate at the top of the ticket. During the campaign, a poll or two can chart its progress and indicate where time and resources ought to be concentrated in its waning days (see box on p. 260).[27]

Parties and candidates have not been uniformly willing or able to avail themselves of such new techniques. Much of the knowledge thus far accumulated, especially about voting behavior, derives chiefly from presidential campaigns and elections and has only limited applicability to less-visible contests. Also, many of the techniques are beyond the resources of local campaigns, although recent technical support efforts by the parties' national committees and congressional campaign committees (reviewed in Chapter 4) have made these new tools of campaigning available to even the campaigns with the slimmest budgets. The difficulty runs deeper, however. American political campaigns, despite popular impressions to the contrary, have rarely been run on a solid

DAILY READINGS OF THE PUBLIC PULSE: THE TRACKING POLLS

One innovation in gathering information about the electorate is the so-called tracking poll, based on the daily monitoring of opinion. The first extensive usage of tracking polls was by campaign consultant Richard Wirthlin's firm Decision/Making/Information for Ronald Reagan's reelection campaign in 1984. D/M/I conducted 250 telephone interviews nationwide per night beginning June 1, 1984. They increased the number to 500 per night on October 5 and then to 1,000 per night on November 1. These daily samples were large enough to be able to detect immediate public reactions to particular campaign events and played an important role in the strategic planning of the Reagan campaign.

base of information. Thousands of party organizations around the country never have kept even basic voting data by precincts, wards, townships, cities, and counties. Thus, such a shift to the "new knowledge" involves a basic commitment to knowledge itself, as well as a willingness to bear the costs of acquiring it.

The New Techniques of Persuasion

Campaigns are basically exercises in mass persuasion, and the commercial arts of persuasion have increasingly been applied to them. There was a time when strong party organizations were the great persuaders in American campaigns. Changes in the organizations and in American politics, however, have greatly diminished that role. Party organizations do not control votes and turn them out as they once did. It is left increasingly to candidates to do their own persuading of voters.

Predominant among the new persuasive techniques are the mass-communications media. Even old-style communications are pursued with the media in mind: A candidate takes the time and effort to address a rally or meeting largely in the hope that it will produce a news report or a brief film clip on the local TV news. (Of course, the question of whether it produces a news report is not left to chance; the staff prepares news releases and copies of the speech for the local media.) Early in the campaign, candidates may vie to commit choice TV time and billboard space for the concluding weeks of the campaign. As the campaign progresses, the candidates' faces, names, and slogans blossom on billboards, newspaper ads, radio and TV spot announcements—even on lawn signs, automobile bumpers, and construction fences.

For the offices for which the new campaigning is most appropriate, television has become the major medium of persuasion. Time on TV may consume the majority of the campaign's funds. In the early and inexpensive days of television, candidates bought large chunks of time for entire speeches that were carried nationwide, but this is no longer done. Increasingly, the political message is compressed into the thirty- or sixty-second spot advertisement that can be run everywhere or targeted to particular areas of the country. The writing, the filming, and the placing of those messages (after the pro football game? before the evening news?) become a major activity of the campaign and, except in the case of the publicly financed presidential campaign, so does the ability to raise the necessary money to pay for them. Thus, what was a long, stem-winding speech by the candidate in a sweaty hall fifty or sixty years ago is now a few carefully crafted visual images and a very simple text put together by professionals. More people depend upon television for their political news than upon any other medium, and the intermediary role between candidates and voters once dominated by local group and party leaders seems to have eroded as well (see box on p. 262).[28]

At the same time, high-speed computers have brought the postal service back to the center of the campaign. Computers can produce personalized, targeted letters by the millions. They are effective both for campaigning and for fund raising; the well-written letter seeking money is indeed also an appeal for the candidate seeking the funds.

> Long gone, of course, are the days when a direct mailer began a form letter with an awkward "Dear Mr. Smith," printed in different type, usually above or below the line. Now, the "computer" types each letter individually, using the receiver's name throughout the text, in exactly the type of the letter body. If a letter to a Congressman is suggested, the computer knows the name of that representative by the person's zip code. The one thing direct mail letters are not is dispassionate. "You've got to have a devil," said Mr. (Roger) Craver. "If you don't have a devil, you're in trouble." . . . "You need a letter filled with ideas and passion. . . . It does not beat around the bush, it is not academic, it is not objective."[29]

Gradually building a list of contributors and supporters—a list that can be returned to with good results—is also building for the political future. It is one of the many advantages an experienced and veteran campaigner enjoys.

All of this is not to argue that the traditional campaign techniques are obsolete. Handshaking on the streets and in the stores, speeches before anyone who will listen, endorsements by local groups and party organizations—all the old ways are very much alive. The new campaigning is too expensive for many candidates, particularly at the local level. Also, these techniques are inefficient for candidates in small constituencies because the radio, television, billboard, and newspaper space they purchase is wasted in great part on readers, viewers, and listeners who cannot vote for them.[30]

THE NEW CAMPAIGNING FOR THE PRESIDENCY

Nowhere are the techniques and technicians of the new campaigning more visible than in the presidential election campaigns. The campaign for the presidency is in many ways the generic American political campaign "writ large." Its main problems and tasks are different in degree but similar in kind. Yet, many of the usual campaign problems are heightened by the nature of the presidential office and constituency. Keeping posted on how the campaign is going is a tremendous problem for the candidate. The vast expanse of the country, the variety of local conditions, and the candidate's isolation from the grass roots make any kind of assessment difficult. To solve this problem, modern presidential candidates have relied on professional poll-

THE MADE-FOR-TELEVISION CANDIDATE

Source: Copyright 1986, Raleigh News and Observer. Distributed by Los Angeles Times Syndicate. Reprinted with permission.

sters to supplement and, increasingly, replace the reports of local politicians. Campaigning across a huge country also places heavy demands on the candidates. Their packed schedules and their need to address the concerns of varied audiences (all within the clear view of a press corps that follows them almost continuously) put exceptional physical and mental strains on a candidate.

Given these difficulties, it is little wonder that presidential candidates find it hard to resist channeling much of their campaign through the mass media, especially television. A media-based campaign possesses a number of advantages for presidential aspirants. Through it, they can communicate efficiently with a national audience, reaching more potential voters than they ever could hope for with any series of local campaign appearances. Nonetheless, these local appearances remain important for the free media coverage they generate. This very fact has fostered a proliferation of campaign activities that are staged mostly, sometimes even wholly, for the media coverage they attract. Presidential candidates also transmit their message through paid media advertising, especially on television. Of course, such extensive usage of the media by presidential candidates is made possible by sums of money that few other candidates can command, but, ironically, it is made necessary by the limits on campaign expenditures that go along with public funding of the presidential campaigns.[31]

TO WHAT EFFECT THE CAMPAIGN?

Many candidates—whether their campaigns are old or new style—have wondered about the impact of a campaign's sound and fury. The barrage of words and pictures is staggering, but is anyone listening or watching? Has the apparent upsurge in negative political advertising turned voters away? Do the spot commercials, the literature, even the canvassing make any difference in the ultimate voting decision? No one really knows for sure.

Selective Exposure

Logical deduction leads to some plausible and probably reliable answers. We know that American voters expose themselves to a campaign with great selectivity. First of all, they tend to surround themselves with friends, literature, and even personal experiences (such as rallies and meetings) that support their perceptions and loyalties. Furthermore, they tend to perceive what they are exposed to through a filter of stable, long-term orientations, the most stable of which is loyalty to a political party for those who have it. What we think of as a campaign may to some extent be two campaigns—one party and its candidates shouting at their supporters and the other party and its candidates doing the same. Thus, a good deal of American campaigning has the effect of stimulating, activating, and reinforcing given political predispositions, as it always has. Much of the campaign, too, is directed as much at getting people out to vote as at influencing their voting decision.[32]

The Dominance of Short-Term Impressions

Yet, in the contemporary environment of weakened partisan loyalties and large numbers of independents, the potential of the campaign for shaping voter perceptions of the candidates may be higher than it has ever been. As long-term voter commitments to party become less important, short-term impressions come to predominate, especially where there is no incumbent candidate in the race. Recent campaigns have witnessed tremendous swings in public support for candidates right up to election day and an increase in the effectiveness of personal attacks by opponents and single-issue groups through negative television advertising (see box on p. 264),[33] both signs of an electorate that lacks deep-seated commitments to candidates or to parties.

The Impact of Television

Now that the traditional intermediaries (local party and group leaders) seem to play a reduced role as cue givers for voters, television has become the primary medium for winning their support. The importance of television for their campaigns is a fact

A CASE STUDY IN NEGATIVE ADVERTISING: THE WILLIE HORTON COMMERCIAL

The most infamous in these negative ads is the thirty-second "Willie Horton" commercial, aired nationally for twenty-eight days on cable television during the 1988 presidential race. In comparing the positions of presidential candidates Bush and Dukakis on crime, it linked Dukakis to a controversial prison-furlough program adopted while he was governor. The ad stated "Bush supports the death penalty for first-degree murderers. . . . Dukakis not only opposes the death penalty, he allowed first-degree murderers to have weekend passes from prison. One was Willie Horton, who murdered a boy in a robbery, stabbing him 19 times. . . . Despite a life sentence, Horton received 10 weekend passes from prison. (He) fled, kidnapped a young couple, stabbing the man and repeatedly raping his girlfriend." As the narrator recounted these details, a glaring Willie Horton was pictured and the words *kidnapping, stabbing,* and *raping* were flashed on the screen. The conclusion left no doubt about what message was to be drawn from the ad: "Weekend prison passes. Dukakis on crime."

The Willie Horton commercial was devastatingly effective. Even though it was not directly attributable to the Bush campaign and was subsequently denounced by Bush and his campaign manager, it redounded to Bush's benefit in the presidential race. The ad was produced, it turned out, by advertising consultants long associated with the Republican party and paid for by an independent conservative political-action committee, which claimed that it had the tacit approval of the Bush campaign organization and had offered Bush campaign leaders the opportunity to veto the ad.

that few modern-day politicians have failed to appreciate. As Austin Ranney has observed, they recognize that in the modern

> world of mass constituencies and of voters who would rather stay home and watch television than attend a political rally in some auditorium, appearing on television is the closest candidates can get to all but a handful of their constituents and provides by far the most cost-effective campaigning device they have. Moreover, . . . while eye-to-eye contact and a warm handshake between politician and voter may be best, having the politician's voice and face appear in living color on the tube a few feet away from the constituent in his own living room is surely second best.[34]

The predominance of television as a source of political information by now is unquestioned, and the data bear this out. By the early 1960s, shortly after virtually all homes had televisions in the United States, Americans reported that television had replaced newspapers as their most important and most credible source of political news, and TV's advantage has remained large ever since.[35] Television also has supplanted the political parties in providing campaign information. Only 22 percent of a national sample of the adult public reported being personally contacted on behalf of a presidential candidate during the 1992 campaigns, and only 39 percent said they received materials supporting a candidate through the mail. By contrast, 94 percent of the respondents paid at least some attention to television news about the campaign.[36] Even if the figures for television may be subject to some inflation, exposure to it is so much more substantial than to any other intermediary that no one, especially not candidates for office, doubts its importance as an information source in the modern political campaign.

In spite of their importance as a source of information about politics, the actual impact of the media on political attitudes and behavior is unclear. There is ample evidence that the media do not directly determine political preferences, in large part because the modern media provide fairly balanced coverage of political candidates.[37] Rather, media influence is more subtle. By the kinds of issues and events it emphasizes, the media affect what people see as important in a political campaign (the process is called agenda setting), and a focus on this "agenda" in turn "primes" candidate evaluations.[38] By its more-or-less balanced treatment of the candidates, however, the media does break the cocoon of homogeneous political views in which many voters otherwise would find themselves and, in that way, it may undermine their traditional political viewpoints.

The Impact of the Campaign

Campaigns attract widespread attention because of their intrinsic drama—the parries and thrusts of competing candidates, the strategic maneuverings of party and campaign organizations, the surprises of the campaign trail, and especially who is winning the "game" among the candidates, which receives heavy coverage by the media.[39] They also are of interest because it is presumed that they matter, that they significantly influence which candidates are chosen to serve in the government. But is this presumption correct?

A few scholars have questioned whether the nature of the campaigns has much effect on the eventual outcomes. Because the results are so well predicted from factors—such as the prevailing distribution of party loyalties, economic conditions, or the standing of incumbents—known long before the campaign has begun, they reason, the events of the campaign itself have little bearing on the outcome. Instead, the function of the campaign is to provide voters with information about these precampaign factors so that they will move to this largely preordained outcome.[40]

Despite these skeptics, the conventional wisdom is that campaigns of course are consequential. Documenting their impact, though, is extremely difficult. For one thing, there are all manner of methodological complications. What we call the campaign is a congeries of events and activities; some of them are the activities of the parties and the candidates, and some are not. Consequently, it is difficult to say what part of the total impact can be attributed to any part of the campaign or its context. It is also difficult to determine what part of the campaign the voter has been aware of and how he or she has perceived it. Finally, as campaigns have come to rely more and more on the media, especially television, the variations in exposure required to identify campaign effects has diminished. The effects of television, for example, could be estimated by comparing those who watch it with those who do not. But is there anyone in the modern electorate who does not pay at least some attention to the medium?

In spite of these difficulties, some empirical evidence documenting effects of the campaign is available—although much of it dates from the period before the new technologies and television were widely used. Early studies showed that traditional grass-roots precinct work by party committee members produced a small, but electorally significant, boost in the expected or usual party vote. The research suggested, furthermore, that the effect of precinct work probably was greater in local elections than in media-centered presidential elections because there were apt to be fewer alternative cues and sources of information.[41] Early studies also indicated which campaign techniques were most effective: personal contacts were found to activate voters more often than did mailed propaganda, and door-to-door canvassing seemed more efficacious than telephone calls.[42] Those conclusions are buttressed by another set of findings—that precinct canvassing in a presidential campaign increases turnout but has little effect on voter choice and that an active local party organization is associated with a vote increase over the expected norm.[43] To these now-dated studies has been added evidence of contemporary effectiveness in party campaign efforts. Where the parties were active, the vote share for that party was enhanced by 2–3 percent—a modest amount perhaps in absolute terms but a critical margin in competitive areas.[44]

Recent trends—in both the decreased party anchoring of voters and the increased professionalization and resources of campaigners—suggest that the campaign might play a more important role now than ever before. Furthermore, while face-to-face personal contact seems to be the most efficacious kind of campaigning, candidates increasingly are relying upon powerful techniques of personalized indirect contact—the personally targeted letter or phone call and, above all, television. Even though scholars know less about the effectiveness of the new techniques, rapid growth in their utilization in political campaigns suggests at the very least that the candidates think they are effective. In the competitive world of politics, candidates cannot wait until the carefully analyzed empirical evidence is in before judging the various campaign techniques. Instead, they must operate with a cruder, but perhaps more practical, measure: What have past winners done? What are their opponents likely to do?

THE PARTY ORGANIZATION'S ROLE IN MODERN CAMPAIGNING

Nothing assures the party organizations a place in the campaign. They must compete constantly for a role in it, just as they fought without much success to control the nominations after the introduction of the direct primary. Their adversaries in this struggle are the candidates, the personal campaign organizations they create, the new professional campaign managers, and the new campaign financiers. Although the realities of American politics usually force candidates to run under party symbols that will help them attract the votes of a party electorate, nothing forces them to let the party organization control or even participate in their campaigns.

In a few places, however, the party organization still retains the traditional assets that made it valuable to candidates and their campaigns. Where it still commands armies of local workers, it can provide the candidate with a campaign vehicle that ensures success but costs very little—in either money or issue commitment. These old-style party organization efforts occur chiefly in a declining number of one-party urban areas, in which parties control primaries and voters habitually vote the party ticket in the general election. Canvassing and turning out the vote are still relevant there. Furthermore, the urban candidate is much more likely to have been nominated by the party organization through its control of the primary and thus to be its creature in the general election campaign.

The Resurgent Party Role

Elsewhere, where parties have retained an important campaign role, they have done so by adapting to the new realities. In place of the traditional grass-roots contacts through precinct organizations and their armies of committed jobholders, they have drawn from the familiar arsenal of modern techniques. Where they relied upon volunteers in the past, many now resort to employing at least some paid campaigners. From primarily in-kind contributions to party effort, they increasingly have turned to a cash economy—paying for the activities they perform with funds from generous state and national organizations. As professional campaign specialists have become more important, the parties often have served as their placement offices, matching them up with needy campaigns and even sustaining them during the lean interelection periods.

In the last few decades, in fact, there is persuasive evidence that the parties at all levels—local, state, and federal—have become more rather than less active in campaigns. But the nature of this activity has changed. Current efforts rely less on face-to-face, personal contacts than in the past; in this sense, the modern party is less "of the community" than the fabled party machine. It is for this reason, perhaps, that it is questionable whether the upsurge in party activity during the past few decades really signifies a more effective grass-roots party.[45]

What is not in doubt, though, is that there has been a resurgence in the involvement of the party organizations in electoral campaigns since the 1950s and 1960s. The large sums of money that have flowed to the national parties have enabled them, through selective investments of money and expertise, to stimulate greater activity in the state and local parties as well as to directly assist candidates in their own campaigns.[46] Moreover, the recent transfusion of millions of dollars in so-called soft money into the coffers of the state and local parties to promote activities on behalf of the party ticket and the increased fund-raising capabilities of the subnational party organizations themselves have enabled the parties at the grass roots to expand their campaign roles even more.[47] With these new financial resources and the efforts they have underwritten, then, the state and local parties no longer seem to be relics of a bygone era. With their new-found wealth and the services it can buy, the national parties have become significant players in political campaigns at all levels as well.

The Continuing Struggle for Control

Behind the struggle of the candidate and the party organization for control of the campaign, there is a basic truth: their interests never completely converge. The candidate, unless he or she has been dragooned to fill a ticket in a lost cause, takes the candidacy seriously. Even the longest shot among candidates expects to win; the degree of ego involvement in the campaign almost demands it. The party, on the other hand, wants to be selective in its use of campaign resources. It may see some races as lost and thus may be glad to turn these candidates loose for their own independent campaigns. Party organizations want to set overall priorities and allocations of scarce resources; they want to eliminate the inefficient and uneconomical parts of the campaign. Furthermore, the party organization wants to activate party loyalty, and candidates may not care to do so. The organization may also want to protect a platform and a program, help a presidential or gubernatorial candidate, or win control of a legislature, but these may not be the goals and interests of individual candidates.

To be sure, there are potent advantages to a party-led series of campaigns on behalf of an entire ticket. Such planning can eliminate the embarrassment and futility of two candidates competing for audiences in the same small town. The party organization can distribute campaign literature for a number of candidates at the same time and mount voter registration drives. Also, it alone can conduct the major election-day activities: setting up operation headquarters, providing cars and baby-sitters, checking voter lists to alert nonvoters late in the day, and providing poll watchers to oversee the balloting and counting. Efficiency and integration of the campaign, however, often threaten the interests of specific candidates. Although the party organization may prefer to raise money and prevent unseemly competition for the political dollar, a candidate may well believe he or she can raise more individually. Although the party may prefer billboard posters that celebrate the full party ticket of candidates, some among them may prefer to go it alone.

In this struggle for control of campaigning, the party organizations have historically been disadvantaged by the very nature of American elections. The sheer number of offices to be contested has forced the parties to surrender control by default. Electoral institutions, from the direct primary to the office-block ballot, have been on the side of the candidates. Now, recent revolutions in the ways of campaigning threaten to set the parties aside further. New sources of political information, political expertise, and political communication are available to the candidate—and so, too, are the sources of money to pay for them. They enable candidates to run campaigns and to communicate with voters without the mediation of the party. Even if the parties have more to offer to candidates for office than they did just a few years ago, many candidates can do quite well on their own.

The competition between the party organizations and the parties in government thus intensifies over the control of nominations and election campaigns. If the American parties are indeed electoral parties, then whoever controls the picking of candidates and the staging of campaigns controls the parties. At stake here is not only pride, but also the fruits of victory. In the old days, the activists of the party organization were satisfied with electoral victory by itself, for their goals were largely satisfied by public office per se and by the patronage and preferments that flowed from it. The new activists, however, seek much more than mere victory: they seek candidates and officials who will pursue specific issues and policy options after victory. Thus, to achieve their own goals, the workers of the party organization need to assert greater control over the party's candidates and officeholders at the very time when it seems harder to do so.

The new campaigning works against the party and the party organization in another way. It reinforces the development of personalism in politics. It is the candidate, not the party, who is "sold." The image transmitted by TV and the other media is of a person, not of the abstraction known as a political party. The campaign techniques, therefore, foster a tie between candidate and voter in which the role of party loyalty is less important. The new campaign techniques thus threaten to displace the party within the voter as well as the party organization in the campaign.

By controlling their own nominations and election campaigns, candidates are free of party organizational dominance and can pursue their own relationships with their constituencies and their alliances with nonparty organizations. The failures of the party organizations also enhance the competitive positions of other groups that want to play electoral politics and influence public policy. At stake in the battle, therefore, are the control and health of the political parties and the very nature of representative government in the United States.

Chapter 12

Financing the Campaigns

To the old adage "money isn't everything," people of practical bent often are inclined to add the coda "but it sure helps in getting what you want." Money has been an important ingredient in successful political campaigns since the beginnings of American politics.

> When [George Washington] ran for the Virginia House of Burgesses from Fairfax County in 1757, he provided his friends with the 'customary means of winning votes': namely 28 gallons of rum, 50 gallons of rum punch, 34 gallons of wine, 46 gallons of beer, and 2 gallons of cider royal. Even in those days this was considered a large campaign expenditure, because there were only 391 voters in his district for an average outlay of more than a quart and a half per person.[1]

But money probably has never been more important to electoral politics than it is today. As the volunteer manpower traditionally supplied by the party organizations has diminished and campaigns have come to depend more on paid professionals and television for transmitting their messages, money has become increasingly crucial in marshaling the resources necessary for serious campaigns. At all levels of government, but especially for the top state and national offices, candidates cannot compete without a substantial campaign bankroll. This chapter is primarily concerned with that money.

Traditionally, manpower was the principal contribution of the party organization to a campaign, and the principal contribution of the candidates was the money they could raise. This division of labor has eroded in recent years. Without vast armies of patronage employees and other dedicated party workers, the party organizations have had less manpower to supply. Furthermore, the rise of issue and ideologically oriented activists, wedded to candidates and causes rather than party, has given the candidates greater access to volunteer workers. Access to money also has broadened. As was shown in Chapter 4, the national party organizations now are able to raise and invest considerable financial resources in political campaigns, and many state organizations have stepped up their campaign-funding efforts as well. Nonetheless, the prime responsibility for financing the campaign still falls upon the candidate. This fact helps to account for the separation of the party organization from the party in government that continues to characterize the American political system.

Until recent times, a forbidding secrecy veiled the budgets of parties and candidates. Contributors were hesitant to be identified publicly, and candidates feared public disapproval of even the most modest expenditures. At the federal level, reforms had banned contributions from corporate treasuries, required public disclosure of receipts and expenditures, and limited the amounts that could be spent by House and Senate candidates. Yet, these regulations, full of loopholes, were easily avoided. In the case of presidential elections, for example, no centralized accounting was required of spending by the myriad campaign and party committees until the 1970s. Also vast sums of money could be raised and spent for many state and local contests without any public accounting of either contributions or expenditures.

This veil of secrecy has been lifted by campaign finance reform at the state and national level since the 1970s. A wealth of campaign finance data is now publicly available—through the Federal Election Commission in Washington on federal contests (see box on p. 272) and in many of the individual states for elections below the federal level. Where once the problem was secrecy, it is now trying to cope with a flood of data.[2]

The mind-boggling complexity of the world of campaign finance, though, makes it difficult to explore even after extensive data on contributions and expenditures have become available. Its practices are governed by the laws of the United States and the fifty states, where there is any regulation at all, and these laws have been in considerable flux. Moreover, even where campaign finance reports are dutifully filed, they lie in raw form in the files of many a state, and extensive effort is required to convert them into comprehensive accounts of campaign contributions and expenditures. There is no state counterpart to the Federal Election Commission in providing citizens, reporters, and scholars with good summaries of state campaign finance data. Finally, as is often the case when human activity is regulated by new and changing rules, candidates and contributors are adept at finding loopholes through which they can pursue their objectives.

Amid all this complexity, the only realistic approach is to seek answers to some basic questions: How much money is spent on election campaigns and by whom? From where does the money come? How have recent reforms changed the practices of campaign contributions and expenditures? Answers to these questions will illuminate the campaign finance picture in the United States and clarify the party's role.

HOW BIG HAS THE MONEY BECOME?

In a series of quadrennial studies, Herbert Alexander, the most authoritative source on the sums of money spent on campaigns, has estimated total campaign expenditures in every presidential year from 1960 through 1992 (see Table 12.1).[3] By his calculations, expenditures for all offices at all electoral levels, including both nominations and general elections, have increased eighteenfold since 1960. Growth in actual expenditures was especially explosive in 1968 and 1972 and again in the 1980s.

A NEW OPENNESS IN CAMPAIGN FINANCE: THE CONTRIBUTIONS OF THE FEDERAL ELECTION COMMISSION

Campaign spending figures for federal elections have become more widely available and more reliable since 1974. That was the year in which the Federal Election Commission was created by the Federal Election Campaign Act to supervise the reporting of campaign expenditures, to disseminate information on these expenditures, and to enforce federal campaign-finance regulations. Through its news releases and reports, the FEC distributes a wealth of data to the public on contributions and expenditures in presidential and congressional election campaigns. Even more information can be gained by delving into the FEC files or by connecting on-line into the FEC's computerized database. Through its provision of information on campaign contributions and spending, the FEC has enabled scholars, the press, and the public to penetrate the shadowy area of campaign finance and to illuminate the role of money in federal campaigns.

Because inflation reduces the purchasing power of the dollar, nominal dollar comparisons give a misleading impression of how much is being devoted to political campaigns. Campaign expenditures have increased in inflation-adjusted constant dollars (see the adjusted column of Table 12.1) by only about fourfold since 1960. As the temporary result of major campaign-financing reforms, they even decreased from 1972 to 1976, although soon thereafter they experienced their greatest surges. In the 1991–92 election cycle, even with the well-funded independent candidacy of Ross Perot, they experienced very little real growth from the previous four years.

Presidential Campaigns

Even with the limits imposed on general-election spending for candidates who accept public funding, the most expensive campaign for public office in the United States is that for the presidency (Table 12.2). While the total costs of those campaigns has varied with the amount of competition in the primaries and the activities of third-party candidates, the reforms stimulated by improprieties in 1972 campaign financing have managed to slow the previously explosive growth in the costs of competing for the presidency. The spirited three-sided contest in 1992, in fact, cost less in inflation-adjusted dollars than the 1988 contest.

Congressional Campaigns

The total cost of the races for the many United States House and Senate seats has come to exceed the presidential total in recent years, even if the expenditures for no single campaign even approach those of a presidential campaign (Table 12.3).[4] Of

Table 12.1 TOTAL CAMPAIGN EXPENDITURES FOR ALL OFFICES IN PRESIDENTIAL YEARS: 1960–92

Year	Expenditures (in millions)		Percentage change since previous election	
	Actual	Inflation Adjusted	Actual	Inflation Adjusted
1960	$ 175	$175	—	—
1964	200	191	+ 14.3%	+ 9.1%
1968	300	255	+ 50.0	+33.5
1972	425	301	+ 41.7	+18.0
1976	540	281	+ 27.1	− 6.7
1980	1200	431	+122.2	+53.4
1984	1800	513	+ 50.0	+19.0
1988	2700	676	+ 50.0	+31.8
1992	3220	679	+ 19.3	+ 0.4

Note: Estimates are for two-year cycles ending in the presidential election years. Inflation adjusted figures are computed by deflating the actual expenditures by changes in the price level as measured by the Consumer Price Index using 1960 as the base year.

Sources: For campaign expenditures, Herbert E. Alexander and Anthony Corrado, *Financing the 1992 Election* (Armonk, N.Y.: M.E. Sharpe, 1995), p. 6. CPI deflator is based on data from U.S. Bureau of the Census, *Statistical Abstract of the United States: 1993* (Washington, D.C.: U.S. Government Printing Office, 1993), Table 756.

Table 12.2 TOTAL SPENDING BY CANDIDATES, PARTIES, AND GROUPS IN PRESIDENTIAL GENERAL ELECTIONS: 1960–92

Year	Expenditures (in millions)		Percentage change since previous election	
	Actual	Inflation Adjusted	Actual	Inflation Adjusted
1960	$ 30.0	$ 30.0	—	—
1964	60.0	57.3	+100.0%	+91.0%
1968	100.0	85.1	+ 66.7	+48.5
1972	138.0	97.7	+ 38.0	+14.8
1976	160.0	83.2	+ 15.9	−14.8
1980	275.0	98.8	+ 61.1	+18.8
1984	325.0	92.6	+ 18.2	− 6.3
1988	500.0	125.1	+ 53.8	+35.1
1992	550.0	116.0	+ 10.0	− 7.3

Note: Estimates are for two-year cycles ending in the presidential election years. Inflation adjusted figures are computed by deflating the actual expenditures by changes in the price level as measured by the Consumer Price Index (yearly averages) using 1960 as the base year.

Source: Herbert E. Alexander and Anthony Corrado, *Financing the 1992 Election* (Armonk, N.Y.: M.E. Sharpe, 1995), Table 2–2, p. 21, for actual spending. CPI deflator is based on data from *Statistical Abstract of the United States: 1993* (Washington, D.C.: U.S. Government Printing Office, 1993), Table 756.

Table 12.3 TOTAL SPENDING BY CANDIDATES IN THE 1994 CONGRESSIONAL
CAMPAIGNS, 1971–72 TO 1993–94

| Year | Expenditures (in millions) | | | | Percentage change since previous election | | | |
| | Actual | | Inflation Adjusted | | Actual | | Inflation Adjusted | |
	House	Senate	House	Senate	House	Senate	House	Senate
1971–72	$ 46.5	$ 30.7	$ 46.5	$ 30.7	—	—	—	—
1973–74	53.5	34.7	45.4	29.4	+15.1	+13.0	– 2.4	– 4.2
1975–76	71.5	44.0	52.5	32.3	+33.6	+26.8	+15.6	+ 9.9
1977–78	109.7	85.2	70.3	54.6	+53.4	+93.6	+33.9	+69.0
1979–80	136.0	102.9	69.0	52.2	+24.0	+20.8	– 1.8	– 4.4
1981–82	204.0	138.4	88.4	60.0	+50.0	+34.5	+28.1	+14.9
1983–84	203.6	170.5	81.9	68.6	– 0.2	+23.2	– 7.4	+14.3
1985–86	239.3	211.6	91.2	80.7	+17.5	+24.1	+11.4	+17.6
1987–88	256.5	201.2	90.6	71.0	+ 7.2	– 4.9	– 0.7	–12.0
1989–90	265.8	180.4	85.0	57.7	+ 3.6	–10.3	– 6.2	–18.3
1991–92	406.7	271.6	121.0	80.9	+53.0	+50.6	+42.5	+40.2
1993–94	405.7	318.4	114.5	90.0	– 0.2	+17.2	– 5.4	+11.2

Note: Estimates are for two-year cycles ending in the presidential and midterm election years. Inflation adjusted figures are computed by deflating the actual expenditures by changes in the price level as measured by the Consumer Price Index (yearly averages) using 1972 as the base year.

Source: Herbert E. Alexander and Anthony Corrado, *Financing the 1992 Election* (Armonk, N.Y.: M.E. Sharpe, 1995), Table 7.1, p. 178, for actual spending through 1991–92; Federal Election Comission for 1993–94. CPI deflator is based on data from *Statistical Abstract of the United States: 1993* (Washington, D.C.: U.S. Government Printing Office, 1993), Table 756, and for 1994 the February 1995 issue of the *Monthly Labor Review*, Table 31.

this total, more is spent on House than on Senate contests; as one would expect, though, the average expenditure for the many fewer Senate contests is higher than that of House contests. Total spending on each set of contests has rather steadily climbed since 1971–72, virtually in tandem, especially in the first decade of the period. Only two campaign cycles for each house registered expenditures below those of the previous cycle. This picture changes, though, when attention turns to inflation-adjusted real dollars. The purchasing power of House expenditures actually declined from one cycle to the next more often than it increased, whereas for the Senate spending increased only somewhat more than it declined. Popular impressions of surging campaign spending are belied by these figures. Instead, it is apparent that expenditures have been relatively constant from year to year in real dollars, with big gains being registered in only the fiercely contested 1978 and 1992 contests.

These, then, are preliminary answers to the question of how big the political money is. They show a level of total campaign expenditures that has grown in recent years, outstripping the costs of most other items in the American economy. Ironically, for all the attention focused on the Washington part of the equation, campaign

CAMPAIGN SPENDING: TOO MUCH OR TOO LITTLE?

The expenditure of $3,220,000,000 on political campaigns in 1992 is a tremendous sum of money by anyone's reckoning. Yet, as Herbert Alexander and Anthony Corrado observe, it is less than the sum that two large corporations, Procter and Gamble and Philip Morris, spent in 1992 on product advertising and a mere fraction of what Americans spend on cosmetics and gambling.[6] To many Americans, distressed at what they see as the low quality of political candidates and political campaigns, these expenditures are surely not worthwhile. Considering the large number of candidates running for office in the United States and the role that advertising plays in the American culture in providing citizens with information that they need to make important decisions about goods or candidates, however, a persuasive case can be made that this key cost of democracy is not at all excessive and may even be insufficient.

costs have swollen more in the states and localities than at the federal level over this period.[5] These numbers alone leave unanswered, though, the question of how big campaign spending really is—that is, how it measures up to the needs for communication in a democracy and the relative values and utilities of Americans. That question undoubtedly requires a more subjective answer (see box above).

WHO SPENDS THE CAMPAIGN MONEY?

The money consumed by American campaigning varies enormously across offices and levels of government, with the costs of the presidency receiving the greatest attention. It also is spent by a variety of individuals and groups. Most attention of course focuses on the candidates for office and their committees: In the American system, unlike the case in most other democracies where parties do the spending, they are responsible for most of the campaign spending. Yet, party committees and nonparty groups, especially political action committees, also invest considerable funds in elections beyond what they may contribute directly to candidates. To understand the flow of money in American campaign politics, it is necessary to disentangle the various actors who disburse it.

Presidential Campaigns

As is understandable given the national scope and importance of the office, the costs of electing the president dominate the campaign finance picture. Just selecting a party candidate for the office requires considerable money, especially when there is open competition for the nomination within both of the major parties and the general election campaigns can cost as much or more.

Most of the presidential spending is done by the candidates for office and their campaign committees. The major party candidates spent 41.5 percent of the total expenditures in the 1992 race, and third-party and independent candidates accounted for an additional 14 percent (Table 12.4). The major party candidates actually spent less in actual dollars in 1992 than they had four years before. With Republican incumbent Bush seeking reelection, the competition and hence the investments were concentrated on the Democratic nomination contests, and nomination expenditures declined. Because of the Perot candidacy, by contrast, third-party and independent candidate spending was fifteen times what it had been in 1988.

Obscured by the aggregated figures are the costs of the presidential race for the individual campaigns. Just winning the party nomination—that is, the right to run in 1992—cost the Clinton campaign $33.9 million and the Bush campaign $37.9 million. Even candidates who experienced little success in the 1992 nominating contests spent considerable sums. Pat Buchanan's unsuccessful bid for the GOP nomination cost $11.6 million, while Democratic hopeful Jerry Brown's total expenditures almost reached $9 million. The record in futility prior to 1996 (see box on p. 278), in terms of dollars per vote in an ill-fated quest for the party nomination, though, was set by Republican Pat Robertson in 1988. He spent a total of $30.9 million to finish first in only three caucuses and no primaries. Similarly, third-party candidate Lenora Fulani invested almost $4.2 million ($2 million of it in public funds) to gain the nomination of her third party (and only $0.2 million in the general election campaign), and it gained her only 73,000 general election votes—at a cost of about $28 per vote.

The general election campaign raises the ante conspicuously. Before the advent of public financing, Richard Nixon set records in his successful campaign in 1972 by spending about $62 million. Because all major party candidates since public funding for presidential campaigns became available in 1976 have accepted the federal funds, they have also accepted the condition that they spend only the public contributions. Thus, in 1992, the Bush and Clinton general election campaigns spent $55.2 million apiece, all of it in public funds. Independent candidate Ross Perot was free to spend $68.3 million in 1992, $63.3 million of it his own money, because he did not accept public funding.

The other categories of expenditure listed in Table 12.4 are less obvious and bear some explanation. The major party organizations and their committees spent substantial sums on their national conventions and directly in the general election to support their party's candidate. Individuals and nonparty groups also made substantial independent expenditures on behalf of or in opposition to a candidate—under the law, this spending is to be done without the knowledge or cooperation of any candidate or party.[7] Communication costs are expenditures made by organizations to urge their workers or members to vote for a particular candidate; labor unions account for most of them. Additional expenditures by labor unions, corporations, and membership associations in "nonpartisan" voter mobilization—largely in voter registration and get-out-the-vote programs—totaled a substantial $55 million in 1992, again most of it spent by labor unions. Finally, compliance costs are expenses (lawyers' and accountants' fees, for example) incurred by the candidates in preparing reports required under the law.[8]

Table 12.4 COSTS OF NOMINATING AND ELECTING A PRESIDENT: 1992

	Amount (in millions)
I. Prenomination	
Spending by major party candidates	$117.6
Compliance costs	8.0
Independent expenditures	1.2
Communication costs	0.7
Labor spending	20.0
Spending by minor party candidates	5.7
Prenomination Total	$153.2
II. Conventions	
Republicans' expenditures	$ 21.0
Democrats' expenditures	38.6
Conventions Total	$ 59.6
III. General Election	
Spending by major party candidates	$110.4
Spending by Perot	68.3
Spending by minor party candidates	2.9
Compliance costs	10.3
Party committee spending	63.4
DNC and RNC media	14.5
Expenditures by labor, corporations, and associations	35.0
Independent expenditures	3.0
Communication costs	2.7
General Election Total	$310.5
Miscellaneous Expenses	$ 26.7
Grand Total	$550.0

Notes: Parties' general-election total includes $43 million in "soft money" expenditures by the DNC and RNC.

Source: Herbert E. Alexander and Anthony Corrado, *Financing the 1992 Election* (Armonk, N.Y.: M.E. Sharpe, 1995), Table 2-1, p. 21.

Congressional Campaigns

Similar analyses of congressional campaigns are possible with the data of the Federal Election Commission. Campaigns for nomination and election to the two houses of the Congress went on simultaneously with the 1992 presidential election. Candidates for Congress that year spent a total of $678.3 million in the primaries and general elections (see Table 12.3). In campaigning for the midterm elections of 1994, the candidates' spending total increased to $724.1. In the congressional contests, absent the expenditure limits which constrain presidential candidates and public funding, candidate spending dwarfs spending by any other campaign actor. Consequently,

SELF-FINANCED CANDIDATES FOR THE 1996 REPUBLICAN PRESIDENTIAL NOMINATION

Two millionaire businessmen, Malcolm S. (Steve) Forbes, Jr., and Maurice (Morry) Taylor, invested considerable amounts of their own personal wealth in their futile quests for the Republican nomination in 1996. In the Iowa caucus alone, Forbes spent about $4 million and Taylor $1 million— or about $408 and $725 per vote, respectively. Taylor never became a viable candidate, and his several million dollar investment did not win him a single delegate. Forbes surfaced as one of the leading early challengers to Bob Dole, drawing twenty-four percent of the vote in February primaries to Dole's thirty-one percent and actually winning the Arizona primary. But with Dole locking up the nomination early, Forbes withdrew from the race on March 14 after investing an estimated $30 million to gain only 70 delegates—at a steep "price" of over $400,000 per delegate. These twin examples in 1996 illustrate how candidates willing to personally finance their own campaigns can enter into the nomination contest without qualifying for federal matching funds, but also that money alone does not produce votes or delegates.

in the campaigns for Congress, it is the candidates who control the money, and our attention should be primarily focused on them.[9]

One of the cardinal rules of modern campaign finance is that incumbent office-holders vastly outspend their challengers in campaigns for Congress. In the 1991–92 electoral cycle, the spending edge for incumbents was almost 1.8 to 1; in 1993–94, it narrowed to 1.5 to 1. A corollary of this rule is that Democrats, who have had more incumbents in modern times, usually—but not always—outspend Republications. This Democratic edge appeared again in 1992 (when it was 1.25 to 1), but in the stunning Republican congressional victory of 1994, the Republicans edged ahead of the Democrats in campaign spending ($371 million to $359 million). Once the dust had settled, it turned out that the Democrats had spent $25 million less than they had spent two years before, while the GOP was increasing its campaign expenditures by $72 million, a boost of almost 25 percent. To the degree that money draws electoral support, the Republicans had gained the advantage in 1994. Their new status as the majority party gave them an even greater financial advantage going into the 1996 House and Senate elections.

As usual, the aggregated figures hide considerable variation in candidate spending on individual campaigns. By now it has become commonplace for a Senate candidate to spend several million dollars, and the average general election expenditure in 1994 was slightly more than $2.0 million. The days of serious Senate campaigns for under a million dollars even in small states seem to have ended, except in the case of token challengers. Among the 1992 and 1994 Senate contests, only in Hawaii did the total spending (a measly, by modern standards, $455,000) fall short of $1 million. New spending records, in fact, were set in the 1994 contests. In the California contest between Republican Congressman Michael Huffington and incumbent Democrat Dianne Feinstein, Feinstein spent $14.4 million to win reelection while Huffington invested $30.0 million in a losing cause. Huffington's record expenditure and Oliver North's allotment of $20.6 million to his unsuccessful Virginia campaign are the largest amounts ever spent by single candidates in a Senate race—far surpassing Jesse Helms' record $13.4 million ten years before.

The average 1994 House general election contest, by contrast, cost less than $320,000—up from an average of $290,000 in 1992. A total of forty-eight candidates in 1994 and more than fifty in 1992, though, spent over $1 million. Leading the way here too was millionaire Michael Huffington, whose successful challenge to an incumbent in his own party and subsequent general election victory cost him a total of $5.4 million.

But the candidates are not the only important spenders in congressional campaigns. The parties invest money in the congressional campaigns beyond what they contribute directly to the candidates. Their House and Senate campaign committees, national committees, and state and local committees spent almost $45 million "on behalf of" candidates of their parties in 1991–92 and another $42 million in 1993–94, with the Republicans considerably outspending the Democrats in this respect over both election cycles. Additional money is invested directly in campaign efforts by corporations, labor unions, and other organizations beyond what they contribute to candidates. It goes to encourage their members (and anyone else who may receive the communication) to oppose or support particular candidates and, in amounts difficult to estimate, to encourage voters to participate in the election.[10]

State and Local Campaigns

Beyond these quests for national office are the thousands of campaigns for state and local offices. Hard information is rare because there are no state or local sources comparable to the FEC, and generalizations are questionable. Many of these campaigns involve almost unbelievably small sums. Each year hundreds of candidates win office in the United States in campaigns that involve cash outlays of a few hundred dollars. On the other hand, the mayoralty campaign in a large American city may cost a candidate and his or her supporters as much as some Senate contests. Edward Koch spent almost $6 million in 1985 in his successful reelection bid for mayor of New York City, and the city's most recent mayoralty candidates spent as much as $8 million between the primary and general elections. In Dallas, a mayoralty candidate spent more than $1 million for a $50 per week part-time job. Campaigns for governor of the larger states typically cost as much as or more than races for the U.S. Senate, with California again setting the records. Successful contests for the state legislature in large states now sometimes require more than $100,000, and spending in these contests seems to be growing more rapidly than for any other office. As usual, the record for campaign spending in these races seems to be set by California. By 1990, the average expenditure per seat in the lower house of the California legislature had surpassed $512,000, and some particularly competitive contests drove that cost up far more.[11]

TO WHAT EFFECT IS CAMPAIGN SPENDING?

Victory is not automatically awarded to the side with the most money. Money is only one of the ingredients for a successful campaign, and how much it contributes to winning votes is not clear. In presidential contests, where both candidates have enough money to reach voters with their messages, the candidate with the largest war chest probably gains no significant advantage. In seeking the presidential nomination, money is undoubtedly more important, especially in buying crucial early visibility for the underdogs. Yet, having a large campaign war chest was not enough for Pat Robertson in 1988 or Steve Forbes in 1996, and similar examples can be found from earlier years. Once the candidate has qualified for federal matching funds, though, the advantage money can confer narrows considerably.

The most systematic studies of the importance of campaign spending have focused on congressional races, where the large number of contests at any one time enables the analyst to control other possible influences on the outcome. It should come as no surprise that these studies conclude that money is important in running for Congress. There is no doubt that the more challengers spend in races against incumbents, the more votes they win and the better their chances of victory become.

The effects of campaign spending, however, are not so clear cut for incumbents. Based on a careful examination of the relationship between spending levels and votes that takes into account other influences, Gary C. Jacobson has concluded that the more incumbents spend, the worse they do. The reason is that high levels of incumbent spending typically come in response to a spirited election challenge. Donald Philip Green and Jonathan S. Krasno, however, have challenged Jacobson's assertion. If the quality of the challenger is taken into account, their analysis finds that increased incumbent spending yields more electoral support for the incumbent. Even though this dispute is mired in thorny questions about the proper way to estimate the impact of spending, two things about the efficacy of incumbent spending seem clear. First, strong challenges to incumbents are infrequent occurrences. Second, when they do occur, representatives may not be able to survive the challenge by pouring more money into their reelection effort.[12]

As these scholars point out, how spending levels affect votes has important implications for current reform efforts to limit campaign spending. If the chances of incumbents and challengers improve equally with spending increases, then spending caps do not particularly benefit either of them. If the chances of challengers increase as they spend more, while those of incumbents decline, then any reasonable ceiling on campaign spending benefits incumbents. In this situation, campaign finance reform that caps spending protects incumbents. This would have favored the Democrats before 1994, but now would benefit the GOP. As we shall see, in recent attempts to reform campaign finance laws, congressional Democrats and Republicans have assumed, following Jacobson and most scholars, that spending limitations do favor incumbents and have divided their votes on that issue accordingly.

It even is questionable that independent expenditures always benefit the candidates they support. This spending favored the Republicans, in both presidential and congressional races, in recent years. Made independently of Republican candidates and committees and of their campaign plans and strategies, however, it may have achieved Republican goals very imperfectly. Sometimes, independent expenditures even backfire, as some observers think happened when the National Conservative Political Action Committee (NCPAC) defeated only one of the thirteen Democratic senators it had targeted for defeat in 1982 when NCPAC support itself became a campaign issue.

Estimating the partisan advantage of other forms of noncandidate spending faces similar problems. The communications costs incurred by organized labor overwhelmingly support Democrats; yet their effectiveness is unclear. When it is seized upon as a campaign issue, in fact, labor support can even be counterproductive in certain locales. Nor is it clear how the effects of "nonpartisan" voter registration and voter activation campaigns should be calculated. They are nonpartisan on the surface, but the unions, corporations, and associations that mount them usually do so in the confidence that they are mobilizing voters strongly in favor of one party or ideological preference.

SOURCES OF FUNDS IN FEDERAL CAMPAIGNS

Beyond questions of how much money is spent, who spends it, and how effective it is lies the fundamental question of where the money comes from. Candidates raise their campaign money from five basic sources: individual contributors, political action committees, political parties, the candidates' own resources, and public funds. For significant amounts of money, there are no possibilities beyond these five. All candidates are limited to them. Anyone who proposes reform in the American system of campaign finance, unless they desire a return to direct contributions from corporations and labor unions, must prescribe a changing role for these sources of money (Table 12.5).

Individual Contributors

It is one of the best kept secrets in American politics that the individual contributor still dominates campaign finance. While public funding of presidential general elections has greatly reduced the role of the individual contributor there (who still can support his or her candidate by contributing to the party or by making independent expenditures), individual contributions dominate the prenomination contests both directly and through the federal matching funds they generate. Almost all money spent in the 1992 primaries came from individuals or the federal treasury in matching the individual contributions. Even though PACs have come to play important roles in the funding of House and Senate races, individual donors still are the dominant contributor of the congressional campaign funds as well. In 1993–94 individuals accounted for 51 percent of the contributions to House candidates and 58 percent of all of the money given to Senate candidates. Although the precise numbers are difficult to come by, it is likely that individual contributors also provide the majority of funds for state campaigns.[13]

Table 12.5   SOURCES OF CAMPAIGN FUNDS FOR PRESIDENTIAL AND
CONGRESSIONAL CANDIDATES (IN MILLIONS)

Presidential, 1991–92

	Democrats		Republicans		Total	
	Nomination	General	Nomination	General	Nomination	General
Individuals	$44.8	0.0	$34.5	0.0	$ 82.6	$ 8.0
Candidates	0.0	0.0	0.0	0.0	0.0	63.3
PACs	0.9	0.0	0.1	0.0	0.9	0.0
Party	0.0	10.3	0.0	10.3	0.0	20.3
Public Funds	24.7	55.2	15.7	55.2	42.7	110.4
TOTAL	$70.4	$65.5	$50.3	$65.5	$126.4	$202.0

Congressional, 1993–94

	Democrats		Republicans		Total		
	House	Senate	House	Senate	House	Senate	Total
Individuals	$100.3	$ 80.4	$114.6	$104.8	$216.1	$186.5	$402.5
Candidates							
Contributions	3.3	7.3	6.1	17.4	10.6	24.9	35.5
Loans	15.0	12.9	28.6	30.2	43.8	43.6	87.3
PACs	88.1	23.7	43.7	23.0	132.1	46.7	178.8
Party	1.5	0.6	2.0	0.7	3.5	1.3	4.8
Public Funding	0.0	0.0	0.0	0.0	0.0	0.0	0.0
Other Loans	0.4	0.6	0.6	2.6	1.0	3.2	4.2
TOTAL	$216.9	$133.5	$201.8	$183.5	$421.5	$319.1	$740.6

Note: The figures are for the two-year cycles ending in the presidential and midterm election years. Candidate loans are personal loans by the candidate to her/his campaign. The total columns include funds for Democratic, Republican, and other candidates; the $63.3 million total in the "candidates" row represents Perot's personal contributions to his campaign.

Source: For President, Herbert E. Alexander and Anthony Corrado, *Financing the 1992 Election* (Armonk, N.Y.: M.E. Sharpe, 1995), Table 2.4, p. 31, and Table 5.6, p. 136. For Congress, Federal Election Commission, April 28, 1995 News Release, p. 4.

The reforms of 1974, by limiting individuals to a maximum of $1,000 in donations to any single candidate for federal office, also changed the nature of the individual contributor in federal races. They ended the era of the big "fat-cat" contributors. Now congressional campaigns are financed by large numbers of people making small contributions rather than a handful of large contributors. Small contributors also dominate in the nomination phase of the presidential campaigns, the only time when individual contributions can be made directly to presidential candidates. Even these small contributors, though, comprise a very unrepresentative slice of the American electorate. Generally speaking, they are older, more involved in politics, more conservative, and more affluent than the average American.[14] Still, they resemble the typical American voter far more closely than did the storied fat cats of a generation ago.

Over the years, the parties and the candidates have devised all manner of ways to separate prospective political contributors from their money (see box on pp. 284–285). Personal visits, phone calls, and conversations with the candidate or the candidate's workers raise substantial sums and are the preferred form of soliciting large contributions. On a grander scale, group events—such as a gala dinner or a briefing from a top advisor—also are important means for reaching the big donors. Aided by computerized mailing lists and the new technology for personalizing letters, though, political money is increasingly raised by mail, especially from small contributors. Mailing lists of dependable donors, in fact, have become one of the most treasured resources in modern campaign politics.

Recent patterns in the partisan direction of individual donations seem to have been disrupted in the 1994 congressional contests. In giving their money, individual donors had been more generous to Democratic candidates than to Republicans in the three previous congressional election cycles. In 1993–94, by contrast, Republican candidates raised 21 percent more from individual contributors than did their opponents. With a continuation of their new edge in congressional incumbency, the retirements of many long-standing popular Democrats, and the new-found aggressiveness of the congressional Republicans, this edge may be maintained for some years.

The Soft Money Loophole

Amendments to the Federal Election Campaign Act in 1979, however, opened up a window through which large individual contributors have been able to reenter federal political campaigns, as contributors to party campaign efforts rather than to the candidates, although they have not been able to resume their previously dominant role. To strengthen parties at the state and local level, the new law exempted from federal regulation money spent by the state/local **parties** for volunteer, voter registration, and get-out-the-vote activities even if they were conducted in support of the presidential or congressional campaigns. This law was interpreted to allow unlimited soft-money contributions—from individuals as well as corporations and labor unions—to pass through the national party committees on their way to the state parties.

Tremendous sums of money have flowed through the soft-money conduit in recent years. In 1992, for example, $151 million in soft money was raised by the major party committees at the state and national levels. Of this total, $88 million was raised by the national party committees, especially by the Democratic National Committee ($31.6 million) and the Republican National Committee ($36.2 million). Former Bush and Clinton campaign staffers who had joined the national committee staffs after the nomination process ended played an important role in this fundraising. A substantial portion of this money came from individuals who had pledged at least $100,000 apiece, but large contributions also were made by corporations, PACs, and labor unions.[15]

PIONEERS IN POLITICAL FUND-RAISING

Perhaps America's most prodigious presidential fund-raiser ever was Ohio industrialist Marcus Alonzo Hanna, who personally financed the nomination campaign of William McKinley in 1896 and then raised most of the reputed $6–7 million (the equivalent of almost $100 million in current dollars) spent in McKinley's successful general-election campaign. Hanna raised the art of extracting campaign contributions from American corporations to a new level. "Assessments were apportioned according to each company's 'stake in the general prosperity.'. . . Banks, for instance, were assessed one quarter of one percent of their capital; Standard Oil contributed about a quarter of a million dollars, and the large insurance companies slightly less. If a company sent in a check Hanna believed to be too small, it was returned; if a company paid too much, a refund was sent out." Hanna's accomplishments fanned the reform flame that led to federal prohibition of corporate contributions in 1907 and a federal campaign fund disclosure law in 1910.

In the 1940 elections, a young congressman from Texas named Lyndon B. Johnson wrote a new chapter in the annals of campaign finance by raising, through the Democratic Congressional Campaign Committee, huge sums of Texas oil and construction money to support Democratic congressional candidates. "Lyndon Johnson's work with Democratic congressional candidates . . . added a new factor to the equation of American politics. The concept of financing congressional races across the country from a single central source was not new, but the Democrats had seldom if ever implemented the concept on the necessary scale or with the necessary energy." This accomplishment catapulted Johnson onto the national political stage, foreshadowed the importance of congressional campaign committees in modern times, and initiated the vital role Texas money was to play in Democratic, and later Republican, politics for many years.

The era of the big contributors ended with the greatest feat of fund raising in this century—the collection of much more than $60 million in support of the reelection campaign of President Richard M. Nixon in 1972. Under the leadership of Maurice Stans and Herbert Kalmbach, much of this sum was raised from a few large contributors before tough campaign-financing laws went into effect on April 7 of that election year. Chicago insurance magnate W. Clement Stone alone contributed $2 million to the Nixon cause, and Mellon-heir Richard Mellon Scaife donated another $1 million. Some of this largesse was illegally diverted to finance the Watergate break-in and related activities, and Stans subsequently was convicted for his role in funding them. The massive size and illegalities of this 1972 effort stimulated reforms of campaign fund-raising practices that ended more than a century's reliance upon large contributors.

The master architect of modern campaign fund-raising techniques is Richard Viguerie, whose direct-mail methods for raising political money

(box continues)

first attracted widespread attention in the ill-fated 1972 presidential campaign of George Wallace. From a base of Goldwater and Wallace contributors, Viguerie built a computerized list of millions of donors to conservative causes and candidates. For a fee (averaging 50 percent of the proceeds) and access to his client's own list of contributors for the purpose of enlarging his master file, Viguerie devoted his fund-raising talents to conservative candidates and causes. The cost of raising money in small amounts from tens and hundreds of thousands of contributors is high, but in the postreform era computerized direct mail has become the principal means of raising campaign funds.[16]

Political Action Committees

Political action committees (PACs) are political committees that are connected with neither parties nor (officially declared) candidates but that raise and spend money to influence election outcomes. The great majority of PACs are the creature of a sponsoring parent organization; that is, they are PACs of corporations, labor unions, and membership associations. Some, however, have no sponsoring organization; these are most likely to be ideological PACs of the right or the left. The PACs spend their money in three different ways: They transfer it to parties or to other PACs, they spend it independently to support or oppose candidates, and they give it directly to candidates. Because the first route (transfers) is negligible, and because we have already discussed independent expenditures, the concern here is with the PACs as contributors to the candidates.

On the last day of 1974, there were only 608 PACs operating in national elections; but by the very end of 1995 that number had climbed to 4,016. The greatest growth over time has come in the number of corporate and independent (typically ideological and issue-oriented) PACs. Corporate PACs climbed from 15 percent of the 1974 total to 42 percent by 1995, and independent PACs grew from 0 to 25 percent during this same period; the number of labor and association PACs increased as well.[17]

A number of factors account for that growth. The decline of the parties and the advent of a more fragmented, issue-centered politics helped to foster it. Most important of all was the reform legislation of the post-Watergate years. The Federal Election Campaign Act of 1974, for example, in its zeal to limit the big individual spenders of American politics, put the limit on individual contributions far below that for the PACs. The new law also explicitly permitted corporations doing business with government to have PACs, which clarified a previous law that had barred direct or indirect contributions to federal election campaigns by government contractors. Furthermore, decisions of the federal courts and the Federal Election Commission made clear the legality of PACs and confirmed the right of sponsoring organizations to pay their administrative and overhead expenses. Their political funds, though, must be collected and kept separately in what federal statutes call a *separate segregated fund;* under federal law, the sponsoring corporation or labor union may not use its regular assets and revenues for political expenditures.

For all of the bad press PACs have received, it may come as a surprise to learn that they do not dominate American campaign finance. Because of public funding, PACs are not direct contributors to presidential general election campaigns. They can contribute to candidates for the presidential nominations, but these contributions have tended to be modest in recent years ($0.8 million in 1991–92). PACs also can make independent expenditures for or against presidential candidates. These independent expenditures totaled $4.0 million in the 1991–92 electoral cycle.

The bulk of PAC contributions instead go to congressional candidates. PACs contributed $186.9 million to congressional candidates in 1991–92 and almost as much in 1993–94 (Table 12.5). Of the 1993–94 total, corporate PACs accounted for 35 percent, associational PACs (a catch-all category containing trade, health, and membership associations) 28 percent, labor PACs 22 percent, and nonconnected PACs (mostly ideological and issue organizations) 10 percent.

Despite all this largesse, political action committees do not dominate congressional fund raising. They accounted for less than a quarter of all the money received by congressional candidates in 1993–94 (24.1 percent). The PACs also make independent expenditures for or against particular candidates to influence the congressional races. This spending reached $6.6 million in 1991–92 but declined to $4.7 million in 1993–94—or less than 3 percent of their direct candidate contributions.

It is important to realize, finally, that these various figures represent the sum of contributions from several thousand different PACs, representing a number of diverse and sometimes even competing interests. There is no monolithic PAC "interest," nor are PACs solely the representatives of business or disproportionately supporters of Republican (or Democratic) candidates and causes. Corporate PACs contributed the most to congressional candidates in 1993–94, with slightly more money going to Republicans than to Democrats. Labor PACs invested less money in the congressional races, but by concentrating almost all of it on Democratic candidates, they more than compensated for the Republican edge in corporate contributions. Associational and unconnected PACs also skewed their money in a Democratic direction, but they made considerable contributions to candidates from both parties.

The objective of most PAC campaign giving is not partisan or ideological but rather is an underwriting of the status quo. Most PAC contributions go to incumbents, and, because there have been more Democratic than Republican incumbents in recent years, Democratic House and Senate candidates have received more PAC money. With their new majorities in both the House and the Senate after the 1994 elections, though, the attraction of money by congressional incumbents should now favor the GOP—just as the election of Bill Clinton in 1992 reversed the flow of PAC party contributions to a Democratic direction. Indeed, toward the end of the 1994 campaign, PAC giving tilted in a Republican direction, as the "safe money" moved to anticipate the election results.

Candidates pursue the PACs just as sedulously as they pursue individual contributors. Both parties' congressional and senatorial campaign committees put their candidates in touch with PACs likely to be sympathetic to their causes, and the parties are increasingly active in channeling PAC money directly to candidates. Candidates and their campaign managers also track the PACs at first hand, assisted by the directories and information services that list PACs by their issue positions, the size of their resources, and their previous contributions. Incumbent members of Congress also invite the PACs or lobbyists of their parent organizations to fund-raising parties in Washington, at which a check earns the PAC people hors d'oeuvres, drinks, and legislative gratitude. On the other hand, the PACs also take the contributing initiative. Unlike most individual contributors, they are in the business of making political contributions, and they don't necessarily wait to be asked.[18]

What do PACs buy with their extensive spending on congressional campaigns? It is unquestionable that their campaign contributions gain them access to lawmakers. What political officials will fail to listen to representatives of interests that have provided financial support for their political campaigns? How hard they listen and how much what they hear changes their legislative behavior, however, are more difficult to determine. Research on the relationship between PAC contributions and subsequent roll call votes has not produced much evidence that contributions influence votes.[19] PAC money does, however, seem to produce greater access to members of Congress and more committee activity by recipients on behalf of issues of PAC concern.[20]

There are ample reasons why the straightforward exchange of votes for PAC money rarely occurs. A single PAC is limited to a contribution of $5,000 per member of Congress in each election or $10,000 for the primary and general election together, which makes it only one of many relatively small contributors. The concentration of PAC money on incumbents, who have the easiest time of raising campaign funds, may also limit its effectiveness. Another factor is that contributions often flow mostly to well-known friends whose support does not need to be won, rather than to those whose support has to be wooed. There even is evidence that PACs are constrained from pursuing the most effective strategies for influence by their need to decentralize efforts in response to the local orientations of their members.[21] Finally, PACs often face formidable competition from party leaders and constituents—and from one another—for the ear and the vote of a legislator. They are most successful in this competition, no doubt, when they represent powerful constituency interests and do not encounter party opposition or when the issue is of little concern to anyone else.

Political Parties

Amidst such a heavy flow of political money, it is easy to lose sight of the party role in campaign financing. Yet, the parties are important players in raising and spending money in political campaigns. They invest considerable resources in conducting party business—on running party conventions and other party processes during the nomination phase. As discussed earlier, they also channel their increasingly rich flow of soft money into supporting the general party ticket in campaigns.

But the parties have only a modest presence when it comes to contributing money directly to the campaigns of specific candidates. Beyond their soft-money expenditures, the dollars they spend in the presidential contests go to run the national conventions. The congressional campaign committees do contribute to specific candidates, with the Republicans providing somewhat more than the Democrats, but the $4.8 million they gave in 1993–94 constituted a paltry 0.6 percent of the congressional candidates' campaign funds. More substantial are the roughly equal amounts the Democratic and Republican congressional committees contributed in coordinated expenditures on behalf of their candidates, but even here the $42 million total in 1993–94 amounted to only 6 percent of the candidates' total. These figures suggest how much more money the parties will have to raise and spend before they can reestablish a major role for themselves in American electoral politics or achieve the position in financing and running campaigns that parties assume in the other democracies of the world. That even these sums now come predominantly from the party committees in the Congress, as vehicles of the party in government rather than the party organizations, also reflects the nature of the party presence in American campaigns.

The Candidates Themselves

One of the most noticeable developments in recent years has been the increasing role of candidates' personal fortunes in funding their campaigns. Candidates' personal wealth always has had a place in American campaigning, but it seems more important today than ever. As with Forbes and Taylor in 1996, Ross Perot's fortune underwrote his presidential campaign in 1992; FEC reports show that he invested more than $63 million of his own money. In 1993–94, the congressional candidates ended up bankrolling their campaigns to the tune of $35.5 million, plus another $87.3 million in loans, and these funds represented 17 percent of all their campaign money (Table 12.5). The aggregate totals provide a misleading impression of the role of personal money, however, because it is more unevenly distributed than other sources of campaign funds. The average figure is greatly inflated by the self-financing of a few relatively wealthy candidates. In 1993–94 congressional fund-raising, for example, just one candidate, Michael Huffington of California, accounted for almost a quarter of the total personal contributions and loans.

Public Funding

Finally, for some campaigns, public funding is available if the candidate wishes to claim it. Claiming it, of course, often means accepting spending limitations as a condition of receiving the money. Public monies are most conspicuously available for the presidential campaigns (see box on following page). In 1992, public matching funds for the preconvention contenders, subsidies for the national conventions, and grants to Bush and Clinton for the general-election campaign totaled $175.4 million, or 32 percent of the total costs in the nomination contests and general election. The full costs of the general election were covered out of the federal treasury except for the money spent by independent Ross Perot, who decided not to request federal matching funds. By contrast, there is no public funding of congressional elections.

THE "CATCH" IN PUBLIC FUNDING

Under public funding provisions for presidential elections, first implemented in 1976, all qualified candidates receive federal money to match individual contributions during the nomination contests and full public funding of their general-election campaign. In exchange for these federal funds, candidates are required to limit their expenditures to prescribed levels in each state and overall in pursuing the nomination and to use only federal funds in their general election campaign. The money to finance public funding is raised through a voluntary income tax checkoff; taxpayers can divert a part of their tax payments, without increasing what they owe or reducing their refunds, to fund the presidential election simply by checking the appropriate box on their tax returns. Through 1992, the checkoff was $1 for individuals or $2 for married persons filing jointly; in 1993, it was raised to $3 and $6, respectively.

The "catch" is that the candidates cannot receive more money than has accumulated in funds dedicated to public funding, even if they are entitled to more. The candidate entitlements are based on a set formula through which a base amount is adjusted for yearly changes in the cost of living. The revenues collected from the checkoff depend, on the other hand, on individual taxpayer decisions to divert taxes for this purpose. In its first decade of operation, about a quarter of all taxpayers used the checkoff; since then, participation has declined to well under 20 percent of taxpayers (17.7 percent in 1992).[22]

In early 1996, the accumulations in the fund were inadequate to cover the legitimate requests for public funding, and candidates for the presidential nomination did not receive all of the federal matching funds for which they had qualified. The Treasury had only $22.4 million in its fund by January 1996 to fill requests from candidates for more than $37 million at the start of the campaign. When such a shortfall occurs, the law requires that money first be set aside for financing the general elections and the party conventions before it can be distributed to candidates in the nomination phase, even if tax payments later in the year would fully replenish the fund. This means that the candidates who agreed to abide by spending limits in exchange for public funds received only a fraction of the public funds they had counted on early in their campaigns, while self-financed candidates Forbes and Taylor were free to spend as much as they wished. With an incumbent Democrat running for reelection without opposition, the consequences of the short fall in 1996 were borne by the various Republican contenders, especially those most in need of public money.[23]

SOURCES OF FUNDS AT THE STATE AND LOCAL LEVEL

The preceding paragraphs have focused on the national funding experience. The picture in the fifty states is, as usual, both more varied and less clear. All evidence suggests that national patterns generally prevail in state and local election campaigns. Individual contributors are the most important source of campaign funds, followed by PAC contributions and then, at greater distance, by party and personal funds. A minority of states and even some cities (for example, New York City) provide public funding, but it generally defrays only a small portion of the campaign costs and often goes to parties rather than candidates.[24]

There are, however, several important departures from federal patterns when one turns to state and local financing. First, individual contributions become relatively more important in local campaigns because the interest of parties and PACs in those campaigns is less lively. Candidates in the localities are also more limited in the ways in which they raise money; fund-raising experts are usually beyond their means, for example, and the practicalities rule out such techniques as telethons and mass mail solicitation. Second, because campaign finance regulations vary enormously from state to state or city to city, there always will be exceptions to the general patterns. For example, in Oregon, Pennsylvania, and Washington, PACs have provided at least a third of the campaign funds for legislative candidates compared to 13 percent in Wisconsin and 12 percent in Missouri.[25] Third, legislative leaders and legislative caucuses in an increasing number of states are supplying campaign funds to their party's legislative candidates. Because many states do not impose low ceilings, or in some cases any limits at all, on campaign contributions in state legislative contests, such donations can play a significant role in a candidate's campaign.[26]

REFORM AND REGULATION

Disgruntlement with the prevailing ways of financing political campaigns has been a longstanding feature of the American political culture. For a long time, the regulation of campaign finance in the United States was a jerry-built structure of assorted and not very well integrated federal and state statutes. Periodically, reformers attempted to bring order out of that legislation and at the same time to strengthen legal controls over the raising and spending of campaign money. A new episode of reform was under way in the early 1970s when the Watergate scandals broke over the country. The result in 1974 was the most extensive federal legislation on the subject in the history of the Republic.

The 1974 law, as many laws are, was set down on an already existing web of legislation, superseding some of it and supplementing some of it. Some of the 1974 law, in turn, was invalidated by the United States Supreme Court in late January 1976. It was then supplemented by amendments passed in the late 1970s. The resulting structure of federal legislation falls into two main categories: the limitations on campaign contributions and spending and the provisions for setting up a system of public funding of national politics.[27]

Limitations on Contributions

The provisions of existing federal law, which apply only to candidates for president and Congress restrict the amounts of money each individual, PAC, and political party can give to a candidate for each election (primary or general) or for the year (see Table 12.6). Corporations and labor unions themselves may not contribute, but they may set up political action committees and pay their overhead and administrative costs.

The new limits on the size of contributions in the 1974 legislation have already curbed the role of the very large contributor. Even with the loopholes (and the possibility that all adults in a family can contribute within the ceiling), under these laws, the large contributors will be unlimited only in their personal, independent efforts on behalf of candidates or their soft money contributions.

Limitations on Expenditures

The federal campaign finance laws also impose restrictions on expenditures for presidential candidates. If they accept federal subsidies for the prenomination and general-election campaigns, they must agree to spend no more than the law permits: a base level established in 1974 of $10 million before the convention and $20 million after it plus cost of living adjustments for each succeeding year. In 1996, presidential candidates were allowed to spend no more than $37.1 million to compete for the nomination and another $61.8 million in the general election. Moreover, candidates must abide by prenomination spending limits in each of the 50 states based on their voting-age populations; these limits ranged from a high of $11.3 million in California to a low of $618 thousand in the smallest states. If presidential and vice-presidential candidates accept the public subsidies, they are also limited to expenditures of no more than $50,000 of their own or their family's money on the campaigns.

Table 12.6   LIMITS ON CAMPAIGN CONTRIBUTIONS UNDER FEDERAL LAW

	Limit on Contributions		
	Individual	Political Action Committee	Party Committee
To candidate or candidate committee per election	$ 1,000	$ 5,000[a]	$ 5,000[a]
To national party committee per year	$20,000	$15,000	no limit
To any nonparty committee (PAC) per year	$ 5,000	$ 5,000	$ 5,000
Total contributions per year	$25,000	no limit	no limit

[a] If the political action committee or the party committee qualifies as a "multicandidate committee" under federal law by making contributions to five or more federal candidates, the limit is $5,000. Otherwise, the PAC is treated as an individual with a limit of $1,000. Party committees can contribute up to $17,500 to Senate candidates.

Source: Adapted from *Federal Election Commission, Campaign Guide* (June, 1985).

The 1974 law's limits on spending in House and Senate campaigns were the chief casualties of a Supreme Court decision in 1976.[28] The challengers to the statutes—an unlikely coalition extending from Senator James Buckley and the conservative *Human Events* magazine to Eugene McCarthy and the New York Civil Liberties Union—had argued that restrictions on campaign expenditures infringed upon the rights of free speech and political activity. The Supreme Court agreed. Expenditure limits, therefore, are permissible only when they are a condition of the voluntary acceptance of public subsidies. Congress could thus reinstate the expenditure limits on its own campaigns only as part of a plan for subsidizing them. Candidates, of course, would have to be free to reject the subsidies, as the presidential candidates are. The restrictions on contributions make rejecting subsidies a hazardous option, however, for the presidential contestants unless they are willing to invest their own fortunes in their campaigns.

Requirements for Accounting and Reporting

Just as important as their limitations have been the requirements for public disclosure of contributions and spending. All contributions to a federal candidate now must go through and be accounted for by a single campaign committee; prior to the reforms, candidates could avoid full public disclosure by using a complex array of committees. Each candidate must file quarterly reports on his or her finances and then supplement them with reports ten days before the election and thirty days after it. All contributors of $200 or more must be identified by name, address, occupation, and name of employer.

The publicity provisions of earlier legislation had not been notably effective. Reports were sketchy at best and missing at worst. The new legislation has improved the quality of reporting, however, by centralizing candidate responsibility in a single committee, by creating a new public interest in reporting, and by setting up an agency (the Federal Election Commission) to collect the data and to make them available. Despite the continuing desire of some members of Congress to undercut the disclosure of campaign finance data by reducing funding for the FEC, so far the commission has been able to publicize contributions and expenditures quickly and comprehensively, and the FEC's public files, now available in computer-readable form, have been a treasure trove of campaign finance information for scholars and journalists.

Public Funding of Presidential Campaigns

Although the Congress has not yet been willing to fund its own challengers from the public treasury, since 1976 it has provided public support for presidential candidates.

Presidential candidates seeking their party nominations are qualified for public funding only if they first pass a private funding test. They have to raise $5,000 in contributions of $250 or less in each of twenty states. If they so establish their eligibility, public funds match every contribution up to $250, to a total of about $37.9 million in 1996. In addition, each of the major parties received $12.364 million that year to offset the costs of its national nominating convention.

Provisions for funding the general-election campaign are somewhat simpler. Candidates may draw on a public fund for some or all of their expenses up to a $20 million ceiling in 1974 dollars. This figure is recalculated for each presidential year according to rises in the consumer price index; the ceiling was $61.82 million in 1996.

Minor parties fare less well. They receive only a fraction of the maximum, and then only *after* the election if they have received at least 5 percent of the vote. If they drew at least 5 percent of the vote in the previous election, however, they can receive their payment before the election. Perot's independent candidacy in 1992 qualifies him for no public money in advance of the 1996 campaign; if he had run as a third-party candidate, he would have received public funding after the 1992 contest and in advance of the 1996 campaign. The section dealing with minor parties has received a major part of the criticism directed at the 1974 statute. Critics charge that it enfeebles minor parties, making it hard for them to reach major party status and, in view of the need to pay cash for many campaign expenses, making it hard for them to finance even a modest campaign.

The Consequences of Reform

The new structure of federal regulation and subsidy worked a number of changes in the campaign finance system and the nature of campaign politics. To a considerable degree, the reforms have achieved their paramount purpose. They have lowered the scale of presidential campaign expenditures. From 1972 to 1992, real expenditures increased by only 19 percent, and in three of the five elections they actually declined. By contrast, the growth in presidential expenditures had been an explosive 225 percent between 1960 and 1972. They also have opened up campaign giving to public scrutiny by removing the veil of secrecy that previously had shielded contributors and their contributions from attention.

The reforms have not been entirely successful, however, in realizing their other paramount goal—ending the role of the giant contributors to both presidential and congressional campaigns. In presidential nominations, the day of the big contributors (when a candidate could raise hundreds of thousands of dollars for a campaign in one Manhattan or Hollywood visit) has ended. Similar activity has been restricted in congressional campaigns as well. The possibility of unlimited soft-money contributions to the parties for "party" activities, however, has opened a window through which "fat cats" have been able to reenter presidential election politics, albeit not in the untrammeled and secret way they once were able to operate (see box on p. 294).

In achieving these purposes, however, the campaign finance reforms of the 1970s have altered the nature of federal campaigning in important and not always desirable ways. First, as large individual donors have become less important in congressional campaigns, alternative sources of money—PACs, wealthy candidates, and small contributors—have become more valuable and plentiful. No one decries the growing importance of the small contributors, although reliance upon them does enhance the influence of the direct mail fund-raising specialists—a prospect some thoughtful observers of politics find disturbing. On the other hand, that PACs and wealthy candidates now play more of a role in congressional campaigns has obviously raised a new set of concerns.

THE NEW FAT CATS: SOFT-MONEY DONORS IN THE 1990s

Both political parties raise millions of dollars in soft-money contributions from a few wealthy individuals, corporations, or organizations. The Republican National Committee has turned to a group of $100,000 contributors, called Team 100, to raise millions for the party. In the 1991–92 election cycle, its largest single contributor was Dwayne Archer and his Archer-Daniels-Midland Company of Decatur, Illinois, who donated $907,000. The Democratic National Committee proved to be even more adept at obtaining money in this fashion. By March 1994, it had attracted huge contributions from a variety of corporations and their executives (for example, $508,333 from Time Warner, $270,000 from the irrepressible Archer-Daniels-Midland, and $250,000 from Walt Disney), associations (for example, $339,950 from the National Education Association) unions ($229,100 from the Communication Workers of America), and individuals ($250,000 from Carl Lindner of American Financial Corporation, $237,200 from Swanee Hunt, and $200,000 from Edgar Bronfman and son of Seagrams)—as well as $300,000 from the Mashantucket Pequot Tribe.[29]

Second, as expenditure ceilings were lowered for the 1976 presidential campaign, the patterns of spending changed. Candidates cut down less on media advertising and more on other advertisements (for example, billboards) and the traditional paraphernalia of campaigns buttons, leaflets, and bumper stickers. Amendments to the Federal Election Campaign Act in 1979 were designed to restore some of these traditional activities by permitting state and local parties to spend unlimited amounts for campaign materials. Still, tighter planning and setting of priorities has become the order of the day in presidential camps; by general agreement, there has been less activity in the smaller states or in states that appeared secure for the opposition. The Bush campaign in 1992 virtually halted its campaign efforts in California, for instance, when pre-election polls showed that they had fallen way behind.

Third, the new limits on spending in the presidential nominations process may be too low. Low state-spending ceilings in the early primary and caucus states may provide insufficient money for the intense campaigning there, especially now that so many nomination contests have crowded to the front of the calendar. Moreover, by spending up to the federal levels in the early states, candidates often reach their overall spending ceiling before the last primaries and caucuses occur. If future nomination contests go down to the last few states in May and June, it is quite possible that they will be waged without candidates being able to spend any money on television and the other usual forms of campaign advertising.

Fourth, regulation and the 1976 Supreme Court decision have clearly stimulated the growth of independent expenditures—initially by individuals and ideological PACs and more recently by business and trade-association committees. Moreover, the clear favoring of Republican causes in those expenditures has introduced a new source of inequality into campaign finance.

Fifth, strict regulations and extensive reporting requirements have increased centralized control of campaigns and have made lawyers and accountants indispensable members of the modern campaign staff. Campaigns rely much less on the loosely coordinated efforts of local campaign organizations and volunteers and much more upon paid professionals than was the case prior to the reforms.

Finally, public funding of the presidential campaigns may have skewed the outcomes in important ways. By providing a sizable financial "grubstake" to the major-party candidates at the beginning of their campaigns and effectively denying it to others until after the election, they have increased the competitive disadvantage of third-party and independent candidates. Ross Perot demonstrated that by bringing to bear great personal wealth this hurdle can be overcome, but it remains imposing for ordinary candidates unless they have the capability to raise extraordinary amounts of money. Moreover, by possibly denying candidates for the party nominations the full matching amounts to which they are entitled because of shortfalls in public funds, public funding provisions seem to further advantage candidates who can raise the most money.

Nor have the reforms been politically neutral in other respects. Most observers thought that the new subsidies and expenditure limits helped Jimmy Carter to the White House in 1976, Gary Hart's challenge to front-runner Walter Mondale in 1984, and perhaps even Pat Buchanan's insurgency against President Bush in 1992. The preconvention grants obviously benefit the less well-known candidates for the presidential nomination, especially the ones with a limited financial base. The grants and limits in the presidential campaign also have erased the usual GOP advantage in spending and have prevented affluent campaigns from developing a late media blitz that conceivably could carry a close election. Contribution limits and the entry of PACs may have redounded to the benefit of the already advantaged incumbents in congressional races.

More generally, as perhaps the recent avalanche of soft-money contributions or the independent expenditures exemplify, we are learning that in a capitalistic society where freedom of speech is constitutionally protected, money always is going to play an important role in the selection of government officials. Campaign finance reforms may erect dikes to contain it, but the dikes then channel the money in other, sometimes equally undesirable, directions. The dikes also inevitably develop leaks that may take some time to close. The lesson is that the role of money can be altered, although not always in predictable ways given human resourcefulness and the necessary incompleteness of laws, but it cannot be eliminated.

In one important way, however, the experience did not have the result many expected. It has not yet led to public subsidies for elections to Congress. The main issues here were two. First, there was a good deal of concern about voter reaction—a concern that voters would view subsidies as an improper use of tax monies or as a congressional raid on the treasury for its own advantage. The second issue concerned a possible incumbent and partisan bias in public funding. A few members of Congress grumbled that they would be subsidizing their own opponents, but the Republicans and many observers thought the plan would further entrench the incumbent

Democrats, at least before 1994. What scholarly evidence there is on the point, however, suggests a significant relationship between a challenger's level of expenditures and his or her ability to give an incumbent a close race, so public funding of congressional campaigns seems likely to stimulate rather than reduce competition.

It is as of yet unclear what effect these reforms have had upon the role of political parties in the electoral process. Two broad questions are involved. Have the reforms strengthened or weakened today's parties in comparison to yesterday's? How have they affected parties in comparison to their competitors—especially the candidates, individual contributors, and organized groups—in influencing the party in government? At first glance, the parties seem to have been victims of the reforms, especially in their role as contributors to federal campaigns. They have been limited in the cash contributions they can make to presidential and congressional candidates. Moreover, direct public funding of candidates rather than parties (which is the common practice in other democracies and some states) enhances the traditional separation between the presidential campaign and the party organization. More important, the absence of limits on independent expenditures by individuals or PACs has given the advantage to the parties' major competitors for influence over candidates.

But this first glance is deceiving. Higher ceilings on contributions to parties than to PACs or candidates give the parties an edge in fund-raising, and both national parties are now more successful fund raisers than they have ever been. Contribution limits on individuals make party funds even more attractive to the congressional candidates. Most important, the parties have been able to circumvent the $5,000 limit on their contributions to candidates by providing valuable services, acting as conduits for individual contributions to candidates (so-called bundling), channeling soft money to the state parties, making coordinated expenditures for the party ticket as a whole, and investing in long-term state and local party building.

Thus, the national party committees now play a much more important role in political campaigns than ever before, which increases the potential of some centralized direction for the American parties and their candidates. There are signs too that the state and local parties, energized by the new funding directed their way from the national parties and by their own successes in fund-raising, are becoming more actively involved in campaigns—especially in the labor-intensive grass-roots work that was the staple of party organizations in an earlier era. Money was not the vital resource that the traditional party organizations brought to political campaigns anyway, so their current financial contributions are a new-found source of influence. Amid this continuing transformation in campaign practices and traditional party roles, though, it is difficult to come to any final conclusion about the impact of campaign-finance reform on the parties. Moreover, it is quite conceivable that the parties' role in campaigns ultimately may depend more upon their own initiative than present financing laws.[30]

State Regulation and Financing

To the maze of federal legislation must be added the even more complicated fabric of fifty different state regulations. The states have long set at least some limits to campaign activity, usually in response to egregious violations of fair campaign practices. Most states, for example, have some law prohibiting certain election-day expenditures; all prohibit bribery and vote buying; and some prohibit such practices as buying a voter a drink on election day. Most states also require that expenditures be made through an authorized campaign treasurer or committee and that contributions and expenditures be reported.

The Watergate scandals spurred a new round of campaign finance legislation in the states after 1972, and the states have continued to be active in this area. The most popular measure is a requirement that campaign contributions be publicly disclosed. Many states also have acted to restrict campaign contributions. In 1992, thirty-two states limited campaign contributions by individuals; twenty prohibited and another nineteen limited contributions by corporations; ten prohibited and twenty-five limited labor union donations to candidates; and twenty-five placed limits on PAC giving. A few even limited contributions from parties (fourteen) or the candidates themselves (eleven).

A minority of states have even ventured into public funding for state elections. A total of twenty-three have some kind of arrangement for allocating money from their treasuries to political campaigns. In ten states the payments go to the political parties, which in turn can spend the money on behalf of candidates. In another ten, they go directly to the candidates, and in three states public funding is provided for both the parties and the candidates. The level of state support for campaigns, though, falls far short of being proportionate to the full funding that is provided by the federal treasury to the presidential general-election campaigns. Moreover, only eight of the states that provided public funding limited candidate expenditures; two other states allowed for voluntary limitations.[31]

The Continuing Quest for Campaign Finance Reform

The burst of post-Watergate legislative activity in the Congress and the states has not put the question of reform to rest. Pressures for new regulations follow changes in the patterns of campaign finance. The growth of the PAC role has spawned a new set of proposed remedies: reduced limits on PAC contributions to candidates or their elimination altogether, a new limit on the total dollar amount congressional candidates could accept from PACs, restrictions on the amount a candidate can raise out of state, and, ultimately, public financing, with its condition of limits on how much the candidate can raise and spend. Similarly, the growth of independent expenditures, especially in national politics, has spurred the search for limitations on them. At a minimum, the reformers would like to tighten the statutory definition of independence to eliminate the possibility of even indirect coordination between candidate or party and the independent spender.

At least three considerations now slow the course of additional reform. First, unless the Supreme Court retreats from its position in *Buckley* and subsequent cases, the reform options are sharply limited. By holding limits on expenditures unconstitutional for independent groups or individuals and for candidates without public funding, for example, the Court sharply curtails the feasible ways for capping the costs of campaigning or independent spending. Second, campaign finance has increasingly become a partisan and ideological issue, with liberals and Democrats favoring one set of restrictions and conservatives and Republicans another. It would thus appear that substantial reform at the national level would be difficult or unlikely unless one party controlled both the Congress and the presidency. Third, even one-party control of all branches of government would not necessarily favor reform. Incumbent legislators are leery about changing the rules under which they have been elected, especially in ways that might give an advantage to challengers. Unless powerful popular pressures for reform return, incumbents feel that certain rules disadvantage them, or the new GOP congressional majorities act to undo reforms imposed upon them by the Democrats, the chances for major changes in current campaign financing laws seem slim.[32]

MONEY, PARTIES, AND POWER IN AMERICAN POLITICS

The status quo in American campaign finance raises a series of questions about power and influence in the American democracy. The first is the basic question of influence in the parties and electoral processes. Political contributors have political goals and incentives, just as do activists who contribute their skills and labor to the party organization or to a candidate's campaign. Large numbers of Americans wonder what kinds of demands or expectations accompany their financial contributions. Money is obviously a major resource of American politics, and its contributors clearly acquire some form of political influence. What is not yet clear is the nature of the influence and the differences, both quantitative and qualitative, between it and the influence that results from nonmonetary contributions to the parties and candidates.

It is not easy to specify with certainty the goals or incentives that motivate the financial contributor. Very likely they come from the same range of incentives that stir the activist to contribute his or her time to the party organization: patronage, preferment, a political career; personal, social, or psychological satisfactions; and interest, issue, and ideology. Unquestionably, the chief incentive is the desire to influence the establishment or administration of some kind of public policy. The concentration of PAC contributions on incumbent members of Congress is a case in point. The contributor's desire may be for direct access or for the ear of the powerful. More commonly, it is only a desire to elect public officials with values and preferences that promise a sympathy for the goals of the contributor. Thus, the demands of the contributor are largely indirect; certainly, very few contributors seek a direct quid pro quo.[33]

Second, in addition to the issue of influence on policy, there is the question of power within the party. The status quo in American political finance supports current officeholders and helps them maintain their independence from the party organizations. So long as candidates and officeholders continue to finance their own primary and general-election campaigns, they block the organizations' control of access to public office. Unquestionably, the reluctance of Congress and state legislatures to disturb the present patterns of political finance grows, in large part, from their satisfaction with the political independence these patterns ensure them. Despite the spate of reforms of recent years, candidate spending as opposed to party organization spending remains entrenched. The candidate, rather than the party, raises and spends large sums of money. Even in the sorties into public financing of campaigns, in contrast to the practice in many other democracies, the funds go to candidates (not to party organizations) in presidential elections and in a majority of states with public funding. To be sure, there has been some indirect support of a party role—the federal legislation permitting party committees to spend beyond candidate expenditure ceilings and the allowance for unrestricted soft-money donations to state parties, for example—but it is far less than would be necessary to establish strong and disciplined parties with sanctions over their candidates and officeholders.

Third, reform in campaign finance, like all other party reform, never affects all individuals and parties alike. It works to some people's advantage and to others' disadvantage. The cumulative effect of the reforms of the 1970s will surely be to diminish the influence of wealthy contributors and to make the "little" contributor more valuable than ever. In that respect, one ought to note, however, that it is hardly certain that one contributor of $10,000 actually made more effective demands on the recipient than ten contributors of $1,000 will and, furthermore, $1,000 is hardly a small contribution. New influence and access also accrue to the technicians who can raise small gifts as well as to group contributors and incumbents. Also, some advantages clearly accrue to candidates who can raise substantially greater sums than their opponents can. Concern over the effect of unequal cash resources cuts two ways, however. Some of the support for public funding comes from those who see it as a way of equalizing resources and thus eliminating unfair advantages; but cash is not the only resource a candidate needs. Incumbent officeholders have all manner of other advantages over challengers—staffs, media access, and name recognition, for example—and challengers may well need to have a cash advantage if they are to have a chance of winning and if elections are to remain competitive.

CAMPAIGN FINANCE: A REFLECTION OF THE AMERICAN WAY

The American way of campaign finance reflects the American way of politics. Campaign costs reflect the vastness of the country, the many elective offices on many levels of government, the localism of American politics, and the unbridled length of our campaigns for office. The domination of spending by candidates reflects our candidate-dominated campaigns and, more generally, the dominance within American parties of the party in government. The importance of the mass media in major American campaigns speaks volumes about the media themselves, while it also reflects the sheer size of our constituencies.

By contrast, campaign finance in Great Britain involves far smaller sums more firmly in the control of the party organizations. Moreover, British campaigns have free time on the government-run BBC and a long-standing, albeit eroding, tradition of the soft sell rather than the American-style hard sell in campaign advertising. The British election campaign runs for only about three weeks, during which paid radio and television political advertising is banned, and the average constituency in the

House of Commons has less than one-fifth as many people as the average American congressional district. Most significantly, there is no office with a constituency as vast as most American states, not to mention the American presidency's national constituency. British campaigns are organized around their national party leaders, to be sure, but they depend upon integration between the local parliamentary candidate and the leader rather than the largely separate campaigns of American congressional and presidential candidates.

Aided by institutions such as the direct primary and the office-block ballot and supported by their ability to recruit the campaign resources they need, the American parties in government thus largely escape the control of party organizations. Two of each party's national organizations, the congressional campaign committees, are under the thumb of elected officeholders rather than party professionals. Even the national committees receive powerful direction from the party's president and presidential candidates, and much of their soft money resources are raised in conjunction with the presidential campaign. In many states and localities, the officeholders also dominate, and legislative leaders are important sources of campaign funds in many of the states.

But what price does the American political system pay for this? Certainly, there is the price of a loss of cohesion as a party in government—for example, in the loss of a unified presence as party representatives in American legislatures. Certainly, too, there is the price of a weakening of party organization, not only vis-a-vis the party in government, but also internally, in terms of its ability to achieve the goals of its activists. Finally, nowhere in the life of the parties is the competition between party in government and party organization any clearer than in the competition for campaign funds and campaign control. As the costs of campaigning rise and as all participants are forced to shift to a cash economy of enormous magnitude, the future is with the sector of the party with access to those cash resources. So far, the advantage is clearly with the candidates and officeholders.

PART
Five

THE PARTY IN GOVERNMENT

America's first political parties, and the first parties in most other democracies as well, were built around opposing factions in the government.[1] Later developing parties here and elsewhere were erected on a broader foundation, in keeping with the more democratic system in which they emerged, but typically at their core before too long also were identifiable factions within the government. With such ancestry, it is little wonder that the party in government so dominates the political party, so structures partisan political conflict, and so profoundly shapes our images of the party.

Yet, unlike their counterparts in parliamentary systems, the American parties in government are notoriously loose coalitions, sometimes even exhibiting little more cohesiveness than a "pick-up" team of playground basketball players. Each party member represents a different constituency and heeds his or her constituency more than the party leaders. Furthermore, the structural separation of legislature from executive denies to the American parties in government the prime unifying activity of governing—the responsibility for creation and maintenance of the government. Few scholars have made this point as pungently as E. E. Schattschneider:

> Yet, when all is said, it remains true that . . . the parties are unable to hold their lines on a controversial public issue when the pressure is on. . . . (This) constitutes the most important single fact concerning the American parties. He who knows this fact, and knows nothing else, knows more about American parties than he who knows everything except this fact. What kind of party is it that, having won control of government, is unable to govern.[2]

Nonetheless, parties—as parties—are critical to the functioning of the American government. Party lines are the chief lines of conflict in American legislatures. There is a degree of intraparty cohesion and interparty division in the legislative roll calls of the states and, especially these days, of Congress that cannot be lightly dismissed. The party winning the presidency even succeeds in carrying out a good portion of its party platform.[3] Furthermore, partisan considerations apply in the staffing of the top, appointive levels of national, state, and local executive offices and in the appointment of judges to the bench. Public-policy making in the United States does vary significantly with the composition of the party in government, however faint its imprint sometimes may be.

Some distinctions are important here. When public officials are elected on a partisan basis, as they are almost always in most democratic systems, including the American, whichever party or coalition of parties can command a majority determines which one is nominally in charge of each governmental institution. Constitutional separation of powers throughout the various levels of the American system complicates this situation by permitting split control of the different governmental institutions. Since 1969, in fact, split party control of the national government has been the norm, not the exception. But nominal control is only the first step in party control over policy making, the initial point on a continuum measuring the extent of **party government**—the ability of public officials of the same party to enact the programs of their party. Political systems can be located at various points along this continuum of party government, and where they are at any one time depends upon the cohesiveness of the party in government as well as whether control of the different institutions is divided.

Furthermore, because it is **party** government about which we speak, which parts of the party do we expect to set the policy by which the party will govern—all three sectors, the party organization, or just the party in government? If the latter, would it be the entire party in government, or is it possible that the executive party has propensities and abilities to govern different from those of the legislative party?

It is well to remember that although the three sectors of the party are brought together in the search for power at elections, each has its own goals and motives. The activists of the party organization may seek to translate a program or ideology into policy, but they may also seek patronage jobs, other forms of reward or preference, the sensations of victory, or the defeat of a hated opposition. The party's voters may be stimulated by an issue, a program, or an ideology, but they also respond to personalities, to incumbency, to abstract and traditional loyalties to a candidate or party, or to the urging of friends and family. The candidates and officeholders seek the office, its tangible rewards, its intangible satisfactions, and its opportunities to make public decisions. The important point is that none of the three sectors is committed wholly or possibly even predominantly to the capture of public office for the purpose of enacting party policies into law.

The classic American statement on party government (or party responsibility) was made in the late 1940s by a committee of the American Political Science Association in a report entitled *Toward a More Responsible Two-Party System.*[4] The report argued that the American parties ought to articulate more specific and comprehensive policy programs, nominate candidates pledged to those programs, and then see to it that their successful candidates enact the programs while they are in office. In other words, the major parties ought to serve as the mechanisms through which American voters can choose between competing programs, and through which the winning majority of voters can be assured of the enactment of its choice.

Put in such terms, the question of party government (or responsibility) concerns not just the nature of the parties but the nature of American democracy itself. If the parties were to become policy initiators, they would assume a central representative role in the American democracy. They would bring great, amorphous majorities in the American electorate into alliance with groups of officeholders by means of some kind of party program or platform. They would forge a new representative link between the mass democratic electorate and the powerful few in government. To put the issue another way, responsible parties would bring electorates closer to the choices of government by giving them a way to register choices on policy alternatives. Those choices might be partly before the fact (in the mobilization of grassroots support behind proposed programs) and partly retrospective judgments on the stewardship of two different, distinguishable parties in government. In both cases, the proposal is an attempt to restore initiative and significant choice to the great number of voters.[5]

The critics of such proposals for party government have concentrated on one insistent theme: the nonideological, heterogeneous, and pragmatic nature of the American parties. They argue that agreement on and enforcement of a coherent policy program is very difficult, if not impossible, in the American setting. Recently, of course, the party organizations are more oriented toward programs and ideology and thus toward the uses of governmental authority for specific policy goals. There was a time when the activists of the party organization contested elections largely for the spoils at stake: jobs, contracts, honors, access, and other forms of special consideration. It made little difference to them what uses public officeholders made of the governmental power in their hands. That time is passing. As more and more citizens are attracted to the party organizations and electorates for reasons of policy, important intraparty pressure builds for some degree of party responsibility.

Discussion of more programmatic and disciplined political parties leads always to the European parties, especially those of England. Parliamentary institutions foster the kind of legislative cohesion and discipline—the sharply drawn party lines—that the advocates of responsible parties have in mind. Giving the House of Commons the power to select the chief executive of the government, the prime minister, from its own ranks and making the prime minister dependent upon command of a legislative majority to continue in office creates powerful incentives for party government.

Party organizations in parliamentary systems seek to enforce the party's program on its legislators. In some cases, they have succeeded—in many of the socialist and communist parties, among others. In others, they have not, but even in these cases the national party leaders speak powerfully for the party's program. One often sees a concerted effort on the part of the party in government (all of which sits in parliament) and the party organization to carry out a program that was adopted with the help of the party members at an earlier party conference. Indeed, so strong has been party discipline in the legislative process in some European countries that scholars complained about the decline of parliaments and journalists wrote darkly of "party-ocracy." Ironically, in these circles, it is not uncommon to hear envious talk of the flexible, nondogmatic American parties and the uncontrolled and deliberative American legislatures.

The European experience is important for perspective and comparison. It is also important because the European variety of party government, with its focus on parliamentary discipline, has dominated the thinking of many Americans about party government. Any change in the American parties toward greater responsibility, however, will probably follow no European route. The role the parties now have in American politics and the roles toward which they move will be as uniquely American as the institutional complex of American federalism, separation of powers, and electoral processes that influence them. Given the power of the executive in American government, its ability to convert party goals or platforms into public policy may be as important as the legislature's.

Beyond this question of the party's contribution to the making of public policy—to the organizing of majority decisions in a democracy—there is another one: the question of the impact of winning office and making policy on the political party. The achievement of party goals (the goals of all three sectors) depends directly on the holding of governmental power—but in what way? To put it bluntly, what does governmental power do for the parties? What kinds of rewards does it generate for the men and women who have invested so much in politics and the party? How does it contribute to the health and vitality of the party and its various sectors?

The chapters in this part address such questions of party influence and party gain. The first two chapters examine the present role of the political party in the organization and operation of the three branches of government. They are primarily concerned with the degrees of party direction or party cohesion in legislative, executive, and judicial policy making. In short, they deal with the impact of internalized party loyalties and external party influences on public officials. The third chapter in this part faces the general question of party government—its desirability and its possibility in the American political setting. It also addresses the question of whether the new programmatic orientations within the parties create conditions hospitable to the development of party government.

Chapter
13

Party and Partisans in the Legislature

The political party assumes an obvious, very public form—yet often a very shadowy role—in American legislatures. The parties organize majority and minority power in the legislatures, and the legislative leaders and committee chairpersons are usually party oligarchs. Yet, despite the appearance and panoply of party power, voting on crucial issues often crosses party lines and violates party pledges and platforms. In short, the party in many forms dominates the American legislatures; yet, the effect of party effort and loyalty often seems small. On this paradox turns much of the scholarly concern and reformist zeal expended on American legislatures.

The character of the American legislative party has been deeply affected by the American separation of powers. In a parliamentary regime, such as that of Great Britain, a majority party (or a multiparty governing coalition) in the legislature must cohere in support of its leaders or it may lose its position. This creates powerful pressures for unity within the legislative party. When the parliamentary majority no longer supports the cabinet, either reorganization of the cabinet or a reshuffling of the legislative coalition supporting it ensues, or else the legislature is dissolved and sent home to face a new election.

No such institutional and constitutional pressures weigh on American legislators. They suffer no great penalty for voting in opposition to their party's legislative leaders. They may divide on, dispute with, or reject executive programs, even if the executive is of their own party, without dire consequences. In American legislatures, the party role is not institutionalized as it is in parliaments. The American legislature may not run so smoothly without high levels of party cohesion and discipline, but it can run, and executives can survive its faithlessness.

PARTY ORGANIZATION AND PARTY POWER IN LEGISLATURES

In forty-nine of the state legislatures and the Congress, almost all members come to their legislative tasks as elected candidates of a political party.[1] The ways in which they form and behave as a legislative party, however, differ enormously. In some states, the legislative party scarcely can be said to exist; in others, it dominates the legislative process through an almost daily regimen of party caucuses. Parties in most of the state legislatures and in the Congress, however, fall comfortably in the territory between these two poles.

Party Organization in the Congress

Party organization in the United States Congress stands as something of a benchmark for observations of the American legislatures because it is the best known of the legislatures.

Organizing the Congress   Both parties in both houses of Congress meet prior to the beginning of each congressional session to select their party leadership. In addition, the party meetings (called *caucuses* by the Democrats or *conferences* by the Republicans) nominate candidates for the position of speaker of the house or president pro tempore of the Senate, and they set up procedures for the appointment of party members to the regular committees of the chamber. In selecting the leadership for the entire House or Senate, of course, the majority party is in control—if it can remain unified, which it virtually always does. In effect, then, the basic unit of party organization conducts the initial business of organizing the chamber. From its decisions rises the machinery of the party as a party (the leaders, whips, policy committees) and the organization of the chamber itself (the presiding officer and the committees).

In this fashion, the organization of the two parties and the organization of the House and Senate are woven into what appears to be a single fabric. This organizational system is dominated by the majority party, which has been the Democratic party for most of time since World War Two but was the Republican party after the 1994 elections. The party with a voting majority has control of the committees and of the floor. It chooses the presiding officer or speaker of the House of Representatives and the chairs of all the standing committees in both houses. It hires (and fires) the staff of these standing committees and of the chambers (see box on following page). The presiding officer of the Senate is the vice-president of the United States, but it is the majority party that manages floor action to the degree that it is managed in that highly democratic institution. A majority of the membership of each committee also comes from the majority party, and by a margin that reflects the majority's margin in the house.

Party Leadership and Party Coordination   These are all positions of considerable power and authority within the party. That their occupants are chosen by the vote of all party members, though, makes their relationship with rank-and-file members more reciprocal than hierarchical. The leaders' power is delegated by the

THE SPOILS OF VICTORY: THE GOP PURGE OF COMMITTEE STAFF IN THE HOUSE OF REPRESENTATIVES

With their nationwide electoral successes in 1994, the Republicans gained majority control of the House of Representatives for the first time in forty years. This meant that they now chose the leaders of the House, determined its rules, and selected the staff for both the chamber and its committees. From the outset, the Republicans were determined to reduce the number of employees in these staff positions—a goal made more desirable by the fact that most existing staffers had been hired by the Democrats—and to exercise their prerogative to staff the House with their own people. They were aided in these efforts by the absence of the job-security protection afforded to workers in the executive branches of federal, state, and local governments. As the new majority took charge in January 1995, with the ruthless efficiency of the old-time patronage system, it summarily dismissed a multitude of mostly Democratic congressional staffers and replaced them with Republicans. In this way, the House continued the partisan turnabout initiated by voters in the 1994 contests and ensured that its staff would be sympathetic to Republican policies and priorities.

Each party fills out its own internal organizational structure as well, which is elected by the entire party membership of the chamber (see Figure 13.1). At the top of the party hierarchy is the party leader (called the majority or minority leader, depending on whether the party controls the chamber). In the House of Representatives, though, it is the speaker who serves as the true leader of the majority party. Beneath these leaders in the party hierarchy come the assistant party leader or "whip" and a panoply of assistant whips, so-called because of their traditional role in mobilizing the party members to vote the way the party leadership wants. Each congressional party also fills some specialized positions—for example, chairs of its caucus or conference (that is, the meeting of all members), its steering and policy committees, its campaign committee, and any other party committees it may create.

party caucus.[2] Consequently, leaders serve subject to the approval of their party—an approval the perquisites of leadership give them great advantage in, but no guarantee of, securing. Some top party leaders, even in the more democratic Congresses of modern times, have wielded more power and authority than others due no doubt to both their personal characteristics and the willingness of the party rank and file to accept strong leadership. Republican Speaker Newt Gingrich, for example, has been the strongest speaker in modern times. Not only have his party colleagues in the House been willing to delegate to him more authority than usual in seeking to fulfill the Republican agenda, but Speaker Gingrich has been more willing than usual to exercise his authority over the party rank and file.

HOUSE OF REPRESENTATIVES

Republicans	Democrats
Speaker Newt Gingrich, Ga.	
Majority Leader Dick Armey, Tex.	**Minority Leader** Richard Gephardt, Mo.
Majority Whip Tom Delay, Tex.	**Minority Whip** David Bonior, Mich.
Conference Chair John Boehner, Oh.	**Caucus Chair** Vic Fazio, Cal.
Steering Committee Chair Newt Gingrich, Ga.	**Steering Committee Co-Chairs** Richard Gephardt, Mo. Steny Hoyer, Md.
Policy Committee Chair Christopher Cox, Cal.	**Policy Committee Chair** Richard Gephardt, Mo.
Campaign Committee Chair Bill Paxon, N.Y.	**Campaign Committee Chair** Martin Frost, Tex.

SENATE

Republicans	Democrats
* **Majority Leader** Bob Dole, Kan.	**Minority Leader** Tom Daschle, S. Dak.
Majority Whip Trent Lott, Miss.	**Minority Whip** Wendell Ford, Ky.
Conference Chair Thad Cochran, Miss.	**Conference Chair** Tom Daschle, S. Dak.
Policy Committee Chair Don Nickles, Okla.	**Policy Committee Chair** Tom Daschle, S. Dak.
Committee on Committees Chair Larry Craig, Id.	**Steering and Coordination** Committee Chair John Kerry, Mass.
	Technology and Communications Committee John D. Rockefeller, W. Va.
Campaign Committee Chair Alfonse D'Amato, N.Y.	**Campaign Committee Chair** Bob Kerry, Neb.

Figure 13.1 Top party leaders in the U.S. Congress: 1995–96.

Note: The leader's state follows his name.

* Resigned his position in June 1996 and was replaced by Trent Lott.

The party leadership often has difficulty, however, in moving beyond organizing the two chambers to mobilize the party members for coordinated action in public-policy making. The policy committees do not necessarily function as broadly based instruments of party policy making or strategy even though they were created for that purpose. Instead of being a collective party leadership, they frequently tend to repre-sent the assorted blocs and wings of the party, which themselves often play the important role of uniting their members on behalf of some policy goal. Nor have the party caucuses or conferences always served to consolidate the party in common cause. When they do meet on important issues during the session, only occasionally do they undertake to bind their members to vote the same way.

Increased Party Coordination   Recent years have witnessed enhanced party coordination in the Congress, especially within the House of Representatives. The Republicans took a first, tentative step in this direction in the late 1960s by giving rank-and-file party members greater opportunity to influence party policy through the party caucus. In the 1970s, under the prodding of its reform-minded Democratic Study Group,[3] the Democrats took more dramatic steps toward the same goal by strengthening both the party caucus (the group of all party members) and the party leadership. Then at the beginning of the 1995 session, the new GOP majority moved toward being the most cohesive party in modern times.

The most visible of the Democratic party reforms early on was the power assumed by the caucus to challenge and even vote out incumbent committee chairs by secret ballot. During the preceding six decades, the position of committee chair went automatically to its most-senior majority-party member. The Democratic reforms of the 1970s changed that. Soon thereafter, not only were some chairs chal-lenged in the caucus, but a few were stripped of their committee positions and replaced by the choice of the party caucus—and not always by the next most-senior party member.[4] This transformation in the basis of a chair's power and other changes designed to give rank-and-file members more committee rights and leaders more control over the floor fundamentally restructured authority within the Democratic-run House—away from aged, sometimes autocratic committee chairs and toward the party caucus.

This enhanced caucus role is not by itself a tool for party centralization or pol-icy coordination. It increases the power and authority of the individual members at the expense of the committee chairs,[5] but it does not necessarily lead the individual members to use their newfound power on behalf of transcending party goals. What was required to turn this decentralization toward party-based centralization and coor-dination were two additional changes: First, a majority of individual members needed to be willing to use the caucus for collective party purposes. Party leaders then had to be willing and able to play an active coordinating role.[6]

When parties become more ideologically cohesive, it is easier for the party cau-cus to articulate a party position on substantive legislation and to pressure straggling party members to come into line. As will be discussed more fully later in the chapter, the membership of both parties in the House has become more ideologically homo-geneous in recent years. As conservative Democrats became less numerous and their committee strongholds were reduced, the Democrats became more cohesively liberal. Over the same period, energized particularly by conservative policy leadership from the White House during the Reagan years, ideological cohesion grew among the Republicans as well. After more than a decade as an increasingly combative minority party, the House GOP in 1995 took party control of Congress to a new level.

The Variable Role of Party Leadership   To the extent that there is party policy in the houses of Congress, though, it is largely set and implemented by the party leadership, although more so in the large and unwieldy House than in the smaller, less centralized upper chamber. The floor leaders and the powerful figures of the party consult widely throughout the party, but the final codification of party policy, the sensing of a will or consensus, rests primarily on their judgment. If they are of the president's party, their actions and decisions are limited by his legislative program and his influence within the Congress. Within the nonpresidential party, the leadership in the House and Senate may act not only without a continuing check by the legislative party but also without a continuing check by any party organ or spokesperson.[7]

What emerge as the decisions and priorities of the party leadership, however, are not really "party policy" except in the sense that they are voiced by leaders of the legislative party. They are, rather, an amalgam of or a negotiated compromise among the goals of the party members who hold committee power, the party leaders themselves, the rank and file of the legislative party, and (in one party) the president. They rarely flow from any national party program or platform. They speak, instead, of the powers and perquisites of the legislature, the need to support or oppose a president, and the demands of the legislative constituencies. The party leaders, in other words, do not enforce a prior party policy. They make policy for and with their fellow legislators in an ad hoc way. Their party policy is purely that of the legislative party and is developed as much to serve the individual reelection needs of each party member as to implement any coherent party philosophy or program.[8]

The authority of the party leadership in Congress has varied considerably over time. Before House members revolted against Speaker ("Czar") Joe Cannon in 1911, power in the House of Representatives was highly centralized in the hands of the speaker. Cannon chaired the Rules Committee through which he could control the flow of legislation to the floor; appointed committees and committee chairs, putting his lieutenants in the key positions; and generally possessed the resources and sanctions necessary for enforcing party discipline. Speakers after Cannon did not command such a powerful institutional position. Instead, they have had to operate in a far more decentralized House in which party discipline could only be maintained through skillful bargaining and strong personal loyalties. Successful speakers during this era, such as Sam Rayburn and Tip O'Neill, were consummate brokers rather than czars.[9]

By the late 1980s, however, it was clear that the seeds had been sown for a resurgence in party leadership power within the House of Representatives. First, Democratic party reforms in the House in the early 1970s provided the levers for a more forceful Democratic leadership. The power to assign members to committees was vested in the new Steering and Policy Committee chaired by the speaker. The speaker also was allowed to choose, subject to caucus ratification, the chair and other Democratic members of the Rules Committee, which serves as the "traffic cop" for legislation on the floor. The whip system was made more responsive to party leaders as well. Second, by 1987 the political context had changed to produce a Democratic majority that, because of its greater ideological cohesiveness and the opportunities provided by the party's recapture of the Senate, was ready for stronger leadership. During his brief tenure as speaker, Jim Wright took advantage of these opportunities to become one of the most assertive Democratic leaders in decades. His successor, Thomas Foley, however, was less inclined to such partisanship and returned to a more collegial style before being defeated for reelection in the Republican surge of 1994.[10]

Given the expansion in the authority of the Democratic leadership throughout much of the 1970s and 1980s, it is ironic that the pinnacle in party leadership power was achieved by a Republican—Speaker Newt Gingrich in 1995. Gingrich's leadership role did not evolve from the gradual effect of procedural reforms, for the minority Republicans had been bystanders to the Democratic changes. Instead it emerged full-born out of Republican determination to enact the comprehensive policy changes promised in the Contract with America around which they had centered their successful 1994 campaign. With a Democrat in the White House and a slender majority in the House, the GOP realized that their only hope of realizing the goals of their contract and of spending cuts to produce a balanced budget lay in unshakable party discipline and strong party leadership. They elected Newt Gingrich to the speakership, ceded to him the authority to select committee and subcommittee chairs who could ensure that the desired legislation came to the floor, and permitted him to challenge the autonomy of committee chairs on substantive legislation in promoting the GOP agenda. What resulted was as remarkable a display of party discipline within the majority GOP as the House has seen since the days of Speaker (Czar) Cannon in the first decade of the twentieth century (see Table 13.1).

Parties in the State Legislatures

Among the state legislatures are those in which daily caucuses, binding party discipline, and autocratic party leadership make for a party every bit as potent as the Republicans in the 1995 session of the U.S. House of Representatives. There are also state legislatures, especially those of the traditional one-party states, in which party organization is perceptibly weaker than it was in the Congress before the reforms of the 1970s. Even in states that have a complete apparatus of party organization, the parties fail more frequently than the congressional parties to make the apparatus operate effectively.

The party caucuses in Congress at least maintain cohesion in their initial organizational tasks; they always agree on candidates for the presiding officers. State legislative parties periodically find themselves too divided by factionalism or ambition even to organize the legislature. In some states with comparatively weak legislative parties such as California, coalitions across party lines to elect legislative leaders have not been rare. The most recent example of this phenomenon was a dramatic running battle over the speakership in the California Assembly in which long-time Speaker Willie Brown first won with the vote of a Republican defector and then engineered the selection of a Republican maverick. Party discipline in selecting the legislative leaders often breaks down under the pressure of electoral realignment as

Table 13.1   PARTY COHESION ON THE REPUBLICAN CONTRACT WITH AMERICA, 1995

Provisions of House Republican Contract with America	Republicans		Democrats	
	For	Against	For	Against
A. Commitments to enact				
1. End of congressional exemptions from workplace laws	218	0	171	0
2. Cuts in committee budgets/staffs	224	0	191	12
B. Commitments to vote on				
1. Balanced-budget amendment	228	2	72	129
Line-item veto	223	4	71	129
2. Anticrime measures	220	9	18	182
3. Welfare reform	225	5	9	193
4. Protection for families/children				
Parental consent for children participating in surveys	225	0	192	7
Increased penalties for sex crimes against children	225	0	191	0
Stronger enforcement of child-support laws	228	0	204	0
5. Tax cuts	219	11	27	176
6. Various national security provisions (prohibit U.S. troops under UN command; reduce U.S. funds for UN peacekeeping; change defense funding priorities)	223	4	18	176
7. Repeal of 1993 tax increase on social security benefits (part of tax cuts in #5 above)	219	11	27	176
8. Reductions in federal regulations	219	8	58	132
9. Changes in liability laws				
Limits on punitive damages in product liability	220	6	45	154
Restrictions on investor suits	226	0	99	98
Institution of "loser pay" rules in certain lawsuits	216	11	16	181
10. Congressional term limits	189	40	38	163

Note: The Contract with America was publicized by the House Republicans during the 1994 congressional campaign. Under its provisions, if they became the majority party in the House, the Republicans promised to enact some procedural changes in Congress (listed under A above) and to bring 10 bills (listed under B above) to a vote on the House floor in the first 100 days of the congressional session. The latest vote taken was on April 4, 1995—well within the 100-day limit. All of the bills were passed by the House, but some of them were defeated or modified in the Republican-controlled Senate, and still others were vetoed by the Democratic president.

Source: Various issues of the *Congressional Quarterly Weekly Report* for the different votes. CQ's "Contract Score Card" was used to identify the various bills and their content.

well, as was demonstrated in several states in the late 1980s. In Florida, for example, conservative Democrats joined with a growing minority of Republicans to choose the leadership of the state senate. Legislative leaders in Illinois, North Carolina, and Oklahoma were similarly elected by a bipartisan coalition rather than a strict party vote.

In one-party states, of course, the party caucus has had little excuse for existing. Disagreement over organization, leadership positions, and policy issues in these states usually has fallen along factional lines within the party. In the heyday of the Long dynasty in Louisiana, one Democratic faction backed the Longs and others supported their opponents. In this particular case and in others, factional lines built on personal and family followings coincided with differing regional loyalties. Alternatively, the legislative caucuses in one-party states may reflect ideological differences; from 1910 to the 1930s in Wisconsin, for example, the La Follette Progressive Republicans organized one legislative caucus, the conservative Republicans another, and the very feeble Democrats a third.

Party leadership in the state legislatures also assumes a number of forms. The traditional floor leaders and whips exist in most. In others, the Speaker of the lower house or a spokesperson for the governor may mobilize the party's legislators. State party officials, unlike national party officials, may have a powerful voice in the legislative party. Whatever their relationship with state party leaders may be, however, the state legislative leaders often enjoy enormous power in the day-to-day workings of the legislature. Their influence on party caucuses is great. They do not often have to defer to steering or policy committees or to independent committees and their chairs, whom they directly appoint.

In many state legislatures, the party leaders also control resources that are vital to the ordinary members. In most, members have little personal staff to do their work, so they are always in need of the labor to perform the tasks of legislative life which a party leader can supply. Campaign funds too usually seem to be in short supply, and through their legislative leadership funds, party leaders are able to help out.[11] Because of campaign contribution limits and the considerable staff provided to each member for use in both the office and the district, members of Congress need few resources from their leaders. Such is not the case in many of the state legislatures, and, where a member depends upon the leadership for critical resources, a leader's pleas for party discipline are likely to be answered.

Modern-day Czar Cannons are to be found, if anywhere, in a few of the state houses—not in the U.S. House of Representatives, at least not before 1995. They may be throwbacks to an earlier era, however, before most state legislatures had achieved a significant degree of professionalization. As this professionalization, along with two-party competition, spreads across the states, legislative practices may become more similar, more homogeneous, and less subject to a high degree of centralized control.

There is also wide range in the importance of the party caucus. Malcolm Jewell and David Olson reported that the caucus was active beyond selecting the leaders in all but seven states in the 1980s. In two states the majority caucus actually bound its members on budget bills, while twenty-eight had caucuses in one or both parties that played a role in policy making by frequently meeting to discuss legislation, take straw votes of their members, and determine what bills should be pushed on the floor. At the other end of the continuum were party caucuses in eleven states whose major purpose was informational and where no attempt was made to either gauge party opinion or build party consensus.[12]

There remains, and probably will remain, wide variation in party legislative organizations across the states. Their structure is fairly uniform—with the familiar panoply of party offices, the appointment to positions of legislative power by the party leaders, and the existence of party caucuses. What differs is their practice. State party leaders differ enormously in power across the ninety-nine state legislative chambers, even between two houses in the same state. So too does the influence and effectiveness of the party caucus.[13]

THE EFFECTS AND INFLUENCE OF PARTY

The shape of party power is clearly evident in American legislatures, especially in the aftermath of the Republican seizure of Congress in 1994, but power for what? Is it power for organizing party support for a set of party programs or merely for parceling out the perquisites of legislative office? Or does the legislative party seek both policy and perquisites? How the legislative parties, typically through their party leadership but also as caucuses, use power is clearly important to understanding the role of party in government.

Effects in the Congress

At first glance, beyond their organizing presence, the parties seem to have little influence over the legislative behavior of their members. Normally American representatives and senators can freely vote against the party's platform, majority, or leadership—or against the program of their party's president. The Republicans who defied President Bush to oppose his tax increases in the late 1980s and the Democratic leaders who led opposition to President Clinton's North American Free Trade Agreement (NAFTA) in the early 1990s—both without any penalties being imposed by their parties—all bear witness to the freedom members of Congress traditionally have had from party discipline.

During the last century, Congress has imposed party sanctions consistently on only one kind of deviation from party regularity: a member's support of the opposing party's candidate for president in the general election. In 1925, the Senate Republican caucus expelled four senators for supporting La Follette's Progressive ticket in the 1924 elections, thereby denying them Republican committee assignments and committee seniority. In 1965, the House Democratic caucus stripped committee seniority from two southern Democrats who had supported the Republican presidential candidate, Barry Goldwater, the year before. In 1968, the same fate befell Representative John Rarick, a Democrat from Louisiana, for supporting George Wallace.

Even the greatest displeasure in legislative parties rarely leads to more than a stripping of seniority or committee assignments. In early 1983, the Democratic caucus removed Representative Phil Gramm from his seat on the House Budget Committee. In view of his Democratic colleagues, Gramm, a conservative Democrat from Texas, had betrayed his party by divulging to the Republicans the proceedings of secret Democratic party meetings on the Reagan budget. His "boll weevil" Democrat colleagues who had **merely** voted for the Reagan budget were not disciplined in any way.[14] In 1995, new Republican Speaker Newt Gingrich made veiled threats to some GOP committee chairs to remove them from their positions when they stood in the way of action on the party's Contract with America, but in the end he backed away from carrying out this action when the chairs became more compliant with his wishes.

The party organizations in Congress rely on carrots much more than sticks to increase party cohesiveness. If they are of the president's party, they convey the president's wishes and with them the president's influence and sanctions. In other instances—not frequently, indeed—legislative leaders report and transmit the feelings of party leaders outside the Congress. Chiefly, however, they depend on their own legislative leverage. Their sympathy to a member's bills or the favors they can bestow—choice committee assignments, help in passing favorite bills or additional office space, for example—can cultivate a measure of party support. So, too, can their political help to their fellow legislators; party leaders give political speeches and raise campaign funds at least in part for that purpose. Moreover, through their control of floor activities, the party leaders can set the agenda in a way to maximize party unity on important matters.[15]

When party leaders fail in their attempts to maintain party unity in the legislature, it is not so much for lack of leverage as for the strength of the pressures from the local congressional constituencies. The chief limit to leaders' persuasion is always the need of the individual member of Congress to satisfy this constituency in order to win reelection. When party and constituency conflict, responsiveness to the folks back home usually outweighs the calls for party unity.

In past years, attempts to build party discipline in Congress also were undercut by the power of the committees and by a tradition of seniority that automatically awarded committee chair positions to the majority party members with the longest continuous service on the committee. Independent committees stand, as a system of influence, squarely in opposition to any influences that the parties might exert. Seniority as a key to committee power puts a premium on getting reelected rather than on party loyalty or regularity within the Congress.[16]

Thus, attempts by a legislative party to reform seniority and the committee system such as those of the House Democrats in the 1970s were nothing less than struggles for control of the business of the Congress. The Democrats of the House succeeded in their reform efforts because they were willing to punish committee chairs—by relieving them of their positions—if they too flagrantly ignored their responsibility to the party and its congressional caucus. As a committee chair's independent power was curbed, one barrier to the influence of party organization was lowered. When the Republicans took over the House in 1995, they continued this practice of deviating from strict seniority rules in choosing committee chairs and, thereby, put in place committee leaders who were sympathetic with the party's policy agenda and leadership (see box on p. 316).

Effects in the State Legislatures

In some state legislatures, party leadership and organization operate far more effectively than they usually have in the Congress—at least before 1995. Positions of party leadership and committee power much more frequently go to legislators loyal

THE REPUBLICAN'S COMPLIANT COMMITTEE CHAIRS

In the year following their stunning takeover of House of Representatives in the 1994 elections, as they rushed to enact their Contract with America into law, the House Republicans centralized power in their speaker, Newt Gingrich, largely at the expense of the committee chairs. Gingrich took into his own hands the legislative leadership on such key issues as Medicare reform, District of Columbia finances, and telecommunications reform—thereby ignoring a long tradition of giving the issue leadership role to the appropriate specialized committees and undercutting the authority of their chairs. Whether out of personal loyalty to the leader credited with the Republicans' 1994 election victory, dedication to the overarching policy agenda of their party, or fear of the personal consequences of resistance, GOP committee chairs were willing to acquiesce to this extraordinary usurpation of committee power—at least for the time being. This significant realignment in the influence of party versus committee leaders may signal yet another step in the long-term enlargement of party powers in the House initiated by the Democratic reforms of the 1970s. It also may be only a short-term response to the partisan zeal of the moment and may give way to normal pressures for committee autonomy as time passes. How favorably the electorate responds to the "Republican revolution" in Congress, especially in the 1996 elections, probably more than anything will determine the fate of this new centralization of party power.[17]

to the party and to its programs. Furthermore, either the party leaders, the party speaking through a periodic caucus decision, or the party's governor or state committee may expect the legislators to support the party program or stand on a particular issue. It is not surprising that state legislators have looked to party leaders for cues and direction much more frequently than have the members of Congress.[18] For excessive lapses in party loyalty, legislators in these states may suffer sanctions that would be inconceivable in the United States Congress. Their influence may wane in the legislature, and they may ultimately lose positions of power. In a state that has numerous patronage jobs, they may find that the applicants they sponsor fare less well than formerly. They may also find in the next election campaign that they no longer receive campaign funds from the state or local party or, worse yet, that the party is supporting competitors in the primaries.

Conditions of Party Power in Legislatures

Clearly, the parties in some of the competitive, two-party state legislatures have advanced the art of discipline far beyond its normal state in the Congress. The reasons for their success tell us a good deal about the building of party power in legislatures. Among the most important factors that provide for strong legislative parties in the states and at various times in Congress are:

Absence of Competing Centers of Power In the Congress, the committees traditionally have been the centers of legislative power, centrifugal forces countering the centripetal tendencies of party. A vast amount of the real business of Congress goes on in them. They are the screens that sift through the great mass of legislative proposals for those relatively few nuggets of legislative metal. The result has been the creation in the Congress of alternative centers of power to that of party. The more committees become autonomous units in which influence derives from seniority or some other criterion independent of party loyalty, the less they owe to the parties and reflect the party organization or aims.

In the typical state, on the other hand, because the legislature is less attractive as a career, legislators accumulate less seniority,[19] and deference to seniority in allocating positions of power is far less common. The parties in the states are freer to appoint their loyalists to positions of legislative power; the committees and other legislative agencies of the states generally operate as instruments of party power in a way previously unknown in the modern Congress. In this respect, the post-1994 Congress may be approaching the pattern of power of many states or of the Congress in late nineteenth and early twentieth centuries.

Availability of Patronage and Preferences Patronage and other forms of governmental preference still exist in some states to a far greater extent than they do in the national government. Especially in the hands of a vigorous and determined governor or state legislative leader, these rewards may be potent inducements to legislative party discipline. Legislators who ignore the needs of their party may not be able to secure the political appointments that their constituents and local party workers have been waiting for. Conversely, the loyal and faithful party legislator is amply rewarded. In the Congress, by contrast, about the only material inducements to party discipline are projects in the member's home district, which can be moved forward or held back with the intercession of a party leader or even a president.

Strong Influences from the Party Organization State and local party organizations exert greater influence on state legislators than does the national committee of the party over the members of Congress. In the states, the party organization and the legislative party are far more likely to be allies. State party leaders may inhibit the political ambitions of party mavericks or deny them advancement within the party, especially in states in which they can influence the nomination processes. They may prevail on local parties to oppose renomination for those who are disloyal, although the spread of nominations through primaries has deprived the party of the control over nominations it once enjoyed. Moreover, it is not rare in the states—as it is in Washington, where serving in Congress is a full-time job—for state and local party leaders also to be legislative leaders.

The state and local parties figure more prominently in the lives of state legislative candidates in another way—the provision of campaign money. State legislative campaigns are more likely to depend upon the party organization for financial support than are congressional campaigns for several reasons. First, the few states that provide public funding for campaigns are as likely to channel that money through the parties as to give it directly to candidates. Second, many states also impose no ceilings on party contributions to campaigns, unlike the situation at the congressional level, and consequently the parties can make substantial investments if they wish. Third, the division of labor between the national party committees and the congressional campaign committees is not paralleled at the state level. Even though more states now have significant legislative campaign committees, many candidates still are forced to look beyond them to the party for campaign funds and services—and the state parties are better prepared to respond than they have been in past years.

Greater Political Homogeneity   Greater party cohesion in some state legislatures also reflects the greater homogeneity of state parties. While a legislative party in Congress reflects the full range of differences within the nation, that same party in any given state embraces a narrower spectrum of interests and ideologies. This greater political homogeneity of the states produces legislative parties in which the ranges of differences and disagreements are smaller and in which there are fewer sources of internal conflict. The political culture of the state also is more homogeneous and, in some cases, more tolerant of party discipline over legislators than the national constituency is. Legislative party strength has traditionally flourished, for example, in the northeastern part of the country (such as in Rhode Island, Connecticut, Pennsylvania, or New Jersey), the states of party organizational strength, patronage, weak primaries, and, one infers, a political culture tolerant of centralized political control.

Lesser Legislative Professionalism   Over the years, the Congress has evolved into a highly professionalized legislative body. Each member controls a sizable and well-paid personal staff and a considerable budget, which are employed to meet personal legislative and reelection needs. Congress now meets almost continuously, and the office has become a full-time job with high pay (an annual salary of $133,600 in 1995–96) and good benefits.

The state legislatures have become much more professional in recent years, but very few provide ordinary members with levels of support that even approach those in the Congress. State legislators are fortunate to have as much as a private office and personal secretary. Staff and budget resources typically are minimal (only a minority of the legislatures provide any personal staff at all), and sometimes they are under the control of the party leadership rather than the individual member. Many state legislatures also have retained their traditional part-time orientation, meeting for only a part of the year and providing such low levels of compensation that most members must hold other jobs and live only temporarily in the capital. As a result of these restrictions, state legislators in most of the states are much less able to operate independently of their party leaders than are members of Congress.[20]

PARTY COHESION IN LEGISLATIVE VOTING

Party organization in Congress and the state legislatures with caucuses, leaders, whips, and policy committees is only the most overt manifestation of the party in the legislature. Its efforts on behalf of party unity and discipline among its legislators are also tangible, if difficult to document. Party influence in legislatures, however, is broader and more pervasive than the enforcing activities of the organized legislative party. Party in a broader, more figurative sense may also operate "within" the legislator as a series of internalized loyalties and frameworks for organizing his or her legislative decisions. To speak of party only in the organizational sense of leaders and caucuses, therefore, is to miss the richness and complexity of party influence on the legislative process.

The political party is only one of a number of claimants for the vote of a legislator on any given issue. The voters of the home constituency make their demands, too, and so do the more ideological and militant workers of the party back home. Nor can the wishes of the president or a governor be easily dismissed. To all of these pressures one must also add those of interest groups, financial contributors, friends and associates in the legislature, and the legislator's own system of beliefs. Happily, all or most of these pressures point in the same direction on many issues. When they do not, party loyalty understandably gives way.

The cumulative consequences of party influence amid the many other sources of voting cues can be gauged by looking at how legislators behave—in the most visible sense, how they vote on legislation. Their formal, recorded roll-call votes on bills, amendments, and resolutions of course are not the only important dimensions of legislative behavior. Yet, the public nature of the roll-call vote makes it a good test of the ability of the party to maintain discipline among its members.

Levels of Party Discipline

Answers always depend on the questions asked. So it is with the question of the amount of discipline the American parties generate in legislatures. The answer depends to a considerable extent on the definition of the term *discipline*.

Party Voting   One classic measure of party voting discipline in legislatures has been the party vote—any nonunamimous legislative roll call in which 90 percent or more of the members of one party vote yes and 90 percent or more of the other party vote no. By such a stringent test, party discipline appears regularly in the British House of Commons but rarely in American legislatures. Julius Turner found that from 1921 through 1948, only 17 percent of the roll calls in the House of Representatives met such a criterion of party discipline.[21] In the 1950s and 1960s, the number of party division roll calls dropped steadily to about 2 or 3 percent.[22] During approximately the same period in the British House of Commons, the percentage of party votes averaged very close to 100 percent.

Although the "90 percent versus 90 percent" standard discriminates well between British and American party cohesion—indeed, between parliamentary and other systems—it is too stringent a standard for comparisons within the American experience. Only three of the seventeen provisions of the House Republican's Contract with America, for example, had 90 percent or more of the Republicans voting yes against 90 percent or more of the Democrats voting no.

Scholars of the American legislatures, therefore, have opted for a less-demanding criterion—the percentage of instances in which the majority of one party

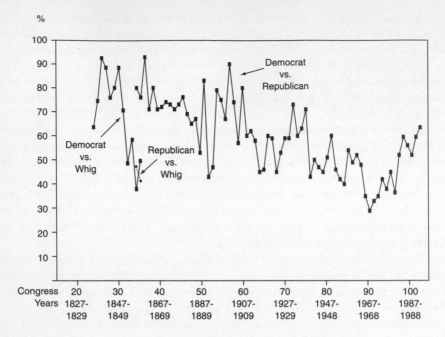

Figure 13.2 Party voting in the House of Representatives: 1835–1994.

Note: Entries are the percentage of roll call votes on which a majority of one party opposed a majority of the other party for both sessions combined.

Source: For 24th through 36th congresses, Thomas B. Alexander, *Sectional Stress and Party Strength* (Nashville, Tennessee: Vanderbilt University Press, 1967). For 37th through 93rd congresses, Jerome B. Chubb and Santa A. Traugott, "Partisan Cleavage and Cohesion in the House of Representatives, 1861–1974," *Journal of Interdisciplinary History* 7 (1977), 382–383. For the 94th through 103rd (1993–94) congresses, *Congressional Quarterly Weekly Report,* December 31, 1994, 3658.

opposed a majority of the other. By this measure the 1990s had produced the highest levels of congressional party voting in years. A majority of Democrats opposed a majority of Republicans in 67 and 52 percent of all contested Senate votes in the 1993 and 1994 sessions, respectively; the 1993 figure was the highest level in the Senate since these measurements started in 1954. Party voting has been even more prevalent in the House in recent years. From its twentieth-century low in 1969–1970, it has climbed steadily to levels not seen since the partisan divisions over New Deal legislation in the 1930s (Figure 13.2). House party voting dropped off somewhat in 1994, as it usually does in both the House and Senate in an election year, but it still reached an impressive 62 percent. In the rancorous 1995 session, party voting was even higher: 69 percent in the Senate and a fifty-year high of 73 percent in the House.[23]

Party voting in the Congress has varied enormously since the beginning of regular two-party competition in the 1830s. In the nineteenth century when interparty competition was high in most congressional districts, party leaders exercised considerable legislative authority, and Congress was far less professional, party voting attained levels comparable to those of the most partisan state legislatures, although still far below those of the British parliament. After 1900, following what Nelson W. Polsby has termed the "institutionalization" of Congress and what Walter Dean Burnham has seen as a "disaggregation" of party,[24] party voting fell off precipitously. Although the New Deal realignment of the 1930s boosted the cohesiveness of the legislative party, the amount of party voting since the early 1900s has not recaptured its nineteenth century levels or approached that of the most party oriented of the states.

Beyond these variations from one party system to another, levels of party voting also have differed considerably within party systems. Samuel Patterson and Gregory Caldeira have examined the period from 1949 through 1984 to determine what accounts for the ebbs and flows of party voting in both the Senate and the House of Representatives. The political and electoral context of Congress proved to be the most significant factor. Party voting peaked when Democrats controlled both the White House and the Congress—conditions under which the polarization inherent in party government flourished—and when the parties exhibited the greatest differences in their platforms. Large and homogeneous majorities in the House also enhanced party voting, while the Senate was found to respond mainly, pro and con, to presidential leadership.[25]

Information on the levels of party voting across the American state legislatures is not available for recent years, as there is no equivalent to the *Congressional Quarterly Weekly Report* at the state level. Studies of selected states in the 1950s and 1960s, supplemented by occasional measurements since, however, suggest great variation in the extent to which their legislatures divide along party lines and their legislative parties exhibit voting cohesiveness. In some states, especially those with strong party organizations, competitive politics, and ideological divisions between the parties, party is the dominant force in legislative voting—attaining a significance that was attained in Congress only in the previous century. In other states, probably most, party voting may be no more, and possibly much less, prominent than in the modern Congress.[26]

Party Cohesion   Party voting, by the measure we have employed, though, does not tell us how united the two party majorities are. For that, one needs to examine how much party members vote with their parties when majorities of one party oppose majorities in another. Such an examination shows that congressional Democrats were more cohesive than the Republicans throughout the 1980s, with the gap between them widening after 1985 (Table 13.2). This reversed the earlier pattern from the 1960s and 1970s when, with conservative Democrats from the South often crossing the aisle to vote with Republicans under a more decentralized party leadership, Democratic cohesion usually was weaker than Republican cohesion. With the beginning of the Clinton presidency, however, even higher levels of party cohesion than in the 1980s were being reached, and the Republicans became as cohesive as the Democrats—and even more cohesive once they took control of the Congress in 1995.

David Rohde has attributed this increased Democratic party cohesiveness to two factors. First, the parties have become more ideologically homogeneous. Changes in

Table 13.2   PARTY COHESION ON PARTY VOTES, 1961–1995

Year	Democrats	Republicans
1961	71%	72%
1962	69	68
1963	71	72
1964	67	69
1965	69	70
1966	61	67
1967	66	71
1968	57	63
1969	62	62
1970	57	59
1971	62	66
1972	57	64
1973	68	68
1974	63	62
1975	69	70
1976	65	66
1977	67	70
1978	64	67
1979	69	72
1980	68	70
1981	69	76
1982	72	71
1983	76	74
1984	74	72
1985	79	75
1986	78	71
1987	81	74
1988	79	73
1989	81	73
1990	81	74
1991	81	78
1992	79	79
1993	85	84
1994	83	83
1995	80	91

Note: Entries are the average percentages of members voting in agreement with a majority of their party on party votes. Party votes are votes in which a majority of one party voted against a majority of the other party. Figures for the House and Senate are combined.

Source: Congressional Quarterly Weekly Report, January 27, 1996, 199.

the composition of the southern congressional delegation, wrought by the Voting Rights Act and growing two-party competition, narrowed the policy differences between northern and southern Democrats. The old "conservative coalition" of northern Republicans and southern Democrats has weakened, leaving the Democratic party more cohesive than it has been in years. This change and the enhanced partisan conflict during the Reagan presidency also sharpened policy differences between the Democrats and the Republicans in Congress. Second, organizational reforms (mainly reducing the power of committee chairs and strengthening the powers of party leaders) have made it easier for the Democratic leadership to unify its party and to fend off Republican appeals to more conservative Democrats.[27]

Occasions for Cohesion

Cohesive voting among members of the same legislative party is greater on some issues and questions than on others. Studies in the Congress and in the state legislatures find that three kinds of legislative concerns are most likely to stimulate high levels of party discipline: those touching the interests of the legislative party as a group, those involving support of or opposition to an executive program, and those concerning the issues and interests that tend to divide the party electorates.

Party-Oriented Cohesion   The interests of the legislative parties as parties— as interest groups, one might say—often spur the greatest party unity in legislatures. The range of such issues is broad. It includes, especially in two-party legislatures, the basic votes to organize the legislative chamber. In the Congress, for example, one can safely predict 100 percent party cohesion on the early-session votes to elect a speaker of the House; Newt Gingrich was elected speaker in at the beginning of the 104th Congress in 1995 with the support of all fellow Republicans and none of the Democrats. Cohesion also tends to be extremely high on issues affecting party strength. In a 1985 vote on whether to award the congressional seat to Democrat Frank McCloskey or Republican Richard McIntyre after a disputed Indiana election, for example, the House of Representatives divided along partisan lines, with Democrats voting 236–10 to seat McCloskey and Republicans voting 180–0 in opposition.

Discipline runs high in the state legislatures over issues such as patronage (and merit-system reform), the laws regulating parties and campaigning, the seating of challenged members of the legislature, election and registration laws, or the creation or alteration of legislative districts. Whatever form these issues take, they all touch the basic interests of the party as a political organization. They threaten some aspects of the party status quo: the party's activists, its internal organizational structure, its system of rewards, its electorate, or its electoral competitiveness.

Executive-Oriented Cohesion   Legislators of a party may also rally around the party's executive or unite against the executive of the other party. Perhaps the reaction to an executive program is not so predictable as it is in a parliamentary system, for American presidents freely court the support of the other party. Nonetheless, it is a significant partisan issue even in the American context. The *Congressional Quarterly Weekly Report* regularly measures the support that each legislative party gives to the president on issues that he has clearly designated a part of his program (Table 13.3). From 1966 through 1995, Republicans supported Republican presidents and Democrats supported Democratic presidents on a majority of votes, except among Democrats in the 1968 Senate as Lyndon Johnson's presidency was eroding.

Table 13.3 PRESIDENTIAL SUPPORT SCORES: 1966–1995

Party of President	Year	Senate		House of Representatives	
		Democrats	Republicans	Democrats	Republicans
Democratic	1966	57%	43%	63%	37%
Democratic	1967	61	53	69	46
Democratic	1968	48	47	64	51
Republican	1969	47	66	48	57
Republican	1970	45	60	53	66
Republican	1971	40	64	47	72
Republican	1972	44	66	47	64
Republican	1973	37	61	35	62
Republican	1974	39	56	44	58
Republican	1975	47	68	38	63
Republican	1976	39	62	32	63
Democratic	1977	70	52	63	42
Democratic	1978	66	41	60	36
Democratic	1979	68	47	64	34
Democratic	1980	62	45	63	40
Republican	1981	49	80	42	68
Republican	1982	43	74	39	64
Republican	1983	42	73	28	70
Republican	1984	41	76	34	60
Republican	1985	35	75	30	67
Republican	1986	38	79	25	66
Republican	1987	36	64	24	62
Republican	1988	47	68	25	57
Republican	1989	55	82	36	69
Republican	1990	38	70	25	63
Republican	1991	41	83	34	72
Republican	1992	32	73	25	71
Democratic	1993	87	29	77	39
Democratic	1994	86	42	75	47
Democratic	1995	81	29	75	22

Note: Entries are percentages of the time that members supported the announced position of the president.

Source: Data from *Congressional Quarterly Almanac* for each year through 1989; for 1990–94, *Congressional Quarterly Weekly Report*, January 27, 1996, 239.

Conversely, support from the opposition party for a president's program fell below the majority mark almost always. Of all these figures, the ones for the first years of the Clinton presidency stand out: Democrats' support for their president was never higher, and Republicans' support was relatively low. The increased partisanship of the Congress which appeared in the party cohesion figures is repeated here.[28]

This executive-oriented cohesion in the Congress, which appears in the state legislatures as well, reflects a number of realities of American politics. It may result from the executive's control of political sanctions—patronage in some states, personal support in fund-raising and campaigning, or support of programs for the legislator's constituency. It also results from the fact that the executive increasingly symbolizes the party and its performance. Legislators of the president's party or the governor's party know that they threaten their party and their own political future if they make the party's executive appear ineffective. Of course, it may also result from the coincidence of preferences and constituencies between the congressional party and its president.

Nonetheless, there are occasions when loyalty to the chief executive of a legislator's party can not withstand other pressures and demands. Although legislative party disloyalty to its president can be particularly embarrassing to the president and a source of tension between the White House and Capitol Hill, it does not carry with it the threat of a new election or a new leader (see box on p. 326) as it does in a parliamentary system, where major opposition to a prime minister's legislation from within his or her party can bring down the government.

Issue-Oriented Cohesion   Legislative cohesion has remained firm for decades on those issues that involve the welfare state, the whole complex debate over government responsibilities that can be summed up as the liberal-conservative dualism which has dominated party conflict since the 1930s. In the states, such issues include labor-management relations, aid to agriculture or other sectors of the economy, programs of social security and insurance, wages and hours legislation, unemployment compensation, and relief and welfare programs. In Congress, a similar set of issues—government management of the economy, agricultural assistance, and social welfare—stimulated the most partisan voting over the years.[29]

The Constituency Basis of Cohesion

The cohesiveness of the legislative parties primarily depends upon how well those parties represent the fundamental differences in interests and values within the electorate. Party cohesion is greatest where politics is most competitive along party lines—along two-party lines in the United States, of course. One-partyism in a legislature invites the disintegrating squabbles of factions and regional or personal cliques within the dominant party. The South, therefore, has been the region of the least cohesive legislative parties. Representatives from the one-party South also were the ones most responsible for undermining the cohesion of the Democratic majority in Congress during much of the post-World War Two period.

Party cohesion, furthermore, typically has reached its maximum in the legislatures of urban, industrialized states. The key here and perhaps the key to the entire riddle of legislative party cohesion is in the types of constituencies the different parties represent. In these urban, industrial states, the parties tend to divide the constituencies along the urban-rural and SES lines that have most differentiated the parties during the New Deal party system, and they develop an issue-oriented politics that reflects those lines. Party cohesion in the legislature, therefore, reflects the relative homogeneity of the interests and constituencies the party represents. Moreover, the legislators of one party usually have different backgrounds and lifestyles from those of the legislators of the other party; that is, differences in their own values and experiences reinforce the party differences in constituencies. Thus, in such state legislatures, an attempt to change eli-

PARTISANS' SUPPORT OF THEIR PRESIDENT: CONTRASTING CASES

Two congressional votes less than a year apart, involving the two most important policy actions of the early Clinton presidency, illustrate how different circumstances can induce divergent levels of loyalty to a president by the members of his party.

On issues involving the president's authority in committing American troops abroad, the congressional party usually gives overwhelming support to its president. Such loyalty was manifested in the October 1993 vote on a GOP measure to pull U.S. forces out of Haiti less than a month after they had been dispatched there. House Democrats voted 223–32 against the pull-out proposal; Republicans were 173–1 in favor. Senate Democrats had voted a unanimous 55–0 against, while the Republicans were 34–10 in favor of, an earlier attempt to tie President Clinton's hands.

On issues triggering powerful district pressures, by contrast, partisans occasionally desert their president. Votes in 1993 on the controversial North American Free Trade Agreement (NAFTA) are an especially relevant case in point. House Democrats voted 156–102 against implementing an agreement the president had championed, whereas Republicans supported the treaty by a 132–43 margin. In the Senate, Republican votes (34 in favor, 10 against) again carried the agreement, while Democrats opposed it 28–27. Negotiated by the Republican Bush Administration and adamantly opposed by organized labor and in many districts, NAFTA had long divided the Democratic party, and this division was reflected in the decision by majorities of Democrats to vote against their president—a situation normally precluded by a parliamentary form of government.

gibility for an unemployment compensation program will put two cohesive parties in sharp opposition, with the prolabor and promanagement sides each reinforced by their roots in their home districts and by their own lives and values.

In the broader historical perspective, the constituency bases of party cohesion have been found to vary with changes in the cleavages underlying the party systems described in Chapter 6. As realignments have transformed the party systems over the course of American history, the issues that dominate interparty conflict and consequently form the bases of legislative party cohesion have changed. Slavery and Reconstruction may have generated the greatest interparty conflict and intraparty cohesion around the time of the Civil War, but they were displaced by issues centered around agrarian-industrial conflicts by the realignment of 1896. If issues of social welfare and government management of the economy have come to produce the greatest party voting since the 1930s, it is because they capture best the differences between the Democratic and Republican parties during the New Deal party system. These issues in turn may give way to a new set of issues (for example, affirmative action, abortion, deregulation, the budget deficit) to define interparty conflict if a new party system emerges. The parties, in short, should not be expected to divide sharply on all issues that come before the legislature. Rather, they will be most distinctive on policy matters closest to the electoral cleavage underlying the current party system.[30]

It also is notable that the party voting in the House described in Figure 13.2 generally has peaked during partisan realignments. By focusing attention on national rather than local issues and thereby overcoming the inherent localism of Congress, as well as inducing membership turnover and a larger majority party, realignments promote party unity on the issues most central to the new party cleavage and thereby permit a degree of party discipline that is rare in the American political system. This newly "responsible" majority party is then in a position to enact the major policy changes that we have come to associate with realignments.[31]

Corresponding declines in party voting and party cohesion are associated with the aging of the prevailing party system and partisan dealignment.[32] Low levels of party voting through the 1970s, therefore, may be attributable to the obsolescence of the New Deal party system and, as a consequence of electoral dealignment, the increasing insulation of incumbents from partisan tides.

The enhanced levels of party voting since the early 1980s, by the same token, may be yet another sign that the long-awaited realignment is finally on its way. The dramatic Republican victory in the 1994 midterm elections and the determined congressional pursuit of the GOP's policy agenda which followed had the clearest earmarks yet of such a change—an election in which national forces dominated, unusually high turnover in legislative seats, a policy-oriented new congressional majority, and a Congress even more sharply divided along partisan lines. If the changes set in motion in 1994 endure, then the nation may be entering another era of constituency-based party cohesion.

While they are the principal basis of party cohesion in the states and Congress, constituency pressures also can form a stubborn barrier to cohesion. On some legislative issues, the representative must bend to constituency wishes in opposition to the party position, acting more or less as an instructed delegate, if he or she wishes to be reelected. Party leaders rarely demand the member's loyalty in this situation. A study of the congruence between constituency opinion and the representative's vote in the 1958 U.S. House of Representatives found delegatelike behavior on civil rights issues, for example, especially in the South where constituency pressures were intense.[33] As long as the American parties cannot protect legislators from such constituency pressures, it stands to reason that party cohesion will suffer.

Other Bases of Cohesion

Clear and unmistakable though the constituency bases of party regularity may be, they do not explain all party cohesion in American legislatures. The parties as operating political organizations account for some. Centralization of the party leadership in Congress has been linked to high levels of party voting during the 1881 to 1911 period and in recent years. The weakening of the party leadership in between surely is in part responsible for the lower levels of party voting during most of the twentieth century. Even if variations in party cohesion and party leadership may be traced to different constituency arrangements, organization and leadership in the Congress are crucial.

Daily caucuses, party representatives roaming the legislative corridors, and the party pressures of a vigorous governor or powerful party leader enhance cohesion in some of the states today. These party leaders often control resources of considerable value to the individual legislator, which can serve as a carrot or stick to secure compliance with the leader's wishes. Assignment as the chair or member of a key committee, campaign contributions at the critical point of a close reelection contest, and endorsements from prominent party leaders are particularly effective at the state level where legislators are less able to go it alone in election campaigns. Whatever actual organizational pressure the legislator feels, however, rarely comes from the local party, which, if it makes any demands at all, generally makes them on purely local, service issues. The local party is much more concerned with matters of local interest and its own perquisites than it is with questions of state or national policy.[34]

Party regularity may also be related to the political competitiveness of the legislator's constituency. Legislators from the unsafe, marginal districts with finely balanced parties are more likely to defect from their fellow partisans in the legislature than are those from the safer districts. To be sure, it is likely that many of these marginal districts are the districts with SES characteristics atypical of the parties' usual constituencies. Marginality may also be a product, however, of the organizational strength of the opposing party or the appeal of its candidates, which in turn forces the legislator to be more than usually sensitive to the constituency.

Finally, as obvious and even banal as it may seem, parties must cohere in order to get the business of the legislature conducted. If bills are to be passed and the public's business done, majorities must be put together. Putting together those majorities is the prime task of the leadership of the majority party. In truth, that leadership is far more likely to be concerned with the smooth operation of the legislative body than with the enactment of some stated party policy, which often leads it to settle for compromise solutions rather than complete policy victories. The leadership is also persuasive and influential at least in part because it dominates the group life of the legislative party and controls access to its esteem and camaraderie.

LEGISLATIVE PARTIES AND PARTY GOVERNMENT

Not so long ago the conventional wisdom among scholars of American legislatures—the textbook account, if you will—was that the centralizing force of party had been undermined by the decentralization of authority and power to committees and individual members, especially in the Congress but even in some other legislative bodies as well.[35] The presumption that parties had given away their policy-making role by delegating their powers to others was always an exaggeration. With the growing importance of congressional parties and the new theoretical approaches that have framed studies of Congress in recent years, this view has now been replaced by one that locates parties at the very center of the legislative process—in the apt metaphor of Cox and McCubbins, as cartels which ". . . usurp the rule-making power of the House in order to endow their members with differential power (e.g., the power of committee chairs) and to facilitate and stabilize legislative trades that benefit their members."[36]

This view accords well with the evidence presented throughout this chapter. Even though party cohesion in American legislatures falls far short of the standards of some parliamentary parties, party remains the most powerful determinant of roll-call voting within them and a constant force throughout the legislative process. Party affiliation goes further to explain the legislative behavior of American legislators than any other single factor in the legislator's environment. Legislators' normal dispositions seem to be to support the leadership of their party unless some particularly pressing consideration intervenes. All other things being equal (that is, being quiescent and not demanding), party loyalty usually gets their votes.[37]

Yet, despite their importance, the fact remains that most American legislative parties achieve only modest levels of cohesion. Party lines are often obliterated in the coalitions that enact important legislation. For several decades, in fact, Congress's conservative coalition of southern Democrats and northern Republicans rivaled the Democratic party as a source of legislative organization. Interest groups, powerful governors, local political leaders, influential legislative leaders all contend with the legislative party for the ability to organize legislative majorities. In this system of fragmented legislative power and local, virtually autonomous constituency pressures, the legislative party dominates only occasionally. It often finds itself in conflict with other voices, in the party and outside of it, in the struggle to mobilize majorities in the legislatures.

Thus, the fragmenting institutions of American government once again have their impact. With the separation of powers, there is no institutionalized need for party cohesion, as there is in the parliamentary systems.[38] It is possible for government in the United States to act, even to govern, without disciplined party support in the legislature. In fact, at those times when one party controls both houses of Congress and the other controls the presidency—or one controls both houses of the state legislature and the other the governorship—it would be difficult to govern if high levels of cohesion behind an *a priori* program did prevail in each party.

Even when one finds high levels of party cohesion or discipline in an American legislature, however, party government need not result. Cohesion is a necessary but not sufficient condition for party-dominated government—and there's the rub. The American legislative party tends to have only the most tenuous ties to the various units of the party organization. The legislative parties of Congress do not recognize the equality—much less the superiority—of the party's national committee. Many state legislative parties similarly escape any effective control, or even any persistent influence, by their state party committees. Nor do the legislative parties have a great deal of contact with local party organizations. Many legislators depend on personal organizations for reelection help, but even those who rely on the party at election time receive no advice from the party back home during the legislative session. Local party organizations do not often sustain enough activity between elections to keep even the most fleeting supervisory watch over their legislators.

The American legislative party, therefore, has often found it easy to remain aloof from and independent of the party organization and its platforms and program commitments. The legislative party creates the major part of its own cohesion, employing its own persuasions, sanctions, and rewards. What discipline it commands generally serves a program or a set of proposals that originates in the executive or within the legislative party itself.[39] Only rarely is the legislative party in any sense redeeming earlier programmatic commitments or accepting the overriding discipline of the party organization. As a legislative party, it is politically self-sufficient; it controls its own rewards to a considerable extent. In some cases, it also attempts to control its own political future; the party campaign committees of both houses of Congress are good examples. So long as the members of the legislative party can protect their own renomination and reelection, they can keep the rest of the party at arm's length.

This freedom—or, if one prefers, irresponsibility to the rest of the party—of the American legislative party grows in large part from its unity and homogeneity of interests in a total party structure where disorder and disunity prevail. Even if local party organizations were to establish supervisory relationships with their legislators, no party responsibility would result unless those relationships were unified and integrated within the state as a whole. In other words, there exists no unified political party that could establish some control over and responsibility for the actions of its legislative party. There is only a party divided geographically along the lines of American federalism, functionally along the dimensions of the separation of powers, and politically by the differing goals and commitments its various participants bring to it.

At the most, therefore, the American legislative parties are tied to the rest of their parties by agreement on an inarticulate ideology of common interests, attitudes, and loyalties. In many state legislatures and in the United States Congress, the mute ideology of one party and its majority districts differs enough from that of the other party to promote the tensions of interparty disagreement and intraparty cohesion. These modal sets of interests and attitudes—we most often give them the imprecise labels *liberal* and *conservative*—may or may not find expression in platforms, and they may or may not be articulated or supported by the party organizations. Legislative parties may even ignore them in the short run. Nonetheless, they are there, and they are the chief centripetal force in a political party that has difficulty articulating a central set of goals for all its activists and adherents. Whether this inarticulate ideology can produce a measure of party responsibility is another question, however, and it will wait until the considerations of Chapter 15.

Chapter *14*

The Party in the Executive and the Judiciary

When offices have important policy-making responsibilities, as the American executives and judiciary do, it probably is inevitable that they will be drawn into partisan politics. The American involvement of the executive and the courts in party politics appeared soon after the beginnings of the Republic, with the battles between supporters of Hamilton and Jefferson within George Washington's administration and the difficult transition from the Federalists to the Democratic-Republicans after the 1800 election. But the real boost to partisanship in these two branches of government came from the traditions of nineteenth-century popular democracy.

The framers of the American Constitution saw to it that the president would be independent from the legislative branch of government to a degree that is unparalleled in a modern-day democratic world dominated by parliamentary governments. But it was not until the emergence of the presidency as a popularly elected office in the early decades of the 1800s that it became possible for the president to be a party leader at the national level as many governors had long been in their states. Today it seems almost unthinkable that a president—or a governor—would avoid the dominant leadership role of her or his political party.

With its appointments for life and its clear separation from the legislative branch of government, the framers also designed an independent federal judiciary, which they hoped would be above the daily battles of partisan politics. But, at least since the historic confrontation between Chief Justice John Marshall and the new Jefferson administration in 1803, the federal judiciary has been unable to remain completely aloof from partisan politics.[1] The conflict over nominations to the federal bench in recent years certainly gives proof to the presence of party considerations in the judiciary.

The forces for popular democracy enabled party politics to penetrate even more deeply into the executive and the judiciary than originally intended. The belief that democratic control can best be guaranteed through the ballot box led to the long ballot, on which judges and all manner of administrative officials at the state and local level were elected. Popular election led easily to party influences in those elections. At the same time, the tenets of Jacksonian democracy supported the spoils system and the value of turnover in office, justifying the use of party influence in appointments to administrative office. Thus, in the name of popular democracy, the access of parties to the executive and judicial branches was established to an extent quite unknown in the other Western democracies. Even subsequent surges of reformist zeal designed to insulate some officials, especially judges and bureaucrats, from partisan pressures have not overcome these tendencies.

It is one thing for the political party to influence or even control the recruitment or selection of officeholders. It is quite another, however, for it to mobilize them in the exercise of their powers of office. The parties have had success in mobilizing American legislatures. The pertinent question here is whether they have had equal success with the executive and judicial branches. In other words, in their policy decisions, has it made any difference that the men and women making them have been selected by a party? Does the pursuit of public office by the political parties serve only their internal organizational needs for rewards and incentives, or does it also promote party positions and programs?

THE EXECUTIVE AS A PARTY LEADER

The twentieth century has been a century of political leadership of mass publics, both in the democracies and in the dictatorships of the world. In the democracies, electorates have expanded to include virtually all adults. At the same time, the revolutions in mass media and communications have brought political leaders closer than ever to the electorates. In the United States, these changes have culminated in the personal leadership of the presidency in the twentieth century—a trend summed up by merely listing such names as Wilson, Roosevelt, Eisenhower, Kennedy, and Reagan, names that signify both executive power and a personal tie to millions of American citizens. The post-Watergate reaction against the "imperial presidency" only temporarily stalled the trend. Even the parliamentary systems and their prime ministers have been energized by the growth of personal leadership, and their election campaigns increasingly center on the potential prime ministers.[2]

Unquestionably, one major ingredient of executive leadership in the United States has been leadership of a mass political party. When Andrew Jackson combined the contest for executive office with leadership of a popular political party, he began a revolution in both the American presidency and the American political party. The presidency ceased to be the repository of elitist good sense and conservatism that Hamilton hoped it would be and became an agency of mass political leadership. Ultimately, it was the president rather than the Congress who became the tribune of the people in the American political system. Popular democracy found its two chief agents—a popularly elected leader and a mass political party—merged in the American chief executive, the power of the office reinforced by the power of the party.

It is easy to speak glibly of the American chief executive as the leader of a party. The specific components of leadership are more elusive, however, for presidents, governors, and mayors rarely are formal party leaders. National, state, and local party chairpersons hold that responsibility. The chief executive's role as party leader is really a subtle, complex combination of a number of overlapping partisan roles. Among them, certainly, are the roles discussed below.

Party Leader as Representative of the Whole Constituency

One of the unique features of the American system is that the president and the Congress represent different constituencies. The national constituency the president represents differs from the sum total of the congressional constituencies. Whereas the congressional constituencies are local and particularistic ones, and in the Senate collectively overrepresent the rural areas of the country, the president's constituency overrepresents the large, urban, industrial states on which the electoral college places such a premium. It is a constituency that often makes its incumbent more committed to government responsibility for solutions to national problems than the congressional party is. Furthermore, because his is the only truly national constituency—especially in contrast to the localism of the congressional party—the president or the presidential candidate is the only candidate of the national party. Apart from the party's national convention, he is its only manifestation.

Many of the same observations may be made of the American governors. They, too, represent the entire state in contrast to the local ties of the state legislators. Other public officials may also have statewide constituencies because the constitution writers of many states have seen fit to elect such officials as treasurers, attorneys general, state insurance commissioners, and even state supreme court justices. Unlike these less-known fellow executives or judges, though, the governor embodies the party on the statewide level—just as most mayors do at the local level. He or she is the political executive and is so recognized by the voters of the states. Like the president, most governors must make political and policy records appealing to the voters of the entire state, and like him, they embody concern for the problems of the whole constituency.

Party Leader as Organizational Leader

At the same time, the American executive may choose to be concerned with the organizational affairs of his political party. Some, like President Eisenhower in the 1950s, may consciously cultivate an image of being above partisan politics.[3] But far more common is the president who recognizes that for millions of Americans he symbolizes his party and who takes seriously his partisan leadership role. Ronald Reagan, for example, championed his party's cause more actively than perhaps any president since Franklin Roosevelt. Lyndon Johnson drew on years of experience in American politics to involve himself in the Democratic National Committee and, through it, in state and local party politics.[4]

The president's greatest influence in the business of the party organization rests in his control of the national party committee. Its chairperson must be acceptable to him and usually is selected by him (see box on p. 335). The president also is free to shape the committee's role, even if only to turn it into his personal campaign organization. Presidents' relationships with state and local party organizations, however, have become increasingly attenuated. Presidents are less and less willing to put their executive appointments to the political uses of those party organizations. They are now virtually unwilling to do the kind of "party building"—strengthening of state parties and their leadership—that presidents routinely did early in the century. While President Reagan campaigned unusually hard for Republican candidates, particularly in the midterm congressional elections, the extensive party-building efforts of the Republican National Committee have been largely independent of the White House. Moreover, the national committee and state party organizations of the president have lost virtually all of their role in making executive appointments to the president's immediate White House staff.[5] Presidents now use their appointments for governing and for protecting their own political positions rather than for rewarding various party factions.

To find a way through all the thickets of party politics, presidents do not usually rely on the national committee or its officers. Earlier in this century, presidents used the cabinet position of postmaster general as the post for an advisor knowledgeable in the intricacies of the party's many organizations. Franklin Roosevelt relied on James Farley, and Dwight Eisenhower chose Arthur Summerfield; each had extensive party organizational experience, and each served simultaneously as the national party chairman. This was the tradition that Lyndon Johnson honored in 1965 by appointing Lawrence O'Brien, his predecessor's shrewdest political counselor, as his postmaster general. Now that the postal service is reorganized and the postmaster general no longer sits in the cabinet, political advisors hold positions on the White House staff. The exception was Lee Atwater, who initially served as President Bush's top political advisor from his position as chairman of the Republican National Committee. After health problems prevented Atwater from continuing in that role, the president returned to the practice of depending upon his immediate staff for political advice.

Party Leader as Electoral Leader

The common sense of the executive's role as electoral leader is that executives, by their successes or failures and by their popularity or lack of it, affect the electoral fortunes of other office seekers of their party. One sees, for example, a strong correspondence between the fortunes of presidents and their parties. Lyndon Johnson's landslide victory over Barry Goldwater in 1964 was accompanied by the election of the largest Democratic majority in the Congress since the 1930s. That landslide also swept Democratic parties to power in the states. The presence of Ronald Reagan on the ticket in both 1980 and 1984 similarly was associated with higher than normal levels of support for other Republican candidates. The Republicans captured control of the Senate in the 1980 election for the first time since the election of 1952. Republican House candidates also received a higher percentage of the votes cast in the two presidential election years than in the preceding and following midterm elections, when Reagan was not on the ballot.

Coattail Effects   The traditional explanation for the relationship between presidential fortunes and party success has employed the old metaphor of presidential

---

PRESIDENT CLINTON ORCHESTRATES CHANGE AT THE DNC

In a political application of the sports maxim "you can't fire the team, so you fire the coach," President Bill Clinton arranged for the replacement of the chairman of the Democratic National Committee in the aftermath of the party's electoral debacle in 1994.

Replacing his hand-picked choice David Wilhelm, who had run Clinton's 1992 election campaign and then moved to chair the DNC in early 1993, were Don Fowler and Christopher Dodd. Fowler, a party official from South Carolina, was chosen to run the daily operations of the party as the DNC Chairman. Dodd, a U.S. senator from Connecticut and son of former Democratic Senator Thomas Dodd, was named as general chairman of the party. A similar tandem arrangement was used by the Republicans in the early 1980s when Senator Paul Laxalt served as general chair and Frank Fahrenkopf as chair of the RNC.

Although the appointments of Fowler and Dodd required confirmation by a vote of the full DNC, just as Wilhelm's had two years before, the White House's orchestration of the change left no doubt about who was in charge. When a party controls the White House, its president is the party leader and the leaders of the national committee are his choices.

---

coattails. Presidents ran "at the top of the ticket," the explanation goes, and the rest of the party ticket came into office clutching and clinging to their sturdy coattails. (Nineteenth-century dress coats did have tails.) Coattail effects seemed especially prominent in the nineteenth century when, in a time when the parties printed their own ballots, it was difficult to split the ticket in voting for candidates from different parties.

Recent research has found that coattail effects in congressional elections remain significant, even though they have declined since World War Two.[6] The decline appears to be related to decreased competitiveness, a result, in turn, of the increased ability of incumbent representatives to insulate themselves from external electoral forces through increased attentiveness to their districts and through their significant advantage in campaign resources over challengers.

Both the significance of coattail effects and their limits can be illustrated in an examination of recent presidential-year election outcomes for the House of Representatives. Sizable Reagan presidential victories in 1980 and 1984 were accompanied by gains in votes for GOP candidates and in GOP seats in the House; the gains were 3 percent of the vote and 34 seats in 1980 and 4 percent of the vote but only 16 seats in 1984. In 1988, even though George Bush defeated Michael Dukakis 54 to 46 percent in the popular vote and the Republican House candidates received a 1 percent gain in votes, the party actually lost two seats in the House of Representatives. In these years, the imperfect translation of vote gains into seat gains moderated the effects of coattails. Finally, 1992 provides a rare example of the apparent absence of presidential coattails. In Bill Clinton's 1992 presidential victory, which was attained with only 43 percent of the vote in a three-way race, the party's House candidates ran well ahead of their standard-bearer. As the Democrats' presidential vote dropped by 3 percent, popular votes for Democratic House candidates fell off by 2 percent—to their lowest level since 1968—and the presidential party lost nine seats.

Presidential coattails have extended beyond House elections to contests for the state legislature and for the U.S. Senate as well.[7] From 1944 through 1984, when a president ran strongly in a state, the president's party typically did better in state legislative contests on the same ballot. The presidential effect on state legislative races, however, was somewhat less than on congressional contests, and of course many states have moved their legislative elections into nonpresidential years to insulate them from presidential forces. That presidential coattails seemed significant in many Senate elections from 1972 to 1988 may be even more surprising, considering the high visibility of contestants for this office.

The importance of presidential coattails also may underlie the remarkable phenomenon of the president's party losing seats in midterm contests for the U.S. House of Representatives. Since 1856, the presidential party's seat share in the House has been reduced by each midterm election with but a single exception—in 1934 at the beginning of the New Deal realignment. Just as a popular presidential candidate can boost the chances of his party's candidates in the presidential year, his absence from the ticket may deprive them of this advantage at midterm.[8]

A Broader Perspective on Electoral Influence   Yet, so prominent is presidential leadership in the eyes of voters that a president can influence election results for other contests even if he is not on the ballot. In the years of the midterm congressional elections, the intention of voters to vote for candidates of the president's party fluctuates during the campaign with the level of their approval of how the president is managing the presidency as measured by questions such as the Gallup organization's familiar "Do you approve or disapprove of the way _____ is handling his job as president?" There has been a substantial relationship between presidential approval and midterm seat gains (or losses) since the late 1930s and early 1940s, which no doubt partially accounts for why midterm Democrats fared so poorly in 1994.[9]

Where does all of this leave the American president as electoral leader of his party? First of all, the fate of a party's candidates for office is unavoidably linked to the standing of their president. Presidential coattails extend to a variety of legislative contests on the same ticket, and the popularity of the president even influences congressional election outcomes when he is not on the ballot. An important component of the president's electoral leadership, then, is the tendency for voters to be influenced by his standing in casting ballots for other offices and, of course, the knowledge that his partisan running mates and their potential challengers have of the significance of the relationship.[10]

Second, while significant, the impact of a president's popularity and coattails seems not to be as strong as it once was. That fact reduces both an important aspect of his party leadership and an important source of his influence over the Congress. Even if presidential influence accounts for only small percentage shifts in the total vote, however, small shifts can have a significant impact on party strength in the Congress. From 1952 to 1970, each shift of one percent in the popular vote added or subtracted about eight seats in the House of Representatives.[11] Even though House seats may have become less responsive to popular vote changes since then, the balance in Congress between conservative and liberal forces and the less-than-perfect levels of party cohesion allow even a small shift in seats to have an important bearing on policy making.

Also, voters do continuously evaluate presidential performance. Popular support is a valuable resource for the chief executive in getting Congress to go along with his programs. In the first year of the Reagan administration, for example, President Reagan's popularity in the country could be credited in part for his considerable success on the Hill, just as President Clinton's unpopularity made it more difficult for him to steer health-reform legislation through a Democratic Congress. There also is some suggestion that voters who disapprove of presidential performance vote in larger numbers in midterm elections than those who approve, and that their negativism leads them to prefer the other party and its candidates.[12] It is also very likely that perceptions and evaluations of a president (and governor) affect the way individuals view the parties. Executive programs are party programs, and the successes and failures of executives are party successes and failures. For a public that views politics chiefly in personal terms, a president or a governor—even a big-city mayor—is the personification of the party. Finally, the fund-raising capabilities of a popular president confer considerable advantages on his party's candidates, especially the ones he favors. This gives the president important leverage over party office seekers.

Limits on Electoral Leadership

Imposing as these ties between the chief executive and the party may be, they are not without real and tangible limits. First of all, the executive may be limited by his own political experience and taste for political leadership. Some presidents and governors do not want to lead a party, or they do not think it proper for an executive to do so. Like Eisenhower, they find it politically advantageous to appear to be above party politics. Even those who do want to be party leaders may find that the representational demands of the office—the pressures to be a president, governor, or mayor of "all of the people"—limit their partisan work and identification.

Chief executives also may lead only part of a party. Governors from one-party states, for example, often lead only a party faction. Executives also may share leadership of the party with other partisans. Presidents who are not especially secure in national party affairs may find the more experienced leaders of the congressional party asserting major leadership in the national party. Governors may find senators, who represent as broad a constituency, and other representatives of their party pressing parallel leadership claims over the state party. These legislators and state party leaders may fear that the governor will use party control for his or her own political ambitions.

The Executive-Centered Party

Nonetheless, the president heads, and occasionally even unifies, the national party. He dominates the national committee and the rest of the national organization, and, through a combination of his powers of office and his party leverage, he often exerts enough mastery of the legislative party to speak for the party in government. Most important, perhaps, for millions of American voters he is the symbol of the party, its programs, and its performance. The national constituency is his, and his nomination and campaign are the chief activities of the national party. They are the only activities with any visibility in this age of media politics. Within the state and local parties, the governors and many mayors have the same unifying, symbolizing role, and they, too, have their leverage on legislative parties and organizations.[13]

Therefore, it is no exaggeration to speak of the American parties as executive-centered coalitions. No alternative leader can compete with the executive in representing the party to the public, in commanding a broad array of tools of influence, or in enjoying as much legitimacy as the center of party leadership. Even in the party out of power, the executive office and its opportunities dominate. Opposition to the other party's executive and his or her coalition, as well as planning for the next election's assault on the office, provide the chief unifying focus. Moreover, it is the headless quality of the party out of power that most typifies its melancholy condition.

To some extent, the executive-centered party is a coalition of the executive-dominated party in government with the party in the electorate. That alliance, of necessity, bypasses the party organization. The identifications and loyalties of voters are not to the party organization but to the party symbols, the meaning for which comes largely from executives and their programs. The men and women of the party in government often build their own supporting organizations and thus bypass the party organizations in their quest for office. Even in the use of patronage, executives maximize support for their programs and their own political futures rather than maintain or rebuild the strength of the party organization.[14]

Once in office, executives generally put the leverage they derive from their position as party leaders into the business of governing, rather than into any concern for the party as an organization. The president, for example, finds himself without sufficient constitutional powers to hold his own in the struggles of the American separation of powers. Indeed, if the proverbial man from Mars should obtain a copy of the United States Constitution, he could not imagine from its niggardly grants of power to the president what the office has come to be. American presidents, faced with that shortage of formal powers, have had to rely heavily on their extraconstitutional powers. They derive an important portion of those powers from party leadership.

PARTY LEADERSHIP AND LEGISLATIVE RELATIONS

The American chief executive does not possess a large area of policy-making autonomy. Aside from the president's primacy in the fields of defense and international relations, which itself is not always exercised without congressional challenges, little major policy-making power is reserved solely for the American executive. What impact the executive is to have on the making of policy or on the enacting of a party program largely must come about through the formal actions of the legislature. In this pursuit of policy by influencing a legislature, the president and other chief executives turn repeatedly to the ties of party.

The Problems of Divided Control of Government

The coordination of legislative and executive decision making under the aegis of a political party is not easily accomplished, however. The possibility of divided control of government in the American system is a formidable obstacle to legislative-executive cooperation. Between 1968 and 1996, for example, the president's party has controlled both houses of Congress for only six years, four under President Carter and two under President Clinton. During the same period, virtually all of the states have experienced divided party control of the legislature and the governorship. At such times, the executives often have no choice but to minimize partisan appeals. In view of the closeness of the party division in many legislatures and the unreliability of some legislators of their own party, they must also curry the favor of some legislators of the opposing party. Thus, the American chief executives must follow a mixed strategy: partisan appeals and sanctions for their own party and nonpartisan or bipartisan politics for those of the opposition.

Tools of Executive Influence

In trying to get the Congress to pursue their objectives, presidents rely upon a variety of different resources. They make constant use of their nonparty sources of leadership of course—their prestige and persuasiveness, their command of the communications media, their own attention and favors. Overtly or not, they also use their identification with the party, whatever lingering patronage or preferments they can command (a judicial appointment here, a government project there), and their ability to influence coming elections. Members of the president's party know that if they make him look bad, to some extent they also make themselves and their party look bad. That awareness surely accounts for their tendency to rally around the president on important votes despite their own legislative preferences. When their president has exercised his veto of congressional bills, for example, members of his party are sometimes even willing to counter their original support for the bill by voting to uphold his veto (Table 14.1).

Nor can they escape the fact that the president heads the party ticket when he runs and that his performance becomes the party's record when he does not. In fact, members of Congress who benefited in the past from presidential coattails are more likely to support the president's program than those who did not. Legislators thus appear both to anticipate and to react to presidential leadership at the polls. The president figures even more prominently in legislators' hopes and fears of a change in the competitive position of their party and, by extension, themselves. Only he has sufficient political visibility to seize the opportunities to move party supporters or opponents into a partisan realignment or, by incautious misstep, to turn the mood of the moment against the party as happened with the Watergate affair.

Legislative Support for Executives

Even so, Congress is often stubbornly resistant to presidential leadership, and recent presidents often have been unsuccessful in securing congressional approval of mea-

Table 14.1   PRE- AND POSTVETO SUPPORT OF PRESIDENT BY HIS PARTY ON
SELECTED VOTES, 1973–92

	Percent of president's party supporting president's position	
	Original passage	Vote on veto override
President Nixon		
Vocational Rehabilitation, Senate, 1973	5	76
Water-Sewer Program, House, 1973	31	87
Cambodia Bombing Halt, House, 1973	66	72
President Ford		
Public-Works Employment, Senate, 1976	44	68
Aid to Day-Care Centers, Senate, 1976	47	70
Hatch Act Revisions, House, 1976	65	84
President Carter		
Weapons Procurement Authorization, House, 1978	26	69
Public-Works Appropriations, House, 1978	18	48
Oil Import-Fee Abolition, Senate, 1980	12	22
President Reagan		
Standby Petroleum Allocation Act, Senate, 1982	13	62
Supplemental Appropriations, House, 1982	27	56
South African Sanctions, Senate, 1986	27	40
President Bush		
FS-X Development Restrictions, Senate, 1989	56	73
Most-Favored-Nation Status for China, House, 1992	8	32
Family Leave, Senate, 1992	65	67

Note: President Clinton vetoed no legislation through his first two years in office.

Source: For presidents Nixon through Reagan: Selections from Randall B. Ripley, *Congress, Process and Policy* (New York: Norton, 1988), p. 189. For President Bush, various issues of the *Congressional Quarterly Weekly Report.*

sures they endorse even when their party controls the Congress. President Carter had only about a 75 percent success rate with a Democratic Congress, while President Clinton scored no more than 10 percent higher during his first two years in office when the Democrats held majorities in Congress. Presidents receive much less support when Congress is in the hands of the opposing party, as the battles between President Clinton and the Republican Congress in 1995 exemplify. Still, there are occasions—the early Nixon years, the early Reagan years—when especially effective presidential leadership is able to get even a Congress controlled by the other party to go along with what he wants. What helped President Reagan in the early 1980s, of course, was the fact that his party had gained a majority in the Senate (Figure 14.1).[15]

Even though they usually can count on a majority of Congress, presidents never have been able to get as much support, even from members of their own party, as

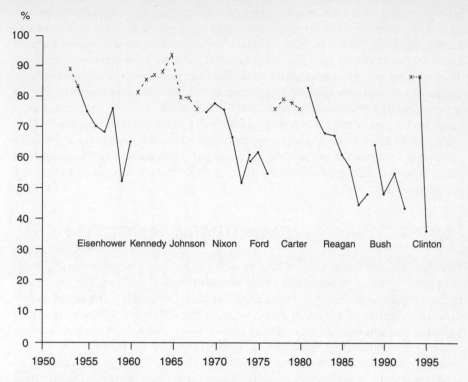

Figure 14.1 Presidential success in the U.S. Congress, 1953–94.

Note: the entry for each year is the percentage of time members of both the House and the Senate voted in support of the announced position of the president. Years in which the president's party controlled both houses of Congress are indicated by an "x" and connected by dotted lines. Years in which opposition party controlled at least one house of Congress are indicated by a "." and connected by solid lines.

Source: Congressional Quarterly Weekly Report, December 31, 1994, 3654.

prime ministers naturally enjoy. Moreover, their influence seems to have diminished in recent decades. One reason is that they have been more likely to face a Congress in which at least one house is controlled by the opposition party. The changing electoral realities for members of Congress surely have played an important role as well. The impact of presidential coattails and presidential influence on congressional elections is somewhat lower than before, and incumbent members of Congress also have been more secure in their constituencies. A congressional politics of cultivating the constituency by greater attention to its interests and increased services to individual constituents secures these legislators' political futures and insulates them from the electoral influences of the presidency.[16] Under modern conditions, then, presidents emphasize their role as party leaders less and are forced back more upon the nonparty components of their influence.

Governors, on the other hand, are frequently in a position to exercise far-greater and more-direct party organizational power over the legislators of their own party. In many states, their legislatures are unbound by the traditions of seniority, and a few governors may even take an active part in selecting committee chairpersons and influential party floor leaders at the beginning of the session. They may view the party's legislative leaders as "their" leaders, chosen to steer their programs through legislative waters. They may also lead powerful, ongoing state party organizations. To cross them may be to run the risk of falling from party favor, which means that a legislator's career in the legislature, not to mention his or her future ambition, may be at the mercy of a determined, politically skillful governor. In short, the average governor has far greater control over party rewards and incentives than a president does. On the other hand, in the symbolic aspects of party leadership, a governor probably exerts less influence than a president. Because governors are less visible and salient than presidents, their coattails and prestige are likely to be less potent than those of presidents.

PARTY POWER AND ADMINISTRATIVE POLICY

The very size and complexity of modern government and modern society necessitates broad exercises of discretion in the administration of the laws. The implementation of programs involves bureaucrats regularly in making important policy decisions. In spite of a burst of deregulation in the 1980s and 1990s, government agencies also still regulate vast areas of the economy—banking, insurance, nuclear energy, prescription drugs, radio and TV, workplace safety, for example—under necessarily vague legislative mandates.[17] Obviously, then, any concept of party responsibility or party government cannot be restricted to legislatures. Administration clearly shapes policy in its applications, and, to be effective, party programs require sympathetic administrative leadership.

Limits on Executive Leadership

However, there are substantial limits, many of them resulting from Progressive reforms enacted decades ago on the executive's ability to unify an administration and hold it responsible to a party program:

- The legislature may place administrative positions outside executive control by stipulating terms of appointment that last beyond a chief executive's term (such as for the governors of the Federal Reserve System, which acts as the nation's central bank), by limiting the executive's power of removal, or by placing policy makers under a merit system.
- Special precautions may also be taken to thwart partisan control of an administrative agency. Some federal agencies, especially regulatory commissions, are headed by five-person boards, but not more than three of the members of each board may be of the same political party. (The Federal Elections Commission is a good example.)
- In a number of states, top administrative positions, in addition to the gubernatorial office, are filled by election. At worst, that places members of both parties—a Republican governor and a Democratic state treasurer, for exam-

ple—in an uncomfortable alliance. Even if the offices are filled by candidates of the same party, they are often politically and constitutionally independent. In many ways, this plural executive system diminishes the authority of the governor.

- Furthermore, American executives suffer some diminution of political power as their terms approach a predetermined end. The Twenty-second Amendment to the United States Constitution limits the presidential term to between eight and ten years, and a majority of the states limit the governor's time in office to one or two consecutive terms.

- Finally, political realities may force executives to share the instruments of party leadership with others. Senatorial courtesy and other political considerations guarantee that the Senate's confirmation of presidential appointments will be more than pro forma. Also, in forming a cabinet, the president cannot ignore the feelings and aspirations of groups within the party that contributed to his victory.

Establishing control of the executive branch, however, is far more complex than simply putting fellow partisans into positions of power. The chief executive faces essentially the same problem in enforcing party discipline on administrative subordinates that a party leader in the legislature faces. In both cases, the problem is loyalty to and the power of a constituency. Just as the legislators identify with the problems and outlooks of the citizens they know and represent, administrators often identify with the problems and outlooks of the groups and individuals with which their agencies deal. Also, just as legislators must depend on the folks back home to protect their political careers, top-level administrators know that the support of client groups is their best personal political protection and the only protection for an agency, its mission, and its budget. In this way, the Department of Veterans Affairs enjoys the protection of the American Legion and the Veterans of Foreign Wars, and the Environmental Protection Agency depends on the support of organized naturalists and environmentalists as well as of the industries it regulates. Only with the greatest difficulty does the pressure of party loyalties and party sanctions overcome the power of these administrative constituencies. In the executive as well as the legislative branch, the party has less to give and less to take away than the constituency does.[18]

Tools of Executive Influence

In that part of the administrative establishment closest to the chief executive lies the greatest chance of party responsibility. At these top administrative levels, the appointee often has been politically active and has associated actively with a political party. He or she has very likely come to recognize the claims of the party organization and has developed a commitment to party goals and programs.

The cabinet of a president such as Bill Clinton (see box on p. 345) suggests the extent to which the political party remains a reservoir of talent, even a recruiter of talent, for modern administrations. It is undoubtedly true that presidents no longer are as explicitly partisan as they once were in their cabinet appointments, that they no longer use them as rewards for party service or as symbolic rewards to some part of the party. Presidents increasingly draw on individuals with standing and experience in the areas of policy they will administer.[19] At the same time, however, presidents largely find their appointees among those who have earlier held partisan public office or who have experience in the affairs of the party itself. Their political careers and their values and commitments often have, to a significant degree, been shaped by their political party.

When one looks a step below in the administrative structure to the assistant secretary level, however, party and governmental experience may dwindle. In many administrations these individuals are most often chosen for their skills and experience in administration and only secondarily for their political credentials. In the selection of many of them, the role of the party organization may not have extended beyond determining whether they were politically acceptable (that is, inoffensive) in their home states. Yet, they continue to come largely from the party of the president. Although these positions no longer serve so frequently as party patronage, the party link is still there to guarantee a commitment to a common outlook.[20]

Administrations with a more ideological mission—the Reagan administration is a good example—have taken great pains to ensure this common political outlook. They recruit ideological sympathizers rather than just fellow partisans into executive positions and charge them with the mission of turning their agencies toward the president's policies. An inevitable result is that a certain tension develops between party loyalists and ideologues in the top leadership circles of the administration—with the former dedicated to long-term party interests and the latter to the president's agenda. While appointing ideological sympathizers produces an even more cohesive administration in terms of policy viewpoints, it can weaken the party link and undermine the president's influence with fellow partisans in the Congress.

All things considered, the problem of political control over the executive bureaucracy is formidable, especially at the national level. Modern presidents are limited to only about 3,000 political appointees, fewer appointive positions than are available to some governors, with which to try to gain control of a federal executive branch containing several million civilian employees. Many of the president's men and women are novices, who have little time to "learn the ropes" and little prospect of gaining the necessary support of career bureaucrats without compromising their commitment to presidential designs. Furthermore, as Hugh Heclo has so convincingly shown, together they comprise "a government of strangers"—a set of executives whose limited familiarity and interaction with one another prevent them from constituting an effective team—which is often overwhelmed by a huge, fragmented, and more or less permanent bureaucracy.[21]

It is little wonder that recent presidents, especially Republican presidents, have relied more and more on their immediate White House staff and the Office of Management and Budget in trying to mobilize the executive branch on behalf of their policy goals.[22] Therefore, even though party is an important instrument for control of the administrative bureaucracy, serving as both a recruitment channel for scarce executive talent and a common bond linking the interests of the chief executive and the top bureaucrats, it is often inadequate for accomplishing the difficult task of executive leadership.

PARTISAN DEMOCRATIC BACKGROUNDS OF THE CLINTON CABINET

All but one of the members of President Bill Clinton's cabinet in early 1996 had some record of activity in Democratic party politics as elected officeholders and candidates for office, appointees to political positions in previous Democratic administrations, or campaign strategists. What follows is a short sketch of the partisan political positions of each.

Bruce Babbitt (Interior): Democratic Attorney General and Governor of Arizona.

Jesse Brown (Veterans Affairs): no previous partisan political experience.

Ronald H. Brown (Commerce): Chairman of the Democratic National Committee; top strategist in presidential campaigns of Ted Kennedy and Jesse Jackson.

Henry G. Cisneros (Housing and Urban Development): Democratic Mayor of San Antonio.

Warren M. Christopher (State): Deputy U.S. Attorney General under President Johnson; Deputy Secretary of State under President Carter.

Dan Glickman (Agriculture): Democratic U.S. Representative from Kansas.

Hazel R. O'Leary (Energy): High-level Energy Department official under President Carter.

Federico Peña (Transportation): Democratic member and leader of Colorado legislature; Democratic Mayor of Denver.

William Perry (Defense): Under Secretary of Defense under President Carter; Deputy Secretary of Defense under President Clinton.

Robert Reich (Labor): Director of Policy Planning, Federal Trade Commission, under President Carter.

Janet Reno (Justice): Democratic State Attorney, Dade County (Miami), Florida.

Richard W. Riley (Education): Democratic member of the South Carolina legislature; Democratic Governor of South Carolina.

Robert Rubin (Treasury): major fundraiser for Democratic presidential candidates since Carter.

Donna E. Shalala (Health and Human Services): Assistant Secretary of Housing and Urban Development under President Carter.

Changing Political Outlooks in the Federal Bureaucracy

Yet, in its own way, the federal bureaucracy (and many of the state bureaucracies as well) is responsive to partisan political forces. With the expansion of the federal government in the 1930s, President Franklin Roosevelt was able to draw into the career-service bureaucracy, especially to agencies handling New Deal programs, personnel committed to his programs and dedicated to implementing them through government service. They constituted a powerful bulwark against subsequent diminution of these programmatic commitments, especially as they were promoted during the years to more and more senior positions in their agencies.

Thus, it should come as no surprise that Republican President Richard Nixon came to perceive that he faced a federal bureaucracy that was unsympathetic, perhaps even hostile, to his more conservative political agenda. Interviews with top career officials in domestic agencies by Joel Aberbach and Bert Rockman in 1970 showed that Nixon's perceptions were to a considerable degree anchored in reality. Just short of a majority of these career bureaucrats proclaimed that they normally voted Democratic, and only 17 percent normally voted Republican. Moreover, in the social service agencies especially, even those officials who were not Democrats tended to favor liberal policy postures. It is little wonder that the Nixon administration devoted considerable energy to trying to control a bureaucracy with "clashing beliefs" to its own through the appointment of White House loyalists to top bureaucratic positions.[23]

By 1992, after the battles of the Nixon years and twelve years of Republican presidencies, including eight years of conservative leadership from Ronald Reagan, the bureaucratic environment had changed. When Aberbach and Rockman returned to interview career administrators in comparable positions to those they talked to in 1970, they found slight Republican and liberal pluralities, although the career executives still were considerably more Democratic and liberal than the Reagan and Bush political appointees. Among the forces to which they attribute change in the partisan tenor of the bureaucracy are the turnover of civil servants, due to both departures and the recruitment to senior executive positions of a new generation less committed to New Deal and Great Society programs, and changes in civil service laws that allowed positions formerly reserved for career employees to be filled by political appointees, who could be carefully screened by the White House. Whatever the cause, what had been "Nixon's problem" of an unsympathetic bureaucracy had now to a considerable degree been overcome, leaving only the inherent difficulties of controlling even a generally sympathetic bureaucracy.[24]

For what purposes, then, do executives use the executive party and their leadership role in it? Their power and influence go chiefly for the tasks of governing, of meeting their executive decision-making responsibilities. Only secondarily can they attend to the goals and interests of the party organization. Many governors use some chunk of their patronage purely for party goals, and presidents may use cabinet appointments to satisfy the need for recognition of various groups or factions within the party. Such concessions may satisfy the political demands of the party and build party cohesion, but they may also undermine the administrative goals of the president. Ultimately, chief executives need whatever party loyalty and cohesion they can build for their own programs and, if they are in their first term, for their own reelection. It is the goals of the office, not of the party, that they pursue.

THE SHADOW OF PARTY IN THE JUDICIARY

While custom and the privacy of decision making have subdued their visibility, political party considerations are hardly absent from the judiciary. Many American judges are political men and women, who are often drawn to the bench after careers that involved them in some aspect of partisan politics. Moreover, as much as judicial reformers have attempted to insulate the bench from politics, especially party politics, the selection of judges in many locales and states and at the federal level continues to be strongly shaped by partisanship through both elections and appointment. The very nature of the judiciary, though, makes demonstrating the influence of party on it no easy task.

Judicial Voting Along Party Lines

Nothing illustrates the difficulties of evaluating the party in office quite so clearly as the examples of cohesive party voting in American appellate courts. Several studies have pointed to the presence of party-rooted blocs in state appellate courts in cases such as those involving workers' compensation, and there is no reason to believe that those partisan blocs have not endured into modern times. Another study, cutting across a number of state courts, found that Democratic and Republican judges differ significantly in the ways they decide certain types of cases. Democrats on the bench, for example, tend to decide more frequently for the defendant in criminal cases, for the government in taxation cases, for the regulatory agency in cases involving the regulation of business, and for the claimants in workers' compensation, unemployment compensation, and auto accident cases.[25] In recent redistricting cases, U.S. District Court judges also have tended to uphold plans enacted by their party more than those enacted by the opposing party.[26]

To be sure, no one suggests that the incidence of party cohesion in judicial decision making approaches that in legislatures. It appears only in certain types of cases; and the amount of disagreement within an appellate court that can be explained by party division falls far below the amount of legislative division that can be explained by partisanship. Yet, there is a trace of party in the American judiciary; Democratic judges render different decisions than their Republican counterparts.

It may infrequently happen that an American judge is swayed by some subtle persuasion by his or her political party. Although explicit partisan activity now violates judicial norms, from time to time judges have continued to be deeply immersed in partisan politics after they have gone on to the bench (see box on p. 348), and occasionally, especially on controversial issues at the state and local levels, partisan politicians will try to influence judges in particular cases. But neither happens frequently enough to explain partisan decision making in the courts.

JUDICIAL INDEPENDENCE: THE NORM AND ITS VIOLATORS

So powerful has the American norm of an independent judiciary become that the few instances of manifest extrajudicial political activity have had serious consequences for the judge involved, especially for justices on the Supreme Court.

This norm was not always so powerful, as Bruce Allen Murphy chronicles in the appendix to *The Brandeis/Frankfurter Connection*.[27] By the 1920s, though, the norms were changing, and involvement by judges in the broader world of politics became increasingly unacceptable—to the political community as well as to the general public.

So it was that Murphy's revelations about the extraordinary behind-the-scenes political involvement of widely revered Supreme Court Justices Louis Brandeis and Felix Frankfurter created such a sensation. More recent extrajudicial political involvement, albeit on a much smaller scale, cost Supreme Court Justice Abe Fortas his seat on the high court. During the Senate confirmation hearings on President Lyndon Johnson's nomination of Fortas to move up to the chief justice position, it was revealed that Justice Fortas had regularly and secretly served as a personal political advisor to Johnson on a variety of important policy matters, including the war in Vietnam. Faced with considerable Senate opposition to his nomination, Fortas asked the president to withdraw it; seven months later, as controversy continued to swirl around him, he resigned from the Court.

The explanation for the effects of party on judicial behavior instead rests in the different sets of values, even the different ideologies, that the major parties and their partisans reflect. Judges of the same party vote together on cases for the same reasons of values and outlook that led them to join the same political party. In other words, two judges will vote together on the issue of administrative regulation of utilities because of deep-seated values they share about the relationship of government and the economy. Those same values or perceptions led them some years earlier to join the same party, or they were developed out of experience in the same political party. In short, it is the party **in** the judge that affects his or her behavior and leads judges with similar partisan backgrounds to the same decisions, not the party as some external pressure.

Partisan Considerations in Judicial Selection

The impact of the party on the decision-making processes of the judiciary, therefore, is indirect. It stems largely from the role of the party as symbol of its members' commitments. This should not surprise anyone, for the selection of judges in the United States traditionally has taken the values and attitudes of judges into account.

Although we have only recently accepted in any overt way the notion of judicial policy making—the notion that, in some instances, judges have options and that in making these choices they may reflect, in part, their own prior experiences, perceptions, and values—we have acknowledged it implicitly for some time. For example, as President Theodore Roosevelt, considering a replacement for Justice Horace Gray on the Supreme Court, wrote to Senator Henry Lodge in inquiring about a certain Judge Oliver Wendell Holmes of the Massachusetts Supreme Court:

> In the ordinary and low sense which we attach to the words "partisan" and "politician," a judge of the Supreme Court should be neither. But in the higher sense, in the proper sense, he is not in my judgment fitted for the position unless he is a party man, a constructive statesman, constantly keeping in mind his adherence to the principles and policies under which this nation has been built up and in accordance with which it must go on.
>
> Now I should like to know that Judge Holmes was in entire sympathy with our views, that is, with your views and mine and Judge Gray's, just as we know that ex-Attorney General Knowlton is, before I would feel justified in appointing him. Judge Gray has been one of the most valuable members of the Court. I should hold myself as guilty of an irreparable wrong to the nation if I should put in his place any man who was not absolutely sane and sound on the great national policies for which we stand in public life.[28]

Selection of Federal Judges Congress, too, has often examined such issues in reviewing presidential nominations to the federal judiciary. In 1969 and 1970, the Senate rejected two Nixon nominees for the Supreme Court (Clement Haynesworth and G. Harold Carswell) at least partly because of the general conservatism of their views on race and labor. The major Supreme Court confirmation battles in recent times were over the nominations of outspoken conservatives Robert H. Bork and Clarence Thomas. Even party platforms occasionally have stipulated ideological criteria for judicial appointments.

Whether or not it should be within the province of a president (or a governor) to consider such matters in proposing judicial appointments, the appointee's political party and ideological loyalties serve as an important indication of her or his values and attitudes. Indeed, it is one of the reasons that, in the last century, American presidents have appointed judges overwhelmingly from their own parties. They have generally chosen fellow partisans for more than 90 percent of their appointees, and in every case, from Cleveland through Bush, the percentage has been above 80 percent (Table 14.2).

Recent presidents have differed in the extent to which ideological and party activism considerations have affected their judicial appointments. The Reagan and Bush appointees to the federal courts have been even more ideological than the average among recent presidents, and they also stand out in the extent to which they have been active in partisan politics over the course of their lives. The Reagan and Bush administrations took special care to screen candidates for the desired judicial philosophy through personal interviews and, if available, evaluations of their judicial records. The old tradition of allowing candidates for district and appellate courts to be identified by the party's senators was modified to ask senators to submit three names for consideration so that the administration had more influence on the final

Table 14.2   PARTISAN APPOINTMENTS TO FEDERAL DISTRICT AND APPELLATE COURTS: PRESIDENTS CLEVELAND THROUGH CLINTON'S FIRST TWO YEARS

	Percentage from the President's Party
Cleveland	97.3
Harrison	87.9
McKinley	95.7
T. Roosevelt	95.8
Taft	82.2
Wilson	98.6
Harding	97.7
Coolidge	94.1
Hoover	85.7
F. Roosevelt	96.4
Truman	93.1
Eisenhower	95.1
Kennedy	90.9
Johnson	95.2
Nixon	93.7
Ford	81.2
Carter	94.8
Reagan	94.4
Bush	93.5
Clinton	88.8

Source: Data through Bush from Harold W. Stanley and Richard G. Niemi, *Vital Statistics on American Politics* (Washington, D.C.: CQ Press, 1994), Table 9–3, p. 292. Stanley and Niemi, in turn, took their figures from Henry J. Abraham, *Justices and Presidents: Appointments to the Supreme Court* (New York: Oxford University Press, 1991), Chapter 4, Table 7 and updated them from personal communications with Abraham. Clinton figures from Sheldon Goldman "Judicial Selection under Clinton: A midterm examination," *Judicature* 78 (1995), pp. 281 and 287.

choices.[29] By contrast, the Clinton administration has given a larger role to the party's senators and other leaders in suggesting judicial nominees and has been less concerned with ideological screening. In his first two years, Clinton also has appointed a somewhat lower percentage of federal judges from his own party and has been less inclined to choose judges with records of party activity (53 percent) than Carter (64 percent), Reagan (61 percent), or Bush (63 percent).[30]

Selection of State Court Judges   There are substantial differences between the federal courts and the state courts in how judges are selected. First, five different selection methods are employed by the states—gubernatorial appointment, legislative election, partisan election, nonpartisan election, and the merit or "Missouri" plan in which judges are first selected (usually by the governor) from a list compiled by a nonpartisan screening committee and then must run in a retention election within several years of their appointment. Second, many states rely upon different methods of judicial selection for different courts. Third, lawyers play a more decisive role in screening candidates in the states, particularly in states using the Missouri plan, where they often are the dominant influence on the ultimate choices.

The states are divided fairly evenly among the different selection methods. Gubernatorial appointment of judges is used in seven states, and in another four the legislature chooses them. Partisanship intrudes directly into the selection process in thirteen states: candidates for at least some of their judgeships must run for office in partisan elections. This partisanship is sometimes illusory, however, as both parties will endorse the same candidate, who often is the choice of the state bar association. In most states, extensive attempts have been made to take the partisanship of appointment by a party leader or of partisan elections out of judicial selection. Ten states, following the Progressive tradition, elect judges on a nonpartisan ballot. But in some of these, such as Ohio, it is common practice for each party to publicly endorse its own slate of candidates, so nonpartisanship is a facade. Merit selection by the Missouri plan is an increasingly popular alternative for taking partisan politics out of the judicial selection process. Sixteen states employed this method as of 1992.[31]

Regardless of the selection process, partisanship is unmistakably present in most of the state judiciaries. Indeed, in a nation where the judiciary plays such an important policy-making role, it may be naive to think that the bench can or should be purged of partisan influences. Many a judge selected on a nonpartisan ballot or through the Missouri plan comes to the bench with the values represented by a particular party, and party lines are often apparent in the divisions on multijudge panels no matter what selection procedure is used.

Judicial terms also tend to be so long that many elective judgeships become appointive. Death or retirement often takes a nonpartisan judge from the bench in midterm, and the vacancy is filled before the next election by a gubernatorial appointment. The political considerations attending such appointments may then prevail: with the advantage of even a brief period of incumbency, the appointee usually wins a full, regular term at the next election. Only the low probabilities of defeat in retention elections may free appointed judges from partisan pressures, but they are so often already internalized in the judge's values and preferences that a long-term judgeship merely allows them to flourish.[32]

The Influence of Party in and on the Judge

The point, then, comes down to this. There is no way to eliminate the important political frames of reference that judges bring to their work. Judges have been men and women of the world; they know the issues of their times and the ways the parties relate to them. Furthermore, given the tradition of political activity of American lawyers, there is a good chance that the judge has had some active political party experience. Beyond this, the political party has an opportunity for active and overt influence in the selection process through the initiatives of governors or the president or through the usual processes of a partisan election. In these selection processes, the party has the opportunity to achieve two goals: the selection of judges who are sensitive to the values for which the party stands, and the appointments of deserving (and qualified) lawyers for service to it.

In some instances, the relationship between judge and party may extend beyond the politics of appointment. In some parts of the country, the local district or county judge sometimes still retains hidden ties to local politics. In a few American counties, the judge is the "eminence grise" of the party, slating candidates behind the scenes, directing party strategy, arbitrating among the conflicting ambitions of the party's candidates. Moreover, the local administration of justice occasionally opens new reservoirs of patronage for the party. The judge who is a loyal member of a political party may parcel out guardianships, receiverships in bankruptcy, and clerkships to loyal lawyers in the party.[33]

How is it that the tie between the judiciary and the parties is so substantial in the United States? The factors are complex and mixed. The phenomenon of the elective judiciary, compounded by the political appointment process, is one factor. Then, too, there is no career vocation, no special training process or examination for the judiciary; any lawyer can be a judge. By contrast, in many continental European countries, the career of judging requires special preparation, study, and apprenticeship, and one enters it by special civil service examination. In the American context, then, the additional factor of the dominance of our politics by the legal profession is free to operate. Lawyers are everywhere in American political and public life, and many of them hope for ultimate reward in appointment to the bench.

THE PARTY WITHIN THE EXECUTIVE AND THE JUDGE

Surprisingly, the influence of the political party on the executives and judiciaries of the American political system differs in degree but not in kind. The main avenue of party influence is indirect, and in both cases it stems from the kinds of commitments and values that loyalty to a party represents. Without the means to enforce party discipline through patronage appointment or removal for partisan disloyalty, it primarily depends, in other words, on the ideological impact or presence of the party *within* the men and women who hold administrative or judicial office. Although attempts have been made to remove partisan considerations from who these men and women are, especially through merit system appointments, their views and values—hence, their partisanship—are significant in their selection for both judicial and administrative offices.

Yet, partisanship is not alone as a factor guiding the selection or confirmation of administrators and judges by partisan executives or legislatures. The demands of the party organization compete with policy purpose—even when pursued within the limits of judicial propriety. On the one hand, the administrative position and the judgeship are two of the few available positions with which to reward party leaders, and the party is not anxious to have them pass to party "nobodies." On the other hand, ability and policy orientations have an importance that goes beyond party to the party leaders who are involved in the selection process. In the filling of positions in both branches, thus, one sees again the struggle between the party's own important need for organizational incentives and the need to recruit people who can best meet the responsibilities of governing. Set in a political culture and an era that disparages parties and partisanship, it is a struggle the parties have great difficulty winning.

Chapter
15

The Quest for Party Government

Political parties are everywhere in American legislatures and executives, and even appear in American judiciaries. Almost all American executives, American legislatures, and most of the American judiciaries are selected in processes that weigh the party affiliation of the office seeker heavily. Moreover, the appearances of party power are plentiful in the party leaders and whips of the legislatures and in the clearly partisan cast of many executive appointments. Even the elemental struggle between government and opposition, between ins and outs, largely follows political party lines in the American system. To a political order designed two hundred years ago to fragment rather than concentrate power, the political parties have brought a vital element of governmental coordination.

Yet, despite the trappings and portents of power, the American major parties do not govern easily. They find it hard to mobilize cohesive groups of officeholders behind programs and ideologies to which their organizations, activists, and candidates have committed themselves. Compared with the tightly disciplined parties that dominate the politics of parliamentary systems, the American parties are weak institutions indeed. Not only do they find it difficult to act cohesively within the various branches of government, but they face considerable limitations on their ability to serve as an ongoing force for the entire political system.

THE DISCONTENT WITH AMERICAN PARTIES

This inability of the American parties to govern is an old source of discontent for many political scientists.[1] The dissatisfactions, however, are with more than the American parties. They extend to the entire American political system and its fragmented centers of authority, its tendency to blur political alternatives and differences, and its built-in barriers to strong and vigorous governmental initiatives—each of them nurtured by the twin constitutional principles of separation of powers and federalism. The critics, motivated by a different model of government embodied in the cohesive parties of the British Parliament, have long hoped that by joining electoral majorities and officeholders to party programs, they could surmount the diffusion of power in the American polity. A 1950 report by a committee of the political-science discipline's leading professional association, written by some of the leading specialists on political parties of their day,[2] has served as the manifesto of the supporters of this model. The controversy it raised and that its ideas continue to raise has kept the question of the proper role of parties in governing at the center of academic discourse, especially as the realities of an alternative model—implicitly arising from the nation's experience with divided government since 1950—have taken hold.[3]

The controversy over party responsibility and party government is more than just an abstract academic argument. From the ideologically oriented activists in both parties have come wails of dissatisfaction with the issuelessness of American politics and the tendency of the major parties to take similar centrist positions.[4] In working for the nomination of Barry Goldwater in 1964, Republican conservatives pleaded for "a choice, not an echo." George Wallace capitalized upon the fact than many people felt there was "not a dime's worth of difference" between the major parties in his third-party candidacy in 1968. In 1972 a similar cry came from the left—in a movement that repudiated the centrist politics of established Democratic leaders and won the Democratic presidential nomination for George McGovern. More recently, in his quest for the presidency, Ross Perot has echoed the theme of both parties being too wedded to the status quo.

The forces for more responsible, more ideological parties have gained an upper hand in recent years. With the demise of the solidly Democratic South has come a more homogeneously liberal Democratic party. Only sixteen years after the smashing Goldwater defeat, Goldwater's ideological heir, Ronald Reagan, won the White House and began to shape a more ideologically distinctive Republican party—a legacy which has been continued through pursuit of an indisputably conservative agenda by the post-1994 Republican majority in the Congress.

At first blush, it may seem that the academic controversy over party responsibility does not have a great deal to do with the distinct programs of the parties. The two questions are to a great extent the same, however. The scholars who favor party government (or responsibility) and the ideologues of the left and right in American politics both want the major American parties to present more specific and differentiated programs. Both groups also want the parties to govern by carrying their programs into public policy. To the extent that such goals require some degree of consensus on basic values and long-term philosophies, they both also want greater ideological clarification and commitment within the parties.

THE DEBATE OVER RESPONSIBLE PARTY GOVERNMENT

Despite the nomenclature, the doctrines of party government (or party responsibility) are only secondarily concerned with political parties. They are fundamentally doctrines of democratic government or, more precisely, doctrines that advocate one particular variety of American democracy. Much of the debate over them has been over the kind of democracy we are to have. The whole movement for party government, in other words, has sprung from discontent over what some have seen as the ills of American democracy.

The Case for Party Government

The case for party government is a complicated one. It is especially difficult to appreciate in an American political culture steeped in concerns for limited government and in aversions to the organizing might of political parties.

Party Government and Positive Political Leadership   Most proponents of party government begin with a belief in strong, decisive government as a necessary force for the solution of problems in the American society and economy. Like so many of the advocates of positive government in the context of the American separation of powers, they see a need for strong executive leadership if the whole complex governmental apparatus is to move forward with vigor and with a semblance of unity. Yet they know all too well that the institutions and traditions of American government diffuse and divide governmental power in ways that prevent the generation of aggressive and responsive governmental programs. Theirs is the old complaint that American political institutions—suited, perhaps, for the limited, gingerly governing of the eighteenth and nineteenth centuries—are far less adapted to the present century's need for government action. Clearly, decentralized political parties, each of them divided by a vast diversity of interests and points of view, only accentuate the problem of diffusion. In a sense, therefore, doctrines of party responsibility are attempts to bind American politics and government into a cohesive and integrated whole of the kind more typical of parliamentary government.

To be sure, the various proponents of party government do not agree on the purposes that a strong, decisive government should serve. Once leery of a powerful and unified central government, many modern-day conservatives nonetheless have come to view untrammeled presidential power as necessary for the conduct of foreign policy. They also had become impatient with the constraining influence a Democratic Congress imposed on the Reagan and Bush attempts to reduce domestic spending and eliminate liberal programs. In 1995, however, they became more cognizant of the virtues of congressional power, while yearning for a president who could finalize the "Republican revolution." By contrast, liberals, who chafed at the bit because of separation of powers in years past, came to look with favor on congressional ability to check presidential initiatives in the Reagan years. Both groups recognize the value of party government if leaders they support are to change the status quo and, by the same token, the danger of party government to their cherished beliefs when the opposition is in charge.

A second thread of argument runs through the political diagnoses of the proponents of party government: concern for the minuscule influence of individuals in a mass, popular democracy. Contemporary government is complex and remote, and indivduals find it hard to have the time, attention, and political knowledge for an active role in it. They find it especially difficult to assess what their elected representatives have been doing in public office. Into the political void resulting from their ineffectiveness and ignorance rush well-organized and well-financed minorities—local elites, interest groups, party bosses, or political action committees. Consequently, so the argument goes, important decisions frequently are made by public officials and organized minorities without the participation or even the retrospective judgment of the great majority of individual citizens. Individuals drift from one meaningless decision to another; they do not know what the candidates stand for when they first elect them, and they have no standards or information for judging their performance in office when they come up for reelection.[5] These tendencies are seen as having been exacerbated in recent decades by a candidate-centered electoral politics fostered by television, individualistic campaigns, the general weakening of the political parties in the electorate, and of course the diffusion of governmental responsibility that divided government brings.

Party Government and Popular Democracy   This sense of alarm about the American democracy is by no means limited to the proponents of party government. It is a more or less standard critique from those quarters of American life committed to beliefs in the value of broad policy change and in the rationality and desirability of citizen involvement in a popular democracy. What sets the school of party government apart is its reliance on the organizing and consolidating powers of the competitive political party. A reconstructed (and responsible) pair of political parties, so the argument goes, would bring together masses of voters behind meaningful party programs and candidates loyal to them, would give one party control of all popular branches of government, would hold their elected candidates to the obligation of carrying those programs into public policy, and then would be held responsible for their programs by the electorate. The responsible political party thus would bridge the gulf between the disoriented individual and the complex institutions of government and stimulate greater participation in electoral politics. It would also bind the divided institutions of government into an operating whole.

In essence, these are proposals for the reinvigorating and animating of popular democratic institutions through the prime organizing role of the political party. Why use the political party for so crucial a role? It is because

> . . . the parties have claims on the loyalties of the American people superior to the claims of any other forms of political organization. . . . Moreover, party government is good democratic doctrine because the parties are the special form of political organization adapted to the mobilization of majorities. How else can the majority get organized? If democracy means anything at all it means that the majority has the right to organize for the purpose of taking over the government.[6]

Only the parties, their supporters believe, are stable and visible enough to carry this representational burden. As the only completely political organization and the only one with a public or semipublic character, the political party alone has the capacity for developing the essential qualities of responsibility. Moreover, parties are seen as much superior as democratic institutions to the pressure groups, their major rivals as intermediaries between citizens and government.[7]

The call for responsible political parties, therefore, is a call for political parties with new capacities and new goals. Specifically, the responsible political party must:

- Enunciate a reasonably explicit statement of party programs and principles.
- Nominate candidates loyal to the party program and willing to enact it into public policy if elected.
- Conduct its electoral campaigns in such a way that voters will grasp the programmatic differences between the parties and make their voting decisions substantially on that basis.
- Guarantee that public officeholders elected under the party label will carry the party program into public policy and thus enable the party to take responsibility for their actions in office.

The entire argument, therefore, rests on replacing individual or group responsibility for governing with the responsibility of the political party.

Concern for developing and enacting programs must infuse all relationships within the party and all steps in the contesting of elections. As the report of the committee of the American Political Science Association (APSA) argues in its very first paragraph:

> While in an election the party alternative necessarily takes the form of a choice between candidates, putting a particular candidate into office is not an end in itself. The concern of the parties with candidates, elections and appointments is misunderstood if it is assumed that the parties can afford to bring forth aspirants for office without regard to the views of those so selected. Actually, the party struggle is concerned with the direction of public affairs. Party nominations are no more than a means to this end. In short, party politics inevitably involves public policy in one way or another.[8]

The whole idea of party government is policy and issue oriented. It is concerned with using public office for predetermined goals, not merely for the thrill of winning, the division of patronage and spoils, or the reward of the office itself. The winning of public office becomes no more than a means to policy ends (see box on p. 358).

The Case Against Party Government

Despite the persuasiveness of the advocates of party government, there still remains a sizable platoon of American political scientists and political leaders who are definitely unconvinced. The journals of American political science, in fact, were dotted with rejoinders for several years after the publication of the report of the Committee on Political Parties in 1950. Their collective case against party government and responsibility divides into two related but independent arguments: the undesirability of party government and its impossibility (or at least its improbability) in the American context. Although the two points are related, both logically and polemically, one does not have to make both in order to venture one.[9]

On the grounds of undesirability, the skeptics raise a number of fundamental issues of political philosophy. They fear that party government would stimulate a more intense politics of dogmatic commitment—one in which the softenings and majority building of compromise would be more difficult. They fear, too, that by making the political party the prime avenue of political representation, the advocates of party government would destroy the richness and multiplicity of representational mechanisms in the American democracy. Interest groups and other nonparty political

THE RESPONSIBLE PARTY, MID-1990s STYLE

In issuing their Contract with America, the House Republicans adhered to many precepts of the responsible party model. As described in the flyers and ads they distributed in advance of the 1994 election, theirs was "A Program for Accountability" that pledged to change long-term congressional practices on the first day of the new Congress and to ensure votes on ten specific pieces of legislation within the first one hundred days—if only the electorate would give them the majority. Furthermore, the Republicans' contract concluded: "If we break this contract, throw us out. We mean it." Given their majority by the electorate, the House Republicans proceeded to honor the terms of their contract through iron control of the House agenda and levels of voting cohesion higher than those seen in decades. At this point, however, their attempts at party responsibility were stymied by a Republican Senate majority that was not committed to the contract and the veto powers of a Democratic president. For responsible party government to be practiced under the American rules of government, in short, requires more than the dedication to responsible party principles of partisans in a single chamber of Congress.

organizations, they feel, are necessary means of political representation in a large and heterogeneous polity. Channeling the representation of such a diversity of interests into the party system would overload two parties and risk the development of multipartyism, which would further fragment the American system. Moreover, the skeptics are concerned lest party government destroy the deliberative quality of American legislatures, for legislators would cease to be free, independent men and women and would become the mandated representatives of a fixed party position. In short, they fear what European critics have called *partyocracy*—the domination of politics and legislatures by a number of doctrinaire, unyielding political parties, none of them strong enough to govern yet none willing to let others govern.

On the related grounds of realism, the critics of responsible parties have argued:

- The American voter remains insufficiently involved in issues to be coaxed easily into viewing politics and electoral choices in programmatic terms.
- The complexity of American society and the diversity of interests it generates are too great to be expressed in the simple set of alternatives a two-party system can frame.
- The parties themselves are too diffuse and decentralized—too lacking in central disciplinary authority—and the nation too large and diverse for the parties ever to take a single national position and then enforce it on their holders of public office.
- The institutions of American government stand in the way at a number of crucial points. The direct primary, for example, makes it difficult for the parties to choose nominees loyal to their programs, and the near-monopoly it has recently achieved over the nomination process makes it impossible for the par-

ties to enforce party discipline. Moreover, the separation of powers and bicameralism often prevent the control of all executive and legislative authority by a single party.

- Americans have distrusted parties too much, as is evidenced by their recurrent attempts to reform politics to reduce rather than increase their influence, to be mobilized in support of institutional changes to increase party power.

In other words, the model of the responsible, governing political party appears to the critics to demand too much of the American voters, of the parties themselves, of the institutions of American government, and of the will of the people in an antipartisan political culture.

Ways of Achieving Greater Cohesion

If the major American parties are to meet the demands and roles of party government, they must find some way to overcome their disunity. The problem is really one of uniting the party organization, the party in the electorate, and the party in office in active and responsible support of a party program—despite their different political goals, different political traditions and interests, and different levels of attention, information, and activity. There are three ways in which the necessary cohesiveness might be achieved: they involve changes in institutional arrangements, organizational discipline, and ideological agreement.

In many systems, party cohesion is promoted by institutional arrangements and their imperatives for political activity. The parliamentary system demands that the majority party maintain cohesion in the legislature—and to a lesser extent in the electorate and the party organization—if it is to stay in office.[10] In the United States, federalism and the separation of powers have just the opposite effect of fragmenting constitutional authority by dividing it among levels and branches of government. Indeed, in the current era of divided government, institutional fragmentation probably has never been greater. It is farfetched to imagine that the Constitution would ever be amended to reduce this fragmentation through, for example, creation of a parliamentary system.

Cohesion may also be promoted by organizational discipline. A strong party organization may impose its discipline and cohesion on balky partisans in office if it can control renomination to office. The proliferation of the American direct primary, however, makes that a hard task. Primaries now enjoy an almost complete hegemony over the nominating process. Alternatively, powerful party leaders or executives may enforce discipline through the manipulation of the rewards they control (patronage, preference, access to authority, and so on). The value of these rewards is shrinking, however, and political ethics in most parts of the United States no longer easily accept an enforced toeing of the line. Still there is a remote possibly that the increased resources of the national (and perhaps even state) party organizations might be employed to enforce some degree of ideological discipline, even if it flies in the face of decades of tradition.

Finally, the cohesion may be produced "naturally" by an all-pervasive, intraparty agreement on ideology or program. All three components of the party may reach some consensus on a basic party ideology or program or at least on a "silent ideology" of commonly held interest. The activists and identifiers of the party would then achieve a cohesion arising from common philosophy and goals, and their cohesion, to a considerable extent, would be a result of internalized and self-enforced commitment to those goals. Distasteful external constraints and restraints would thus be less necessary.

Because it seems that only the third avenue to party government is a likely one for contemporary American parties, the issue of party government for the United States becomes one of ideological—or at least more ideological—politics and parties. A pervasive ideological commitment appears to be the necessary condition for party cohesion in the American system, which in turn is a necessary condition for responsible governing parties. Organizational discipline may supplement and buttress the ideology, but it does not appear to be a realistic alternative to it.

IDEOLOGICAL PARTIES IN THE UNITED STATES?

Throughout their long histories, the American political parties have been remarkably nonideological. Even the Republican party, born out of the impassioned abolitionist movement of the 1850s, soon moved away from its ideological roots as slavery ended and it attempted to hold together a national constituency as a majority party.

The reasons for the pragmatic nature of American parties are several. First and perhaps foremost, there are only two of them to divide up the political world. The parties in a multiparty system, by contrast, can cater to a special ideological niche within the electorate in a way that parties in a two-party system cannot if they wish to survive. The very size and diversity of the American nation itself also limit the ideological purity of its parties. With so many different interests and people to represent, it is little wonder that they are wide coalitions of office seekers and organizational activists, the epitome of what Otto Kirchheimer so aptly called "catch-all" parties.[11] Finally, of course, one is led back to the American people themselves, whom scholars agree have been unusually free of the kinds of deep-seated animosities that fuel an ideological politics in other democratic systems.[12]

The Nature of Party Differences

This is not to say, however, that there are no important differences of principle between the parties. They clearly diverge on specific policy questions. These differences appear in the platforms they adopt every four years at their national nominating conventions (see box on pp. 361–363), in the speeches of their candidates for president and other offices, and in the policies they pursue when they occupy governmental office—as became apparent in the battles between the Republican Congress and President Clinton over House Republican Contract with America in 1995.[13] The roots of such differences are to be found in the nature of the party coalitions, particularly as they were shaped in the realigning periods that have defined the different American party systems (see Chapter 6).

But the policy stands and even principles that have been identified with the American parties fall short of being ideologies in the conventional sense because

WHAT THE DEMOCRATS AND REPUBLICANS STAND FOR: KEY ELEMENTS OF THE 1992 PARTY PLATFORMS

Party platforms are not binding upon their candidates or their followers, and they sometimes mask more than they reveal. Nonetheless, they do express the sentiments of the national party conventions about what the parties stand for at a particular time and, in this sense, serve as a valuable encapsulation of party positions on the issues of the day. Below are the party platform pronouncements on a dozen important contemporary issues, chosen so as highlight some of the current differences between the parties. Some of these differences are clear-cut; others are reflected in the subtle contrasts in emphasis that these selections are meant to convey. For more detail on them, see the full text of the party platforms. They are reprinted in the *Congressional Quarterly Weekly Report:* July 18, 1992, for the Democratic platform and August 22, 1992, for the Republican platform.

PARTY DIFFERENCES ON KEY ISSUES, 1992

1. Abortion

Democrats: "Democrats stand behind the right of every woman to choose, consistent with *Roe v. Wade,* regardless of ability to pay, and support a national law to protect that right."
Republicans: "We believe the unborn child has a fundamental individual right to life that can not be infringed. We therefore reaffirm our support for a human life amendment to the Constitution . . . and oppose using public revenues for abortion."

2. The Arts

Democrats: "We believe in public support for the arts, including a National Endowment for the Arts that is free from political manipulation and firmly rooted in the First Amendment's freedom of expression guarantee."
Republicans: "Government has a responsibility to ensure that it promotes the common moral values that bind us together as a nation. We therefore condemn the use of public funds to subsidize obscenity and blasphemy masquerading as art. . . . We believe a free market in art—with neither suppression nor favoritism by government—is the best way to foster the cultural revival our country needs."

3. Budget Deficit

Democrats: ". . . the Democratic investment, economic conversion and growth strategy will generate more revenues from a growing economy. We must also tackle spending by putting everything on the table; eliminate non-productive programs; achieve defense savings; reform entitlement programs . . . ; and make the rich pay their fair share in taxes. These

(box continues)

choices will be made while protecting senior citizens and without further victimizing the poor."

Republicans: "The only solution is for the voters (to elect) . . . a Republican Congress (which) can enact the balanced-budget amendment . . . and adopt a line-item veto for the presidency. . . . (Republicans) will consider non-social security mandatory spending portions of the federal budget when looking for savings."

4. Civil Rights

Democrats: "We support ratification of the Equal Rights Amendment, affirmative action, stronger protection of voting rights for racial and ethnic minorities . . . , and continued resistance to discriminatory English-only pressure groups."

Republicans: "Asserting equal rights for all, we support . . . vigorous enforcement of statutes to prevent illegal discrimination on account of sex, race, creed or national origin. Promoting opportunity, we reject efforts to replace equal rights with quotas or other preferential treatment."

5. Defense Spending

Democrats: "A post-Cold-War restructuring of American forces will produce substantial savings beyond those promised by the Bush Administration, but that restructuring must be achieved without undermining our ability to meet future threats to our security."

Republicans: "U.S. defense spending already has been reduced significantly. . . . Yet any defense budget, however lean, is still too much for the Democrats. They want to start by cutting defense outlays over the next four years by nearly $60 billion. . . . This is folly."

6. Educational Funding

Democrats: "We oppose the Bush Administration's efforts to bankrupt the public school system . . . through private school vouchers."

Republicans: ". . . the most important goal . . . (is) helping middle- and low-income families enjoy the same choice of schools—public, private or religious—that families with more resources already have. . . . The GI Bill for Children will provide $1,000 scholarships to middle- and low-income families, enabling their children to attend the school of their choice."

7. Firearms Regulation

Democrats: "We support a reasonable waiting period to permit background checks for purchases of handguns, as well as assault weapons controls to ban the possession, sale, importation and manufacture of the most deadly assault weapons."

Republicans: "Republicans defend the constitutional right to keep and bear arms."

8. Health Care

Democrats: "All Americans should have universal access to quality, affordable health care—not as a privilege but as a right."

(box continues)

Republicans: "Republicans believe that government control of health care is irresponsible and ineffective. . . . We endorse (a plan) which will make health care more affordable through tax credits and deductions that offset insurance costs for 95 million Americans; and make health care more accessible . . . by reducing insurance costs and eliminating workers' worries of losing insurance if they change jobs."

9. International Cooperation

Democrats: "The United States must be prepared to use military force decisively when necessary to defend our vital interests. The burdens of collective security in a new era must be shared fairly, and we should encourage multilateral peacekeeping through the United Nations and other international efforts.

Republicans: "Republicans understand that (our post-Cold War) objectives cannot be pursued by the United States alone. We therefore have harnessed the free world's strength to American leadership. . . By forging consensus whenever possible, we multiply the impact of our nation's power and principles. But if necessary we will act alone to protect American interests. . . . Consistent with our policy and traditions, we oppose any actions that would undermine America's sovereignty, either in political or economic terms."

10. Market System

Democrats: "We believe in free enterprise and the power of market forces. But economic growth will not come without a national economic strategy to invest in people. . . . The only way to lay the foundation for renewed American prosperity is to spur both public and private investment."

Republicans: "Republicans believe that the greatest engine for social change and economic progress is the entrepreneurial economy. . . . We believe that positive change can occur and benefit all Americans if we continue to remove governmental barriers to entrepreneurship and, thus, economic growth."

11. Taxes

Democrats: "We will relieve the tax burden on middle-class Americans by forcing the rich to pay their fair share."

Republicans: "We will oppose any attempt to increase taxes. . . Reducing the tax on investment will be the biggest possible boost for the new technologies, businesses, and jobs we need for the next century."

12. Welfare

Democrats: "Welfare should be a second chance, not a way of life. We will continue to help those who can not help themselves. . . . We'll invest in education and job training, and provide the child care and health care they need to go to work and achieve long-term self-sufficiency."

Republicans: "Today's welfare system . . . must be re-created by states and localities. . . . (It) can no longer be a check in the mail with no responsibility."

they are not sharply articulated or codified as all-encompassing political philosophies, such as those found in the old-style Communist or Socialist parties of Europe or the Moslem fundamentalist parties that have arisen in the Middle East, nor do the American parties insist upon faithful obedience to these principles from their members. They permit, and the localism inherent in the American system encourages, their leaders and their followers alike to be drawn into the party on their own terms, for their own reasons, rather than having to pass some sort of ideological "litmus test" for involvement.

Some kind or degree of ideology, however, is implicit in every demand for party government. In a heterogeneous society of many conflicting interests, parties cannot take stands on ten or fifteen separate issues if there is no similarity among the coalitions on each issue. There must be some clustering of one group of voters, as well as politicians, on one set of issue positions and of another group on the opposing sides, and issues that crosscut the party coalitions must be relegated to a remote position on the political agenda. That alignment of voters along a single axis presumes, in turn, some kind of ideology, some basic commitments or values that connect separate issues into logical structures and govern stands on a number of them. Thus, call it what one will (the APSA report refers at several points to general party principles), programmatic commitment in the American parties depends on underlying values or philosophies to reduce the vast number of policy issues to one or at least a few dimensions.

At certain points in American political history, the parties seem to have moved in the direction of the kind of programmatic unity necessary for responsible parties. During periods of partisan realignment, the party coalitions achieve their sharpest definition along a single line of political cleavage, and their respective members exhibit their greatest agreement with one another and their greatest differences with the other party.[14]

Yet, even during realignments, partisan cohesion in adherence to common ideological principles has fallen short of what is necessary for truly responsible parties. The realignment of the 1930s, for example, produced a majority Democratic party by joining a liberal northern wing, attracted to the party because it gave voice to the aspirations of disadvantaged groups and championed the developing welfare state, with a conservative southern wing that often opposed both of these policy directions. His congressional majority was large enough for Franklin Roosevelt to achieve many of his policy goals as president, but throughout he was faced with persistent and outspoken opposition within his own party.

In short, even at the peak of their unification around a single political agenda during times of realignment, American parties have been broad coalitions. They have never been sufficiently consolidated around common principles to completely overcome the powerful centrifugal effects of constitutionally-imposed federalism or separation of powers.

The Rise of More Ideological Parties

Attention to issues and even ideology within the parties, though, has risen over the past several decades. Both major parties seem to have become more cohesive and, as a consequence, more ideological. As new issues have emerged as important subjects of policy debate, particularly involving civil rights for blacks, white southerners have deserted the Democratic party. While this has eroded that party's electoral strength, it also has reduced the principal barrier to Democratic party cohesiveness along more or less ideological lines.[15] One major consequence is the greater voting cohesiveness within the congressional Democratic party. With the demise of the liberal northeastern wing of the party (led for many years by people such as Governor Nelson Rockefeller of New York), the Republicans too seem to have become more homogeneous on key party principles.

Men and women also are increasingly being drawn to party work out of their involvement with issues and ideologies. The triumph of political ideas and values thus becomes a major incentive to party activity. To some extent, it replaces the older incentives of patronage and preference, which have been waning on their own accord (as discussed in Chapter 5).

Another clear symptom of this ideological renaissance in American party politics has been the elevation of more ideological partisans to leadership positions where they have been able to pursue an ideologically driven policy agenda. The election and reelection in the 1980s of Ronald Reagan, a candidate well identified with the conservative wing of his party, demonstrated the attractiveness of noncentrist politicians. His principled assault on the role of government as it had developed since the New Deal, an effort redoubled by the Republican congressional majority in 1995, gave a more ideological tone to American politics than it had witnessed in decades.

Most of these signs of increased ideological concern are visible chiefly among the activists of the party organization. What of the American voters, however, especially the less partisan electorate? It may very well be that the small core of party activists will bring their new involvement to a deaf or hostile public and that their "ideologizing" will only bore or alienate the majority of the electorate. Moreover, the issue of the differences in ideological concern between activists of the party organization and the electorate is not merely a scholarly one. The ideologues of American politics have long claimed that a horde of ideological voters is increasingly alienated by parties unwilling or unable to give them clearly defined ideological alternatives. Are the American parties, then, reflecting a nonideological electorate or suppressing an ideological one?

IDEOLOGY IN THE AMERICAN ELECTORATE

It is commonplace to characterize the American electorate, or any electorate for that matter, in ideological terms. Many political analysts have depicted the public as liberal or conservative at particular times and have attributed changes in party control of government and its consequent policy directions as the result of swings from liberal to conservative or vice versa within the public. The Republican successes of the last two or three decades and the emergence of a new breed of "neoliberal" Democratic leaders, for example, is often attributed to a more conservative mood within the American electorate.[16]

How Ideological Is the American Public?

Careful study of the political attitudes of the American electorate since the 1950s, though, makes one question just how ideological the public really is. For one thing, only a small minority—never more than a quarter of the electorate, and often less— seem to base their political evaluations on easily identifiable liberal or conservative principles. The electorate is much more inclined to evaluate candidates and parties based on the interests of their group, a single issue, or personal characteristics of the candidates. Many Americans do show the attitude consistency produced by an ideology in the interrelationship among their positions on the issues of the day. Yet, the scope of this consistency often is narrow; it holds up within many an issue area but evaporates when issues are chosen from diverse issue areas, such as welfare and foreign policy or economic policy and civil rights.[17]

Many more Americans are able to identify themselves in ideological terms. In a 1994 CBS News/*The New York Times* national survey, for example, 50 percent of the respondents called themselves either liberals or conservatives, and another 44 percent thought of themselves as moderates. The acceptance of such labels is easy, but it tells us nothing about how much ideological thinking underlies them. It is difficult to imagine what a moderate political ideology is; to take that position is probably another way of saying that one has no ideology. Moreover, people often mean very different things when they say they are liberals or conservatives, and the label they choose may have little to do with the positions they take on specific issues or their party orientation. In this same survey, for instance, only 50 percent of the Republicans called themselves conservatives. Even today it seems likely that many adopting a liberal or conservative label lack the consistent, programmatic thinking of the ideologue.[18]

Ideological thinking, in short, has not been prevalent enough within the American electorate to provide a dependable foundation for responsible parties. To be sure, the electorate does exhibit conservative or liberal moods at different times.[19] They may be more supportive at some times than at others, for example, of a major role for government in the economy or in providing a "safety net" for the elderly or disadvantaged. But their thinking is more concrete than abstract, more pragmatic than ideological. In constructing winning electoral coalitions, parties and candidates stitch voters together through a variety of appeals—for example, popular candidates, group interests, particular issues, negative reactions to the party in power—but rarely through widespread appeals along ideological lines.

The Electoral Basis for More Ideological Parties in Recent Years

Even in the more ideologically charged 1980s and 1990s, the evidence suggests that American voters were not turning to ideology as the principal guide in their voting. For example, Ronald Reagan's popularity and electoral success were achieved almost in spite of his conservative policy positions. In both 1980 and 1984, the voting public on balance preferred the policy positions of Reagan's presidential opponent. What benefited Reagan, instead, was his relative standing in retrospective eval-uations of presidential performance—that is, how well things had turned out rather than exactly what policies he had pursued. Negative appraisals of the Carter presi-dency had led voters to turn to Reagan in 1980, and favorable evaluations of his per-formance in office promoted his reelection in 1984.

Performance-based evaluations have continued to be important in American presidential elections. George Bush was able to capitalize upon his association with the popular Reagan administration in 1988. But Bush's advantage had eroded by 1992, as dissatisfaction with his performance led the electorate to reject him in favor of Democrat Bill Clinton. In each case, these were results-oriented **retrospective** evaluations, not **prospective** ideological or policy judgments. Thus, even with the rise in ideological conflict at the elite level, the American electorate could hardly be characterized in ideological terms.[20]

The reality is that responsible party governments are based on institutional arrangements and elite orientations rather than an ideological citizenry. Even in nations characterized by highly ideological party systems, it is the rare citizen whose political thinking is as highly structured as that of the elite political actors.[21]

THE DILEMMA OF IDEOLOGY

In general, the uneven and uncertain rise of ideology risks a discontinuity between the ideological minority within the parties and the essentially nonideological major-ity in the electorate. At best, the full electorate is only sporadically given to ideolo-gies. It responds selectively to issues, to be sure, but it also responds to a personality, a deeply felt personal interest, a campaign, a group loyalty, an enduring tradition, or an incumbent's performance in office. The parties and their candidates may respond to that gulf between the ideological minority and the nonideological majority with appeals on a number of levels—ideological arguments for some parts of the audi-ence, nonideological arguments for others. Always, however, there is danger of alien-ating a majority irritated and ultimately repelled by a discourse they find obscure, irrelevant, and sometimes even frightening.

The Differential Spread of Ideological Thinking

Thus, the establishment of an ideological party is impeded, first of all, by the fact that only some Americans see party politics consistently in issue or ideological terms. Those ideological concerns are spread unevenly across American social classes. Because they are so strongly associated with higher levels of formal education, one finds them disproportionately among higher SES Americans. They are, in a sense, the political preoccupations of an affluent, well-educated, upper-middle-class elite in American politics for whom the abstractions and verbal content of ideology come easily. Thus, they increasingly tend to be the preoccupations and even the political incentives of the middle-class activists within each party's organization.

Differences Between Activists and Voters

The gulf between an ideological elite of activists and a less ideological party electorate would pose problems for the parties in itself. That problem is made even more serious, however, by the fact that the party activists tend to take more extreme ideological positions than the party voters on many issues. Careful scholarly studies both of officials in the party organizations and of delegates to the two national parties' nominating conventions have consistently found the electorates of both parties close to the center on the left-right continuum, with the activists of the Democratic party farther to the left and the Republican activists and officials farther to the right. In some years and on some issues, moreover, the party activists are farther away from their own rank-and-file supporters on this continuum than are the activists of the opposing party (see Figure 15.1).[22] In short, the activists and voters in the two parties differ both in the extent and in the direction of their ideologies. Caught in the middle of these differences are the party candidates and officeholders. The only alternatives open to them—conflict with the party's activists, lack of candor with the electorate, or defeat at the next election—are hardly attractive. It is no wonder that the party in government so strongly resists fixed issue and ideological commitments within the parties and is inclined toward ideological ambiguity in political campaigns.[23]

Differences Between Party Sectors

A major American party, faced with the development of a cadre of ideological activists, may develop an internal, private ideology or issue consensus at odds with the stance necessary to win elections. That divergence aggravates, in yet another way, the tensions and strains among the party organization, the party in government, and the party in the electorate. There are periodic eruptions of dissatisfaction among the ideologues of both parties with the moderation of the party in office. For example, in the 1970s, even so conservative a "moderate" as President Gerald Ford found himself rejected by many of the organization Republicans in favor of the more conservative Ronald Reagan. Conservative Republicans were never comfortable with George Bush and his more pragmatic approach to policy making, and many of them bitterly opposed the possible candidacy of "Rockefeller Republican" Colin Powell for the presidency in 1996, even though polls showed him to be the most electable of all their candidates. By the same token, liberal Democrats have exhibited great dissatisfaction with the centrist policies of Democratic Presidents Carter and Clinton.[24]

Regional Differences

Beyond these differences in levels of ideological commitment and in distances from the political center, ideologies within each party differ from state to state and from region to region. A persistent ideological factionalism in both parties has been evident in the behavior of state delegations to the two national party conventions over recent decades. Those differences obviously reflect the different economies and demographies of the states, as well as different state political cultures.[25] Thus, lack-

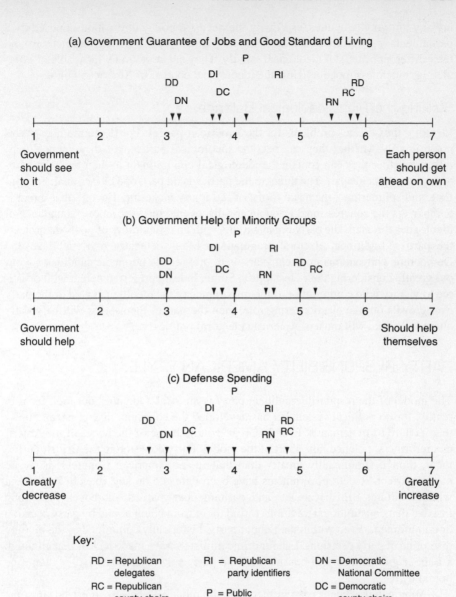

Figure 15.1 Party elites, party identifiers, and the public on key issues, 1984.

Source: Denise L. Baer and David A. Bositis, *Elite Cadres and Party Coalitions* (New York: Greenwood, 1988), pp. 192, 202, 204.

ing any unifying structures, especially the need for policy unification imposed by a parliamentary government, the two national parties speak in a babel of voices around their different centers of ideological gravity. They are structurally incapable of articulating, much less monopolizing, the ideological content of American politics.

Striking the Right Ideological Balance

Ideology thus creates problems for the American parties. For them, the question is not primarily whether they can become ideological parties, for they cannot. It is, rather, whether they can contain the ideological commitment to their activists without it tearing them apart. The threat to the parties is, in part, one of factionalism, conflict, and splintering—the usual forms of intraparty bickering. Beyond that threat is another. As the congressional Republicans discovered in 1996, an overabundance of ideologues threatens the party organizations with an inflexibility of goals that rejects the parties' traditional electoral pragmatism. Many delegates to Republican and Democratic conventions in recent years were prepared to nominate candidates without greatly considering their electability. Some, indeed, preferred defeat with principle to victory with compromise. If the importance of the ideological goal of the party ever crowds out the electioneering role, then the parties themselves will be greatly altered. So, too, will most of American electoral politics.

PARTY RESPONSIBILITY AMERICAN STYLE

The model of the responsible political party is an ideal. One does not look for it in reality, for no political system yet has developed the cohesion, discipline, and unity that its pure form demands. Even in Great Britain, home of the hopes of the American reformers, practice falls short of the model. Party cohesion in the British Parliament, though significantly greater than that in the American Congress, is by no means perfect. Recent governments have been defeated on key votes in Parliament without falling. British cabinets and parliamentary parties, moreover, have long insisted that constitutional traditions forbid them from being bound by party decision or commitment. Even within the Labour party, historically committed to the binding discipline of party decisions, Labour prime ministers have made it clear that although a Labour government will consult with the party's national executive, it cannot be bound by it.[26]

American practice is even further from the model. To be sure, one finds in some state legislatures a high order of party discipline behind or in opposition to a party program. The programs or principles, however, spring not so much from a party organization or from the decision of the electorate as from the initiative of the governor or the party's legislative leadership. What responsibility there is to the voters for their program is established at later elections, when the voters reward or punish their programmatic stewardship.[27] Even when sophisticated voters may be able to identify a past policy or decision with a party, such a quasi responsibility diverges from the model in one major way: There is little role in it for the party organization because the legislative party or the executive originates the program and enforces discipline behind it. The responsibility rests not on the overt program of party activists and organizations but on the homogeneous interests of the voters, party leaders, and constituencies that support the legislative and executive parties. It is a cohesion and responsibility that springs essentially from the coalescing of common interests in electoral politics.

Crisis-Stimulated Responsibility

Occasionally, American politics approaches the model of party responsibility. In the presidential election of 1936, for example, the Democrats and the Republicans were identified with sharply differing solutions to the nation's economic woes. If their positions were not truly ideological, they were at least determinedly programmatic. The burdens of the Depression may have focused voter attention on the hopes and remedies of policy to an unusual degree. Much of the campaign oratory centered on the Roosevelt program for social and economic change and on his opponent's charges that Roosevelt was proposing radical changes in the American polity and economy. The programmatic rhetoric and identification, combined with high voter attention, may well have produced something close to a mandate election and a mandated congressional contingent of Democrats. That election of 1936 suggests that the kind of ideology or programmatic concern necessary for "pure" party responsibility may be a product of crisis conditions that have prevailed only for short periods in American experience.

Presidential-Centered Responsibility

More common than the case of crisis-stimulated responsibility is the type of responsibility that results from presidential government. Strong presidential leadership, especially when aided by majorities of the same party in the Congress, produces a somewhat cohesive program that becomes the program of the president's party. Indeed, some presidents, such as Lyndon Johnson and Ronald Reagan, have been able to organize the enactment of large parts of the party platform on which they ran for office. Presidential government, however, produces only the kind of post hoc responsibility noted earlier in which presidential performance rather than policy guides voter decision making. It need not produce the kind of clear programmatic alternative the reformers want. Presidential government does stamp some differences on the parties, however, and it does fashion points of reference for the approval or disapproval of voters.

Realignment and Responsibility

As a more general rule, it is during the periods of partisan realignment, when party loyalties most parallel opposite sides on the dominant policy conflicts of the day, that the American system has most closely approached the requirements for party government. Realignments sustain a unified federal government with the same party controlling both houses of Congress and the presidency and a judiciary that, through the appointment power, subsequently comes to reflect the new majority. On only five occasions in American history has one party enjoyed control of Congress and the presidency continuously for more than a decade, and each time this control was initially established during a realignment.

Although such party control is certainly no guarantee of cooperation among the policy-making branches of the national government, it is far easier for a president to deal with a majority of his own party in Congress—especially if its members feel they owe their positions to their party label, as often is the case during a realignment—than with opposition majorities. Moreover, during realignments, party cohesion in the Congress is especially high. Therefore, it should come as little surprise to find that major bursts of comprehensive policy change typically have followed realignments.[28] It is the wholesale realignments of the party system, as well as the atmosphere of crisis and the strong presidential leadership that have accompanied them, that produce the highest levels of responsible party government in the United States. Even during realignments, when the conditions for responsible parties are most propitious, however, the American version of party government is a pale imitation of its European counterparts.

Barriers to Party Responsibility

Outside of the infrequent periods of crisis, strong presidential leadership, and realignment, the achievement of party responsibility is stymied by any number of barriers, which have seemed especially imposing in recent years.

The most formidable, of course, are the classic American institutions that fragment the powers of government—federalism and the separation of powers—and thereby disconnect the parties that would govern in them. Circumstances that can unite what the Constitution has separated are rare and ephemeral. The fragmenting effects of these institutional arrangements are exacerbated by frequent insulation of legislative from executive elections, which is accomplished by holding elections for each office on separate schedules. This practice limits the possibility that the governor's and especially the president's coattails might produce the kind of unified government and cohesive party that is the almost automatic result of elections in a parliamentary system.

Even when there is a rise of ideological and issue concerns in the electorate, the American parties face severe tests and strains in converting themselves into ideological parties. The proliferation of single-issue groups in recent years, in fact, further divides the parties as different groups and individuals within them attach themselves to the party for different causes. Moreover, American electoral politics has developed in directions not easily compatible with party government. The parties have lost control of nominations and find it increasingly hard to manage election campaigns and to establish election programs in ways that promote a unified party "team." The new campaigning and its new campaign finance have freed candidates and officeholders even more from the party organization; even legislators who are at odds with the platforms of their party and the programs of their party's executive do not find it hard to survive. Finally, more Americans today than just a few decades ago resist giving loyalty to or taking cues from a party, which makes it more difficult for transcending party programs to bind candidates and voters together.

The weakness of American party organization, in spite of the unprecedented strength of the national organizations, is apparent to all observers. It does not involve large numbers of Americans—even the most politically involved Americans—either as members or as officials or volunteer activists. Its eclipse by the party in government leaves it woefully short of the authority necessary to integrate a political party and to police its use of public office.

DIVIDED GOVERNMENT: THE ANTITHESIS OF THE RESPONSIBLE PARTY MODEL

Beyond these factors is another—divided party control of government—that makes the goal of responsible party government seem especially distant in modern times. Since 1950, much more often than not control of the federal government has been shared by the two parties rather than vested in a single party (see Table 15.1). Moreover, during this same period, one-party control has declined rather steadily from a characteristic of around 75 percent of the state governments to that of fewer than 45 percent.[29]

Divided control of the national government appeared in earlier times but with much less frequency and under very different conditions than in recent decades. Only nine presidents in two hundred years have been elected at the same time that voters were giving the other party control of one or both houses of the Congress, and four of them came after 1950. Three others all won office in that post-Civil War era when the two major parties were almost evenly balanced nationwide. Rutherford B. Hayes gained the presidency while losing the popular vote contest; James Garfield and Grover Cleveland registered the narrowest popular vote pluralities (1,600 and 24,000 votes respectively) in American history. The more common source of divided government for the first 160 years of the Republic—occurring seventeen times before 1951—was the presidential party's loss of control of at least one house of Congress in the midterm election.

The divided governments of modern times, by contrast, have been the result of less partisan voter behavior rather than midterm reversals or razor-thin electoral margins. At the national level, many voters have been willing to split their votes between Republican presidential candidates and Democratic candidates for Congress, most of them incumbent members seeking reelection. Similar tendencies towards widespread ticket splitting, with the same results in divided control of government, have been evident at the state level.[30] At the same time, the pattern midterm losses by the president's party has continued into the present era—although, until 1994, when this occurred it involved increases in Democratic control of Congress two years after a Republican had gained the White House.

Divided government makes responsible party government impossible. By giving control of different branches of government to opposing parties, it requires agreement between the parties for successful policy making—or what James Sundquist has so appropriately labeled "coalition government."[31] Negotiation and bargaining are of course necessary ingredients for governmental action in any democratic system, especially the American one. But when opposing parties are the prime actors in such a process, it changes the very nature of the policy-making process. In key respects, then, divided government is the antithesis of responsible party government (see box on p. 375).

Table 15.1 PARTY CONTROL OF GOVERNMENT AT THE NATIONAL LEVEL, 1951-96

Year	Party in control of the: President	House	Senate	Divided Government
1951–52	D	D	D	
1953–54	R	R	R	
1955–56	R	D	D	x
1957–58	R	D	D	x
1959–60	R	D	D	x
1961–62	D	D	D	
1963–64	D	D	D	
1965–66	D	D	D	
1967–68	D	D	D	
1969–70	R	D	D	x
1971–72	R	D	D	x
1973–74	R	D	D	x
1975–76	R	D	D	x
1977–78	D	D	D	
1979–80	D	D	D	
1981–82	R	D	R	x
1983–84	R	D	R	x
1985–86	R	D	R	x
1987–88	R	D	D	x
1989–90	R	D	D	x
1991–92	R	D	D	x
1993–94	D	D	D	
1995–96	D	R	R	x

Note: D=Democratic control; R=Republican control; and X=president, House, and Senate controlled by different parties.

Concern over the consequences of continued divided government has extended far beyond the small circle of scholars and political activists who have advocated responsible parties. The barriers to government action imposed by separation of powers are made far more formidable when the Congress and the presidency are controlled by different political parties. Government's failure to address pressing domestic problems—from foreign-policy stalemates over Vietnam and Bosnia to the spiraling public debt—are attributed by many but not all scholars to the division of authority and the consequent bickering between Republicans and Democrats that has become a familiar feature of our time.[32]

Some even feel that divided government undermines the democratic process itself. The lack of clarity about which party is responsible for governing, they observe, strips the electorate of its most effective instrument of popular control of public policy—the ability to blame the party in charge for unsatisfactory governmental policies and to ensure policy change by replacing that party with the opposing party. It is debatable how much the American national government is malfunctioning due to prolonged divided government, and a few pundits even credit

POLICY MAKING UNDER DIVIDED GOVERNMENT: ENACTING THE FY96 FEDERAL BUDGET

With a Democratic policy activist in the White House and the Republican opposition unified around its Contract with America, more responsible parties than seen in some time had emerged by the mid-1990s. The problem was that after 1994, while Republican majorities ran the Congress, the Democrats controlled the presidency. This set the stage for intense partisan conflict across a wide policy agenda, especially over how to reduce the large federal budget deficit. But it denied either party the means to determine federal policy on its own.

Because of an unresolved battle between the parties over budget priorities, the 1996 fiscal year was more than half gone without an officially approved budget, and the federal government was twice shut down with a significant number of its workers furloughed. Ultimately, the radically different approaches of the two parties were compromised, and a budget was adopted. This was not accomplished, however, without an elaborate partisan dance between the parties—carefully choreographed by the leaders of each to maximize its future electoral standing while avoiding the stigma of government shutdown and policy paralysis which would make both parties look bad with a Perot-led third party standing in the wings.

These struggles between President Clinton and the Republican Congress in 1995 and 1996, then, illustrate the problems of relatively responsible parties in an institutional situation in which true party responsibility is denied. They echo the battles between President Reagan and a Democratic Congress from more than a decade before, when the two parties' pursuit of competing principles led to a ballooning of government debt.

the public with consciously seeking divided government to check and balance parties they equally distrust.[33] What is undeniable, however, is that America's unique brand of "coalition government" has ushered in a kind of governmental politics that is the opposite of what is intended under the responsible party model.

THE CONTINUING SEARCH FOR RESPONSIBLE PARTY GOVERNMENT

In this era of divided government, with an electorate that seems increasingly removed from party commitment and regularity and a nomination system more dependent upon primaries than ever before, responsible party government seems even more distant than it was a half-century ago. Yet, the cry for more responsible parties continues. Scholars have been joined by many political leaders and ordinary citizens in seeking parties that are more ideologically distinctive and governments that are more responsible for their policy directions.[34]

In some important ways, the parties have responded to this cry. The national party committees never have been stronger than they are today or more active in coordinating the activities of the state and local parties. The various national committees also play a larger role in financing both federal and nonfederal campaigns than they ever have. The parties in the electorate, and especially the congressional parties, are more cohesive philosophically and ideologically than they have been in decades. Moreover, throughout the American system, but especially in Washington and in the party platforms, the level of party conflict over basic principles of public policy is at what may be an all-time high.

Yet, these changes are not sufficient to satisfy the recurrent cry for party responsibility. For all their ideological cohesiveness in recent years, party candidates remain pretty much on their own when it comes to both acquiring the party nomination and winning the general election. The contemporary realities of campaign finance, in which the individual candidates have the responsibility for raising most of the funds for their campaigns, accentuate candidate independence from parties to an extent that a few thousand dollars of party organization money cannot overcome. As the party rank and file has become more involved in selecting party candidates, furthermore, its size—and its satisfaction with the results—seems to have declined. Above all, the institutional realities of separation of powers and federalism impose constraints on party responsibility that even ideologically-driven voters would have difficulty in overcoming. Moreover, the American electorate in recent years appears to have become more responsive to individual candidate appeals than party programs and to antiparty impulses, including independent or third party candidates such as Ross Perot, than parties.

For the immediate future, barring a wholesale partisan realignment of traditional proportions,[35] then, it seems likely that the American parties will achieve no more, and sometimes even less, than to continue the modest governing role that has characterized them during most of the twentieth century—a post hoc responsibility for carrying out programs that generally promote the interests of the party's activists and loyal electorate. Neither the American parties nor the voters can at present meet the demands that the classic model of party responsibility would impose on them. Rather, the various sectors of the party are bound together by only a loose commitment to a set of issue positions that separates the activists, candidates, and voters of one party from those of the other. That tentative and limited agreement on issues, reinforced by executive leadership of the party in government or an occasional surge of programmatic direction from congressional leaders, may produce enough cohesion for a modest degree of responsibility. Ironically, such a degree of party responsibility must be achieved without the central role—drawing up a program and enforcing it on candidates and officeholders—that the reformers envisioned for party organizations, often in the frustrating presence of divided party control of government. Whether this level of party responsibility will be sufficient for democratic accountability or adequate to the task of solving pressing national problems are vexing questions indeed for the 1990s and beyond.

PART Six

POLITICAL PARTIES IN THE AMERICAN SETTING

The preceding chapters have reviewed in fine detail the various facets of the American parties and party system. It is now appropriate to step back from the detail to gain a broader view of political parties in America. This is the task of the concluding Chapter 16.

Political parties are complex institutions, and they operate in an even more complex political setting. They also are live entities that cannot be understood if observed in isolation from their natural habitat in the controlled situations that enable scientists to study other complex phenomena. The study of parties and party systems instead must progress by the slow process of comparison and contrast, by observing how they have changed and what else has changed in their environment over the course of their lives—by taking advantage of the possibilities for comparison across different stages in their two hundred years of development and, where it is possible, with other democratic nations.

As the parties develop new activities, depend on new incentives, take new organizational forms, for example, one is naturally led to wonder how and why the changes came about. What changes in the parties' environment accompanied those changes in the parties? Is there a causal relationship between changes in the parties and those outside them? For example, if the decline of patronage accompanies the decline of the old-style urban machine, is it the cause or the effect of change in party organization? Is the decline of party loyalties in the electorate the result of an eviscerated party organization or one of its causes? We learn much about the parties if we put the changes together into a pattern and adduce explanations for them.

Chapter 16 undertakes this analytical task by examining the changes presently under way in the American parties. It brings together the trends and transformations that have been mentioned throughout the book and then ventures a series of projections of what's ahead for the American parties. The central theme already more than hinted at in earlier chapters is that the powerful, predominant role of the major parties in American politics has eroded but that the parties have adapted to the new realities. The questions of what produced these changes, how the parties responded to them, and how the landscape of American politics has been altered by the changes and the party responses, therefore, are addressed as well.

Chapter 16 then expands the analysis beyond the specific changes presently abroad in the American parties to consider the broader question of what accounts for the particular form of the American parties and the party system they have defined. Parties are creatures of their environments. Their longevity in American political life and their centrality to democratic politics in the United States and throughout the world can be attributed to their remarkable adaptivity to changing conditions—much more than to their ability to shape that environment to their liking.

The goal for the tentative suggestions that follow is a modest one: to raise the understanding of American political parties beyond description of specific events to a more general knowledge of how parties have operated and will operate in the American system. After a journey through a book such as this, one at least ought to be able to explain why parties differ from one place or one time to another and especially why the American parties are what they are and do what they do. With this understanding should also come a better appreciation of the place of parties in the American political system.

Chapter
16

The Place of Parties in American Politics

The American parties have experienced considerable change in the last several decades. By the 1970s, they appeared to be in decline on a number of fronts, and the decay in their performance received a good deal of the blame for the general malaise and decline of public confidence in many institutions that has beset American society since that time. Because their troubles had started a decade or two earlier in response to long-term changes in American society and politics, it was easy to conclude that the decline was permanent. By the time their decay had become the central theme of chronicles of the parties, however, signs of party resurgence had begun to emerge. Although this resurgence seems to have fallen short of restoring parties to the place in American politics they once enjoyed, it signals that they are likely to remain an important part of the American political landscape in the years to come. Any concluding assessment of the American parties, therefore, must begin with the direction of recent trends and how these trends have changed the parties.

An assessment of the parties is incomplete, though, without viewing them from an even broader perspective. Political parties influence the world around them in important ways to be sure, but they also are powerfully shaped by that world. This perspective is sometimes lost by those who have wanted to reform the parties. The Progressives were wont to attribute many of the ills they saw in the American political scene to the parties, just as the responsible party theorists seemed to think that the system would function more to their liking if only they could make American parties more like British parties. Yet the persistent urges to reform them by their very nature assume that the parties can be transformed by changes in their environment—and the accomplishments of some of these reform efforts are testimony to how malleable, in the end, they are. Parties do, indeed, have an impact on political processes and institutions, but other political and nonpolitical forces, in turn, have powerful effects on the parties.

This interaction between parties and their environments—with parties buffeted by, adapting to, and even changing the external forces around them—has been a prominent theme throughout this book. As the ultimate step in its treatment, therefore, it is only appropriate that the concluding chapter returns to this theme in a more comprehensive way.

THE DECAY OF PARTIES IN THE 1960S AND 1970S

The American parties have long been characterized by the loose set of relationships that have bound the three party sectors together. That looseness, or lack of integration, is indeed one of their most fundamental features. The party organization has never been able either to bring a substantial part of the party electorate into membership or to assert its leadership or discipline over the campaigns and policy making of the party in government. It is not surprising, therefore, that the decline of parties which had become apparent by the 1960s hit the three sectors quite differently.

The Parties in the Electorate

The American electorate experienced a substantial weakening of its long-run attachments and loyalties to the American parties through the late 1960s and into the 1970s. More and more American adults considered themselves independents rather than identifiers with a major party. Even among those who professed a loyalty or attachment to a party, that attachment no longer dominated the decision on how to cast the vote, as it once did. The result, obviously, was a shrinking of the size of party electorates and an eroding of fidelity to the parties even among their followers.

If the American electorate in the 1960s and 1970s was not responding eagerly to its party loyalties, to what did it respond? Some segments were attuned to the appeals of program and ideology. The Goldwater campaign of 1964, the McCarthy and Wallace appeals of 1968, the McGovern candidacy of 1972—along with those of many state and local issue-oriented candidacies—drew on and activated higher levels of issue awareness. For less-sophisticated voters, the appeals that registered most effectively were those of candidate personality and image. The handsome faces, ready smiles, and graceful lifestyles that television screens so fully convey attracted some of the support that party symbols once commanded. Because candidates and issues change far more frequently than parties, the consequence was an unstable, less predictable pattern of voting.

The decline of party as a prominent guide to voter choice in the 1960s and 1970s was clearly manifested in electoral results. The electorate became more inclined to respond to candidates as individuals than as members of a particular political party. At the presidential level, this phenomenon was manifested in the rising fortunes of independent presidential candidates Eugene McCarthy in 1976 and John Anderson in 1980 and the rise in successful independent candidates for governor. Even the strong third-party candidacy of George Wallace in 1968 fit the pattern of diminished party-based voting, because the American Independent (the name says it all!) party was more a vehicle for him as an individual candidate than an effort to build a base of loyalists for a new political party.

Such candidate-centered voting also is illustrated by the inordinate amount of split-ticket voting. Beginning in the late 1960s, the percentage of respondents to the

ANES surveys who reported voting for a presidential candidate of one party and a House candidate of the other began to move upward—to the point where it had doubled by 1980, and parallel increases appeared in Senate-House and state-local splits. Moreover, the number of congressional districts awarding victories to presidential and congressional candidates of different parties topped 30 percent for the first time in history in 1964 and only twice since has fallen below that level.[1]

The Party Organizations

In the party organizations during the 1960s and 1970s, the last of the party machines were passing from the scene, and with them their activists and incentives. The famous Daley machine in Chicago was ripped apart in a series of tumultuous struggles after Richard Daley's death in 1976 and then stripped of its patronage base. Many organizations of all kinds no longer could depend on the patronage and preferments or the guaranteed election to public office that once recruited their full-time, vocational activists. Instead, they were drawing a better educated, part-time leadership who were attracted to the party because of issues or ideology and who brought with them new demands for intraparty participation. Some among the new activists rejected the politics of compromise, accommodation, and pragmatism that resulted from the assumption that the capture of public office is the highest goal of American politics. If their ideological goals were not satisfied or even recognized within the party, they stood ready to leave it for particular candidates or issue organizations.

Increasingly too, the internal, intraorganizational processes ceased to be under the organization's control. Under the force of growing participatory expectations, these processes became more open, and the private sphere of the party organization shrank accordingly. The direct primary long had been taking decisions from the party organization, and its dominance now became virtually complete. The presidential convention ceased to be a device for the organization's deliberation and choice making. Its options were sharply restricted by the activities of the would-be candidates in the preconvention politicking. Even the preconvention scramble for presidential votes was increasingly removed from the hands of party organizations, as almost all convention delegates came to be chosen through presidential primaries. By the 1970s, candidate strategy and money overwhelmed whatever role the party organization may once have played, as was evidenced by the Democrats' nomination of candidates in 1972 and 1976 who were well outside of the organizational mainstream of their party.

By the 1960s and 1970s, the party organizations had lost whatever capacity they may once have had for controlling electoral politics. Not only were they no longer able to exert much influence over nominations thanks to the direct primary, but they also lost their central role in election campaigning. Candidates typically built their own campaign organizations, raised their own campaign funds, and went on their own merry ways in the campaign. The campaign assets they once received from the local party organizations and their workers—skills, information, pulse readings, manpower, exposure—they now were able to get directly from pollsters, the media, public relations people, volunteer workers, or even by "renting a party" in the form of a campaign management firm.

Especially because the local party organizations were unwilling or unable to provide the new arts for the candidates, they waned in influence in the contesting of elections. Their fairly primitive campaign skills were superseded by a new campaign technology, and more and more they found themselves among the technologically obsolescent. Even though by the 1970s the national parties were becoming more important suppliers of campaign expertise and resources and were increasingly sharing this wealth with the state and local parties (at least as far as stringent post-1974 campaign finance restrictions would permit), the party organization could not regain its once central role in electoral campaigns.

In spite of the new vigor in their national committees, through the 1970s the American party organizations remained considerably more decentralized than life and politics in the United States. The electorate had been looking more and more to national political symbols and figures, but the party organizations still tended to be collections of state and local fiefdoms. The national committees and the national conventions have always been loose confederations of local organizations and, despite stronger national committees and more central authority, they seemed destined to remain so.

The Party in Government

The men and women of the party in government, freed from reliance on the party organizations by the direct primary, by access to the media, by independent sources of funds, and by supportive personal followings, came to depend more than ever upon direct appeals to voters in the 1960s and 1970s. No longer able to rely so heavily on abstract party loyalties, through personal services, personal appeals, personal style, physical appearance, even what personal magnetism they could generate, they developed a "personal vote"[2] independent of party. Incumbents became more difficult to dislodge than ever before, and office holding became more of a lifetime career or profession—even at the state and local level where professionalism had been rare.

Among the successful candidates are the parties' contingents in American legislative bodies. There, reflecting the decline of party loyalties among voters and the decline of party organizations' power over legislators, it became more difficult to harness partisans on behalf of party causes, and party-line voting in the Congress fell to an all-time low in the late 1960s and early 1970s. Freed from the party demands of both voters and the party organizations, legislators became more exposed to the nonparty pressures—the local interests of the constituency primarily, but also of interest groups. More important, perhaps, with the decline of competition (especially for incumbents) in congressional elections, they were not often exposed to serious challengers, even though most perceived their hold on office as precarious no matter how wide their previous victory margin.

When the legislative party lacks cohesion and strength, the executive party rushes into the vacuum. Presidents and governors enjoyed increased power and leadership at the very time at which they increasingly represented the party and its programs to so many voters. More than anyone else, they came to personify the party and give tangible content to its labels and symbols. In a period when many partisans sought programmatic goals, they alone formulated programs and controlled policy initiatives.

Therefore, it was no exaggeration to speak of the parties as executive-centered coalitions during the late 1960s and 1970s. Nowhere was the phenomenon clearer than in the ability of presidents to dominate the national party organization of their parties, to give life and meaning to the symbol of their parties, and, with the help of federal subsidies after 1974, to mount campaigns free of obligation to the party organization at any level. Ironically, though, just as the party dominance of chief executives became clear, the upsurge in divided governments beginning in 1960s often denied them unquestioned leadership of their governments by forcing them to negotiate their policies with the opposing party.

Shifting Power Centers in the Tripartite Party

The foregoing is merely a summary of what has been said in greater detail in earlier chapters about the patterns of American party politics through the 1960s and 1970s. The changes they represented cumulated in a vast shift of power within the American political party from the decentralized party organization to the individual members of the party in government, especially the executives, and made responsible party government more difficult. These changes also reflected—and accentuated—a shift in influence away from the parties to rival political intermediaries, especially interest groups and the mass media.

At the core of these changes was the progressive isolation of the party organization in the American parties. The organizations had enjoyed their days of glory, but they ultimately failed to retain the unquestioned loyalty of any significant measure of the party electorate. Isolated from the electorate and without its broad-based support or participation, they became even more vulnerable to suspicions that they were run by irresponsible oligarchies. The smoke-filled room myths have never died, and the cries of bossism were as alive at party conventions in the 1960s and 1970s—particularly the 1968 and 1972 Democratic conventions—as they were at the turn of the twentieth century.

What assets the party organizations once had were substantially eroded by the 1960s and 1970s. In most locales, even many bastions of their former strength, they no longer controlled the chief incentives for political activity, as they did when it was patronage and preference that mobilized the activists. The party organizations had lost their monopoly of the resources and technology of campaigning and of electoral politics. Also, they no longer invoked strong feelings of party loyalty in their electorate or controlled the tangible rewards for political support.

What kind of party is it, however, in which the party organization loses its central position? Is not the party organization the only sector of the party that has more at stake than the winning of individual elections, that offers some possibility of life and principle beyond specific elections and even beyond electoral defeat? Without some semblance of a party organization, what will keep officeholders and office seekers from setting up shop on their own, ignoring the calls for collective action that have justified political parties? The decline of the party organizations surely accentuated the decline of the parties more generally.[3]

A RENAISSANCE OF THE PARTIES

The American party system and the American parties have shown a remarkable ability to adapt to changing circumstances in the past, so it is reasonable to expect them to have responded to these new challenges in ways that sought to maintain their centrality in American politics. The 1980s and 1990s indeed have witnessed such adaptations and changes. With them has come an end to the decay of parties—and even a kind of renaissance. Yet, there are also signs that the parties have been unable to recover from some of the changes in the 1960s and 1970s and have had to accommodate themselves to a new—and less central—role in American politics.

Toward a Realignment of the American Electorate

Recent years have produced changes in the party coalitions and have rekindled talk of party realignment. The external symptoms that ordinarily precede realignment have been evident since the 1960s: low turnout levels, support for third-party or independent candidates, a widely fluctuating presidential vote from one election to the next, extensive ticket splitting, the diluted effects of party loyalties on the voting of individuals, and divided government.[4]

With the surge of Republican fortunes in the 1980s and again in the 1994 election, some have concluded that this long-awaited realignment has finally taken place. The party coalitions are now quite different—with black Americans steadfastly Democratic, white southerners disproportionately Republican, and religious conservatives now a vital force within the GOP—from what they were during the height of the New Deal era. The electoral ascendancy of the Republican party in the 1980s reversed the decline of party loyalties and brought the number of GOP loyalists up to the level enjoyed by their Democratic opponents for the first time in fifty years. Yet, it left the parties, even the ascendent Republican party, with far weaker bases of loyal supporters than previous parties, especially the leading party, have enjoyed. By 1992, in fact, the GOP gains of the previous decade appeared to have vanished in the stunning defeat of President Bush—only to resurface two years later in the first Republican takeover of Congress in forty years. Even this latest sign of realignment, though, failed to induce any significant growth in Republican (or, for that matter, Democratic) party loyalties, as the American electorate remained disenchanted with both major parties and drawn to the prospect of new parties and independent candidates.

There is no guarantee of course that even a full-fledged realignment of the party coalitions, much less the kind of incomplete realignment experienced so far, will restore the parties to their previous political preeminence. Realignment is not a solution to an erosion of the party's organizational capacity to nominate and elect candidates—and to the more candidate-centered electoral world that has created. Nor does it even ensure that large numbers of Americans will return to an unswerving partisanship or that they will again mark the straight party ticket. The truth is that a party realignment is only a readjustment of the parties to new cleavages in the society. It does not necessarily renew the strength of one or more of the parties in the electorate.[5]

With the passage of time, in fact, it seems increasingly clear that the 1960s and 1970s produced an irreversible "sea change" in the role of party loyalties within the American electorate. Large numbers of voters now have cues and sources of information outside the parties. These information intermediaries—a nonpartisan mass media, single-issue pressure groups, increasingly heterogeneous primary groups— also may fail to provide the reinforcement for partisan views they once did.[6] Many Americans seem less and less inclined to accept the omnibus commitments that party loyalty implies. They want to pick and choose among issues and candidates, and they are encouraged to do so by the low profile of party labels in modern campaigns. Party loyalty demands that they buy a whole collection of commitments; in effect, it asks them to divide the political world into two simple categories, ours and theirs. The simple, dichotomized choice that party loyalty within a two-party system demands may no longer appeal to an educated, issue-oriented electorate.[7]

The Rise of More Cohesive Parties in Government

If voters have remained mired in nonpartisanship, the opposite has occurred among the governmental parties. By the 1970s, party cohesion in Congress had halted its long period of decline, and the organizational seeds had been sown for even stronger parties. By the 1980s, the congressional parties had emerged as more cohesive and their leadership stronger and more assertive than they had been since the early part of the century. With the arrival of interparty competition in the South and other historically one-party areas in the last few decades, the party coalitions in both the electorate and the government have become more homogeneous, which makes it easier for them to offer clearly alternative programs and policies. The epitome of the new congressional parties appeared with the 104th (1995–96) Congress in its new Republican majority united around the House GOP's Contract with America. Similar ideologically-unified legislative parties at the same time appeared with more frequency in the states.

Party considerations also seemed to have grown within the federal executive and even the judiciary by the 1980s. The new Reagan administration in 1981 came to office as the most ideologically committed in decades. Its programmatic leadership accentuated the conservative tenor of the GOP and solidified the hold of conservatives on the party; its agenda was dominated by a desire for a more conservative executive and judiciary. Faced with a more ideological opponent in the White House and in the Congress, amidst a steady decline in the influence of conservative southern Democrats, the Democratic party too became more cohesive—although intraparty philosophical disputes have continued to plague them even into the Clinton presidency. By the time a less ideologically oriented George Bush inherited the presidency, the ideological lines had become so sharply drawn in Washington that the ultimate dissatisfaction with the Bush administration pervaded even his own party.

By the mid-1990s the partisan warfare in Washington, between an programmatically committed Republican majority in the Congress and an activist Clinton White House, had intensified. The battle over the FY97 budget signaled the sharpest party divide in decades, and it crystallized the philosophical and programmatic differences between the parties. Ironically, the fact of divided government, which has become the dominant institutional form since the 1950s, has exacerbated these party differences, but it also has prevented them so far from yielding responsible party government of the kind reformers would have applauded a half-century before. That these battles will in turn lead to a more partisan electorate and bring an end to the norm of divided government remains questionable, as the immediate response of the electorate has been further dissatisfaction with the major parties rather than a rallying to their banners.

The New "Service" Parties

Nowhere has the renaissance of parties been more apparent than in the party organizations. Out of the ashes of the traditional urban machines have arisen impressive new national "service" parties—financially well-to-do, staffed with skilled professionals applying the latest campaign technologies, dedicated to distributing their resources to candidates and organizations nationwide, and active in recruiting candidates for office. With the assistance of the national parties, as well as the existence of their model to emulate, the state and local parties also seem to have become stronger in recent years—at least in comparison to just a decade or two before. In particular, the infusion of soft money into the state party organizations has enabled them to step up their role in political campaigns. The spread of two-party competition into formerly one-party strongholds has surely accelerated these trends, as more than a modicum of party organization now is required in many locales just to keep up with the competition.

Yet, the new service party is no substitute for the grass-roots organizations of an earlier era. The party organizations remain aloof from the voters, much of the time in an almost invisible support role. In the world of campaign finance, they do not bring enough money to the table in a fashion that matters for the individual candidates to assert much influence over the campaigns. Amidst the wide variety of campaign professionals available "for hire" to the candidates, the parties no longer are distinctive, no longer provide campaign resources that no one else can deliver.[8]

Thus, the party organizations remain alive in America and are involved in political life with a renewed vigor. Their renewal has been achieved through creative adaptations to new conditions, however, rather than through a return to previous practices. They have come back to a political world in which they increasingly compete with other entities (for example, the mass media, interest groups and PACs, candidate organizations, and ideological and single-issue movements) as transmitters of political communications to the public—and often as funding sources for candidates and, through registration and get-out-the-vote campaigns, as citizen mobilizers as well.[9]

THE FUTURE OF PARTY POLITICS IN AMERICA

Gauging the future is always difficult, especially for institutions that are so profoundly influenced by their environments. Nonetheless, there are features of recent party politics and trends in the historical development of parties that are so persistent that they seem destined to give shape to the future.

A Dwindling Intermediary Role

Among political organizations, the parties alone attach their names to candidates for public office. The willingness or need to respond to that label on the part of large numbers of Americans is what has made the party label so valuable. Political parties originated in large part from the need of voters for a guide, a set of symbolic short-cuts, to the confusing and often trackless political terrain. The labels, activities, and personages of the parties ran as a clearly perceptible thread through the jumble of political conflict and the baffling proliferation of American electoral contests. When that cue giving also produced loyalties and identifications with the parties, when those loyalties were stable and enduring, and when they dominated so many voting decisions, the conclusion was inescapable that political parties were the key interme-diaries between citizens and the wider political world.

The parties' symbolic importance, the value of their labels in elections, is great-est in meeting the informational needs and problems of a new, relatively nonpoliti-cized mass electorate. As the electorate matures, however, its needs change. One explanation for the reduced incidence of and reliance on party loyalties in the Amer-ican electorate of recent years is that voters are better educated and better informed than they were sixty or eighty years ago. Citizens now are more attracted to alterna-tive sources for political messages—especially those of the personalities and per-sonal images that the mass media carry so effectively. The net effects are a reduced need for the simplifying shorthand of the party label and less reinforcement for par-tisan views of the political world.[10]

This is not to say that American voters no longer need cues or labels. Rather, it seems to be the case that they increasingly seek the differentiated cues that can be provided by interest groups or the mass media—not by a party. The traditional party may have been suited to an earlier American electorate seeking a single, consistent cue to a great many political decisions and judgments. As voters become more sophisticated, however, they are better prepared to handle a wider range of political perceptions and loyalties and to sift through a greater variety of political messages. They may form an attachment to an issue or two or to an entire ideology, and they are not prepared to surrender those loyalties to an overriding loyalty to a political party. In short, voters increasingly are not willing to buy the whole packages of candidates offered by parties, preferring instead to pick and choose from among them in making their political decisions.

The present diversity of goals in the American electorate, multiplied by the intensity of feelings about them, cannot easily be handled even by two pragmatic, compromising political parties—much less more ideological ones—unless the elec-torate sharply realigns along a new dominant line of cleavage. Voters instead seem to want more specialized cues for political choice and action and have developed a deepening suspicion of political parties. The activists among them, moreover, want to discriminate among the causes and people for whom they will work.

The result of these changes is that the parties' traditional dominance as interme-diaries has been eroded by competition from other powerful intermediaries.[11] A huge array of specialized interest groups offers guidance on the issue and ideological side. On the other side is a nonpartisan, even antipartisan, mass media which encourages voters to differentiate among candidates on the basis of their personal characteristics or their media style rather than their party. Between pressures to vote their narrow issues and interests and presentations of candidates as individuals, it is little wonder that the message carried by the parties—for voters to support a coalition of interests and a smorgasbord of personalities and styles—seems so unattractive.

Domination by the Party in Government

When measured by the roles and influence of their sectors, political parties in democratic regimes have tended to fall into two groups: those dominated by the party organization and those dominated by the party in government. From the beginning more candidate centered than most democratic parties, the American parties have become increasingly more ruled by the party in government—that is, by the party's candidates and officeholders. In their glory days at the turn of the twentieth century, one might have argued that their organizations directed them, but no longer. The American party in government increasingly determines the party candidates, contests the elections, controls the party image and reputation, supplies the campaign resources, and governs in office without important constraints from the party organizations.

Differences between Contrasting Types   A party dominated by its office-holders and office seekers differs in several very fundamental ways from the party led by its organization (Table 16.1). Where the party in government dominates, almost by definition, the party's focus is electoral. The concerns of the party's office-holders are in winning elections, and they establish both the priority of the electoral mission and their control over the resources and choices for it. Once elected, they govern in response to the need for securing reelection and for making a record of accomplishment in governance.

The alternative—the party dominated by its organizational sector—is best typified by the early working-class parties of the European parliamentary democracies, although even they have come under more control by their officeholders in recent years. The issue commitments or ideologies of the organization's activists assume a greater importance in the life of this kind of party. They have such an impact within the party precisely because the organization speaks for the party, picks its candidates, and maintains some degree of leverage over its parliamentarians.[12]

One can summarize many of the differences between the party models in terms of their ability to integrate their three sectors. In the organization-centered model, the three sectors are bound closely by ties of loyalty and discipline. A substantial part of the party electorate, in fact, joins the organization as members, and the debts of candidates for nomination and election assistance bind them to the party organization. The key to the organization-centered party lies in the ability of the organization to unite the party in government to it and to the goals of its activists. In the classic urban machine of patronage and preference, both sectors were united in the overarching goal of electoral victory and the electoral pragmatism it demanded. In the now dated "textbook" model of the British parties, the party organization's ability to discipline officeholders by denying them renomination was the glue that held the two sectors together. Alternatively, the two sectors might be united, as the responsible party advocates argue, by loyalty to the same principles or issue positions.

Table 16.1 CHARACTERISTICS OF ALTERNATIVE TYPES OF POLITICAL PARTY STRUCTURES

Party organization dominates	Party in government dominates
1. Party in electorate assumes a membership role in the organization	1. Little or no membership component in party organization
2. Party organization controls nomination of candidates and much of election campaign	2. Party in government largely free from organizational control in nomination and election
3. Relatively high degree of cohesion in legislative party	3. Relatively low degree of cohesion in legislative party
4. High degree of integration of three sectors	4. Low degree of integration of three sectors
5. Unified by goals of party organization's activists	5. Unified (if at all) by goals and programs of executive party
6. Activities substantially electoral, but programmatic as well	6. Activities almost exclusively electoral

In the party controlled by the party in government, by contrast, everything depends on the pragmatic alliances of convenience at election time. The dominant party in government is free to form alliances with nonparty organizations, such as interest groups, rather than working with its own party organization. Indeed, it is free to ally with members of the opposition party, as Republicans did with southern conservative Democrats in the 1950s and 1960s in what was called the "conservative coalition."[13]

The eviscerated American party organization has had so little to offer to the candidate running for office that it has been virtually ignored at election time and consequently has less influence thereafter. The distance between the congressional parties, which have created their own campaign committees, and the national party committees illustrates this point, as does the tendency of recent presidential candidates to keep their election campaigns independent from the national committee. Under this model, the party in government establishes contact with the party electorates without relying greatly on the party organization.

Obviously, the differences between these two varieties of political party run to deeper, more basic issues. Should a political party be something more than the sum total of the candidates who choose to run on its label? At the very least, it seems unlikely that a party led by its party in government can provide the continuity and breadth that distinguishes the party from other political organizations. The parties that are strong in their ability to monopolize certain forms of activity have been those led by the organizational sector. Only the party organization has the range of skills and resources, as well as the commitment to all party goals and even to the party itself, to fill this leadership role within the party. Only such a party can approach the model of the responsible party. Only strong parties that exert policy leadership as well as leadership in the recruitment of public officials and in providing a stable cue to millions of voters can augment or support the officeholder's responsibility to his or her electorate.

Sources of the Different Types   These two kinds of parties do not occur without reason or explanation. What differences are there in the different environments from which they come that will explain their differences? One can also put the question in more parochial terms. Because the American party is the archetype of parties controlled by the party in government, what accounts for the differences between the American parties and parties dominated by their organizations? Some persuasive answers to these questions are:

- Scholar after scholar has noted that American parties are not found in nations with parliamentary forms of government and that the organization-dominated parties are.
- The very nature of a parliamentary system demands discipline and integration of the parties; the American separation of powers does not.
- American electoral law (primaries and the regulation of finance, for example) is all on the side of the party in government, giving it easy access to nomination and great freedom from the party organization in waging campaigns.
- State regulation of and legislation on parties has placed a set of heavy constraints on the party organization; the reformist urge has indeed been heavily antiorganization in its goals and has virtually ignored the party in government. The states have imposed cumbersome forms and a weakening openness and permeability on the organizations, while making it difficult for them to develop large memberships.

Once one part of the party comes to dominate, moreover, it usually has been able to perpetuate its control through the laws and customs that govern party practices. In the United States, for example, the new campaign arts and technologies have provided the party in government with an alternative to party organizations by destroying the organization's monopoly over election campaigning. The new campaigning is available in other democratic nations, however, and one must ask why it has freed the parties in government in the United States but not elsewhere. The answer, of course, is that where there are parliamentary institutions and election legislation which limit the freedom of candidates and restrict their access to the tools of the new campaigning, it is the party organization that has administered the new technologies, thus buttressing its central role.[14]

Other forces in the political environment have reinforced the hegemony of the party in government. Reacting to the ills of organizational control, the party organizations have been a perennial target of American reformers, most notably the Progressives. By "reforming" the parties to weaken their organizational component, a decided advantage was given to the party in government. Even the increasing role of rival intermediaries further undercuts the organizations. Under such an assault, what is remarkable perhaps is that the organizations have survived, not that their role has eroded.

Toward a Politics without Parties?

With the recent renaissance of American parties, it is much less likely now than it was just a decade or so ago that the foreseeable future will contain a politics without parties, or at least a politics in which parties play a significantly lesser role than they have. Political life in the United States without the guiding dominance of the two major political parties, however, is not unthinkable in these times of independent candidacies, fleeting third parties, and divided government. Much of American local politics has been nonpartisan in reality as well as in name for some time. At the national level and in the states, moreover, extensive experience with divided government has produced a level of interparty coalitional politics that has been unprecedented on the American scene.

An increasingly diminished role for the parties throughout electoral politics, however, suggests impacts of a greater magnitude. The consequences, not only for the political processes but for the quality of American democracy, trouble many observers. For one thing, it would reduce the capacity of American citizens to combine with their leaders in collective action on public policy issues. To be sure, public policy would still be made, albeit perhaps less often, but the coalitions producing it— for example, interest groups, candidate-centered organizations—would be far less permanent or identifiable to the public than the parties have been.[15]

The displacement of parties as the central mechanism for collective action might also profoundly affect who gets what from American politics.

> Political parties, with all their well-known human and structural shortcomings, are the only devices thus far invented by the wit of Western man which with some effectiveness can generate countervailing collective power on behalf of the many individually powerless against the relatively few who are individually—or organizationally—powerful. Their disappearance could only entail the unchallenged ascendancy of the latter unless new structures of collective power were somehow developed to replace them and unless conditions in the social structure and political culture were such that they could be effectively used.[16]

The American parties—and most others for that matter—mobilize sheer numbers against organized minorities who possess other political resources, and they do so in the one forum of political action in which sheer numbers of individuals count most heavily: elections. Thus, the parties traditionally were the mechanisms by which newly enfranchised and powerless electorates rose to power. The old-style urban machine in the United States, for example, was the tool by which the recently arrived, urban masses won control of their cities from older, largely white Anglo-Saxon Protestant (so-called WASP) elites. In a more fluid politics of bargaining among a larger number of political organizations and millions more uncommitted voters, the worry is that the advantage will be on the side of the well-organized minorities that possess such critical political resources as money, prominent names, and insider knowledge.

The present movement toward ideology and away from electoral pragmatism in weakened parties might have additional elitist consequences. The educated, sophisticated, and involved political minority may impose a new kind of political tyranny on the less-involved, lower SES segments of the electorate. Its brand of ideological politics may lack salience and be incomprehensible to the less sophisticated. At the same time, it may accelerate the decline of the most useful cue giver, the major political party. The removal of the political party as an organizer and a symbol in nonpartisan elections, for example, has probably helped upper SES elites, both of the right and the left, to dominate those politics.[17] Similar circumstances might come to prevail on a national scale as well.

The political party, in other words, historically has been the form of political organization most available to those citizens who lack the cues and information as well as the political resources of status, skills, and money to make a major impact on public decisions via other means. A diminution of the power of the parties makes the game of politics more difficult for these people to play and to win. That may be one reason why the participation declines of the last few decades have come somewhat disproportionately from lower status and less-educated Americans, disenfranchised so to speak by a growth of politics less and less linked to parties.[18]

Finally, weakened parties would rob the political system of an effective vehicle for the construction of majorities. Although imperfectly, the major American parties have helped piece together governing coalitions. American presidents have enjoyed the legitimacy of majority coalitions much of the time, and the party majority in legislatures has permitted them to organize for action. Without at least moderately strong parties, the problem of creating majorities in a fragmented politics becomes even more formidable. One alternative is to rely on the personal appeals and promises of individual national candidates, even independents like some state governors, but this solution lacks the continuity or the discipline that parties bring. Another alternative is the kind of political immobility that has resulted elsewhere from the splintering of majorities into intransigent groups with deeply felt loyalties and sentiments. Divided government is the recent American manifestation of this phenomenon, and it threatens policy paralysis and delay—and the open displays of what is commonly disdained as partisan bickering which undermine the confidence in democratic politics.

To be sure, one must be careful not to exaggerate what the parties traditionally have contributed to democratic politics. But the contributions, if more modest than many want to believe, are still real and important. Certainly a mature political system can and will work out its adaptations. There are, indeed, workable alternatives to stable, two-party systems that dominate electoral choice, although no democracies so far have survived without parties. The issue for the United States is whether any of the alternative organizations could pull together the pieces of a fragmented politics and separated political institutions across a broad and diverse nation as effectively as the parties have. What is a danger for the future of course is that the disadvantages of a politics without parties would not be known until it was too late for them to avoided.[19]

WHAT SHAPES THE PARTIES? A REPRISE

One thing that has become apparent throughout this consideration of the American parties is how much they are influenced by external forces. Of course, the parties are hardly helpless in molding this environment to their advantage. They participate in making public policy to determine, among other things, who votes, what kinds of ballots voters use to mark their choices, and how candidates will be nominated. They influence, by education and through their own performance, public attitudes about the parties themselves and about politics more generally. Moreover, they play an

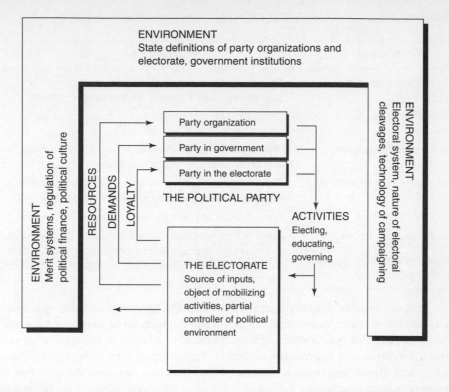

Figure 16.1 The political party as a conversion mechanism within a broader environment.

important role in mobilizing the electorate by converting citizen resources, demands, and loyalties into goal-seeking activities (Figure 16.1).

Yet, over the course of their history, parties have had to be more responsive to their environments than their environments are to them. Three types of influences have been especially important in shaping the outlines and dimensions of political parties in the United States as well as other Western democracies. They are those that define the electorate, those that set the basic electoral and governmental structures of the political system, and, finally, those that mold the broader society (Table 16.2).[20]

The Definition of the Electorate

The first set of influences—the one defining the electorate—is in fact made up of a number of components. It includes the legal statements, both constitutional and legislative, that define which individuals will be in the electorate. It contains the social conditions that determine the numbers, the age distribution, the education, the affluence, and the other social characteristics of the electorate. It also encompasses the factors that shape the levels of political awareness and information, the attitudes and expectations, and the sheer political understanding of the electorate. Finally, it includes the political cleavages that divide the electorate into the various parties and therefore define the party systems.

Table 16.2 MAJOR CATEGORIES OF INFLUENCES IN THE ENVIRONMENT OF THE AMERICAN PARTIES

Influences	Examples
1. Political institutions	Federalism, separation of powers, development of presidency, judicial review, single-member districts
2. Statutory regulation	Legislation on campaign finance, structure of party organization, merit system
3. Electoral processes	The direct primary, office block ballots, nonpartisan elections, definition of the franchise
4. Nature of the electorate	Democratization and politicization of citizenry, social character of the electorate, lines of political division
5. Political culture	Attitudes toward parties, politics, and politicians
6. Nonpolitical forces	State of economy, war, current problems, sources of division among citizens, influence of interest groups, importance of television, affluence and education of population

The nature of the electorate, in all of these facets, changes over time. In particular, the changes from lesser to greater politicization, from fewer to more democratic and participatory expectations, and from a limited to a larger or universal adult suffrage are obviously interrelated, although they happened at different rates and sequences in different political systems. Taken together, they constitute the rise of mass popular democracy—a process that began in the United States at the beginning of the Republic and has expanded virtually to this day with the enfranchisement of southern blacks, and the consequent reshaping of the party system in that region, coming as recently as the 1960s. Only one trend in the American electorate appears to have moved in the opposite direction—rates of voter turnout. The downturn of turnout since 1960 may be temporary (especially if the increase in 1992 proves to be lasting), or it may signal a fundamental, long-term change in the electorate—perhaps involving the withdrawal of the lower classes from an increasingly middle-class politics.

The nature of the electorate impinges on the parties principally by shaping the distribution of party loyalties and the reliance on the parties for political cues and information. It also affects the nature of campaigns and candidates, the relationship of the officeholders to the parties and to their constituencies once they are elected, and the kinds of activists who are drawn to the parties. Thus, the shape of electoral politics depends to a great extent on the nature of the electorate—something which the parties can help to shape, especially early in their lives, but mostly have to take as given.

The Governmental and Electoral Institutions

The second cluster of influences on the parties includes the chief governmental institutions and structural constraints within which the parties work. Foremost within this cluster is the basic configuration of political institutions—federalism or unitary government, parliamentary forms or a separation of powers, the nature of the executive, and the extent of governmental authority. Second, it includes the myriad laws and constitutional provisions that define the election processes (and those for nominations, too, where that is a matter of public policy). Finally, there are the regulations of the parties per se and of the activities carried out under their labels. They run the gamut from laws creating party organizational structure to those regulating the spending of money in campaigns. Often, too, they merge almost imperceptibly into the legislation creating election machinery. The impact of all this on the parties is an old subject involving, for example, the effect on the democratic parties and party systems of the separation of powers, the impact on party organizations of the direct primary as a way of choosing party candidates, and the use of plurality elections in single-member districts rather than proportional representation from multimember constituencies.

These segments of the parties' environments change too. Constitutions and electoral systems are often replaced, though not usually in the United States. If one compares the United States and Great Britain to the nations of continental Europe on this point, the contrast is striking. Although their basic systems change and adapt, there have not been any abrupt breaks with the past in the last hundred years in either Britain or the United States. In that time, however, France has launched five entirely separate republics, each one intended to be a break with, even a repudiation of, its predecessor. Similarly, large numbers of European countries (most recently Italy) have tinkered with various election systems, whereas Britain and the United States have stayed with plurality elections from single-member constituencies.[21]

On the other hand, the American parties have been subjected to more regulation of themselves and their activities than have parties anywhere else. The direct primary constrains their selection of candidates to a degree unknown elsewhere, and American state laws defining the party organizations have no parallel in the democratic world. The effect, and in most cases the intention, of such regulation is to restrict the party organization; an unintended consequence is that they boost the party in government. What is more, the reformist zeal behind much of this legislation lives on—in, for example, reform of the national party conventions.

These two sets of variables interact in a special way on the American parties to produce their rather different, special qualities. First of all, many of the important institutional-structural influences on the parties are almost uniquely American: the direct primary, the separation of powers, the nationally elected executive, and the network of regulatory legislation on the parties. It is precisely these factors that are instrumental in shaping the American two-party system and in vaulting the parties in government to dominance at the expense of the party organizations. Second, although the first set of influences—those shaping the electorate—has changed over time both in the United States and in the other democracies, the second set has remained fairly constant in the United States. For that reason, changes in the American parties seem more directly related to changes in the electorate than to institutional changes, with the major exception being the advent of the direct primary.

Nonpolitical Forces in the Environment

There is also a third set of environmental variables that ought to be mentioned: variables of the nonpolitical environment. These are the events and trends beyond the political system that nonetheless shape politics in any particular year or era. Their effect is not really on the parties, except insofar as they shape the electoral coalitions that define the parties. They define the policy issues of a time, and thus they shape the demands and goals that individuals try to achieve through the parties. They originate outside the parties and the political system, and they are to a significant extent beyond their influence. The ultimate impact of these variables is beyond the parties. It is not primarily on the parties as conversion mechanisms but on the goals for which the mechanisms are employed.

Finally, it is important to appreciate how much the parties compete with other organizations and avenues for representing large numbers of individuals. If there are other more effective ways for individuals to seek their political goals than through political parties, they will use them. If a relationship with a particular member of congress and the member's attentive staff secures a social security check or access to federal contracts, or if an interest group is more forthright and effective in opposing abortion or gay rights, why work through a party? What the parties are at any given time, therefore, is determined, in part, by the alternatives to them that are available and how they respond to their competitors.

Indeed, the major problem for the American parties today arises from the increased differentiation of American aggregative politics. As the American electorate continues to develop more complex interests and a greater sense of individualism evolves from the breakdown of traditional group ties, it acquires more differentiated loyalties and responds to more complex and differentiated cues. The electorate may maintain identifications with parties, but it also responds to candidates and to issues, programs, and ideologies. It responds differentially to different elections and even to the choice between electoral and nonelectoral politics. The ultimate consequence is a more diverse, complex politics that no single set of loyalties, and thus no single set of political organizations, can easily contain.

CONCLUSION: THE PARTY DILEMMA

The American parties cannot be all things to all citizens. It is difficult for them to represent the narrow interests of a self-oriented citizenry effectively while trying to build a majority coalition. They cannot be pure in their ideology and still make the compromises that are necessary for coalition-building and governing. They find it hard to pursue their programmatic goals and offer policy alternatives to the electorate without engaging in the partisan conflict and competition many Americans find so distasteful. They cannot unite their officeholders and office seekers in common cause while giving candidates full electoral independence and freedom. They cannot depend upon unwavering party loyalty in an electorate that wants to choose candidates individually.

The American parties seem fated to have to endure the conflicting, even contradictory expectations contained in their environment for some time to come.
Their continuing challenge is how to adapt to these realities without losing the
distinctive character that has sustained them over the long course of democratic
politics. For the American democracy, the continuing challenge is how to function
effectively for its citizens given this new, more problematic place for its life-long
ally, the political party.

End Notes

Part One

1. The phrase comes from the title of Harold Lasswell's pioneering book *Politics: Who Gets What, When, How* (New York: McGraw-Hill, 1936).
2. C. Wright Mills, *The Power Elite* (New York: Oxford University Press, 1956), offers the best-known example of such "elitist" interpretations of American politics. The alternative "pluralist" perspective adopted by most political scientists is well illustrated in Robert A. Dahl, *Who Governs?* (New Haven: Yale University Press, 1961).
3. E. E. Schattschneider, *Party Government* (New York: Rinehart, 1942), p. 1.
4. Illustrations of this favorable treatment of parties as crucial to the democratization of new nations may be found in David Apter, *The Politics of Modernization* (Chicago: University of Chicago Press, 1965), Chapter 6; and Joseph LaPalombara and Myron Weiner, *Political Parties and Political Development* (Princeton: Princeton University Press, 1966).
5. Austin Ranney provides an excellent account of these antiparty attitudes and reforms in *Curing the Mischiefs of Faction* (Berkeley: University of California Press, 1975).
6. See Anthony King, "Political Parties in Western Democracies," *Polity* 2 (1969): 111–41, for a similar note of caution about the role of parties generally.

Chapter 1

1. These definitions are taken from: John H. Aldrich, *Why Parties? The Origin and Transformation of Party Politics in America* (Chicago: University of Chicago Press, 1995), pp. 283–84; Edmund Burke, "Thoughts on the Cause of the Present Discontents" (1770), in *The Works of Edmund Burke* (Boston: Little, Brown, 1839), vol. I, pp. 425–26; William Nisbet Chambers, "Party Development and the American Mainstream" in William Nisbet Chambers and Walter Dean Burnham, eds., *The American Party Systems* (New York: Oxford University Press, 1967), p. 5; Anthony Downs, *An Economy Theory of Democracy* (New York: Harper and Row, 1957), p. 24; Leon Epstein, *Political Parties in Western Democracies* (New Brunswick, N.J.: Transaction Books, 1980; originally published in 1967), p. 9; and V. O. Key, *Politics, Parties, and Pressure Groups* (New York: Crowell, 1958), pp. 180–82. For an extended discussion of key issues in defining political parties, see Giovanni Sartori, *Parties and Party Systems* (New York: Cambridge University Press, 1976), pp. 3–38; Leon Epstein, *Political Parties in Western Democracies;* Gerald M. Pomper, *Passions and Interests: Political Party Concepts of American Democracy* (Lawrence: University of Kansas Press, 1992); and Joseph Schlesinger, *Political Parties and the Winning of Office* (Ann Arbor: University of Michigan Press, 1991), pp. 5–10.
2. This treatment hardly exhausts the various notions of political parties that have frequented the American scene. In a recent treatment of American parties, for example, Gerald Pomper identifies at least eight different party models—governing caucus, ideological community, cause advocate, social movement, bureaucratic organization, urban machine, rational team of office seekers, and personal faction—by differentiating between a mass vs. elite focus, collective vs. coalitional goals, and instrumental vs. expressive modes of operation. His approach recognizes the cacophony of party images in the American political tradition. See Pomper, *Passions and Interests.*
3. This account of the Mountaineer "party's" misfortune draws upon a report in *Ballot Access News,* August 23, 1994.
4. In a recent work on political parties that is sure to prove very influential, John Aldrich views parties as enduring organizations through which teams of ambitious politicians combine to solve collective action problems in achieving their goals. Although he appreciates that voters may be a

valuable component of a party and were from the 1830s to about 1960, he does not see a mass base as fundamental for an organization to constitute a political party. See his *Why Parties?*, especially Chapter 1.

5. This tripartite conception of the political parties is attributed to V. O. Key, Jr., who uses it to organize his classic political parties textbook, *Politics, Parties, and Pressure Groups*. Key attributes the concept of party-in-the-electorate to Ralph M. Goldman, *Party Chairmen and Party Factions, 1789–1900* (Chicago: University of Chicago Ph.D. dissertation, 1951), Chapter 17.

6. This point is emphasized by a number of critics of the tripartite approach. See especially Denise L. Baer and David A. Bositis, *Elite Cadres and Party Coalitions: Representing the Public in Party Politics* (Westport, Conn.: Greenwood Press, 1988), pp. 21–50; and Pomper, *Passions and Interests*, pp. 3–5.

7. The failure to recognize that political parties do not single-mindedly seek only to win office but also are motivated by the benefits that can be derived from control of office has led to some confusion about the electoral goals of parties. For clarification, see Joseph A. Schlesinger, "The Primary Goals of Political Parties: A Clarification of Positive Theory," *American Political Science Review* 69 (1975): 840–49.

8. On the party as a series of task-oriented nuclei see Joseph A. Schlesinger, "Political Party Organization," in James G. March, ed., *Handbook of Organizations* (Chicago: Rand McNally, 1965), pp. 764–801; and "The New American Political Party," *American Political Science Review* 79 (1985): pp. 1152–69.

9. Theodore Lowi has brought together a number of descriptions of party functions in his article "Toward Functionalism in Political Science: The Case of Innovation in Party Systems," *American Political Science Review* 57 (1963): 570–83. See also A. James Reichley, *The Life of the Parties: A History of American Political Parties* (New York: Free Press, 1992), pp. 1–2 and 414–15.

10. John Aldrich sees parties as organizations that are created by rational politicians to solve their most challenging collective action problems: (a) to organize political officeholders into an enduring and cohesive group in support of key policy principles, (b) to forge durable majorities, and (c) to mobilize voters in elections and political activity on behalf of their cause. See Aldrich, *Why Parties?*, especially Chapters 2 and 9.

11. There are, of course, many histories of the development of American political parties. Most devote virtually all their pages to the candidates and platforms of the parties; few discuss the parties qua parties. The most notable ones that do are William N. Chambers, *Political Parties in a New Nation* (New York: Oxford University Press, 1963); Chambers and Burnham, *The American Party Systems;* Everett C. Ladd, Jr., *American Political Parties* (New York: Norton, 1970); Reichley, *The Life of the Parties;* and John H. Aldrich, *Why Parties?*

12. See John H. Aldrich, and Ruth W. Grant, "The Antifederalists, the First Congress, and the First Parties," *Journal of Politics* 55 (1993): 295–326; Aldrich, *Why Parties?*, Chapter 3; Chambers, *Political Parties in a New Nation;* Joseph Charles, *The Origins of the American Party System* (New York: Harper & Row, 1961); John F. Hoadley, *Origins of American Political Parties 1789–1803* (Lexington: University of Kentucky Press, 1986); and Reichley, *The Life of the Parties*, Chapters 3 and 4.

13. See *The Federalist* (New York: Mentor Books, 1961), p. 77, for the quoted material. What is referred to as *The Federalist* is the collection of eighty-five essays written to justify the new constitution that was undergoing ratification in the states and published as letters to the editor in New York newspapers in 1787 and 1788 under the pseudonym of Publius. Their authors were Alexander Hamilton, James Madison, and John Jay; Madison clearly was the author of essay number 10. Partly because of the powerful justification for it fashioned by Hamilton, Jay, and Madison, the new Constitution was adopted and has served the nation ever since.

14. For a detailed account of the extension of the suffrage, focusing on the separate actions of the states, see Chilton Williamson, *American Suffrage: From Property to Democracy* (Princeton: Princeton University Press, 1960).

15. For a more complete account, see Neal R. Peirce and Lawrence D. Longley, *The People's President: The Electoral College in American History and the Direct Vote Alternative* (New Haven: Yale University Press, 1981).

16. Both Aldrich, in *Why Parties?,* Chapter 4, and Reichley, *The Life of the Parties,* Chapter 5, provide excellent descriptions of how mass parties first appeared in the decades after the 1820s. Martin Van Buren, leader of the Albany, New York's Regency machine and the eighth president of the United States, is credited as being the lead architect in the creation of the first of the mass parties, the Democratic party, which itself was a direct descendent of the Democratic-Republican party.

17. For a more complete account of parties during their golden age, see Reichley, *The Life of the Parties,* Chapters 6–11.

18. A spirited account of the development of American parties and party organizations into their golden age from a disapproving normative perspective is found in Moisei Ostrogorski, *Democracy and the Organization of Political Parties, Volume II: The United States* (Garden City, N.Y.: Anchor Books, Doubleday and Company, 1964; originally published in 1902).

19. On the various episodes of party reform in American history and their effects, see Austin Ranney, *Curing the Mischiefs of Faction* (Berkeley: University of California Press, 1975). A good account of the Progressive movement may be found in Richard Hofstadter, *The Age of Reform* (New York: Vintage Books, 1955).

20. So extensive is government regulation of political parties that Leon Epstein was moved to characterize them as public utilities rather than as the private associations they were during the nineteenth century. See his *Political Parties in the American Mold* (Madison: University of Wisconsin Press, 1986), pp. 155–99.

21. The best discussions of the concept of political culture remain Gabriel Almond and Sidney Verba, *The Civic Culture* (Princeton, N. J.: Princeton University Press, 1963) and Lucian W. Pye and Sidney Verba, *Political Culture and Political Development* (Princeton, N. J.: Princeton University Press, 1965). For an interesting application of the political culture concept to American state and local politics, see Daniel Elazar, *American Federalism: A View from the States* (New York: Crowell, 1972), Chapter 4.

22. The results of this July 1994 survey conducted for the Times Mirror Center for People and the Press are reported in *The New York Times,* September 21, 1994, p. A12.

Chapter 2

1. For comprehensive studies of other party systems, see, *inter alia,* Kenneth Janda, *Political Parties: A Cross-National Survey* (New York: Free Press, 1980); and Arend Lijphart, *Electoral Systems and Party Systems: A Study of Twenty-Seven Democracies, 1945–1990* (New York: Oxford University Press, 1994).

2. For a sophisticated critique of the traditional classification and analysis of party systems, see Giovanni Sartori, *Parties and Party Systems* (New York: Cambridge University Press, 1976).

3. Other relevant records in presidential elections are the greatest electoral college vote—Ronald Reagan in 1984, with 525 votes—and the greatest percentage of the two-party popular vote—Calvin Coolidge in 1924, with 65.2 percent.

4. Historical studies of competition for the House of Representatives show that the high and increasing level of competitiveness through the mid-1890s was replaced by a steady decrease in competitiveness for the next 90 years. See James C. Garand and Donald A. Gross, "Changes in the Vote Margins for Congressional Candidates: A Specification of Historical Trends," *American Political Science Review* 78 (1984): 17–30; and Donald A. Gross and James C. Garand, "The Vanishing Marginals, 1824–1980," *Journal of Politics* 46 (1984): 224–37.

5. The original measurements were presented for 1946–63 by Austin Ranney, "Parties in State Politics," in Herbert Jacob and Kenneth Vines, eds., *Politics in the American States* (Boston: Little, Brown, 1965), p. 65. For an alternative index, based on state legislative races, see Thomas M. Holbrook and Emily Van Dunk, *American Political Science Review* 87 (1993): 955–62.

6. Harvey J. Tucker, "Interparty Competition in the American States," *American Politics Quarterly* 10 (1982): 93–116; and Patrick J. Kenney and Tom W. Rice, "Party Composition in the American States: Clarifying Concepts and Explaining Changes in Partisanship since the 1950s," *Political Behavior* 7 (1985): 335–51.

7. These were the results of a study relating the Ranney index for the 1970–80 period to various characteristics of the states. See Samuel C. Patterson and Gregory A. Caldeira, "The Etiology of Partisan Competition," *American Political Science Review* 78 (1984): 691–707.

8. The figures on incumbency success rates are drawn from Paul R. Abramson, John H. Aldrich, and David W. Rohde, *Change and Continuity in the 1992 Elections* (Washington, D.C.: Congressional Quarterly Press, 1994), pp. 255–80 and especially Tables 9–1 and 9–6. On the influence of incumbency in general, see, *inter alia,* Garand and Gross, "Changes in the Vote Margins for Congressional Candidates;" Gross and Garand, "The Vanishing Marginals, 1824–1980;" David R. Mayhew, "Congressional Elections: The Case of the Vanishing Marginals," *Polity* 6 (1974): 295–17; Gary C. Jacobson, *The Politics of Congressional Elections* (Boston: Little, Brown, 1987); and L. Sandy Maisel, Linda Fowler, Ruth S. Jones, and Walter J. Stone, "Nomination Politics: The Role of Institutional, Contextual, and Personal Variables," in L. Sandy Maisel, ed., *The Party Responds* (Boulder, Colo.: Westview Press, 1994), pp. 145–68. On incumbency in state legislative elections, see Malcolm Jewell and David Breaux, "The Effect of Incumbency on State Legislative Elections," *Legislative Studies Quarterly* 13 (1988): 495–514.

9. Gary C. Jacobson, "The Marginals Never Vanished: Incumbency and Competition in Elections to the U.S. House of Representatives, 1952–82," *American Journal of Political Science* 31 (1987): 126–41, quotation from p. 138. On how redistricting and scandals make incumbents vulnerable, also see Monica Bauer and John R. Hibbing, "Which Incumbents Lose in House Elections: A Response to Jacobson's 'The Marginals Never Vanished'," *American Journal of Political Science* 31 (1987): 262–71.

10. The original development of this "law" is found in Maurice Duverger, *Political Parties* (New York: Wiley, 1954); for an even earlier illustration of the institutional explanation, see E. E. Schattschneider, *Party Government* (New York: Rinehart, 1942). For more recent evidence of the influence of electoral institutions on the size of the party system, see Arend Lijphart, "The Political Consequences of Electoral Laws, 1945–85," *American Political Science Review* 84 (1990): 481–96; Douglas Rae, *The Political Consequences of Electoral Laws* (New Haven, Conn.: Yale University Press, 1967); William Riker, "The Two-Party System and Duverger's Law," *American Political Science Review* 76 (1982): 753–66; and Lijphart, *Electoral Systems and Party Systems.*

11. In the past, many states have had multimember districts for one or both houses of the state legislature. As recently as 1955, 58 percent of all state legislative districts were multimember compared to 10 percent by the 1980s. See Theodore J. Lowi, "Towards a More Responsible Three Party System," *PS* 16 (1983): 699–706. On competition in multimember districts, see Richard Niemi, Simon Jackman, and Laura Winsley, "Candidates and Competitiveness in Multimember Districts," *Legislative Studies Quarterly* 16 (1991): 91–109.

12. This statement requires some qualification to be wholly accurate. The presidency goes to the party whose candidate has won a majority of the electoral votes; a state's electoral votes almost always have gone to the candidate who has won a **plurality** of the votes in the state. Gubernatorial victors in most states are the simple plurality winners; some southern states, however, require the winner to attain a majority of the votes and provide for a run-off between the top two vote-getters if no candidate receives a majority in the first round. On these run-off elections, see Charles S. Bullock, III, and Loch K. Johnson, *Runoff Elections in the United States,* Knoxville: University of Tennessee Press, 1991.

13. Leon Epstein, *Political Parties in the American Mold* (Madison: University of Wisconsin Press, 1986), pp. 129–32.

14. See, for example, V. O. Key, Jr., *Politics, Parties and Pressure Groups,* 5th ed. (New York: Crowell, 1964), pp. 229ff.; and Seymour Martin Lipset, Martin A. Trow, and James S. Coleman, *Union Democracy* (New York: Free Press, 1956), especially Part III.

15. Louis Hartz, *The Liberal Tradition in America* (New York: Harcourt, Brace, and World, 1955).

16. The clearest statements of this view are found in Oliver P. Williams and Charles Adrian, "The Insulation of Local Politics Under the Nonpartisan Ballot," *American Political Science Review* 53 (1959): 1052–63; and Willis D. Hawley, *NonPartisan Elections and the Case for Party Politics* (New York: Wiley, 1973).

17. Susan Welch and Timothy Bledsoe, "The Partisan Consequences of Nonpartisan Elections and the Changing Nature of Urban Politics," *American Journal of Political Science* 30 (1986): 128–39.

18. A list of these third-party and independent governors through 1992 is provided by J. David Gillespie, *Politics at the Periphery* (Columbia: University of South Carolina Press, 1993), Appendix 5, pp. 302–05.

19. The literature on American third parties is rich and varied. The best general treatments of third parties may be found in Daniel A. Mazmanian, *Third Parties in Presidential Elections* (Washington, D.C.: Brookings Institution, 1974); Steven J. Rosenstone, Roy L. Behr, and Edward H. Lazarus, *Third Parties in America* (Princeton: Princeton University Press, 1996); and Gillespie, *Politics at the Periphery.*

20. For more on the Libertarian party, see Gillespie, *Politics at the Periphery,* pp. 174–78; and especially Joseph M. Hazlett II, *The Libertarian Party* (Jefferson, N.C.: McFarland and Company, 1992).

21. Evidence of the effects of voter skepticism about their chances is the fact that almost all third-party presidential candidates in this century have received less support on election day than they had exhibited in public-opinion polls prior to the election. See Rosenstone, Behr, and Lazarus, *Third Parties in America,* p. 41. The Perot candidacy in 1992 continued this pattern.

22. Ibid., p. 162.

23. On the attitudes and preferences of Perot voters, see Paul R. Abramson, John H. Aldrich, and David W. Rohde, *Change and Continuity in the 1992 Elections* (Washington, D.C.: CQ Press, 1994). For the argument that Perot voters were less drawn to him than repulsed by the major party candidates, see Herbert B. Asher, "The Perot Campaign," in Herbert Weisberg, ed., *Democracy's Feast: The 1992 U.S. Elections* (Chatham, N.J.: Chatham House, 1994), Chap. 6.

24. Federal Election Commission figures show that the Perot organization invested almost $73 million in the 1992 campaign (June 28, 1994, report). Richard L. Berke reported in *The New York Times* (October 27, 1992, p. A11) that as much as $46 million of this money may have been spent on television.

25. This claim is made by David Gillespie, as quoted in *The Washington Post National Weekly Edition,* September 19–25, 1994, p. 13.

26. Third parties and independents have compiled a checkered record of success in ballot-access cases. State laws requiring filing fees and petitions signed by large numbers of voters before such candidates are allowed on the ballot have been overruled in some cases but upheld in others. On balance, the courts have made access to the ballot for third parties and independents easier in recent years. But this action has been taken on a piecemeal basis that requires petitioners to raise the challenge in each state and has left in place many curbs on access to the ballot as reasonable state efforts to avoid voter confusion and frustration when faced with a long ballot. See Clifton McCleskey, "Parties at the Bar: Equal Protection, Freedom of Association, and the Rights of Political Organization," *Journal of Politics* 46 (1984): 346–68; John Moeller, "The Federal Courts' Involvement in the Reform of Political Parties," *Western Political Quarterly* 40 (1987): 717–34; and Lee Epstein and Charles D. Hadley, "On the Treatment of Political Parties in the U.S. Supreme Court, 1900–1986," *Journal of Politics* 52 (1990): 413–32. For regular reports on access to the ballot by minor parties and independents, see Richard Winger's *Ballot Access News,* published in San Francisco, California.

27. For an account of how New York election laws permitting multiple nominations and multiple ballot placement foster minor parties, see Howard A. Scarrow, *Parties, Elections, and Representation in the State of New York* (New York: New York University Press, 1983).

28. There are signs that this space may be increasing in the 1990s, although it remains small. Christian Collet and Jerrold R. Hansen, writing in *Vox Pop,* the Newsletter of Political Organizations and Parties (volume 14, issue 2, p. 2), describe an upturn in independent and third-party voting in the 1990s in statewide, state legislative, and U.S. House contests.

29. The case was Williams v. Rhodes, 393 U.S. 23 (1968).

30. This account of Anderson's efforts to gain access to the ballot draws upon Jack W. Germond and Jules Witcover, *Blue Smoke and Mirrors: How Reagan Won and Why Carter Lost the Election of*

1980 (New York: Viking, 1981), pp. 236–37. The Supreme Court case was Anderson v. Cele-brezze 460 U.S. 780 (1983).

Part Two

1. Maurice Duverger, in *Political Parties* (New York: Wiley, 1954), inaugurated the distinction between cadre and mass membership parties. For an expansion of that analysis and a comparison of the American parties with those of other Western democracies, see Leon D. Epstein, *Political Parties in Western Democracies* (New Brunswick, N.J.: Transaction, 1980).
2. These reformers viewed the political party organizations, especially the urban political machines, as powerful (and baneful) entities and were devoted to destroying them. For a charac-teristic treatment of party organizations by reform-minded observers, see Moisei Ostrogorski, *Democracy and the Organization of the Political Parties,* Volume II (New York: Anchor, 1964; first published in 1902 and now available in an edition edited and abridged by Seymour Martin Lipset).

Chapter 3

1. The results of this study are reported in Timothy Conlan, Ann Martino, and Robert Dilger, "State Parties in the 1980s," *Intergovernmental Perspective* 10 (1984): 6–13, 23; and *The Transforma-tion in American Politics* (Washington, D.C.: Advisory Commission on Intergovernmental Rela-tions, 1986), pp. 95–162.
2. The case citations are *Tashjian v. Republican Party of Connecticut,* 479 U.S. 1024 (1986); and *Eu* (Secretary of State of California) *v. San Francisco County Democratic Central Committee et al.,* 103 L. Ed. 2nd 271 (1989). The injunction against enforcement of the endorsements law was issued on August 5, 1994, in *California Democratic Party v. Lungren,* no. C94–1703–WHO, Northern District. For a review of earlier federal court decisions in this area, see Clifton McCleskey, "Parties at the Bar: Equal Protection, Freedom of Association, and the Rights of Political Organizations," *Journal of Politics* 46 (1984): 346–68. On deregulation of parties in California, see Roy Christman and Barbara Norrander, "A Reflection on Political Party Deregu-lation Via the Courts: The Case of California," *Journal of Law and Politics* 6 (1990): 723–742.
3. Within the same state, the various intermediate committees may cover geographical areas of varying sizes and thus may occupy different positions in the organizational pyramid. Congres-sional districts, for example, may be smaller than a city or larger than a county, depending on the density of population.
4. The results of this survey are reported on p. 22 of John F. Persinos, "Has the Christian Right Taken Over the Republican Party?" *Campaigns and Elections,* September 1994, pp. 20–24.
5. Leon Epstein, *Political Parties in the American Mold* (Madison: University of Wisconsin Press, 1986), pp. 155–99.
6. V. O. Key, Jr., *Politics, Parties and Pressure Groups* (New York: Crowell, 1964), p. 316.
7. Samuel J. Eldersveld, *Political Parties: A Behavioral Analysis* (Chicago: Rand McNally, 1964).
8. The organization of American political parties leads one to question whether Michels' "iron law of oligarchy"—that organizations are inevitably controlled from the top—is really an iron law after all. See Robert Michels, *Political Parties* (Glencoe, Ill.: Free Press, 1949; originally pub-lished in 1915), and Eldersveld, *Political Parties.*
9. These estimates on the number of machines governing American cities at various times during their heyday come from M. Craig Brown and Charles N. Halaby, "Machine Politics in America, 1870–1945," *Journal of Interdisciplinary History* 17 (1987): 587–612.
10. These are the characteristics David Mayhew uses to define traditional party organizations, which when they hold overall control of a city or county at the local level are synonymous with machines. See Mayhew's *Placing Parties in American Politics* (Princeton, N.J.: Princeton Uni-versity Press, 1986), pp. 19–21. This book provides excellent descriptions of traditional party organizations in a variety of states through the 1960s.

11. For an interesting comparison of reform movements in three cities, see Kenneth Finegold, *Experts and Politicians: Reform Challenges to Machine Politics in New York, Cleveland, and Chicago* (Princeton, N.J.: Princeton University Press, 1995).

12. The colorful politics of Chicago has stimulated a rich literature, probably the richest on the subject of party politics in any American city. An early study of the Chicago machine is Harold Foote Gosnell's classic *Machine Politics: Chicago Style* (Chicago: University of Chicago Press, 1939). Good studies of the Daley years are Edward C. Banfield, *Political Influence* (New York: The Free Press, 1961); Milton Rakove, *Don't Make No Waves, Don't Back No Losers* (Bloomington, Ind.: Indiana University Press, 1975); and Thomas M. Guterbok, *Machine Politics in Transition: Party and Community in Chicago* (Chicago: University of Chicago Press, 1980). For perspectives on the post-Daley years and their roots in earlier times, see Paul Kleppner, *Chicago Divided: The Making of a Black Mayor* (DeKalb, Ill.: Northern Illinois University Press, 1985), William J. Grimshaw, *Bitter Fruit: Black Politics and the Chicago Machine* (Chicago: University of Chicago Press, 1992), and Kenneth Finegold, *Experts and Politicians.*

13. Steven P. Erie makes a persuasive argument that the great urban machines were principally organizations of, by, and for the Irish that proved unwilling to accommodate other ethnic groups. See his *Rainbow's End: Irish-Americans and the Dilemmas of Urban Machine Politics, 1840–1985* (Berkeley: University of California Press, 1988). The mobilization of ethnics, including the non-Irish, however, required the right kind of political leadership. On how such an ethnic group coalition was built by the Tammany Hall political machine in New York, see Martin Shefter, "The Electoral Foundations of the Political Machine: New York City, 1884–1897," in Joel H. Silbey, Allan G. Bogue, and William H. Flanagan, eds., *The History of American Electoral Behavior* (Princeton, N.J.: Princeton University Press, 1978), pp. 263–98.

14. For an insightful discussion of the conditions for machine politics here and abroad, see James C. Scott, "Corruption, Machine Politics, and Political Change," *American Political Science Review* 63 (1969): 1142–58. On the importance for party development of an autonomous bureaucracy, insulated from being used for patronage by a political party in its quest for votes, see the rich comparisons among Britain, Germany, Italy, France, and the United States by Martin Shefter, *Political Parties and the State* (Princeton, N.J.: Princeton University Press, 1994), Chap. 2. A useful perspective on the development of American machines also is provided by Amy Bridges, *A City in the Republic: Antebellum New York and the Origins of Machine Politics* (New York: Cambridge University Press, 1984).

15. On the Nassau County machine, see Anne Freedman, *Patronage: An American Tradition* (Chicago: Nelson-Hall, 1994), Chap. 5. One of its leaders, U.S. Senator Alphonse D'Amato, remains one of the most powerful figures in New York politics.

16. Kenneth R. Mladenka, "The Urban Bureaucracy and the Chicago Political Machine: Who Gets What and the Limits to Political Control," *American Political Science Review* 74 (1980): 991–98.

17. Michael Johnston, "Patrons and Clients, Jobs and Machines: A Case Study in the Uses of Patronage," *American Political Science Review* 73 (1979): 385–98.

18. A few thoughtful scholars have resisted the stampede to sound the death knell for political machines. See Raymond Wolfinger's "Why Political Machines Have Not Withered Away and Other Revisionist Thoughts," *Journal of Politics* 34 (1972): 365–98. Others also have questioned whether the replacement of the machines by more-bureaucratic and less-centralized government has been beneficial for American cities. See Theodore Lowi, "Machine Politics—Old and New," *Public Interest,* Fall 1967, pp. 83–92.

19. The results of this survey are reported in James L. Gibson, Cornelius P. Cotter, John F. Bibby, and Robert J. Huckshorn, "Whither the Local Parties?" *American Journal of Political Science* 29 (1985): 139–60, and Cornelius P. Cotter, James L. Gibson, John F. Bibby, and Robert J. Huckshorn, *Party Organization in American Politics* (New York: Praeger, 1984).

20. Cotter et al., *Party Organization in American Politics,* pp. 49–53. The states with strong and weak local organizations, respectively, are virtually the same ones cited in Mayhew's survey of party strength in the late 1960s. See Mayhew, *Placing Parties in American Politics.*

21. James L. Gibson, John P. Frendreis, and Laura L. Vertz, "Party Dynamics in the 1980s: Change in County Party Organizational Strength, 1980–1984," *American Journal of Political Science* 33 (1989): 67–90.

22. See Cotter et al., *Party Organization in American Politics,* p. 54, for the 1964–80 comparison. The 1964 figures come from Paul Allen Beck, "Environment and Party," *American Political Science Review* 68 (1974): 1229–44. The 1988 figures are from a study conducted by John Kessel and William Jacoby and are reported in Charles E. Smith, Jr., "Changes in Party Organizational Strength and Activity 1979–1988," The Ohio State University, unpublished manuscript, 1989. On Detroit and Los Angeles, see Samuel J. Eldersveld, "The Party Activist in Detroit and Los Angeles: A Longitudinal View, 1956–1980," in William J. Crotty, ed., *Political Parties in Local Areas* (Knoxville: University of Tennessee Press, 1986), pp. 89–119.

23. This study of local party organizations was conducted by Paul Allen Beck, Russell J. Dalton, Audrey Haynes, and Robert Huckfeldt as a part of the American component in the Cross-National Election Project. The forty counties were selected to represent, with probabilities proportionate to size, the locales of voters in the 1992 election. Democratic and Republican county chairs or their equivalents were contacted by phone or by mail in all forty counties, and information on their organization and its activities was collected from all but one respondent. For early reports on the results of this study, see Beck, Dalton, Haynes, and Huckfeldt, "Local Party Organizations in the 1992 Presidential Elections," paper presented at the 1993 Annual Meeting of the Southern Political Science Association; and "Party Effort at the Grass Roots: Local Presidential Campaigning in 1992," paper presented at the 1994 Annual Meeting of the Midwest Political Science Association.

24. Increased levels of local party activity in 1992 also are reported in a study of the party role in legislative campaigns in eight states. See John Frendreis, Alan R. Gitelson, Gregory Flemming, and Anne Layzell, "Local Political Parties and the 1992 Campaign for the State Legislatures," paper presented at the 1993 Annual Meeting of the American Political Science Association.

25. For excellent descriptions of these traditional organizations before they suffered their recent declines, see Mayhew, *Placing Parties in American Politics.*

26. These notes of caution, among others, are sounded by John J. Coleman in "The Resurgence of Party Organization? A Dissent from the New Orthodoxy," in Daniel M. Shea and John C. Green, eds. *The State of the Parties: The Changing Role of Contemporary American Parties* (Lanham, Md.: Rowman and Littlefield, 1994), pp. 282–98.

27. A. James Reichley cites Illinois, Michigan, Ohio, Pennsylvania, and Wisconsin as states with powerful state organizations near the turn of the twentieth century. They had been fueled by the federal patronage allocated by the state's U.S. senators, one of whom typically served as their leader, since the time of the Grant presidency. Probably the most powerful state organization ever, though, was that built by Governor (then Senator) Huey Long in the 1920s and 1930s using **state** government powers and patronage. See Reichley's *The Life of the Parties* (New York: Free Press, 1992), pp. 144–60 and 268–72.

28. These estimates come from Robert J. Huckshorn and John F. Bibby, "State Parties in an Era of Political Change," in Joel L. Fleishman, ed., *The Future of American Political Parties* (Englewood Cliffs, N.J.: Prentice-Hall, 1982), pp. 70–100; and James L. Gibson, Cornelius P. Cotter, John F. Bibby, and Robert J. Huckshorn, "Assessing Party Organization Strength," *American Journal of Political Science* 27 (1983): 193–222.

29. These figures come from a survey conducted by the Brookings Institution and reported in Reichley, *The Life of the Parties,* p. 388.

30. For an account of these legislative campaign committees, see Anthony Gierzynski, *Legislative Party Campaign Committees in the American States* (Lexington, Ky.: University of Kentucky Press, 1992).

31. See John F. Bibby, "State Party Organizations: Coping and Adapting," in L. Sandy Maisel, ed., *The Parties Respond* (Boulder, Colo.: Westview, 1994), pp. 21–44.

32. The 1979–80 study is Cotter et al., *Party Organizations in American Politics.* The 1984 study is Advisory Commission on Intergovernmental Relations, *The Transformation in American Politics.*

33. For an account of how one of the pioneers of effective state party organization operated, see John H. Kessel, "Ray Bliss and the Development of the Ohio Republican Party During the 1950s," in John C. Green, ed., *Politics, Professionalism, and Power* (Lanham, Md.: University Press of America, 1994), pp. 48–61.

34. These were identified as the strongest state organizations in 1979–80 by Cotter et al., *Party Organizations in American Politics,* pp. 28–29.

35. Soft money refers to campaign contributions raised by the national parties and presidential candidates that would be illegal under federal law if they remained at the national level but become legal when they are directly funneled to the state parties for use in nonfederal elections and for generic party activities. For more on soft money, see Chapter 12.

36. On the role of the national parties in state-party building, see Bibby, "State Party Organizations: Coping and Adapting," especially pp. 36–43. (The funding figures are reported in his Table 2.2.) Also see, Robert Biersack, "Hard Facts and Soft Money: State Party Finance in the 1992 Federal Elections," in Shea and Green, *The State of the Parties,* Chapter 7.

37. Walter Dean Burnham, *Critical Elections and the Mainsprings of American Politics* (New York: Norton, 1970), p. 72.

38. For an intensive examination of how factors such as these undermined Democratic organizations in three different locales, see Alan Ware, *The Breakdown of the Democratic Party Organization 1940–80* (Oxford, England: Oxford University Press, 1985).

39. This notion of the state and local parties fits Mildred Schwartz's conceptualization of the party as a network of interactions in *The Party Network: The Robust Organization of Illinois Republicans* (Madison: University of Wisconsin Press, 1990). She found that the most central actors within the modern Illinois Republican party were financial contributors, interest groups, advisors, state senators and representatives, county chairs, and the governor—not solely the occupants of the formal party organization.

Chapter 4

1. Cornelius P. Cotter and Bernard C. Hennessy, *Politics without Power: The National Party Committees* (New York: Atherton, 1964). For a comprehensive history of the national committees, see Ralph M. Goldman, *The National Party Chairmen and Committees* (Armonk, N.Y.: M. E. Sharpe, 1990).

2. E. E. Schattschneider, *Party Government* (New York: Rinehart, 1942), pp. 129, 132–33.

3. Leon D. Epstein, *Political Parties in the American Mold* (Madison: University of Wisconsin Press, 1986), pp. 200–238; and Gary D. Wekkin, "National-State Party Relations: The Democrats' New Federal Structure," *Political Science Quarterly* 99 (1984): 45–72.

4. Cotter and Hennessy, *Politics without Power,* p. 39.

5. James W. Ceaser, "Political Parties—Declining, Stabilizing, or Resurging," in Anthony King, ed., *The New American Political System* (Washington, D.C.: American Enterprise Institute, 1990), pp. 87–137 at pp. 114–117. For a more general treatment of how American parties have become more tightly linked to the president as they have become more nationalized, see Sidney M. Milkis, *The President and the Parties: The Transformation of the American Party System Since the New Deal* (New York: Oxford University Press, 1993).

6. For illustrations of these antithetical views of party strength, compare David Broder's *The Party's Over,* an early chronicle of the decline of parties thesis, with *The Party Goes On* by Xandra Kayden and Eddie Mahe, Jr. (New York: Basic Books, 1985) or Larry J. Sabato, *The Party's Just Begun* (Glenview, Ill.: Scott Foresman/Little, Brown, 1988).

7. Their ability to raise substantial sums of money directly through individual contributions has contributed to the national parties increased power by freeing them from their previous dependence on assessments upon the state parties, another characteristic of a confederated structure, and from the resultant state party influence. For a description of this earlier system, see Cotter and Hennessy, *Politics without Power,* pp. 180–182. For more on modern party finance, see Frank J. Sorauf and Scott A. Wilson, "Political Parties and Campaign Finance: Adaptation and Accommodation Toward a Changing Role," in L. Sandy Maisel, ed., *The Parties Respond: Changes in American Parties and Campaigns,* Second Edition (Boulder, Colo.: Westview Press, 1994), pp. 235–53; and David B. Magleby and Candice J. Nelson, *The Money Chase* (Washington, D.C.: Brookings, 1990).

8. John H. Kessel, "Organizational Development of National Party Committees: Some Generalizations and Supporting Evidence," *Vox Pop: Newsletter of Political Organizations and Parties,* vol. 7, no. 3, p. 1.

9. F. Christopher Arterton calls them "service vendor" parties, while Paul Herrnson refers to them as "broker" parties. See Arterton's "Political Money and Party Strength," in Joel Fleishman, ed., *The Future of American Political Parties* (Englewood Cliffs, N.J.: Prentice-Hall, 1982), pp. 101–39; and Herrnson, "National Party Organizations and Congressional Campaigning: National Parties as Brokers," paper presented at the 1986 Annual Meeting of the Midwest Political Science Association, Chicago.

10. Excellent accounts of the roles of Brock and especially Bliss in party building at the national level are contained in various chapters of John C. Green, ed., *Politics, Professionalism, and Power: Modern Party Organization and the Legacy of Ray C. Bliss* (Lanham, Md.: University Press of American, 1994). On the role of Manatt and the others, see A. James Reichley, *The Life of the Parties* (New York: Free Press, 1992), pp. 353–81.

11. On Democratic party reform, see Austin Ranney, *Curing the Mischiefs of Faction: Party Reform in America* (Berkeley: University of California Press, 1975); William J. Crotty, *Decisions for the Democrats: Reforming the Party Structure* (Baltimore: Johns Hopkins University Press, 1978); and Byron E. Shafer, *The Quiet Revolution: The Struggle for the Democratic Party and the Shaping of Post-Reform Politics* (New York: Russell Sage Foundation, 1983).

12. A reform committee, the Rule 29 Committee, was mandated by the 1972 Republican National Convention, but its recommendations for RNC review of state party "positive action" programs were rejected by the RNC and later by the 1976 convention. In general, the GOP has been far more protective of states' rights for the parties than have the Democrats. See John F. Bibby, "Party Renewal in the Republican National Party," in Gerald M. Pomper, ed., *Party Renewal in America* (New York: Praeger, 1981), pp. 102–115.

13. Comprehensive recent accounts of the increased strength of the national parties include A. James Reichley, *The Life of the Political Parties* (New York: Free Press, 1992), pp. 353–81; and Paul S. Herrnson, "The Revitalization of National Party Organizations," in Maisel, *The Parties Respond*, pp. 45–68.

14. For a good description of the traditional relationships of state party leadership and the national parties, see Robert J. Huckshorn, *Party Leadership in the States* (Amherst: University of Massachusetts Press, 1976), Chapter 8.

15. See Epstein, *Political Parties in the American Mold*, p. 237; and Xandra Kayden, "The Nationalization of the Party System," in Michael J. Malbin, ed., *Parties, Interest Groups, and the Campaign Finance Laws* (Washington, D.C.: American Enterprise Institute, 1980), pp. 257–82.

16. This incident and the policy change it induced are described in Kayden and Mahe, *The Party Goes On*, pp. 78–79.

17. Party-presidential relations during the Reagan years are discussed in A. James Reichley, "The Rise of National Parties in John E. Chubb and Paul E. Peterson, eds., *The New Direction in American Politics* (Washington, D.C.: Brookings Institution, 1985), pp. 175–200. The traditional relationship between the president and his party's national committee is discussed in Cotter and Hennessy, *Politics without Power*, pp. 81–94.

18. The national committees may, however, exert considerable influence over the management of a campaign, particularly for nonincumbents, who are most in need of their assistance, through their power to withhold services and funds. See Paul S. Herrnson, *Party Campaigning in the 1980s* (Cambridge, Mass.: Harvard University Press, 1988), p. 59.

19. Herrnson, *Party Campaigning in the 1980s*, pp. 41–42.

20. This observation is made by Reichley, *The Life of the Party*, pp. 377–81. It echoes a challenge to the presumption that local parties are now more effective by John J. Coleman, "The Resurgence of Party Organization? A Dissent from the New Orthodoxy," in Daniel M. Shea and John C. Green, eds., *The State of the Parties* (Lanham, Md.: Rowman and Littlefield, 1994), pp. 311–28.

21. Epstein, *Political Parties in the American Mold*, p. 200.

22. This point is made by Ceaser in "Political Parties—Declining, Stabilizing, or Resurging?" p. 120.

Chapter 5

1. A 1992 national survey of county party organizations conducted by Paul Allen Beck, Russell J. Dalton, Audrey Haynes, and Robert Huckfeldt found that only 24 percent of the county organi-

zations had paid staff and fewer than 4 percent had paid chairs. This is higher than in 1980 when a national survey put these figures at 10 percent and 2 percent, respectively, but it still shows how reliant the local parties are on volunteers. See Cornelius P. Cotter, James L. Gibson, John F. Bibby, and Robert J. Huckshorn, *Party Organizations in American Politics* (New York: Praeger, 1984), pp. 42–43, for a report on the 1980 study.

2. See Peter B. Clark and James Q. Wilson, "Incentive Systems: A Theory of Organizations," *Administrative Science Quarterly* 6 (1961): 129–66, for the original development of this theory; and James Q. Wilson, *The Amateur Democrat* (Chicago: University of Chicago Press, 1960) and *Political Organizations* (New York: Basic Books, 1973), Chapter 6, for the application of this typology to political organizations. Also on this subject, see M. Margaret Conway and Frank B. Feigert, "Motivation, Incentive Systems and the Political Party Organization," *American Political Science Review* 62 (1968): 1159–73.

3. For a lively account of the use of patronage and preferments, see Martin and Susan Tolchin, *To the Victor* (New York: Random House, 1971).

4. Insightful treatments of the development of patronage practices in the United States and attempts to reform them can be found in A. James Reichley, *The Life of the Parties* (New York: Free Press, 1992), pp. 55–56, 67–68, 88–92, and 202–20; Martin Shefter, *Political Parties and the State* (Princeton: Princeton University Press, 1994); and Anne Freedman, *Patronage: An American Tradition* (Chicago: Nelson-Hall, 1994). Shefter contends that the conditions for patronage were especially ripe in the nineteenth-century United States. Lacking the tradition of a strong professional bureaucracy, patronage was used freely by parties in power, especially in American cities, to recruit new voters into their ranks. By contrast, patronage practices never became embedded in those European nations where professional bureaucracies already were established or where, as in the case of the European socialists, the lack of access to government forced parties to appeal to constituents along ideological rather than material lines.

5. These figures are cited in Stephen Skowronek's study of the reform of the federal bureaucracy. See his *Building a New American State* (New York: Cambridge University Press, 1982), p. 69.

6. All are listed in a publication, unofficially known as the "Plum Book" (its official title is *U.S. Government Policy and Supporting Positions*), compiled by the House Committee on Post Office and Civil Service.

7. The 1976 case is *Elrod v. Burns,* 427 U.S. 347; the 1980 case is *Branti v. Finkel,* 445 U.S. 507; and the 1990 case is *Rutan v. Republican Party of Illinois,* 111 L. Ed. 2d 52.

8. For a full account of the Shakman decrees and their effect, see Freedman, *Patronage: An American Tradition,* Chapter 2. The term *patronage army* is hers.

9. On the problems of using patronage, see Frank J. Sorauf, "State Patronage in a Rural County," *American Political Science Review* 50 (1956): 1046–56; W. Robert Gump, "The Functions of Patronage in American Party Politics: An Empirical Reappraisal," *Midwest Journal of Political Science* 15 (1971): 87–107; and Michael Johnston, "Patrons and Clients, Jobs and Machines: A Case Study of the Uses of Patronage," *American Political Science Review* 73 (1979): 385–98.

10. The case for patronage, grounded essentially on its utility for democratic control of the bureaucracy, has been articulated over the years in *The Washington Monthly* and in the dissenting opinions to the Supreme Court's *Elrod, Branti,* and *Rutan* decisions. The case against patronage is well put in Freedman, *Patronage: An American Tradition,* Chapter 5.

11. For the 1979–80 results, see Cotter et al., *Party Organizations in American Politics,* p. 42; the figures on state chairs are for 1962–72 and come from Robert J. Huckshorn, *Party Leadership in the States* (Amherst: University of Massachusetts Press, 1976), p. 37.

12. This point is made by A. James Reichley in *The Life of the Parties,* p. 313.

13. A 1980 collaborative study of local parties in five cities, based on interviews with precinct and ward committee members, found that social incentives figured prominently among the motivations for activity. See the chapters by Richard W. Murray and Kent L. Tedin on Houston (p. 51), Anne H. Hopkins on Nashville (p. 74), Samuel J. Eldersveld on Detroit and Los Angeles (pp. 104–5), and William Crotty on Chicago (p. 174) in William Crotty, ed., *Political Parties in Local Areas* (Knoxville: University of Tennessee Press, 1986). For a general treatment of solidarity incentives, especially in political club life, see Wilson, *The Amateur Democrat.* The importance of solidary incentives is illustrated well in George V. Higgins' novel, *Victories* (New York: Holt, 1991).

14. John Fischer, "Please Don't Bite the Politicians," *Harper's* (November 1960), p. 16. The classic treatment of the psychological roots of political behavior is Harold Lasswell's *Psychopathology and Politics* (Chicago: University of Chicago, 1931).

15. A 1988 study of county leaders of the Bush campaign organization found that 32 percent of them had switched to the GOP from the Democratic party, typically to align their ideological convictions with their party. John A. Clark, John M. Bruce, John H. Kessel, and William Jacoby, "I'd Rather Switch than Fight: Lifelong Democrats and Converts to Republicanism among Campaign Activists," *American Journal of Political Science* 35 (1991): 577–97. Studies of conversions among Democratic and Republican state party convention delegates in 1980 and 1984 corroborate the strong ideological bases of party switching. See Mary Grisez Kweit, "Ideological Congruence of Party Switchers and Nonswitchers: The Case of Party Activists," *American Journal of Political Science* 30 (1986): 184–96; and Dorothy Davidson Nesbit, "Changing Partisanship among Southern Party Activists," *Journal of Politics* 50 (1988): 322–34.

16. Samuel Eldersveld, *Political Parties: A Behavioral Analysis* (Chicago: Rand McNally, 1964), p. 278 and Chapter 11.

17. Lewis Bowman, Dennis Ippolito, and William Donaldson,"Incentives for the Maintenance of Grassroots Political Activism," *Midwest Journal of Political Science* 13 (1969): 126–39; Charles W. Wiggins and William L. Turk, "State Party Chairmen: A Profile," *Western Political Quarterly* 23 (1970): 321–32; Conway and Feigert, "Motivation, Incentive Systems and the Political Party Organization;" Dwaine Marvick, "Party Organizational Personnel and Electoral Democracy in Los Angeles, 1963–1972," in William Crotty, ed., *The Party Symbol: Readings on Political Parties* (San Francisco: Freeman, 1980), pp. 63–86; Barbara C. Burrell, "Local Political Party Committees, Task Performance and Organizational Vitality," *Western Political Quarterly* 39 (1986): 48–66; and the various city studies contained in Crotty, *Political Parties in Local Areas.*

18. The fact that Eldersveld finds little change between 1956 and 1980 in the incentives for party activity (except the expected declines in party loyalty) in Detroit and Los Angeles, though, should rein in sweeping generalizations about motivational change. It is possible that what may distinguish modern from traditional party workers is the direction of their ideology, not its intensity. See Samuel J. Eldersveld, "The Party Activist in Detroit and Los Angeles: A Longitudinal View, 1956–1980," in Crotty, *Political Parties in Local Areas,* Chapter 4.

19. Among others, see Conway and Feigert, "Motivation, Incentive Systems, and the Political Organization."

20. Phillip Althoff and Samuel C. Patterson, "Political Activism in a Rural County," *Midwest Journal of Political Science* 10 (1966): 39–51; Lewis Bowman and G. R. Boynton, "Recruitment Patterns among Local Party Officials," *American Political Science Review* 60 (1966): 667–76; and Samuel J. Eldersveld, *Political Parties in American Society* (New York: Basic Books, 1982), p. 175.

21. Paul Allen Beck and M. Kent Jennings found that strong conservatives were the most active participants in the 1956, 1960, and 1964 campaigns but that strong liberals matched their activism in 1968 and then surpassed it from 1972 through 1980. See their "Political Periods and Political Participation," *American Political Science Review* 73 (1979): 737–50, and "Updating Political Periods and Political Participation," *American Political Science Review* 78 (1984): 198–201. Steven E. Finkel and Gregory Trevor, "Reassessing Ideological Bias in Campaign Participation," *Political Behavior* 8 (1986): 374–90, attribute the hyperactivity of strong liberals in 1984 to the competitiveness of the Democratic primaries that year.

22. For similar theories of recruitment, see Bowman and Boynton, "Recruitment Patterns;" and C. Richard Hofstetter, "Organizational Activists: The Bases of Participation in Amateur and Professional Groups," *American Politics Quarterly* 1 (1973): 244–76.

23. Eldersveld, *Political Parties,* pp. 142–43.

24. Cotter et al., *Party Organizations in American Politics,* p. 42.

25. On the prominence of lawyers in American politics, see Heinz Eulau and John D. Sprague, *Lawyers in Politics* (Indianapolis: Bobbs-Merrill, 1964).

26. The relatively high status of party activists is documented in Sidney Verba and Norman H. Nie, *Participation in America* (New York: Harper Row, 1972), Chapter 8, for campaign activists; in Crotty, *Political Parties in Local Areas,* pp. 45, 72, 94–95, 162–63, and Cotter et al., *Party Orga-*

nizations in American Politics, p. 42, for local leaders; in Wiggins and Turk, "State Party Chairman: A Profile," for state chairmen; in Ronald Rapoport, Alan I. Abramowitz, and John McGlennon, *The Life of the Parties* (Lexington: The University of Kentucky Press, 1986), Chapter 3, for state convention delegates; and in Warren E. Miller and M. Kent Jennings, *Parties in Transition* (New York: Russell Sage Foundation, 1986), pp. 67–85, for national convention delegates. For many years, Republican activists came from higher SES groups than did their Democratic counterparts, reflecting the social-class differences between the two party coalitions. These differences have considerably narrowed in recent years.

27. Michael Margolis and Raymond E. Owen, "From Organization to Personalism: A Note on the Transmogrification of the Local Political Party," *Polity* 18 (1985): 313–28.

28. These assertions are supported by a potpourri of data. See Martin Plissner and Warren J. Mitofsky, "The Making of the Delegates, 1968–1988," *Public Opinion* 11 (September/October 1988): 45–47, on characteristics of delegates to the national nominating conventions through 1988; data from *The New York Times* survey of convention delegates in 1992 show that the Democrats remained highly atypical of the rank and file of their party and more like Republicans in both income and education. See Cotter et al., *Party Organizations in American Politics,* p. 42, and the 1988 study of presidential campaign leaders conducted by John Kessel and William Jacoby on the characteristics of the county chairs.

29. This distinction between amateurs and professionals is developed in Clark and Wilson, "Incentive Systems;" Wilson, *The Amateur Democrat;* Aaron Wildavsky, "The Goldwater Phenomenon: Purists, Politicians, and the Two-Party System," *The Review of Politics* 27 (1965): 386–413; and John W. Soule and James W. Clarke, "Amateurs and Professionals: A Study of Delegates to the 1968 Democratic National Convention," *American Political Science Review* 64 (1970): 888–98.

30. Walter J. Stone and Alan I. Abramowitz, "Winning May Not Be Everything But It's More Than We Thought: Presidential Party Activists in 1980," *American Political Science Review* 77 (1983): 945–56.

31. Michael A. Maggiotto and Ronald E. Weber, "The Impact of Organizational Incentives on County Party Chairpersons," *American Politics Quarterly* 14 (1986): 201–18.

32. The 1992 national survey of county party organizations was conducted by Paul Allen Beck, Russell J. Dalton, Audrey Haynes, and Robert Huckfeldt.

33. On traditional differences among organizational activists, see Robert H. Salisbury, "The Urban Party Organization Member," *Public Opinion Quarterly* 29 (1965–66): 562, 564; Lewis Bowman and G. R. Boynton, "Activities and Role Definitions of Grass Roots Party Officials," *Journal of Politics* 28 (1966): 132–34; Eldersveld, *Political Parties,* p. 348; and Burrell, "Local Political Party Committees . . . ".

34. On the effects of party effort, see Phillips Cutright and Peter Rossi, "Grass Roots Politicians and the Vote," *American Sociological Review* 63 (1958): 171–79; Daniel Katz and Samuel J. Eldersveld, "The Impact of Local Party Activity upon the Electorate," *Public Opinion Quarterly* 25 (1961): 1–24; Raymond E. Wolfinger, "The Influence of Precinct Work on Voting Behavior," *Public Opinion Quarterly* 27 (1963): 387–98; Gerald H. Kramer, "The Effects of Precinct-Level Canvassing on Voter Behavior," *Public Opinion Quarterly* 34 (1970–71): 560–72; William J. Crotty, "Party Effort and Its Impact on the Vote," *American Political Science Review* 65 (1971): 439–50; David E. Price and Michael Lupfer, "Volunteers for Gore: The Impact of a Precinct-Level Canvass in Three Tennessee Cities," *Journal of Politics* 35 (1973): 410–38; and John P. Frendreis, James L. Gibson, and Laura L. Vertz, "The Electoral Relevance of Local Party Organizations," *American Political Science Review* 84 (1990): 225–35.

35. See Daniel Elazar, *American Federalism: A View from the States* (New York: Crowell, 1972), Chapter 4, for the distribution of individualistic, moralistic, and traditionalistic political cultures throughout the nation.

36. V. O. Key, Jr., *American State Politics* (New York: Knopf, 1956), Chapter 6.

37. The most notable fictionalized accounts of real-life "bosses" are to be found in Edwin O'Connor, *The Last Hurrah* (Boston: Little, Brown, 1956); and Robert Penn Warren, *All the King's Men* (New York: Harcourt, Brace, 1946). See also William L. Riordon, *Plunkitt of Tammany Hall* (New York: Dutton, 1963; first published in 1906).

38. Wilson, *The Amateur Democrat,* Chap. 5. These reform orientations sometimes are rooted as much in the deprivations of being out of power as in principled opposition to the concentration of power in a political machine. For some evidence of this in a Chicago reform club, see David L. Protess and Alan R. Gitelson, "Political Stability, Reform Clubs, and the Amateur Democrat," in William Crotty, ed., *The Party Symbol* (San Francisco: Freeman, 1980), pp. 87–100.

39. This theory is elaborated in Anthony Downs, *An Economic Theory of Democracy* (New York: Harper & Row, 1965).

40. Key, *American State Politics;* and Walter Dean Burnham, *Critical Elections and the Mainsprings of American Politics* (New York: Norton, 1970), p. 75.

41. Robert Michels, *Political Parties* (Glencoe, Ill.: Free Press, 1949; originally published in 1915), p. 32.

42. The quotations in this paragraph come from Eldersveld, *Political Parties,* pp. 99–100.

Part Three

1. The different wordings of partisanship questions, especially the different time horizons imposed by using "as of today" versus "generally speaking," seem to have only minor effects on the estimated levels of partisanship and its stability over time even though the "as of today" prompt shows slightly more sensitivity to current political events. See George Bishop, Alfred J. Tuchfarber, and Andrew E. Smith and Paul Abramson and Charles W. Ostrom, "Question Form and Context Effects in the Measurement of Partisanship: Experimental Tests of the Artifact Hypothesis," *American Political Science Review* 88 (1994): 945–58.

2. The concept of party identification and the most familiar measure of it were introduced in Angus Campbell, Philip E. Converse, Warren E. Miller, and Donald E. Stokes, *The American Voter* (New York: Wiley, 1960), Chapter 6.

3. For an examination of some alternatives in identifying party adherents, see Everett C. Ladd and Charles D. Hadley, "Party Definition and Party Differentiation," *Public Opinion Quarterly* 37 (1973): 21–34; and Steven E. Finkel and Howard A. Scarrow, "Party Identification and Party Enrollment: The Difference and the Consequence," *Journal of Politics* 47 (1985): 620–42.

Chapter 6

1. The most common definition of a *realignment,* and the one adopted here, involves changes in the party coalitions or parties in the electorate. For elaborations of this conceptualization, see V. O. Key, Jr., "A Theory of Critical Elections," *Journal of Politics* 17 (1955): 3–18; Walter Dean Burnham, *Critical Elections and the Mainsprings of American Politics* (New York: Norton, 1970); and James L. Sundquist, *Dynamics of the Party System* (Washington, D.C.: Brookings Institution, 1973). For one alternative view of what constitutes a realignment, see Jerome M. Clubb, William H. Flanigan, and Nancy H. Zingale, *Partisan Realignment: Voters, Parties, and Government in American History* (Beverly Hills, Calif.: Sage, 1980). They emphasize the importance of control of the national government in defining a realignment. Each of the party systems we have designated began with more than a decade of unbroken unified control of the national government by the new majority party. Another view is that realignment is elite rather than mass based—the product of the changing party loyalties of American industrial and business interests. See Thomas Ferguson, *Golden Rule: The Investment Theory of Party Competition and the Logic of Money-driven Political Systems* (Chicago: University of Chicago Press, 1995).

2. Because aggregate election returns (typically reported on county or state units) reflect differential levels of turnout, candidate appeal, and issue salience in the short term as well as long-term party loyalties and portray geographical divisions of the electorate more clearly than coalitions built upon class and other lines, these data do not always sharply define realignment periods and the ensuing party systems and must be interpreted in conjunction with other political patterns.

3. Not all scholars are persuaded that the notion of periodic party realignments captures the essence of American electoral change, especially in recent years. These doubts are expressed in the essays by Joel Silbey, Everett Carll Ladd, Byron Shafer, and Samuel T. McSeveney in Byron E.

Shafer, ed., *The End of Realignment? Interpreting American Electoral Eras* (Madison: University of Wisconsin Press, 1991). See also Allan J. Lichtman, "The End of Realignment Theory— Toward a New Research Program for American Political History," *Historical Methods* 15 (1982): 170–88; and, for a view that the important changes are subnational rather than national in scope, Peter F. Nardulli, "The Concept of a Critical Realignment, Electoral Behavior, and Political Change," *American Political Science Review* 89 (1955): 10–22.

4. For similar periodizations of American political history from the realignment perspective, see Burnham, *Critical Elections;* William Nisbet Chambers and Walter Dean Burnham, eds., *The American Party Systems* (New York: Oxford University Press, 1967); Clubb, Flanigan, and Zingale, *Partisan Realignment;* Charles Sellers, "The Equilibrium Cycle in Two-Party Politics," *Public Opinion Quarterly* 30 (1965): 16–38; and Sundquist, *Dynamics of the Party System.*

5. Because the realignments that transform one party system into another take place during a period of time rather than occur sharply, the exact beginning and end of a party system can not be reduced to a single year. For convenience, though, the beginning of each party system must be located at a particular time—the year in which the new majority party coalition first took office (having been elected at the end of the previous year) to begin the period of undisputed control of government which began each of the first five party systems.

6. In the two-party competition that has characterized the American party system since its inception, these coalitions are never simple or predictable on issue grounds. What gave the Democrats their dominance was the unification of their western, populist supporters with the New York political organization run by Martin Van Buren, who was attracted to the party because of interstate rivalries and the promise of political patronage. Such odd alliances have been a hallmark of the American two-party system.

7. From the end of the Civil War in 1865 through 1876, Democratic voting strength in the South was held in check by the occupation Union army and various Reconstruction policies and laws. Thus, in presenting party control figures that reflect the true party balance during the third party system, it is necessary to differentiate between 1861–76 and the more representative 1877–96 period.

8. Comprehensive treatments of the different party systems may be found in Paul Goodman, "The First Party System," in Chambers and Burnham, *The American Party Systems,* pp. 59–89; Richard McCormick, *The Second American Party System: Party Formation in the Jacksonian Era* (Chapel Hill: University of North Carolina Press, 1966); and, for the party systems since the 1850s, Sundquist, *Dynamics of the Party System.* Especially valuable (because they are used to explain why parties emerge and change) accounts of the development of the first three party systems may be found in John H. Aldrich, *Why Parties? The Origin and Transformation of Party Politics in America* (Chicago: University of Chicago Press, 1995), Chapters 3–5.

9. See Paul Allen Beck, "The Electoral Cycle and Patterns of American Politics," *British Journal of Political Science* 9 (1979): 129–56. This view of recent nonpartisanship as largely a result of neutrality toward the parties rather than negative rejection of them is developed in Martin P. Wattenberg, *The Decline of American Political Parties, 1952–92* (Cambridge: Harvard University Press, 1994). For evidence that Americans also have become more negative toward the parties, see Stephen C. Craig, "The Decline of Partisanship in the United States: A Reexamination of the Neutrality Hypothesis," *Political Behavior* 7 (1985): 57–78.

10. Burnham, *Critical Elections,* Chapters 4 and 5.

11. The seminal work on party identification is based on survey data from the 1952 and 1956 elections. See Angus Campbell, Philip E. Converse, Warren E. Miller, and Donald E. Stokes, *The American Voter* (New York: Wiley, 1960). Since this first full-gauged presidential-year survey in 1952, scholars at the University of Michigan have continued to conduct surveys of the American electorate in presidential and midterm election years, most recently under National Science Foundation auspices as the American National Election Studies (ANES).

12. This description of the changes in partisanship since 1952 is justified regardless of whether partisans are defined as strong identifiers, strong plus weak identifiers, or all respondents who indicate some kind of preference for one of the parties.

13. Paul Allen Beck and M. Kent Jennings, "Family Traditions, Political Periods, and the Development of Partisan Orientations," *Journal of Politics* 53 (1991): 742–63.

14. Fred I. Greenstein, *Children and Politics* (New Haven: Yale University Press, 1965). See also Robert D. Hess and Judith V. Torney, *The Development of Political Attitudes in Children* (Chicago: Aldine, 1967), especially pp. 80–81.

15. For recent evidence on the partisan homogeneity of social networks, see Robert Huckfeldt and John Sprague, *Citizens, Politics, and Social Communication* (New York: Cambridge University Press, 1995), especially Chapter 7; and Robert Huckfeldt and Paul Allen Beck, "Contexts, Intermediaries, and Political Behavior," in Lawrence C. Dodd and Calvin Jillson, eds., *The Dynamics of American Politics: Approaches and Limitations* (Boulder, Colo.: Westview Press, 1994), pp. 252–76.

16. Arthur S. Goldberg, "Social Determinism and Rationality As Bases of Party Identification," *American Political Science Review* 63 (1969): 5–25.

17. Morris P. Fiorina, *Retrospective Voting in American National Elections* (New Haven: Yale University Press, 1981), p. 102. For an application of retrospective voting theory to recent elections, see Paul R. Abramson, John H. Aldrich, and David W. Rohde, *Change and Continuity in the 1992 Elections* (Washington, D.C.: Congressional Quarterly Press, 1995), especially Chapter 7. For an analysis of the role contemporary issues may play in disrupting the transmission of partisanship from parents to children, see Robert C. Luskin, John P. McIver, and Edward G. Carmines, "Issues and the Transmission of Partisanship," *American Journal of Political Science* 33 (1989): 440–58; and Richard G. Niemi and M. Kent Jennings, "Issues and Inheritance in the Formation of Party Identification," *American Journal of Political Science* 35: 970–88.

18. See William Claggett, "Partisan Acquisition vs. Partisan Intensity: Life-Cycle, Generational, and Period Effects," *American Journal of Political Science* 25 (1981): 193–214. On how much partisanship strengthens as the voter ages, see Philip E. Converse, *The Dynamics of Party Support* (Beverly Hills, Calif.: Sage, 1976); Paul R. Abramson, "Developing Party Identification: A Further Examination of Life-Cycle, Generational, and Period Effects," *American Journal of Political Science* 23 (1979): 78–96; and W. Phillips Shively, "The Development of Party Identification among Adults," *American Political Science Review* 73 (1979): 1039–54.

19. For the view that realignments are attributable to mobilization of the young and other new voters, see Kristi Andersen, *The Creation of a Democratic Majority 1928–1936* (Chicago: University of Chicago Press, 1979); Paul Allen Beck, "A Socialization Theory of Partisan Realignment," in Richard G. Niemi, ed., *The Politics of Future Citizens* (San Francisco: Jossey-Bass, 1974), pp. 199–219; and James E. Campbell, "Sources of the New Deal Realignment: The Contributions of Conversion and Mobilization to Partisan Change," *Western Political Quarterly* 38 (1985): 357–76. For an alternative view, emphasizing partisan conversions among older voters, see Robert S. Erikson and Kent L. Tedin, "The 1928–1936 Partisan Realignment: The Case for the Conversion Hypothesis," *American Political Science Review* 75 (1981): 951–63. The role of the young in contemporary partisan change is discussed in Helmut Norpoth and Jerrold G. Rusk, "Partisan Dealignment in the American Electorate: Itemizing the Deductions Since 1964," *American Political Science Review* 76 (1982): 522–37; and Warren E. Miller, "Generational Changes and Party Identification," *Political Behavior* 14 (1992): 333–52.

20. For a comprehensive treatment of these various cleavages, see Seymour Martin Lipset and Stein Rokkan, "Cleavage Structures, Party Systems, and Voting Alignments," in Seymour Martin Lipset and Stein Rokkan, eds., *Party Systems and Voter Alignments* (New York: Free Press, 1967), pp. 1–67.

21. The classic statement of the role of social class in the elections of the western democracies appears in Seymour Martin Lipset, *Political Man* (New York: Doubleday, 1960), especially Chapter 7. Also see Richard Hamilton, *Class and Politics in the United States* (New York: Wiley, 1972).

22. See Madison's *Federalist* 10: "The most common and durable source of factions has been the various and unequal distribution of property."

23. See Robert A. Alford, *Party and Society* (Chicago: Rand McNally, 1963); and Russell J. Dalton, Scott C. Flanagan, and Paul Allen Beck, eds., *Electoral Change in Advanced Industrial Democracies* (Princeton, N.J.: Princeton University Press, 1984). For an appraisal of class voting in the western world during the past century from the perspective of working-class support for a left-

wing party, see Adam Przeworski and John Sprague, *Paper Stones: A History of Electoral Socialism* (Chicago: University of Chicago Press, 1986).

24. So powerful have these southern ties to the Democratic party been that some voters, termed *split-level partisans,* have retained their Democratic loyalties in state and local politics even after rejecting them for the purpose of national politics. For more on this phenomenon, see Charles D. Hadley, "Dual Partisan Identification in the South," *Journal of Politics* 47 (1985): 254–68; and Richard G. Niemi, Stephen Wright, and Lynda W. Powell, "Multiple Party Identifiers and the Measurement of Party Identification," *Journal of Politics* 49 (1987): 1093–1104.

25. Richard Rose and Derek Urwin have shown that religion rivals social class as a basis for partisan loyalties in the western democracies. See their "Social Cohesion, Political Parties and Strains in Regimes," *Comparative Political Studies* 2 (1967): 7–67.

26. Lawrence Fuchs, *The Political Behavior of the American Jews* (Glencoe, Ill.: Free Press, 1956). For a somewhat more recent treatment, see Milton Himmelfarb, "The Case of Jewish Liberalism," in Seymour Martin Lipset, ed., *Emerging Coalitions in American Politics* (San Francisco: Institute for Contemporary Studies, 1978), pp. 297–305.

27. See Ted G. Jelen, *The Political Mobilization of Religious Belief* (Westport, Conn.: Praeger, 1991); David C. Leege and Lyman A. Kellstedt, eds., *Rediscovering the Religious Factor in American Politics* (Armonk, N.Y.: M.E. Sharpe, 1993); and Kenneth D. Wald, *Religion and Politics in the United States* (New York: St. Martin's, 1987).

28. On black political behavior, see Patricia Gurin, Shirley Hatchett, and James S. Jackson, *Hope and Independence: Blacks' Response to Electoral and Party Politics* (New York: Russell Sage Foundation, 1989); and Katherine Tate, *From Protest to Politics* (Cambridge, Mass.: Harvard University Press, 1994).

29. The gender gap in presidential voting widened in the 1992 election in comparison with the contest between Bush and Dukakis four years before. See Paul R. Abramson, John H. Aldrich, and David W. Rohde, *Change and Continuity in the 1992 Elections* (Washington, D.C.: Congressional Quarterly Press, 1995), pp. 136–37. On the gender gap in 1992, see Elizabeth Adell Cook and Clyde Wilcox, "Women Voters in the 'Year of the Woman'," in Herbert F. Weisberg, ed., *Democracy's Feast* (Chatham, NJ: Chatham House, 1995), 195–219.

30. Data from 1960 are more appropriate for this comparison than data from 1964, when the Democratic landslide victory produced a temporary surge in Democratic partisanship across most of the social groups. The 1960 figures are taken from Warren E. Miller and Santa A. Traugott, *American National Election Studies Sourcebook, 1952–1986* (Cambridge, Mass.: Harvard University Press, 1989).

31. On social group changes in the party coalitions in recent years, see John R. Petrocik, *Party Coalitions* (Chicago: University of Chicago Press, 1981); Robert Axelrod, "Where the Votes Come From: An Analysis of Electoral Coalitions, 1952–1968," *American Political Science Review* 66 (1972): 11–20, and "Presidential Election Coalitions in 1984," *American Political Science Review* 80 (1986): 281–90; and Harold W. Stanley and Richard G. Niemi, "The Demise of the New Deal Coalition: Partisanship and Group Support, 1952–1992," in Weisberg, *Democracy's Feast,* pp. 220–40. Stanley and Niemi, in particular, feel that the New Deal coalition has eroded so much that it no longer exists.

32. For demonstrations of how attitudinal and behavioral deviance from one's partisanship can undermine it, see Fiorina, *Retrospective Voting in American National Elections;* and Benjamin I. Page and Calvin C. Jones, "Reciprocal Effects of Policy Preferences, Party Loyalties and the Vote," *American Political Science Review* 73 (1979): 1071–89.

33. On this point, see David O. Sears, Richard R. Lau, Tom R. Tyler, and Harris M. Allen, Jr., "Self-Interest vs. Symbolic Politics in Policy Attitudes and Presidential Voting," *American Political Science Review* 74 (1980): 670–84. For an alternative view, see Paul Sniderman and Thomas Piazza, *The Scar of Race* (Cambridge, Mass.: Harvard University Press, 1993).

34. For a discussion of the cross-cutting nature of some of these issues, see Warren E. Miller and Teresa E. Levitin, *Leadership and Change: The New Politics and the American Electorate* (Cambridge, Mass.: Winthrop, 1976).

35. For more on the case for dealignment, see Paul Allen Beck, "Incomplete Realignment: The Reagan Legacy for Parties and Elections," in Charles O. Jones, ed., *The Reagan Legacy* (Chatham,

N.J.: Chatham House, 1988); Walter Dean Burnham, *The Current Crisis in American Politics* (New York: Oxford University Press, 1982); and Wattenberg, *The Decline of American Political Parties.*

36. The Watergate affair began in 1972 with the arrest of burglars with ties to the Nixon reelection campaign for breaking into the offices of the Democratic National Committee and culminated with the resignation of President Nixon in the face of sure impeachment by the House of Representatives for trying to cover up his role. The unpopularity of the subsequent pardon of Nixon by his former vice-president and successor Gerald Ford played a key role in the 1976 presidential campaign and may have cost Ford the presidency.

37. For more on the case for realignment, see John Aldrich, *Why Parties: The Origin and Transformation of Party Politics in America* (Chicago: University of Chicago Press, 1995), Chapter 8; Earl Black and Merle Black, *Politics and Society in the South* (Cambridge, Mass.: Harvard University Press, 1987); and Edward G. Carmines and James A. Stimson, *Issue Evolution* (Princeton, N.J.: Princeton University Press, 1989).

38. On the party loyalties of the young, see Helmut Norpoth, "Under Way and Here to Stay: Party Realignment in the 1980s?" *Public Opinion Quarterly* 51 (1987): 376–91; and Warren E. Miller, "Party Identification, Realignment, and Party Voting: Back to Basics," *American Political Science Review* 85 (1991): 557–70.

39. The ANES figures from immediately after the 1994 midterm election were 34.3 percent weak and strong Democrats, 30.4 percent weak and strong Republicans, and 35.3 percent independents.

Chapter 7

1. See John R. Petrocik, "An Analysis of the Intransitivities in the Index of Party Identification," *Political Methodology* 1 (1974): 31–47; Ralph W. Bastedo and Milton Lodge, "The Meaning of Party Labels," *Political Behavior* 2 (1980): 287–308; and Herbert F. Weisberg, "A Multidimensional Conceptualization of Party Identification," *Political Behavior* 2 (1980): 33–60.

2. Paul Allen Beck, "The Dealignment Era in America," in Russell J. Dalton, Scott C. Flanagan, and Paul Allen Beck, eds., *Electoral Change in Advanced Industrial Democracies* (Princeton, N.J.: Princeton University Press, 1964), pp. 244–46.

3. Philip E. Converse and Gregory B. Markus, *"Plus ça change. . . :* The New CPS Election Study Panel," *American Political Science Review* 73 (1979): 32–49. Even greater stability in partisanship, as expected because of the shorter time period, was found from January to November during the 1980 presidential campaign. See Donald Philip Green and Bradley Palmquist, "Of Artifacts and Partisan Instability," *American Journal of Political Science* 34 (1990): 872–902, and "How Stable is Party Identification?" *Political Behavior* 16 (1994): 437–66.

4. On the political impact of the psychological processes of projection and persuasion, see Bernard R. Berelson, Paul F. Lazarsfeld, and William N. McPhee, *Voting* (Chicago: University of Chicago Press, 1954), pp. 215–33; and Benjamin I. Page and Richard A. Brody, "Policy Voting and the Electoral Process: The Vietnam War Issue," *American Political Science Review* 66 (1972): 979–95.

5. Donald E. Stokes, "Some Dynamic Elements of Contests for the Presidency," *American Political Science Review* 60 (1966): 23.

6. In this respect, partisanship functions as an information shortcut, or what social psychologists call a heuristic, for making sense of the complex political world. On the use of shortcuts in voter decision making, see Samuel L. Popkin, *The Reasoning Voter* (Chicago: University of Chicago Press, 1991), Chapter 3. On the importance of party as a shortcut in candidate evaluations, see Pamela J. Conover and Stanley Feldman, "Candidate Perceptions in an Ambiguous World: Campaigns, Cues, and Inference Processes," *American Journal of Political Science* 33 (1989): 912–40; and Wendy M. Rahn, "The Role of Partisan Stereotypes in Information Processing about Political Candidates," *American Journal of Political Science* 37 (1993): 472–96.

7. Roberta A. Sigel, "Effects of Partisanship on the Perception of Political Candidates," *Public Opinion Quarterly* 28 (1964): 483–96.

8. See Morris Fiorina, *Retrospective Voting in American National Elections* (New Haven, Conn.: Yale University Press, 1981); Benjamin I. Page and Calvin C. Jones, "Reciprocal Effects of Policy Preferences, Party Loyalties and the Vote," *American Political Science Review* 73 (1979): 1071–89; and Michael B. MacKuen, Robert S. Erikson, and James A. Stimson, "Macropartisanship," *American Political Science Review* 83 (1989): 1125–42.

9. Arthur H. Miller, "Partisan Cognitions in Transition," in Richard R. Lau and David O. Sears, eds., *Political Cognition* (Hillsdale, N.J.: Erlbaum, 1986), Chapter 9.

10. An examination of patterns across the ballot in voting for five state executive offices in Ohio found party identification to be the principal predictor of straight-ticket voting. See Paul Allen Beck, Lawrence Baum, Aage R. Clausen, and Charles E. Smith, Jr., "Patterns and Sources of Ticket Splitting in Subpresidential Voting," *American Political Science Review* 86 (1992): 916–28.

11. The unexpectedly greater partisan voting of the independent identifiers compared to the weak partisans, and similar "intransitivities" in the relationship between partisanship and political involvement shown later, are commonly cited as evidence of the weakness of the party-identification measure. This anomaly may appear because independents asked to indicate which party is closer will name the one for which they intend to vote that year. A truer indication of their partisan strength, instead, is found in their straight-ticket voting patterns. For a persuasive case that the independent leaners are really partisans, see Bruce E. Keith, David B. Magleby, Candice J. Nelson, Elizabeth Orr, Mark Westlye, and Raymond E. Wolfinger, *The Myth of the Independent Voter* (Berkeley, Cal.: University of California Press, 1992).

12. Beck, Baum, Clausen, and Smith, "Patterns and Sources of Ticket Splitting in Subpresidential Voting."

13. Philip E. Converse, "The Concept of a Normal Vote," in Angus Campbell, Philip E. Converse, Warren E. Miller, and Donald E. Stokes, eds., *Elections and the Political Order* (New York: Wiley, 1966), pp. 9–39.

14. *Split-ticket voting,* defined as supporting candidates from different parties on the same ballot, also has been higher since the mid-1960s than it was in the 1950s for both president-House and Senate-House combinations. See Martin P. Wattenberg, *The Decline of American Political Parties: 1952–1992* (Cambridge, Mass.: Harvard University Press, 1994), Chapters 9 and 10.

15. See Norman H. Nie, Sidney Verba, and John R. Petrocik, *The Changing American Voter* (Cambridge: Harvard University Press, 1976), Chapters 10, 16, and 20 (especially pp. 373–78); and Frederick Hartwig, William R. Jenkins, and Earl M. Temchin, "Variability in Electoral Behavior: The 1960, 1968, and 1976 Elections," *American Journal of Political Science* 24 (1980): 353–58.

16. For the classic view, see Angus Campbell, Philip E. Converse, Warren E. Miller, and Donald E. Stokes, *The American Voter* (New York: Wiley, 1960); and Arthur S. Goldberg, "Discerning a Causal Pattern among Data on Voting Behavior," *American Political Science Review* 60 (1966): 913–22.

17. Page and Jones, "Reciprocal Effects of Policy Preferences, Party Loyalties and the Vote."

18. Gregory B. Markus and Philip E. Converse, "A Dynamic Simultaneous Equation Model of Electoral Choice," *American Political Science Review* 73 (1979): 1055–70.

19. Overall turnout in 1992 among citizens of voting age was estimated at 58.5 percent. Reported turnout levels in the 1992 ANES survey are considerably higher for reasons specified in Chapter 8.

20. These differences are documented in Paul R. Abramson, John H. Aldrich, and David W. Rohde, *Change and Continuity in the 1992 Elections* (Washington, D.C.: CQ Press, 1995), Chapter 8, especially Figure 8–1 and Tables 8–5 to 8–7.

21. On similar Republican hyperactivity in the 1960s, see Verba and Nie, *Participation in America,* (New York: Harper & Row, 1972), Chapter 12. The varying relationships between ideology and campaign activity over a longer period are examined in Paul Allen Beck and M. Kent Jennings, "Political Periods and Political Participation," *American Political Science Review* 73 (1979): 737–50.

22. For comparisons of the support for Wallace, Anderson, and Perot among white party identifiers, see Abramson, Aldrich, and Rohde, *Change and Continuity in the 1992 Elections,* Table 8–9, p. 245. For more on the Perot candidacy, see Herb Asher, "The Perot Campaign," in Herbert F. Weisberg, ed., *Democracy's Feast* (Chatham, N.J.: Chatham House, 1995), Chapter 6.

23. Although it is easy to picture independents as providing a ready constituency for a new party or independent candidacy, the truth is that their heterogeneity on issues and in other sources of political orientation makes them an unlikely electoral coalition. On their heterogeneity, see Keith, Magleby, Nelson, Orr, Westlye, and Wolfinger, *The Myth of the Independent Voter.*

24. See Keith, Magleby, Nelson, Orr, Westlye, and Wolfinger, *The Myth of the Independent Voter.* The myth of independence as the posture toward politics of the highly informed, sophisticated voter (in contrast to the slavish partisan) is effectively laid to rest for the 1952 and 1956 elections by Campbell, Converse, Miller, and Stokes, in *The American Voter.*

25. V. O. Key, Jr. (with the assistance of Milton C. Cummings), *The Responsible Electorate* (Cambridge: Harvard University Press, 1966).

26. The necessity of revisions in the portrait of independents is largely obscured when independent leaners and pure independents are combined, as was the case in *The American Voter.* When they are treated as separate categories, the attitudinal and behavioral differences among them and thereby the distinction between two types of independents becomes clear. See Petrocik, "An Analysis of Intransitivities in the Index of Party Identification," pp. 31–47; and Keith, Magleby, Nelson, Orr, Westlye, and Wolfinger, *The Myth of the Independent Voter.*

27. V. O. Key and Frank Munger characterized the century-long stable voting patterns of Indiana counties as "standing decisions" to support a particular party. See their "Social Determinism and Electoral Decision," in Eugene Burdick and Arthur J. Brodbeck, eds., *American Voting Behavior* (Glencoe, Ill.: Free Press, 1959), pp. 281–99.

28. See Martin P. Wattenberg, *The Rise of Candidate-Centered Politics: Presidential Elections of the 1980s* (Cambridge, Mass.: Harvard University Press, 1991); and Morris P. Fiorina, "The Electorate at the Polls in the 1990s," in L. Sandy Maisel, ed., *The Parties Respond* (Boulder, Colo.: Westview, 1994), pp. 123–42.

Chapter 8

1. Because of the difficulties in estimating American turnout, most "official" turnout figures *underestimate* it. The figures cited here, compiled by Walter Dean Burnham, carefully correct for this underestimation and, consequently, will be higher than the widely reported turnout figures. Their denominator is based on the adult population of voting age minus the number of aliens restricted from voting by state law, which since 1924 has included all aliens. The numerator of the turnout fraction is the number of voters who cast a vote for president or for the office with the highest vote in midterm elections. Estimated turnout would be slightly higher if there was a reliable way to include in the numerator blank or spoiled ballots, write-in votes for the office with the highest vote total, and voters who did not vote for that office and to exclude from the denominator citizens who are ineligible under the laws of the various states because they are institutionalized in prisons or mental hospitals. For a discussion of the pitfalls in estimating turnout, see Walter Dean Burnham, "The Turnout Problem," in A. James Reichley, ed., *Elections American Style* (Washington, DC: Brookings Institution, 1987), pp. 97–133, especially footnote 1.

2. On the normative problems nonvoting may pose for democracy, see Benjamin Barber, *Strong Democracy: Participatory Politics for a New Age* (Berkeley: University of California Press, 1994). For an empirical examination of some of these normative issues, and a discounting of the threat to democracy posed by nonvoters, see Stephen Earl Bennett and David Resnick, "The Implications of Nonvoting for Democracy in the United States," *American Journal of Political Science* 34 (1990): 771–802.

3. The classic examination of turnout over the course of American history is Walter Dean Burnham, "The Changing Shape of the American Political Universe," *American Political Science Review* 59 (1965): 7–28.

4. Data on turnout in other democracies are presented and analyzed in G. Bingham Powell, Jr., "American Voter Turnout in Comparative Perspective," *American Political Science Review* 80 (1986): 17–44. Also see Burnham, "The Turnout Problem," p. 107. Only Switzerland has had lower national turnout levels than the United States, but national elections are less important than local contests there.

5. On the early development of the American electorate, see Chilton Williamson, *American Suffrage: From Property to Democracy* (Princeton, N.J.: Princeton University Press, 1960).

6. The Supreme Court case overturning the poll tax was *Harper v. Virginia State Board of Elections,* 383 U.S. 633 (1966).

7. *Oregon v. Mitchell,* 400 U.S. 112 (1970).

8. The legal and constitutional issues involved in defining the electorate through the 1960s are covered in Richard Claude, *The Supreme Court and the Electoral Process* (Baltimore: The John Hopkins University Press, 1970).

9. See Stephen Knack, "Does 'Motor Voter' Work? Evidence from State-Level Data," *Journal of Politics* 57 (1995): 796–811.

10. Paul Kleppner, *Continuity and Change in Electoral Politics, 1893–1928* (Westport, Conn.: Greenwood Press, 1987), pp. 165–66.

11. The landmark Supreme Court cases dealing with residency requirements are *Dunn v. Blumstein,* 405 U.S. 330 (1972); and *Burns v. Fortson,* 410 U.S. 686 (1973).

12. U.S. Bureau of the Census, *Statistical Abstract of the United States,* 113th edition (Washington, D.C.: U.S. Government Printing Office, 1993), Table 34, p. 32.

13. Peverill Squire, Raymond E. Wolfinger, and David P. Glass, "Residential Mobility and Voter Turnout," *American Political Science Review* 81 (1987): 45–65.

14. See Philip E. Converse, "Change in the American Electorate," in Angus Campbell and Philip E. Converse, eds., *The Human Meaning of Social Change* (New York: Russell Sage Foundation, 1972), pp. 263–337; Walter Dean Burnham, "Theory and Voting Research: Some Reflections on Converse's 'Change in the American Electorate'," *American Political Science Review* 68 (1974): 1002–23; and Frances Fox Piven and Richard A. Cloward, *Why Americans Don't Vote* (New York: Pantheon Books, 1988).

15. A state-by-state list of registration requirements is reported each year in *The Book of the States* (Lexington, Ky.: The Council of State Governments).

16. The most recent estimates—that turnout would be 7.8 percent without the most burdensome requirements—are provided by Ruy A. Teixiera, *The Disappearing American Voter* (Washington, D.C.: Brookings Institution, 1992), Chapter 4. For similar estimates from earlier years, see Raymond E. Wolfinger and Steven J. Rosenstone, *Who Votes?* (New Haven, Conn.: Yale University Press, 1982), pp. 61–78; and Glenn E. Mitchell and Christopher Wlezien, "The Impact of Legal Constraints on Voter Registration, Turnout, and the Composition of the American Electorate," *Political Behavior* 17 (1995): 179–202.

17. The story of black disenfranchisement in the South is well told by V. O. Key, Jr., in *Southern Politics in State and Nation* (New York: Knopf, 1949). See also J. Morgan Kousser, *The Shaping of Southern Politics* (New Haven: Yale University Press, 1974); and Donald R. Matthews and James W. Prothro, *Negroes and the New Southern Politics* (New York: Harcourt, Brace and World, 1966).

18. The white primary was finally overturned by the Supreme Court in *Smith v. Allwright,* 321 U.S. 649 (1944). Not only is this a landmark case in the area of black voting rights, but it also is significant in establishing that political parties, in spite of their right to handle their own affairs under the freedom of association guaranteed in the Bill of Rights, are not free to violate constitutional prohibitions on discrimination.

19. Pat Watters and Reese Cleghorn, *Climbing Jacob's Ladder* (New York: Harcourt Brace Jovanovich, 1967), pp. 122–23.

20. For a review of the impact of the Voting Rights Act of 1965 and its extensions, see Chandler Davidson and Bernard Grofman, eds., *Quiet Revolution in the South* (Princeton, N.J.: Princeton University Press, 1994). On black turnout in the South generally, see Harold W. Stanley, *Voter Mobilization and the Politics of Race* (New York: Praeger, 1987).

21. See Matthews and Prothro, *Negroes and the New Southern Politics;* H. Douglas Price, *The Negro and Southern Politics* (New York: New York University Press, 1957); David Campbell and Joe R. Feagin, "Black Politics in the South: A Descriptive Analysis," *Journal of Politics* 37 (1975): 129–62; and Lester M. Salamon and Stephen Van Evera, "Fear, Apathy, and Participation," *American Political Science Review* 67 (1973): 1288–1306.

22. The case is *Miller v. Johnson,* decided on June 29, 1995.

23. The fall-off in voting for issues is especially pronounced among lower socioeconomic status voters. For an extensive review of voting on ballot propositions, see David B. Magleby, *Direct Legislation: Voting on Ballot Propositions in the United States* (Baltimore: The Johns Hopkins University Press, 1984); and Thomas E. Cronin, *Direct Democracy* (Cambridge: Harvard University Press, 1989).

24. For systematic explanation of variations in turnout across the election calendar and for different combinations of contests, see Richard W. Boyd, "Election Calendars and Voter Turnout," *American Politics Quarterly* 14 (1986): 89–104; and "The Effects of Primaries and Statewide Races on Voter Turnout," *Journal of Politics* 51 (1989): 730–39.

25. Jae-On Kim, John R. Petrocik, and Stephen N. Enokson, "Voter Turnout among the American States: Systemic and Individual Components," *American Political Science Review* 69 (1975): 107–23.

26. See Steven J. Rosenstone and John Mark Hansen, *Mobilization, Participation, and Democracy in America* (New York: Macmillan, 1993), pp. 177–88; Gregory A. Caldeira and Samuel C. Patterson, "Contextual Influences on Participation in U.S. State Legislative Contests," *Legislative Studies Quarterly* 3 (1982): 359–81; Samuel C. Patterson and Gregory A. Caldeira, "Getting Out the Vote: Participation in Gubernatorial Elections," *American Political Science Review* 77 (1983): 675–89; and Gregory A. Caldeira, Samuel C. Patterson, and Gregory A. Markko, "The Mobilization of Voters in Congressional Elections," *Journal of Politics* 47 (1985): 490–509.

27. This thesis is expounded in the work of Walter Dean Burnham. In particular, see his "The Changing Shape of the American Political Universe" and "Theory and Voting Research: Some Reflections on Converse's 'Change in the American Electorate'," *American Political Science Review* 68 (1974): 1002–23. Also see Paul Kleppner, *Who Voted?* (New York: Praeger, 1982).

28. The challenge to Burnham is raised primarily by Converse, "Change in the American Electorate;" and Jerrold G. Rusk, "The American Electoral Universe: Speculation and Evidence," *American Political Science Review* 68 (1974): 1028–49. The colloquy between Burnham and his critics is continued in this 1974 issue of the *American Political Science Review;* see also later works by Burnham, especially *The Current Crisis in American Politics* (New York: Oxford University Press, 1982), pp. 121–65.

29. At least this is the conclusion reached by scholars who have attempted to explain why American turnout levels are so much lower than those in other democratic nations. See Sidney Verba, Norman H. Nie, and Jae-on Kim, *Participation and Political Equality* (Cambridge: Cambridge University Press, 1978) and Powell, "American Voter Turnout in Comparative Perspective."

30. Of course, this is why turnout may change as the result of a realignment. For an insightful discussion of how the nature of political conflict affects participation, see E. E. Schattschneider, *The Semi-Sovereign People* (New York: Holt, Rinehart, and Winston, 1960).

31. The importance of political mobilization, often neglected in research on American turnout, is the main theme of Rosenstone and Hansen, *Mobilization, Participation, and Democracy in America.*

32. On the mobilization of black voters, see Rosenstone and Hansen, *Mobilization, Participation, and Democracy in America,* pp. 188–96 and 219–24; Lawrence Bobo and Franklin D. Gilliam, Jr., "Race, Sociopolitical Participation, and Black Empowerment," *American Political Science Review* 84 (1990): 377–94; Frederick C. Harris, "Something Within: Religion as a Mobilizer of African-American Political Activism," *Journal of Politics* 56 (1994): 42–68; and Katherine Tate, "Black Political Participation in the 1984 and 1988 Presidential Elections," *American Political Science Review* 85 (1991): 1159–76. In "Mass Mobilization or Governmental Intervention: The Growth of Black Registration in the South," *Journal of Politics* 57 (1995): 425–42, Richard Timpone shows that significant black mobilization in the South was attributable to both organizational mobilization efforts and federal intervention under the Voting Rights Act of 1965.

33. From the perspective of strict rationality, some theorists have argued, it is paradoxical that people do vote in a large electorate. For a careful review of these arguments and a theory of why it may be rational to vote under these conditions nonetheless, see John H. Aldrich, "Rational Choice and Turnout," *American Journal of Political Science* 37 (1993): 246–78.

34. Sidney Verba and Norman H. Nie, *Participation in America* (New York: Harper and Row, 1972), pp. 125–37. See also Teixiera, *The Disappearing American Voter,* Chapter 3.

35. Verba, Nie, and Kim, *Participation and Political Equality.*
36. Wolfinger and Rosenstone, *Who Votes?* pp. 35–36.
37. Verba and Nie, *Participation in America,* pp. 145–47. Of course, chronological age indexes the varying political experiences of different generations in addition to stage of the life cycle, but scholars have found little evidence that generation exerts an independent impact on turnout. On this point, see Rosenstone and Hansen, *Mobilization, Participation, and Democracy in America,* pp. 136–41.
38. Bobo and Gilliam, "Race, Sociopolitical Participation, and Black Empowerment."
39. Verba and Nie, *Participation in America,* Chapter 11, examine the effects of organizational membership. See Laura Stoker and M. Kent Jennings, "Life-Cycle Transitions and Political Participation: The Case of Marriage," *American Political Science Review* 89 (1995): 421–36, for the salutary impact of getting married; and Rosenstone and Wolfinger, *Who Votes?,* on the detrimental effects of losing a spouse among the elderly.
40. See Rosenstone and Hansen, *Mobilization, Participation, and Democracy in America,* pp. 141–56; and Verba and Nie, *Participation in America,* pp. 133–36.
41. See Richard A. Brody, "The Puzzle of Participation in America," in Anthony King, ed., *The New American Political System* (Washington, D.C.: American Enterprise Institute, 1978), pp. 287–324.
42. The emphasis on efficacy and partisanship appears in Paul R. Abramson and John H. Aldrich, "The Decline of Electoral Participation in America," *American Political Science Review* 76 (1982): 502–21; and Paul R. Abramson, John H. Aldrich, and David W. Rohde, *Change and Continuity in the 1992 Election* (Washington, D.C.: CQ Press, 1995), pp. 114–20.
43. Studies by Teixeira, *The Disappearing American Voter,* Chapter 1, and Rosenstone and Hansen, *Mobilization, Participation, and Democracy in America,* Chapter 7, echo the emphasis on efficacy but attribute the greatest additional effects to declines in social connectedness (both studies) and electoral mobilization (Rosenstone and Hansen). For a general account of the deterioration of social connectedness in the United States, see Robert D. Putnam, "Bowling Alone: America's Declining Social Capital," *Journal of Democracy* 6 (1995): 65–78.
44. See Stephen M. Nichols and Paul Allen Beck, "Reversing the Decline: Voter Turnout in the 1992 Election," in Herbert F. Weisberg, ed., *Democracy's Feast* (Chatham, N.J.: Chatham House, 1995), Chapter 2.
45. On this point, see Edward G. Carmines and James A. Stimson, *Issue Evolution* (Princeton, N.J.: Princeton University Press, 1989).
46. The youngest voters were key actors in the last clear-cut realignment, casting heavily Democratic first votes during the New Deal realignment of the 1930s, so their apparently pro-Democratic behavior in 1994 gives one pause in announcing that election as the first stage of a realignment.
47. *Congressional Quarterly Weekly Report,* January 13, 1996, pp. 97–100.
48. On this point, see Verba and Nie, *Participation in America,* Part III; and Bennett and Resnick, "The Implications of Nonvoting for Democracy in the United States."
49. Wolfinger and Rosenstone, *Who Votes?,* Chapter 6; and Teixeira, *The Disappearing American Voter,* Chapter 3.
50. See James DeNardo, "Turnout and the Vote: The Joke's on the Democrats," *American Political Science Review* 74 (1980): 406–20; the exchange between DeNardo and Harvey J. Tucker and Arnold Vedlitz, "Does Heavy Turnout Help Democrats in Presidential Elections?" *American Political Science Review* 80 (1986): 1291–1304; and Teixeira, *The Disappearing American Voter.*

Part Four

1. In recent years, Louisiana has broken the tradition of separate nomination and election steps. For races other than those for the presidency, it now holds a single election, a so-called blanket primary. All candidates of all parties run in it and are designated by party on the ballot. If one candidate wins a majority of the vote, he or she is elected to the office. If not, the top two candidates,

regardless of their party, face each other in a runoff election. See Chapter 9 for more on this peculiar feature of Louisiana politics.

Chapter 9

1. For the story of the convention system and the early years of the direct primary, see Charles E.
   Merriam and Louise Overacker, *Primary Elections* (Chicago: University of Chicago Press,
   1928). For a discussion of the early spread of the direct primary, see V. O. Key, Jr., *American
   State Politics: An Introduction* (New York: Knopf, 1956), pp. 87–97. For the operations of the
   direct primary in the South, see V.O. Key, Jr., *Southern Politics in State and Nation* (New York:
   Knopf, 1949), Chapters 19 and 20.
2. The methods for selecting delegates to the national nominating conventions also vary across the
   states, and, as we shall see, they are not always the same as the methods employed for choosing
   party nominees for statewide office.
3. Some states allow third parties to nominate their candidates through conventions.
4. *The Book of the States 1994–95* (Lexington, Ky.: The Council of State Governments, 1994), pp.
   234–35. For a general discussion of the various methods, see Malcolm E. Jewell and David M.
   Olson, *Political Parties and Elections in American States* (Chicago: Dorsey, 1988), pp. 94–97.
5. For an account of variations within these broad categories, see Craig L. Carr and Gary L. Scott,
   "The Logic of State Primary Classification Schemes," *American Politics Quarterly* 12 (1984):
   465–76; and Steven E. Finkel and Howard A. Scarrow, "Party Identification and Party Enrollment: The Difference and the Consequence," *Journal of Politics* 47 (1985): 620–52.
6. The Republican party's challenge primary in Connecticut (in which the convention's choice of a
   nominee can be challenged by a loser who gained at least 15 percent of the convention vote) also
   can be opened to independents as the result of a 1986 Supreme Court decision (*Tashjian v.
   Republican Party of Connecticut,* 106 S.Ct. 783 and 1257) which upheld the party's attempts to
   override the state's closed-primary law. This decision affirms the authority of the party, rather
   than the state, to control its own nomination process and may clear the way for other state parties to regulate participation in their primaries as they wish.
7. See David Adamany, "Cross-over Voting and the Democratic Party's Reform Rules," *American
   Political Science Review* 70 (1976): 536–41. Also see Ronald D. Hedlund and Meredith W.
   Watts, "The Wisconsin Open Primary: 1968 to 1984," *American Politics Quarterly* 14 (1986):
   55–74; and Gary D. Wekkin, "The Conceptualization and Measurement of Crossover Voting,"
   Western Political Quarterly 41 (1988): 105–14.
8. Alan Abramowitz, John McGlennon, and Ronald Rapoport, "A Note on Strategic Voting in a Primary Election," *Journal of Politics* 43 (1981): 899–904; and Gary D. Wekkin, "Why Crossover
   Voters Are Not 'Mischievous' Voters," *American Politics Quarterly* 19 (1991): 229–47.
9. Access to the major-party ballot has become easier as a result of court action in recent decades.
   In key early cases, the United States Supreme Court invalidated a Texas law requiring candidates
   to pay both a flat fee for candidacy and a share of the cost of the election (up to $9,000) and over-
   turned the California scale of filing fees because they did not provide an alternative means of
   access to the ballot (such as a petition) for candidates unable to pay. The cases were *Bullock v.
   Carter,* 405 U.S. 134 (1972); and *Lubin v. Panish,* 415 U.S. 709 (1974). The monthly newsletter
   Ballot Access News chronicles continuing efforts to regulate ballot access, especially for third
   parties and independents.
10. That blacks are disadvantaged by runoff primaries is challenged by Charles S. Bullock, III, and
    A. Brock Smith in "Black Success in Local Runoff Elections," *Journal of Politics* 52 (1990):
    1205–20. For more on the discriminatory impact of runoff primaries, see Harold Stanley, "The
    Runoff: The Case for Retention," *PS* 18 (1985): 231–36; and Charles S. Bullock, III, and Loch
    K. Johnson, *Runoff Elections in the United States* (Knoxville: University of Tennessee Press,
    1991). For the argument that blacks are not necessarily advantaged by maximizing the number
    of offices they can win, see Carol Swain, *Black Faces, Black Interests* (Cambridge, Mass.: Har-
    vard University Press, 1993).
11. Theodore H. White, *The Making of the President 1960* (New York: Atheneum, 1961), p. 78.

12. On the behavior of activists, see Donald B. Johnson and James L. Gibson, "The Divisive Primary Revisited: Party Activists in Iowa," *American Political Science Review* 68 (1974): 67–77; and Emmett H. Buehl, Jr., "Divisive Primaries and Participation in Fall Presidential Campaigns," *American Politics Quarterly* 14 (1986): 376–90; Walter J. Stone, "The Carryover Effect in Presidential Elections," *American Political Science Review* 80 (1986): 271–80; and Martin P. Wattenberg, "The Republican Presidential Advantage in the Age of Party Disunity," in Gary W. Cox and Samuel Kernell, eds., *The Politics of Divided Government* (Boulder, Colo.: Westview, 1991), Chapter 3.

13. The most recent and comprehensive studies have found that divisive primaries depress general-election support for most offices, except for the House of Representatives. See Patrick J. Kenney and Tom W. Rice, "The Relationship between Divisive Primaries and General Election Outcomes," *American Journal of Political Science* 31 (1987): 31–44; Patrick J. Kenney, "Sorting Out the Effects of Primary Divisiveness in Congressional and Senatorial Elections," *Western Political Quarterly* 41 (1988): 765–77; Patrick J. Kenney and Tom W. Rice, "Presidential Prenomination Preferences and Candidate Evaluations," *American Political Science Review* 82 (1988): 1309–19; and James I. Lengle, Diana Owen, and Molly W. Sonner, "Divisive Nominating Mechanisms and Democratic Party Electoral Prospects," *Journal of Politics* 57 (1995): 370–83.

14. See V. O. Key, *American State Politics: An Introduction*, Chapter 6. It is ironic that direct primaries, designed by southern Democrats and northern Progressives to solve problems of one-partyism, contribute to the very evil they were designed to combat by making interparty competition in the general election even less likely in one-party areas.

15. The party's role in recruiting candidates for office varies with how much control it has over the primary, which in turn is affected by the type of primary. For example, one study found that parties were more active in recruiting and endorsing legislative candidates and in scaring off challengers in closed primary than in open primary states. See Richard J. Tobin and Edward Keynes, "Institutional Differences in the Recruitment Process: A Four-State Study," *American Journal of Political Science* 19 (1975): 667–82.

16. Followers of Lyndon LaRouche cleverly have taken advantage of these situations by filing as the only candidates for minority party nomination in one-party areas. If the major-party candidate subsequently stumbled on the way to what seemed to be sure victory, this put them in position to win the office.

17. About a third of all state legislative races have been uncontested in recent years. On the phenomenon of uncontested races, as well as candidate recruitment more generally, see L. Sandy Maisel, Linda L. Fowler, Ruth S. Jones, and Walter J. Stone, "Nomination Politics: The Roles of Institutional, Contextual, and Personal Variables," in L. Sandy Maisel, ed., *The Parties Respond* (Boulder, Colo.: Westview, 1994), pp. 148–52.

18. See Jewell and Olson, *Political Parties and Elections in American States*, pp. 94–104; and Maisel, Fowler, Jones, and Stone, "Nomination Politics," pp. 155–56.

19. Craig H. Grau, "Competition in State Legislative Primaries," *Legislative Studies Quarterly* 6 (1981): 35–54.

20. In a survey of gubernatorial primaries in forty-nine states from 1960 to 1986, Malcolm Jewell and David Olson found that the major parties had contests for the gubernatorial nominations 74 percent of the time overall. See their *Political Parties and Elections in American States*, pp. 104–6.

21. On the factors that promote or suppress competition in the primaries, see Tom W. Rice, "Gubernatorial and Senatorial Primary Elections: Determinants of Competition," *American Politics Quarterly* 13 (1985): 427–46; Harvey L. Schantz, "Contested and Uncontested Primaries for the U.S. House," *Legislative Studies Quarterly* 4 (1980): 545–62; and Jewell and Olson, *Political Parties and Elections in American States*, pp. 104–18.

22. Jewell and Olson, *Political Parties and Elections in American States*, p. 110.

23. Malcolm E. Jewell, "Northern State Gubernatorial Primary Elections: Explaining Voting Turnout," *American Politics Quarterly* 12 (1984): 101–16; and Patrick J. Kenney, "Explaining Turnout in Gubernatorial Primaries," *American Politics Quarterly* 11 (1983): 315–26.

24. The early studies are Austin Ranney and Leon D. Epstein, "The Two Electorates: Voters and Non-Voters in a Wisconsin Primary," *Journal of Politics* 28 (1966): 598–616; and Austin Ranney,

"The Representativeness of Primary Electorates," *American Journal of Political Science* 12 (1968): 224–38. Similar results appear for turnout in more recent Senate primaries; see Patrick J. Kenney, "Explaining Primary Turnout: The Senatorial Case," *Legislative Studies Quarterly* 11 (1986): 65–74. On different results in presidential primaries, see John G. Geer, "Assessing the Representativeness of Electorates in Presidential Primaries," *American Journal of Political Science* 32 (1988): 929–45.

25. Jewell and Olson, *Political Parties and Elections in American States*, pp. 112–13.

26. Key, *American State Politics*, p. 195.

27. In this vein, to avoid collusion between parties in interactive general election Prisoner's Dilemma "games," intraparty democracy actually may contribute to electoral responsiveness. See John G. Geer and Mark E. Shere, "Party Competition and the Prisoner's Dilemma: An Argument for the Direct Primary," *Journal of Politics* 54: 741–61.

28. On the relationships among party, mechanism of nomination, and primary competition, see Andrew D. McNitt, "The Effect of Preprimary Endorsement on Competition for Nominations: An Examination of Different Nominating Systems," *Journal of Politics* (1980): 257–66.

29. A study of gubernatorial nominations in 1982 suggests this by showing that more money was spent on campaigns and the spending was more related to the outcome in the contests in states where party organizations did not make preprimary endorsements. Sarah M. Morehouse, "Money versus Party Effort: Nominating for Governor," *American Journal of Political Science* 34 (1990): 706–24.

Chapter 10

1. With the movement to direct primaries for nominations of state officials beginning in 1902, it seemed only natural to involve voters in the selection of presidential candidates as well. But the national conventions remained in place, and even where presidential primaries were adopted they only supplemented rather than displaced the traditional convention system.

2. For an excellent account of this episode, a rare event of political leaders willingly giving up power, see Byron E. Shafer, *Quiet Revolution* (New York: Russell Sage Foundation, 1983). Other useful sources on the reform of the presidential nomination process are James W. Ceaser, *Presidential Selection* (Princeton, N.J.: Princeton University Press, 1979); William J. Crotty, *Party Reform* (New York: Longman, 1983); Nelson W. Polsby, *The Consequences of Party Reform* (Oxford: Oxford University Press, 1983); and Austin Ranney, *Curing the Mischiefs of Faction: Party Reform in America* (Berkeley, Calif.: University of California Press, 1975).

3. In a case involving the Wisconsin open primary, the Supreme Court upheld the power of the national party to refuse to seat delegates chosen under a state law which violated its rules. See *Democratic Party of the United States v. La Follette,* 450 U.S. 107 (1981).

4. See Robert J. Huckshorn and John F. Bibby, "National Party Rules and Delegate Selection in the Republican Party," *PS* 16 (1983): 656–66.

5. The parties in a few states have held both primaries and caucuses. Texas Democrats select some delegates through primaries and some through caucuses. In recent years the Democrats in four other states have held preference primaries called "beauty contests" because their results have no bearing on delegate selection, which is done through the caucus-convention system.

6. Because of these so-called "loophole" primaries, caucus results in the past tended to represent popular votes more proportionally than primary results, and, as he charged, Jesse Jackson in 1988 did receive fewer delegates than he would have earned under a strict proportional representation system. See Stephen Ansolabehere and Gary King, "Measuring the Consequences of Delegate Selection Rules in Presidential Nominations," *Journal of Politics* 52 (1990): 609–21.

7. On the shift to candidate-oriented delegate loyalties, see Byron E. Shafer, *Bifurcated Politics: Evolution and Reform in the National Party Convention* (Cambridge, Mass.: Harvard University Press, 1988), pp. 181–84.

8. For an account of the struggle between the Wisconsin Democrats and the national party over open primaries, see Gary D. Wekkin, *Democrats versus Democrats* (Columbia: University of Missouri Press, 1983).

9. On the Iowa caucuses, which have received more media coverage than any other caucus and most primaries, see Peverill Squire, ed., *The Iowa Caucuses and the Presidential Nominating Process* (Boulder, Colo.: Westview, 1989).

10. For a discussion of these various strategic considerations, see John H. Aldrich, *Before the Convention* (Chicago: University of Chicago Press, 1980). For a more recent account, emphasizing the strategic trade-off between winning delegates and gaining momentum through media coverage, see Paul-Henri Gurian, "Candidate Behavior in Presidential Nomination Campaigns: A Dynamic Model," *Journal of Politics* 55 (1993): 115–39; and Paul-Henri Gurian and Audrey A. Haynes, "Campaign Strategy in Presidential Primaries," *American Journal of Political Science* 37 (1993): 335–41.

11. Studies of the effect of primary divisiveness on the presidential races are cited in footnotes 12 and 13 of Chapter 9.

12. On the Super Tuesday contests, see Barbara Norrander, *Super Tuesday: Regional Politics and Presidential Primaries* (Lexington, Ky.: University of Kentucky Press, 1993).

13. Differences between "superdelegates" and regular delegates are examined in Richard Herrera, "Are 'Superdelegates' Super?" *Political Behavior* 16 (1994): 79–92; and Priscilla L. Southwell, "The 1984 Democratic Nomination Process: The Significance of Unpledged Superdelegates," *American Politics Quarterly* 14 (1986): 75–88.

14. Turnout rates in nomination contests are exceedingly difficult to estimate, even when the actual number of participants (the numerator) is known. The denominator of this fraction is the number of voters eligible to vote in the particular primary or caucus. But what is this number? Is it the voters registered with that party? That number does not exist in states without party registration, and it understates the potential electorate where primaries are open to independents or partisans of the other party. Is it the potential general election electorate for that party? That number surely is affected by who the nominee is. Is it the total voting-age population? Party turnout from that base depends upon how much competition there is in each party's primary or caucus. The best estimate of turnout under these circumstances, although hardly ideal, is a comparison of two different calculations—the one based on general election voters for that party, the other on the voting-age population.

15. See Jack Moran and Mark Fenster, "Voter Turnout in Presidential Primaries: A Diachronic Analysis," *American Politics Quarterly* 10 (1982): 453–76; Patrick J. Kenney and Tom W. Rice, "Voter Turnout in Presidential Primaries: A Cross-Sectional Examination," *Political Behavior* 7 (1985): 101–12; and Barbara Norrander and Gregg W. Smith, "Type of Contest, Candidate Strategy, and Turnout in Presidential Primaries," *American Politics Quarterly* 13 (1985): 28–50.

16. See Barbara Norrander, "Selective Participation: Presidential Voters as a Subset of General Election Voters," *American Politics Quarterly* 14 (1986): 35–54.

17. Evidence on the representatives of primary electorates may be found in Larry M. Bartels, *Presidential Primaries and the Dynamics of Public Choice* (Princeton, N.J.: Princeton University Press, 1988), pp. 140–48; John G. Geer, "The Representativeness of Presidential Primary Electorates," *American Journal of Political Science* 32 (1988): 929–45; and Barbara Norrander, "Ideological Representativeness of Primary Voters," *American Journal of Political Science* 33 (1989): 570–87. The classic case for the unrepresentativeness of primaries is made by V. O. Key, Jr., *American State Politics: An Introduction* (New York: Knopf, 1967), pp. 133–68.

18. The most severe indictment of the primaries on these grounds appears in Scott Keeter and Cliff Zukin, *Uninformed Choice* (New York: Praeger, 1983). On the restricted influence of ideology and issues, see John G. Geer, *Nominating Presidents: An Evaluation of Voters and Primaries* (New York: Greenwood Press, 1989) and Barbara Norrander, "Correlates of Vote Choice in the 1980 Presidential Primaries," *Journal of Politics* 48 (1986): 156–66. Also see J. David Gopoian, "Issue Preferences and Candidate Choice in the 1980 Presidential Primaries," *American Journal of Political Science* 26 (1982): 523–46.

19. Samuel L. Popkin, *The Reasoning Voter* (Chicago: University of Chicago Press, 1991), especially Chapters 6–8.

20. Bartels, *Presidential Primaries and the Dynamics of Public Choice.*

21. For a persuasive analysis of strategic voting in primaries, in which voters temper their "sincere" preferences with calculations of their candidate's viability, see Paul R. Abramson, John H.

Aldrich, Phil Paolino, and David W. Rohde, "'Sophisticated' Voting in the 1988 Presidential Primaries," *American Political Science Review* 86 (1992): 55–69.

22. A similar blend of preferences and strategic calculations has been found to influence the decisions of participants in the Iowa caucuses and convention. See Walter J. Stone, Ronald B. Rapoport, and Alan I. Abramowitz, "Candidate Support in Presidential Nomination Campaigns: The Case of Iowa in 1984," *Journal of Politics* 54 (1992): 1074–97.

23. Credit for the national party-convention idea can be claimed by a long-forgotten minor party, the Anti-Masons, who brought together their supporters in a Baltimore meeting in 1831 to nominate a candidate for president. But it is the major parties that have made the convention a familiar institution of American politics.

24. The best account of the evolution of the national party conventions is Byron E. Shafer, *Bifurcated Politics.* Shafer contends that the central role of the conventions—nominating a president—was eroding with the nationalization of American politics prior to the post-1968 reforms. On pre-1960 conventions, see Paul T. David, Ralph M. Goldman, and Richard C. Bain, *The Politics of the National Party Conventions* (Washington, D.C.: Brookings Institution, 1960).

25. Party platforms first appeared in the 1840s, and all of them through 1976 are available in one volume: Donald B. Johnson, *National Party Platforms, 1840–1976* (Urbana: University of Illinois Press, 1978). For summaries of more recent platforms, see the *Guide to U.S. Elections* (Washington, D.C.: Congressional Quarterly, 1985) and postconvention issues of the *Congressional Quarterly Weekly Report.*

26. Gerald Pomper, *Elections in America* (New York: Dodd, Mead, 1968), p. 201.

27. The candidates, especially the winning candidate, play a more important role in platform development now than ever before. See L. Sandy Maisel, "The Platform-Writing Process: Candidate-Centered Platforms in 1992," *Political Science Quarterly* 108 (1993–94): 671–99. On the sometimes conflicting goals of candidates and issue-oriented delegates, see Byron E. Shafer, *Bifurcated Politics*, Chapters 4 and 6.

28. On pp. 333–37 of *Bifurcated Politics,* Shafer discusses the possibility, in a "deviant" year, of the nomination decision returning to the convention.

29. On the representativeness of convention delegates, see Howard L. Reiter, *Selecting the President* (Philadelphia: University of Pennsylvania Press, 1985), Chapter 4.

30. Information on the party activities and offices of delegates to the 1992 Democratic Convention is provided by *The New York Times* from the *Times*/CBS News Democratic Delegate Poll conducted with a random sample of delegates between June 18 and July 2, 1992. Information on Republican delegates comes from a survey conducted by CBS News.

31. The classic account of this relationship, in which delegates to the 1956 conventions are compared to Democratic and Republican identifiers from a national survey, is found in Herbert McClosky, Paul Hoffman, and Rosemary O'Hara, "Issue Conflict and Consensus among Party Leaders and Followers," *American Political Science Review* 54 (1960): 406–27. For a replication and extension with similar results, see David Nexon, "Asymmetry in the Political System: Occasional Activists in the Republican and Democratic Parties, 1956–1964," *American Political Science Review* 65 (1971): 716–30.

32. These were the findings and the conclusion of Jeane Kirkpatrick, *The New Presidential Elite* (New York: Russell Sage Foundation and Twentieth Century Fund, 1976).

33. For comparisons of post-1972 convention delegates with their respective party rank and files, see John S. Jackson III, Barbara L. Brown, and David Bositis, "Herbert McClosky and Friends Revisited: 1980 Democratic and Republican Party Elites Compared to the Mass Public," *American Politics Quarterly* 10 (1982): 158–80; Warren E. Miller and M. Kent Jennings, *Parties in Transition* (New York: Russell Sage Foundation, 1986), Chapters 7–9; Denise L. Baer and David A. Bositis, *Elite Cadres and Party Coalitions* (New York: Greenwood Press, 1988), Chapter 8; and Shafer, *Bifurcated Politics*, (1988), pp. 100–107.

34. See John W. Soule and Wilma E. McGrath, "A Comparative Study of Presidential Nomination Conventions: The Democrats 1968 and 1972," *American Journal of Political Science* 19 (1975): 501–17. The seminal study is John W. Soule and James W. Clarke, "Amateurs and Professionals: A Study of Delegates to the 1968 Democratic National Convention," *American Political Science Review* 64 (1970): 888–98.

35. For subsequent studies of amateurs and professionals among convention delegates, see Dennis G. Sullivan, Jeffrey L. Pressman, Benjamin I. Page, and John J. Lyons, *The Politics of Representation: The Democratic Convention 1972* (New York: St. Martin's, 1974); Kirkpatrick, *The New Presidential Elite;* Thomas H. Roback, "Motivations for Activism among Republican National Convention Delegates," *Journal of Politics* 42 (1980): 181–201; and Denise Baer and David Bositis, *Elite Cadres and Party Coalitions*, Chapter 7.

36. The seating of superdelegates as almost 20 percent of the total delegates in 1996 has made the Democratic convention more representative of its elected national officeholders and its party officials. Ironically, it also has given members of Congress more of a chance to participate in the nomination process than at any time since the congressional caucus reigned supreme before 1832.

37. See Shafer, *Bifurcated Politics,* especially Chapter 5.

38. Shafer carefully details the decreasing media coverage of the conventions and their declining ratings through 1984 in Chapter 8 of *Bifurcated Politics*. Since then, network coverage has decreased even more.

39. See the figures cited in Shafer, *Bifurcated Politics,* Chapter 8, especially p. 280.

40. The fact that Iowa and New Hampshire, two unrepresentative states containing a mere 2.9 percent of the U.S. population, garner such a disproportionate share of the media coverage reflects the powerful role a few contests can play in the nomination process. On media coverage of these states in 1984, see William C. Adams, "As New Hampshire Goes. . . ," in Gary R. Orren and Nelson W. Polsby, eds., *Media and Momentum* (Chatham, N.J.: Chatham House, 1987), pp. 42–59.

41. A good statement of the case against recent party reforms may be found in Polsby, *Consequences of Party Reform*. The case for party reforms is best articulated in William J. Crotty, *Decision for the Democrats* (Baltimore: The Johns Hopkins University Press, 1978).

42. See Michael W. Traugott and Margaret Petrella, "Public Evaluations of the Presidential Nomination Process," *Political Behavior* 11 (1989): 335–52.

Chapter 11

1. *National Observer,* September 26, 1966.

2. Jerrold G. Rusk found that the introduction of the Australian ballot was accompanied by an increase in split-ticket voting. See his article, "The Effect of the Australian Ballot Reform on Split Ticket Voting: 1876–1908," *American Political Science Review* 64 (1970): 1220–38.

3. The best account of the effects of ballot form on voting remains Angus Campbell, Philip E. Converse, Warren E. Miller, and Donald E. Stokes, *The American Voter* (New York: Wiley, 1960), Chapter 11. For an inventory of ballot provisions in the various states, see *The Transformation in American Politics: Implications for American Federalism* (Washington, D.C.: Advisory Commission on Intergovernmental Affairs, 1986).

4. Provisions for write-ins allow access to the ballot by candidates who have not been nominated by any of the parties. As was shown in Chapter 2, the states typically have protected the parties by making it difficult for such candidates to earn a position on the ballot. Moreover, a majority of states have so-called sore-loser laws that prevent candidates who have lost in the contest for their party's nomination from qualifying for the general-election ballot as an independent. For comprehensive coverage of actions affecting ballot access in general and write-in provisions specifically, see Richard Winger's *Ballot Access News,* published by the Coalition for Free and Open Elections.

5. Delbert A. Taebel, "The Effect of Ballot Position on Electoral Success," *American Journal of Political Science* 19 (1975): 519–26.

6. The introduction of the secret ballot at the end of the nineteenth century increased roll-off by requiring that voters actually mark their choices for each office or, where it was permitted, consciously cast a straight-ticket vote. See Walter Dean Burnham, "The Changing Shape of the American Political Universe," *American Political Science Review* 59 (1965): 7–28. The effects of the secret ballot on roll-off, though, have been dampened by ballot forms that encourage straight-ticket voting. See Rusk, "The Effect of the Australian Ballot Reform on Split Ticket Voting," p. 1237; and Jack L. Walker, "Ballot Forms and Voter Fatigue: An Analysis of the Office Block and Party Column Ballots," *Midwest Journal of Political Science* 10 (1966): 448–63. A recent study also has shown that roll-off is decreased by electronic voting machines that use a blinking light to call voter attention to their failure to vote the entire ballot. See Stephen M. Nichols and Gregory A. Strizek, "Electronic Voting Machines and Ballot Roll-off," *American Politics Quarterly* 23 (1995): 300–18.

7. For a good survey of the effects of various types of districts, see Howard D. Hamilton, "Legislative Constituencies: Single-Member Districts, Multi-Member Districts, and Floterial Districts," *Western Political Quarterly* 20 (1967): 321–40.

8. For an excursion into some of the complexities of proportional representation, see Douglas W. Rae, *The Political Consequences of Electoral Law* (New Haven: Yale University Press, 1967), and Arend Lijphart, *Electoral Systems and Party Systems: A Study of Twenty-Seven Democracies, 1945–1990* (New York: Oxford University Press, 1994).

9. The classic study of presidential coattails is Warren E. Miller, "Presidential Coattails: A Study in Political Myth and Methodology," *Public Opinion Quarterly* 19 (1955–56): 353–68.

10. Walter Dean Burnham, *Critical Elections and the Mainsprings of American Politics* (New York: Norton, 1970), p. 94; and V. O. Key, Jr., *American State Politics: An Introduction,* (New York: Knopf, 1967), pp. 41–49 and 52–84.

11. For an analysis of the relative importance of states in presidential elections due to the electoral college, see George Rabinowitz and Stuart Elaine MacDonald, "The Power of the States in U.S. Presidential Elections," *American Political Science Review* 80 (1986): 65–87. Several studies have shown that presidential candidates concentrate their campaign resources on the most populous and the most competitive states, which are often the same. See especially Claude S. Colantoni, Terrence J. Levesque, and Peter C. Ordeshook, "Campaign Resource Allocation under the Electoral College," *American Political Science Review* 69 (1975): 141–54; and Larry M. Bartels, "Resource Allocation in Presidential Campaigns," *Journal of Politics* 47 (1985): 928–36.

12. Walker, "Ballot Forms and Voter Fatigue," makes the latter point.

13. Ibid., pp. 448–49.

14. The landmark Supreme Court cases striking down, as unconstitutional, malapportioned congressional and state legislative districts are *Baker v. Carr,* 369 U.S. 186 (1962); *Reynolds v. Sims,* 377 U.S. 533 (1964); and *Wesberry v. Sanders,* 376 U.S. 1.

15. In *Karcher v. Daggett* (462 U.S. 725 [1983]), the Supreme Court struck down a New Jersey plan because, by creating districts that differed in population size by seven-tenths of one percent from the average, it violated the constitutional requirements of "precise mathematical equality." While ruling that partisan gerrymanders may be challenged in the courts, however, the Supreme Court refrained from invalidating the notoriously gerrymandered Indiana (*Davis v. Bandamer,* 478 U.S. 109 [1986]) and California redistricting plans (*Badham v. Eu,* 488 U.S. 1024 [1989]). Some years before, however, in *Gomillion v. Lightfoot,* 364 U.S. 339 (1960), the Court had struck down an Alabama gerrymander in which the municipal boundaries of a city were redrawn to exclude blacks.

16. On the Voting Rights Act and Justice Department involvement in preclearance of electoral laws, see Chandler Davidson and Bernard Grofman, eds., *Quiet Revolution in the South* (Princeton, N.J.: Princeton University Press, 1994), especially Chapter 1.

17. The original quotation comes from Charles Ledyard Norton in his 1890 book, *Political Americanisms;* quoted in William Safire, *Safire's Political Dictionary* (New York: Random House, 1978), pp. 254–55.

18. In its 1993 decision on the North Carolina districting plan (*Shaw v. Reno,* 113 S Ct 2816), the Supreme Court seemed to be disturbed by the bizarre shape of the district. In its 1995 decision on the Georgia districting plan (*Miller v. Johnson,* 115 S Ct 2475), the court took issue with political boundaries drawn with racially based representation in mind to create a majority-minority district of rather conventional shape. A subsequent redistricting plan drawn up by a panel of federal judges eliminated two of Georgia's three majority-minority districts for the 1996 elections.

19. On the effects of redistricting, see Amihai Glazer, Bernard Grofman, and Marc Robbins, "Partisan and Incumbency Effects of 1970s Congressional Redistricting," *American Journal of Political Science* 31 (1987): 680–707; Richard Born, "Partisan Intentions and Election Day Realities

in the Congressional Redistricting Process," *American Political Science Review* 79 (1985): 305–19; and Richard G. Niemi and Laura R. Winsley, "The Persistence of Partisan Redistricting Effects in Congressional Elections in the 1970s and 1980s," *Journal of Politics* 54 (1992): 565–72. For somewhat contrary evidence of more than minimal effects in 1972 and 1982 but not in 1992, see Richard G. Niemi and Alan I. Abramowitz, "Partisan Redistricting and the 1992 Congressional Elections," *Journal of Politics* 56 (1994): 811–17. On California, see Bruce E. Cain, "Assessing the Partisan Effects of Redistricting," *American Political Science Review* 79 (1985): 320–34; on Indiana, see John D. Cranor, Gary L. Crawley, and Raymond H. Scheele, "The Anatomy of a Gerrymander," *American Journal of Political Science* 33 (1989): 222–39. Finally, a comprehensive study covering all state lower-house redistricting from 1968–1988 found significant partisan advantages even while affirming that redistricting fostered greater responsiveness; see Andrew Gelman and Gary King, "Enhancing Democracy Through Legislative Redistricting," *American Political Science Review* 88 (1994): 541–59.

20. For systematic empirical evidence showing partisan gains from the creation of more minority districts, see Kimball Brace, Bernard Grofman, and Lisa Handley, "Does Redistricting Aimed to Help Blacks Necessarily Help Republicans," *Journal of Politics* 49 (1987): 169–85; and Kevin A. Hill, "Does the Creation of Majority Black Districts Aid Republicans? An Analysis of the 1992 Congressional Elections in Eight Southern States," *Journal of Politics* 57 (1995): 384–401.

21. An example of the how-to-do-it genre is Joe Napolitan, *The Election Game and How to Win It* (Garden City, N.Y.: Doubleday, 1972). Also, the magazine *Campaigns and Elections* contains valuable articles on the art and practice of campaigning. More scholarly analyses may be found in Paul S. Herrnson, *Congressional Elections: Campaigning at Home and in Washington* (Washington, D.C.: CQ Press, 1995); and John H. Kessel, *Presidential Campaign Politics* (Chicago: Dorsey, 1988). Case studies of particular campaigns round out the literature on campaigning. See Lucius J. Barker and Ronald W. Walters, *Jesse Jackson's 1984 Presidential Campaign: Challenge and Change in American Politics* (Champaign: University of Illinois Press, 1979); Sidney Blumenthal, *Pledging Allegiance: The Last Campaign of the Cold War* (New York: HarperCollins, 1990); Marjorie Randon Hershey, *Running for Office: The Political Education of Campaigners* (Chatham, N.J.: Chatham House, 1984); L. Sandy Maisel, *From Obscurity to Oblivion: Running in the Congressional Primary* (Knoxville: University of Tennessee Press, 1986); David R. Runkel, *Campaign for President: The Managers Look at '88* (Dover, Mass.: Auburn House, 1989); Jack W. Germond and Jules Witcover, *Mad as Hell: Revolt at the Ballot Box, 1992* (New York: Warner Books, 1993); Mary Matalin and James Carville, *All's Fair: Love, War, and Running for President* (New York: Random House, 1994); and the best-selling novel *Primary Colors* (NY: Random House, 1996), written by an anonymous author, who later identified himself as Joe Klein.

22. For an examination of how presidential candidates allocated one scarce resource, campaign visits, among various constituency groups, see Darrell M. West, "Constituencies and Travel Allocations in the 1980 Presidential Campaign," *American Journal of Political Science* 27 (1983): 515–29.

23. Susan E. Howell, "Local Election Campaigns: The Effects of Office Level on Campaign Style," *Journal of Politics* 42 (1980): 1135–45.

24. For a colorful account of American campaign professionals in other foreign nations, see John M. Russonello, "The Making of the President . . . in the Philippines, Venezuela, France. . . ," *Public Opinion* 9 (1986): 10–12.

25. Among the many books on the subject, see especially Sidney Blumenthal, *The Permanent Campaign* (New York: Simon and Schuster, 1980); and Larry J. Sabato, *The Rise of Political Consultants* (New York: Basic, 1981).

26. Described in Ithiel de Sola Pool, Robert P. Abelson, and Samuel Popkin, *Candidates, Issues, and Strategies* (Cambridge, Mass.: MIT Press, 1964). A fictionalized version can be found in Eugene Burdick, *The 480* (New York: McGraw-Hill, 1964).

27. Although soundings of public opinion have been a staple of political campaigns from the beginning, the first use of a more or less "scientific" public opinion poll on behalf of a candidate appears to have been in advance of the 1936 presidential election. Campaign strategists for President Franklin Roosevelt, hiding the poll's true sponsor, mailed out quite a few more than 100,000 straw ballots and used the returns to help position Roosevelt for the presidential contest.

See Edwin Amenta, Kathleen Dunleavy, and Mary Bernstein, "Stolen Thunder? Huey Long's 'Share Our Wealth,' Political Mediation and the Second New Deal," *American Sociological Review* 59 (1994): 678–702, especially 687–91. For an interesting study of the use of private polls in the 1960 presidential campaign, see Lawrence R. Jacobs and Robert Y. Shapiro, "Issues, Candidate Image, and Priming: The Use of Private Polls in Kennedy's 1960 Presidential Campaign," *American Political Science Review* 88 (1994): 527–40.

28. On the use of television advertising in modern campaigns, see Kathleen Hall Jamieson, *Packaging the Presidency: A History and Criticism of Presidential Campaign Advertising* (New York: Oxford University Press, 1996); Montague Kern, *Thirty-Second Politics: Political Advertising in the Eighties* (New York: Praeger, 1989); and Darrell West, *Air Wars: Television Advertising in Election Campaigns, 1952–92* (Washington, D.C.: CQ Press, 1993).

29. E. J. Dionne, Jr., in *The New York Times,* September 7, 1980. Copyright 1980 by *The New York Times* Company. Reprinted by permission.

30. About 9 percent of the $3.22 billion spent on 1992 campaigns went for television. The presidential candidates spent 57 percent of their money on TV in the fall campaign—Clinton (59%), Bush (69%), and Perot (47%). See Herbert E. Alexander and Anthony Corrado, *Financing the 1992 Election* (Armonk, N.Y.: M. E. Sharpe, 1995), pp. 6, 115, 136, 233, 235, and 237.

31. Thoughtful reflections on how television is used in presidential campaigns are contained in Mathew D. McCubbins, ed., *Under the Watchful Eye* (Washington, D.C.: CQ Press, 1992), and Thomas E. Patterson, *Out of Order* (New York: Knopf, 1993).

32. The classic studies of the mobilizing effects of a political campaign were conducted in the 1940s before the appearance of television. See Paul Lazarsfeld, Bernard Berelson, and Hazel Gaudet, *The People's Choice* (New York: Columbia University Press, 1948); and Bernard Berelson, Paul Lazarsfeld, and William McPhee, *Voting* (Chicago: University of Chicago Press, 1954). Evidence that most voters continue to be found in highly homogeneous political environments and consequently are more likely to be mobilized than persuaded may be found in Robert Huckfeldt and John Sprague, "Networks in Context: The Social Flow of Political Information," *American Political Science Review* 81 (1987): 1197–1216; and Paul Allen Beck, "Voters' Intermediation Environments in the 1988 Presidential Contest," *Public Opinion Quarterly* 55 (1991).

33. For an illuminating examination of how negative advertising by single-issue groups defeated four of six targeted Senate incumbents in 1980, see Marjorie Hershey's, *Running for Office.* On negative campaigning generally, see Kathleen Hall Jamieson, *Dirty Politics: Deception, Distraction, and Democracy* (New York: Oxford University Press, 1992). One recent study of negative campaigning suggests that its major effect is to demobilize voters, especially supporters of the target of the ads; see Stephen Ansolabehere, Shanto Iyengar, Adam Simon, and Nicholas Valentine, "Does Attack Advertising Demobilize the Electorate?" *American Political Science Review* 88 (1994): 829–38: and Stephen Ansolabehere and Shanto Iyengar, *Going Negative: How Campaign Adversing Shrinks and Polarizes the Electorate* (New York: Free Press, 1995).

34. Austin Ranney, *Channels of Power: The Impact of Television on American Politics* (New York: Basic Books, 1983), p. 90.

35. These figures come from Harold W. Stanley and Richard G. Niemi, *Vital Statistics on American Politics* (Washington, D.C.: CQ Press, 1994), Table 2–12, p. 74.

36. These were the responses of a national sample of the American electorate interviewed after the 1992 campaign in a study directed by Paul Allen Beck, Russell J. Dalton, and Robert Huckfeldt.

37. Various studies of media content have demonstrated that the media do not systematically favor either candidate in presidential elections. Content analyses of ABC, CBS, and NBC evening news by the Center for Media and Public Affairs during the 1992 presidential campaign found that Clinton and Perot received only a slightly higher percentage of positive assessments than Bush—and that a majority of the assessments of each were negative. See Stanley and Niemi, *Vital Statistics on American Politics,* Table 2–10, p. 71. Similar findings for earlier years are reported in Doris A. Graber, *Mass Media and American Politics* (Washington, D.C.: CQ Press, 1989); C. Richard Hofstetter, *Bias in the News* (Columbus: Ohio State University Press, 1976); Thomas Patterson, *The Mass Media Election* (New York: Praeger, 1980); and Michael J. Robinson and Margaret A. Sheehan, *Over the Wire and On TV: CBS and UPI in Campaign '80* (New York: Russell Sage Foundation, 1983). For the first time in the sixty years that records have been

kept, a majority of newspapers even failed to endorse a candidate for president in 1992—and those that did favored the Democrat more than the Republican for the first time since 1964. See Stanley and Niemi, *Vital Statistics on American Politics,* Table 2–15, pp. 77–78.

38. For evidence on the agenda-setting effects of the media, see Donald Shaw and Maxwell E. McCombs, *The Emergence of American Political Issues: The Agenda-Setting Function of the Press* (St. Paul, Minn.: West, 1977); Lutz Erbring, Edie Goldenberg, and Arthur Miller, "Front-Page News and Real-World Cues: A New Look at Agenda-Setting by the Media," *American Journal of Political Science* 24 (1980): 16–49; and Shanto Iyengar and Donald Kinder, *News That Matters* (Chicago: University of Chicago Press, 1987). For evidence on priming, also see Iyengar and Kinder, *News That Matters.*

39. Media scholars for years have depicted the media as covering elections as if they were strategic games or horse races. The most recent case for this is made by Thomas E. Patterson, *Out of Order,* pp. 53–133. In the 1992 election, for example, a content analysis of the evening network news conducted by the Center for Media and Public Affairs showed that 29 percent of all news coverage of the presidential campaign focused on the "horse race." This figure is reported in Stanley and Niemi, *Vital Statistics on American Politics,* p. 63, Table 2–6.

40. Andrew Gelman and Gary King, "Party Competition and Media Messages in U.S. Presidential Elections," in L. Sandy Maisel, ed., *The Parties Respond* (Boulder, Colo.: Westview), pp. 255–95; and Thomas M. Holbrook, "Campaigns, National Conditions, and U.S. Presidential Elections," *American Journal of Political Science* 38 (1994): 973–98.

41. Phillips Cutright and Peter H. Rossi, "Grass Roots Politicians and the Vote," *American Sociological Review* 23 (1958): 171–79; Daniel Katz and Samuel J. Eldersveld, "The Impact of Local Party Activity upon the Electorate," *Public Opinion Quarterly* 25 (1961): 1–24; and Raymond E. Wolfinger, "The Influence of Precinct Work on Voting Behavior," *Public Opinion Quarterly* 27 (1963): 387–98.

42. Samuel J. Eldersveld, "Experimental Propaganda Techniques and Voting Behavior," *American Political Science Review* 50 (1956): 154–65; and John C. Blydenburg, "A Controlled Experiment to Measure the Effects of Personal Contact Campaigning," *Midwest Journal of Political Science* 15 (1971): 365–81.

43. Gerald H. Kramer, "The Effects of Precinct-Level Canvassing on Voter Behavior," *Public Opinion Quarterly* 34 (1970): 560–72; and William J. Crotty, "Party Effort and Its Impact on the Vote," *American Political Science Review* 65 (1971): 439–50.

44. John P. Frendreis, James L. Gibson, and Laura L. Vertz, "The Electoral Relevance of Local Party Organizations," *American Political Science Review* 84 (1990): 225–35.

45. Such skepticism, for example, is expressed by A. James Reichley in *The Life of the Parties* (New York: The Free Press, 1992), pp. 377–81.

46. An excellent account of these developments is provided by Paul S. Herrnson, *Party Campaigning in the 1980s* (Cambridge, Mass.: Harvard University Press, 1988). See also Paul Allen Beck, Russell J. Dalton, Audrey Haynes, and Robert Huckfeldt, "Party Effort at the Grass Roots," paper delivered at the Annual Meeting of the Midwest Political Science Association, Chicago, 1994.

47. Soft money refers to contributions to the national parties that would be illegal under federal law if they stayed at the national level. Acting under the aegis of a 1979 amendment to the federal campaign-finance laws, the parties have been able to make these contributions legal by passing them on to the states for party-building and voter mobilization activities. See Frank J. Sorauf, *Inside Campaign Finance* (New Haven, Conn.: Yale University Press, 1992), pp. 146–52.

Chapter 12

1. George Thayer, *Who Shakes the Money Tree?* (New York: Simon and Schuster, 1973), p. 25.

2. Readers interested in comprehending the mysteries of modern campaign finance should start with Frank J. Sorauf, *Inside Campaign Finance: Myths and Realities* (New Haven, Conn.: Yale University Press, 1992). The standard accounts of campaign finance before modern times are Louise Overacker, *Money in Elections* (New York: Macmillan, 1932) and *Presidential Campaign Funds* (Boston: Boston University Press, 1944); and Alexander Heard, *The Costs of Democracy*

(Chapel Hill: The University of North Carolina Press, 1960). Estimates of presidential campaign spending back as far as 1860 may be found in Erik W. Austin, *Political Facts of the United States since 1789* (New York: Columbia University Press, 1987), Table 3.9.

3. Herbert E. Alexander's studies are: *Financing the 1960 Election* (Princeton: Citizens' Research Foundation, 1962); *Financing the 1964 Election* (Princeton: Citizens' Research Foundation, 1966); *Financing the 1968 Election* (Lexington, Mass.: Heath, 1971); *Financing the 1972 Election* (Lexington, Mass.: Heath, 1976); *Financing the 1976 Election* (Washington, D.C.: Congressional Quarterly, Inc., 1979); *Financing the 1980 Election* (Lexington, Mass.: Heath, 1983); (with Brian A. Haggerty) *Financing the 1984 Election* (Lexington, Mass.: Heath, 1987); (with Monica Bauer) *Financing the 1988 Election* (Boulder, Colo.: Westview Press, 1991); and (with Anthony Corrado) *Financing the 1992 Election* (Armonk, N.Y.: M.E. Sharpe, 1995).

4. This table does not include quite all of the spending on congressional elections. While most of the money spent by the congressional campaign committees goes directly to the candidates and is therefore reflected in their totals, these committees also make so-called coordinated expenditures for multiple campaigns. In 1993–94, the Democratic committees spent $21.1 million and the Republican committees spent $20.4 million in this fashion. In addition, much smaller amounts were spent by nonparty organizations or independents for or against particular candidates and on communication expenditures.

5. The state and local totals can be estimated fairly precisely (except for the spending noted in footnote 4 above) by subtracting the presidential expenditures in Table 12.2 and the congressional expenditures in Table 12.3 from the overall totals in Table 12.1.

6. See Alexander and Corrado, *Financing the 1992 Elections,* pp. 3–4.

7. The costs of the Willie Horton commercial discussed in Chapter 11 are included in this independent expenditure category. They were paid for by a political action committee that was, technically speaking, independent from the Bush campaign or the Republican party and did not count against the Bush campaign expenditure limit. Constitutional protection for such independent expenditures was provided by the United States Supreme Court in *Buckley v. Valeo,* 424 U.S. 1 (1976).

8. For more on 1992 presidential campaign finance, see Clifford W. Brown, Jr., Lynda W. Powell, and Clyde Wilcox, *Serious Money: Fundraising and Contributing in Presidential Nomination Campaigns* (New York: Cambridge University Press, 1995), and Alexander and Corrado, *Financing the 1992 Elections,* Chapters 3–6. Specific spending figures cited in the text come from Alexander and Corrado.

9. Just because money is spent "by" the campaign does not mean that it is spent "on" the campaign itself. Campaigns have considerable expenses beyond those which are directed to persuade voters to support their candidate. On this point, see Stephen Ansolabehere and Alan Gerber, "The Mismeasure of Campaign Spending: Evidence from the 1990 U.S. House Elections," *Journal of Politics* 56: 1106–18. For further insight into how the campaigns spend their money, see Sara Fritz and Dwight Morris, *Handbook of Campaign Spending: Money in the 1990 Congressional Races* (Washington, D.C.: CQ Press, 1992), and Dwight Morris and Murielle E. Gamache, *Handbook of Campaign Spending: Money in the 1992 Congressional Races* (Washington, D.C.: CQ Press, 1994).

10. The specific spending figures cited in the text come from news releases of the Federal Election Commission dated March 4, 1993, for the 1991–92 election cycle, and April 28, 1995, for the 1993–94 election cycle. For more on recent congressional campaign spending, see Alexander and Corrado, *Financing the 1992 Election,* Chapter 7; and Paul S. Herrnson, *Congressional Elections: Campaigning at Home and in Washington* (Washington, D.C.: CQ Press, 1995), especially Chapter 6.

11. The figures for Koch are reported in *The New York Times,* March 21, 1988; on the Dallas race, in *The New York Times,* April 4, 1987; for the 1990 California gubernatorial race, in *The New York Times,* October 14, 1990; and for the California house races, in Frank J. Sorauf, *Inside Campaign Finance,* p. 36.

12. The divergent conclusions reached from analysis of spending levels and outcomes for congressional races are well represented in an exchange in the *American Journal of Political Science.* See Donald Philip Green and Jonathan S. Krasno, "Salvation for the Spendthrift Incumbent:

Reestimating the Effects of Campaign Spending in House Elections," 32 (1988): 884–907; Gary C. Jacobson, "The Effects of Campaign Spending in House Elections: New Evidence for Old Arguments," 34 (1990): 334–62; and Donald Philip Green and Jonathan S. Krasno, "Rebuttal to Jacobson's 'New Evidence for Old Arguments'," 34 (1990): 363–72.

13. For a discussion of campaign spending in the states, see Ruth S. Jones, "State Election Campaign Financing: 1980," in Michael J. Malbin, ed., *Money and Politics in the United States* (Chatham, N.J.: Chatham House, 1984), pp. 172–213; and Frank J. Sorauf, *Money in American Elections* (Glenview, Ill.: Scott, Foresman, 1988), Chapter 9.

14. Ruth S. Jones and Warren E. Miller, "Financing Campaigns: Macro Level Information and Micro Level Response," *Western Political Quarterly* 38 (1985), 187–210.

15. On soft-money contributions in the 1992 campaign, see Alexander and Corrado, *Financing the 1992 Election,* Chapter 6.

16. On Hanna, see Thayer, *Who Shakes the Money Tree?,* pp. 48–52; the quotation is taken from pp. 49–50. On Johnson, see Robert A. Caro, *The Years of Lyndon Johnson: The Path to Power* (New York: Alfred A. Knopf, 1982), pp. 606–64; the quote is from p. 662. For a discussion of campaign financing in the 1972 election, see Thayer, *Who Shakes the Money Tree?,* pp. 108–16; and Michael J. Malbin, "Looking Back at the Future of Campaign Finance Reform," in Malbin, *Money and Politics in the United States,* pp. 245–47. The discussion of Richard Viguerie is based on Nick Kotz, "King Midas of 'The New Right'," *The Atlantic* 242 (1978): 52–61.

17. The figures are for the number of PACs registered at the federal level and come from the end of year reports of the Federal Election Commission, typically dated in early January.

18. For a more extensive discussion of the role of PACs in campaign financing, see Sorauf, *Inside Campaign Finance,* Chapter 4. See also Larry J. Sabato, *PAC Power: Inside the World of Political Action Committees* (New York: Norton, 1984).

19. The conclusion that PAC contributions do not influence voting is reached by, among others, Janet M. Grenzke, "Shopping in the Congressional Supermarket: The Currency is Complex," *American Journal of Political Science* 33 (1989): 1–24; and John R. Wright, "PACs, Contributions, and Roll Calls: An Organizational Perspective," *American Political Science Review* 79 (1985): 400–14. A good summary of the studies on the effects of campaign contributions may be found in Sorauf, *Inside Campaign Finance,* Chapter 6.

20. On access, see Laura I. Langbein, "Money and Access: Some Empirical Evidence," *Journal of Politics* 48 (1986): 1052–64. On committee involvement, see Richard L. Hall and Frank W. Wayman, "Buying Time: Moneyed Interests and the Mobilization of Bias in Congressional Committees," *American Political Science Review* 84 (1990): 797–820.

21. Wright, "PACs, Contributions, and Roll Calls."

22. For figures on participation in the tax checkoff and a general discussion of that program, see Alexander and Corrado, *Financing the 1992 Election,* pp. 10–14.

23. This discussion of the shortfall in public funds is based on an article in the Congressional Quarterly *Weekly Report,* January 6, 1996, pp. 63–64.

24. On the state experience with public funding, see Ruth S. Jones, "State Public Campaign Finance: Implications for Partisan Politics," *American Journal of Political Science* 25 (1981): 342–61; and Jack L. Noragon, "Political Finance and Political Reform: The Experience with State Income Tax Checkoffs," *American Political Science Review* 75 (1981): 667–87.

25. The figures come from William E. Cassie, Joel A. Thompson, and Malcolm E. Jewell, "The Pattern of PAC Contributions in Legislative Elections: An Eleven State Analysis," paper delivered at the Annual Meeting of the American Political Science Association, Chicago, 1992.

26. For a general review of state campaign financing, see Malcolm E. Jewell and David M. Olson, *Political Parties and Elections in American States* (Chicago: Dorsey, 1988), pp. 154–73. On the regulation of PAC contributions in the states, see Arnold Fleischmann and David C. Nice, "States and PACs: The Legacy of Established Decision Rules," *Political Behavior* 10 (1988): 349–63. On legislative caucus and leadership funds in the states, see Anthony Gierzynski, *Legislative Party Campaign Committees in the American States* (Lexington: University of Kentucky Press, 1992).

27. Good accounts of federal campaign-finance reform legislation may be found in Sorauf, *Inside Campaign Finance,* Chapter 7; and Robert E. Mutch, *Campaigns, Congress, and the Courts* (New York: Praeger, 1988).
28. *Buckley v. Valeo,* 424 U.S. 1 (1976).
29. The contribution figures come from the files of the Federal Election Commission as reported in *The New York Times,* July 10, 1992, and May 31, 1994.
30. Particularly useful treatments of the effects of campaign-finance reforms on the parties can be found in F. Christopher Arterton, "Political Money and Party Strength," in Joel L. Fleishman, ed., *The Future of American Political Parties* (Englewood Cliffs, N.J.: Prentice-Hall, 1982), pp. 101–39; and Sorauf, *Inside Campaign Finance,* Chapter 7.
31. The data on state campaign finance provisions are drawn from *The Book of the States: 1994–95* (Lexington, Ky.: Council of State Governments, 1994), pp. 254–78.
32. Some of the most interesting new proposals for campaign-finance reform include reduced broadcast and postal rates for candidates, free broadcast time for parties to be used by their candidates, and exemptions from spending limits for some part of the contributions from the candidate's home state. They were key recommendations in a 1990 report of the Campaign Finance Reform Panel established by Democratic and Republican party leaders of the U.S. Senate. This report and subsequent proposals by party leaders, as well as a public agreement to pursue reform between Republican House Speaker Newt Gingrich and President Bill Clinton, however, have not led to any changes in campaign finance laws so far. For additional proposals for reform, see Alexander and Corrado, *Financing the 1992 Campaign,* Chap. 9.
33. For an interesting analysis of who the more "serious" (with donations of more than $200) of these individual contributors were and why they gave in 1988 and 1992, see Brown, Powell, and Wilcox, *Serious Money.*

Part Five

1. See John F. Hoadley, "The Emergence of Political Parties in Congress, 1789–1803," *American Political Science Review* 74 (1980): 757–79.
2. E. E. Schattschneider, *Party Government* (New York: Rinehart, 1942), pp. 131–32.
3. Gerald M. Pomper, *Elections in America* (New York: Dodd, Mead, 1968), Chapter 8.
4. The report was published in New York by Rinehart in 1950. It also appears as a supplement to the September 1950 issue of the *American Political Science Review.*
5. The Republican's 1994 *Contract with America* gives us a modern-day glimpse of how responsible party government might work. It became the centerpiece of the 1994 midterm elections and the Republican-dominated Congress that followed. That Republican control did not encompass the presidency and the Democratic opposition did not present an alternative policy vision, though, shows the limits of this model for American government.

Chapter 13

1. The Nebraska legislature is chosen in nonpartisan elections, although the partisan affiliations of its members usually are no secret. Of the 7,343 legislators in the remaining states and the 535 members of Congress, only 25 were neither Democrats nor Republicans in 1992.
2. The view of leadership power as authority *delegated* to leaders by the party caucus is one of the cornerstones of a new principal-agent conceptualization of Congress. In this view, the majority party is the principal, and its power to make policy is delegated to agents such as the leadership, the committees, the president, and even the bureaucracy. The effectiveness of the majority party lies less in how much authority is delegated, for delegation is necessary in modern governments, and more in how well delegation helps the congressional party to carry out its policy goals. For a clear articulation of this view and a compelling argument that the congressional party has delegated much better than is commonly supposed when it comes to the appropriations process, see D. Roderick Kiewiet and Mathew D. McCubbins, *The Logic of Delegation: Congressional Parties and the Appropriations Process* (Chicago: University of Chicago Press, 1991).

3. On the Democratic Study Group, see Arthur G. Stevens, Arthur H. Miller, and Thomas E. Mann, "Mobilization of Liberal Strength in the House, 1955–1970: The Democratic Study Group," *American Political Science Review* 68 (1974): 667–81. For more on the reforms, see Leroy Reiselbach, *Congressional Reform* (Washington, D.C.: CQ Press, 1986).

4. For a list of the cases between 1947 and 1988 when the Congress violated seniority in allocating committee positions, see Gary W. Cox and Mathew W. McCubbins, *Legislative Leviathan: Party Government in the House* (Berkeley and Los Angeles: University of California Press, 1993), pp. 279–82. Once open to challenge in the party caucus, especially after a few of their number had been stripped of committee positions in 1975, it should hardly be surprising that committee chairs became more solicitous of their committee and party colleagues. One study finds that the reforms increased party loyalty in roll-call voting among House Democrats who chaired committees or subcommittees or who were next in line to be a chair. See Sara Brandes Crook and John R. Hibbing, "Congressional Reform and Party Discipline: The Effects of Changes in the Seniority System on Party Loyalty in the U.S. House of Representatives," *British Journal of Political Science* 15 (1985): 207–26.

5. On this point, see Steven S. Smith, "New Patterns of Decisionmaking in Congress," in John E. Chubb and Paul E. Peterson, eds., *The New Direction in American Politics* (Washington, D.C.: Brookings institution, 1985), pp. 203–33.

6. This account of how the reforms provided the conditions under which more ideologically homogeneous congressional parties would support stronger leadership and in turn be more cohesive draws heavily from David W. Rohde, *Parties and Leaders in the Postreform House* (Chicago: University of Chicago Press, 1991). Also see Barbara Sinclair, *Legislators, Leaders, and Lawmaking: The U.S. House of Representatives in the Postreform Era* (Baltimore, Md.: Johns Hopkins University Press, 1995).

7. There is a rich literature on party leadership in the Congress. Among the best works are Ralph K. Huitt, "Democratic Party Leadership in the Senate," *American Political Science Review* 55 (1961): 333–44; Charles O. Jones, *The Minority Party in Congress* (Boston: Little, Brown, 1970); Robert L. Peabody, *Leadership in Congress* (Boston: Little, Brown, 1976); Randall B. Ripley, *Party Leaders in the House of Representatives* (Washington, D.C.: Brookings Institution, 1967); Barbara Sinclair, *Majority Leadership in the U.S. House* (Baltimore: John Hopkins University Press, 1983); Rohde, *Parties and Leaders in the Postreform House;* and Barbara Sinclair, "The Emergence of Strong Leadership in the 1980s House of Representatives," *Journal of Politics* 54 (1992): 657–84.

8. That the activity of Congress is organized around the election needs of its members is a view powerfully articulated in David R. Mayhew, *Congress: The Electoral Connection* (New Haven, Conn.: Yale University Press, 1974).

9. See Joseph Cooper and David W. Brady, "Institutional Context and Leadership Style: The House from Cannon to Rayburn," *American Political Science Review* 75 (1981): 411–25.

10. On Wright, see Rohde, *Party and Leaders in the Postreform House,* pp. 105–18; and Barbara Sinclair, "House Majority Party Leadership in the Late 1980s," in Lawrence C. Dodd and Bruce I. Oppenheimer, eds., *Congress Reconsidered.* (Washington, D.C.: CQ Press, 1989), pp. 307–30. On the transition in styles from Wright to Foley, see Rohde, *Party Leaders in the Postreform House,* pp. 184–89.

11. On the activities of legislative leadership campaign committees, see Anthony Gierzynski, *Legislative Party Campaign Committees in the American States* (Lexington, Ky.: University of Kentucky Press, 1992); and Daniel M. Shea, *Transforming Democracy: Legislative Campaign Committees and Political Parties* (Albany, N.Y.: State University of New York Press, 1995).

12. Malcolm E. Jewell and David M. Olson, *Political Parties and Elections in American States* (Chicago: Dorsey, 1988), pp. 235–44.

13. For more on parties and party leadership in state legislatures, see Keith E. Hamm and Robert Harmel, "Legislative Party Development and the Speaker System: The Case of the Texas House," *Journal of Politics* 55 (1993): 1140–51; and Malcolm E. Jewell and Marcia Lynn Whicker, *Legislative Leadership in the American States* (Ann Arbor, Mich.: University of Michigan Press, 1994).

14. Gramm resigned his seat shortly thereafter and was reelected to it as a Republican in a special election some weeks later. In 1984, he was elected as a Republican U.S. senator from Texas.

15. See Barbara Sinclair, "Majority Party Leadership Strategies for Coping with the New U.S. House," *Legislative Studies Quarterly* 6 (1981): 391–414. On the favors leaders can bestow, see Roger Davidson, "Senate Leaders: Janitors for an Untidy Chamber?" In Dodd and Oppenheimer, eds., *Congress Reconsidered*, pp. 225–52. On leaders' control of the floor through the Rules Committee and other devices, see Steven Smith, *Call to Order: Floor Politics in the House and the Senate* (Washington, D.C.: Brookings Institution, 1989).

16. The rise of seniority as a principle for allocating committee positions in the House of Representatives can be traced to the period around the turn of the twentieth century, when House members became more likely spend a long career in the chamber, and especially to the weakening of the speaker after 1911. See Nelson W. Polsby, Miriam Gallaher, and Barry Spencer Rundquist, "The Growth of the Seniority System in the U.S. House of Representatives," *American Political Science Review* 68 (1969): 787–807.

17. This discussion draws upon Jackie Koszczuk, "Gingrich Puts More Power Into Speaker's Hands," *Congressional Quarterly Weekly Report,* 53 (October 7, 1995): 3049–53.

18. Eric M. Uslaner and Ronald E. Weber, *Patterns of Decision Making in State Legislatures* (New York: Praeger, 1977).

19. Membership turnover in state legislatures varies considerably across the states. From one session to the next in 1990 and 1992, upper-house turnover ranged from a low of 4 percent in Maryland and Pennsylvania to a high of 70 percent in Alaska; average turnover was 29. Lower-house turnover varied between a low of 2 percent in Alabama to a high of 58 percent in Alaska during the same period, with an average of 31 percent.

20. The influence of party in the states, though, should not be exaggerated. In one survey, state legislators were asked who made the most significant legislative decisions. A majority cited the party leadership in sixty-seven of ninety-nine legislative chambers and the party caucus was important in fifty chambers, but committees were significant in eighty-seven. The party leadership was perceived to dominate only five chambers at that time. The party leaders and party caucus shared dominance in twelve more. But, in most state legislatures, committee and party shared the stage as important centers of decision making. Of course, committee power is allocated by the party leadership, rather than by strict seniority rules, in many states, so party power may have an indirect influence as well. See Wayne L. Francis, "Leadership, Party Caucuses, and Committees in the U.S. State Legislatures," *Legislative Studies Quarterly* 10 (1985): 243–57.

21. Julius Turner, *Party and Constituency: Pressures on Congress,* rev. ed. by Edward V. Schneier (Baltimore: The Johns Hopkins University Press, 1970), pp. 16–17.

22. The corresponding number of uncontested or "universalistic" votes, in which 90 percent of Congress votes the same way, conversely, increased steadily from the late 1940s to 1980. See Melissa P. Collie, "Universalism and the Parties in the U.S. House of Representatives," *American Journal of Political Science* 32 (1988): 865–83.

23. To even out this "session effect," the data in Figure 13.2 are averaged across the two sessions of each Congress. The downturn in party voting in the even years, when House members stand for election, goes back as far as the 1830s. The 1995 figures come from the *Congressional Quarterly Weekly Report,* January 27, 1996, p. 199.

24. Institutionalization is the term Polsby uses to characterize the development of a professionalized Congress, with greater specialization of party and committee roles, established norms, deference to congressional experience, and greater longevity in office. Nelson W. Polsby, "The Institutionalization of the United States House of Representatives," *American Political Science Review* 62 (1968): 144–68. By disaggregation, Burnham means a decline in the party-based linkage among candidates for various offices. Walter Dean Burnham, *Critical Elections and the Mainsprings of American Politics* (New York: Norton, 1970), pp. 91–134.

25. Samuel C. Patterson and Gregory A. Caldeira, "Party Voting in the United States Congress," *British Journal of Political Science* 18 (1988): 111–31.

26. On party voting in state legislatures, see Jewell and Olson, *Political Parties and Elections,* pp. 246–49. Data on party voting and cohesion in selected state legislatures from 1959 to 1974 are provided by Malcolm E. Jewell and Samuel C. Patterson, *The Legislative Process in the United States* (New York: Random House, 1977), pp. 384–85. For recent data on one state, South Car-

olina, see Cole Blease Graham, Jr., and Kenny J. Whitby, "Party-Based Voting in a Southern State Legislature," *American Politics Quarterly* 17: 181–93.

27. Rohde, *Parties and Leaders in the Postreform House,* especially Chapter 3. On changes in the South, also see Franklin D. Gilliam, Jr., and Kenny Whitby, "A Longitudinal Analysis of Competing Explanations for the Transformation of Southern Politics," *Journal of Politics* 53 (1991), 504–18.

28. For more on presidential support in Congress and the conditions under which it varies, see Jon R. Bond and Richard Fleisher, *The President in the Legislative Arena* (Chicago: University of Chicago Press, 1990); Mark A. Peterson, *Legislating Together: The White House and Capitol Hill from Eisenhower to Reagan* (Cambridge, Mass.: Harvard University Press, 1990); and Cary R. Covington, J. Mark Wrighton, and Rhonda Kinney, "A 'Presidency-Augmented' Model of Presidential Success on House Roll Call Votes," *American Journal of Political Science* 39 (November, 1995): 1001–24.

29. See Aage Clausen, *How Congressmen Decide* (New York: St. Martin's, 1973). Political ideology also provides a powerful explanation of legislators' votes, and some scholars have even argued that it can account for most voting behavior in the Congress. See Keith T. Poole, "Recent Developments in Analytical Models of Voting in the U.S. Congress," *Legislative Studies Quarterly* 13 (1988): 117–33; and Jerrold Schneider, *Ideological Coalitions in Congress* (Westport, Conn.: Greenwood Press, 1979).

30. This theme underlies such diverse historical studies of party voting in the House of Representatives as Jerome M. Clubb and Santa A. Traugott, "Partisan Cleavage and Cohesion in the House of Representatives, 1861–1974," *Journal of Interdisciplinary History* 7 (1977): 374–401; David W. Brady and Philip Althoff, "Party Voting in the U.S. House of Representatives, 1890–1910: Elements of a Responsible Party System," *Journal of Politics* 36 (1974): 752–75; and Barbara Sinclair, "Party Realignment and the Transformation of the Political Agenda: The House of Representatives, 1925–1938," *American Political Science Review* 71 (1977): 940–53.

31. David W. Brady, "A Reevaluation of Realignments in American Politics: Evidence from the House of Representatives," *American Political Science Review* 79 (1985): 28–49; and *Critical Elections and Congressional Policy Making* (Stanford, Calif.: Stanford University Press, 1988).

32. Paul Allen Beck, "The Electoral Cycle and Patterns of American Politics," *British Journal of Political Science* 9 (1979): 129–56.

33. Warren E. Miller and Donald E. Stokes, "Constituency Influence in Congress," *American Political Science Review* 57 (1963): 45–57.

34. David M. Olson, "U.S. Congressmen and Their Diverse Congressional District Parties," *Legislative Studies Quarterly* 3 (1978): 239–64.

35. This view echoed earlier laments voiced by congressional scholar and later president Woodrow Wilson at the height of committee power in 1800s and by a committee of political parties specialists sixty-five years later. See Woodrow Wilson, *Congressional Government* (New York: Meridian Books, 1956; originally published in 1885); and the Committee on Political Parties of the American Political Science Association, *Toward a More Responsible Two-Party System* (New York: Rinehart, 1950).

36. The quotation is from Cox and McCubbins, *Legislative Leviathan,* p. 278. Their book is one of several important studies in recent years that have shown the majority party to be the prime actor in the House of Representatives—a veritable "legislative leviathan." Other key works in this genre are Kiewiet and McCubbins, *The Logic of Delegation;* Rohde, *Parties and Leaders in the Postreform House;* and Sinclair, *Legislators, Leaders, and Lawmaking.*

37. A valuable insider's perspective on the role of party in Congress is provided by political scientist and U.S. Representative David E. Price in *The Congressional Experience* (Boulder, Colo.: Westview, 1992).

38. Studies of legislative party voting in Britain and Canada suggest that it is the parliamentary form more than anything else that accounts for greater party discipline there than in the United States. On Britain, see Austin Ranney, "Candidate Selection and Party Cohesion in Britain and the U.S.," in William J. Crotty, ed., *Approaches to the Study of Party Organization* (Boston: Allyn and Bacon, 1968), pp. 139–68; and Gary Cox, *The Efficient Secret* (New York: Cambridge University Press, 1987). On Canada, see Leon D. Epstein, "A Comparative Study of Canadian Par-

ties," *American Political Science Review* 58 (1964): 46–59; and Allan Kornberg, "Caucus and Cohesion in Canadian Parliamentary Parties," *American Political Science Review* 60 (1966): 83–92.

39. Even the vaunted *Contract with America* was the creation of only House Republicans, especially party leaders Newt Gingrich and Dick Armey—not its party organization, national party convention, or even its senators.

Chapter 14

1. In the landmark *Marbury* case, Federalist Chief Justice Marshall refrained from ordering the new Jefferson administration to deliver a commission to Marbury that had been approved by the previous Federalist administration. In so doing, though, he claimed for the Supreme Court the power to judge congressional actions as to their constitutionality and used this power to rule that Congress had (wrongly) authorized the Supreme Court to exercise powers denied to it by the Constitution. This case is regarded as the key precedent for the Court's power of judicial review. See *Marbury v. Madison* 1 Cranch 137 (1803).

2. For this point, see Clive Bean and Anthony Mughan, "Leadership Effects in Parliamentary Elections in Australia and Britain," *American Political Science Review* 83 (1989): 1165–80.

3. Fred I. Greenstein finds persuasive evidence that Eisenhower's public avoidance of partisan politics masked, in his characteristic "hidden hand" fashion, an abiding sense of partisanship and a commitment to strengthening the Republican party. See his "Eisenhower as an Activist President: A Look at New Evidence," *Political Science Quarterly* 94 (1979–80): 575–99, as well as his *The Hidden-Hand Presidency: Eisenhower as Leader* (New York: Basic Books, 1982). Also see Cornelius P. Cotter, "Eisenhower as Party Leader," *Political Science Quarterly* 98 (1983): 255–83.

4. Franklin Roosevelt is considered the consummate party leader as president in the twentieth century. For a comprehensive study of him in this role, see Sean J. Savage, *Roosevelt: The Party Leader, 1932–1945* (Lexington: University Press of Kentucky, 1991). On the legacy Roosevelt left and how subsequent presidents have tried to use it, see Sidney M. Milkis, *The President and the Parties* (New York: Oxford University Press, 1993).

5. Roger G. Brown, "Party and Bureaucracy: From Kennedy to Reagan," *Political Science Quarterly* 97 (1982): 279–94.

6. On presidential coattails in U.S. House elections, see Randall L. Calvert and John A. Ferejohn, "Coattail Voting in Recent Presidential Elections," *American Political Science Review* 77 (1983): 407–19; John A. Ferejohn and Randall L. Calvert, "Presidential Coattails in Historical Perspective," *American Journal of Political Science* 28 (1984): 127–46; Richard Born, "Reassessing the Decline of Presidential Coattails: U.S. House Elections from 1952–80," *Journal of Politics* 46 (1984): 60–79; and James E. Campbell, "Predicting Seat Gains from Presidential Coattails," *American Journal of Political Science* 30 (1986): 164–83.

7. See James E. Campbell, "Presidential Coattails and Midterm Losses in State Legislative Elections," *American Political Science Review* 80 (1986): 45–63; and James E. Campbell and Joe A. Sumners, "Presidential Coattails in Senate Elections," *American Political Science Review* 84 (1990): 512–24. The first Campbell study finds evidence of gubernatorial coattails as well.

8. Angus Campbell attributed this phenomenon to the absence in midterm elections of the short-term forces that had favored the president two years earlier. This in turn led to declines in turnout among those without strong partisan loyalties. See his "Surge and Decline: A Study of Electoral Change," in Angus Campbell, Philip E. Converse, Warren E. Miller, and Donald E. Stokes, eds., *Elections and the Political Order* (New York: Wiley, 1966), pp. 40–62.

9. This view that midterm congressional contests are in part a referendum on presidential performance was initially offered by Edward R. Tufte, "Determinants of the Outcomes of Midterm Congressional Elections," *American Political Science Review* 69 (1975): 812–26; and *Political Control of the Economy* (Princeton, N.J.: Princeton University Press, 1978), Chapter 5. Even more persuasive evidence of the relationship between presidential approval and midterm congressional outcomes may be found in Robin F. Marra and Charles W. Ostrom, Jr., "Explaining

Seat Change in the U.S. House of Representatives, 1950–86," *American Journal of Political Science* 33 (1989): 541–69.

10. An attractive "strategic politicians" explanation for this relationship has been offered by Gary Jacobson. Rather than voters explicitly linking presidents to legislators, the Jacobson thesis is that presidential popularity and other factors impinging upon the standing of the party determine the quality of candidates (especially challengers) in the president's party which, in turn, affects outcomes in the fall election. See his "Strategic Politicians and the Dynamics of U.S. House Elections, 1946–86," *American Political Science Review* 83 (1989): 773–93.

11. This translation of votes into seats, called the "swing ratio," is calculated by Edward R. Tufte in "The Relationship between Seats and Votes in Two-Party Systems," *American Political Science Review* 67 (1973): 540–54. The swing ratio declined sharply to a low of 0.71 in 1966–70 and may have stayed around that level since, which means that only 0.71 percent of 435 seats (or 3 seats) changed hands for each 1 percent vote change.

12. Samuel Kernell, "Presidential Popularity and Negative Voting: An Alternative Explanation of the Midterm Congressional Decline of the President's Party," *American Political Science Review* 71 (1977): 44–66. The negative voting thesis, though, has been challenged by Richard Born, who concludes that it is the return of presidential defectors to their home party and not negative voting that accounts for the presidential party's loss of seats at midterm. See his "Surge and Decline, Negative Voting, and the Midterm Loss Phenomenon: A Simultaneous Choice Analysis," *American Journal of Political Science* 34 (1990): 615–45.

13. On the role of the governor in party leadership, see Alan Rosenthal, *Governors and Legislatures: Contending Powers* (Washington, D.C.: CQ Press, 1990).

14. How operational control of presidential appointment powers has changed over time, moving from the White House to the party and now back to the White House, is considered by G. Calvin MacKenzie, "Partisan Leadership Through Presidential Appointments," in L. Sandy Maisel, ed., *The Parties Respond* (Boulder, Colo.: Westview, 1994), pp. 341–62.

15. In addition to the figures in Figure 14.1, see George C. Edwards III, "Measuring Presidential Success in Congress: Alternative Approaches," *Journal of Politics* 47 (1985): 667–85.

16. See Bruce Cain, John Ferejohn, and Morris Fiorina, *The Personal Vote: Constituency Service and Electoral Independence* (Cambridge: Harvard University Press, 1987).

17. In *The End of Liberalism: The Second Republic of the United States* (New York: Norton, 1979), Theodore J. Lowi criticized Congress for delegating so much authority to the executive branch bureacracy that they have compromised the democratic nature of the American political system. In their *The Logic of Delegation: Congressional Parties and the Appropriations Process* (Chicago: University of Chicago Press, 1991), D. Roderick Kiewiet and Mathew D. McCubbins have defended these large grants of discretion by congressional "principals" to bureaucratic "agents" as reasonable, and controllable, exercises of majority party power. Whether bureaucratic discretion is too large or about right, there is no question that it is considerable in the American system—or, for that matter, any modern government.

18. In his *Building a New American State* (Cambridge, U.K.: Cambridge University Press, 1982), Stephen Skowronek shows how a federal regime dominated by political parties (through Congress and patronage) and the courts turned into government by a professional bureaucracy around the turn of the twentieth century. This change has made the executive branch bureaucracy less responsive to the political parties per se but probably more responsive to the president.

19. Hugh Heclo, "Issue Networks and the Executive Establishment," in Anthony King, ed., *The New American Political System* (Washington, D.C.: American Enterprise Institute, 1979), pp. 87–124.

20. Dean E. Mann, *The Assistant Secretaries* (Washington, D.C.: Brookings Institution, 1965); and Brown, "Party and Bureaucracy."

21. Hugh Heclo, *A Government of Strangers: Executive Politics in Washington* (Washington, D.C.: Brookings Institution, 1977).

22. See Terry M. Moe, "The Politicized Presidency," in John E. Chubb and Paul E. Peterson, eds., *The New Direction in American Politics* (Washington, D.C.: Brookings Institution, 1985), pp. 235–71.

23. Joel Aberbach and Bert A. Rockman, "Clashing Beliefs Within the Executive Branch: The Nixon Administration Bureaucracy," *American Political Science Review* 70 (1976): 456–68.

24. Joel D. Aberbach and Bert A. Rockman, "The Political Views of U.S. Senior Federal Executives, 1970–1992," *Journal of Politics* 57 (1995): 838–52. For a similar report through 1987, see Joel D. Aberbach and Bert A. Rockman with Robert M. Copeland, "From Nixon's *Problem* to Reagan's *Achievement:* The Federal Executive Reexamined," in Larry Berman, ed., *Looking Back on the Reagan Presidency* (Baltimore: Johns Hopkins University Press, 1990), pp. 175–94.

25. See Sidney Ulmer, "The Political Party Variable on the Michigan Supreme Court," *Journal of Public Law* 11 (1962): 352–62; Stuart Nagel, "Political Party Affiliation and Judges' Decisions," *American Political Science Review* 55 (1961): 843–50; Glendon A. Schubert, *Quantitative Analysis of Judicial Behavior* (Glencoe, Ill.: Free Press, 1959), pp. 129–42; and David W. Adamany, "The Party Variable in Judges' Voting: Conceptual Notes and a Case Study," *American Political Science Review* 63 (1969): 57–73. For a review of party influence in the federal courts, see Robert A. Carp and Ronald Stidham, *The Federal Courts* (Washington, D.C.: CQ Press, 1985), pp. 142–48.

26. See Randall D. Lloyd, "Separating Partisanship from Party in Judicial Research: Reapportionment in the U.S. District Courts," *American Political Science Review* 89 (1995): 413–20.

27. Bruce Allen Murphy, *The Brandeis/Frankfurter Connection* (New York: Oxford University Press, 1982).

28. The Roosevelt letter is quoted more fully in Walter F. Murphy and C. Herman Pritchett, *Courts, Judges, and Politics* (New York: Random House, 1961), pp. 82–83.

29. Sheldon Goldman, "The Bush Imprint on the Judiciary: Carrying on a Tradition," *Judicature* 74 (1991), 294–306.

30. Sheldon Goldman, "Judicial Selection under Clinton: a midterm examination," *Judicature* 78 (1995): 276–91.

31. These data on judicial selection in the states come from the *Book of the States: 1992–93* (Lexington, Ky.: Council of State Governments, 1992), p. 233.

32. On the political effects of different state selection systems, see Henry R. Glick and Craig F. Emmert, "Selection Systems and Judicial Characteristics: The Recruitment of State Supreme Court Judges," *Judicature* 70 (1987), 228–35.

33. On judicial patronage, see Herbert Jacob, *Justice in America* (Boston: Little, Brown, 1965), pp. 87–89; and Martin and Susan Tolchin, *To the Victor . . . : Political Patronage from Clubhouse to White House* (New York: Random House, 1971), pp. 131–86.

Chapter 15

1. Austin Ranney, *The Doctrine of Responsible Party Government* (Urbana: University of Illinois Press, 1962).

2. Committee on Political Parties of the American Political Science Association, *Toward a More Responsible Two-Party System* (New York: Rinehart, 1950).

3. *Divided government* refers to a government in which different parties control the different centers of power. At the national level in recent decades, divided government has almost invariably had a Democratic Congress and a Republican president—except in 1995–96 when Republicans held the Congress for the first time in years. Divided government forces interparty cooperation or coalition in the making of public policy, which is exactly the opposite of how government operates under the responsible party model. For an introduction to the divided government model, see James L. Sundquist, "Needed: A Political Theory for the New Era of Coalition Government in the United States," *Political Science Quarterly* 103 (1988): 613–35.

4. The distinguished British observer of American politics, Lord Bryce, long ago made the same complaint about American parties. See James Bryce, *The American Commonwealth* (New York: Macmillan, 1916).

5. See Ranney, *The Doctrine of Responsible Party Government,* Chapters 1 and 2, for an analysis of what party government presumes about democracy.

6. E. E. Schattschneider, *Party Government* (New York: Rinehart, 1942), p. 208.

7. This point is made in E. E. Schattschneider, *The Semi-Sovereign People* (New York: Holt, Rinehart, and Winston, 1960).

8. Committee on Political Parties, *Toward a More Responsible Two-Party System,* p. 15.

9. The literature critical of the concept of party responsibility is a large one. Pendleton Herring's *The Politics of Democracy* (New York: Rinehart, 1940) presented an early argument against the reformers. Also see Julius Turner, "Responsible Parties: A Dissent from the Floor," *American Political Science Review* 45 (1951): 143–52. An excellent evaluation of this debate is provided in APSA Committee on Political Parties member Evron Kirkpatrick's "Toward a More Responsible Two-Party System: Political Science, Policy Science, or Pseudo-Science?" *American Political Science Review* 65 (1971): 965–90. A more contemporary discussion of responsible parties in the American context may be found in the various chapters of John Kenneth White and Jerome M. Mileur, eds., *Challenges to Party Government* (Carbondale and Edwardsville, Ill.: Southern Illinois University Press, 1992).

10. See Leon D. Epstein, "A Comparative Study of Canadian Parties," *American Political Science Review* 58 (1964): 46–59; Leon D. Epstein, *Political Parties in Western Democracies* (New Brunswick, N.J.: Transaction Books, 1980; originally published in 1967); and Austin Ranney, "Candidate Selection and Party Cohesion in Britain and the U.S.," in William J. Crotty, ed., *Approaches to the Study of Party Organization* (Boston: Allyn and Bacon, 1968), pp. 139–68.

11. Otto Kircheimer, "The Transformation of the Western European Party Systems," in Joseph LaPalombara and Myron Weiner, eds., *Political Parties and Political Development* (Princeton, N.J.: Princeton University Press, 1966), pp. 184–92.

12. On the consensus among Americans on the basic principles of politics, see Louis Hartz, *The Liberal Tradition in America* (New York: Harcourt, Brace, 1955).

13. Ian Budge and Richard I. Hofferbert have demonstrated that, for the 1948–1985 period, important differences existed between the platforms of the two major American parties and the policies the parties enacted, as measured by federal expenditures when they controlled the presidency. See their "Mandates and Policy Outputs: U.S. Party Platforms and Federal Expenditures," *American Political Science Review* 84 (1990): 111–32.

14. See Paul Allen Beck, "The Electoral Cycle and Patterns of American Politics," *British Journal of Political Science* 9 (1979): 129–56; and James L. Sundquist, *Dynamics of the Party System* (Washington, D.C.: Brookings Institution, 1983).

15. On the importance of racial issues in the changing nature of the party coalitions among both voters and political leaders, see Edward G. Carmines and James A. Stimson, *Issue Evolution: Race and the Transformation of American Politics* (Princeton, N.J.: Princeton University Press, 1989).

16. Leading examples of the view that the American public alternates between different ideological postures are Arthur M. Schlesinger, Jr., *The Cycles of American History* (Boston: Houghton Mifflin, 1986) and Samuel P. Huntington, *American Politics: The Promise of Disharmony* (Cambridge, Mass.: Harvard University Press, 1981.) For a more contemporary account based on systematic empirical analysis, see James A. Stimson, *Public Opinion: Moods, Cycles, and Swings* (Boulder, Colo.: Westview, 1991).

17. The seminal study, based on surveys conducted in 1956, 1958, and 1960, is Philip E. Converse, "The Nature of Belief Systems in Mass Publics," in David Apter, ed., *Ideology and Discontent* (New York: Free Press, 1964), pp. 206–61. For subsequent years, see Norman H. Nie, Sidney Verba, and John R. Petrocik, *The Changing American Voter* (Cambridge, Mass.: Harvard University Press, 1976), Chapters 7–9; Philip E. Converse, "Public Opinion and Voting Behavior," in Fred I. Greenstein and Nelson W. Polsby, eds., *Handbook of Political Science,* Volume 4 (Reading, Mass.: Addison-Wesley, 1975); and John L. Sullivan, James E. Piereson, and George E. Marcus, "Ideological Constraint in the Mass Public: A Methodological Critique and Some New Findings," *American Journal of Political Science* 23 (1978): 233–49.

18. The survey results are reported in *The New York Times,* November 13, 1995, p. A7. On ideological self-identification, see Pamela Conover and Stanley Feldman, "The Origins and Meaning of Liberal/Conservative Self-Identification," *American Journal of Political Science* 25 (1981): 617–45. On its relationship to positions on issues, see Lloyd A. Free and Hadley Cantril, *The Political Beliefs of Americans: A Study of Public Opinion* (New Brunswick, N.J.: Rutgers University Press, 1968).

19. On mood changes in the electorate, see Stimson, *Public Opinion: Moods, Cycles, and Swings.*

20. See Thomas Ferguson and Joel Rogers, *Right Turn: The Decline of the Democrats and the Future of American Politics* (New York: Hill and Wang, 1986), especially Chapter 1; Paul R. Abramson,

John H. Aldrich, and David W. Rohde, *Change and Continuity in the 1988 Elections* (Washington, D.C.: CQ Press, 1989), Chapter 6; and Abramson, Aldrich, and Rohde, *Change and Continuity in the 1992 Elections* (Washington, D.C.: CQ Press, 1995), Chapters 6 and 7.

21. For evidence on the ideological nature of the electorate in political systems with more responsible parties, including Britain which often is thought of as the apotheosis of party government, see David Butler and Donald Stokes, *Political Change in Britain* (New York: St. Martin's, 1969), Chapter 9; and Philip E. Converse and Roy Pierce, *Political Representation in France* (Cambridge, Mass.: Harvard University Press, 1986), Chapter 4.

22. See Herbert McClosky, Paul J. Hoffman, and Rosemary O'Hara, "Issue Conflict and Consensus among Party Leaders and Followers," *American Political Science Review* 54 (1960): 406–27; Jeane Kirkpatrick, "Representation in the American National Conventions: The Case of 1972," *British Journal of Political Science* 5 (1975): 265–322; Robert S. Montjoy, William R. Shaffer, and Ronald E. Weber, "Policy Preferences of Party Elites and Masses: Conflict or Consensus?" *American Politics Quarterly* 8 (1980): 319–44; John S. Jackson III, Barbara L. Brown, and David Bositis, "Herbert McClosky and Friends Revisited: 1980 Democratic and Republican Party Elites Compared to the Mass Public," *American Politics Quarterly* 10 (1982): 158–80; Warren E. Miller and M. Kent Jennings, *Parties in Transition* (New York: Russell Sage Foundation, 1986), pp. 189–219; and Denise L. Baer and David A. Bositis, *Elite Cadres and Party Coalitions* (New York: Greenwood Press, 1988), pp. 100–107. Evidence that party activists have become even more polarized ideologically is found in John M. Bruce, John A. Clark, and John H. Kessel, "Advocacy Politics in Presidential Parties," *American Political Science Review* 85 (1991): 1089–1105.

23. On the use of ambiguity as a political strategy, see Benjamin Page, *Choices and Echoes in Presidential Elections* (Chicago: University of Chicago Press, 1978).

24. The tendency for candidates seeking office in the general elections to converge upon the center in a two-party system is given theoretical expression in Anthony Downs, *An Economic Theory of Democracy* (New York: Harper & Row, 1957). Rebecca B. Morton has shown that ideological candidates and parties will still diverge to some degree in spite of the pressures to converge upon the center; see her "Incomplete Information and Ideological Explanations of Platform Divergence," *American Political Science Review* 87 (1993): 382–92.

25. David Nice, "Ideological Stability and Change at the Presidential Nominating Conventions," *Journal of Politics* 42 (1980): 847–53; and Howard L. Reiter, "Party Factionalism: National Conventions in the New Era," *American Politics Quarterly* 8 (1980): 303–18.

26. For a discussion of the British responsible party model as an ideal and a reality, see Leon D. Epstein, "What Happened to the British Party Model?" *American Political Science Review* 74 (1980): 9–22.

27. This is largely the point V. O. Key makes in *The Responsible Electorate* (Cambridge: Harvard University Press, 1966). Alternatively, retrospective policy voting may be viewed from the Downsian perspective in which the past is the best rational guide to the future. See Downs, *An Economic Theory of Democracy*. For a contrast between these two types of retrospective voting and a powerful application of the Downsian approach, see Morris P. Fiorina, *Retrospective Voting in American National Elections* (New Haven: Yale University Press, 1981).

28. For further development of these points, see Paul Allen Beck, "The Electoral Cycle and Patterns of American Politics;" and Jerome M. Clubb, William H. Flanagan, and Nancy H. Zingale, *Partisan Realignment* (Beverly Hills, Calif.: Sage, 1980), pp. 155–88.

29. On divided government in the states, see Morris Fiorina, *Divided Government* (New York: MacMillan, 1992), Chapter 3; and "Divided Government in the American States: A Byproduct of Legislative Professionalism," *American Political Science Review* 88 (1994): 304–16.

30. On the causes of divided government, see the essays by Gary C. Jacobson, John Petrocik, Martin Wattenberg, Morris Fiorina, and Charles Stewart in Gary Cox and Samuel Kernell, eds., *The Politics of Divided Government* (Boulder, Colo.: Westview, 1991); Gary Jacobson, *The Electoral Origins of Divided Government: Competition in U.S. House Elections, 1946–1988* (Boulder, Colo.: Westview, 1990); and Paul Allen Beck, Lawrence Baum, Aage Clausen, and Charles E. Smith, Jr., "Patterns and Sources of Split-Ticket Voting," *American Political Science Review* 86 (1992): 916–28.

31. Sundquist, "Needed: A Political Theory for the New Era of Coalition Government in the United States."

32. On the consequences of divided government, see Alberto Alesina and Howard Rosenthal, *Partisan Politics, Divided Government, and the Economy* (New York: Cambridge University Press, 1994); James E. Alt and Robert C. Lowery, "Divided Government, Fiscal Institutions, and Budget Deficits: Evidence from the States," *American Political Science Review* 88 (1994): 811–28; the essays by Samuel Kernell, Mathew McCubbins, and Gary Cox and Mathew McCubbins in Cox and Kernell, eds., *The Politics of Divided Government;* and Fiorina, *Divided Government,* Chapter 6. For a contrary view that divided government has not made much difference for federal policy making, see David R. Mayhew, *Divided We Govern* (New Haven, Conn.: Yale University Press, 1991).

33. See Fiorina, *Divided Government,* Chapter 5. Also see Richard Born, "Split-Ticket Voters, Divided Government, and Fiorina's Policy-Balancing Model," *Legislative Studies Quarterly* 19 (1994): 95–115.

34. The reform-minded commitment of the 1950 APSA Committee on Political Parties lives on in state and national chapters of the Committee for Party Renewal, which has joined scholars and political leaders in the quest for more responsible parties. Also the bipartisan blue-ribbon Committee on the Constitutional System, deeply concerned about the deadlock produced by divided government, offered a number of recommendations to strengthen parties in its 1987 report. Their recommendations included increased collaboration between Congress and the president through, among other things, scheduling all congressional elections in presidential election years and allowing members of Congress to serve simultaneously in the executive branch; public financing of congressional campaigns with party leaders controlling half of the funds; and a presidential nomination system in which congressional nominees had more influence over who the presidential nominee would be. For more on the Committee's report, see an article by Stuart Taylor, Jr., in *The New York Times,* January 11, 1987, p. 1.

35. It is of course possible—perhaps even more likely in the wake of the 1994 Republican gains—that a partisan realignment will arrive to provide that strong bond of partisan unity across party organizations, party officials, and party voters that the current system lacks. Yet, current appraisals of the prospects for realignment view it as surely less encompassing than even the realignments of earlier eras, which themselves produced only pale imitations of responsible parties. John H. Aldrich sees the newly invigorated parties of recent years as lacking their traditional base in the electorate. Walter Dean Burnham calls the new order, with "divided government as a natural condition," a form of "postpartisan politics." The 1994 elections rekindled hope (or, as the case may be, dismay) about the onset of a new realignment, but there is no reason to believe that, even if it has arrived, it will bring about the kind of responsible party government its champions envision. See Aldrich, *Why Parties? The Origin and Transformation of Party Politics in America* (Chicago: University of Chicago Press, 1995), Chapter 9; and Walter Dean Burnham, "Critical Realignment: Dead or Alive," in Byron E. Shafer, ed., *The End of Realignment? Interpreting American Electoral Eras* (Madison, Wisc.: University of Wisconsin Press, 1991), pp. 101–39.

Chapter 16

1. These figures are taken from Harold W. Stanley and Richard G. Niemi, *Vital Statistics on American Politics* (Washington, D.C.: CQ Press, 1994), Tables 4–7 (on ticket splitting) and 4–8 (on split-district outcomes), pp. 146–47.

2. See Bruce E. Cain, John Ferejohn, and Morris P. Fiorina, *The Personal Vote: Constituency Service and Electoral Independence* (Cambridge, Mass.: Harvard University Press, 1987).

3. The voluminous literature on the "decline of parties" during the 1960s and 1970s has been cited at the appropriate points in earlier chapters. Most representative of these works are David S. Broder, *The Party's Over* (New York: Harper & Row, 1972); Nelson W. Polsby, *Consequences of Party Reform* (New York: Oxford University Press, 1983); Alan Ware, *The Breakdown of the Democratic Party Organization: 1940–1980* (New York: Oxford University Press, 1985); and Martin P. Wattenberg, *The Rise of Candidate-Centered Politics* (Cambridge: Harvard University Press, 1991).

4. For a discussion of these characteristics of dealignment and how they might serve as necessary, though not sufficient, conditions for a subsequent realignment, see Paul Allen Beck, "The Electoral Cycle and Patterns of American Politics," *British Journal of Political Science* 9 (1979): 129–56.

5. On the apparent failure of recent signs of realignment to fulfill the normal conditions of a realignment, see Martin P. Wattenberg, "The Hollow Realignment: Partisan Change in a Candidate-Centered Era," *Public Opinion Quarterly* 51 (1987): 58–74; and Paul Allen Beck, "Incomplete Realignment: The Reagan Legacy for Parties and Elections," in Charles O. Jones, ed., *The Reagan Legacy* (Chatham, N.J.: Chatham House, 1988), pp. 145–71. In *Critical Elections and the Mainsprings of American Politics* (New York: Norton, 1970), Chapter 5, Walter Dean Burnham contends that antiparty political reforms probably prevent present or future realignments from attaining the completeness of past realignments. A similar point is made in John H. Aldrich, *Why Parties: The Origin and Transformation of Party Politics in America* (Chicago: University of Chicago Press, 1995), Chapter 9.

6. For a discussion of information intermediaries in American election campaigns, see Robert Huckfeldt and Paul Allen Beck, "Contexts, Intermediaries, and Political Activity," in Lawrence C. Dodd and Calvin Jillson, eds., *The Dynamics of American Politics: Approaches and Interpretations* (Boulder, Colo.: Westview Press, 1994), Chapter 11.

7. For an elaboration of this view, see W. Phillips Shively, "The Development of Party Identification among Adults: Exploration of a Functional Model," *American Political Science Review* 73 (1979): 1039–54.

8. Such skepticism about the capacity of the new "service" party to fully restore the party organization to its earlier prominence is best expressed in John J. Coleman, "The Resurgence of Party Organization: A Dissent from the New Orthodoxy," in Daniel M. Shea and John C. Green, eds., *The State of the Parties: The Changing Role of Contemporary American Parties* (Lanham, Md.: Rowman and Littlefield, 1994), Chapter 20.

9. The renewed strength of the parties since the late 1970s triggered a shift in the emphasis of scholarly studies of parties from decay to renewal. Most representative of this approach are Cornelius P. Cotter, James L. Gibson, John F. Bibby, and Robert J. Huckshorn, *Party Organization in American Politics* (New York: Praeger, 1984); Xandra Kayden and Eddie Mahe, Jr., *The Party Goes On* (New York: Basic Books, 1985); David E. Price, *Bringing Back the Parties* (Washington, D.C.: CQ Press, 1984); Larry J. Sabato, *The Party's Just Begun* (Glenview, Ill.: Scott Foresman/Little, Brown, 1988); and Joseph A. Schlesinger, "The New American Political Party," *American Political Science Review* 79 (1985): 1152–69.

10. On the greater sophistication and politicization—or what is called cognitive mobilization—of western electorates and the consequent decline of "blind" party loyalists, see Ronald Inglehart, *Culture Shift* (Princeton, N.J.: Princeton University Press, 1990), especially Chapters 10 and 11.

11. The growing strength of competitors to political parties has been found throughout the western world. See Kay Lawson and Peter H. Merkl, *When Parties Fail: Emerging Alternative Organizations* (Princeton: Princeton University Press, 1988).

12. On the centrality of the organization in these working-class parties, especially the British Labour Party, see Leon D. Epstein, *Political Parties in Western Democracies* (New York: Praeger, 1967), Chapter 11.

13. The so-called *conservative coalition* is the term used to characterize the congressional voting alliance of Republicans and southern Democrats against northern Democrats. This alliance became conspicuous as early as the 1930s and reached its pinnacle in the 1950s and 1960s. Formed on about a quarter of all votes in the 1970s, its appearance has declined to about 10 percent of all votes in recent years.

14. In most other democracies, it is the parties rather than the candidates who control television time and receive the public financing for campaigns. American parallels to these practices may be found in the (now dwindling) coverage television networks give to the national *party* conventions and in financing for parties in a few of the states.

15. For a compelling argument that parties emerge to solve persistent collective action problems, see Aldrich, *Why Parties?*, Chapter 2.

16. Burnham, *Critical Elections and the Mainsprings of American Politics,* p. 133.

17. Willis D. Hawley, *Nonpartisan Elections and the Case for Party Politics* (New York: Wiley, 1973).

18. A slight SES bias of the decline in turnout in recent decades is described in Ruy A. Teixeira, *The Disappearing American Voter* (Washington, D.C.: Brookings Institution, 1992), Chapter 3. Broader studies of voter participation in the United States and elsewhere demonstrate the importance of the political parties for mobilizing the lower status groups into politics. See Steven J. Rosenstone and John Mark Hansen, *Mobilization, Participation, and Democracy in America* (New York: Macmillan, 1993), especially Chapter 8; and Sidney Verba, Norman H. Nie, and Jae-On Kim, *Participation and Political Equality* (Cambridge, U.K.: Cambridge University Press, 1978).

19. With a little imagination and knowledge of historical experience, including current electoral politics in the former communist nations of Eastern Europe, it is easy to conceive of a few alternative forms this politics without parties might take. At one extreme, it might take on a plebiscitary form in which a dominant national leader (today a president, a popular monarch in an earlier day) faces an up or down vote at regular intervals. The leader's command of television, whether he or she was a partisan or an independent, and how the country was faring under her or his stewardship might figure most prominently in how both other political leaders and voters would respond. At the other extreme, one can imagine a multiplicity of narrow interests vying with one another for political dominance, with no one of them strong enough to hold the reins of government alone or pragmatic enough to be willing to join with other interests in enduring governing coalitions. Under either of these alternatives, it is not difficult to envision how some of the basic functions we take for granted that parties will perform—for example, selecting candidates for office, organizing the electorate, coordinating the government, and simplifying policy alternatives—might be performed in ways that favor a few people at the expense of others and that are, in the end, quite inimical to political democracy.

20. For a systematic attack on these explanatory problems, see Robert Harmel and Kenneth Janda, *Parties and Their Environments: Limits to Reform* (New York: Longman, 1982).

21. It should not be overlooked, though, that considerable change has occurred in American electoral districts, even beyond the decennial battles over redistricting. For example, multimember districts were once common for the American state legislatures, but their number has dwindled in recent years (to fifteen for lower chambers and seven for upper chambers in 1990). See Richard Niemi, Simon Jackman, and Laura Winsky, "Candidates and Competitiveness in Multimember Districts," *Legislative Studies Quarterly* 16 (1991): 91–109; and Theodore J. Lowi, "Toward a More Responsible Three-Party System," *PS* 16 (1983): 699–706.

Index

Witcover, Jules, 403, 429
Wlezien, Christopher, 419
Wolfinger, Raymond, 405, 411, 417, 419
    431
Workers' League, 47
Wright, Jim, 311
Wright, John R., 433
Wright, Stephen, 415
Wrighton, J. Mark, 437
Wyoming
    franchise for women, 171
    party competition, 37
    party legislation, 68

Yeutter, Clayton, 91
Young Democrats of America, 93
Young Republican National Federation,
    93

Zingale, Nancy H., 412, 442
Zukin, Cliff, 425